THE CAMBRIDGE HISTORY OF
LATIN AMERICA

VOLUME IV

c. *1870 to 1930*

THE CAMBRIDGE HISTORY OF
LATIN AMERICA

VOLUME I *Colonial Latin America*

VOLUME II *Colonial Latin America*

VOLUME III *From Independence to* c. *1870*

VOLUME IV C. *1870 to 1930*

VOLUME V C. *1870 to 1930*

THE CAMBRIDGE
HISTORY OF
LATIN AMERICA

VOLUME IV

c. *1870 to 1930*

---

edited by

LESLIE BETHELL

Reader in Hispanic American and
Brazilian History at University College London

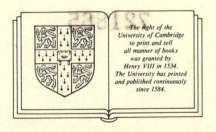

The right of the
University of Cambridge
to print and sell
all manner of books
was granted by
Henry VIII in 1534.
The University has printed
and published continuously
since 1584.

CAMBRIDGE UNIVERSITY PRESS

Cambridge

London   New York   New Rochelle
Melbourne   Sydney

Published by the Press Syndicate of the University of Cambridge
The Pitt Building, Trumpington Street, Cambridge CB2 1RP
32 East 57th Street, New York, NY 10022, USA
10 Stamford Road, Oakleigh, Melbourne 3166, Australia

First published 1986

Printed in Great Britain at the University Press, Cambridge

British Library cataloguing in publication data

The Cambridge history of Latin America.
Vol. 4: c. 1870–1930
1. Latin America – History
I. Bethell, Leslie
980   F1410

Library of Congress cataloguing-in-publication data

Main entry under title:
The Cambridge history of Latin America.
Includes bibliographies and indexes.
Contents: v. 1–2. Colonial Latin
America – – v. 4. c. 1870–1930.
1. Latin America – History – Collected works.
I. Bethell, Leslie.
F1410.C1834 1984   980   83–19036

ISBN 0 521 23225 2

721865

CONTENTS

Contents

ix

MAPS

GENERAL PREFACE

In the English-speaking and English-reading world the multi-volume Cambridge Histories planned and edited by historians of established reputation, with individual chapters written by leading specialists in their fields, have since the beginning of the century set the highest standards of collaborative international scholarship. *The Cambridge Modern History*, planned by Lord Acton, appeared in sixteen volumes between 1902 and 1912. It was followed by *The Cambridge Ancient History*, *The Cambridge Medieval History* and others. The *Modern History* has now been replaced by *The New Cambridge Modern History* in fourteen volumes, and *The Cambridge Economic History of Europe* has recently been completed. Cambridge Histories of Islam, of Iran and of Africa are published or near completion; in progress are Histories of China and of Judaism, while Japan is soon to join the list.

In the early 1970s Cambridge University Press decided the time was ripe to embark on a Cambridge History of Latin America. Since the Second World War and particularly since 1960 research and writing on Latin American history had been developing, and have continued to develop, at an unprecedented rate – in the United States (by American historians in particular, but also by British, European and Latin American historians resident in the United States), in Europe (especially in Britain and France) and increasingly in Latin America itself (where a new generation of young professional historians, many of them trained in the United States, Britain or Europe, had begun to emerge). Perspectives had changed as political, economic and social realities in Latin America – and Latin America's role in the world – had changed. Methodological innovations and new conceptual models drawn from the social sciences (economics, political science, historical demography, sociology, anthropology) as well as from other fields of historical research were increasingly being adopted by historians of Latin America.

The Latin American Studies monograph series and the *Journal of Latin American Studies* had already been established by the Press and were beginning to publish the results of this new historical thinking and research.

In 1974 Dr Leslie Bethell, Reader in Hispanic American and Brazilian History at University College London, accepted an invitation to edit *The Cambridge History of Latin America*, and he began work on the project two years later. For the first time a single editor was given responsibility for the planning, co-ordination and editing of an entire *History*.

The Cambridge History of Latin America, to be published in eight volumes, is the first large-scale, authoritative survey of Latin America's unique historical experience during almost five centuries from the first contacts between the native American Indians and Europeans (and the beginnings of the African slave trade) in the late fifteenth and early sixteenth centuries to the present day. (The Press will publish separately a Cambridge History of the Native Peoples of the Americas – North, Middle and South – which will give proper consideration to the evolution of the region's peoples, societies and civilizations, in isolation from the rest of the world, during the several millenia before the arrival of the Europeans, as well as a fuller treatment than will be found here of the history of the indigenous peoples of Latin America under European colonial rule and during the national period to the present day.) Latin America is taken to comprise the predominantly Spanish- and Portuguese-speaking areas of continental America south of the United States – Mexico, Central America and South America – together with the Spanish-speaking Caribbean – Cuba, Puerto Rico, the Dominican Republic – and, by convention, Haiti. (The vast territories in North America lost to the United States by treaty and by war, first by Spain, then by Mexico, during the first half of the nineteenth century are for the most part excluded. Neither the British, French and Dutch Caribbean islands nor the Guianas are included even though Jamaica and Trinidad, for example, have early Hispanic antecedents and are now members of the Organisation of American States.) The aim is to produce a high-level synthesis of existing knowledge which will provide historians of Latin America with a solid base for future research, which students of Latin American history will find useful and which will be of interest to historians of other areas of the world. It is also hoped that the *History* will contribute more generally to a deeper understanding of Latin America through its history in the United States and in Europe and, not least, to a greater awareness of its own history in Latin America.

Contributors have been drawn from the United States and Canada, from Britain and Europe, and from Latin America.

For the first time the volumes of a Cambridge History will be published in chronological order: Volumes I and II (Colonial Latin America – with an introductory section on the native American peoples and civilizations on the eve of the European invasion) in 1984; Volume III (from Independence to *c.* 1870) in 1985; Volumes IV and V (*c.* 1870 to 1930) in 1986; and Volumes VI–VIII (1930 to the present) in 1988 or as soon as possible thereafter. Each volume or set of volumes examines a period in the economic, social, political, intellectual and cultural history of Latin America. While recognizing the decisive impact on Latin America of external forces, of developments within what is now called the capitalist world system, and the fundamental importance of its economic, political and cultural ties first with Spain and Portugal, then with Britain, France and, to a lesser extent, Western Europe as a whole, and finally with the United States, the emphasis of the *History* will be upon the evolution of internal structures. Furthermore, the emphasis is clearly on the period since the establishment of all the independent Latin American states except Cuba at the beginning of the nineteenth century, which, compared with the colonial and independence periods, has been relatively neglected by historians of Latin America. The period of Spanish and Portuguese colonial rule from the sixteenth to the eighteenth centuries is the subject of two of the eight volumes. Six are devoted to the nineteenth and twentieth centuries and will consist of a mixture of general, comparative chapters built around major themes in Latin American history and chapters on the individual histories of the twenty independent Latin American countries (plus Puerto Rico), and especially the three major countries – Brazil, Mexico and Argentina. In view of its size, population and distinctive history, Brazil, which has often been neglected in general histories of Latin America, written for the most part by Spanish Americans or Spanish American specialists, will here receive the attention it deserves.

An important feature of the *History* will be the bibliographical essays which accompany each chapter. These will give special emphasis to books and articles published during the past 15–20 years, that is to say, since the publication of Charles C. Griffin (ed.), *Latin America: a guide to the historical literature* (published for the Conference on Latin American History by the University of Texas Press, Austin, Texas, 1971) which was prepared during 1966–9 and included few works published after 1966.

PREFACE TO VOLUMES IV AND V

Volumes I and II of *The Cambridge History of Latin America* published in 1984 were largely devoted to the economic, social, political, intellectual and cultural history of Latin America during the three centuries of Spanish and (in the case of Brazil) Portuguese colonial rule from the European 'discovery', conquest and settlement of the 'New World' in the late fifteenth and early sixteenth centuries to the late eighteenth and early nineteenth centuries, the eve of Latin American independence. Volume III published in 1985 examined the breakdown and overthrow of Spanish and Portuguese colonial rule in Latin America during the first quarter of the nineteenth century and, the main focus of the volume, the economic, social, political and cultural history of the independent Spanish American republics and the independent Empire of Brazil during the half-century from independence to *c.* 1870. With Volumes IV and V *The Cambridge History of Latin America* moves on to the period from *c.* 1870 to 1930.

During the first half-century after independence Latin America experienced, at best, only very modest rates of economic growth and, at least in Spanish America, violent political and ideological conflict and considerable political instability. Besides the war between Mexico and the United States (1846–8) and frequent foreign, especially British, interventions in Latin America, there were also at the end of the period two major wars between Latin American states: the Paraguayan War (1865–70) and the War of the Pacific (1879–83). In contrast, the following half-century, and particularly the period up to the First World War, was for most Latin American countries a 'Golden Age' of predominantly export-led economic growth, material prosperity (at least for the dominant classes and the urban middle classes), ideological consensus and, with some notable exceptions like Mexico during the

Revolution (1910–20), political stability. Moreover, although there was continued foreign intervention in Latin America – mainly US intervention in Mexico, Central America and the Caribbean – throughout the period, there were no major international conflicts in Latin America between the end of the War of the Pacific (1883) and the outbreak of the Chaco War (1932).

Volume IV, the first of these two volumes on the period *c.* 1870 to 1930, consists of twelve general chapters on the economic, social, political, intellectual and cultural history of Latin America as a whole. Two chapters examine the growth of the Latin American economies, the first in the period 1870–1914, the second in the period from the First World War to the eve of the World Depression of the 1930s. This growth was largely a result of the greatly accelerated incorporation of the Latin American economies as primary producers into the expanding international economy and significant inflows of foreign capital, particularly from Britain and, in the twentieth century, from the United States. At the same time domestic markets and domestic capital accumulation are not neglected. Latin America's political relations with the major European powers and, above all in Central America and the Caribbean, with the increasingly expansionist United States receive separate treatment. Another chapter analyses the growth of Latin America's population (from 30 million in 1850 to 105 million in 1930), in part the result of mass European immigration especially in Argentina and Brazil. The profound impact of capitalist penetration of the countryside is the subject of two chapters, one concentrating on the traditional highland areas of Mexico, Central America and the Andes, the other on the Spanish Caribbean. The first of these, while claiming that rural economies and societies underwent greater change in the period 1870–1930 than in any previous period except the Conquest, also seeks to show that in many rural areas, especially in the Andes, the forces of change were resisted and pre-capitalist structures survived. Urban society also experienced rapid change in this period, and there are separate chapters on the growth of Latin American cities, especially primary cities like Buenos Aires, Rio de Janeiro and Mexico City, all of which had between one and two million inhabitants by 1930 and rivalled the major cities of Europe and the United States; on the beginnings of industry, especially in Brazil, Argentina, Chile, Colombia and Mexico; and on the emergence of an urban working class as a significant force in many republics and the history of the early Latin American labour movements. Two chapters treat separately the evolution of political and social ideas in Latin America in this period (and in particular the adaptation of liberalism to highly stratified societies with under-developed economies and an authoritarian political tradition, and the influence of positivism on the governing and intellectual elites), and major movements and notable individual achievements in Latin American literature, music and art (as well as the early days of the cinema in Latin America). Finally, the volume concludes with a chapter which examines how the Catholic Church in Latin America adjusted to the decline in its power and privileges in a secular age while retaining the adherence of the vast majority of Latin Americans.

Volume V consists of twenty-one chapters on the economic, social and, above all, political history of the various Latin American countries from *c.* 1870 to 1930. Part One deals in some detail with the history of Mexico in this period. There are chapters on the Porfiriato (the thirty-five-year dictatorship of Porfirio Díaz, 1876–1911), on the Mexican Revolution and on reconstruction under the 'Sonoran dynasty' during the 1920s. Part Two, 'Central America and the Caribbean', has a single chapter on the five republics of Central America and separate chapters on Cuba, Puerto Rico, the Dominican Republic and Haiti. Part Three, 'The River Plate Republics', has four chapters on the economic, social and political evolution of Argentina, which had become in many respects Latin America's most advanced nation by 1930, as well as chapters on Uruguay and Paraguay. Part Four, 'The Andean Republics', has separate chapters on Chile, Bolivia and Peru in the half-century following the War of the Pacific and a single chapter on Colombia, Ecuador and Venezuela. Finally, Part Five is devoted to Brazil. There are chapters on Brazil's coffee-dominated economy in this period, on the political system and the politics of reform during the late Empire (1870–89) and on the social and political structure of the First Republic (1889–1930).

Many of the historians who contributed chapters to these two volumes – twelve of them North American, eight Latin American (three from Brazil, two each from Argentina and Cuba and one from Uruguay), eight British, four continental European and one Puerto Rican – also read and commented on the chapters of their colleagues. I am especially grateful in this respect to Malcolm Deas, Ezequiel Gallo and Colin Lewis. In addition, Christopher Abel, Alan Knight and Rory Miller provided critical assessments of more than one of these chapters. A number of

Latin American historians and historians of Latin America have given valuable advice and encouragement from the very beginning of this project. I would like to take the opportunity here to thank, in particular, John Lynch, Richard Morse and John Womack.

At the Cambridge University Press Elizabeth Wetton was the editor responsible for these volumes of *The Cambridge History of Latin America*. Cynthia Postan was the subeditor of Volume IV, Elizabeth O'Beirne-Ranelagh of Volume V. The index to Volume IV was prepared by Hilda Pearson, the index to Volume V by Ann Hudson. As in the case of the three volumes of the *History* already published Nazneen Razwi at University College London gave invaluable secretarial assistance.

United STATES
of AMERICA

ATLANTIC

OCEAN

Rio Grande

MEXICO · Monterrey

Guadalajara

BAHAMA
ISLANDS

Havana

Mérida

Puebla

México · VeraCruz

CUBA

DOMINICAN
REPUBLIC

JAMAICA

HAITI

PUERTO
RICO

HONDURAS

GUATEMALA Tegucigalpa

San Salvador NICARAGUA

EL SALVADOR Managua

S.José

COSTA RICA

PANAMA

Caracas

TRINIDAD

VENEZUELA

Medellín

R. Orinoco

Bogotá

COLOMBIA

Quito

ECUADOR

Guayaquil

R. Amazon

Manaus

Belém

PERU

BRAZIL

Recife

Callao

Lima

BOLIVIA

La Paz

PACIFIC

Salvador

R. São Francisco

PARAGUAY

São Paulo

Asunción

Rio de Janeiro

OCEAN

R. Paraná

CHILE

Valparaíso

Santiago

Rosario

URUGUAY

Buenos Aires

Montevideo

ARGENTINA

N

Land over 2000 metres

0   1500 km

0   1000 miles

Latin America in 1900

1

LATIN AMERICA AND THE INTERNATIONAL ECONOMY, 1870–1914

INTRODUCTION

The half-century following the wars of independence in Latin America, that is to say, the period from the 1820s to the 1860s or 1870s, had been generally disappointing in terms of economic growth, although here and there, in the niches of a somewhat ramshackle but nevertheless changing structure, modest material and organizational gains were made. Over the region as a whole, the uneven diffusion of commercialization during the colonial period had left a complex mosaic of capitalist and non-capitalist relations of production, ranging from reciprocal labour networks, slavery, other compulsory labour regimes and debt peonage to share-cropping and various forms of tenant farming, wage labour and small-scale commodity production by artisans and smallholders. Communal ownership of land still existed alongside privately held properties both large and small, while other rural holdings were controlled by ecclesiastical and public authorities. Gradually, however, over the course of several decades, relationships more compatible with capitalist modes of interaction gained ground as long established colonial mechanisms for allocating resources fell into disuse and the world capitalist system expanded. A half-century of incremental change had not been enough to transform the economic organization of Latin America, but it did sufficiently alter conditions for the more sweeping institutional and technological developments of 1870–1914 to get under way.

The regulatory systems established during the colonial period were being dismantled at the same time as public administration was breaking down and new, sometimes contested, national boundaries were being drawn. These developments disrupted local commerce and in many instances halted the former inter-regional (but by then inter-country) currents of trade within Latin America, while the strong gravitational pull of the expanding North Atlantic economies reoriented economic life towards a slowly growing participation in global trade no longer determined by Iberian commercial policy. For example, an export boom in Peruvian guano had begun in the early 1840s; in the same decade Chilean mineral and Argentinian wool exports also began their rapid growth; Brazilian coffee exports also gathered momentum; and some other notable gains, mostly in agricultural exports, were registered elsewhere before 1870.

Even as they brought important new opportunities for growth, the dislocation of trade following in the wake of this reorientation entailed costs for several elements in the regional economy: dwindling artisan production and the virtual extinction of manufacturing workshops or *obrajes*, economic decline for some areas, a decay of inter-regional transport systems. But what was perhaps in the long run one of the most significant institutional losses could hardly have been foreseen at the time. The integration of the region into the world economy and the corresponding ease of borrowing from abroad helped to stifle whatever potential for a local production of technology might have survived the Spanish crown's attempts at modernization in the closing decades of the colonial era, as well as to hinder the development of manufacturing experience within the Continent. Such technological transfers as did occur raised productivity in the Americas and thus undoubtedly increased aggregate output more rapidly than would have happened in their absence. But the fact remains that this type of cross-cultural borrowing did not succeed in persuading or helping the borrowing countries to undertake their own home-grown technological improvement. Cost–benefit relations made it far easier – and more rational – in the short term to acquire new 'off the shelf' methods of production from Europe rather than to establish the kind of social milieu that would have encouraged local generation.

As control and use of the economic surplus shifted from the imperial rulers into the hands of the new national governments, factional disputes combined with interregional rivalries and political-administrative inexperience to breed policy conflicts that were fully as disabling for the conduct of business as the almost complete breakdown of the colonial financial structure had been. Punctuated by repeated *coups d'état* and military uprisings, the aftermath of independence had been, in fact, a period of exceptional political fluidity. It is not always easy to ascertain the correlation of social forces that shaped the somewhat erratic national economic policies of the post-independence period. New currency systems interjected new uncertainties, as did the frequently disordered state of public finance. The inefficiency, indiscipline and corruption which plague so many of today's new states were no less baleful and widespread then. And these were to some extent the cause of the not inconsiderable instability and insecurity that afflicted the contractual-legal environment, especially for larger-scale operations and transactions extending over longer periods of time.

Unfortunately, such institutional disturbances had handicapped Latin America during a period in which the real volume of world trade was rising and, after 1850, increasing at a possibly more rapid rate than even that which obtained between 1870 and 1914. Population growth in Europe and North America, the investment accelerator effects of this growth, together with changes in the technology of production and transport, interacted on the metropolitan economies to increase the capacity to export and import. With the passage of time, this would open up ever more attractive trading opportunities for Latin America when its political environment should improve. Until that moment came, and despite the many failed ventures of the pre-1870 period, much information of eventual economic value on the resources and production possibilities of the region was being accumulated. European mercantile beachheads had been established in the major ports and other principal population centres, new shipping routes connected Latin America with North Atlantic growth centres and, increasingly, the means were at hand for tapping European, and, to a lesser extent, U.S., capital and money markets. All the while, influential segments of Latin American society were acquiring a fuller appreciation of what might be in store (for them, at least) if ties could be successfully consolidated with the vanguard of the industrial revolution.

As Latin America moved into the last third of the nineteenth century, the business climate, which since independence had for the most part been disturbed by political instability, began to acquire a more settled character. So, too, did the transaction of framework derived from law and public policy. This is not to say that the dominant atmosphere of Latin American political life was one of serene sobriety. Flamboyant individuals still thronged the political stage of *fin de siècle* Latin America, and its salient characteristic was often a disequilibrating factionalism. Manipulation of electoral processes was commonplace. More than just occasionally, political life harked back to the earlier part of the century. Yet, notwithstanding episodic disputes among regions, classes and factions, government authority gradually came to be more stable and more comprehensive. Moreover, serious international conflicts were, perhaps surprisingly, few, the most consequential being the War of the Pacific, 1879–83, in which hapless Bolivia lost its access to the sea and both Bolivia and Peru were relieved by Chile of their major nitrate deposits.

Brazil, Chile, Argentina and Mexico stood out from most of the other Latin American nations in the degree to which domestic political stabilization allowed the machinery of state to be devoted to securing the policy basis of material prosperity. In the case of Brazil, which had escaped the earlier troubled times of Spanish America, the long rule of a progressive and enlightened monarch of the best nineteenth-century European type culminated, during 1888–9, in a remarkably peaceful abolition of slavery and the inauguration of a republic. Save for a short civil war in the early 1890s, stability was never seriously shaken and reasonably constructive political guidance enabled a favourable investment climate to be maintained to a degree that attracted much foreign notice and enabled the economy to derive considerable gain from the new export boom that was transforming the economic and geographical patterns of the nation. Chile, too, relatively stable even before 1850, had had a head start in building an economic and social environment relatively conducive to material progress. Interruptions came in the form of the War of the Pacific (although this considerably augmented the Chilean resource base) and in the civil war in 1891 that terminated the nationalistic and interventionist Balmaceda administration. But there, as in Argentina, which until 1880 was subject to extreme internal conflict, a class of improving landlords joined forces with a plutocracy of mercantile and financial origin (and, in the case of Chile, of mineowners) to establish a coalition that presided over a long wave, albeit subject to fluctuation, of economic expansion. So successful was oligarchic rule in Argentina that an area which had been largely empty at the close of the colonial period emerged as an economic heartland remarkably receptive to the new ideas, attitudes and modes of conduct, and the new methods of production which were promoted by the country's international economic contacts. In Mexico, the other major locus of economic growth in the 1870–1914 period, which had suffered a half-century of almost unrelieved turmoil after separating from Spain, an increasingly autocratic period of liberal rule known as the *Reforma* gave way in 1876 to the Porfiriato, a firmly authoritarian administration that enforced political stability on the country and wooed foreign business until its collapse in 1911. While the government of Porfirio Díaz left much to be desired from the standpoint of liberal democracy, it was received with accolades by the foreign investors of the day who perceived the fortunes to be made from linking the diverse resources of Mexico with the rapidly growing markets of the United States and Europe.

The record elsewhere in Latin America during this period was uneven. Most often, where some semblance of political order was attained it came about under the aegis of dictators, some of whom proved to be quite durable, for example, Antonio Guzmán Blanco (1870–87) and Juan Vicente Gómez (1908–35) in Venezuela, Justo Rufino Barrios (1871–85) and Manuel Estrada Cabrera (1898–1920) in Guatemala. Even in the more politically disordered states, however, the expected rates of return on at least some business ventures and bond issues evidently reached the level necessary to induce entrepreneurs and investors, both domestic and foreign, to shoulder the tasks of setting up new trading, agricultural and small industrial enterprises, if only firms catering for the more affluent consumers of the capitals and other major urban centres.

In other words, by the 1870s, major portions of Latin America came to offer a much more hospitable – which is to say reliable – investment climate for foreign capital than they had hitherto, reinforcing the basic cultural affinity that gave Latin America closer and broader links with the capital-exporting countries than were enjoyed by Asia, Africa or the Middle East. (In these areas, political subjugation was a partial substitute for cultural affinity in establishing the economic intelligence systems and common framework of transactions and expectations associated with the spread of a world market.) Greater stability in the institutional framework of business not only increased the attractiveness of Latin America for foreign investments, it also aided domestic capital accumulation and local private investment. It had as well a direct bearing, through effects on risk calculations and debt amortization experiences, on the not inconsiderable flow of capital moving from the capital markets of the North Atlantic economies to the public sectors of Latin America, a flow which was probably much more profitable to the financial intermediaries and political insiders who put these deals together than it was to either the ultimate borrowers or the ultimate

lenders. While the years from 1870 to 1914 were clearly those of high
capitalism, with all that this implied for reliance on the private sector, it
should not be overlooked that these massive transfers of resources also
occurred through the mechanism of government borrowing, with a
substantial improvement in the region's infrastructure (and the growth
of its external debt) as the result.

Further, while governmental improbity and a certain suppleness in
fiscal administration were far from being eradicated anywhere in the
region, regime stability, whatever its human costs, tended to raise the
effectiveness with which long-term capital transfers were put to use, if
only because there was less of the wastage and pilfering associated with
frequent and irregular changes of government, and because there was
rather more opportunity for administrative competence to build up
through learning by doing. There can be little doubt that social
investment was more efficiently carried out in, say, Argentina or Chile
than it was in Bolivia or Ecuador, in Mexico or Brazil than it was in Haiti
or El Salvador, although this is not to deny that, from the standpoint of
long-run growth capabilities, substantial amounts of resources were
misallocated, by governments and markets alike, in even the leading
economies of the area.

If more stable political conditions contributed to the growth of
investment, production and trade, the relation was not only
unidirectional but also interactive inasmuch as the growth of export
earnings and hence the capacity to import eased the collection of
resources for government-sponsored investment and current expenditures alike. The long-term rise in trade taxes, chiefly from duties on
imports, gave governments a far more ample fiscal base than they had
enjoyed previously, both directly in the form of the revenues themselves
and indirectly in the form of the increased volume of loans which could
be floated abroad thanks to projected tax receipts. The public finances
generated by external sector growth, in turn, not only enabled
governments more readily to purchase the means of repression (an aspect
that has probably been overplayed in political history) but also provided
the wherewithal for avoiding recourse to a heavier burden of internal
taxation, always the occasion for political conflict, and for generating
the employment and profits that would increase regime acceptability
among important local constituencies. The swelling of public payrolls
may have been decried as *empleomanía* by more than one contemporary
critic, but it afforded a politically convenient way of dealing with those

who, if left to their own devices, might have proved troublesome.

In the long run, it was resource complementarities with the world market that played a major role in governing how the individual Latin American economies would respond to the opportunities presented by the growth in world trade. The entire nineteenth century was marked by general export expansion, with world trade in primary products growing more rapidly than the world trade in manufactures until the last quarter of the nineteenth century, during which period the two rates of expansion were approximately equal, at around 3 per cent annually. After the turn of the century, trade in manufactures grew more rapidly, at a rate of 4.5 per cent per annum compared with around 3 per cent for primary commodities. The regional impact of these trends was substantial, if so diverse, however, that increasing heterogeneity was already characteristic of the region as it approached the last quarter of the century. Yet the wide divergence of experiences among the Latin American countries in exporting basic commodities was only partly explicable in terms of national resource endowments and the social implications of differing production methods in export industries. Institutional conditions within the republics also helped to pattern their differential economic performances. It was in this connection that political stability and continuity were such influential factors, not least because they were so intimately related to the international movements of capital, technology and, in some instances, labour that created resources out of the natural endowments of land, minerals and climate.

What happened in Latin America between 1870 and 1914 is, in one sense, indisputable. The principal engine of growth in this period was industrial production in countries of the economic centre, with its concomitant social and economic changes. The aggregate growth rate in these advanced economies was largely determined by the rate of growth of industrial output, which in turn determined the rate of increase in the demand for exports from the peripheral economies, including those of Latin America. At the same time, gains in the size of the centre's economic surplus, as well as changes in its composition, gave industrially advanced regions the technical and economic means for drawing peripheral regions ever more closely into that economic field of gravity, the capitalist world market.

As part of this global process, Latin America became increasingly integrated, or, as it is more commonly expressed in Latin America, 'inserted', into the overarching structure of articulation provided by the world market system. Among some scholars this process is thought to have begun with the Conquest; for others, around the middle of the eighteenth century. The degree to which the economic systems of Latin America and those of North Atlantic capitalism were engaged before the middle of the nineteenth century, however, need not concern us here. What is more important for present purposes is that by 1870 the process was, for most of Latin America, well under way and, indeed, even accelerating. That the growth rate of world trade in primary products may have averaged somewhat higher before 1870 (e.g., around 4.3 per cent per annum from 1853 to 1872) than it did thereafter (around 3 per cent per year from 1872 to 1913) does not contradict the increasing influence of the world market on domestic patterns of resource allocation in Latin America. For one thing, the absolute size of increases in the global commerce in primary commodities was generally rising even when, for reasons of an expanded statistical base, the rate may have slipped. For another, world commerce in manufactures increasingly incorporated trade in investment goods, with which substantial portions of the production systems of Latin America were transformed between 1870 and 1913.

The growth of the Latin American external sectors was not a steady process, for it was hindered by periodic instability in the core economies of capitalism. The post-1873 crisis, for instance, brought some weakening of export prices and necessitated a rescheduling of the foreign debt of Honduras, Costa Rica, the Dominican Republic, Paraguay, Bolivia, Guatemala, Uruguay and Peru. Argentina, Chile and Colombia were also deeply affected. The recession in the British and French economies in the middle to late 1880s had a lesser impact, but the economic crisis in most of the advanced industrial countries during the early to mid-1890s coincided with the Baring crisis, default by Argentina, and a big dip in foreign lending generally. Mexico, with its increasingly unpopular political regime, suffered particularly from the 1907–8 recession, a slowdown which was also felt elsewhere. Export price instability further complicated the picture. Cotton, wool and wheat prices, for example, generally declined from the late 1860s to the mid-1890s. Coffee prices fell in the early 1880s, rose sharply thereafter, then declined even more to the early 1900s. More comprehensively, the terms of trade for primary products moved somewhat adversely in the 1880s and 1890s, but improved in the early 1900s. The external sector, then, was not an unfaltering source of support, even before the severe crises of the twentieth century.

Variations in trade volume and prices aside, however, the fact was that Latin American economic expansion in the period under review remained overwhelmingly export-led and therefore primarily induced by the pull of demand in the advanced industrial economies. To this impetus the Latin American economies reacted in varied fashion, with the result that structural differentiation among the countries and regions of the hemisphere, which of course existed before 1870, increased even further. By 1914 the economic contrasts in Latin America were far sharper than they had been a half-century or so earlier. A reorientation of economic processes to the world market and unequal development across sectors and regions were both, in fact, defining characteristics of the era. On this much there is more or less general agreement. Where scholars part company, however, is in interpreting the details of how this process came about in the first place and in assessing its implications for future policy alternatives in the area. The chapter will conclude with an examination of these differences of interpretation. First, however, it is useful to look more closely into the specific ways the international economy impinged on economic organization in Latin America. Product markets, above all export product markets, inasmuch as it was the swelling demand of the North Atlantic industrial centres for imports that propelled Latin American economic life forward, will be considered first. The adaptive response of the Latin American economies will then be reviewed through an exploration of changes in factor markets: land, labour and capital.

EXPORT MARKETS

As Latin America was drawn more deeply into the Atlantic economy, far-reaching changes in the pattern, and in some cases the geographical location, of production occurred in response to overseas demand for the area's minerals and its pastoral and agricultural products. Both consumption goods and industrial raw materials were shipped abroad in rising volume.

In the River Plate, a region that had counted for little, commercially speaking, even at the very end of the period of Spanish imperial rule, the opening up of Argentina and, on a smaller scale, Uruguay produced a stream of temperate zone commodities, notably livestock products and cereals. Improvements in sheep herds, through the importation of blooded stock and cross-breeding, combined with a substantial spread of sheep grazing to yield notable results even before mid-century; the growth of the industry continued at a rapid pace thereafter. From an export of only 1.6 million kilograms in 1840, for example, Argentina was able, on average, to export nearly 45 million kilograms of wool annually during the decade 1860–9. By the 1880s, wool exports averaged well over 100 million kilograms a year, and the annual average for 1895–9 reached 211 million kilograms. Wool exports subsequently fell, however, to an average of only 137 million kilograms in 1910–14. In Uruguay, foreign sales of wool and other products of sheep-farming tripled between 1876–80 and 1896–1900. While the total volume of Uruguayan production was much smaller than that of Argentina, the industry figured much more prominently in the export lists down to the end of the period. Wool exports from the two countries went mostly to the continent of Europe – chiefly France, Germany, Belgium and Austria. In 1913 a little under a fifth of the wool exported from the River Plate entered the British market.

In Argentina other export industries were experiencing substantial growth as well. Hides, a traditional product, earned about two-thirds the value of wool exports over most of the period and almost doubled in aggregate value from the mid-seventies to 1910–14. It was the development of refrigerated shipping in the 1870s, however, that paved the way for the swift rise of meat shipments from Argentina, and, to a lesser extent, Uruguay. Mutton was at first favoured, but by the turn of the century beef began to overshadow the volume of mutton being shipped out, thanks to an upgrading of the quality of herds and other technical improvements made after the 1860s. By 1910–14 the value of frozen and chilled beef exports, two relatively new products, had grown from the very small fraction of mutton exports that frozen beef shipments had represented as late as 1890–4 to six times the value of mutton exports. In volume, frozen mutton and lamb exports grew from 36,486 tons in 1894 to 58,688 tons in 1914; frozen beef, from 267 tons in 1894 to 328,287 tons in 1914. In 1914 there were also chilled beef exports amounting to 40,690 tons. And canned meat exports rose over the same interval from 1,374 tons to 13,590 tons. At the close of the period Uruguay was selling abroad about a fifth of the Argentine volume of frozen beef exports and about 15 per cent of the Argentine exports of mutton. Europe was the destination of virtually all shipments of meat exports from both Uruguay and Argentina, as it was for a variety of by-products of cattle-ranching.

It was during the late 1870s that Argentina became a net exporter of grains, a trade which began on a small scale but which quickly gained momentum. Between 1872 and 1895, the amount of pampa acreage under cultivation in all crops, especially grains, grew fifteen times, and in the next decade, the amount of acreage planted in wheat and maize alone more than doubled. Between 1880–4 and 1890–4 wheat was the major gainer, increasing twenty-three times in export value. In the next decade, however, the value of maize exports rose more rapidly, with a nearly six-fold gain. Rapid growth continued thereafter. From 1900–4 to 1910–14, maize exports more than doubled again, while wheat exports rose in value by approximately 42 per cent. By this last quinquennium the value of maize exports was just under that of wheat, and together they were almost three times as valuable as foreign sales of wool. In terms of export volumes, shipments of both wheat and maize moved erratically, reflecting both the natural production variability of agricultural goods and responses to price fluctuations. By 1911–13, however, wheat exports attained a level of 2.3–2.8 million tons, while maize exports peaked at around 4.8 million tons in 1912–13. Considering the modest amounts of both grains shipped abroad in the mid-1870s, the figures represent impressive increases in Argentine production.

Just before the First World War, Argentina's principal exports were, in descending order of importance (with values given in millions of gold pesos): wheat (78.1), maize (72.4), frozen and chilled beef (54), wool (51.9), hides (44) and linseed (41.0). Lesser exports included: mutton and lamb, other grains (oats, barley and rye) and quebracho extract and logs. From 1875 to 1914, according to estimates made by Carlos Díaz Alejandro, both the quantum and value of Argentine exports rose at a rate of at least 5 per cent a year.

Within the country the geographical distribution of economic activity had been almost wholly rearranged. The north-western region – in colonial times the principal zone for farming, ranching and artisan trades – had greatly declined in relative importance despite a sugar industry that served the growing domestic market and became the economic mainstay for part of the region. Instead, the pampa and areas to the west and north of Buenos Aires had been opened up as the main zones for colonization, with wheat-growing in turn shifting from the areas of agricultural colonization towards the pampas south and west of Buenos

Aires and wool production shifting from the pampas into Patagonia.

More than any other Latin American country, Argentina was almost wholly given over, directly and indirectly, to the export economy, thanks to which the Argentines attained an average standard of living notably higher than that achieved by citizens of the other Latin American republics. The Buenos Aires of 1914 symbolized the changes. In place of the primitive outpost of empire that stood beside the Río de la Plata as the nineteenth century began, there had grown up a burgeoning, cosmopolitan metropolis managing a hugely increased flow of goods in and out of the country. Only Uruguay approached Argentina in the comprehensiveness of its involvement in world trade and in its Europeanization.

Chilean participation in the international economy also underwent sweeping changes between 1870 and 1914, albeit with rather fewer domestic repercussions than in Argentina, owing partly to the nature and location of the principal export industries and partly to the fact that Chile carried into the nineteenth century a denser institutional structure from the colonial era than did its neighbours to the east. At the outset of the period silver, wheat and copper headed the country's export lists, mostly coming from firms under national ownership. For copper, in fact, Chile was the world's largest producer until 1880. The peak years of production were 1869–76, when a production level of around 52,000 tons was attained. Some 43.6 per cent of world copper production came from Chile as late as 1878, although after a swift decline the Chilean share of world production had fallen to 25.3 per cent in 1880, with a further slump thereafter to 9.7 per cent in 1890 and only 4.3 per cent in 1900. The lowest point in this production drop was reached in 1897, whereupon production remained stagnant until 1906 at around 26,000 tons. High-grade ore deposits had been exhausted, and the modest technical capacity of small and medium-sized Chilean mining companies proved inadequate to reverse this trend. Shortly after the opening of the twentieth century foreign mining engineers and capital had entered Chile to inaugurate a new era in copper: the age of large-scale, mass mining techniques. Under new management, huge deposits of low-grade ores were opened up and the modern Chilean copper industry got under way. By 1908 production had risen to 42,000 tons, its highest level since 1884; by 1917 it was 102,500 tons.

Had Chile been monocultural in its export structure, the interval between copper booms would have been one of acute depression, but the country's resources together with the buoyancy of world market demand afforded a number of other options. Wheat exports, which were not unimportant by mid-century, contributed greatly to foreign exchange earnings over the next seventy-five years, with the grain going primarily to Europe and, in smaller volume, to elsewhere in Latin America. Although it was highly unstable in a cyclical manner, the wheat export trade was gradually expanding up to 1893, with a long-term decline, masked partly by a continuing high level of instability, visible in the twentieth century. The average annual volume of wheat exports for 1870–4 was just over one million metric tons; a decade later it averaged 1.25 million metric tons; for 1910–14, however, only 395,000 metric tons. Wool, too, was shipped abroad in fairly substantial quantities. About 18,780 metric tons were exported annually from 1870–4; approximately 28,860 metric tons in 1890–4; with a jump to over 120,000 metric tons annually from 1912. The quantity sold in the U.K. in 1913, for example, represented more than a third of that supplied by Argentina and was more than Uruguay was shipping at the time. Frozen mutton was being exported on about the scale of Uruguay's sales abroad. Some silver was sold to the world market, as was tin, although Chilean exports of tin were only about one-sixth those of Bolivia. From around 1900, after the decline of silver, Bolivia's export sector depended over-whelmingly on tin.

It was nitrates, however, that supplied the main impetus to keep the Chilean export sector so markedly expansive between copper booms. Destined chiefly for continental European markets – especially the German and, to a lesser degree, the French – and for the North American market, the exportation of nitrates had begun long before the period under review and had reached 59,000 metric tons in 1879. But the real export bonanza, one of unprecedented magnitude for Chile, followed the War of the Pacific. Production (and exports) from northern Chile soared, from 356,000 metric tons in 1881 to 1.5 million in 1900 and 2.7 million metric tons in 1913. According to an estimate by Marcos Mamalakis, nitrates (and iodine) export taxes financed over 50 per cent of total government expenditures for the three decades following 1900, while the resource surpluses of the nitrate sector averaged 14 per cent of gross domestic product in Chile between 1882 and 1930. Although the export-induced transformation of the Chilean economy was less comprehensive than that of Argentina or Uruguay, it unarguably became more 'modernized' than did, say, Mexico, Brazil, or Colombia, let alone such countries as Peru, Bolivia, or Ecuador.

Brazilian experience between 1870 and the First World War was focused mainly on the coffee export boom which had started in the 1820s, 1830s, and 1840s. An immense supply of suitable land, with appropriate climate, was available in a relatively unoccupied state, as had been the case when Argentine cereal and livestock production was growing so rapidly. Consequently, supply conditions were highly elastic. From 216,120 tons annually in 1871–5, coffee exports rose to 311,760 tons annually in 1881–5 and to 740,280 tons in 1901–5. During this last quinquennium a crisis in the market led Brazil to institute the first of the coffee valorization schemes that were to play such a prominent role in organizing the marketing of subsequent increases in production. Thanks in part to the valorization scheme and other control efforts, and to a recovery of demand, the value of the 826,908 tons annually exported in 1906–10 reached an average of £27,877,000, a marked gain on the previous peak in coffee export earnings of £20,914,000 during 1891–5, not to mention the £10,487,800 the export crop fetched, on average, between 1871 and 1875. From the 1870s to 1911, coffee exports accounted for more than half the value of all Brazilian exports, reaching nearly two-thirds of the total in the 1890s. The largest market for the product was in the United States, but substantial amounts were shipped to Germany and to France.

Other Brazilian products were exported during this period, some increasing and others declining in value and volume. The impact on Brazil of these developments was quite limited, however, in comparison with the leading position the country commanded in the world coffee market. Sugar was one of the losers. Sugar exports rose, irregularly, from an average of 169,337 tons annually in 1871–5 to 238,074 in 1881–5, but afterwards the figures show a substantial decline, to only 51,338 tons annually for the 1906–10 period. Beet sugar and Caribbean, especially Cuban, cane production had gained a strong edge in the major world markets, notwithstanding the efforts, only partially successful, of the Brazilian government to promote the modernization of this traditional export industry. By value, sugar shipments fell from nearly 12 per cent of all Brazilian exports in the 1870s to under 2 per cent in the decade 1901–10.

Tobacco production for sale abroad made some gains in the north-east during the latter half of the 1880s; exports in 1913, mostly to Germany, reached 29,388 tons, a figure which represented around 2.5 per cent of aggregate Brazilian exports. Cacao, another north-eastern Brazilian export, enjoyed a boom of sorts, especially after the introduction of high-yielding varieties of the crop in the early 1900s. France, Germany, and the United States provided the chief markets, as they did for the rising cacao exports in the same period from Ecuador, the Dominican Republic and Venezuela. Of the Latin American exporters of cacao, Brazil, which sold just under 17,000 tons in 1900, lagged slightly behind Ecuador, which sold almost 19,000 tons in that year. By 1914, the cacao export figures for Brazil and Ecuador were 40,766 and 47,210 tons respectively. Of major importance in Ecuador's foreign trade, cacao accounted for a little under 4 per cent of Brazilian exports in the pre-war years. Neither tobacco nor cacao, however, could offset the depressive effect of sugar's decline on the enfeebled economic structure of the populous north-east.

Brazil had begun the period under discussion with sizeable cotton exports, due largely to the stimulus provided by the Civil War which had drastically curtailed exports from the United States. Nearly 109 million lb of cotton were exported by Brazil annually between 1871 and 1875. Then the recovery of North American production and growing output elsewhere cut into Brazil's markets, with the result that by 1896–1900, the average annual export of raw cotton had dropped to only 24.6 million lb. A recovery ensued, with Brazilian cotton exports climbing to over 36 million lb in 1912, but a considerable portion of Brazilian cotton production was increasingly retained for use in the growing textile industry of the country, which as early as 1904, for instance, took some 35,000 tons of the fibre. Only around 2 per cent or so of the value of Brazilian exports came from cotton sales by the second decade of this century.

Rubber provided the last major Brazilian export surge before the First World War, a development in which Peru and Bolivia also shared. From the Amazon region occupied in 1880 by the three countries came 8,635 tons, overwhelmingly Brazilian in origin. By 1910 the comparable figure stood at 26,693 tons, with shipments going to the industrial centres of North America and Europe. In 1914 Brazilian production alone was more than 70,000 tons, with additional gains negated by continually falling prices, thereafter. Prices had climbed almost steadily until 1910, but Brazilian rubber output kept rising even after the market price began to weaken. For the decade 1900–10 rubber yielded 28 per cent of aggregate Brazilian export earnings, compared with only a little over 5 per cent in the 1870s. By the onset of the First World War, however, the rubber boom, a stunning export performance while it lasted, was over and with it vanished hopes for prosperity in the vast forests of Amazonia.

None of the export expansion which affected the parts of Brazil north of Rio de Janeiro, however, was to prove anything like as consequential as the coffee boom, which started around Rio and then spread through São Paulo, with spillover effects in other southern states. A secondary impetus to the region's economic expansion came from shipments of hides, which were around 5 per cent of Brazilian exports just before the First World War. A great deal of the country, therefore, experienced only marginally the transforming impact of export-propelled growth. It could be said, with only slight exaggeration, that the region benefiting from the major coffee boom was virtually a new country. Unlike northern and central Brazil, the south had lingered in economic obscurity until nineteenth-century capitalist expansion distributed a new set of production possibilities around the globe. When this occurred, the south left the older parts of the country far behind.

With the extraordinary economic changes it underwent during the Porfiriato, Mexico provides the other striking case of national participation in export commodity markets. Attributable to the country's ample resource endowment and its advantageous location, this growth owed much also to the supportive policies of the Porfiriato. Located in the northern hemisphere, Mexico was relatively close to major shipping routes to Europe, the market for some 22 per cent of its exports by the end of the Porfiriato (the U.K. chiefly, but with smaller amounts going to France, Germany and other countries). It was adjacent to the expanding U.S. market, to which transport costs were low, and which consequently took three-quarters of Mexican exports at that time. Doubtless the size and rate of growth of that market and the diversity of Mexican resources interacted to account for the salient feature of the Mexican export pattern: namely, the large number of products composing the trade. Silver exports rose from 607,000 kilograms in 1877–8 to 2.3 million kilograms in 1910–11, by which time they accounted for approximately a third of Mexican exports. Gold production, which had grown from just over one thousand kilograms in 1877–8 to 37,100 kilograms in 1910–11, accounted for another sixth, while copper and henequen each represented nearly a tenth. But a wide range of products each contributed between one and 5 per cent of aggregate export value at the close of the Porfiriato: rubber, hides, coffee, lead, cattle, vanilla, chick peas, ixtle, fine woods. Still lesser amounts of export earnings came from such products as fruits, chile, beans and vegetables, honey, beer, tobacco, straw hats, chicle, zinc, antimony and mercury, and a number of others. In the opening decade of the twentieth century, a phenomenal export growth began in the petroleum industry so that by the time Díaz left office Mexico ranked third among the world's petroleum producing nations.

The volume and prices of many of the products Mexico sent abroad exhibited a great deal of instability, and even the long-term trends were mixed. For example, coffee more than doubled in export volume between 1877–8 and 1910–11, but grew no more until the end of the period. While cattle exports were 11,300 head in 1878–9 and 170,200 head in 1910–11, the peak year had been 1896–7 when 313,600 head had been shipped north. Sugar exports varied widely, peaking in 1904–5, while other crops such as vanilla, chick peas and henequen were shipped out in far greater volume at the end of the period than they had attained at the beginning and experienced a generally rising production trend throughout the period. Henequen exports, for instance, had reached 13.3 million kilograms in 1878–9, but rose to the level of 123 million kilograms in 1910–11. Minerals, too, were being sold abroad in growing volume over most of the period.

Except for the repercussions of major business cycles in export markets, the very diversity of Mexican exports tended to provide somewhat more stability for the external sector as a whole than would have come from a more concentrated export pattern. From the 1870s to 1910 the aggregate volume and value rose markedly. Between 1877–8 and 1910–11 the change in aggregate value was, in constant pesos, from 29.3 million to 293.7 million. And since not all of the resources tapped by export expansion were located near each other, many regions were touched by the flourishing foreign trade. Minerals and ranching, for example, drew business northward; the henequen trade, to Yucatán; oil, to the Gulf coast. Although none of these regions was changed sufficiently to create a virtually new subnational economy, as happened in Brazil, the wonder is that material progress was not more pervasive than it was. For all practical purposes most Mexicans were as much by-passed by external sector growth as were the Brazilians of the north-east who remained on the sidelines when coffee pulled the economic centre of gravity southwards.

Peru launched its nineteenth-century export expansion on the basis of guano and, later, nitrates. Brought to an abrupt end by ineffective national policies and the War of the Pacific, this early phase was superseded by a second, longer period of expansion that began in the early 1880s and carried well beyond the First World War. In this second export phase, the product base was broader. From the sierras came wool (sheep and alpaca), along with silver, gold, copper and other minerals; from the interior, coffee, coca and rubber; from the coast, sugar and cotton. The total value of these exports fell from £1.9 million in 1880 to £1.4 million three years later, but gradually, on an uneven path, the export sector recovered by 1889 and eleven years later the total value amounted to £3.8 million. By 1910, the value of Peruvian exports stood at £6.2 million.

Sugar and copper led Peruvian exports in the 1890s; cotton and rubber gained in relative weight during the following decade. In the decade of the First World War, petroleum rose in relative importance while rubber quickly declined to only 5 per cent of Peruvian exports in 1915, compared with 18 per cent in 1910. From 1890 to 1915, there was an overall decline in the relative importance of silver. From 33 per cent of exports in the former year, it fell to 5 per cent in the latter. Yet, except for a decline in gold production in the early 1900s, the output of most export products rose, with fluctuations, up to 1914, demonstrating the growing productive capabilities of the Peruvian economy. Nevertheless, despite growth, product diversification and a geographical distribution of export industries, the export expansion of Peru appears to have wrought even fewer beneficial changes domestically than did Mexico's similarly diversified and dispersed export pattern.

Elsewhere in Latin America, the late nineteenth-century export economy tended to produce a simpler structure, often on the basis of a monocultural pattern of development. In Colombia, for example, coffee was the mainstay of the external sector from the late 1880s. There had been a notable growth in coffee production in the 1860s and early 1870s, a period in which the tobacco export cycle that had begun in the 1840s had faltered. Thereafter, exports of coffee from Colombia had fallen, but by 1880 the exports had recovered to 107,600 bags (of 60 kilograms each). It remained around this level until it started upwards again in the late 1880s. By 1889, after a phase of strong price recovery that peaked in the early 1890s, exports rose to 475,400 bags, or approximately 70 per cent of aggregate Colombian exports; in 1898, to 531,400 bags. A steep decline in world coffee prices discouraged further growth in the volume of exports for several years, but eventually output resumed its rise, and by 1913 and 1914 exports were just over a million bags each year. For the decade 1905–14, coffee exports amounted to between 40 and 46 per cent of Colombian exports. By the turn of the century, banana exports had also entered the picture, thanks partly to the organization of foreign enterprise in that field (United Fruit began operating in Colombia in 1901). Exports rose from 263,000 bunches in 1901 to 1,400,000 bunches in 1906, to slightly more than three million bunches in 1909. For the decade 1910–14, they made up 9 per cent of Colombian exports. But neither bananas nor other export products – gold, hides, chinchona, cotton, tobacco – whose market behaviour could, for the most part, be best described as fitful, could overcome the basic instability of an export economy based so heavily on coffee.

From the 1830s, when it replaced cacao, until the 1920s, when it was replaced by oil, coffee was also Venezuela's principal export. Indeed, until the First World War when it was overtaken by Colombia, Venezuela was, after Brazil, the region's leading coffee exporter. The export sectors of the Central American and Caribbean economies were dominated by a variety of tropical agricultural goods; notably, bananas, coffee, sugar and tobacco.

DOMESTIC MARKETS

Changes in domestic product markets, while no less momentous, may be treated somewhat more simply at the regional level; there was less inter-country variation than was the case with export product markets. In every country, these markets were influenced by pronounced changes in consumption habits (the result, doubtless, of new product availabilities) among the rapidly expanding urban populace. To this must be added, in the case of southern South America, the new consumption preferences which came with relatively large-scale immigration, a phenomenon which installed European tastes also among rural people in contrast to the marked urban/rural cultural cleavage that prevailed over most of Latin America. In no few instances, the growth of urban markets for foodstuffs provided a stimulus of some significance for rural production in outlying areas: e.g., the Mendoza wine region and the Tucumán sugar region in Argentina, the Morelos sugar region in Mexico.

Urban consumer markets for manufactures were supplied heavily by British exporters, but with strong challenges from Germany and the United States and with contributions from France and, in lesser amounts, many other countries. A whole host of products either appeared for the first time or came to be consumed in notably larger volume than previously. Cotton manufactures from Europe, Britain in particular, played a conspicuous role in the consumer product markets of Latin America, but on a smaller scale came also imports of woollen piece goods (where climate permitted), linens, silks and a limited volume of footwear and ready-made clothing. Fine ceramic ware, jewelry and household furnishings also were imported along with soaps and toiletries, drugs, paper and a wide variety of hardware goods. Automobiles were added to the import lists toward the end of the period – and even, in the case of sixteen units shipped to Brazil from France and Italy in 1913, aircraft.

Not all such manufactured products, however, came from abroad. In the old colonial heartlands, artisan industries never entirely died out in the face of factory-made imports, especially as a supply source for the interior rural and provincial markets. And in nearly all the republics there were established before the First World War some local factories producing ironware, tobacco products, textiles (cottons and woollens) and soft goods in the coarser grades, furniture, glassware, matches, candles, perfumes, pharmaceuticals, paints, saddles, shoes and boots, other leather goods, foodstuffs and beverages, soaps, some hardware and so on. In at least the major countries, evidence of this incipient industrialization was reflected in changes in the structure of import schedules. To be sure, local industrialization was both limited and scattered, and production was not continuously expanding. Experience in this respect was quite mixed from country to country. Nevertheless, the years 1870 to 1914 may appropriately be called the dawn of the factory age in Latin America – and with it came the new social relations implied by trade union organizations and imported European varieties of social criticism.

Besides shifts in consumer tastes, however, striking changes in production methods brought additional changes in internal product markets by dramatically enlarging the market for factory-made capital goods over what it had been earlier in the nineteenth century, when more archaic, and locally provided, production technologies were nearly all-pervasive. Indeed, the growing prominence of producer goods in the import trade is one of the features that most distinguished the 1870–1914 period from, say, the import structure of a half-century earlier. That most of the new types of producer goods were imported simply meant that the export industries had begun to function as a capital goods sector, not merely as a means of paying for consumer speciality imports.

Producer goods markets also became far more complex. Some such goods came from Latin American manufacturers of construction materials and newly established local foundries, iron works and machine shops, some of which had been originally set up to handle repairs and maintenance on imported products. The great bulk of the newer producer goods, however, came, as mentioned previously, from abroad, chiefly from Britain, Germany, the U.S. and France. Chemicals and dyestuffs, paints and varnishes, yarns and threads, lubricating oil and grease, coal and coke, iron and steel in a variety of forms (sheets and plates, bars and rods, structural forms), copper (plates, ingots, wiring, moulded forms), other metals in intermediate states of processing, rolling stock for railway and tramway companies, machine belting, tools and implements, electrical machinery and instruments, and engines, motors, machinery of all sorts for mining, agriculture, local factories and new municipal activities (e.g., waterworks and gasworks, light and power companies) – all came in a generally growing volume to hasten the absorption of Latin America into industrial society, long before deliberate import-substituting industrialization programmes were launched. It should not pass unnoticed that new producer services also entered the market, financial and insurance services especially, but others as well: business information, new marketing channels, grain elevators and cold storage facilities, construction firms and so on. The increased commercial sophistication of the area was, in fact, one of the most striking transformations of the age.

Finally, another category of product market, that for collective goods and services, merits mention. More technically advanced military equipment, and sometimes the training services to go with it, figured among the consumption mix of the Latin America of 1870 to 1914. In the case of armaments, imports continued to supply a portion of the market, as they had for decades, but state arsenals and local manufactories were of some consequence in the larger countries. One should not exaggerate the weight of militarism in the economy, however, for all the prominence of military leaders in politics; the real resources actually devoted to weaponry were trifling compared with the practice in most countries of Europe at the time. Far more significant were collective services for the civilian economy. Municipal services (e.g., gasworks, tramways, street lighting, waterworks and sanitation), telecommunications systems, rail transport and modern port facilities were among the more innovative collective goods in this period, and in the major cities of all countries they were supplied by a mixture of domestic and foreign inputs. In most instances, foreign capital participated in the provision of these services through both direct and portfolio investments, while the requisite engineering and managerial skills were similarly, on many occasions, brought from far afield. Yet local investors also put their savings to work in these attractive new fields of endeavour, and native engineers, lawyers, accountants and others were usually numbered among the employees of such firms.

No country was left untouched by these changes in internal product markets, although the scope of the transformation was especially great in the River Plate area, southern Brazil, Chile, and to a lesser extent, Mexico. Moreover, not only were the items traded in these markets changing but it was also the case that, on account of new telegraphic communication systems and new transport facilities, the articulation of local and regional markets within the larger system was being altered substantially.

THE CHARACTER AND FUNCTIONS OF NEW PRODUCT · MARKETS

What stands out clearly in the nature of product markets is that Latin America came to be doubly joined to the world market. On the one hand, this engagement is manifest in the very substantial commitment of resources that was necessary to develop the supply of commodities shipped to export product markets. In view of how elastic the long-term supply conditions turned out to be for most of Latin America's export products, despite the limitations of an economic structure which carried over from colonial times and deteriorated badly during the first half of the nineteenth century, one must conclude that this process of organizing for export expansion must have supplied the central dynamic for national resource allocation processes during the period under review. True, regional agricultural development was, here and there, stimulated by population growth and a rising urban demand in the national markets, and most of the scattered instances of nineteenth-century industrialization – textile mills, food and beverage industries, paper factories, ironworks and so on – were based upon these local and regional gains. Such instances aside, however, it was nevertheless the case that foreign, not domestic, demand called the tune. For the volume, value and variety of Latin American exports to have increased as they did, a great deal in the way of possible alternatives in resource use must have been subordinated to this overriding consideration.

On the other hand, changes in domestic product markets also reveal how heavily committed to participation in foreign trade the aggregate consumption patterns of the different Latin American nations came to be. For a few export products, a portion of the growing total output was diverted to meeting increases in domestic demand. But there were not many parallels to Brazilian or Mexican cotton, in which more and more of the volume of the commodity produced came to be absorbed by local manufacturing set up to satisfy domestic markets. Important though incipient industrialization was, for the most part the paramount development of the age in domestic product markets was the growing and increasingly varied supply of goods and services procured from abroad. Indeed, one of the many as yet insufficiently researched topics in Latin American economic history is the extent to which small factories established earlier in the nineteenth century to supply fabricated goods for local and regional use were, with the spread of rail transport (and a consequent reduction of the protection afforded by high overland shipping costs), displaced by factories more centrally located or by imports.

The composition of Latin American imports yields further insight into the institutional mechanisms at work. In effect, a safeguard for continuity of the system was provided through the large portion of foreign exchange devoted to purchasing foreign-supplied consumer superfluities. By providing a cushion for absorbing fluctuations in export earnings, this use of foreign exchange in effect shielded from such fluctuations the capacity to import producer goods. So long, in other words, as consumption could be treated as a residual claim on export earnings, the system could reproduce itself and the prevailing set of relationships was more assured of survival. It was only later that this structure came to be undermined when debt management finally fell victim to the disordered state of public finance, when shortfalls in foreign exchange earnings could no longer, because of the political consequences, be so readily dealt with by import curtailment and when a changed structure of imports caused the current levels of national production to depend more heavily on a continuing stream of imported fuels, raw materials and intermediate goods.

Broadly speaking, the supply of new products to Latin American markets seems to have been reasonably competitive, the more so by the end of the period when German, U.S. and French exporters had gained on their British counterparts. This is not to say that, locally, the sale of goods to ultimate consumers always took place under conditions resembling pure competition, or that elements of monopolistic competition were absent from the larger scene. Far from it. Buyers' knowledge of market alternatives, one may safely assume, was often far from complete at the retail level and the local marketing networks into which imports fed were often constricted and sometimes subject to intermediary manipulation. Buyer (or middleman) attachment to certain styles and grades of imports, or to particular supply sources, appears also to have been present. In the case of domestic manufactures, there were also monopoly profits created by an early, somewhat sporadic drift into protectionism. While the liberal economic model tended to dominate policy formation in this period, it is by no means true that an open economy growth model was universally and continuously accepted by Latin American elites throughout the period. In Mexico and Uruguay, after the turn of the century, and even earlier in Argentina, Brazil, Chile, Colombia and Peru, the liberal growth pattern was questioned and modifications were made in *laissez-faire* policies: to cover higher local costs of production and yield a measure of monopoly profit.

Yet the kinds of 'monopoly profits' Latin American social critics have decried, retrospectively, in addressing the historic role of the world market were probably not those that sprang from supplier collusion, from overwhelming supplier control of a broadly defined product market, let alone from protectionist policies. Rather, since very nearly all product innovation originated abroad, it was European and U.S. suppliers who were in a position to harvest the steady stream of temporary monopoly profits that came from bringing new products to market before imitating rivals could catch up. In this sense it seems incontrovertible that practically all innovational profits realized during the period accrued to Latin America's trading partners and that foreigners, taken as a whole or as a category (not as individual firms), did indeed monopolize the process of innovation. With some licence, then, one can speak of substantial foreign monopoly profits as a factor of reckoning throughout the period.

Less frequently did Latin American suppliers enjoy a similar advantage in their export markets, although there were some cases of this. Chinchona (for quinine) from Colombia, coca (for cocaine) from Peru and Bolivia, rubber from Amazonia, nitrates from northern Chile and Bolivian tin were instances in point, to which one might conceivably add bananas and coffee. But by the early 1890s Colombian chinchona had been displaced by Asian production, rubber suffered a similar fate a couple of decades later, the demand for coca was not great, and marketing intermediaries, rather than growers, were the ones best able to garner the banana profits. For a while, an element of monopoly profit doubtless accrued to the Brazilian coffee industry as a whole by virtue of that country's early predominant position in the world coffee market, but the need for a valorization scheme soon after the turn of the century showed how much this position had been eroded by an expanding supply of the crop, both in Brazil and elsewhere in Latin America. In tin, too, the structure of the market, thanks to a running down of European sources, long gave leadership to Bolivian suppliers, with lesser amounts coming from Chile and Mexico. By the twentieth century, however, Asia was gaining in prominence as a source of this metal, and while local ownership was at first dominant in the industry of Bolivia, this ownership was, in effect, later to denationalize itself by moving the seat of organization abroad. Nitrates probably represented the most durable market advantage held by Latin American suppliers, with Chile the chief exporter. There were, however, some substitute sources of the fertilizer even before European technical advances in the production of synthetic nitrates undercut the industry so dramatically after the First World War.

FACTOR MARKETS

Land

The far-reaching changes in product markets would, of course, have been unthinkable in the absence of correspondingly extensive transmutations in factor markets. Of these, it seems reasonable first to consider land, using the term in its economic sense to designate all natural resources. These resources were (*a*) fundamental to the nature of the export economies that arose and (*b*) critical in conditioning the social and political arrangements of the period. For all of the alterations in economic structure, land, in its narrower agricultural sense, remained the basic means of production for the majority of the population in every country, and virtually all Latin American exports (crops, livestock products and minerals) could be characterized as being primarily land-intensive products, even when, as in the case of twentieth-century

Chilean copper, capital-intensive methods were employed in their production.

In some ways, the single most striking economic change for the period as a whole was the massive increase in the supply of land as a mainspring for capitalist development. This came principally from three sources and as a function of both substantial increases in demand for the products of land and a considerable extension and improvement of transport networks, international as well as national.

A large part of the new supply came from private appropriations of the vast public domain. In northern Mexico and southern South America, the indigenous population had, early on in this period, been pushed aside, sometimes with armed force, to make way for the installation of land management more attuned to the exigencies of market conditions. In between these two extremities of Latin America, the frontier of economic appropriation was similarly pushed back, into regions either only sparsely settled or regions before that time only loosely integrated, if at all, into the capitalist institutional fabric. In Mexico and Central America, for instance, the extensive margin of cultivation spread out from the fringes of the already developed highland zones and spilled into sub-tropical areas and coastal territories, whence came much of the tropical produce being shipped abroad in increasing quantity. A similar diffusion of commercial production occurred in Venezuela, Colombia and Ecuador, with the added feature that in the first two there was an extension of ranching-based settlement into interior savannahs known as *llanos*.

At least two types of frontier expansion can be discerned. In the first case, settlement along the extensive margin corresponded directly to the climb in production of export commodities, as in the southern Brazilian coffee frontier or the Patagonian wool frontier. In other instances, however, a displacement effect was in evidence. Just as, for example, the eighteenth-century indigo boom in Guatemala and El Salvador had shifted cattle production to Nicaragua and Costa Rica, the spread of Central American coffee cultivation in the nineteenth century pushed food production and cattle ranching to even more outlying zones in the region. Similar displacement shifts can be observed elsewhere. Together, the export impetus and cultivation displacement reworked the settlement map of the continent.

In Peru, the margins of commercial agriculture were pushed out along the coast with the extension of irrigation, enlarged in scattered pockets of the highlands or sierras and, during the rubber boom especially, extended into the Amazonian interior. This last development was replicated in Colombia and Ecuador, but the chief locus of Amazonian expansion was, of course, in Brazil. Meanwhile, in Brazil, the coffee frontier advanced southward, precipitating a related agricultural expansion that moved into the interior, towards Paraguay and Bolivia, along a coastal zone that extended from Rio de Janeiro to well below Porto Alegre. In Argentina, besides the already noted southward movement of commercialization, which Chile, too, experienced, the rural economy incorporated additional new land to the west and the north-west of Buenos Aires, extending to the zones of new cultivation lying along the Andes in one direction and to the Mesopotamian region between Uruguay and Paraguay on the other. Uruguay gradually filled out its borders with the spread of ranching, and there was even some enlargement of the areas under cultivation or in ranching in Bolivia and Paraguay. An increase in the commercialization of forest products affected portions of Brazil, southern Chile, Paraguay and the Caribbean coast of Central America, among other places.

Subsoil natural resources were brought into the scheme of production from deposits scattered over a considerable portion of Latin America, but especially in north and north-central Mexico (where portions of the Gulf coast were also opened up with petroleum finds) and the sierra of Peru, Bolivia and Chile. The northern desert of Chile also acquired economic significance with the rise of the nitrate industry.

The institutional mechanisms for bringing these lands and mineral resources into production varied, although in mining the customary procedure was an official concession of usufruct. As for the surface of the land, part of the public domain was disposed of in concessions to railway companies to help pay for the construction of lines. Part went as payment to land survey companies. Part went to land colonization companies and projects, either *bona fide* schemes, such as were prevalent in Argentina and southern Brazil, or thinly disguised frauds and misguided projects which never reached fruition. Other portions of the public domain were alienated through land grants and sales at nominal prices: in medium-sized parcels in some instances, such as occurred in the coffee zones of Colombia and Costa Rica, but often in large grants to individuals and land companies. Occasionally, the holders of government bonds were compensated with titles to land, while in other cases, land grants were made with the hope of promoting new cultivations, especially of export crops. In more than a few instances land in the public domain was simply occupied and later claimed by force of possession, legal chicane, or a type of squatters' rights – an expedient more likely to be successful when the claimants were wealthy and/or politically influential. It goes without saying that by no means was all of the 'vacant' public land so claimed actually unpopulated.

By means both questionable and legal, huge amounts of land formerly held by the state and most of the then-known commercial deposits of minerals fell under private control, a control that was sometimes exercised by an individual or a family and sometimes by a corporate enterprise. The latter form of business organization predominated in mining. Owing to the size of many Latin American landowning families, however, the corporate device was also resorted to with some frequency as a means of apportioning land rights among numerous heirs. So far as large rural properties and the corporately held mines are concerned, actual managerial control, in either corporate or non-corporate properties, was, in most instances, likely to be exercised on behalf of absentee owners, but there were also a fair number of cases in which large landholders took at least a regular, if not necessarily continuous, hand in the organization of production and marketing. In the cases of corporate land ownership, the ownership group sometimes comprised European or U.S. investors who never actually saw their distant properties; this was true, for example, of some of the British-owned cattle companies of the River Plate, or American-held banana and sugar companies in Central America and the Caribbean. The situation was usually similar for the larger foreign corporations that operated mining properties, some of which had been put together by acquiring smaller, nationally owned concessions. But in other cases the foreign owners actually took up residence in Latin America, as happened with the Gildemeister properties in Peru, the Hochschild holdings further south, more than a few estancias in Argentina and Uruguay, and northern Mexican ranches. From southern Brazil southwards, there were a great many instances in which European immigrants became rural property holders, either on arrival or at some subsequent date. Elsewhere as well, albeit much less frequently, immigrants became the owners or owner-managers of farms and ranches, as, for instance, in the case of Guatemalan coffee *fincas*.

The huge scale of the new properties carved out of the public domain has received a great deal of attention, and properly so; it was a factor in virtually every country, but reached particularly notable proportions in

Argentina, Mexico and Brazil. But this should not lead one to overlook the other places in which land colonization projects and spontaneous migration led to a spread of farming by smallholders or to relatively modest medium-sized farms and ranches. Moreover, size was a distinctly relative matter. The large agricultural estates of, say, highland Guatemala or parts of the Ecuadorian or Peruvian sierra were hardly on a par with the vast livestock ranches of the pampa or Patagonia or with those of the northern reaches of Chihuahua or Durango.

Mining, a field in which the largest operations were almost invariably foreign controlled, save perhaps for the early years of the Patiño tin empire in Bolivia, was similarly varied in respect of the scale of ownership units. Small mines were to be found throughout the mineral-bearing portions of Latin America, generally operated by nationals. Medium-sized mining properties were somewhat more likely to involve foreign participation, albeit they were usually immigrants who had come to seek their fortunes in Latin America, some with the thought, not always realized, of eventually returning to their homelands. It was this medium-sized mining property which typically formed a basis for some of the more prominent local accumulations of wealth: e.g., the families of Proaño, Fernandini, Gallo, Rizo Patrón, Boza, Bentín and Mujica of Peru, or Ossa, Puelma, Cousiño and Errazuriz in Chile. In no few instances, though, local owners were eventually bought out when their mining properties looked particularly promising, with such concessions forming the basis of the holdings of large foreign-owned companies. For Latin America as a whole, this process of denationalization was probably much more significant in mining than it was for rural properties, even though non-resident foreign ownerships of agricultural land did loom prominently in certain regions: e.g., Cuban sugar plantations, the banana plantations of Central America and Colombia, Mexican ranching and so on.

The second major source of land expansion came from the conversion to more commercially efficient use of lands belonging to the traditional estates, or haciendas, to use the customary generic term for them. Most commonly, this conversion was triggered when railway lines were laid into new regions; sometimes, when coast-wise shipping was improved, or when new national or regional markets opened up. This happened, for instance, with the growth of capital cities and major ports or with the upsurge of mining activity, or with the growth of new provincial market centres on the basis of new transport patterns. Sometimes this commercialization entailed bringing previously unused estate land into cultivation or into use as pasture with the help of hired labour, *peones*, or tenant farmers and sharecroppers of one sort or another, depending on circumstances. At other times, conflicts arose over attempts by landowners to wrest a larger demesne from the parcels occupied by tenants with various types of claims. If intrusions into the public domain represented expansion at the extensive margin, this second process of land conversion represented a growth of land supply along the intensive margin. The process tended to be concentrated in the long-settled parts of the continent, mostly, but not always, in agricultural regions serving inland markets.

This commercialization of traditional landholdings had in some places the effect of creating a rather more active market in land than had existed during the long colonial era. The results, however, were quite mixed, reflecting the extraordinary diversity of conditions among the productive regions of Latin America. In some places, the Mexican Bajío and central Chile, for example, haciendas (and smaller farming units) appear to have undergone a process of subdivision between 1870 and 1914, so that there were more units in the picture by the end of the period than there had been at the beginning. Agricultural estates were also bought and sold so that subdivision was not simply associated with inheritance transfers. In scattered parts of Latin America, there was even a tendency for a yeomanry to proliferate, either through settlement of new land or through a redistribution, via the market, of older land titles. This is not to say that the large hacienda disappeared, for a concentration in large holdings was still characteristic of the land tenure system over most of Latin America, but it does serve to indicate the spreading impact of commercialization in this factor market.

On the other hand, there were also older areas where the pull of market demand and changes in production technology seem to have precipitated a very strong drive toward land concentration, through the amalgamation of properties into ever larger production units. The sugar-producing areas of north-eastern Brazil and coastal Peru exemplified this development, but were by no means the only areas where this occurred. In some sections of central Chile and Mexico, the enlargement of initially large properties also took place, as it did in portions of Ecuador, highland Peru and elsewhere. Further, while a shift toward larger sugar mills seems to have provided the impetus for land concentration wherever sugar cultivation and milling came to be combined with rail transport of cane and steam engines in processing, the land tenure consequences of developments in other crops were not necessarily uniform. The advancing coffee frontier in Colombia and Costa Rica, for example, spawned more smallholder properties than were to be found among the coffee *fincas* of Guatemala, while the coffee *fazendas* of southern Brazil tended on the whole to be larger still. Typical cereal cultivation in Argentina was carried out, most often by tenant farmers, on larger holdings than was the case in, say, southern Chile, Rio Grande do Sul in Brazil, Michoacán in Mexico, or the Mantaro Valley in Peru.

A third source of agricultural land for the land market came from corporate holdings in the more traditional areas: lands belonging to the church or to assorted religious or welfare organizations (such as the *beneficencias públicas* of Peru) and land belonging to both indigenous communities and Spanish-founded communities. In Mexico, for example, liberal-inspired legal reforms paved the way from the 1850s on for an alienation of many of these properties into private hands, while laicist movements elsewhere – e.g., Colombia in the 1860s, Guatemala and Venezuela in the 1870s, Ecuador in the 1890s – also sought to diminish ecclesiastical ownership of real property. Market purchase as well as legal manoeuvre and simple seizure were all employed to transfer land claims from institutions which did not primarily exist for profit to capitalistic enterprises, and where property title remained with such institutions, leasing was generally the means of bringing them under commercial management – not always on an open bidding basis, it might be added. Here and there lands of this sort passed into the hands of smaller and medium-sized farm operators, but in many areas these old corporate holdings fell into the lands being amassed by large landowners, either individuals and families or commercial corporations. Even where communal lands did not altogether vanish as such, it was often the case that they suffered private encroachment owing to the value they derived from being located in proximity to established population centres.

The workings of the land market during this period have still to be clarified, and it is obvious that a great deal of further research is needed to distinguish more precisely the evidently broad range of variations and to specify more exactly the factors that accounted for this variation. As in so many aspects of Latin American economic history, any generalizations must be quite provisional in nature, subject to reformulation as new findings come to light. This *caveat* in mind, however, there do seem to be a few observations to be made about the land market to characterize its operations.

Three situations seem to have favoured the small and medium-sized cultivators in the allocation of land resources. In some of the older areas of settlement where the land tenure system was a complex overlay of traditional claims and legal rights and where the chief impetus to commercial expansion came from a growth of local and provincial markets, there seems to have been some room in the system for individuals to acquire or add to farms and ranches of modest scale. Such transactions involved purchases of acreage from others, inheritance of portions of subdivided estates, the conversion of pasturage to cropland, or the acquisition of parcels from land in the public domain, especially the more outlying lands of settled districts. Such properties also were carved out of communal holdings (or those of non-profit making corporations) where the strength of community institutions was being eroded. Generally speaking, these cases were not located in the zones of strongest commercial expansion where export markets dictated patterns of resource use, and not where they were involved in types of cultivation or livestock raising in which the capital and technology requirements were substantial. The second circumstance favouring land cultivation on a sub-latifundian scale seems mainly to have taken place in coffee-growing regions of the Andes and Costa Rica, and to some extent Panama, Nicaragua and Honduras. Here the cash crop was cultivated primarily for the export market, but relative labour scarcity and the technical conditions of production made smaller-scale production an option. The third situation giving rise to moderate farm size was to be found in those comparatively few regions to which European immigrants came to settle the land: the southernmost states of Brazil and parts of Argentina and southern Chile. As for mineral resources, the concessions taken up by nationals and operated on a medium- or small-scale were primarily those whose nature and location meant that they could be worked with a relatively small labour force and moderate capital.

Aside from situations such as these, conditions in general acted to give large landowners the upper hand, just as concessions to exploit the larger and geologically more complex deposits of minerals, those requiring sophisticated production technologies for their extraction, went increasingly to foreign-owned concerns. The rich and influential were the ones who could swing official favour in their direction when governments were doling out the larger mineral concessions and grants of land. When large blocks of land were sold or when expensive land came onto the market (land values were rising sharply in quite a few parts of Latin America), it was they who could secure the mortgage credit or who had the other financial backing to buy it up. Where export market opportunities beckoned, the shift to modern livestock raising or more advanced farming practices created a high demand for land and drove land values up, pricing smaller farmers, peasants and landless workers, practically none of whom had access to bank credit, out of the market or onto sub-marginal lands on the fringe of the money economy. Such, for instance, appears to have happened on the southern Peruvian altiplano as wool prices rose in the late 1890s and early 1900s, although other processes such as abrogation of traditional grazing rights on hacienda land and encroachment on communal property were also at work.

By these means the consolidation and growth of larger holdings took on a certain cumulative aspect over much of Latin America. In this as in other operations of the institutional structure, it is possible to discern how the configuration of social forces within Latin America was strongly influenced by conditions prevailing externally in the system of world capitalism. The spread of capitalist relations of production through Latin America did not eliminate all pre-capitalist corporate and communal holdings, peasant cultivators and customary usufructary claims on latifundian land, but the position of all such cultural survivals was given a largely different meaning in the new social and economic matrix of the day.

Labour

Labour markets were no less affected than product markets by the growing interpenetration of the economic structures of the region and those of the world economy. At one extreme, the case of the *golondrinas*, the migrants who came to work in sparsely settled Argentina between intervals of employment in the Mediterranean, the new labour market operated with a remarkable sensitivity to the seasonally differentiated rhythms of labour demand in the northern and southern hemispheres. In what may be taken as the opposite limiting case, the internal labour markets of Peru were so insensitively structured, so unresponsive to new needs, that coolie labour had to be imported all the way across the Pacific, at first on an indentured basis, to supply the manpower for coastal agriculture and railway construction. For that matter, there were even some situations in which manpower located within national boundaries participated not at all in any of the labour markets of a country. Many of the tribal aboriginals of the Amazonian hinterland were totally beyond the reach of the labour mobilization systems of Brazil, Peru and Colombia – thanks to which isolation they escaped the horrors perpetrated on less fortunate native labour during the rubber boom.

The participation of Latin America in the massive emigrations from Europe in the nineteenth and early twentieth centuries, while smaller than the comparable figures for the United States, was substantial and had a profound effect on the location and character of certain of the region's labour markets. To be sure, the intercontinental movement of people did not begin during the period in question. Immigration from Spain and Portugal had commenced with the Conquest, and even during the years 1820 to 1840 there was a scattering of migrants, from Germany and elsewhere, to Brazil, Argentina, Chile and a few other locations. The slave trade had introduced millions of Africans into Latin America and was not abolished until as late as 1850–1 in the case of Brazil and 1865–6 in the case of Cuba. Nearly 50,000 Chinese had come to Cuba as contract labour between 1847 and 1860, and by 1862 there were over 60,000 Chinese in that country. It was after 1870, however, that the really strong currents of European migration began to have a substantial impact on major Latin American labour markets, although, like everything else, this impact was exceedingly uneven in its distribution throughout the region.

Argentina was the major beneficiary of this aspect of the international economy. The annual average for immigration into that country reached 30,000 in 1871–5, and while it fell to an annual average of 22,000 during 1876–80, this figure subsequently climbed to 51,000 in 1881–5 and to 117,000 for 1886–90. Economic crisis dampened the flow for 1891–5 to an annual average of 47,000. But thereafter the level recovered, reaching an average of 248,000 annually for 1906–10 and 202,000 for 1911–15. Not all of the 4.5 million who came to Argentina stayed, even apart from the seasonal immigrants, but the net immigration for 1871–1915 reached almost 2.5 million. By 1914, almost 30 per cent of the population of Argentina was foreign-born. More tellingly in what it reveals about the spatial distribution of economic opportunity, for over sixty years some 70 per cent of the adult population of Buenos Aires was foreign-born.

Italians and Spaniards made up the overwhelming bulk of this overflow, almost four-fifths of the total between them, with Italians outnumbering those from Spain. Smaller percentages came from France, Russia, the Levant, Germany, Austro-Hungary, and Britain, in descending order of importance. It would scarcely be an exaggeration to say that most of the labour power and skills for building the modern Argentine economy was provided by this huge movement of people. This was also the reason why the quality of the labour force available to the Argentine economy by the onset of the First World War was considerably higher – more literate, more skilled, healthier – than that of any other Latin American country. Not only that, by all accounts the labour market operated far more smoothly there than elsewhere to effect those shifting allocations that are essential to steadily rising levels of productivity; both the transatlantic seasonal migration and the substantial amount of non-seasonal remigration are evidence of the effectiveness of market guidance. All sectors of the economy were aided by this infusion of quality labour power and the substantial subsidy from the sending countries it implied. The littoral zone, as the new home of the great majority of immigrants, emerged as a country of distinctly European attributes in most of the ways that mattered.

Brazil, the second Latin American beneficiary, received a total of some 3.2 million persons from abroad between 1871 and 1915. As in the Argentine case, not all of them remained in Brazil, evidence that here, as in the River Plate, a labour market of some sensitivity was operating. But on the basis of fragmentary data on remigration it may be somewhat crudely but reasonably assumed that between 1.7 and 2 million did put down roots in the country. Italians constituted the largest share of this stream, with Portuguese and Spaniards standing in second and third place, respectively. As for others, Germans and Russians came next, with a fairly wide assortment of nationalities from Europe and the Levant making up the rest. Japanese immigration began in 1907. The largest number of immigrants were drawn to São Paulo state where they represented as much as a fifth of the total population from the 1890s to the First World War. A considerable portion of the rest went to the other southern states of Brazil and to Rio de Janeiro. Only a scattering went to other parts of Brazil. Compared with the total population of the country, however, the immigrant population was much smaller than it was in the case of Argentina.

As in Argentina, some of the newcomers to Brazil came as settlers in the various rural colonies that were organized, not uncommonly with government subvention. The rest came as individuals or in families, also, in some instances, with assistance from governments interested in increasing the supply of labour to the export sector. In the case of Brazil both national and state governments adopted policies designed to attract immigrants. In Argentina and Brazil alike, public leaders saw immigration and colonization as a means of occupying key vacant or sparsely populated regions of their respective national territories, and both appear to have been well aware of the improved skills and Europeanized habits and attitudes the immigrants would bring to their new homelands. Immigrant labour power was properly viewed as critical in building the coffee-based economy of Brazil and the cereals-and-livestock economy of Argentina. Not only did the rural sectors of both rely on the labour power of the immigrants, but so did the work of building the infrastructure and the conduct of a large portion of the expanding urban sector that contributed to the export booms while using its surplus in elaborating a more complex domestic economic structure. Indeed, the relatively high real wage level these two centres of export expansion and immigration enjoyed was itself a factor in this derivative growth of the internal sector.

Of the other countries, Uruguay received a fair number of immigrants, from Spain and Italy especially, in relation to its small population, and a few other places such as Chile, Cuba and Mexico received most of the rest who came to Latin America. The number who came to Mexico, however, was quite small in relation to its population. Only in Uruguay, Chile and Cuba did the influx of Europeans have much notable effect on the labour force, in spite of the sporadic but generally nugatory efforts to attract Europeans to the other republics. For the most part, the chief impact of the comparatively small number who came to countries other than Brazil, the River Plate republics, Chile and Cuba was felt in the realm of business, into which the immigrants went as manufacturing entrepreneurs, merchants, financiers, engineers and other professional and technical specialists. Their contributions in these capacities were sizeable, though, and quite disproportionate to their numbers.

Throughout Latin America, interrelations between the international economy and regional labour markets were quite varied, reflecting a medley of several influences: differences in regional factor endowments other than labour, the differing force of traditional institutions in regulating the relations of production, variations in the structure of production in different export industries and the volume of immigration.

The rate and magnitude of economic change in any given region was a further conditioning variable, as was the demographic trend that operated independently of international migration. Thus it should not be overlooked that there was a secular rise in population during the 1870–1914 era even in countries little affected by the larger-scale movement of people. Precise figures are elusive, but the number of Mexicans, for example, may have doubled between 1850 and 1930, while it is possible that the Chilean population tripled in the same interval, and Peruvian population growth may have been higher still. The general effect of this demographic development was to increase the domestic demand for foodstuffs (and hence the profitability of commercial farming), to intensify the competition for access to land (and hence conflicts between haciendas and indigenous communities) and to drive up land prices while enabling landowners to appropriate more of the product of labour (through labour service requirements, rents and wage levels) than would otherwise have been possible.

About the only generalizations that can be made are that slavery as a formal institution was finally eliminated from Latin America – it was finally abolished in Cuba in 1880–6 and in Brazil in 1888 – and that the very heterogeneity of labour market conditions throughout the continent reflected the numerous imperfections of the market as a connective institution among different regions and production processes. To these generalizations a third may be added: in general, urban labour markets functioned much more freely than did rural markets where the encrustation of archaic practices and relationships was likely to be considerably more pronounced. No less than in Europe of an earlier age could it be said that *Stadtluft macht frei*.

Labour mobilization measures, as might be expected, covered a whole spectrum. In some places, such as Guatemala and highland Peru and Bolivia, compulsory labour obligations were still employed, for local public works in the main but, particularly in Guatemala, also as a technique of conscripting labour for private farmers during the early part of this period. In Peru and Bolivia, assignment of labourers to mining, the old colonial practice, was not unknown, while in some countries with a large indigenous population vagrancy laws were used to steer workers into coerced employment, although this seems not to have been an invariably successful practice. (Evidence for this expedient comes from places as far-flung as Mexico, Guatemala, Colombia and Tucumán in Argentina.) More prevalent, however, was debt bondage whereby the impecunious native population could be pressed into peonage until such time as debts were discharged. Control by landowners of the notorious *tienda de raya*, the company store of the haciendas and plantations, as well as moneylending at usurious rates were employed to try to ensure that the level of debt peonage would be consistent with the labour requirements of the rural estates. In Mexico – particularly in Yucatán – as well as in Guatemala, the rubber-gathering regions of Amazonia and parts of the Andean highlands, where it existed in a modified form known as the *enganche* system, debt peonage served mainly to recruit workers from pools of native labour with access to their own lands.

Just how prevalent these kinds of labour recruitment systems actually were cannot be determined until a great deal more is known about the workings of regional labour markets. Present evidence does suggest, however, that these types of coerced labour were by no means so prevalent as was once thought, particularly outside of Middle America. In some localities, it was simply not necessary, given the limited interregional mobility of labour; latifundian expansion gave the large landed estates control over most of the available means of production, certainly over the best land in the vicinity, and enabled landowners to foreclose most of the more promising employment options for the surrounding population. In the heyday of large land grants, it was not unusual for the scattered inhabitants of sparsely settled frontier regions to have the experience of discovering that distant transactions had converted them into a resident work force for new rural enterprises. In older, more settled regions, too, this pre-emption of employment alternatives by latifundian appropriation of the means of production, especially the absorption of village lands by haciendas, played a role. Under similar circumstances, landowners were also able to revise customary tenancy arrangements to exact a greater contribution of labour service on the demesne and to increase the estate's portion of crops collected from those farming on shares.

Although parts of Latin America, like Eastern Europe, experienced a sort of second enfeudation with the spread of a capitalistic market for rural products, in more than a few regions – probably many more than was once supposed – the demand for labour generated by attractive opportunities in export markets for crops, livestock products and minerals exceeded the labour needs of the rather low level on which many regional economies operated during the colonial period and the long period of economic dislocation that followed independence. This resulted in a reorganization of the various categories of tenancy and an alteration of sharecropping agreements, alongside a discernible growth in wage labour. There is, in fact, mounting evidence that here and there a strong, export-induced demand for labour combined with relative scarcity of workers to improve the terms of tenancy, converting labour obligations and rentals-in-kind into cash payments, and raising the real wages of hired labour as rural employers sought to attract and retain workers. (Real income changes for the rural population were also influenced by the amount of obligatory time spent on hacienda labour.)

The commercial means of eliciting a greater supply of labour, it should be added, could be found in countries other than those of the southern cone where capitalist relations of production were firmly rooted, although the exact extent to which these newer labour systems spread through the rest of the Latin American rural sector has yet to be established. What is clear is that the demand expansion which ensued from increases in income and population in the North Atlantic region had, through its strongly favourable impact on Latin America's foreign trade, repercussions that pervaded many if not most of the labour markets of the continent, in one form or other. That the improvement in real wages, where it occurred, was decidedly modest outside the favoured zones of southern Brazil and Argentina–Uruguay, however, is patent from the almost negligible attraction these other regions had for the European emigrants who were flocking abroad in such numbers in search of remunerative employment.

Capital

That Latin America's evolving relation with the world economy was the central feature of the period after 1870 was nowhere more clearly manifested than in the region's capital markets. The connection of the industrial centre with Latin America was the driving force behind the capital accumulation process throughout the continent. International capital transfers fuelled the process, but by no means did they constitute its entirety. As catalysts for local capital formation they were perhaps even more significant.

The four or five decades before the First World War, the era of high capitalism, were a golden age for foreign investment in Latin America. Conditions for the reception of foreign capital were, as we have seen, much improved over earlier decades and the movement of capital across national borders was as yet almost entirely free of formal restriction. Taking advantage of conditions then developing in product markets, foreign capital poured into Latin America in unprecedented amounts. The process was not always smooth. There had been waves of defaults on government securities in the 1860s and 1870s, and the Baring crisis of 1890–1 occasioned a further interruption. Nor were issues of public securities the only ones that ran into difficulty. Many mining ventures came to grief, and some of the banking shares also failed to live up to expectations. But the flow continued in spite of interruptions. Throughout the period Great Britain supplied the largest portion of this capital transfer, with other European economies, chiefly France and Germany, also playing a significant role.

Up to the 1890s, United States investment was small and mostly in rails and gold and silver mines in Mexico, Cuban sugar plantations, a few railway lines and plantations in Central America and a scattering of other railway companies (in Ecuador and Colombia), forest products enterprises, agricultural operations and mercantile establishments. During the 1890s, further U.S. investment was placed in Mexican copper and lead mining, Central American banana plantations, as well as an assortment of ventures in Colombia and Peru. As late as 1897, however, 80 per cent of U.S. direct investments (the bulk of total U.S. capital abroad was in direct investments) in Latin America were concentrated in Mexico and Cuba, both of which received substantial further capital from the U.S. in the following years. By 1914, U.S. investments had also risen markedly in Chilean and Peruvian mining, so that almost 87 per cent of U.S. direct investments were located in only four countries: Mexico, Cuba, Chile and Peru. From around $300 million in 1897, the total of U.S. holdings rose to almost $1.6 billion in 1914, taking direct investments (nearly $1.3) and portfolio investments together.

European investments in Latin America, aside from having commenced earlier and having risen to a much larger aggregate amount by 1914 (some $7 billion) were different from U.S. investments in two other significant respects. In the first place there was much greater geographical dispersion: for most of the countries for most of this period Europe was the key supplier of capital. Secondly, a considerably larger portion came as portfolio investments: especially into infrastructure-type operations such as railways, ports, tramways, power and light companies, and other utilities. Almost a third, moreover, was placed in government bonds, so that quite substantial sums of capital were transferred to the public sector despite the pre-eminence of private enterprise in the macro-economic organization of the day. To be sure, no small portion of these public sector funds was ploughed back into subsidizing private-sector investments, but it seems not unreasonable to suppose that the political palatability of the heavy infusion of foreign investment derived, at least in part, from the portion of it that was channelled to national authorities.

British investments, though touching every country on the continent, were also somewhat concentrated in their distribution. Argentina had received over a third of the total of nearly $5 billion by the close of the period, and Brazil had received somewhat under a quarter. Mexico was in receipt of about 16 per cent of British investments, and thus these three countries accounted for just over three-quarters of the aggregate British holdings in Latin America. Chile, Uruguay, Cuba and Peru were next in order, composing between them another 18 per cent of the total. Aside from the fields of investor preference indicated earlier, British capital was also found in such activities as mining, navigation and banking.

French investments were clustered in Brazil, with large holdings also in Argentina and Mexico in about equal amounts. The fields of preference were also government securities, railways, mining, banking and finance and so on, although most public utilities appear to have been rather less attractive to French investors than they were to British. German investors, who supplied less capital than did the French, favoured Argentina, Brazil and Mexico, and put comparatively little into either rails or public utilities.

A number of questions can be raised about these and similar estimates of the size of capital flows to Latin America, and the figures should really only be taken as indicative of rough orders of magnitude. Still, of themselves, even allowing for errors of measurement, they are impressive testimony of the extent to which Latin America was prepared for participation in world capitalism and to the strength of the attachment of Latin America to the North Atlantic centres of that capitalist system. Two aspects besides magnitude, however, merit comment.

In the first place, it was this flow of capital, from the relatively well-organized capital markets of the capitalist centre to the almost non-existent capital markets of Latin America, that enabled the region to respond as it did to the new sales opportunities in export product markets. The new cable and telephone companies, economic intelligence systems and faster shipping services, for instance, knitted the scheme of production decisions in Latin American economies ever more securely into the fabric of the world market. The shipping lines provided, thanks to technical improvements, steadily faster and cheaper conveyance of Latin America's goods to the major consuming centres and delivered the counterflow of imports to distribution centres in Latin American ports.

Railways were of particular importance for assessing the repercussions of real capital movements, as well as in the accounting for financial flows. The new railway lines which fanned out from the ports into the interior were designed to collect the exportable surpluses of minerals and agricultural goods and to move them to the water's edge – or, in the case of Mexico, to the northern border of the Republic as well. Not only was the geographical layout of the systems arranged to reinforce the comparative advantages of the region in producing minerals, fibres, food products and the like for export but freight rate structures were also developed to favour the same ends. In consequence, the railway lines, competing nearly everywhere with much more costly methods of overland transport rather than with waterways, played a strong catalytic role by yielding great savings on the unit costs of shipping goods once the subsequent growth of production had been stimulated. The questions that have been raised about the social savings of the early rail systems in the U.S. or Europe are less cogent in Latin America.

This is not to argue that railways were invariably a success in either pecuniary or social terms. There were undoubtedly some lines, particularly in the Andean region, which failed to meet expectations when the very high costs of construction and maintenance were not covered by subsequent savings to producers, marketing institutions and consumers. Additionally, in the freewheeling and speculative business environment of the age, other lines suffered from a poor financial structure or from deficiencies in their construction and maintenance. Thus, even where social savings as usually computed may have been generated, these were less than they might have been had public authorities been more attentive in their supervision, and some lines proved unprofitable to their shareholders – though perhaps immensely profitable to their promoters and to the investment bankers who floated their securities.

Construction on the first rail lines, it should be noted, had begun in the late 1840s and on others in the 1850s. But it was really after 1860, and especially after 1870, that the major era of railway development occurred, amid an atmosphere of almost feverish promotion, financing and building. In 1870 the total distance of railway tracks laid down in South

America stretched over some 1,770 miles. By 1900, the figure exceeded 26,000 miles. Argentina, Mexico and Chile were the nations that ended the period with the most comprehensive railway networks though, on account of such matters as a lack of standardization in rail widths and rolling stock, the coverage, even in these countries, was less comprehensive than a look at a rail map might suggest.

The beneficial technological effects of international capital transfers were comprehensive, for new methods of production were introduced from abroad into all the export sectors of Latin America – into mining, ranching, farming, milling and the like – and in no few instances production intended for domestic product markets was technically upgraded as well. Aided by the shelter provided by transport costs and, often, by tariffs that had moved to protective levels, small local factory industries appeared with increasing frequency in all of the larger countries and most of the smaller ones. Their growth was abetted, in some instances, by overvaluation of imports at customs and by the depreciation to which most Latin American currencies were subject in the closing decades of the century. In most instances these new manufacturers used production technologies imported from abroad.

The second aspect to be emphasized concerns the social conveyance of capital. The capital from abroad came embodied in an organizational matrix, and this circumstance may well have provided the most valuable contribution of the capital movements. While precise data are not available it seems probable that a very large portion of the 'foreign' capital stake in Latin America by 1914 represented not the initial international capital transfers but reinvested earnings; the foreign companies were, in other words, functioning as agencies for local capital formation in a major way. Further, such capital-forming organizations could be emulated. Up-to-date business methods, systems of credit ratings, modes of management and production organization, advertising and promotion became more familiar to Latin Americans, many of whom (from the more privileged segments of society) went abroad for a practicum in mercantile experience. While study abroad, prompted by an admiration for the material achievements of the more industrially advanced countries, had initially led Latin American students into such practical fields as civil engineering, applied sciences and mining engineering, by the last quarter of the century schools in a number of the republics were beginning to cultivate these skills locally. Moreover, in numerous instances, an on-the-job commercial education was obtained, as by the famous Brazilian entrepreneur, the barão de Mauá, through employment in one of the foreign enterprises operating in the region. The proliferation of foreign concerns throughout the region, of course, greatly increased the exposure to this type of business apprenticeship. Much has been made of the supposed bias in the hiring preferences of foreign firms, the expansion of which in the latter half of the nineteenth century greatly exceeded the capacity of national education systems in Latin America to supply specialized personnel. This situation may have been particularly acute in Mexico, where it proved relatively easy to bring in technical and pecuniary specialists from across the border. The fact is, however, that over the whole continent many nationals held jobs with foreign-owned railways, mining ventures, public utility companies and the like, learned the ways of joint-stock companies and other aspects of capitalist management – and in time provided the basis for questioning how socially necessary the continued recruitment of foreigners might be.

This formation of human capital was part and parcel of the operation of the new institutions which took root in Latin America during this period. Mercantile houses established by foreigners played a crucial role in the organization of the export and import trade. British firms took an early lead, but they were joined, and sometimes displaced, by increasing numbers of German, French, Belgian, North American and other foreign firms. Some of the larger of these mercantile firms, which had early performed quasi-banking functions, later participated in the establishment of banks and, alongside their financial interests, were instrumental in promoting industrial, land and mining concerns. Among the many commercial names that could be cited to exemplify this tendency to branch out are those of Duncan Fox, Antony Gibbs, H. S. Boulton, Balfour Williamson, Gildemeister, Tornquist, Graham Rowe and A. and F. Wiese. New marketing channels were opened up between Latin American markets and U.S. and European manufacturers, while with the advent of improved local transport local merchants, especially those located up-country, were able to effect substantial savings on inventories, releasing capital for other uses. Wholesaling/warehousing operations sprang up in the major urban centres while sales agents fanned out into the hinterland. Networks of mercantile credit were established, sometimes with the backing of special banking houses in Europe, and spread their coverage inland.

Ever since independence had been attained, Latin America had lacked an institutional base in the strategic field of finance, and conditions were, for long, hardly propitious for the establishment of durable financial intermediaries. Here and there efforts had been made, but rarely were they successful for long. Brazil had, perhaps, progressed furthest in this respect, for it was there that the spectacular business empire of Mauá had flourished with its extensive banking operations. During the 1860s several British banks were initiated, bringing standard British banking practices to the region: the London and Brazilian Bank (1862), the London and River Plate Bank (1862), the London Bank of Mexico and South America (1863–4), the British Bank of South America (1863), the English Bank of Rio de Janeiro (1863). Joined later by the Anglo South American Bank (an amalgamation of two banks established in 1888 and 1889), these and other British banks gradually spread their operations over an ever wider territory through their branch networks. With some lag, the British banks were followed by continental banks, such as the Deutsche Überseeische Bank, the Brasilianische Bank für Deutschland, Deutsche Süd Amerikanische Bank, the Banque Française pour l'Amérique du Sud and the Banque Argentine et Française. A number of Italian banks and a few banks with connections in Holland, Belgium and Switzerland began business as well. These, too, multiplied their branches through the decades, especially those of French and German origin. With the continental banks, it should be added, came an approach to banking that was different from British practice, that of the *crédit mobilier* type of institution with its roots in Saint-Simonism.

Most of the funds of these banks were raised locally, illustrating the important function of these institutional transplants, like the foreign merchant firms and the factories and mining companies established by immigrant capitalists and entrepreneurs, as residentiary agencies of capital accumulation. From the 1850s through the 1880s and later, additional financial mechanisms for accumulation and the provision of other services were established in the form of mortgage companies and insurance firms. This is not to say that all the new Latin American banks were foreign. But even in many of the banks organized locally, immigrants and foreign-initiated firms had a hand in setting them up and in virtually all cases the institutional prototypes were those supplied from Europe.

Finally, attention should also be called again to yet another aspect of the organizational capital transferred to Latin America during this period: namely, industrial entrepreneurship. As noted previously, a fair number of tariffs had become protectionist, sometimes by design as free trade was by no means universally accepted in Latin American policy-making circles even during the high tide of liberalism. Other promotional measures were sometimes tried as well, and a measure of administrative protection was added when customs procedures were made especially complicated and imports were overvalued for assessing tariffs. When, after 1873, local currency depreciation occurred in relation to the gold standard countries of Western Europe, exporters were favoured (as their costs of production tended to rise more slowly than the gold price of their currencies fell) and would-be local producers enjoyed some relief from the competition of imports whose prices in local currency were rising.

While the evidence is quite fragmentary, it does seem warranted to say that immigrant entrepreneurs contributed disproportionately to the establishment of the hundreds of small local factories which were set up in Argentina, Brazil, Mexico, Chile, Peru and elsewhere, though in Colombia nationals of the country may perhaps have relied somewhat less on foreign *empresarios* and technicians. The view that Latin American industrialization got its start during World War I (not to mention the assertion, sometimes made, that it sprang up still later) is patently incorrect; an incipient phase is clearly visible in the record of what went on between 1870 and 1914, especially in those fields mentioned during the discussion of product markets. On the basis of population growth and export-induced expansion of incomes, local urban markets for common goods and producer goods were growing and new firms were set up in response. That these were not more numerous can be attributed to the limited size of the home markets in spite of export growth, to the elasticity of import supply on advantageous terms and to the very rudimentary state of domestic venture-capital markets, among other elements in the entrepreneurial support system. Investable funds of local origin were still exceedingly scarce and in many instances the pull of export industries, with their strong overseas markets and well-developed information networks and marketing channels, proved irresistible.

CONCLUSION: THE EVOLUTION OF CAPITALISM IN LATIN
AMERICA

Between 1870 and 1914 Latin America not only exhibited increasing regional differentiation but also evolved quite a different endowment of factors of production, thanks to the demand-induced (but not solely demand-constrained) development of the period. The resource patterns which underlay the region's economies on the eve of the First World War differed notably from those on which the economic process rested at the outset of the period. Labour was more abundant, of decidedly higher quality, and more diversified in the array of skills it embodied. Land, including subsoil wealth, had been subject to sizeable expansion. Accumulation and transfer had added, to a certain extent everywhere, to the stock of capital on which the region counted, but of greater consequence still were improvements in its quality. Much had been done to alleviate the technological backwardness under which Latin America laboured even as late as the middle decades of the nineteenth century, although the region still lay outside the mainstream of the scientific and engineering knowledge by which industrial society was nurtured. Although the decisive points in this development cannot be precisely determined, the accumulation of quantitative changes during the period between 1870 and 1914 gave rise to important qualitative changes in systemic organization, particularly in Argentina, Brazil, Mexico, Chile and Uruguay. There were also major modifications in systemic functioning elsewhere.

With few exceptions, the region's governing elites appear to have been enthusiastic about the benefits of what they perceived to be modernization, a modernization which was, considering the vast new resources the process provided, essentially self-financing. Indeed, the prosperity enjoyed by the elites and the middle classes in government and business could only have validated this attachment to the global economy and strengthened the policy of commitment to it. Legitimation of the new order, insofar as such was sought, was forthcoming from two other imports from Europe: liberalism and positivism. For the inhabitants of the sparsely populated River Plate area, where modernization assumed capitalist forms *ab initio*, the new policies were presented as those of 'civilization', in contrast to the 'barbarism' of strong-man rule and a low-level regional economic self-sufficiency. There, the prevailing attitude was caught by Alberdi's dictum *gobernar es poblar*, and the expanding waves of commercially-based colonization that opened up the pampa and beyond became almost the central mission of government. In Brazil, 'order and progress' were emblazoned on the national flag and the state set itself to the task of promoting both – with an enthusiasm that even led it to embark on a moderate interventionism. Elsewhere, as in the more densely settled highlands of Guatemala, Ecuador, Mexico and Peru, the new economic forms were praised by those who deplored alike the alleged feudalism of the Spanish empire and the even more archaic elements carried over from pre-Columbian times.

Praise, however, did not in most cases seem to make for any greater inclination to alter patterns of social investment and institutions so as to confer the benefits of modernization on substantially broader segments of the population. An increasing cosmopolitanism of the elite strata in society, especially in respect of consumption preferences, was more often the socially favoured course of action. And by and large the institutional environment of the colonial heartland areas remained relatively uncongenial for the spread of new business ideas and practice even where these were, in principle, admired. Over much of the continent, even in Mexico where during the Porfiriato the capitalist order was embraced with a fervour tempered by interventionary caution only in its closing decade, the assimilation of traditional and latifundian society to capitalist modes of production was far from complete.

Here and there, in spite of the brightening material prospects, contemporary social critics pointed to contradictions in the prevailing scheme of development, as did, for example, González Prada in Peru or Molina Enríquez in Mexico. And in the southern cone countries where the character of society was much more suffused with European norms, a fledgling labour movement made its appearance seeking redress under the banners of anarcho-syndicalism and socialism, themes echoed in the generally weaker proletarian organizations of the other countries. In southern South America, middle-class radicalism, in more or less the French sense, had begun to agitate for programmes of moderate social and political reforms, carrying the laicism and secularism of the older and more widespread liberalism one step further. The international economy, in other words, both generated the socio-economic changes that had transformed Latin America and supplied contrasting interpretations of their significance.

But what, retrospectively considered, was the significance of these changes? If one may turn the Fabian expression round, it seems indisputable that, at the very least, capitalism gained control of the commanding heights of the economy, orchestrating the region's new resources to respond primarily to the needs of the core economies of the capitalist world system. Further, while they were by no means universal in their influence, economic forces emanating from the process of capitalist expansion undoubtedly penetrated far into the hinterland, reaching, for instance, even Amazonian tribesmen who, as Roger Casement showed, were dragooned with notorious brutality into the rubber trade. Older systems of production organization persisted, but capitalism came to be installed as the hegemonic mode of production among the several coexisting types.

According to some scholars, well exemplified by Jonathan Levin's *The export economies; their pattern of development in historical perspective* (1960), the result was an enclave type of development within which the forces of economic transformation were concentrated and, to some extent, contained, albeit with gradual encroachment on the surrounding field of economic activity. Outside the enclave, social organization was less touched by externally induced changes – left on one side, as it were, beyond the reaches of the market system. In this dualistic reading of historical experience, the external sector appears almost as an odd protuberance set off against a background of incomplete socio-economic transformation. The implication of most such interpretations is that there was little interaction between the two sectors, the capitalist enclave and the more archaic or 'traditional' sector, and that the two stood in a relationship of mutual exclusion. Given more time and a continuation of the economic dynamics of market forces, however, the institutional topography was destined eventually to become more uniform through gradual absorption of the pre-capitalist residue into the vortex of modern economic expansion. Where the transformation of the economic system was manifestly incomplete, this could be attributed less to deficiencies in the transmission mechanisms linking the export and traditional, or domestic, sectors than to the still relatively small size of the export sector and to an insufficiently high rate of growth in the value of per capita exports. In other words, there was, even with all the growth and accumulation of the age, still an insufficiently large surplus available to effect the dissolution of non-capitalist forms in the social organization of production which, as the modern sociology of development has shown, were in any case imbued with the inherent conservatism and inertia of traditional institutions generally.

A revisionist body of scholarship of somewhat more recent (and largely Latin American) origin has suggested that this essentially neo-classical and dualistic portrayal of growth dynamics may well miss significant economic and social relationships in the process of capitalist expansion. Discounting, or at least reconceptualizing, the significance of non-capitalist modes of production in colonial Latin America and the scattered instances in which, even after 1850, an increase of production for the market appears to have strengthened servile relationships rather than hastened their dissolution, some expositors of this *dependencia* school of thought have dated Latin America's insertion into the capitalist order from 1492. In their view, instead of a dualism which grew more accentuated from 1850 onwards, but which was presumably intended for eventual resolution, the various sectors and regions of Latin America exhibited, from the early decades of the Conquest, an overall unity that derived from their common articulation into the capitalist market system. According to this later reading of history, what the conventional interpretation masked by calling it dualism was simply a structure of unequal power and exchange.

The relation between the two sectors was therefore symbiotic, not one of separation. As a mechanism for labour control and the restriction of popular consumption, social stratification and organizational segmentation served to mobilize and protect the economic surplus thus placing it at the disposition of the favoured classes. More than this, traditional society and its economic underpinnings even helped to nourish the growth of the capitalistically appropriated surplus by absorbing labour reproduction costs and supplying social welfare functions without direct charge to the accumulation process. It is perfectly obvious, when the experience of the period is refracted through this analytical perspective, that the persisting institutional distance between the lauded ideal of liberal economy and practical reality is insufficiently explained – and is perhaps even obfuscated – by the conventional dualistic interpretation. The fact is that a serious commitment of resources to resolving the dualism and an institutional reorganization designed to make Latin American society conform to the norms of the liberal vision (as expressed, for example, in the ill-fated Mexican *Reforma*) would, in most cases, have been utterly inconsistent with the maintenance of accustomed relations between dominant (hence decision-taking) and subordinate groups. The evidence is unmistakable that it was the use of the surplus, not its size, that blocked significant change in what may be called the inter-class terms of trade.

Even though these competing theoretical approaches are too general – both too disparate and too abstract – to permit the framing of tight hypotheses and really rigorous cross-testing in a formal way, the socio-economic relations they postulate can, nevertheless, be used as general guidelines to direct attention to important matters in the history of the region. Particularly is this the case if the attempt to fit all parts of the richly complex historical experience of Latin America into a single overarching, coherent, theoretical structure is abandoned and if, more modestly and eclectically, such broader theorizing is mainly drawn upon in order to organize hypotheses to guide inquiry, to impose some order on history and to form the basis of a comparative method of analysis.

For example, the revisionist claim that Latin America was totally absorbed into the capitalist system after 1492 could easily seem to some a rather extravagant assertion in spite of the undoubtedly pivotal role of foreign trade in the organization of the two Iberian empires, especially the Portuguese. But, since for present purposes nothing very important hinges on the proposition that capitalism was enthroned in Latin America with the arrival of the Spaniards and Portuguese, the issue of whether it came then or much later may be safely disregarded. By the same token, the view of some revisionist analysts that a hampering state of dependency termed 'underdevelopment' is produced by the integration of peripheral economics into world capitalism would seem to suggest that Argentina was somehow more disadvantaged than, say, 'undeveloped' Paraguay because of the former's much greater involvement in global trade and capital movements. Yet, for all its twentieth-century afflictions, Argentina would appear to be far more capable than Paraguay of effecting a broad improvement in the social and economic welfare of its people and much ahead in the political awareness and participation of its citizenry – i.e., more 'developed' by almost any understanding of that term. The special use of the concept of under-development may also be discarded as not a marked improvement on such standard concepts as vested interests, spheres of influence, political alliances and class aggrandizement, or even on the earlier insights of Marx himself. At the same time, dependency analysis is of considerable value in drawing attention to the policy preferences of privileged groups. As it points out, resources are likely, from a social point of view, to be allocated suboptimally insofar as policy is responsive mainly to the wishes of certain social segments. With these and similar deletions on both sides, it is not clear that the two explanatory approaches are necessarily competitive; indeed, more cautiously applied, they may mainly shed light on different aspects of the same social complexity and be, therefore, fundamentally complementary.

On the one hand, the dependency critique does serve to explain the overtly conflictive character of twentieth-century development, with its more covert nineteenth-century counterpart, and to expose the simplistic and misleading picture portrayed in the more conventional analytical approach of dualism and enclave theory. The latter seems too capital-centred, and too mechanistic, in its view of the nexus between markets and other institutions and posits a vision of reality in which it is very hard indeed to recognize the intricately structured pluriform economy of Latin America. Yet, for its part, the enclave perspective does highlight quite well the contrasting rates of growth in productivity between the external sector and the several domestic sectors, and helps to identify the implications of significant differences in their respective organizational characteristics. The neo-classical dualistic approach also helps to identify the emerging, demand-defined growth points in Latin American economic structure, on which the increasing but still very limited supply of capital was concentrated to increase output and productivity, and also to account for differences between the paths of development followed by the various countries. Cost–price considerations, for example, dictated that the major avenues of growth should be, by and large, those investment and production opportunities that were defined, on the one hand, by a rapidly expanding demand in the industrially advanced economies of the North Atlantic regions and, on the other, by changes in technology and a lowering of international and internal transport costs which helped bring new areas into cultivation and opened up new mining sites. New production options generated for the Latin American economies in the much weaker demand patterns coming out of the derivative local expansion triggered by export growth were only of secondary importance. As noted earlier, however, all these factors varied considerably from region to region, depending, among other things, on the size of the internal market, the technologies of different export industries and the relations of production prevailing in the regions in which export industries arose.

Conditions of supply were instrumental in producing the lopsided development of the period. Most influential were the restricted coverage provided by the modern transport system then being built, and the low quality and poor distribution of coal and iron, the key natural resources of the age. The transport network, linked as it was to the external sector since foreign capital figured prominently in railway development and lines primarily served the export trade, severely circumscribed the areas that could be harnessed as supply regions for both foreign and domestic markets. Away from the districts served by rail, overland transport costs remained forbiddingly high. For its part, the unfortunate shortage of coal and iron prevented any significant local appropriation of the most critical backward linkage opportunities created by the new economic structure: industries producing machinery and engineering goods. It is worth noting that only on the northernmost margin of Latin America, at Monterrey, had an integrated iron and steel industry come into being before the close of the period under review. Both circumstances, of course, militated against a diffusion throughout the region's national economic systems of the stimulus to development originating in foreign trade and very probably, in the case of the transport limitations, worked against export diversification as well. Mexico, the exception, seems to confirm the particular importance of the transport variable. Thanks to the comprehensive rail network acquired during the Porfiriato, a considerable variety of natural resources could be tapped for the export markets. Further, even though the distribution of income severely constricted the size of the home market, a modest degree of industrial development could nevertheless occur because the transport system allowed national producers to reach such demand as existed. Had the Mexican national market been more fragmented than it was, had the rail lines not been so extensive, it is extremely doubtful whether so many small factories could have been established.

The effect on the range of development options of other supply factors was more problematical. Where demand in home markets was, as in Brazil, Mexico and Argentina, comparatively broad, and where routine cost–price relationships favoured the provision of manufacturing facilities to serve local markets, the requisite capital, labour, and entrepreneurship seem to have been forthcoming – through immigration if not through domestic generation – to get production started on some scale. Quite possibly had there been a more ample supply of entrepreneurship and more efficiently functioning factor markets (to raise more capital locally, for instance), marginal improvements in the situation could have been brought about. Food-processing factories were quite widespread; foundries and machine shops somewhat less so. Textile mills were largely concentrated in Brazil and Mexico, but they were also found in other countries, too. Perhaps this incipient industrialization indicated that still other opportunities were there to be tapped had investors and entrepreneurs been more numerous. Certainly, no one could claim that the institutions of the capital market operated comprehensively and impartially, i.e., solely on the basis of commercial investment criteria. On the contrary, whole regions and segments of the population were cut off from access to the still embryonic institutional development in this field. Yet, within the existing institutional framework, it is likely that weak demand and limited transport coverage, allied with such other infrastructural characteristics of the business environment as deficient educational systems and communications services, constituted the overriding obstacles because they made cost–return ratios unfavourable and kept the level of risk and uncertainty too high.

In stressing the key role of foreign trade as a dynamic force, of exports as a source of income growth and of some of the structural changes associated with development, it is not meant to imply that Latin American economic behaviour was merely reflexive. It is not possible altogether to disregard the extent to which favourable supply conditions based on internal factors enhanced market responsiveness and differentiated those regions in which export expansion stimulated a more general growth from those in which it precipitated the enclave type of economic structure. The experiences of Argentina and southern Brazil stand out sharply in this regard. But in these instances the inter-relatedness of trade and capital movements, not to mention the international mobility of labour and entrepreneurship, serve to point up the fact that the favourable internal supply conditions were themselves hardly independent of the operations of the external sector. The expansion in southern Brazil and Argentina of the domestic market for manufactures that led, with assistance from government policy, to local industrial development was doubly linked to the external sector: to the relatively higher wage level that was associated with large-scale trans-oceanic immigration and to the production functions of export industries for which a significant part of the technology and management could be supplied locally.

At the same time, it also seems clear, thanks to research informed by the revisionist analytical orientation, that international trade could produce the skewed sort of growth most of Latin America experienced precisely because of the nature of the socio-economic structures that were subordinated to the dominant internationally-related economic interests. While production organization frequently tended to be pluriform in character, with more archaic modes and relations of production prevailing outside the external sector and its supporting infrastructure, there were, nevertheless, as noted earlier, critical linkages between the different parts of the economy. For one thing, the same institutions which established the social and political subordination of much of the population – in Mexico, most of Central America, the Andean republics and north-eastern Brazil – tended to hold down money incomes and, by linking economic with political disenfranchisement, protected both the exportable surplus and foreign-instigated, capital-accumulation processes from the erosion that might have ensued from either higher popular consumption levels or from claims for a greater amount of social investment. The consumption claims of the privileged classes were, of course, no less well protected. That this came at the expense of the material and human capital formation which might have been locally encouraged outside the external sector (and was encouraged in a few regions) by stronger home markets was not a particular disadvantage from the viewpoint of those groups whose fortunes were wedded to importing luxury and semi-luxury products, to the export industries, and to industries supporting (and supported by) the export sector – those which attracted so much foreign, and domestic, capital into their expansion. On the contrary, the compatibility of these arrangements with preservation of the established positions of privilege meant that the elites were generally in no haste to invest significant portions of the surplus in general improvements and in reforming or up-dating the structure.

The subjugated position of so much of the domestic economy meant also lower opportunity costs for the local factors of production employed in the external sector. In other words, the external sector enjoyed favourable bidding terms for the available productive factors, or at least it obtained them more cheaply than would have been the case had the domestic sector been vigorously expanding and diverting land, labour and capital away from uses connected with foreign trade and its local auxiliary activities. Under the prevailing institutional dispensation, the domestic sector, by its sparing use of capital, enabled the available capital supply to be concentrated in the service of export expansion while maintaining the labour force at such low levels of real remuneration that, outside the River Plate area and southern Brazil, the supply price of labour to the externally oriented centres of growth tended to be comparatively low. In many rural areas, the subsistence agricultural sector functioned as a type of labour reservoir, raising a native work force and supporting it between intervals of seasonal migratory employment in commercial agriculture, as, for example, on the coastal cotton plantations of Peru or the coffee *fincas* of Guatemala. In like manner, the rural sector often provided temporary workers for mining enterprises, inhibiting development of a permanent agricultural or industrial proletariat. Peasant agriculture, practised on independently held parcels and communal lands as well as through various tenancy arrangements on large estates, commonly served also as the mainstay of the domestic agricultural markets, supplying foodstuffs for urban centres and the mining operations scattered throughout the hinterland without making substantial inroads on the scarce supplies of capital. For that matter, through taxation and the structure of marketing channels, a substantial share of the modest economic surplus generated in peasant agriculture, artisan industries and petty trade was probably siphoned out of the sector and into the urban centres. Incontrovertibly, the peasant sector commonly received very little by way of return, either in the form of social investment or as factor rewards.

Both the conventional and the *dependencia* interpretations of the economic history of the period 1870–1914, however, coincide on several points. As export growth gathered momentum, the experience profoundly altered the connections between the several Latin American regional economies with other parts of the world, the North Atlantic economies in particular. Pre-capitalist forms of economic and social organization remained conspicuous in many areas of Latin America, in some instances reinforced, but the mode and relations of production characteristic of modern capitalism provided a new overlay that subsumed all the other sectors to its logic, controlling and organizing most local-level processes even when the maintenance of older forms of production organization served as a convenience for the systems then taking shape. In 1870, these systems were still in a formative state. By 1914, the new regime was fully consolidated and already propagating the conditions that would, in time, reshape it further.

2

LATIN AMERICA AND THE INTERNATIONAL ECONOMY FROM THE FIRST WORLD WAR TO THE WORLD DEPRESSION

The periodization of Latin American economic history around 'external shocks' has been increasingly rejected in recent years. Yet if we wish to explore – as an open question – the role of the international economy in the economic development of Latin America, the First World War and the World Depression enclose a significant period. It bridges the gap between the first major 'external shock' of the twentieth century and the final breakdown of the export-led growth mechanism of the 'Golden Age' whose starting point had been around 1870. The period also represents the key years in the changeover from one hegemony to another: Britain's decline as a major economic power was hastened by the war (when Germany was eliminated) and the United States was thrust into the role of Latin America's major investment and trade partner. Nevertheless, generalizations about Latin America as a whole, dangerous at the best of times, are particularly difficult in such a period of transition. Change occurs at different rates in different countries and perceptions vary: in some countries the 'Golden Age' clearly continues until 1929; in others fundamental changes occur between 1914 and 1929 and the period is aptly characterized the 'Great Delay'; and in others the roots of change were there well before 1914.

In this chapter we first describe the major characteristics of the changing world economy between the First World War and the World Depression. Then we explore the impact of these changes on the Latin American economies. The conclusion attempts an evaluation of the extent of change and the long-term significance of the period. We try to show how internal forces for change were stimulated by the First World War and its aftermath, and how further important changes were effected during the 1920s which conditioned Latin America's response to the World Depression.

CHANGES IN THE WORLD ECONOMY

Although the outbreak of the First World War was clearly of great
significance in the breakdown of the classical capitalist world economy
based on the dominating role of Britain and the operation of the gold
standard, it is easy to overstress its importance. Certainly, up to that
point the system had worked very smoothly, though the reasons why are
still not clear. There is much controversy over whether the efficiency of
the system was due to wage and price flexibility allowing deflation and
adjustment, to *ex ante* avoidance of substantial disparities in competitiveness, or to the efficiency of interest rate mechanisms and hence
equilibrating capital flows.[1] But from well before 1913, forces making
for change and threatening this harmony had been gathering strength.
There were two main areas of change. First was the already-occurring
shift in trade and investment structures. Britain's initiating role in trade
in manufactures implied that as other members of the trading community
developed her share would have to fall; this was aggravated by the
decline in competitiveness in certain lines. Increasingly her declining
industries lost ground, although her growing role as a key currency and
the corresponding role of sterling liabilities held abroad covered this and
allowed an 'Indian summer' of expansion, a classic example of 'deficit
without tears'.[2] But though Britain remained predominant, the role of
the United States in trade and in investment was increasing rapidly from
the turn of the century: by 1913 Mexico, all the republics of Central
America and the Hispanic Caribbean, Venezuela, Colombia, Ecuador
and, marginally, Peru were already importing more from the United
States than from the United Kingdom (see below Table 4) – which
represented a major switch compared with the 1890s. United States
investment was making rapid headway in, for example, Mexican mining
and railways, Peruvian copper, Chilean nitrates, Colombian bananas and
Cuban sugar, as well as in a number of Central American economies.
Secondly, changes were already under way leading to a growing over-
supply of primary products, and to increasing market instability. These
were trends on the side both of demand and of supply. On the demand

[1] See J. R. Zecher 'How the Gold Standard worked, 1880–1913', in D. N. McCloskey and J. R.
Zecher, *Enterprise and trade in Victorian Britain* (London, 1981), for a recent summary of
alternative views and an interpretation based on the monetary theory of the balance of payments.
See also P. H. Lindert, *Key currencies and gold 1900–13* (Princeton, 1969).
[2] Lindert, *Key Currencies*, 75.

side, population growth in the developed countries was slowing down, and rising income was leading to a proportionately slower growth in the demand for food. On the supply side, technical change and modernization were leading to greater productivity and also in certain cases to increased short run rigidity in supply, as production became more capital-intensive. These trends were only offset in the case of a few primary products (oil, copper) by technical change which led to new demands – a factor which would be of more importance by the 1920s.

During the war, the shift in trade and investment structures was sharply accelerated, since on the one hand Britain's position in world trade declined, never to recover fully, while on the other the opportunities for exporting by the United States were correspondingly transformed. Her geographical position meant that she gained relative to distant countries such as Australia when shipping was at a premium. Her trading surplus swelled: by the end of 1919 the U.S. was a net long-term creditor of over $3.3 billion as compared with a similar net debtor status in the pre-war period.[3] U.S. private foreign investment overseas rose from $3.5 billion in 1914 to $6.4 billion in 1919.[4] Her determined pursuit of the exporting opportunities offered by the war is reflected in the huge growth of trade with Latin America (Table 1) and in the infrastructure which began to grow around it, as U.S. banks sought to establish themselves abroad and as flows of information, etc. were built up. Handbooks of advice for exporters appeared on all sides, with Latin America as the key focus of interest.[5] In 1914 U.S. federal regulations were changed so as to permit the expansion of U.S. branch banking overseas; between 1914 and 1918 the First National City Bank alone set up a dozen branches in Latin America.

The war also stimulated an increase in productive capacity in many primary products where there was already danger of excess supply. Sugar was perhaps the most outstanding example, but the same was true of many foodstuffs and raw materials where European domestic production was temporarily disrupted.

---

[3] D. Aldcroft, *From Versailles to Wall Street, 1919 to 1929* (London, 1977), 239.

[4] C. Lewis, *America's stake in international investments* (Brookings Institute, Institute of Economics, publication 75, Washington, 1938), 449.

[5] A good (and amusing) example is E. Filsinger, *Exporting to Latin America* (New York, 1916): 369 pages of detailed instructions on every aspect of business, including advice on 'the value of moving pictures' in advertising, and covering such practical details as the need for proper saddles when venturing into the Andes, and for 'a liberal quantity of a preparation with which to anoint the body against insects'.

Table 1. *U.S. Trade with Latin America as percentage of total*
Latin American Trade 1913, 1918 and 1927

	1913	1918	1927
South America			
Imports from U.S.	16.2	25.9	26.8
Exports to U.S.	16.8	34.8	25.2
Mexico, Central America and the Caribbean			
Imports from U.S.	53.2	75.0	62.9
Exports to U.S.	71.3	73.4	58.4

Source: M. Winkler, *Investments of U.S. capital in Latin America*, (World Peace Foundation, Boston, 1929); James W. Wilkie, *Statistics and national policy*, Supplement 3 (1974) UCLA, *Statistical abstract of Latin America*, UCLA Latin American Center, University of California, Los Angeles.

There were also more specific effects of the war. Germany's trading and investment links were abruptly ended, so providing a gap into which the U.S. was quick to expand. In the very short term the whole system of banking, credit and the organization of money markets was suspended, producing for Latin America an acute crisis of liquidity and financial panic in 1913–14. Throughout the war period the disruption of imported supplies provided both opportunities and handicaps, the detailed implications of which we consider later. On another level, throughout the Western economies there were abrupt changes in the role of the state, resulting from the sudden need to regulate war economies. Nationalism also became a more potent force, and there were important developments in labour movements.

With the old system in disarray, and new forces for change emerging in forms such as an expanded role of the state, there was in 1919 an opportunity for fresh thinking and for an attempt to appraise and handle the underlying problems. But the problems were not perceived. The accepted wisdom of the post-war period, at least in the U.S. and the U.K., was the need to return to the old system – in particular to the gold standard and as far as possible to pre-war exchange rate parities. From the U.S. came a strong move to reduce again the role of the government: to drop price controls and any interference with trade or exchange rates and to return as nearly as possible to 'healthy' 'free' competition.[6] The

---

[6] See the *Annual Report of the Secretary of the Treasury on Finances for the fiscal year ended June 30, 1920* (Washington, 1921), p. 81: '.... The Governments of the world must now get out of banking and trade ... The treasury is opposed to governmental control over foreign trade and even more

haste to return to market forces was particularly imprudent given the extent of pent up war-time demand: the result was the badly mismanaged boom and crash of 1919–22, largely speculative in nature.[7] The boom further worsened the problem of excess supply of agricultural goods. From 1922 there was sustained economic expansion in the U.S. and many European countries – though Britain was struggling with deflation in the attempt to restore and maintain the pre-war parity. But the system was basically unsound, with capital movements only temporarily papering over the cracks. The reinstituted gold exchange system never worked well: there were too many centres, the U.S. lacked experience, and neither France nor the U.S. was committed to making the new system work. There was also a new instability arising from the increased volume of short-term and volatile funds, and parities for the major currencies were seriously misjudged. Further, the size of the American surplus was such that it urgently required policies for promoting imports and capital export which would ease the payment problems of the recipients. But trade was not the important factor to the U.S. which it had been to the U.K.; policies, in fact, were exactly the reverse of what was needed. The U.S. continued its protectionist policies, dating back to the Civil War, and its capital export policies created major problems for the recipient countries. The 1920s saw a bonanza of private foreign lending on the part of the U.S. Salesmen pressed loans on unwary governments, borrowers were positively encouraged to over-extend themselves. The money tended often to go either to unproductive uses or to increase further the supply of already dangerously surplus agricultural commodities.

Aided by such credits, the volume of primary production continued to expand. Meanwhile the forces operating on supply and demand continued and strengthened. The 1920s were years of particularly rapid technical progress in agriculture: for the first time in history the pace caught up with industry, with the mechanisation of farming and the introduction of new plant strains and fertilizers. There were also major structural changes in primary product markets with substitutes damaging nitrates and rubber. Price behaviour in the decade is complicated to review, since the sudden boom of 1920 was followed by as sudden a crash, to be followed in its turn by recovery for all commodities by 1925, then an uneven weakening of many markets. But underlying this was an

opposed to private control . . . They look towards the removal of governmental controls and interferences, and the restoration of individual initiative and free competition in business . . . strict economy in public expenditure . . .'
[7] See W. A. Lewis, *Economic survey 1919–1939* (London, 1949), for a detailed and coherent account.

Table 2. *Implicit price indices for selected
primary products, 1928*

(1913 = 100)

Crude petroleum	158
Iron ore	142
Copper ore	119
Cotton	149
Coffee	137
Meat	129
Tin	102
Wheat and flour	104
Sugar	84
Cocoa	68

Source: Calculated from P. L. Yates, *Forty years of
foreign trade: a statistical handbook with special
reference to primary products and underdeveloped countries* (London, 1959)

unfavourable long-run trend; by 1926–9 the terms of trade for all primary
products had fallen significantly below their 1913 level.[8] Data on
individual commodities are given in Table 2; it will be seen that against
the background of rise, fall and recovery, fuels and minerals were
basically in strong demand, as was meat. Cotton was aided by disease
problems in the south of the United States. Coffee was only sustained at
the level shown because of the Brazilian coffee valorization scheme: by
the mid-twenties stocks were at a dangerously high level, as they were for
wheat and sugar. The low price of tin was a result principally of the rapid
expansion of low-cost mines in the 1920s.[9]

By 1928 the stresses and strains in the different commodity markets
were beginning to be felt – most markedly in the case of wheat. The
World Depression was in part, then, the result of deep disequilibria in the
international system; its severity was, however, considerably aggravated
by the policy mismanagement which ensued within the United States. As
the boom in the U.S. rose to dizzy heights in 1928, capital was drawn in
from all sides, and many countries in Latin America began to suffer

---

[8] J. F. Rowe, *Primary commodities in international trade* (Cambridge, 1965), 83.
[9] On raw materials, see M. T. Copeland, *A raw commodity revolution* (Business Research Studies, No.
19, Harvard University Graduate School of Business Administration, Cambridge, Mass., 1938).

balance of payments problems as capital ceased to flow in and even began to flow out in the opposite direction. In October 1929 came the Wall Street crash. Commodity prices plummeted, and as they fell faster than the average price level so the terms of trade turned against primary producers. The remaining capital inflows stopped. The result, as is well known, was a seizing up of world trade and investment. Europe was to recover from the recession with some speed – but the U.S. did not really recover throughout the next decade. The consequences for Latin America were serious. At the same time, the further shock of the World Depression forced the fundamental change of economic direction which the First World War had shown was needed, but for which the internal forces were insufficiently strong during the 1920s.

IMPACT ON LATIN AMERICA

We now turn to review the immediate implications for the countries of Latin America, which were still almost exclusively primary producers and exporters, first of the changing structure of world trade and investment, then of the weakening and unsettled behaviour of commodity markets during the period from the First World War to the World Depression. We also consider the deeper question of the kind of response that was possible to the various indicators of the need for a new direction, reviewing institutional developments and industrialization.

The most dramatic shift in this period occurred in investment: as Table 3 shows, the share of the U.S. in the total of U.K. and U.S. invested capital in South America rose in many cases by over 30 percentage points; British investment barely increased while U.S. investment soared. In this major development, the relative roles of British lack of interest, North American dynamism and official U.S. backing are still not clear. Between 1924 and 1928 Latin America absorbed 24 per cent of the new capital issues floated in the U.S. for foreign account and took 44 per cent of new direct foreign investment.[10] The inflow apparently exceeded that received from the U.K. during the peak years 1904–14 – even allowing for price movements.

Direct investment was the smaller of the two components. Minerals, oil and public utilities drew the greatest amounts, though industry in the largest countries was also attractive. Throughout the 1920s, Chile

[10] United Nations, Economic Commission for Latin America, *Foreign capital in Latin America* (New York, 1955), 7.

Table 3. *Nominal capital invested in South America by the U.S. and U.K.,*
1913 and 1929[a]

(million dollars)

	U.S. Investments		U.K. Investments	
	1913	1929	1913	1929
Argentina	40	611	1861	2140
Bolivia	10	133	2	12
Brazil	50	476	1162	1414
Chile	15	396	332	390
Colombia	2	260	34	38
Ecuador	10	25	14	23
Paraguay	3	15	16	18
Peru	35	151	133	141
Uruguay	5	64	240	217
Venezuela	3	162	41	92

	Ratio of U.S. Investment to Sum of U.S. + U.K.	
	1913	1929
Argentina	2.1	22.2
Bolivia	83.3	91.7
Brazil	4.1	39.3
Chile	4.3	50.1
Colombia	5.5	88.1
Ecuador	41.7	53.2
Paraguay	16.7	45.5
Peru	20.8	51.7
Uruguay	2.0	22.8
Venezuela	6.8	54.9

Source: M. Winkler, *Investments of U.S. capital in Latin America* (World Peace Foundation, Boston, 1929).

[a] Note that exact separation by nationality is impossible. S. G. Hanson, 'The Farquhar Syndicate in South America', *Hispanic American Historical Review* (Aug, 1937) cites the Brazil Railway Co.: 'American registration, Canadian association promoters, Brazilian properties, financed in the London market, and funds largely furnished by French and Belgian investors'. For an earlier period, D. C. M. Platt, 'British portfolio investment overseas before 1870, some doubts', *Economic History Review* XXXIII (1980), has argued that this phenomenon may have led to serious exaggeration of the U.K. figures. However, the *shift* in *relative* importance is the key point which emerges from this table.

attracted more U.S. mining investment than any other country in the world. Even Mexico continued to draw foreign money: the immediate post-revolutionary governments maintained a hands-off policy in regard to American property, and the potential threat posed by the 1917 Constitution was not taken very seriously in the decade of the 1920s.

The expansion of direct investment was of course closely associated with indirect inflows. The role of the banks became increasingly important: by 1926 there were 61 branches of U.S. banks in Latin America.[11] United States construction companies frequently worked in close association with a group of bankers, as for example the U.S. Foundation Company in Peru. By these and other means, the 1920s saw an extraordinary expansion of external financing of Latin American governments. It was the age of aggressive salesmanship, with few holds barred. A senate investigating committee found 29 representatives of American financial houses in Colombia alone, trying to negotiate loans for national and departmental governments. Rivalry was unscrupulous and bribery widely used: giving the son-in-law of the Cuban president a well-paid position in the Cuban branch of a U.S. bank while it was successfully competing against other banks, was one of the more innocent ploys.[12] The fortune made by the son of the Peruvian president, Augusto Leguía (1919–30), is a well-known story.[13] Juan Leguía's best-known coup was the collection of $520,000 in commissions in 1927 from Seligmans, the New York investment bankers, as payment for his assistance in passing them two large foreign loan contracts.

With the rise in investment went a rise in U.S. trade with the region (see Table 4). The gains made by the U.S. in wartime were consolidated in the 1920s as her competitive advantage strengthened in the new dynamic products of the period (automobiles, above all). This resulted in interesting shifts in relationships and a new potential for disequilibrium, vividly illustrated by the case of Argentina. In 1913 Argentina, like Brazil, had only limited trade and investment links with the U.S., unlike Peru and Ecuador for example, which were already importing both goods and capital from their northern neighbour. During the 1920s Argentina began increasingly to want to buy modern agricultural and other machinery from the U.S., but was still tightly tied into and

[11] C. W. Phelps, *The foreign expansion of American banks* (New York, 1927), 211–12.
[12] Lewis, *America's stake*, 377.
[13] R. Thorp and G. Bertram, *Peru 1890–1977. Growth and policy in an export economy* (London, 1978), 376 n. 13.

Table 4. *Latin American Imports from U.S. and U.K. as percentage of total imports, 1913 and 1927*

	Imports from U.S.		Imports from U.K.	
	1913	1927	1913	1927
South America				
Argentina	14.7	19.8	31.0	20.7
Bolivia	7.4	28.8	20.3	19.4
Brazil	15.7	28.7	24.5	21.2
Chile	16.7	29.7	30.0	18.4
Colombia	26.7	40.0	20.5	12.8
Ecuador	31.9	58.5	29.6	18.4
Paraguay	6.1	18.6	28.9	11.0
Peru	28.8	42.3	26.2	15.8
Uruguay	12.7	30.3	24.4	15.7
Venezuela	39.0	45.9	21.5	13.5
Mexico, Central America and Caribbean				
Costa Rica	60.4	50.3	15.0	14.9
Cuba	53.7	61.8	12.3	4.5
Dominican Republic	62.9	66.5	7.9	5.6
El Salvador	39.5	46.3	27.2	16.1
Guatemala	50.2	44.1	16.4	9.4
Honduras	67.4	79.8	14.6	7.0
Mexico	49.7	66.7	13.0	6.5
Nicaragua	47.2	66.4	20.0	11.5
Panama	54.8	69.0	21.9	9.0

Source: M. Winkler, *Investments of U.S. capital in Latin America* (World Peace Foundation, Boston, 1929).

constrained by her trading and investment relations with the U.K.[14] Uruguay, too, was constrained by a growing trade dependence on Britain as chilled beef exports became a large proportion of exports.[15]

Turning next to the implications of unfavourable trends and growing instability in commodity markets we have shown that primary product prices were responding to strong disequilibrium forces. As a result most Latin American economies experienced a new level of instability in

[14] See J. Fodor and A. O'Connell, 'La Argentina y la economía Atlántica en la primera mitad del siglo XX', *Desarrollo Económico*, 13 (1973), 13–65, for the original 'triangle' analysis; and Marcelo de Paiva Abreu, 'Argentina and Brazil during the 1930s: Impact of British and American international economic policies' in Rosemary Thorp (ed.), *Latin America in the 1930s: the role of the periphery in world crisis* (London, 1984), for a stimulating use of it in the case of Brazil.

[15] M. H. J. Finch, *A political economy of Uruguay since 1870* (London, 1981), 133.

export proceeds, vividly evidenced in the boom and crash of 1921–2 but continuing throughout the 1920s. For Argentina this is argued by one author so strongly that he is *almost* inclined to suggest that the 1929 Depression was little more than another cycle;[16] for Chile it is argued to differentiate these years significantly from the early Golden Age.[17] Cuba is perhaps the most extreme example with the Dance of the Millions – the sugar madness of 1921, followed by massive bankruptcies and foreign takeovers of the banking system as well as sugar plantations.[18]

This varying experience in terms of export fortunes is vividly illustrated in Table 5, where we see that in terms of the real purchasing power of exports only four Latin American countries (all of them producers of oil, along with a range of minerals, the product in strongest international demand) achieved satisfactory rates of growth.

Three principal sets of economic forces worked, in varying degrees, to bring to an end the 'Golden Age' of export-led growth. The first and most obvious was an early weakening in demand, or even its total collapse. The second was growing resource constraints: it is clear that the remarkable expansion following 1840 was largely 'extensive', incorporating more land, labour or other resources in a process requiring little or no increase in productivity. The third factor was a shift in the composition of exports toward those that were foreign-owned and returned a relatively low proportion of export value to the local economy, which could not only slow down the rate of growth but also introduce distributional tensions.

Chile was the most severe example of export collapse, with the fall in nitrates dating from the First World War. The coffee market, on the other hand, continued to grow, but only slowly. The meat market suffered from Britain's slow growth in the 1920s, affecting Uruguay more than Argentina, since meat was 33 per cent of her exports compared with 15 per cent for Argentina. But what differentiated these two more sharply was the resource constraint: Uruguay had no 'open frontier' while Argentina was only to begin to feel that constraint by the 1930s. In Central America the competition for use of land was beginning to result in increased food imports by this period, as it had done for some years in

16 A. O'Connell, 'Argentina into the depression: problems of an open economy', in Thorp (ed.), *Latin America in the 1930s*, 188–9.

17 J. G. Palma, 'From an export-led to an import-substituting economy: Chile 1914–39', in Thorp (ed.), *Latin America in the 1930s*, 50–74.

18 H. C. Wallich, *Monetary problems of an export economy. The Cuban experience 1914–47* (Cambridge, Mass., 1950), 52–3.

Table 5. *Real purchasing power of Latin America exports[a] 1917–18
and 1928*

(1913 = 100)

	Av. 1917–18	1928	Main exports 1923–5[c]
High growth,[b] > *5% p.a.*			
Venezuela	37	281	copper, petroleum
Colombia	54	276	coffee
Mexico[d]	178	251	petroleum, silver
Peru	106	198	petroleum, cotton
Moderate growth, 2–5% p.a.			
Paraguay	96	174	quebracho, timber
El Salvador	82	167	coffee
Brazil	48	158	coffee
Argentina	60	146	wheat, maize
Guatemala	34	139	coffee, bananas
Low/negative growth, ⩽ *1% p.a.*			
Costa Rica	52	118	coffee, bananas
Cuba	118	118	sugar
Chile	78	108	nitrates, copper
Nicaragua	43	104	coffee, bananas
Uruguay	87	100	meat, wool
Ecuador	48	93	cocoa
Bolivia	95	82	tin
Panama	46	56	bananas

Source: Capacity to import. Brazil: A. V. Villela and W. Suzigan, 'Government policy and the economic growth of Brazil 1889–1945', *Brazilian Economic Studies* (I.P.E.A., Rio de Janeiro), 3 (1975); Chile: J. G. Palma, 'Growth and structure of Chilean manufacturing industry from 1830 to 1935', unpublished D. Phil. thesis, Oxford, 1979; Argentina and Mexico: E.C.L.A., *Economic survey of Latin America 1949* (New York 1951); Other countries: dollar values from J. W. Wilkie, *Statistics and national policy*, (Los Angeles, 1974), and League of Nations, *Balance of payments yearbooks*, deflated by an average of U.S. and U.K. price indices. Main exports: League of Nations, *Memorandum on trade and balance of payments 1911–1925.* (Geneva, 1926)
[a] The product of quantum indices for exports and the terms of trade.
[b] The data for Honduras place it in this group, with by far the best export performance. But with the only export of significance being bananas, the data must surely be inaccurate.
[c] In order of size of share. Where the second export is less than 10% of the total, it is omitted.
[d] 1910–12 = 100. No data are available for 1913–17.

Peru. In Central America this was beginning to generate a tension focused on foreign capital: in Costa Rica the United Fruit Company, for example, controlled 274,000 hectares but worked only 20,000.[19]

Of the four apparent success stories during the period 1913–28 Mexico's performance is particularly notable despite the turmoil and destruction of the revolutionary decade. Oil, minerals and henequen production all expanded during the First World War, for example, to yield the strongest rise in real purchasing power of exports of any country by 1918. Oil was largely responsible for the remarkable export performance of Venezuela in the 1920s, as it was to a lesser extent in the case of Peru – and even Colombia. (By the late 1920s oil was a significant Colombian export – the U.S. interest in Colombian oil had been a major reason for the settlement of the issue of compensation for the loss of the Panama Canal – although most of the Colombian success, as we shall see, is explained by her ability to take advantage of Brazil's self-imposed restrictions on coffee sales.) Oil and minerals are, however, precisely the products with relatively low returned value (that part of export proceeds retained locally through taxes, wages, construction or other expenditures) owing to the capital intensive nature of their production process and to foreign ownership. In one case – Peru – the effect of this factor was enough to reduce the rate of growth of returned value to almost zero during the 1920s, despite the apparently healthy performance of exports in dollar values.[20] By contrast, the significance for growth of Argentina's 46 per cent expansion in the real purchasing power of its exports from 1913 to 1928 was considerably greater, based as it was on commodities with high returned value.

In explaining the development of problems which, whether external or internal, were signalling the end of the 'Golden Age' of exported growth, we have also suggested in several instances potential sources of conflict or tension over issues of distribution or resource use. This might appear to suggest that forces might have emerged in one form or another signalling to policy makers the need for change, or in some way forcing some resolution of the problem. But it is precisely the difficulty of this period that a number of factors operated to suppress or in some way reduce the level of the signal. Among these, one was the high level of

[19] V. Bulmer-Thomas 'Central America in the inter-war period', in Thorp (ed.), *Latin America in the 1930s*, 309, n. 12.

[20] The divergence between export proceeds and returned value in the 1920s is measured for Peru in Thorp and Bertram, *Peru 1890–1977*, ch. 6.

capital inflows, in particular loans, and another was the behaviour of prices.

In part, though it was typically always associated in this period with waste, diversion to luxury consumption, bribery, etc., the inflow of foreign money still played its traditional role in the model of easing the resource constraint. For example, in Colombia the expansion of coffee and other products urgently required massive investment in infrastructure; if foreign loans had not been available it is hard to see how the expansion and improvement of the transport system and port facilities could otherwise have been carried out, enabling efficient access to the Pacific and the development of a whole new area. In many other cases, however, and also in Colombia in considerable measure, the money was so badly used as to bear little relation to supply constraints. The classic story is that of the building of the Cuban national highway: it was prolonged and prolonged, with good business for everyone all round, and 'ornamental parks and some embellishments' and so on, until $100 million of securities were involved – and still the highway was not complete.[21] But the tales are endless.[22] However, what these loans did in the short term was to sustain demand, stimulate construction booms, and remove any sense of an imminent foreign exchange constraint. In the process they provided opportunities for investment or speculation for those who, lacking opportunities in the export sector, in principle might in other circumstances have sought, say, protection to create for themselves profit opportunities.

The second factor concealing the underlying reality was international price behaviour. We have suggested that with hindsight and a long-run view, we can see a weakening in many markets and an unfavourable long-run trend developing in prices. However, the instability which we have described successfully concealed this for these decades. First came the huge price increases of the First World War. Import prices rose very fast also, but since imports were largely unavailable, large export surpluses tended to accumulate, sometimes in the form of stocks sold but unable to be transported. These events were followed by the highly speculative and mismanaged boom of 1920–1. Then *some* commodities still experienced distinctly favourable, if uneven, price trends until 1925

[21] Lewis, *America's stake*, 384–6.
[22] Lewis, *America's stake*, offers numerous examples. On Bolivia, see M. Marsh, *The bankers in Bolivia* (New York, 1928).

or 1926. The movement of prices hid the sometimes slow rates of growth in volume. Uruguay was one example, Brazil another.

This explains in part why even policy innovations directly aimed at sustaining traditional export sectors were limited in number and reach. The best known and most significant was the Brazilian scheme for maintaining the price of coffee. The first scheme dated from 1906; in the 1920s a 'permanent' valorization scheme was introduced. Unfortunately, the scheme maintained prices only too successfully, without achieving either a restriction of Brazilian planting, which *expanded* in the 1920s, or the collaboration of other producers: Colombia took advantage of the maintained price to treble the area under coffee between 1915 and 1925. It has been argued that Brazil's actions would have provoked a crisis in coffee markets even without the World Depression.[23]

Another area where there was some limited innovation in the role of the state in response to the needs of the export sector was in state ownership of various sectors. Here the lead came from Uruguay, a very special case among Latin American countries at this time because of the unusual characteristics of José Batlle y Ordóñez, who first came to power in 1903, who was president in 1903–7 and again 1911–15, and whose policies prevailed until his death in 1929. Controversy reigns over the relative roles of his personal views and of deeper forces in Uruguayan society, severely limited and frustrated by small size and lack of resources in the face of a highly urbanized and abnormally middle-class population: in the 1920s such frustrations were accentuated as beef prices weakened and were channelled against the foreign houses who were seen as distributing a smaller cake unfairly. The state-owned Frigorífico Nacional, formed in 1928, was the answer, designed to compete with foreign companies and so force policies more into accord with the national interest. However, a similar initiative in Argentina needed the conditions of the 1930s to produce action.

Such responses to the role of the foreigner would seem a logical consequence both of the growing pressures on resources, and of the First World War itself, which is generally considered to have stimulated both the growth of nationalism and increased acceptance of the role of the state, the two aspects being interrelated and responding in part to the changes in the international climate described above. The war convinced many that heavy reliance on foreign capital might be unwise. The

[23] C. M. Palaez, 'An economic analysis of the Brazilian coffee support program 1906–1945; theory, policy and measurement', in Palaez (ed.), *Coffee and economic development* (São Paulo, 1973).

military and others became more preoccupied with national control of strategic sectors. At the same time government revenues were rising with exports and providing the means to become independent of foreign interests.

However, what prevented either the wartime developments or the new potential for tensions over resource use from leading to more than the level of conflict which had always been a characteristic of foreign economic presence, was the positive role that the inflow of foreign capital was seen as playing. Generally speaking, governments were keen to welcome and encourage new inflows, and particularly the new and lively interest being shown by the United States – which limited the practicality of distributional conflicts. There were, of course, some serious conflicts; Uruguay was one example. And some others, at least, surged up from a grassroots level; for example, the banana strike in Colombia in the late 1920s. In such a case government might well side *with* foreign capital.

It is no surprise, then, to find the bulk of the institutional innovation of this period precisely in those measures designed to introduce order and to make the economies in question more 'suitable' to foreign investment. This was particularly notable in the field of banking and finance. The 1920s was the decade of the Kemmerer Missions. Dr Edwin Kemmerer was a U.S. financial expert called in to various Latin American economies in turn to assist in the reform of monetary institutions. He was largely responsible for the widespread creation of central banks on the pattern of the Federal Reserve. Significant progress was made in institutional development, but the context of the 1920s had implications for this type of development. Kemmerer's presence was usually requested as part of a strategy to encourage foreign investment, and reforms were geared to that purpose. Kemmerer himself was active in encouraging and arranging loans. We have shown how on the international scene the accepted wisdom of this period was the need to return to at least a modified form of the old gold standard; this extended to Latin America and was a powerful motive behind the pressure for financial reforms, added to the desire on the part of the international financial community to secure a climate of order and good health for their increasing financial interests in Latin America. The result was first that many countries had as a policy goal a return to par value, requiring appreciation of the exchange rate: in Peru for example in 1922 the Central Bank sold off a large part of its reserves in an attempt to bring the exchange rate back up to par, and one of the explicit goals of the huge loans raised in the mid-1920s was exchange stabilization.[24] Secondly, there was a widespread adoption of a gold exchange standard; by early 1926, it had been restored in twelve Central and South American republics.[25] This did not work well; it was a crude mechanism when the refinements of developed countries' financial markets were missing, nor did it take into account that the major debtor to the banking system might be the government, incapable of reducing its expenditure according to the classical prescription, or that the volatility of private capital might equally undermine its operation.

With these reforms, it is clear, went the development of techniques of control and influence. In Central America and the Caribbean – Haiti, the Dominican Republic, Nicaragua – this tended to go as far as U.S. occupation. In South America, techniques of financial control were less direct, but far from subtle. To achieve a loan of $33 million in 1922, Bolivia had to commit not only all customs revenue plus a number of direct taxes, but had to allow a Permanent Fiscal Commission of three members, two appointed by the foreign banks, to manage her fiscal affairs throughout the twenty-five year loan period.[26] In Peru, American officials administered the customs, and an American managed the central bank. Such examples are typical of all but the largest Latin American republics during this period. In other words, the American presence was becoming even more obtrusive and more blatantly interested in control than the English had been earlier. Attempts at control from the Latin American side were weak: for example, in 1928 Colombia did pass a law requiring that provincial and municipal governments should obtain authorization from the central government before negotiating further foreign loans[27] – but only after the damage had been done. In 1927 the president of the Central Bank of Peru went to New York to tell the American banks that the loan being negotiated was too large – but his advice was disregarded.[28]

There is, however, one critical area we have still to explore: that of industry and the development of policies favouring its growth. In studying the relationship between Latin America and the international economy, one of the most intriguing questions is always, how during a period of strong integration into that system via primary products, new

---

[24] Thorp and Bertram, *Peru 1890–1977*, 129.   [25] Aldcroft, *From Versailles to Wall Street*, 151.
[26] Marsh, *Bankers in Bolivia*, 100.   [27] Lewis, *America's stake*, 381.   [28] *Ibid.*, 380.

domestic groups and policy bases can gradually grow – or not grow – to
provide a base for alternative policies as the growth mechanism weakens.

Clearly, in view of the confusing nature of the signals given during the
period by the international economy and by domestic events, radical and
coherent changes of direction and economic policy towards, for
example, protectionism were not to be expected. There were, however,
some important developments in regard to industry.

The immediate impact of the outbreak of the First World War was an
acute financial crisis in Latin America. British banks and discount houses
feared pressure at the London end and began calling in loans and
reducing advances; in the first instance panic and illiquidity were the
most notable results. But by 1915 exports were rising strongly and trade
balances were moving heavily into surplus. Import prices rose very
sharply with international inflation, and domestic prices only followed
with a lag. Thus there was a strong protective effect in a period of
expanding demand, an unusual conjuncture. The problem, however, lay on
the side of supply: clearly normal sources of capital goods were not
available any more from Europe.

How these contradictory issues balanced out has provoked an unusual
concentration of literature, its proliferation aided by unclear data. The
early view, stemming from the writings of Celso Furtado and ECLA,
favoured the view that the War provided a positive stimulation of
industrial growth in Latin America. This line of argument was first
challenged for Brazil by Warren Dean, followed by a number of other
writers.[29] Dean actually suggested that the war interrupted a rather
impressive growth process. Careful later work has concluded that there
was growth of output during the war in the Brazilian case (the earlier
arguments arising partly from differences in the weight given to export-
processing in the figures), but that it was based on fuller utilization of
existing capacity. In other words, the war was not a major discontinuity,
but built on an expansion already under way.

The war was also important, it is suggested, because of the extent to
which necessity stimulated small repair shops to broaden their activities
and to provide thereby a base for an incipient capital goods sector. One
plausible view stresses the long-run tendency for periods of increase in
capacity (when imports are cheap and available) to alternate with periods
of rapid increase in output (when imports are expensive and/or

---

[29] Warren Dean, *The industrialisation of São Paulo 1880–1945* (Austin, 1969). For the subsequent debate
on Brazilian industrialization, see *CHLA* IV, bibliographical essay 2.

Table 6. *Imports from the U.K. and the U.S., 1912–20*

(at 1913 prices)

	Argentina	Brazil	Chile	Colombia	Peru
Share of imports from U.K. in U.K. + U.S. imports, 1912	66	60	66	51	54
Indices of imports from U.S. and U.K. (1912 = 100)					
1913	108	97	100	115	115
1914	64	52	69	83	85
1915	63	52	54	94	78
1916	68	57	32	119	112
1917	59	52	95	76	123
1918	57	45	101	55	109
1919	72	70	73	105	121
1920	90	90	74	229	192

Source: R. Thorp and G. Bertram, *Peru 1890–1977: growth and policy in an open economy* (London, 1978), 128.
Note: The figures have been deflated by export or wholesale price indices for the U.S. and the U.K.

unavailable). Thus, in economies such as Brazil, with a prior industrial base and pre-existing capacity, it seems now to be agreed that the war led to some acceleration of output – some 8 or 9 per cent a year. This view is accepted also for Chile and Uruguay.

However, other economies were already more closely tied into other import sources – the United States and to a much lesser extent Japan. Table 6 shows how West Coast economies, such as Peru and Colombia, already had significant trading links with the U.S., and during the war were able rapidly to build on them – with correspondingly less stimulus to import substitution than, for example, in Brazil. The same factor might have been true for Mexico, but here internal disturbances overrode all other considerations. Despite interesting suggestions that even in the short run the Revolution was not such an economic disaster as has usually been claimed,[30] manufacturing had only just regained its 1910 level by 1920. The surprising case, perhaps, is Argentina, given its size, previous industrial base and relative lack of links with the United States. The fact that by 1918 production was only 9 per cent above the 1914 level

[30] See J. Womack, 'The Mexican economy during the Revolution, 1910–1920: historiography and analysis', *Marxist Perspectives*, 1/4 (1978).

appears to be explained by the high level of stocks at the start of the war and the slow growth of internal demand.[31] The smallest economies, such as those of Central America, were in no position to find the war an opportunity, and their elites are usually described as only waiting for the end of disruption to return wholeheartedly to the export model.

During the 1920s, we again find forces working in different directions, and considerable ambiguities and difficulties of interpretation. Of the immediate economic variables affecting industrial growth, we have to consider first demand, and, secondly, relative prices as they resulted from the combined effect of the exchange rate, tariffs, non-tariff restrictions and movements in international price levels relative to domestic. Demand remained extremely important in this period: industrialists generally still identified their health as dependent on the growth of the export sector. As we have seen, where export growth, or at least returned value, was tailing off, some compensation was typically felt in the stimulus to the level of activity from foreign loans and the accompanying construction booms. In Uruguay, where this did not happen, the redistributive policies of 'Battllismo' were a deliberate substitute. In Brazil, restrictive monetary policy in the years 1924–5 hampered the growth of textiles in particular: the policy was successfully opposed by industrialists and export interests together. As for the exchange rate, we have seen how the ideology of the period – the desire to return to the gold standard, the influence of Kemmerer and orthodox financial policies generally – led to exchange appreciation, thereby discouraging industry. On the other hand, however, once the war was over, there was some tendency to mitigate the disastrous effects of inflation on tariff systems relying heavily on 'specific' tariffs – i.e. per unit of volume and therefore subject to erosion in yield as prices rose. Figure 1 attempts to show the changing level of tariffs as a percentage of import value in four major Latin American countries. It must be stressed that this is difficult evidence to interpret: very successful protection of certain groups of products, of course, would lead to a *fall* in tariff revenues. 'Effective' protection, perhaps the most accurate indicator since it takes account of the effect of exemptions from tariffs on a producer's imported inputs as well as the protection at the level of final sales, is not widely or reliably available. And even here there are such difficulties of measurement ('world prices' and input-output relationships must be established) that it

---

[31] CEPAL (ECLA), *Análisis y proyecciones del desarrollo económico; V: el desarrollo económico de la Argentina* (Mexico, 1959).

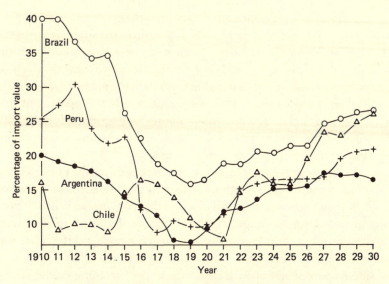

Tariffs as a percentage of import value, 1910–30
Sources: C. Díaz Alejandro, *Essays on the economic history of the Argentine Republic* (New Haven, 1970); A. V. Villela and W. Suzigan, 'Government policy and the economic growth of Brazil 1889–1945', *Brazilian Economic Studies* (I.P.E.A., Rio de Janeiro, 1975); C. Humud, 'Política económica Chilena desde 1830 a 1930', *Estudios de Economía* (Santiago), 3 (1974); *Extracto Estadístico del Perú* (Lima).

can be argued that it is no more reliable a measure than nominal protection.

Making what we can of the evidence, it seems fair to say that the increase in protection in the 1920s did not on the whole even compensate for the previous declines and that the period is perhaps best characterized as weakly protectionist. In Brazil, textiles in particular suffered from increased competition from the combined effect of international price trends and revaluation; this was not compensated adequately by tariff increases. The generally protectionist policies followed in Argentina did not raise tariff incidence to its pre-war level. Peru has been carefully evaluated in the only study which takes full account of non-tariff measures such as government monopolies, as well as attempting to balance out quantitatively the favourable effect of rising tariffs and the unfavourable effect of the appreciation of the exchange rate.[32] It argues

---

[32] C. Boloña, 'Protectionism and liberalism in Peru 1880–1980', unpublished D.Phil. thesis, Oxford, 1981. His study is at variance with some early analyses such as Thorp and Bertram, *Peru 1890–1977*.

that the net effect of changes after 1923 does in fact compensate for the earlier erosion. In Chile, under Ibañez at the end of the 1920s, reforms did take tariff incidence above what it had already been in the 1900s. But the exchange rate was again moving in the opposite direction. (It is interesting that it is suggested that in Colombia Kemmerer did not fight hard for tariff reduction, for the very reason that he appreciated that exchange rate policies were undermining any potential protective effect.[33]) In Chile, the policies did balance out to a net protective effect; the same conclusion is reached for Uruguay.

What clearly never existed was a coherent industrial policy. This is widely accepted, even by authors who find the evidence for increased protection quite convincing, and even for the most seriously protectionist country – Uruguay under Batlle y Ordóñez. Increases in rates were usually a result of individual piecemeal negotiations (and the more able to be successful because they were that) and many elements now considered part of an industrialisation policy (concerning credit, labour training, technology etc.) were completely lacking. Nor surprisingly, it is in this period then that we can date the beginning of many later problems, as the sophistication of international technology was rising fast and the entire spirit of the time was one of acceptance of things foreign. Modern technology is described by a contemporary observer as 'adapted through simple imitation, without sharing its spirits, applying only the results of procedures invented in other nations. (There was) no desire to innovate and improve'.[34] One further point is perhaps worth mentioning, as indirect confirmation of the unattractiveness of industry: the *export* of *local* capital. At a time when foreign capital was flowing in readily, it was nevertheless a matter for frequent comment that domestic capital was moving elsewhere.

Given this analysis, it is no surprise to find the industrial growth of the war years tailing off in Brazil and Chile during the 1920s. In the case of Brazil, the textile sector, suffering severely from relative price trends, stagnated, while other sectors performed less poorly. There was, however, significant growth in capacity during this period. In Chile, the growth rate of industry in real terms was 1.9 per cent a year between 1918 and 1929, compared with 9 per cent between 1913 and 1918.[35] In Peru,

[33] M. Palacios, *El café en Colombia 1850–1970: una historia económica, social y política* (Bogotá, 1979), 292.
[34] Cited in J. G. Palma, 'Growth and structure of Chilean manufacturing industry from 1830 to 1935', unpublished D.Phil. thesis, Oxford, 1979, 307.   [35] *Ibid.*, appendix 47.

there was very little growth in industry: stagnation of returned value from exports combined with a weak reversal of unfavourable relative price trends and worsening income distribution to produce little or no growth in the industrial sector. The exception was Argentina, whose export experience was probably one of the healthiest, and where the industrial sector had not grown at all during the war period. 'Catching up' plus buoyant demand meant that industry grew at 8 per cent a year 1917–29.[36] Colombia also grew quite fast, partly reflecting the previous underdevelopment of industry.

Such a lack of a coherent industrial policy is entirely consistent with the stage of development even the larger economies had reached. There was simply no basis yet for anything more. The surprise is often rather how countries with dominant export elites managed to secure the degree of protection that they did. This appears to come from the fact that exporters quite often *preferred* tariffs on imports to taxes on themselves even though in the long run such an attitude might threaten their own position. This explanation has been argued both for Brazil and Chile. And in fact industry was not always seen as such a threat: in Chile traditional agrarian groups found their export markets weakening and looked increasingly to the domestic market. In Brazil industry used those products which did not have a major market abroad, and the blending of interests was aided by intermarriage and interlocking directorates. The piecemeal nature of tariff changes also helped. This degree of overlap and blending of interests both encouraged a degree of protection to develop and inhibited the clear emergence of an industrial 'consciousness'.

CONCLUSION

What then is the significance of the period from the First World War to the World Depression? Does it have characteristics which distinguish it from the preceding forty years, the so-called 'Golden Age'? We have argued that it does, not only because the international economy was so much less healthy in the latter years, but also because the differentiation significantly changes our evaluation of the impact of the World Depression on Latin America. We have shown how in a number of ways weaknesses and tensions were developing in the 1920s in the export-led model that had appeared to serve the continent well for a long time, at

---

[36] Carlos Díaz Alejandro, *Essays on the economic history of the Argentine Republic* (New Haven, 1970), 52.

least in terms of growth. In part these problems were themselves the
products of the same forces that were to lead to the World Depression. In
part they were related to resource constraints or distributional issues. In
due course, they actually produced in many instances a slow down *before*
1929, as we have seen. For Argentina the wheat market was in decline
from 1928 and the balance of payments was further damaged when
capital outflow occurred in the same year in response to the boom in the
U.S. economy. Such a capital outflow was significant for many countries.
Colombia, Peru, Chile are all described as feeling it, and the effect was
probably still wider. Other export sectors also weakened before 1929: we
have cited the stagnation of returned value in Peru; Central America
experienced recession from 1926; Mexico likewise, accentuated by
contractive internal policies. Colombia, too, was affected by disputes
over foreign capital. To ignore all this would be to exaggerate the
abruptness of the break in 1929.

But this is not to imply that the post-war period can simply be merged
with the decades that followed the depression. There has been a tendency
to see the war as a major favourable impulse to development. Yet on the
whole little was made in the 1920s of the opportunities opened up by the
war, and some of the changes that did occur brought new forms of
vulnerability and external control.

This limited impact arose partly from the simple fact that the First
World War was an external shock which produced a *rise* in exports; even
today it remains true that rising exports are liable to erode the motivation
for a national development effort. Furthermore, its main significance
was the acceleration of the decline of the U.K. and the removal of
Germany as a trading or investing partner: the opportunities this offered
Latin America were seriously reduced by the presence in the wings of the
United States, more than ready to take over trade and investment
opportunities. (We have seen that on the whole the strength of this effect
overwhelmed the differential effect of the degree of prior integration to
the United States – with certain exceptions). Thus, as old links weakened,
new links were formed with often sharper and certainly more obvious
aspects of dependency and control. This would condition the use made
of the options opened up by the depression in 1929.

Despite the incipient tensions and weaknesses which we have shown
to be appearing in the export model it was to require more time and louder
signals before the major economic groups could perceive their interests
as significantly distinct from those of foreigners. In a sense also, the

changes that did occur during the war were premature, lacking the necessary base in the prior extension of the industrial sector and the growth
of a middle class or other groups prepared to see their interests as
lying with the growth of industry. For both kinds of reasons, Latin
America had to await the depression before the forces for change could
coalesce in a manner which made a real alternative policy possible.

This period of delay is, however, critical in explaining why when the
depression came, although its severity is undoubted, Latin America was
able to recover remarkably quickly. In some cases, notably in Brazil and
Colombia, this recovery even preceded any upturn in exports. Industrial
growth after 1929 was to be surprisingly rapid.[37] Again, this illustrates
how wrong it is to see 1929 as too much of a turning point; it was the
outcome of all that had happened – or did not happen – during the
previous fifteen years, and was to be the basis of what was to follow.

[37] See the various essays in Thorp (ed.), *Latin America in the 1930s*.

3

LATIN AMERICA, THE UNITED STATES AND THE EUROPEAN POWERS, 1830–1930

ANGLO-AMERICAN RIVALRIES AFTER INDEPENDENCE

The newly independent Latin American nations found themselves in 1830 in a world of international rivalries and power politics. The European powers, especially Britain which had played at times a decisive part in the struggle for Latin American independence, continued to play a significant political as well as economic role in Latin America until well into the twentieth century. After independence the British showed special concern for Brazil, the Río de la Plata region, Chile, Central America and Mexico. To a lesser degree the French demonstrated an interest in the Río de la Plata and Mexico. And the Caribbean remained a European-dominated lake with Spain, Britain, France, the Netherlands, Sweden and Denmark holding the many islands as colonies.

Between 1830 and 1890 European powers on numerous occasions directly intervened in the hemisphere with varying degrees of military force. Some of these interventions were directed at maintaining influence by aiding friendly Latin American countries in their rivalries with hostile neighbours as well as protecting their own nationals when they were ill used by Latin American governments. These elements were combined in the various British and French interventions in the Río de la Plata between 1836 and 1850, two of which, the French blockade of Buenos Aires in 1836 and the joint British–French blockade in 1845, lasted over two and a half years. The Argentinian dictator, Juan Manuel de Rosas, who was hostile towards both foreign interests and the neighbouring states of Uruguay and Brazil, was the main cause of these interventions.

According to the established international practice of the nineteenth century, great powers had to be able to protect the lives and property of their citizens abroad, and to enforce what were regarded as civilized standards of behaviour. The latter ranged from such actions as the suppression of the transatlantic slave trade to the punishment of those who attacked foreigners or interfered with international commerce. The financial claims of foreign nationals provoked several interventions. In April 1838 the French blockaded the port of Veracruz following Mexico's refusal to pay a bill for assorted claims of 600,000 pesos. Since these included a claim for 800 pesos for pastries devoured by a Mexican army officer in a raid on a shop owned by a French citizen the episode was called the 'Pastry War'. The French navy shelled the fortress of San Juan de Ulua and landed marines, but the claims were merely renegotiated, not paid. More seriously, in 1861 France, Britain and Spain intervened to force collection of some 80 million pesos in debts and claims. Napoleon III of France had greater ambitions than debt collection, and Britain and Spain withdrew from the operation when he landed troops and installed Maximilian of Austria as emperor. The puppet regime survived as long as 34,000 French regulars and the Foreign Legion remained. The victory of the North in the American Civil War, which freed a substantial army for duty elsewhere, combined with growing European complications, convinced Napoleon III that the revival of the French empire in America was too risky. French troops left Mexico in 1867, and subsequently Maximilian went before the firing squad and the Empress Carlota to the madhouse.

It was during the American Civil War that Spain tried to reassert an imperial role in the hemisphere. In 1861 Spain took control of Santo Domingo and remained there until 1865. In 1863 the Spanish also seized control of the Chincha Islands off the coast of Peru to redress claims of Spanish citizens. The Spaniards mined and marketed the guano while fighting a naval war with Chile which joined its rival Peru and, later, Ecuador and Bolivia in a common front against the old enemy. In 1866 the Spanish fleet bombarded both Callao and Valparaíso. During the following three decades claims by European nationals produced minor interventions, or threats of force, by Britain, France, Spain, Germany, Italy, Denmark and Russia on at least sixteen occasions involving Venezuela, Nicaragua, Colombia, Santo Domingo and Haiti.

The United States gradually became involved in the international rivalries of the hemisphere, for many years at least primarily out of concern over the European role in the region. At the time of Latin American independence the policy of the United States was to prevent the restoration of the old colonial order of economic mercantilism and political authoritarianism. As Secretary of State John Quincy Adams noted in May 1823, American policy should be designed 'to counteract the efforts which it cannot be doubted European negotiations will continue to make in the furtherance of their monarchical and monopolizing contemplations'. To promote these goals Adams hoped to negotiate treaties with the new republics that would be based upon 'the broad and liberal principles of *independence, equal favors*, and *reciprocity*'.[1] President Monroe's statement of December 1823 envisioned an 'American System' based not only on liberal economic principles but also on civil, political and religious liberty. In practice these ideals would be modified, and even distorted, when buffeted by the storms of international power politics. The Monroe Doctrine was in any case a declaration of future hopes rather than a direct plan of action. United States involvement in Latin America was for a long time restrained by fear of getting into a war with Britain or France, by domestic political preoccupations and conflicts and by limited military capabilities.

Rivalry between Britain and the United States in Mexico flared up during the mid-1840s. British agents were active in Texas after the province seceded from Mexico in 1836, and encouraged the Texans not to join the United States. In 1844 the British chargé persuaded the Mexican government to recognize the independence of Texas if the latter would agree to remain independent. In the event the Texas government accepted annexation to the United States, and war between the United States and Mexico followed. One of the arguments used by President James K. Polk to justify the annexation of both Texas and California was that Britain (and in the latter case France also) was trying to exert influence in ways hostile to the United States. To American expansionists, the vast territory between Texas and the Pacific, largely unsettled and ungoverned, offered a tempting opportunity for European ambitions. Thus, the 'Manifest Destiny' of the nation to spread from the Atlantic to the Pacific would be blocked if the United States did not incorporate it into the Union.

At the end of the war between the United States and Mexico (1846–8), the Caribbean became an area of confrontation with the British. In 1839 a royal agent had seized the island of Ruatan (off the northern coast of Honduras), and in 1843 the British government had revived the

---

[1] Walter LaFeber (ed.), *John Quincy Adams and American continental empire* (Chicago, 1965), 123.

protectorate over the Mosquito Indians along the east coast of Nicaragua
and Honduras. At the same time United States interests in Central
America were stimulated by the prospect of expansion to the Pacific.
Transit routes across Central America became an item of prime interest
to American officials, and in 1846 the United States negotiated the
Bidlack treaty with New Granada (Colombia). The British and French
had refused a Colombian proposal for international neutralization of the
Isthmus of Panama. Under the Bidlack treaty American citizens were
granted the right of transit under the same conditions as citizens of New
Granada, and the United States guaranteed the neutrality of the isthmus
in order to preserve free transit. In addition, the United States
guaranteed New Granada's rights of sovereignty over the territory. In
1848 the British occupied the town of San Juan at the mouth of the San
Juan river in order to consolidate the Mosquito protectorate; it was
renamed Greytown. Then in October 1849 a British naval officer seized
Tigre Island in the Gulf of Fonseca. This act was repudiated by the
British government, but the ensuing outcry in the United States led to
negotiations. The Clayton–Bulwer treaty, signed on 19 April 1850,
provided that neither party would 'occupy', 'colonize', or exercise
'dominion' over any part of Central America. The treaty also stipulated
that in the event of a canal being built neither country would fortify or
exercise exclusive control over it.

Initially the Clayton–Bulwer treaty settled nothing since the British
argued that it enshrined the *status quo* while the Americans held that it
mandated a reduction in British control; especially over the Mosquito
coast. In 1852 the British government consolidated Ruatan and adjacent
islands into the Colony of the Bay Islands and Americans cried betrayal.
After a ship of the United States navy blew apart Greytown in 1854 to
avenge a mob attack on a diplomatic official, war talk was in the air. In
actuality Central America was not a high priority area for British
interest, and the Crimean War was one war enough. Tempers cooled,
and in 1856 another treaty was signed under which the British agreed to
relinquish the Mosquito protectorate and to cede the Bay Islands to
Honduras. Due to a minor reservation the United States refused to ratify
it, but the British proceeded to settle the Central American question
along the lines of the treaty. All claims were given up except Belize,
which was turned into the Colony of British Honduras in 1862.
Unofficially British officials accepted the idea that sometime in the future

the United States would be the dominant power in the region. Some forty years passed, however, before the United States in fact exercised such a role.

President James Buchanan (1857–61) believed that the United States should exercise a police role in Central America and the Caribbean to ensure that disorderly conditions did not threaten foreign nationals or the transit routes across Central America. He argued that the United States must do this or European powers would intervene. His requests for authority to use the armed forces in such interventions were denied by the Congress. Almost fifty years would pass before President Theodore Roosevelt would enshrine this assertion of American police power in the Caribbean as a corollary to the Monroe Doctrine.

During the second half of the nineteenth century various Latin American states called on the United States for protection. In 1857 Nicaragua signed a protectorate treaty, which the United States Senate refused to approve. And on at least three occasions between 1868 and 1892 Santo Domingo offered to lease or cede a naval base (and even the country itself) to the United States. These offers were rejected, as were similar ones made by Haiti. The United States was also called on to mediate conflicts between Latin American states and European nations attempting to collect debts.

In 1878 the French Panama Canal Company obtained the right to build an isthmian canal. The United States government objected, but to no avail. Yet, from this moment on pressure developed in the country for a more active role in the Caribbean–Central American region. The United States navy conducted surveying expeditions on the isthmus, and a joint Congressional resolution of 1880 urged the abrogation of the Clayton–Bulwer treaty. In 1884 Secretary of State Frederick Frelinghuysen negotiated a treaty with Nicaragua providing for joint United States–Nicaraguan ownership of a canal. The treaty would have unilaterally abrogated the 1850 treaty with Great Britain, but the Senate failed to approve it by five votes.

In 1881 Secretary of State James G. Blaine tried to implement a more active Latin American role for the nation. The United States government issued invitations to an International American Conference, but Secretary Blaine resigned his position for political reasons. His replacement, Frelinghuysen, cancelled the conference even though several Latin American nations had already accepted the invitation. Blaine had hoped the conference would create a system to bring peace and stability to the hemisphere, and that such conditions would help the United States challenge European economic supremacy.

Most Latin American countries not only looked to Europe for markets but also for governmental financing and capital for economic development projects. There was a brief investment boom during the 1820s, but most of these ventures were wiped out by bankruptcy or liquidation. Another era of large-scale investment began after the 1860s with most of the capital coming from Britain, France and Germany. With some fluctuation, British investment grew from £85 million in 1870 to about £750 million ($3.7 billion) in 1914. By this date French investment was approximately six billion francs ($1.2 billion), and German investment was 3.8 billion marks (about $900 million). British capital generally flowed into railway building, mining (Chilean nitrates) and manufacturing (meat packing in the Río de la Plata). French investments went into railways as well as real estate, banking, mining and manufacturing. The Germans were more interested in mortgage banks and plantations (especially in Central America).

During the latter part of the nineteenth century investors in the United States began to look south; especially to Cuba and Mexico. The major flow of American capital, however, did not begin until after 1900, and European capital would predominate (especially in South America) until well into the twentieth century. American entrepreneurs, utilizing European capital, made some contributions to economic development. For example, Henry Meiggs and Minor C. Keith built railways in Peru and Central America. Keith also started the large-scale cultivation of bananas in Costa Rica and Guatemala.

THE UNITED STATES AND LATIN AMERICA IN THE LATE NINETEENTH CENTURY

During the 1880s and 1890s the competition for empire between the major European powers increased sharply. Africa was divided and a race for the final division of Asia seemed to be under way. To many informed people it appeared certain that competition for control of the world's territory, resources and markets had entered its final stage. In turn, this rivalry was enhanced by different versions of the civilizing and Christianizing mission of each nation. Closely related to, and exacerbated by, the imperial perception of national power and prestige was an intensified commercial rivalry even in non-colonial areas.. Driven by a fear of dropping behind and being shut out in the race for markets, national leaders made every effort to improve the marketing position of their country. Protectionism at home and special unilateral economic arrangements abroad (especially commercial agreements that discriminated against third parties) characterized these efforts.

The United States economy had had an important foreign trade component since the colonial period; commerce was considered a vital part of the national interest. Americans in the late nineteenth century became increasingly convinced that their export trade was threatened by the new imperial world order. In 1880 the United States imported goods worth $176 million from Latin America, for example, but exported only $58 million. Thus the country seemed to be falling behind even in what it regarded as its own backyard. And this anxiety was intensified when Americans considered the decay of their once flourishing merchant marine. In 1850 over 50 per cent of all tonnage carried from American ports was carried by American ships; in 1900 this had plummeted to only 17 per cent. In the United States a growing number of influential citizens and political leaders were coming to the conclusion that the nation would have to reorient its foreign policies to meet the changing world conditions and effectively confront the challenges posed by imperial rivalries. Frederick B. Emory, of the Bureau of Foreign and Domestic Commerce, expressed some of the new concerns when he reported in 1898:

It may be said that the chief business of European diplomacy at the present day is to secure 'spheres of influence' and wider opportunities for trade, as well as suitable territory for occupation by the overflow of population from the more densely inhabited countries . . . The partition of Africa among the European powers offers considerations of an economic character of almost equal magnitude while the plans of the more active commercial nations for increasing their respective shares of the trade of the Latin American markets, affect us even more seriously in the development of our commercial intercourse with the southern half of the Western Hemisphere.[2]

James G. Blaine had been an early articulator of these ideas and fears. He believed that in the western hemisphere peaceful relations, mediation of conflicts, the reduction of European influence and the increase of the United States export trade were all inextricably tied together. Although his first effort to convene an inter-American conference to achieve these

[2] Frederick Emory, *Commercial relations of the United States during the years 1896 and 1897* (Washington: 1898), I, 19–22.

721865

goals had failed, his views on hemispheric relations and the need for a more active role by the United States government gained support during the 1880s. In May 1888 the Congress requested President Grover Cleveland to issue invitations to such a conference. As a result of a shift in party control during the 1888 presidential election Blaine once again became Secretary of State and presided over the conference that convened in Washington in 1889.

Before settling down to business the Latin American delegates were taken on a rigorous rail excursion through the industrial areas of the United States. They visited 41 cities, looking at factories and demonstrations of American technological prowess, and listening to innumerable speeches and band concerts. The London *Spectator* commented that the trip was designed to instil respect for a nation, 'so fearfully energetic that it considers a journey of six thousand miles by rail an entertainment'.[3] The excursion and the conference were clearly designed to encourage Latin American nations to look to the United States rather than to Europe for economic and political leadership.

The conference re-convened in November 1889 and Blaine introduced measures to create a hemispheric customs union and provide for arbitration for the settlement of disputes between nations. Argentina led the efforts to oppose the first proposal, and Chile, which had made important territorial conquests in the War of the Pacific, objected to the second. None of the customs union proposals were adopted; a compromise treaty on arbitration was approved by only eleven nations (and none ratified it). The conference did, however, create the International Union of American Republics with a Commercial Bureau of the American Republics, which was authorized to collect and disseminate information concerning tariffs and commercial regulations.

Blaine's vision of a truly functional inter-American system foundered on the myth that the potential for a genuine community of interests existed in the hemisphere and could be brought to reality by American leadership. In the twentieth century many of Blaine's successors would try a variety of policies in attempts to create a system that would solve most, if not all, of the problems of inter-American relations. Their efforts would have limited results because some basic conflicts of interest simply could not be resolved by professions of Pan American harmony. In turn, many Latin American leaders adopted their own version of a special hemispheric relationship in attempts to impose utopian standards of

[3] Quoted in Thomas A. Bailey, *A diplomatic history of the American people*, (9th edn, Englewood Cliffs, NJ., 1974), 408.

international conduct on the United States. Their efforts also would have mixed results.

The inter-American conference of 1889 where the United States was denied the role of elective leader of the hemisphere did nothing to assuage the growing American anxiety over European dominance in the hemisphere and the increased sense of commercial rivalry. The belief that the United States had to play a greater role in Latin America and gain more prestige, helped to set the stage for crises with Chile (1891–2) and Great Britain (1895). In both cases the United States government, under both Republican and Democratic administrations, reacted with an emotional, nationalistic posture conditioned by sharpened feelings of international rivalry. A kind of 'crisis mentality' began to characterize American views of the hemisphere.

The Chilean crisis grew out of an incident in October 1891, when 120 sailors from the U.S.S. *Baltimore* were attacked while on shore leave in Valparaiso. Two were killed, seventeen injured and others were beaten and jailed. According to testimony at a board of inquiry, the Chilean police participated in the attacks. The Chilean regime which had recently come to power through a revolution was antagonistic towards the United States because of its normal diplomatic support of the former (Balmaceda) government. Chilean officials did not express regrets and their first diplomatic efforts were ambiguous and quite critical of President Benjamin Harrison. War fever flared in the United States as the body of one of the sailors lay in state in Independence Hall, Philadelphia. Harrison's ultimatum to the Chilean government in January 1892 was reinforced with a special message to the Congress. A new Chilean foreign minister sent an acceptable apology and reparations were paid for the deaths and injuries. Under the exaggerated rhetoric of national pride the Harrison administration was in effect declaring that the United States was a major power in the hemisphere and must be accorded the same treatment as Great Britain. Its national symbols must be treated with respect, and its official representatives must not be mistreated or the offending nations would be held to account. For their part the Chileans increasingly now looked to Germany for military and economic assistance.

The crisis between Britain and the United States erupted over the long-term boundary dispute between Venezuela and the colony of British Guiana. For years the Venezuelan authorities had tried to enlist the support of the United States to force arbitration. In 1887 the British had declined the offer of American good offices. In 1894 the Venezuelans hired a former American diplomat, William L. Scruggs, as a lobbyist, and his pamphlet 'British Aggressions in Venezuela, or the Monroe Doctrine on Trial' circulated widely. Due in part to his efforts a resolution urging arbitration of the dispute was introduced in Congress and subsequently adopted with the unanimous approval of both houses.

The atmosphere of heightened concern over European influence and power in the hemisphere was further exacerbated in April 1895 when the British occupied Corinto, Nicaragua and took control of the customs house to force payment for damages to the property of British citizens. The force was withdrawn after a reparations agreement was made, but many Americans viewed the incident as more evidence of the ineffectiveness of the Monroe Doctrine. Writing in the *North American Review*, Senator Henry Cabot Lodge of Massachusetts exemplified the crisis mentality when he linked the situation in Nicaragua, the Venezuelan boundary dispute and fears of European imperial expansion:

If Great Britain is to be permitted to occupy the ports of Nicaragua and, still worse, take the territory of Venezuela, there is nothing to prevent her taking the whole of Venezuela or any other South American state. If Great Britain can do this with impunity, France and Germany will do it also.[4]

In a note to the British government of 20 July 1895, Secretary of State Richard Olney gave expression to a rather exaggerated vision of a hemisphere allied with the United States by ties of 'geographical proximity . . . natural sympathy . . . similarity of government'. This alliance gave the protection of the Monroe Doctrine to all the nations of the hemisphere, the Secretary noted. To underline the 'right' of the United States to demand arbitration in the Venezuelan boundary dispute Olney made his famous declaration, 'Today the United States is practically sovereign on this continent, and its fiat is law upon the subjects to which it confines its interposition.'

In late November the British Foreign Secretary, Lord Salisbury, replied to Olney's vastly exaggerated definition of American power in a note that was almost as undiplomatic as the one it answered. Salisbury corrected Olney's errors of history, gave him a lecture on international law and the Monroe Doctrine, and flatly rejected the arbitration demand. President Grover Cleveland was so infuriated that he went before Congress to request funds for a boundary investigation commission. A cheering Congress approved Cleveland's proposal that the United States unilaterally establish the boundary and enforce it regardless of British policy.

[4] *North American Review*, 160 (June 1895), 658.

War talk was heard in both countries, but the Boer crisis in South Africa, combined with the growing British perception of a German threat, prompted a decision to accept the American demand. With the good offices of the United States, Venezuela and Great Britain signed an arbitration treaty in February 1897. The United States government had to apply pressure to Venezuela to accept a compromise exempting territory that had been held by either party for a fifty-year period. In the final settlement of October 1899 the Venezuelans retained control of the mouth of the Orinoco River, buts its leaders were unhappy over the refusal of the United States to support their most extreme claims. Other Latin American leaders were displeased with Olney's statement about American power, although in reality this assertion was largely bluster, designed for local consumption. For the British government, this controversy marked an important turning point. In order to court American friendship in the face of a growing rivalry with Germany, the British took a large step towards accepting United States political predominance in the Western hemisphere. Economic predominance was another matter.

In the United States in the 1890s an increasing number of private citizens and public officials believed that the world was being closed by expanding empires and that the United States could find itself isolated. The United States would then be at the mercy of the most powerful nations in the world. The country could choose not to play in the game of international power politics, but it could not avoid the military, political, economic and ideological consequences of such a decision. An important part of this game was ensuring peace, order and stability in what were called backward nations. In such areas the power that provided the police function was the one that exerted major influence. By the 1890s a number of prominent Americans had adopted this European view of international relations. They believed that if the nation wanted to be taken seriously, and have its interests treated with respect by other powers, then it had to assert the police function to restore and maintain peace and order in those parts of the world considered to be especially vital to American interests. The Caribbean and Gulf of Mexico had long been considered part of the American security zone, as it was the access route to the nation's soft underbelly and the Mississippi–Ohio rivers transportation system. Central America had been added to the zone as American leaders accepted the idea that the United States must build and control an isthmian canal. Such a canal would be militarily and economically vital for any expanded American role in South America

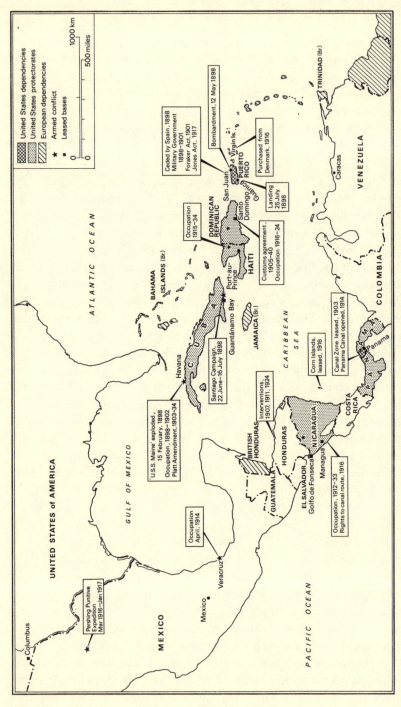

The United States in the Caribbean, 1898–1934

and Asia. In the modern world of steel and steam navies it could mean the difference between isolation and access. But, if the United States failed to maintain peace and order in its own backyard, it could not expect effectively to protect a canal and its access routes. Thus, the argument ran, the United States had to assert a policing role in the Caribbean–Central American region, or else some other power would. In the context of events in Africa and Asia many American leaders believed the country had to act to preclude greater European influence and/or control.

This general point of view did not prescribe any particular policy for implementation. Americans were severely divided over the question of specific policies and especially over the use of military force. The debate was further complicated by the resurgence of an ideological element in the nation's heritage. This was the belief that the country – sometimes in conjunction with other Anglo-Saxons – had a destiny (sometimes called manifest) to redeem the world by spreading Anglo-American civilization, republican government and Protestant Christianity. Many included under civilization the promotion of economic development, education and sanitation.

All of these issues and arguments emerged during the public debate over the United States role in the Cuban war for independence which had begun in 1895. President William McKinley did not want war, but he had accepted the idea that the United States was ultimately responsible for law and order in the Caribbean. When Spain could not settle the war by either winning or withdrawing, McKinley asked the Congress for authority to step in and pacify Cuba. Public enthusiasm for such a move had already been aroused by stories of Spanish atrocities and was further sharpened by the sinking of the U.S.S. *Maine* in Havana harbour in February 1898. The president requested the Congress to grant him authority to carry out the international duty of the United States; the peacekeeping function of all civilized powers:

. . . to take measures to secure a full and final termination of hostilities between the Government of Spain and the people of Cuba, and to secure in the island the establishment of a stable government, capable of maintaining order and observing its international obligations, insuring peace and tranquility and the security of its citizens as well as our own . . .[5]

Some congressmen wanted the authorization to recognize the independence of Cuba under the auspices of the Cuban provisional government. McKinley and his advisers did not believe that this

[5] *A compilation of the messages and papers of the presidents* (New York, 1922), XIII 6292.

'government-in-the-woods', as some called it, was a functional entity capable of governing Cuba in peacetime. They feared that an independent Cuba under this regime would become another Haiti or Dominican Republic and create more temptations for European intervention. If the United States brought peace to Cuba, McKinley believed that the nation had an obligation to prepare the island for self-government and protect it in its republican infancy. The president stated that he would veto any resolution recognizing the independence of Cuba. But, he accepted the compromise Teller Amendment which stated that the United States would not annex Cuba and would 'leave the government and control of the island to its people' after pacification had been accomplished.

As a result of the war with Spain and the Treaty of Paris (1898) the United States took its first step towards establishing a sphere of interest in the Caribbean. Puerto Rico became an American colony, and passed into a kind of limbo – forgotten by most American leaders except for occasional bouts of liberalization when the colonial status would be modified. Cuba, however, was the key to the Gulf–Caribbean, and the status of the island and the role of the United States in Cuban affairs would be debated for several decades. The results, like those of the broader debate over predominance in the Caribbean–Central American region, would be a mixture of policies and actions characterized by paradox and ambiguity; a kind of ambivalent imperialism continually modified by guilt, domestic politics and the lack of a true colonial drive.

To American leaders, pacification of Cuba meant establishing a republican government, providing economic stability and creating the infrastructure for an orderly society. Cuba was ruled by an American military government from 1898 to 1902, and this experiment in nation building would influence United States policies in the region for the first quarter of the twentieth century. General Leonard Wood became the second military governor in December 1899. Under his and Secretary of War Elihu Root's direction extensive programmes of sanitation, school building, teacher training, disease control, prison and mental hospital reform, judicial system reforms and developing governmental structures were implemented. Wood believed that stable government and orderly society required, '. . . good schools, good courts, a system of public works, means of communications, hospitals, charities, etc., etc . . .', and that these could only be provided through economic development. As he told President Theodore Roosevelt:

. . . inasmuch as her geographical position compels us to control and protect her, why not stimulate by moderate assistance those industries which will make her so prosperous and contented that she will be always friendly and a source of strength to us? This certainly is better than having at our doors a demoralized, poverty stricken island, such as Santo Domingo or Hayti [sic] existing under conditions which endanger the lives of millions of our citizens.[6]

Wood articulated a concept of dollar diplomacy that would be increasingly utilized by the United States after 1900. In this view, economic development, sound government and social order were all tied together. A sound government exercised fiscal prudence and created a situation that would attract foreign (preferably American) capital at reasonable rates of interest. This capital would promote economic development, which in turn would strengthen the government and produce social harmony. Peace, order and stability would be ensured by the continuing process of economic development coupled to sound government. Wood and others believed that this would prove mutually beneficial, and that the United States would enjoy increased trade with the developing country.

General Wood and President Roosevelt were convinced that this process was well under way in Cuba by 1902. The United States army withdrew from the island, and the new republic formally came into existence on 20 May 1902. The constitution of Cuba contained several articles (known as the Platt Amendment since they were added to the Army Appropriations Act of 1901) that the Cuban constitutional convention had been required to adopt as the price of American withdrawal. These articles placed certain limitations on the actions of the new government in the areas of contracting public debt, making military arrangements with foreign powers and repudiating acts of the U.S. military government. In addition, the amendment gave the United States the right to intervene in Cuba under certain conditions and stipulated that Cuba would sell or lease 'lands necessary for coaling or naval stations . . .' Secretary Root promised a Cuban delegation that the United States would only intervene under the most extreme conditions of anarchy, and he pledged the Roosevelt administration's support for special treatment for Cuban sugar in the American market; the latter was implemented in 1903 after a hard battle with domestic protectionists.

The Platt Amendment was the product of many minds and was a compromise between those who wanted to exercise a decidedly imperial role in the Caribbean and those who wanted a rather general kind of predominant American influence. Root considered the 1903 treaty with

---

[6] Wood to Roosevelt, 28 October 1901, box 29, Leonard Wood MSS, Library of Congress (Washington).

Cuba embodying the Platt Amendment as the incorporation of the Monroe Doctrine into international law. In historical terms it was the interpretation of the Monroe Doctrine that had been gradually emerging since the 1880s. It certainly embodied the widespread belief that, in the words of General Wood, '. . . there is no escaping the fact that, even if we do not own the island, we are responsible for its conduct, the maintenance of a stable government, and the just and equitable treatment of foreigners residing thereunder'.[7] The basic ideas involved helped to shape the Caribbean policies of the United States for the next three decades.

EUROPE, THE UNITED STATES AND LATIN AMERICA BEFORE THE FIRST WORLD WAR

The United States was not the only country taking an increased interest in Latin America at the turn of the century. Imperial Germany was also becoming involved not only economically, but demographically and militarily. By 1900 over 350,000 Germans had migrated to southern Brazil, and some 120,000 were living in Chile. There were other settlements of Germans in Argentina and Central America. The German government actively encouraged these settlers to preserve and extend German traditions, and financed German-language schools and churches. The imperial navy stepped up its operations in the waters of the hemisphere and in 1900 Admiral von Tirpitz told the Reichstag budget committee that eventually Germany would require an armed naval station on the coast of Brazil.[8] Kaiser Wilhelm II did not hide his belief that Germany had a major role to play in the western hemisphere. He regarded Cuba as a 'European state', but failed in his efforts to rally European opposition to the United States during the war with Spain. In 1900 the German Ambassador to Mexico noted in a dispatch that a German colony in Latin America would be of more value than all of Africa. The Kaiser wrote in the margin: 'Correct, that is why we must be the "paramount power" there.'[9] The Kaiser consistently refused to recognize the Monroe Doctrine and pointedly asserted the right of European nations to intervene in the hemisphere.

The German military presence in Latin America became increasingly

[7] *Ibid.*
[8] Holger H. Herwig, *Politics of frustration: the United States in German naval planning, 1889–1941* (Boston, 1976), 73.   [9] *Ibid.*, 21 and 68.

noticeable. German army officers began to instruct the Chilean army in 1896 and by 1900 the German military mission had founded the Chilean Academy of War. The Chilean army adopted Prussian-grey uniforms and coal-scuttle helmets. Before 1914 Germany had sent military missions to Argentina, Bolivia and Paraguay. The Mexican government had seriously considered such an arrangement. The only comparable effort was the French military mission in Peru (1895).[10]

In 1903 the German Admiralty prepared Operations Plan III; a contingency plan for war against the United States, fought in the western hemisphere. This plan envisaged the occupation of Puerto Rico by an army of 12,000 to 15,000 men (the number increased between 1903 and 1906), and the utilization of bases on the island to conduct a naval offensive against the United States. In 1906 the plan was scrapped as German plans and attentions were directed more to Europe and the shifting alliance structure.[11]

German ambitions in the hemisphere continued and these stimulated American fears of possible European control of parts of the hemisphere. Thus, German–American rivalry was an important factor underlying the expanded role of the United States in the Caribbean–Central American region. The German Admiralty did not hide its desire for bases in the Caribbean to control an isthmian canal, and to American leaders it seemed that the German–American naval confrontations that had occurred in the Samoan Islands (1888) and Manila Bay (1898) might be repeated much closer to home.[12] Rumours of a possible war with Germany periodically circulated in the United States during the early years of the century. Senator Lodge confided to President Roosevelt his belief that the German emperor, 'has moments when he is wild enough to do anything. If it [war] comes at all it will come through some attempt in South America, probably Brazil.'[13] In 1913 the United States navy General Board formulated its Black War Plan; a defensive operation based on a German attack against the western hemisphere. The Board stressed the point that when strong enough, 'Germany will insist upon the occupation of Western Hemisphere territory under the German flag,

[10] 'Foreign Military Training Missions in Latin America', 28 December 1944. Office of Plans and Development (OPD), file #336 Latin America, case 74. RG 165, Records of the War Department General and Special Staffs; National Archives of the United States (Washington).
[11] Herwig, *Politics of frustration*, 85–92.   [12] *Ibid.*, 68–72.
[13] Henry Cabot Lodge, *Selections from the correspondence of Theodore Roosevelt and Henry Cabot Lodge, 1884–1918* (New York and London, 1925), I, 487–8.

and the United States will then have to defend her policy by force, or acquiesce in the occupation'.[14]

The Venezuelan crisis of 1902 provided a new stimulus to German–American rivalry and convinced Theodore Roosevelt, and others, that the United States had to extend its power beyond Cuba and Puerto Rico. Roosevelt had previously stated that Latin American nations could not abuse foreign interests and expect to hide behind the Monroe Doctrine; in cases of misbehaviour by a South American country, '. . . let the European country spank it'.[15] And at first Roosevelt seemed to acquiesce in the British–German–Italian pacific blockade of Venezuela, instituted on 9 December 1902. Several Venezuelan ships were sunk or captured, and some coastal forts were shelled by the combined squadrons. The Venezuelan dictator, Cipriano Castro, accepted the international arbitration he had earlier rejected, but the blockade was turned into an official wartime blockade pending a final settlement. Then, on 17 January 1903, a German gunboat levelled Fort San Carlos guarding the Straits of Maracaibo. Other incidents followed, and Roosevelt informed the German Ambassador that Admiral George Dewey (with a fleet of 54 ships at Culebra Island, Puerto Rico) had secret orders to be prepared to sail for Venezuelan waters on an hour's notice. On 13 February the British and German governments signed a protocol lifting the blockade.

During the year 1901 to 1902 Roosevelt had been engaged in a variety of efforts to strengthen the American position in the Caribbean. Besides assembling a fleet at Culebra and transferring the island to the Navy Department, he had attempted to purchase the Danish Virgin Islands, dispatched a secret expedition to scout the Venezuelan coast for possible landing sites and sent a naval envoy to help Venezuela prepare for an invasion. This burst of activity and veiled show of force was related not only to the Venezuelan crisis but also to the fact that United States' efforts to acquire an isthmian canal site were in the final stages. The second Hay–Pauncefote Treaty between the United States and Great Britain was signed in November 1901. This treaty superseded the Clayton–Bulwer Treaty (1850) and gave the United States the right to build, control and fortify any canal. The search for a suitable route had been going on for some time, but the United States Congress (after some astute lobbying by Philippe Bunau-Varilla of the French New Panama Canal Company) opted for Panama in June 1902 – if the president could

---

[14] Quoted in Herwig, *Politics of frustration*, 105.   [15] Quoted in Bailey, *Diplomatic history*, 502.

secure the right-of-way, 'within a reasonable time and upon reasonable terms'.

Treaty negotiations between Colombia and the United States had been under way for almost two years. They had begun at the behest of Colombia, and Roosevelt and Secretary of State John Hay believed that the final terms of the Hay–Herrán Treaty met the wishes of the Colombian government. But the Colombian president convened a special congress that, under his leadership, stalled for weeks and finally rejected the treaty. The Panamanians revolted and Roosevelt responded by invoking the 1846 Bidlack treaty to prevent Colombia from landing additional troops. Recognition quickly followed the establishment of the Republic of Panama and a canal treaty between the United States and Panama was signed twelve days later. The Colombian president now offered to approve the earlier treaty, but Roosevelt ignored him. The Colombians then cried 'foul' and accused the United States of theft. But Colombia had only exercised intermittent control over Panama and had always relied on United States intervention to maintain some semblance of sovereignty. (There had been some 53 uprisings on the isthmus since 1846 and Colombia had invited American intervention on at least six occasions.) Theodore Roosevelt wanted a canal built as soon as possible. The Hay–Bunau–Varilla treaty of November 1903 provided for an American-controlled canal zone ten miles wide. It also made Panama a virtual protectorate.

With the securing of the canal zone, construction of the waterway to join the Atlantic and Pacific Oceans began, and the United States acquired a stake in Central America that strengthened the belief in the country that it must exercise more control in the region. In December 1902 the British prime minister, Arthur Balfour, had quietly slipped the word to Roosevelt that his government would be more than happy to see the United States police the 'troublemakers' in Latin America. In 1904, when the Dominican Republic went bankrupt, Roosevelt accepted the opportunity to assert a doctrine of preventive intervention, which became known as the 'Roosevelt corollary' to the Monroe Doctrine. He explained to Congress:

If a nation shows that it knows how to act with reasonable efficiency and decency in social and political matters, if it keeps order and pays its obligations, it need fear no interference from the United States. Chronic wrongdoing, or an impotence which results in a general loosening of the ties of civilized society, may in America, as elsewhere, ultimately require intervention by some civilized nation, and in the Western Hemisphere the adherence of the United States to the Monroe Doctrine may force the United States, however reluctantly, in flagrant cases of such wrongdoing or impotence, to the exercise of an international police power.[16]

Thus, Roosevelt extended the basic premise behind the Cuban pacification and the Platt Amendment to the Caribbean–Central American region as a whole, and clearly staked out a United States sphere of interest. In the case of the Dominican Republic, Roosevelt signed a pact giving control of customs collecting to American authorities. They in turn would handle the country's revenues so as to provide a portion to settle the scaled-down debt. The Senate did not approve the original pact, so Roosevelt had to proceed under an executive agreement until a modified treaty was approved in 1907.

Under the conservative guidance of Elihu Root, domestic opposition and the frustrations of the 'civilizing mission' itself, Roosevelt came to accept that there were limitations on the extent to which the American sphere of interest could be enforced. For example, he was most reluctant to send troops to Cuba in 1906 when the Cuban politicians brought the government to a halt. Another attempt at republic building in the Caribbean was to be made, but Roosevelt confided to the editor-diplomat Whitelaw Reed in 1906 that he could see many difficulties in 'the control of thickly peopled tropical regions by self-governing northern democracies . . .'[17] To effect the peaceful settlement of disputes, the Central American Conference was held in Washington in 1907. This conference created the Central American Court of Justice to adjudicate disputes and also formulated policies that were intended to discourage the periodic barrack revolts that were so prevalent in the region.

In similar fashion, Roosevelt's successor William Howard Taft proclaimed a policy of substituting 'dollars for bullets'. He and Secretary of State Philander C. Knox believed that fiscal stability was the key to economic development and stability. The administration encouraged American bankers to refinance the bonds of several countries in order to remove the potential cause for European intervention. American bankers did invest in the Haitian National Bank and loaned money to Nicaragua to pay off British bonds. In Nicaragua the United States took

[16] *Messages and papers of the presidents*, Vol. xiv, 6923.
[17] Quoted in Allan Reed Millett, *The politics of intervention: the military occupation of Cuba, 1906–1908* (Columbus, Ohio, 1968), 251.

over the customs collections as well. Taft and Knox hoped to forestall large-scale interventions by using American dollars to support the financial integrity of governments in the American sphere. The Taft administration also tried to promote the peaceful settlement of disputes by mediating several controversies and sponsoring a series of arbitration treaties.

During this period of American sphere-of-interest diplomacy, the major Latin American nations reacted in various ways. After 1900, Brazil adopted a policy of friendship with the United States as a counterweight to Argentina. On the other hand, Mexico, which had developed very close relations with her northern neighbour, increasingly began to court Britain and Germany. (The United States State Department even suggested in 1907 that Mexico might share the policing duties in Central America. But, Mexican ambitions in the area did not necessarily accord with those of the United States, and the prospect of co-operation evaporated.)[18] Some Latin American nations adopted at this time two doctrines formulated by Argentinians and tried to have these accepted as inter-American and international law. In a series of volumes published between 1868 and 1896 Carlos Calvo argued for an absolute version of national sovereignty and applied this to the national treatment of foreigners and foreign interests. He stated that foreigners must be treated exactly as nationals, they must be subject to national laws and courts, and they had no right to appeal to their home governments for support. He was reacting to the doctrine of extra-territoriality which had been instituted by the developed, industrial nations to protect their nationals from the caprices of rulers, different legal systems and the ravages of political upheaval. The western nations argued that principles such as the sanctity of contracts and due process of law were international law and protected foreigners and their property regardless of what rulers did to their own citizens. This principle of extra-territoriality had been abused in practice and had been used to demand privileged treatment for foreign interests. But Calvo went to the other extreme and argued that nations could do anything they wanted, even change the rules of the game under which foreigners had come to a country and invested. In a peculiar sense Calvo wanted to establish as a principle of international law the idea that there was no such thing as international standards of behaviour. After 1890 the Calvo doctrine became the legal and

18 See Daniel Cosío Villegas, *La vida política exterior, parte primera*, vol. 5 of *Historia moderna de México: El Porfiriato* (Mexico, 1960), 620–92.

ideological battle cry of those Latin American nations that wanted to prevent the industrial powers from protecting their nationals and their interests. This was the classic debate between debtors and creditors, the developed and the underdeveloped, the weak and the strong. The battle about this doctrine would appear in some form in almost every inter-American conference. At the Second International Conference of American States (Mexico City 1901–2) a resolution on the treatment of aliens (similar to the one adopted at the first conference and rejected by the United States) embodying the Calvo Doctrine was proposed. As expected, the United States voted against any idea that states had no responsibilities for damage sustained by foreigners during civil wars, or that aliens had no right to appeal to their home governments.

The second doctrine (based on the first) was enunciated by Luis Drago in 1902, and simply stated that debts owed by one nation to another must not be collected by force. The United States was more sympathetic to this doctrine so long as it did not provide for the absolute right of a debtor to default with no consequences – which was precisely the meaning intended by some debtor states. At the Third Conference of American States held in Rio de Janeiro (1906) the United States agreed to a resolution recommending discussion of the doctrine at the Second Hague Conference. This conference met in 1907 and due to Secretary Root's efforts all the Latin American nations were invited. Drago attended as a delegate from Argentina. The United States delegate supported the adoption of the Drago Doctrine, with the important amendment that non-intervention was to be predicated on the acceptance of arbitration. In this form the Hague Conference adopted the doctrine, but only six Latin American nations ratified the protocol.

At the Fourth International Conference of American States held at Buenos Aires (1910), the Pan American Union was formed as a permanent body with the Secretary of State of the United States as the permanent chairman. The dominant position of the United States in the organization was clear, but the body had little real power. Not all Latin American leaders were enthusiastic about the new Pan American Union, but some believed it had the potential for exerting influence on the policies of the United States.

Meanwhile, after 1898 American capital had flowed south in an ever increasing volume. Much of it went into private business enterprises producing raw materials for export and was concentrated in Cuba and Mexico. Direct American investment in Cuba went primarily into sugar production. In 1909, 34 per cent of Cuban sugar was produced by

American-owned mills. Some direct capital investment also went into mining, tobacco and public utilities. Between 1896 and 1915, American investments in Cuba increased from about $50 million to $265 million, though European capital still predominated. As Cuban sugar production increased after 1900, the Cuban share of the American sugar market jumped to 50 per cent by 1913. American exports to Cuba followed the same trend and by 1914 Cuba was in sixth place among the customers of the United States. In Mexico American capital generally flowed into mining and petroleum enterprises. Companies such as American Smelting and Refining, Phelps-Dodge, Greene-Cananea Copper and the Southern Pacific Railroad acquired a dominant position in the mining of copper, lead, zinc and gold. By 1908 American companies owned three-quarters of the dividend-paying mines in Mexico. In 1901 Edward L. Doheny and his associates brought in the first oil well, and foreign capital poured into the area now dubbed the 'Golden Lane'. Doheny's Huasteca Petroleum Company expanded operations, but its British rival El Aguila (owned by Weetman Pearson – later Lord Cowdray) grew more rapidly thanks to favourable treatment by the Mexican government. American enterprise also expanded in Central America. The United Fruit Company moved into several countries, and in 1899 two Italian immigrant families organized the Standard Fruit and Steamship Company in New Orleans. In South America in the period before 1914 Chile received more United States capital than any other country.

By 1904 the Chilean copper industry had fallen to sixth place among world producers, and the government encouraged North American companies to revive it. Braden Copper Company was organized in 1904 and the Guggenheims started the Chilex Company in 1912. In 1914 neither company had yet recorded a profit but they had together poured a total of $169 million into the industry. Several American companies began to build branch factories in Latin America after 1900. The United Shoe Machinery Company, the Singer Sewing Machine Company, some drug and cosmetic firms, and several Chicago meat packing companies were the most notable examples. In spite of this increased economic activity European capital and enterprise were still dominant prior to World War I.

THE UNITED STATES AND LATIN AMERICA, 1913–21

In 1913 Thomas Woodrow Wilson became president of the United States. His administration was deeply rooted in the secularized,

Calvinistic vision of the redeemer nation with a peculiar mission and destiny. One of the twentieth-century manifestations of this tradition was the Progressive movement with its urge to reform the world. Wilson's Secretary of the Interior, Franklin K. Lane, succinctly expressed this vision and its link with a belief in racial superiority: 'There is a great deal of the special policeman, of the sanitary engineer, of the social worker, and of the welfare dictator about the American people. . . . It is one of the most fundamental instincts that have made white men give to the world its history for the last thousand years.'[19] To Lane, and other believers in this new version of Manifest Destiny, the 'white man's burden' was the noble task of nation building and peace keeping.

In this spirit several key figures in the new administration tried to implement a plan for co-operative policing of the backward areas of the world. Colonel Edward M. House suggested this course of action to German and British officials during his 1913 tour of Europe. During a conversation with Count Johann von Bernstorff, German Ambassador to the United States, House stated that England, Germany, Japan and the United States should work together to, '. . . ensure peace and the proper development of the waste places, besides maintaining an open door and equal opportunity to every one everywhere'. The Ambassador expressed his agreement. And when House visited England in 1914 he described the reaction of British officials as 'enthusiastic'.[20]

As the Colonel reported to President Wilson, he envisaged an extensive plan by which the 'money-lending and developing nations' would be encouraged 'to lend money at reasonable rates and to develop, under favorable terms, the waste places of the earth, and on the other hand to bring about conditions by which such loans may be reasonably safe.'[21] The outbreak of the war in Europe limited the promotion of this co-operative dollar diplomacy to curtail rivalry in the underdeveloped areas of the world. House, however, continued to promote a limited version of the plan that he hoped would form the nucleus for the larger system after the war. This would involve the nations of South America in a Pan American Pact that House also believed would help settle a 'Mexican problem' (a reference to the revolution that had been raging since 1911). The Wilson administration actively worked for this pact as a

[19] *New York World*, 16 July 1916.
[20] Charles Seymour (ed.), *The intimate papers of Colonel House, arranged as a narrative by Charles Seymour* (Boston, 1926), I, 240–4, 264–7.   [21] *Ibid.*, 264–5.

co-operative means of enforcing the Monroe Doctrine. Opposition by Argentina and Chile blocked its consummation, and the proposal was shelved when the United States entered the war in 1917.

Woodrow Wilson firmly believed in the national mission to bring peace, order and stability to the world. And he emphasized the role of Anglo-American political institutions in establishing these conditions. In his view, revolutions occurred either because bad men were trying to usurp power through unconstitutional means, or because the people were unable to vote in free elections. Revolutions would not occur when elections were held, constitutional provisions obeyed and bad men removed from power. To Wilson, constitutional order underlay order and stability. The president placed much emphasis on rule by good men who followed constitutional procedures. But countries did not always choose such men as leaders. Thus, when Sir William Tyrrell, in November 1913, asked Wilson to explain his Mexican policy, the president replied: 'I am going to teach the South American republics to elect good men.'[22]

Under the guidance of the stern professor Wilson, the United States became more actively and militarily involved in the Caribbean–Central American region than at any time in its previous history. In part this was a reflection of the war in Europe that not only exacerbated the fear of Germany but also presented an opportunity to reduce overall European influence. In 1915 the new Secretary of State, Robert Lansing, wrote (with Wilson's approval) that the 'national safety' of the United States depended upon intervention to suppress insurrections and aid the people in 'establishing and maintaining responsible and honest governments . . .'[23] After disorders had broken out in Haiti and the Dominican Republic and the French and Germans had hinted at possible landings, the United States intervened – in Haiti in 1915 and in the Dominican Republic in 1916. Both countries were placed under U.S. military government. Each country was provided with a constitution written by Americans and the adoption of the document in each case was facilitated by the presence of the Marine Corps. A variety of sanitation, public health, education and communication projects were undertaken in both, as the reforming zeal of the Yankee was once more turned to nation

---

[22] Burton J. Hendrick (ed.), *The life and letters of Walter H. Page*, (Garden City, N.Y., 1923), I, 204–5.

[23] Memorandum, 'Present Nature and Extent of the Monroe Doctrine', 24 November 1915; file # 710.11/188½; RG 59, Records of the Department of State, National Archives of the United States (Washington). Hereafter cited as SD and file number.

building. Not that everything that took place during the attempts to create constitutional republics was necessarily planned or approved by officials in Washington. And in Haiti there was armed resistance resulting in the deaths of approximately 3,250 Haitians.[24]

In 1916 the United States purchased the Danish Virgin Islands, and thereby occupied a vantage point controlling every major passage into the Caribbean. The same year the Bryan–Chamorro Treaty with Nicaragua was approved by the United States Senate, though only after Platt Amendment elements had been eliminated – due in part to the efforts of Senator Elihu Root, who took a conservative view of intervention. This treaty gave the United States an exclusive option in perpetuity for a canal route, a 99-year lease on the Great and Little Corn Islands in the Caribbean, and on a possible naval base in the Gulf of Fonseca on the Pacific side – for which concessions the Nicaraguan government was paid. The Senate, however, only took action when Nicaraguan leaders said that Germany was trying to obtain the canal route. Nicaragua's neighbours claimed some of the territory allocated in the treaty and took their case to the Central American Court of Justice. The court ruled in their favour but neither Nicaragua nor the United States accepted the decision. As a result the court lost any meaning and went out of existence.

The Mexican Revolution proved to be a perpetual headache for the Wilson administration. The violence of the struggle directly affected Americans residing in Mexico and continually spilled over the border into the United States. Some of the raids across the border were carried out in the name of the Plan of San Diego, a scheme calling for an uprising in the United States by racial minorities to be followed by the detachment of California, Colorado, Arizona, and New Mexico. During the First World War the Germans became involved in the intrigues, hoping to provoke the United States into a massive intervention in Mexico. If the United States went to war with Germany, the imperial government proposed in the Zimmermann telegram (1917) a military alliance with Mexico and assistance in regaining the territories lost in 1848.[25]

The Wilson administration had first tried to influence Mexican affairs by trying to undercut Victoriano Huerta who, in part supported by the previous U.S. Ambassador, had deposed Francisco Madero, the

24 Hans Schmidt, *The United States occupation of Haiti, 1915–1934* (New Brunswick, N.J., 1971), 103.
25 Charles H. Harris III and Louis R. Sadler, 'The Plan of San Diego and the Mexican–United States war crisis of 1916: a reexamination', *Hispanic American Historical Review*, 58/3 (1978), 381–408.

'apostle of democracy' and 'father' of the Revolution. This led to the occupation of the port of Veracruz in April 1914 as the United States attempted to block the flow of arms to Huerta. The subsequent withdrawal was mediated by Argentina, Brazil and Chile. After Huerta's defeat, Wilson tried to effect a compromise among the warring revolutionary chiefs, finally throwing American support behind Venustiano Carranza. This provoked Pancho Villa's raid on Columbus New Mexico in March 1916. Wilson dispatched a punitive expedition, commanded by General John J. Pershing, with instructions to capture Villa. The expedition did not accomplish this mission, although it did force the dispersal of Villa's band. The United States and Mexico came close to war in May–June 1916. The European situation, however, precluded any substantial involvement in Mexico and Pershing was ordered to return to the United States. When the war in Europe ended some Americans renewed their calls for the pacification of Mexico by armed force, but most officials knew that such an operation would be extremely difficult and command little popular support.

As if United States–Mexican relations were not agitated enough by violence and foreign intrigue, the question of the treatment and status of foreign property emerged as another irritant. The nationalist–reformist element in the revolutionary leadership demanded land reform and some type of national control of foreign investments – especially in the petroleum industry. The demands were vividly documented in the Constitution of 1917, which embodied the Calvo Doctrine in several key sections affecting land ownership, control of mineral rights and rights of aliens. Article 27 contained the doctrine that all sub-surface mineral rights belonged to the nation, and for the next twenty years the foreign oil companies and the Mexican government would be periodically locked in battle over the interpretation and implementation of the article.

By virtue of the new constitution the Mexican Revolution became the first national movement effectively to pose a substantial threat to foreign investments and to the very legal principles upon which such invest-ments were based. The United States government recognized the right of expropriation, provided that 'prompt, adequate, and effective' compen-sation was made. But, there was a vast twilight zone of regulatory implementation before actual nationalization took place, and the real problem of sub-surface ownership revolved around the retroactive application of the national ownership principle. Did the various new taxes, regulatory decrees and (most important) demands that the oil companies exchange their deeds for new confirmatory concessions apply to interests acquired prior to 1917? This issue provoked a wave of private and diplomatic protests in 1918 and 1919. As a result, the Mexican government retreated from most efforts to implement article 27 of the Constitution until the 1920s.

The United States government faced a major dilemma in protecting the investments of its citizens and those of other countries as well. In the traditional view, any respectable nation extended protection to its citizens and their property abroad. But, should the United States go to war with Mexico over its investments? Most Americans answered no, but still wanted to protect their national companies.

Oil was becoming an increasingly vital element for navies, merchant marines, and domestic power and heating. This meant that the question of controlling petroleum went beyond the issue of protecting investments since it was now vital to the operations of industrial nations and their navies. The British government had agreed in 1914 to follow the leadership of the United States in Mexican matters, but would expect the Americans to ensure the flow of oil to the Royal Navy and to protect the British oil companies. This policy continued, although the British believed that the Wilson administration was too soft with Mexico. The oil, however, continued to flow throughout the Revolution, thanks in part to the fact that the Tampico field was controlled by the maverick General Manuel Pelaez; he in turn was supported through arms and cash by the British and American oil companies.

Wilson did not really trust the British and feared that after the war they would effect a separate settlement with the Mexican nationalists that would jeopardize American interests. In 1918 the State Department asked Thomas W. Lamont of J. P. Morgan & Co. to form an international committee of investment bankers in order to tie British and French economic interests to American leadership. The International Committee of Bankers on Mexico was intended to be an unofficial arm of the United States government in co-ordinating matters concerning the Mexican bonded debt, possible loans and other foreign investments. This in turn would limit the ability of governments or private interests to make separate settlements with Mexico. For the most part British and French interests accepted the American leadership, but little was done for several years to settle the problem of the defaulted Mexican debt.

Wilson and Secretary of State Lansing believed that European economic involvement in the hemisphere was a basic cause of political turmoil leading to interventionism which challenged the Monroe Doctrine. In the case of Mexico, Wilson was convinced that the actions of the British oil magnate Weetman Pearson (Lord Cowdray) were behind the 'usurpation' of Huerta. Some of the problems of Haiti were ascribed to French bankers, and German interests were believed to be involved in various Caribbean intrigues. Lansing proposed an American effort to reduce European economic involvement and he suggested a restatement of the Monroe Doctrine to '. . . include European acquisition of political control through the agency of financial supremacy over an American Republic'.[26] Various State Department officials argued that the government should primarily give its support to the extension of American banking institutions, promotion of American goods and the Americanization of communications facilities. The war seemed to offer a good opportunity to encourage Latin American countries to reduce their European economic ties and make new arrangements with American groups.

Specific governmental efforts to promote these changes met with limited success. Although the United States pressed for the liquidation of German interests in those nations that declared war on Germany, only some banana plantations in Guatemala and some properties in Haiti were expropriated. The economic dislocations of the war did, however, promote a distinct alteration in the international economic relations of Latin America. For example, before the war the American-based Central and South American Telegraph Company laid cables along the Pacific coast of South America. A British company had a monopoly concession that prevented the American company from extending its line from Buenos Aires through Uruguay and Brazil. The Americans began court proceedings in Argentina and Brazil in 1917 and, with State Department support, finally broke the British cable monopoly in 1919. American branch banking operations in Latin America also moved ahead after 1914. By 1919 American banks had ten branches in Brazil, for example. After the war Britain was still the dominant economic power in most of South America but the United States was rapidly catching up.

The United States met with only limited success in its efforts to mobilize Latin American support in the war with Germany. Brazil declared war, but the other seven nations that followed this course were

[26] Memorandum, 11 June 1914: SD 710.11/185½.

Caribbean–Central American states. Bolivia, Ecuador, Peru and Uruguay broke diplomatic relations with Germany. Argentina, Chile, Colombia, Mexico, Paraguay, El Salvador and Venezuela declared their neutrality. The Mexican government had tried to form a neutral bloc early in 1917. When this effort failed, President Carranza attempted to unify the other Latin American nations under the banner of the 'Carranza Doctrine by calling for an anti-Yankee bloc championing the Calvo Doctrine and non-intervention. This bloc would 'non-recognize' the Monroe Doctrine and make alliances with powerful nations in other parts of the world. Nothing came of this effort either, and the specific doctrine died with Carranza in 1920. But the ideas and expressions would become part of the left wing variants of anti-Yankee nationalism.

THE UNITED STATES AND LATIN AMERICA IN THE 1920S

During the 1920s the economic stake of the United States in Latin America expanded rapidly. Investments grew from nearly $1.5 billion in 1924 to a little over $3 billion in 1929. In 1929 the British were still ahead of the United States in terms of total investment, but the gap was closing. In the case of Brazil, British investors held much of the pre-1914 bonded debt, but the United States had become the primary source for new capital. American companies also became dominant in the fields of radio, telegraph, motion pictures and newspaper wire services. In air transportation, however, the United States lagged far behind the Germans. This raised the old spectre of the German threat, especially when these airlines flew routes near the Panama Canal. Some American officials wanted to push the country into what was regarded as a strategic industry, but nothing came of these efforts until the eve of World War II.

In 1921 the United States government tried to institute a policy of exercising some supervision over foreign loans. The reasons varied, but for Latin America the most important factors were to prevent loans, (1) for armaments, (2) to countries already too deeply in debt and (3) to countries where funds would be wasted by political corruption. In general, the State Department hoped to encourage the use of American capital to promote sound economic development. Since the advice of the government was not binding the programme had limited success, but some dubious lending ventures in Central America were dropped.

Wartime dislocations had shifted Latin American trade relations away from Europe. Germany, Britain and France recovered some of their lost commerce during the 1920s, but the United States remained the most important country for hemispheric commerce. The main exception to this was Argentina's trade relations with Britain.

Between 1918 and 1930 various kinds of American enterprise in Latin America expanded rapidly. The most important characteristic of this era of investment was the movement into public utilities and manufacturing. Much of the latter was concentrated in Argentina, Brazil, Cuba and Uruguay. The American & Foreign Power Company was organized in 1923 by General Electric and acquired properties in Panama, Guatemala and Cuba from another G.E. subsidiary. By 1929 it had obtained control of the electric power industry in eight additional Latin American countries. In all of these the company instituted operations to develop modern systems with ample plant capacity matched by transmission and distribution facilities. In addition to selling power and light the company also ran street cars, made ice, pumped water and manufactured gas. The International Telephone and Telegraph Company was organized in 1920 by Sosthenes Behn and within a decade had acquired control of the leading telephone companies of Argentina, Chile, Peru and Mexico. Americans also took the lead in building wireless communications systems throughout the hemisphere. The Radio Corporation of America, American Telephone & Telegraph and the United Fruit Company were the principal corporations involved. American automobile companies began to build assembly plants in several countries. By 1926 General Motors had facilities of this kind in Argentina, Brazil and Uruguay. Ford Motors also entered the Latin American field and even built a tractor plant in Mexico; a country not generally considered to be a good credit risk in the 1920s. Leading American banks, such as National City and Chase, entered the branch banking field beginning in December 1913. By 1930 they could be found in most of the major cities of the hemisphere. In addition, some investment firms (such as J. P. Morgan & Company, Chase Securities Corporation and the Equitable Trust Company) began to float governmental bond issues.

The United States government followed a more co-operative policy with regard to other aspects of inter-American relations during the 1920s. Between 1921 and 1933 the United States participated in 41 out of 44 conferences involving nations of the western hemisphere, in contrast to its participation in 23 out of the 50 such conferences held between 1889 and 1921. The Inter-American High Commission was involved in several of these conferences and in addition carried on a general programme of settling problems of a commercial nature. The actions of this group during a typical year included: negotiation of conventions concerning arbitration of commercial disputes, protection of trade marks, protection of commercial travellers and uniform classification of merchandise. This lower-level, non-crisis diplomacy by a quasi-governmental body was indicative of the general trend of the policy – multilateral co-operation to clear the highways for commerce.

The Republican leadership did try to restrict military activity in the area, even though it did not repudiate such action. Marines were removed from Cuba in 1922, the Dominican Republic in 1924 and Nicaragua in 1925 (only to return in 1927). The Haitian occupation continued, but plans for withdrawal had been made by 1933. The use of temporary 'landing parties' was also placed under certain restraints. Moreover, during the numerous revolts that occurred between 1929 and 1933, the State Department refused all requests for armed intervention. President Hoover stated frankly that he did not want the United States represented abroad by marines.

In 1923 President Warren Harding issued orders to the Secretaries of War and Navy prohibiting the sale, or transfer by third parties, of United States military equipment to any foreign country. He was especially concerned with arms build ups in Latin America. And this policy was reiterated by President Hoover in 1931.[27] The United States sent a small naval mission to Brazil in 1919, and two army officers were assigned to Guatemala in 1930 where they were put in charge of the national military academy. Germany for its part was prohibited from sending missions by the Treaty of Versailles, but the French government stepped up its military activities. In 1919 the first French mission arrived in Brazil, and by 1927 it consisted of seventy officers commanded by a major general. Brazil also purchased most of its arms from France during this period. The French continued their Peruvian mission and maintained a mission in Paraguay from 1926 to 1930. United States military intelligence attributed the increased French activity to a desire to offset British influence in the League of Nations by increasing French influence in Latin America. The Italian government sent a mission to Ecuador in 1922, and several small missions were dispatched by the Spanish government.[28]

[27] Memorandum by Joseph C. Green, 18 September 1937; box 2, RG 59, SD Memoranda of the Office of American Republic Affairs, 1918–47.
[28] War Department, Report of 28 December 1944, OPD 336 Latin America, case 74.

As in other parts of the world, United States leaders devised a treaty system to settle disputes peacefully and to promote political order. The Gondra Convention of 1923 called for a cooling-off period during international disputes; this was institutionalized at the Washington Conference on Conciliation and Arbitration, which met in late 1928. Charles Evans Hughes provided active leadership at this conference, and President Calvin Coolidge and Secretary of State Frank B. Kellogg supported his advocacy of American acceptance of the resulting treaties – with reservation. The United States ratified the treaties and joined the Inter-American Court of Arbitration. In addition to these measures, the State Department acted as a kind of one-nation inter-American court by arbitrating numerous boundary disputes. By 1933 the United States had performed this role in regard to disputes involving almost three-quarters of the Latin American nations.

Most officials regarded Central America as the most unsettled part of the hemisphere and the one most requiring a system of order; almost all of the independent Caribbean states were already bound by individual treaty arrangements and loan agreements. In 1923, under the guidance of the United States, the Central American nations signed a Treaty of Peace and Amity. This revived the General Treaty of 1907, which had utilized the Tobar Doctrine of discouraging coups and revolts by non-recognition of the resulting governments. The 1923 treaty added even more restrictive conditions for recognition. The system was intended to discourage revolutions of any kind. During the 1920s many members of the conservative Central American elite groups eagerly supported such a treaty, especially since they feared the spread of revolutionary nationalism from Mexico. Although the United States did not sign the treaty, it was nonetheless an instrument of American policy and the United States provided the leadership in enforcing the treaty.

Nicaragua provided the most important, and controversial, challenge to the treaty system. The United States decision to intervene in 1927 was based in part on the determination to enforce the rules even though the challenger, Emiliano Chamorro, was a conservative supported by some officials and by various business groups with Nicaraguan holdings. Coolidge and Kellogg decided, however, that the status quo throughout Central America could be best preserved by forcing Nicaragua to follow 'constitutional procedures' for political change. There were other factors involved in the intervention. American properties were potentially threatened by the civil war between the political factions, and Mexico was giving aid to elements of the Liberal Party. The administration wanted to prevent any expansion of Mexican influence.

The Nicaraguan intervention, coupled as it was with the possibility of war with Mexico, provoked heated debate. With mounting opposition from Congress, Administration leaders realized that they could not sustain any extensive military operation. Henry L. Stimson was sent as a mediator to arrange a constitutional settlement. The marine corps was given the job of building a national guard rather than pacifying the country. Some marine officers wanted to wipe out the anti-American guerrilla forces of Augusto Sandino, but the administration had decided that United States forces were not to be involved in Nicaraguan politics.[29] The idea was to construct a legal compromise as quickly as possible, provide a politically neutral national guard to sustain the treaty system and then to remove the United States presence.

Actually, adverse reaction (both in the United States and in Latin America) to the Nicaraguan venture and the wave of successful revolts in Latin America after 1928, prompted Hoover and Secretary of State Stimson to further modify their tactics. The rules for recognition would be officially maintained, and 'new governments' would be asked to furnish some 'legal' proof of constitutional continuity. However, this would be interpreted rather broadly. Stimson also ruled out military actions and tried to curtail political meddling by diplomats and businessmen.

One major problem faced by the United States was revolutionary nationalism in Mexico. The new Mexican leaders were much less radical than some officials believed, but they did want to assert some control over the economy, especially in regard to natural resources such as oil and land. The Wilson Administration had refused to recognize the government that replaced Venustiano Carranza in May 1920, and the Republicans continued this policy until September 1923. The State Department also discouraged loans to Mexico. Negotiations between the International Committee of Bankers and Mexico produced an agreement in 1922 on Mexico's foreign debt, and this in turn helped set the stage for negotiations concerning recognition. Part of the increasing support for recognition of the government of Alvaro Obregón came from American exporters. Secretary Hughes concluded that Mexico was actually enjoying a high degree of stability and that in reality investors had not

---

[29] Robert E. Olds to General Frank R. McCoy, 13 April 1928; RG 59, SD Francis White's Files.

suffered very much. Relations deteriorated after 1925 when President Plutarco Calles tried to implement Article 27 of the 1917 Constitution. The situation was not improved by the anti-Mexican attitude of Ambassador James Rockwell Sheffield. He and a few other officials wanted a militant policy, even if it ultimately led to war. Behind-the-scene negotiations, however, between the bankers and Mexican officials led to the compromise arrangements worked out in 1927–8 by the new Ambassador Dwight W. Morrow (a former partner of J. P. Morgan & Co.). As Thomas W. Lamont, the head of the International Committee of Bankers, noted: 'Millhauser [Speyer & Co.] talks glibly about wielding the big-stick or kicking them in the stomach. There is no big stick to wield and we have no boot that could possibly reach their remote and very tough stomach.'[30]

As far as some American officials were concerned the situations in Mexico and Nicaragua were complicated by the existence of Communist parties there. The Latin American Communist parties were tied to the Soviet Union and its foreign policy through the Comintern, and this was seen as a new type of outside intervention in the hemisphere. In 1926 the Communist Party of the United States was assigned the special responsibility of organizing and directing the Latin American parties. To the Communist International the United States was the main enemy in Latin America, and American officials correctly assumed that a Communist party victory in any country would link it to the Soviet Union and turn it against the United States. In the words of the Comintern directive to the Mexican C.P. in 1923: 'the destruction of the last stronghold of capitalist imperialism, the overthrow of the North American bourgeoisie, is the task of the workers and peasants of all the American countries'.[31] But American officials tended to exaggerate the power and influence of the Communists, and this distorted their perception of some political developments like the insurrection led by Sandino in Nicaragua.

The first Latin American Communist Congress was held in 1929 in Buenos Aires with delegates from the fourteen Latin American parties, the United States and France. The Congress adopted the Soviet line of 'extremist intransigence' and pledged itself to pursue militant revo-

[30] Lamont to Vivian Smith and J. R. Carter (Paris Office of J. P. Morgan & Co.), n.d. (probably November 1928), Thomas W. Lamont Manuscripts, Baker Library, Harvard University (Cambridge, Mass.).
[31] Stephen Clissold (ed.), *Soviet relations with Latin America, 1918–1968: a documentary history* (London, 1970), 86.

lutionary tactics. In 1929 the Comintern directed the Mexican C.P. to order the armed Peasant Leagues to attack the government, and it issued a manifesto calling on the Mexican people to wage all-out war. The Mexican government accused the Soviet Union of financing and inciting the subversive movement, and in January 1930 it severed diplomatic relations with Russia. In 1930 the Communist movement in Latin America was small but growing, and with it the Soviet Union was becoming a factor in the international relations of the hemisphere.

Some Latin American leaders saw the League of Nations as a possible factor in hemispheric relations during the 1920s. Nine Latin American nations were charter members and others joined in the course of the decade. At the first assembly Argentina moved to strike the reference to the Monroe Doctrine from the covenant. When this failed, Argentina withdrew for the rest of the decade. The Monroe Doctrine issue surfaced again in 1928. Brazil had left the league when it did not receive a permanent seat on the council, and Costa Rica had dropped out for failure to pay its dues. In inviting them to rejoin Costa Rica was assured by the Council that all nations had equal rights and responsibilities and that the covenant did not confirm the validity of the Monroe Doctrine. Peru and Bolivia had withdrawn from the League in 1921 when it refused to consider the question of Tacna–Arica, held by Chile since the War of the Pacific. They returned in 1929 after the dispute had been mediated by the United States. In 1928 the League issued a warning against aggression in the Chaco dispute between Bolivia and Paraguay, and attempted mediation, but this ended in failure and war erupted a few years later. For the most part the League ignored Latin America and did not prove to be a counter-weight to the United States.

The growing power of the United States and its creation of a Caribbean–Central American sphere of interest provoked some hostility in Latin America, especially among the intelligentsia. Some developed the concept of Latin *Versus* Anglo Saxon civilization and culture, and promoted the idea of Latin unity against the 'Colossus of the North.' The classic work, which most subsequent writers tried to emulate, was *Ariel* (1900), in which José Enrique Rodó personified the North Americans as materialistic and the Latin Americans as idealistic. J. M. Vargas Vila of Colombia carried this theme somewhat further in his book, *Against the barbarians. The Yankee – behold the enemy* (1919). By the 1920s anti-Yankeeism was not only a familiar current in Latin American universities, where it became part of the emotional fervour of nationalistic reform movements, but a regular feature of political rhetoric throughout Latin America.

On the whole, except in Mexico and among Latin American communists, anti-United States feeling did not focus on economic issues, but rather on the problem of military intervention in the Caribbean and Central America. These sentiments came to a head at the Havana Conference of 1928, as representative after representative poured out the vial of aggrieved nationalism upon the heads of the United States delegation. Former Secretary of State Charles Evans Hughes turned the tide, however, with a masterpiece of oratory that placed definite limits on the intervention doctrine. The State Department then decided to issue a white paper clearly separating the Monroe Doctrine from armed intervention. J. Reuben Clark's memorandum was published in 1930 and was testimony to the growing sensitiveness of United States' officials to Latin American criticism.

By 1930 the United States was clearly the predominant power in the western hemisphere. Yet the nations of Latin America were more secure in their independence than they had been in 1830, and the United States was moving away from military intervention in the Caribbean–Central American region. The leaders of the United States were not prepared to renounce their general sphere-of-interest policy in the area and Secretary Stimson articulated this when he wrote in 1931: 'That locality has been the one spot external to our shores which nature has decreed to be most vital to our national safety, not to mention our prosperity.'[32] Still, many United States officials recognized the problems that the maintenance of this sphere posed for inter-American relations in general, and most of them wanted to work out some kind of compromise position. New international rivalries during the following decades would undermine these developments in the relations between the United States and Latin America.

[32] *The United States and other American republics*, Department of State Latin American Series, no. 4 (Washington: 1931), 5.

4

THE POPULATION OF LATIN AMERICA, 1850–1930*

GENERAL TRENDS

During the period from independence until the middle of the nineteenth century – in general a period of economic stagnation, or only modest economic growth – the population of Latin America as a whole grew at a rate of about one per cent per annum. This was in line with the rate of growth of the more developed European countries but less than that of the United States. It was also lower than the rate of growth during the late colonial period, a rate which had been expected to continue or even to accelerate after independence. In Mesoamerica and the Andes, where subsistence agriculture predominated and where the population was predominantly Indian, population growth was slow, hindered by conditions which can only be described as Malthusian. For example, after 1825 the population of the central states of Mexico grew at annual compounded rates which varied between 0.4 and 1 per cent; the north-eastern states of Veracruz and Chiapas experienced somewhat higher rates of population growth; the population of the north-west and Yucatán decreased consistently until the 1870s.[1] The regions of Latin America suitable for the cultivation of staples in demand in the industrializing European countries witnessed somewhat more dynamic demographic growth. Although the population there was generally sparse, it tended to increase faster. For example, the expansion in cattle raising was responsible for populating the pampas of the River Plate area. The rural population of the province of Buenos Aires – excluding the capital – increased at a staggering annual rate of 4.2 per cent between 1836 and 1855. On a national scale, the population of Argentina

---

* Translated from the Spanish by Dr David Brookshaw; translation revised by the Editor.
[1] Viviane Brachet, *La población de los estados mexicanos (1824–1895)* (Mexico, 1976), 105.

Table 1. *The population of Latin America, 1850–1930*

(total figures in thousands; growth rates in percentages)

	1850	1900	1930	1850–1900	1900–1930
Temperate South America					
Argentina	1,100	4,693	11,936	2.9	3.1
Chile	1,443	2,959	4,365	1.4	1.3
Uruguay	132	915	1,599	4.0	1.9
Paraguay	350	440	880	0.4	2.3
Subtotal	3,025	9,007	18,780	2.2	2.4
Tropical South America					
Brazil	7,230	17,980	33,568	1.8	2.1
Colombia	2,065	3,825	7,350	1.2	2.0
Peru	2,001	3,791	5.651	1.3	1.4
Venezuela	1,490	2,344	2,950	0.9	0.8
Ecuador	816	1,400	2,160	1.1	1.5
Bolivia	1,374	1,696	2,153	0.4	0,8
Subtotal	14,976	31,036	53,832	1.5	1.9
Caribbean					
Cuba	1,186	1,583	3,837	0.6	3.0
Puerto Rico	495	959	1,552	1.4	1.6
Dominican Republic	146	515	1,227	2.4	2.9
Haiti	938	1,560	2,422	1.0	1.5
Subtotal	2,763	4,617	9,038	1.0	2.3
Mexico and Central America					
Mexico	7,662	13,607	16,589	1.0	0.8
Guatemala	850	1,300	1,771	0.9	1.0
El Salvador	366	766	1,443	1.0	2.1
Honduras	350	500	948	0.7	1.5
Nicaragua	300	478	742	0.9	1.5
Costa Rica	101	297	499	2.2	1.7
Panama	135	263	502	1.4	2.7
Subtotal	9,764	17,211	22,494	1.1	0.9
Total	30,530	61,871	104,144	1.4	1.7

Sources: In general, for 1850, Barón Castro, Radofo, 'El desarrollo de la población hispanoamericana (1491–1950)', *J. of World History*, 5 (1959), 325–43; for 1900, Miró, Carmen A., *La población de América Latina en el siglo XX* (CELADE, Santiago de Chile, 1965); for 1930, CELADE (Centro Latinoamericano de Demografía), 'América latina: población total por paises. Año 1970', *Boletin demográfico*, 6 (1970). Also, for Argentina, Recchini de Lattes, Zulma and Lattes, Alfredo E. (eds.), *La población de Argentina* (Instituto Nacional de Estadística y Censos, Buenos Aires, 1975); for Chile, Mamalakis, Markos, *Historical statistics of Chile*, vol. II (Westport and London, 1980) (1850 adjusted);

increased at a little over 2 per cent per annum, a similar rate to that of Brazil and Cuba where the large-scale importation of African slaves continued until the third quarter of the nineteenth century.

In contrast, during the second half of the nineteenth and the early decades of the twentieth centuries – in general, a period of rapid, export-led economic growth – Latin America experienced a considerable growth of its population. Table 1 provides an overall summary. For practical reasons, the figures for only three dates – 1850, 1900 and 1930 – are shown. The table also shows the respective growth rates. It is these, more than the population figures themselves, which give the clearest indication of trends in Latin America's population. Between 1850 and 1900 the population of Latin America doubled, from a total of 30.5 to 61.9 million inhabitants. From 1900 to 1930, it increased by a further 68 per cent, reaching 104.1 million. The annual growth rate in the first period was 1.4 per cent, while in the second, it rose to 1.7 per cent. This overall growth, however, includes different rhythm patterns, and even opposing trends.

The region which experienced the most dynamic growth was the temperate zone of South America: between 1850 and 1900, the population increased almost threefold, and in the following thirty years it more than doubled. Within this area, the population of Argentina first quadrupled, and then increased by 250 per cent. The growth of the population of Uruguay was even more rapid during the first period,

Notes to Table 1 (cont.)
for Uruguay, Rial, Juan, *Estadísticas históricas de Uruguay, 1850–1930* (Centro de Informaciones y Estudios del Uruguay, Cuaderno no. 4, Montevideo, 1980); for Paraguay, 1850, estimate based on Kegler de Galeano, Anneliese, 'Alcance histórico-demográfico del censo de 1846', *Revista Paraguaya de Sociología* 35 (1976), 71–121; for Brazil, Merrick, Thomas W. and Graham, Douglas H., *Population and economic development in Brazil. 1800 to the present* (Baltimore and London, 1979); for Colombia, 1900, Collver, O. Andrew, *Birth rates in Latin America: new estimates of historical trends and fluctuations* (Institute of International Studies, Berkeley, 1965); for Peru, 1850, Centro de Estudios de Población y Desarrollo, *Informe demográfico del Perú, 1970* (Lima, 1972); for Dominican Republic, estimates based on Moya Pons, Frank, 'Nuevas consideraciones sobre la historia de la población dominicana: curvas, tasas y problemas', in *Seminario sobre problemas de población en la República dominicana* (Universidad Autónoma de Santo Domingo, Santo Domingo, 1975), 37–63; for Costa Rica, 1900, Casey Gaspar, Jeffrey, *Limón: 1880–1940. Un estudio de la industria bananera en Costa Rica,* (San José, 1979); for Panama, 1850, Urrutia, Miguel and Arrubla, Mario (eds.), *Compendio de estadísticas históricas de Colombia* (Bogotá, 1970); for the rest of Central America, 1850 and 1900, estimates based on Cardoso, Ciro F. S. and Pérez Brignoli, Héctor, *Centro América y la economía occidental (1520–1930)* (San José).

when it increased sevenfold. The population of Chile experienced a more leisurely though regular rate of growth, which was rather higher in the first period than in the second. On the other hand, the population of Paraguay hardly increased at all during the second half of the nineteenth century. The War of the Triple Alliance, which was followed by a severe epidemic of cholera, had a catastrophic effect on Paraguay. It has been claimed that Paraguay lost more than half of its population although this is perhaps an exaggeration. Sixteen years after the end of hostilities, the census of 1886 still recorded 70 per cent fewer men than women between 15 and 45 years old, the age bracket most deeply affected by war. Furthermore, the children born during the war, contrary to any normal age distribution, were 17 per cent fewer than those born before.[2] The country's population growth only began to recover after the turn of the century.

Tropical South America does not present a consistent pattern. Brazil followed a path similar to that of Argentina and Uruguay, though the growth rate was slower. The population of Colombia grew more slowly at first, particularly towards the end of the century, because of civil war and the consequent economic disorder. In the twentieth century it picked up again. Peru and Equador experienced regular growth. The population of Bolivia and Venezuela remained stagnant, more so in the former than in the latter. Nevertheless, Bolivia managed to double its rate of growth in the first three decades of the twentieth century, while Venezuela's growth declined slightly.

In the Caribbean the population of the Dominican Republic, starting from a very low level, multiplied three and a half times during the first period, and two and a half times during the second. In eighty years, the population of Puerto Rico tripled. Conversely, revolts and wars hindered population growth in Cuba during the second half of the nineteenth century. The census of 1899 reveals even a decrease of 59,482 inhabitants in relation to the census of 1887. After independence (1898), immigration caused the population to increase at a fairly dynamic rate. Emigration, on the other hand, was responsible for the comparatively contained growth in the population of Haiti.

In Mesoamerica the population grew at a more modest rate. Population growth in Mexico, the largest country, proceeded smoothly until the Revolution. Between 1910 and 1921, the population fell from

2 Domingo M. Rivarola, *et al.*, *La población del Paraguay* (Asunción, 1974), 13.

15.1 million to 14.3 million, representing a loss of 825,000 inhabitants. Apart from deaths through war, there were considerable losses resulting from the epidemic of 1917 and emigration to the United States, all of which came on top of a temporary drop in the birthrate. The North American census of 1920 records the presence of 651,000 Mexicans north of the Rio Bravo. A third of these had probably arrived before the Revolution, but the rest crossed the frontier between 1910 and 1920. Although emigration continued to drain the population, the Mexican growth rate soon began to pick up again. In Central America the great period of growth occurred, as elsewhere, during the twentieth century, except in Costa Rica. The banana plantations there drew both foreigners and natives to the west coast. In nine years (1883–92), the population of the district of Limón, for example, grew at an annual rate of 12 per cent, while the national rate stood at 3 per cent.[3] In Panama, the construction of the canal and the increased shipping, along with the banana plantations, attracted immigrants. As a result, the population grew quite rapidly.

Brazil replaced Mexico as the most populous Latin American nation during this period. However, it was Argentina which advanced at the most spectacular rate. In 1850, its population was one-tenth the size of Mexico's. Eighty years later, it had risen to some seven-tenths. In 1850, Argentina ranked lower than Cuba, Peru, Venezuela, Bolivia, Chile and Colombia in population, but by 1900, it had overtaken all these countries to rank third behind Brazil and Mexico.

At the conclusion of this brief survey, it should be mentioned that rapid population growth was to a large extent associated with agricultural exports. The River Plate area was a producer of grain, meat, wool and leather on a large scale. Brazil and Colombia exported coffee, Costa Rica bananas as well as its traditional staple, coffee. Santo Domingo entered the highly competitive market as a sugar producer. Cuba and Puerto Rico continued to be committed to sugar. On the Pacific coast, cases of specialized commercial crop cultivation were fewer and confined to specific areas: coffee in Guatemala and El Salvador, and sugar in northern Peru. These crops gave impetus to the rise of services and the growth of domestic markets. Mining, on the other hand, did not require such a large labour force. It encouraged population movements, but on a national scale it did not push up the rate of growth. Copper in

[3] Jeffrey Casey Gaspar, *Limón: 1880–1940. Un estudio de la industria bananera en Costa Rica* (San José, 1979), 215.

Chile and Peru, nitrates in Chile, or the later discovery of oil in Mexico and Venezuela, cannot compare in their effect on population with that which coffee had in Brazil, or cereals in Argentina. Whenever the economy grew, to wait for the population to adjust by itself to the new opportunities would have delayed development, and meant some of those opportunities would have been missed. If labour had remained scarce, wages would have rocketed at a time when the export economy depended on the ability to sell products cheaply on the world market. Entrepreneurs, legislators and ideologists therefore all agreed on the need to attract immigrants.

IMMIGRATION

The newly independent Latin American states for the most part lifted the colonial restrictions on the entry of foreigners and opened their doors to European immigrants in particular. European, especially British, merchants and soldiers of fortune reached all parts of Latin America, though not many stayed. Some countries also embarked on agricultural colonization schemes in the period after independence. Swiss and German colonists, in particular, were established in southern Brazil, Peru, Nicaragua, Venezuela and, most notably, in southern Chile. From 1862 Welsh colonists settled in the lower reaches of the River Chubut in Patagonia where, like the Germans in the forests of Araucania, they prospered and preserved their language and culture. Not all immigrants settled in colonies. Several thousand more Europeans, impelled by poverty in their own countries, found employment in Latin America: for example, Canary Islanders in Venezuela, Azoreans in Brazil, Basques and Irish in the River Plate. And the towns as well as the countryside attracted immigrants. While only 10 per cent of the population of the interior of Buenos Aires province was of foreign origin in 1855, the immigrant population of the capital amounted to 35 per cent. The immigrants were involved in crafts, trade and the liberal professions, while the native-born were rather employed in public administration, or in unskilled work. An extreme case was that of Uruguay, and in particular, its capital Montevideo. In 1843, 63 per cent of the nation's population had been born abroad. While the proportion of foreigners decreased to 45 per cent and 48 per cent in 1852 and 1860, it rose again to reach 68 per cent in 1868. During these thirty key years in the nation's development, about half of those who resided in the most economically active and heavily populated area of the country had been born outside its frontiers. Many of them were Basques from both sides of the Pyrenees and therefore of Spanish or French nationality.

With the ending of the transatlantic slave trade in 1850–1, and given the low birthrate of the slave population, the labour needs of Brazil's expanding coffee region were to some extent supplied by the inter-provincial trade in slaves. It has been estimated that between 1850 and 1881 some 200,000 slaves were transferred from the north and north-east, where the fall in the price of sugar and cotton called for a widespread restructuring of the agricultural export economy, and to a lesser extent from the south and west, to the provinces of Rio de Janeiro and São Paulo. By 1873 the slave population of Brazil had been redistributed in such a way that two-thirds of the total number of slaves were located in the centre-south. Cuba, on the other hand, where the slave trade came to an end in 1865–6, turned in the short run to Chinese coolie labour, imported, allegedly under contract, but in fact under coercion and with little freedom of movement. Between 1853 and 1874, 124,000 Chinese arrived at Havana.[4] Between 1859 and 1874, 87,000 Chinese also entered Peru bound for the sugar plantations of the north and the guano islands of the south. (Polynesians and Hawaians were also imported into Peru, under various dubious schemes, on Chilean ships.) In 1876, almost 2 per cent of the population of Peru was of Chinese origin, and in 1877, 3 per cent of the population of Cuba. Chinese labourers also worked in the nitrate mines of northern Chile, in the building of railways in Colombia and, later, in the construction of the Panama Canal. At the first opportunity, however, the Chinese would escape from their bondage and take refuge in the cities, where most of their descendants now reside.

In the 1870s and 1880s mass European immigration to Latin America began. The prejudices with which certain native elements had received the first foreigners had by now been dissipated. As news of the first settlers began to spread through the Old World, ties of blood and friendship began to draw people to America. The exodus was occasion-ally boosted by occurrences of a political or religious nature, such as the persecutions after the crushing of the Paris Commune, or the pogroms in the Ukraine. However, the main cause of expatriation seems to have been economic. The opportunities which Latin America offered in various areas were, at the time, exceptional. They occurred precisely at the

---

[4] Juan Pérez de la Riva, 'Demografía de los culíes chinos en Cuba (1853–1874)', *Revista de la Biblioteca Nacional José Martí*, 57 (1966), 3–32.

time when agriculture in southern and eastern Europe was in a state of crisis, due in part to the availability of cheap foodstuffs from the New World. The period of greatest need for manpower in Latin America, made more acute by the abolition of the slave trade, coincided with the period of its greatest availability in Europe. Latin America was therefore in a position to compete with the United States, which already had a long experience in attracting immigrants. At the same time, the availability of manpower determined the class and national origin of the immigrants, which were, of course, the same as those of the 'new wave' in North America.

There is no agreement on the actual number of migrants to Latin America in the period 1870–1930. The word 'immigrant' has a clear meaning in common language, but not in statistics. Furthermore, the statistics of the countries of origin do not match those of the receiver countries. Not all migrants settled permanently, while others arrived unofficially. One obvious advantage in calculating immigration in this period is that migrants normally arrived from Europe by ship, and maritime migration is far more easily monitored than that over land frontiers. In some statistics, however, only second and third class passengers are assumed to have been migrants, while others make no distinction. Some only consider arrivals and not departures. In the case of Argentina and Uruguay it was not unusual for immigrants to try their luck in one of these countries first before eventually settling in the other. A proportion of the arrivals in Chile and Paraguay were similarly products of re-migration.

Unlike other published tables, those below sum up data on net migration (arrivals less departures) and, to avoid long series of numbers, condense the information into five-year periods. However, in the case of Brazil there is no way of subtracting departures. Brazil only recorded first-time arrivals, excluding from its records even readmissions who eventually accounted for 10 per cent of all arrivals. Fortunately, over half of all immigrants went directly to the state of São Paulo. Its port of entry, Santos, recorded both arrivals and departures. With regard to this half of the migration to Brazil, therefore, the net figure can be calculated.

By working on the basis of net balance, temporary admissions of foreigners, returning nationals who might have slipped into the figures as well as tourists, who became an important factor in the River Plate during the 1920s, are excluded. That is to say, these figures include only those who took up permanent residence. Since they even include those registered in censuses carried out while they resided in Latin America, they represent an absolute minimum and, it can legitimately be argued, play down the role of migration. Permanent settlement, which demographically counts the most, is, however, more accurately expressed in this way.

Only a few Latin American countries benefited from mass European migration. In order of importance, these were Argentina, Brazil, Cuba, Uruguay and Chile. Approximately 4 million Europeans settled in Argentina, followed by 2 million in Brazil, if one takes the rate of settlement in São Paulo as representing that of the entire country. A little less than 600,000 people settled in Cuba and the same number in Uruguay, although since the population of Uruguay in 1930 was half that of Cuba, the demographic impact had inevitably been far greater there. Net migration to Chile, which was inadequately recorded before 1907, probably amounted to about 200,000 far below the figures for the other countries considered above (see Tables 2, 3 and 4). Immigrants entering Paraguay appear as a footnote in Table 2 as they form part of the process of re-migration in the region. Few arrived directly from Europe and the numbers were in any case small, not even enough to compensate for the exodus of rural labourers to the neighbouring countries. Mexico, with the second largest population in Latin America, witnessed the arrival of only 33,980 settlers from across the Atlantic between 1904 and 1924. The years to which these figures correspond were, of course, not favourable for immigration given the political instability of the country. However, the total is equally low if one compares it with the number of people leaving Mexico during the period. Venezuela, on the other hand, admitted some 300,000 foreigners between 1905 and 1930, but only managed to retain a tenth.

The mass exodus from Europe had in fact begun ten years earlier than 1881, the first date featured in these tables. Between 1871 and 1880, 100,000 foreigners settled in Argentina, and a similar number were admitted into Uruguay. Some 200,000 foreigners entered Brazil for the first time between 1872 and 1880. In Cuba, national statistics only began in 1902. Before that date, it is difficult to distinguish settlers from those sent to the colony as administrators or military personnel. Independence in 1898 saw the repatriation of large numbers of Spaniards.

The fluctuations in the migratory flow are, of course, partly concealed by our division into five-year periods. The seventies experienced a general and sustained increase which reached its climax at the end of the

Table 2. *Net immigration: Argentina, Uruguay and Chile 1881–1930**

(in thousands)

	Argentina	Uruguay	Chile	Total
1881–1885	191.0	26.7	4.3	222.0
1886–1890	489.4	42.1	23.9	555.4
1891–1895	156.1	13.8	2.8	172.7
1896–1900	303.9	33.9	4.1	341.9
1901–1905	329.3	43.8	3.6	376.7
1906–1910	859.3	92.8	35.6	987.7
1911–1915	490.4	101.0	53.3	644.7
1916–1920	2.4	53.1	14.8	70.3
1921–1925	510.2	70.0	34.3	615.5
1926–1930	481.6	102.6	6.3	590.5
	3,813.6	579.8	183.0	4,576.4

Sources: For Argentina, 1881–1930, Recchini de Lattes, Zulma and Lattes, Alfredo E. (eds.), *La población de Argentina* (Instituto Nacional de Estadística y Census, Buenos Aires, 1975), 200; for Uruguay, 1881–92, Willcox, Walter F., *International migrations* (National Bureau of Economic Research, New York, 1929), 568, *Anuarios estadísticos*; for Chile, 1882–1907, Young, George F. W., *The Germans in Chile: Immigration and colonization* (Center for Migration Studies, New York, 1974), 6; also Mamalakis, Markos, *Historical statistics of Chile*, vol. II (Westport and London, 1980), 109;

* Immigrants entering Paraguay

1818–1885	0.8	1900–1905	2.3	1921–1923	1.6
1886–1890	4.7	1906–1910	5.1	1926–1930	1.7
1891–1895	1.8	1911–1915	4.6		
1896–1900	1.2	1916–1920	1.6	1881–1930	25.6

Source: Pidoux de Drachenberg, Lyra, 'Inmigración y colonización en el Paraguay, 1870–1970', *Revista Paraguaya de Sociología* 34 (1975), 65–123.

following decade. In Argentina the crisis of 1890 abruptly interrupted this growth; indeed more foreigners left than entered the River Plate. Brazil, however, did not experience such a fall. Italian emigration to Brazil was at the time prohibited as a result of a disagreement between the two governments, but when Rome authorized its resumption in 1891, many Italians eagerly seized the new opportunity to move to Brazil, especially to work on the coffee plantations of São Paulo. Italian migration then remained high for the next two decades. By the beginning of the twentieth century, Argentina was again widely preferred by immigrants. During the years 1900–10, it received some 300,000

Table 3. *Net immigration: Brazil, 1881–1930*

(in thousands)

| | Brazil | | | | | | State of São Paulo | | | |
| | First time arrivals | Percentage | | | | | Arrivals | % of Brazil | Departures[1] | Rate of perm. settlement |
		Portug.	Ital.	Span.	Germ.	Jap.				
1881–1885	133.4	32	47	8	8	—	19.02[2]		—	
1886–1890	391.6	19	59	8	3	—	199.4	51	—	84
1891–1895	659.7	20	57	14	1	—	413.4	63	65.5[3]	56
1896–1900	470.3	15	64	13	1	—	281.6	60	122.9	12
1901–1905	279.7	26	48	16	1	—	194.3	69	171.4	9
1906–1910	391.6	37	21	22	4	1	190.2	49	173.6	49
1911–1915	611.4	40	17	21	3	2	339.0	55	173.9	30
1916–1920	186.4	42	15	22	3	7	99.9	54	69.5	51
1921–1925	386.6	32	16	12	13	5	222.7	58	108.5	46
1926–1930	453.6	36	9	7	6	13	263.4	58	141.4	
	3,964.3	29	36	14	5	3		56[4]		46[4]

[1] From port of Santos: third class passengers.
[2] 1882–1885
[3] 1892–1895
[4] 1892–1930, only

Sources: For Brazil, Levi, Maria Stella Ferreira, 'O papel da migração internacional na evolução de população brasileira (1872–1972)', *Revista de saúde pública*, 8 (suppl.) (1974), 49–90, esp. 71–2; for São Paulo, Holloway, Thomas H. *Immigrants on the land. Coffee and society in São Paulo, 1886–1934* (Chapel Hill, 1980), 179.

Table 4. *Net immigration: Cuba, 1902–30*

(in thousands)

	Passengers. Balance of arrivals and departures	Rate of settlement[1]	Immigrants admitted Spaniards	Antilleans
			(percentages)	
1902–1905	64.3	57	81[2]	1[2]
1906–1910	66.9	41	71	14
1911–1915	72.0	40	75	11
1916–1920	253.1	63	52	37
1921–1925	158.7	53	50	37
1926–1930	−18.9	−16	30	58
Total	596.1	47	58[3]	31[3]

[1]Residue of arrivals and departures in relation to immigrants admitted (in percentages)
[2]1904 and 1905 only
[3]1904–30.
Source: Cuba, Secretaría de Hacienda, *Inmigración y movimientos de pasajeros, 1902–1930.*

Europeans annually, although only a proportion of these settled permanently. The current to Brazil meanwhile slackened, and the crisis of 1903–4 caused many to return home. The European war caused further repatriation generally. Argentina lost some 87,000 foreigners, although immigrants from the non-belligerent nations continued to arrive. São Paulo and Chile recorded smaller negative balances, while arrivals in Uruguay only fell slightly. The war had the opposite effect in Cuba. With the rise in sugar prices, immigration reached new heights, but did not last. The crisis of 1920 sent back home many recent arrivals. In 1927, 1928 and 1929, departures exceeded arrivals on the island. Finally, sixty years of mass immigration to Latin America came to an end with the onset of the world crisis in 1929–30.

The nations of southern and eastern Europe contributed in varying degrees to this mass migration. Among the 4 million foreigners admitted into Brazil between 1881 and 1930, the Italians ranked first with 36 per cent of the total. The high point of Italian emigration to Brazil was the period between 1896 and 1900. After that, the proportion of Italians fell to a modest 9 per cent during the years of Fascism. As it decreased, its regional composition varied. Italians from the north of Italy were replaced by those from the south on the eve of the First World War. The second largest group of immigrants was that originating from the old mother country. The Portuguese, who had always constituted the majority before the onset of mass migration, conceded primacy to the Italians. The agricultural crisis came later in Portugal, and the Portuguese took to the sea when the flood of Italians was beginning to recede. From 1906, they once again regained their position, representing 29 per cent of immigrants. Spain came third after Italy and Portugal: a total of half a million Spaniards represented one-seventh of the total. The years of greatest influx were those between 1906 and 1920, when Spaniards exceeded Italians in numbers, although during the 1920s Spanish immigration declined. Portuguese and Spaniards made up two-thirds of the total number of immigrants entering Brazil between 1906 and 1920. Immigration from Germany picked up considerably following the First World War. Most Germans made for the states of Rio Grande do Sul, Santa Catarina and Paraná, where they joined the descendants of the pioneers who had settled there during the empire. The war was also responsible for increasing the quota of Slavs, whether Yugoslavs, Poles or Russians by nationality, and of various creeds, including Jews, as well as the quota of Syrians and Lebanese, who were known there, as elsewhere in Latin America, as Turks. Indeed, before the war they had entered the country on Ottoman passports.

Barred from Hawaii and the United States, Japan set its sights on Brazil. From 1908, Japanese emigration companies placed several thousand families at the disposal of the coffee planters. Lacking cohesion (it became clear that many of these 'families' had, in fact, no family ties), and frustrated in their expectations, the Japanese colonies proved unstable. They migrated to the suburbs of cities, especially São Paulo, where they became involved in market gardening, or otherwise made for the pioneer frontiers, where they became independent cotton growers. When Brazilian subsidies were cut, the Japanese government assumed responsibility for financing emigration in 1924. Under these conditions, some 70,000 Japanese entered Brazil before 1930. Japanese even ranked first in numbers between 1932 and 1934. The Japanese migrated to various countries in Latin America, but never in such numbers as to Brazil.

In the River Plate as in Brazil the Italians constituted the largest immigrant group. Between 1860 and 1900, they represented more than half of the total. As the new century got under way, their numbers fell, though never so low as in Brazil. Their regional origin also changed. On the eve of the World War, the Neapolitans, or southerners, outnumbered the immigrants from the north. The *tano* therefore replaced the *gringo* as the popular stereotype of the Italian. Spaniards ranked second in Argentina. Portuguese immigrants were very few. In the ten years between 1911 and 1920, incoming Spaniards managed to top the poll. They made up a third of all immigrants. In terms of regional origin, most of them came from the northern coastal area. Russians (Slavs) and Turks (Syrians, Lebanese and Armenians) also crossed the Atlantic to Argentina. Migration to Argentina, however, differed from that to Brazil in three ways: the French came in greater numbers from 1871 to 1890; national minorities from the British Isles, such as the Irish and the Welsh, also preferred this part of the continent; and Japanese and Germans were not present in any significant numbers. Two factors distinguished Uruguay from Argentina. The number of Spanish immigrants was close to that of Italians, and the French were even more prominent, possibly because, having constituted the largest contingent during the 1840s, the tradition had continued.

In Cuba, Spanish immigrants outnumbered all others by far. Paradoxically, their numbers increased after the withdrawal of the colonial army and administration. In terms of intercontinental migration, that is, excluding those from other Caribbean islands and from North and Central America, Spaniards accounted for some 85 per cent of the total number of immigrants.

Arrival, as we have seen, did not necessarily mean permanent residence. Argentina at the turn of the century, in particular, received large numbers of 'seasonal' workers, who came for the harvest. This was due to the fact that the low season for agricultural activity in the Mediterranean area coincided with the busiest period on the pampas. Because of cheap passages, the farmworker could return home with some savings, while his own lands had not been neglected. Other immigrants simply came with the intention of making enough money to buy property in their village, or with the greater ambition of 'doing America'. If their luck held out, they returned to their native land. The Cantabrian coast of Spain is dotted with houses built by returning 'Americans', with exotic palm trees in the gardens which attest to the incurable nostalgia of their owners. In São Paulo, only 46 per cent of those arriving between 1892 and 1930 actually settled (see above Table 3). In Argentina, the figure fell to 34 per cent between 1881 and 1930.

And not all nationalities settled in the same proportions. Distance travelled and the cost of the passage affected any final decision. For the Japanese, a change of plan proved far more costly than for the Italians. Between 1908 and 1932, 92 per cent of the Japanese who landed at Santos, settled in São Paulo, compared with only 13 per cent of the Italians. For a Yugoslav to transplant himself overseas to a country with a foreign language and foreign habits involved making a more final decision than it did for a Portuguese. About 80 per cent of the former, as opposed to only 42 per cent of the latter, settled permanently. The rates for Poles and Germans were 50 per cent and 18 per cent respectively.[5]

The propensity to settle also varied according to time and destination. 74 per cent of the Italian immigrants arriving in Argentina between 1881 and 1890 put down roots. In the following decade, the proportion fell to 47 per cent. In general, Italian migration, more than any other, seems to have been particularly sensitive to the short-term economic factors. Spaniards, for their part, showed a greater propensity to settle, as the figures of 85 per cent and 56 per cent for the same period seem to indicate.

Permanent residence, however, did not necessarily mean assimilation. A high proportion of Japanese women in São Paulo married their compatriots. The men, on the other hand, given the shortage of women of their own origin, often married Brazilian women. The tendency towards endogamy varied depending on sex and nationality. Although less marked than among Japanese women, it was nevertheless a common feature among all foreign women. Among men, on the other hand, it was lower. The first to turn away from endogamy were the Italians. And the propensity to assimilation through marriage was, generally speaking, higher in the cities than in the rural areas.

Men and women did not cross the Atlantic in equal numbers. The archetypal immigrant was adult, male and single. For immigration to Cuba in the period 1904–28, for example, see Table 5. The Cuban census of 1907 shows a male ratio of 110.3, i.e. for every hundred females on the island there were ten more males. In 1919 and 1931, the male ratio was 112.7 and 113.1 respectively. Table 6 distinguishes between the native and foreign population of Argentina. Whereas in the first group there appear to have been more females than males, due possibly to the higher death rate among males (male ratio of 90 in 1895), the opposite was the case among foreigners (male ratio of 173 in 1895). Apart from this, the

---

[5] Alfredo Ellis, Jr, *Populações paulistas* (São Paulo, 1934), 135.

Table 5. *Sex, age and civil status of immigrants: Cuba, 1904–28*

(in percentages)

Periods (years)	Men	Persons aged between 14 & 45 years	Single people
1904–1908	82.6	82.0	70.7
1909–1913	81.2	83.4	70.4
1914–1918	83.7	90.1	76.4
1919–1923	88.6	95.4	86.0
1924–1928	83.5	91.9	79.1

Source: Centro de Estudios Demográficos, *La población de Cuba* (Havana, 1976), 75.

same table indicates that there was a higher proportion of adult males among foreigners than among natives.

What was the effect of mass European immigration on overall population growth? The populations of Argentina, Uruguay, Brazil and Cuba increased at a rate which cannot be accounted for by reproduction alone. While the rate of increase for every thousand Argentines was 32.5 per year between 1880 and 1930, the balance of births and deaths was in the order of 18.1 per thousand. The difference of 14.4 therefore corresponds to immigration. Immigration, it is important to note, represents 44 per cent of the average increase in each year and about 80 per cent of the natural growth.[6] Over the same period, the endogenous contribution was of the same order in Brazil (18.1), but immigration there only added 3.3 per thousand more, i.e., about 15.4 per cent of the total growth.[7] According to the above estimates, immigrants were three times more important to the growth of Argentina than they were to that of Brazil. If one compares Argentina with the United States, one notes a similar discrepancy. While the North American census of 1910 shows 14.7 per cent of the population as being of foreign origin, the Argentine census of 1914 shows twice that figure.

Sooner or later, all Latin American countries passed immigration laws or financed colonization programmes. The state of São Paulo spent considerable sums of money on subsidizing sea passages, either through

[6] Zulma L. Recchini de Lattes and Alfredo E. Lattes, (eds.), *La población de Argentina* (Buenos Aires, 1975), 34.
[7] Thomas W. Merrick and Douglas H. Graham, *Population and economic development in Brazil. 1800 to the present* (Baltimore, 1979), 38.

Table 6. *Foreigners in the population of Argentina*

	Male ratio			% aged 14–64			Foreigners aged 14–64 as % of total pop.
	Total pop.	Argentine	Foreign	Total pop.	Argentine	Foreign	
1869	1.06	0.94	2.51	56.5	—	—	12.1
1895	1.12	0.90	1.73	57.9	48.6	85.0	25.5
1914	1.16	0.98	1.71	61.4	50.3	87.4	29.9

Source: Gino Germani, 'Mass immigration and modernization in Argentina', in I. L. Horowitz (ed.), *Masses in Latin America* (New York, 1970), 297.

the Society for the Promotion of Immigration, an organization created by the large coffee *fazendeiros*, or through contracts drawn up between the shipping companies and the Department of Agriculture. In addition, the state authorities built a reception centre for immigrants in the capital, the dormitories and refectory of which were used by a good half of the total number of immigrants. It was here that they were issued with rail tickets to the 'Planalto'. The state ploughed 5.2 per cent of its fiscal revenue into promoting immigration between 1892 and 1930, an investment which yielded high returns.[8]

Some nations spent money in vain or to little effect. Porfirio Díaz drew up ambitious plans with a view to populating the northern frontier, which was too exposed to the expansionist tendencies of the United States, the southern and eastern coastal areas, where land was being given over to the cultivation of export crops, and the central region where agricultural production was being modernized. The Italian colonies founded in 1881 proved a failure and ended up by using Mexican labour. Indeed, there was no shortage of labour in Mexico. Soon, the opposite would be the case, although labour was poorly distributed and slow to answer the call for recruitment. The only successful examples of colonization were those organized privately, such as that of the Mormons. In number, however, they counted for very little. Despite this, the foreign population of Mexico was on the increase. The census of 1910 recorded a total of 116,527 foreign residents in the country. Among these were the Chinese fishing community in Sonora, a handful of Puerto

[8] Thomas H. Holloway, *Immigrants on the land. Coffee and society in São Paulo, 1886–1934* (Chapel Hill, N.C., 1980), 56–7.

Ricans involved in the production of henequen and Jamaicans employed in the construction of railways. Spaniards and other Europeans preferred the cities and jobs in trade and services.

In Central America and the Andean countries, there was no mass influx of Europeans. Those who did go to these areas did not integrate into society via the bottom rung, but via the top. Europeans, for example, were heavily represented among the coffee planters of Costa Rica and the bankers of Peru. Entering society at the bottom were Asians, other Latin Americans and immigrants originating from Jamaica and the Lesser Antilles. When the sugar industry failed to keep up with technological innovation, many people in the Caribbean islands were laid off at a time when these islands were severely overpopulated due to rapid population growth. Some 145,000 Jamaicans left their island to build railways, dig the Panama Canal, or harvest the bananas of the United Fruit Company in Central America. As plantation labourers, they also flocked to Cuba and Santo Domingo at harvest time. A fair number of Jamaicans ended up by settling in compact communities in the country of their destination. English can still be heard, for example, along the Atlantic coast of Panama and Costa Rica. The islands which stretch in an arc from Venezuela to Puerto Rico also lost many of their inhabitants. In Santo Domingo, plantation labourers from the French Antilles were soon swallowed up by a flood of 'cocolos', the term by which British West Indians were known there. These were later replaced by Haitians in Santo Domingo and Cuba. Puerto Ricans, for their part, migrated to Santo Domingo, Cuba and Yucatán, not to mention the more unusual destination of Hawaii. Similarly, several thousand Guatemalans settled in Mexico, as did Colombians in Venezuela.

Argentina, Uruguay, Chile and Brazil were not only able to attract Europeans; they also drew people from neighbouring countries. Brazilians migrated to the northern departments of Uruguay where, in 1908, they constituted between one-seventh and one-fifth of the total number of inhabitants.[9] The forests and empty wastes of Patagonia witnessed the arrival of Chileans, while Peruvians and Bolivians settled in the far north of Argentina.

Immigration had a strong cultural as well as demographic impact, though not always the one aspired to and pursued in the beginning. Earlier in the nineteenth century governments had aspired to populate

---

[9] Juan Rial and Jaime Klaczko, *Uruguay: el país urbano* (Montevideo, 1981), 75.

their countries with northern Europeans, Anglo-Saxons or Germans, who were admired for their industry and sense of civic responsibility. Rather than a necessary source of labour, they were seen as instruments of social change and modernization. Moreover, European immigration was not so much viewed as a means to speed up economic growth, but often appeared to be a formula which spared governments the effort of mobilizing their population through education and health policies. This attitude denoted a certain fear or bias directed against the popular classes of their own nations. At times, this policy was tinged with racism. The Argentine constitution of 1853 in effect instructs the federal government to encourage immigration, but it stipulates that it should be of Europeans. Sixty years later, the immigration law of 1912 in the Dominican Republic established a preference for Caucasians. Racial bias even went as far as to only approve of certain Europeans. It was, however, economic need which prevailed over laws and ideologies. The foreigners admitted were those who were then available. Rather than the coveted northerners, it was the less prized Latins who arrived. Caribbean blacks and Asians were also admitted, albeit reluctantly.

If the speed of economic growth did not allow time for any discrimination by the receiving countries, the immigrants, for their part, had plenty of places to choose from. North America had already been a focus of attraction for some time. In Latin America itself, several doors opened at the same time. Whether their decision was made individually or collectively, cultural, linguistic and religious factors no doubt influenced prospective immigrants. The fact that the Portuguese overwhelmingly preferred Brazil supports this argument. That Spaniards turned to Cuba after independence can similarly be explained by their traditional ties with that country. Nevertheless, affinities such as these do not fully explain these or other cases. Much less do they explain the chronology and rhythm of the influx of immigrants.

More recently, historians have focused their attention on the socioeconomic conditions which constituted the yardstick of mass migration. The difference in real wages goes a good way towards explaining the to-ing and fro-ing between Italy and Argentina. Foreign investment and trade also explain the direction and fluctuations in the migratory current. The correlation between migration and these variables is very high, but it is not sufficient to explain the choice between Brazil and Argentina. Variations in the local labour market would seem to have been a decisive factor.

MORTALITY

Immigration explains only part of the demographic growth of several Latin American countries during the period 1870–1930. Natural growth accounted for the rest, that is, the greater part. And mortality and fertility combined in differing degrees to determine this growth.

The populations of Latin America had regularly been subject to a high rate of mortality which at times, as a result of wars, epidemics and poor harvests, sharply increased. The effect of the Paraguayan War on the population of Paraguay, for example, has already been commented upon. More frequent and less erratic were the epidemics, some of which were endogenous, such as smallpox, measles, or yellow fever, while others, such as cholera, were imported.

Cholera was the curse of the nineteenth century, due mainly to the greater intensity of transoceanic communications. Its incubation occurred in the delta of the Ganges, from where it usually spread to the Middle East and then to Europe. After three or four years, this infection from distant Bengal reached the American coast after crossing another ocean. Cholera visited America on five separate occasions: 1833, 1856, 1867–70, 1887 and 1894. The exact time and severity of the epidemic varied from place to place. It has been estimated that cholera claimed 150,000 lives in Brazil, for example, during the second half of the nineteenth century. The first and most severely affected places were the ports. Cholera would then spread inland, affecting above all the cities, or would appear wherever there were concentrations of people, such as in the trenches during the Paraguayan War. On the other hand, distance and poor communications were factors protecting the interior of the continent from the risk of contagion. Indeed, isolation proved to be the best insurance against the disease spreading. Maritime quarantine and other internationally adopted measures succeeded in putting a halt to its recurrence towards the end of the century. The great cholera epidemics were over.

Yellow fever was another common disease. It had existed in the Caribbean for some time in larval form. One less deadly variety may even have been native to the rain forests of America. During the nineteenth century it struck frequently (seven times in seventy years in Havana). The mosquito responsible for transmitting it spread outside its native habitat, and in the hulls and the rigging of sailing ships reached the temperate lowlands. Yellow fever, however, never affected lands situated more than 1,000 metres above sea level. During the 1840s, the fever attacked Lima, while on the other coast it was carried by ship from New Orleans to Bahia from where it spread to Rio de Janeiro. From Rio it moved south during the following decade. In 1857, it reached Montevideo and a year later it crossed to Buenos Aires. Its most devastating effects were felt in 1871 when nearly one-tenth of the population of Buenos Aires died from the disease, a fact which left a deep imprint on the memory of the survivors.[10] It is worth noting that yellow fever was more lethal in Brazil among new arrivals from Europe than among blacks or Brazilian-born whites, and news of this in Europe put off many potential emigrants.

Yellow fever was also a factor behind the failure of the first attempt to dig the Panama Canal at the end of the nineteenth century. The North Americans resumed work on the canal only after a campaign of intensive fumigation aimed at stamping out the disease. The Cuban doctor, Carlos Finlay, had identified the carrier mosquito. Systematic fumigation succeeded in freeing Cuba and Panama from yellow fever and, at the same time, from other diseases such as malaria. Elsewhere, the fever continued to attack. At Santa Cruz, in Bolivia, there were five thousand cases recorded as late as 1932.

Apart from these great epidemics, there was the 'flu pandemic of 1917–19 as well as local scourges such as the outbreak of bubonic plague which affected Santos in 1899. Other infectious illnesses which constantly occurred, but which were, for the most part, selective in that they attacked children, sometimes achieved epidemic proportions. Smallpox and measles continued to claim victims, especially among the rural population. And a wide range of pulmonary, intestinary or parasitic infections for a long time claimed many lives.

Children represented a high proportion of those who died through disease during the nineteenth century. Between 1899 and 1931, Cuba reduced its infantile mortality rate by a quarter, to a still high figure of 168 per thousand. Mexico reduced its rate by more than half: from 324 per thousand between 1896 and 1898, child deaths decreased to 146 in the period 1929–31. In the same period, child mortality in Uruguay had reached an all-time low and almost stationary figure of 98 per thousand, the minimum national rate in the region. Between 1865 and 1895, the life expectancy of a child at birth – which is another way of analysing the mortality rate – did not exceed 26.9 years in the majority of Latin

[10] See Miguel Angel Scenna, *Cuando murió Buenos Aires. 1871* (Buenos Aires, 1974).

American countries (Brazil, Chile, Colombia, Costa Rica and Panama). By 1930 life expectancy had reached no more than 36.1 years, a slow advance of 2.2 months per year over a fifty-year period. In the more backward countries like the Dominican Republic, Guatemala and Nicaragua, life expectancy rose to 27.1 years by 1930, a figure in line with that of the other countries some fifty years before.[11]

Figures for life expectancy are still tentative. Nevertheless, they reveal trends in Latin American mortality during the period. Generally speaking, there was no spectacular improvement; life expectancy remained at a precariously low level. Moreover, conditions in some countries were clearly bad. In Argentina, however, as early as 1914, life expectancy reached 48 years, just below the standard of the most developed countries, although this figure conceals wide regional differences. A strong contrast developed between Buenos Aires and the north-west, where the figures were 51 and 38 years respectively. As far as infant mortality was concerned, the difference was also considerable. Indeed it varied by as much as 200 per cent.[12]

Only the River Plate managed to raise itself in terms of life expectancy to a level close to that of European countries. Significantly, Argentina, along with Uruguay, was the most urbanized country in Latin America. And a considerable part of its population lived in the capital. At a time when antibiotics were still unknown, prevention of contagion depended to a large extent on the standard of hygiene and the availability of public and private health services. Public works and services mushroomed at this time, particularly in the cities. This was the age when most Latin American cities were endowed with drinking water and sewerage systems, when municipal, state, or public hospitals were built, and when the medical profession grew in size and received better training. According to the censuses, the number of doctors in Montevideo, for example, increased from 150 to 243 between 1889 and 1904. However, the most spectacular advances were not made at this level. Rather, they occurred at the more modest, but nevertheless equally efficient level of the auxiliary personnel. Nurses increased from 3 to 250 in the same period. From a ratio of one nurse per 71,687 inhabitants, the situation had improved by 1908 to reach an acceptable ratio of one nurse per 1,237 inhabitants.[13] Improving standards of hygiene, by now more universally

11 Eduardo A. Arriaga, *Mortality decline and its effects in Latin America* (Berkeley, 1970).
12 Jorge L. Somoza, *La mortalidad en la Argentina entre 1869 y 1960* (Buenos Aires, 1971).
13 Juan Rial, *Estadísticas históricas de Uruguay, 1850–1930* (Montevideo, 1980), 137.

practised in the cities, also contributed to reduce the incidence of disease, and deaths. Around 1914 in Argentina, foreign women enjoyed a life expectancy which was some 15 per cent higher than their native-born counterparts.[14] The difference was not so much due to better status, for this was not necessarily the case, but rather to education and customs. Urban centres with a strong European presence experienced a generally earlier decrease in the death rate, similar to that which was occurring in Europe. This could therefore be considered a further effect of immigration on demographic trends.

Nutrition also contributed to the fall in the death rate, especially in the rural areas. As the domestic market developed, food crises became less sharp and frequent, though malnutrition and hunger did not disappear completely. In the River Plate area, which was a large food producer, the diet was abundant and varied, and this explains the better state of health enjoyed by its population. In this respect it was privileged by comparison with the countries of the Pacific coast. Here, the expansion of export crops in various areas occurred at the expense of subsistence agriculture. Nutrition therefore would not have improved. On the contrary, it must have worsened. And the death rate here fell hardly at all.

In conclusion, the mortality rates seem to have levelled out through the gradual elimination of death peaks caused by epidemics and famine. Meanwhile, a gap widened between countries, regions, localities and social strata. Some countries were not able to overcome the traditional causes of high death rates and short life expectancy at birth. A select few embarked on a phase of transition to modernity. However, it was only after the 1940s that drastic action was taken against infectious diseases and a more general, accelerated improvement took place.

FERTILITY

At the beginning of the twentieth century, all Latin American nations evinced high birth rates. Of the twelve countries which, in terms of population and area, accounted for most of Latin America, all but one exceeded the ratio of 40 births per one thousand inhabitants, and the single exception, Uruguay, was not far behind (see Table 7). Two decades previously, the rates for which there is evidence had even been a point or two higher.

[14] Somoza, *La mortalidad en la Argentina*, 165.

Table 7. *Birth rates in Latin America during the first quarter of the 20th century century*

(per thousand population)

	1900–4	1910–14	1920–4
Uruguay	38.9	36.5	30.1
Argentina	44.3	40.3	35.0
Cuba	44.6	44.7	36.7
Panama	40.3	42.0	40.0
Venezuela	41.8	44.5	41.2
Chile	44.7	44.4	42.2
Colombia	43.0	44.1	44.6
Costa Rica	46.9	48.9	44.9
Mexico	46.5	43.2	45.3
El Salvador	43.8	44.7	46.6
Guatemala	45.8	46.6	48.3
Brazil	45.7	47.3	48.6

Source: O. Andrew Collver, *Birth rates in Latin America: new estimates of historical trends and fluctuations* (Berkeley, 1965).

However, within this relatively homogeneous pattern of high fertility rates, it is possible to differentiate between three groups of countries during the first quarter of the century. In the first there was a slight fall in the birth rate. In some countries (Panama, Venezuela and Costa Rica) this fall occurred at the end of a short phase of growth. In Mexico, the opposite happened: the lower rate occurred after the sharp decline which took place during the Revolution, and in this sense, it represented a recovery. In Chile, the birth rate fell rather slowly. In the second group (Colombia, El Salvador, Guatemala and Brazil), there was a slight growth in the birth rate. Though small, this coincided with a decrease in the death rate, and the population increased therefore at a fairly rapid rate. A third group of countries (Uruguay, Argentina and Cuba) had, by 1920, a fertility rate of less than 40 births per thousand inhabitants. It has to be kept in mind that rates in Table 7 tend to overstate the case for a purely mathematical reason. When dividing the number of births by a higher denominator (population on the increase due to the arrival of immigrants and the lowering of the death rate), the quotient logically falls. If, however, the fertility rate is measured by the number of girl children born to women of a fertile age, the fall is less steep.

We do not know yet why immigration caused the birth rate to fall, if indeed this was the cause. Most immigrants came from southern Europe, an area where concepts of family and reproduction prevailed which favoured large families. In Buenos Aires, foreign women at first bore more children than Argentine women, but soon the opposite occurred. Why did this happen? Was the simultaneous fall in the birth rate in the River Plate and in southern Europe the result of a simultaneous improvement in the standard of living and education in the two regions?

In all this, urbanization seems to have been a decisive factor. Cities seem less fertile than the countryside. If a woman in rural Argentina had an average of 4.4 children in 1895, her city-dwelling counterpart had only 4. Equally, the birth rate in the interior of Uruguay was 33 per thousand, and that of the city of Montevideo 22 per thousand. From the cities, urban attitudes and values spread to the surrounding areas. Birth rates in the interior of Uruguay and in the province of Buenos Aires were lower than those of other rural areas in Latin America. The high birth rate in Latin America as a whole can be attributed mainly to the rural character of the region as late as the 1920s.

Among this rural population, marriage was certainly not widespread; free unions were common practice. The offspring of such relationships, which were not necessarily unstable, were considered illegitimate by law. Illegitimacy, which had been high ever since the colonial period, endured, with its fluctuations and local variations. On the Atlantic coast of Costa Rica, for example, 630 out of a thousand births occurred outside matrimony between 1915 and 1917. Only recently populated, the area housed a mainly floating population. Instability bred illegitimacy, but the national average was only 200 per thousand. The lower rate still was rather high.[15] On the other hand, marriage and birth rates did not go hand in hand. As the rate of marriage increased in the interior of Uruguay, the birth rate fell. The same happened in Argentina.

While one part of Latin America, therefore, followed an expected slow pattern of reproduction, the other was giving free reign to a certain capacity for generation which, up until then, had been contained. One factor may have been a reduction in the age at which couples married or began a sexual relationship. This seems to have happened, for example, in Mexico between 1905 and 1925. Finally, another area, more open to external influences, was beginning to adopt more modern habits and

---

[15] Casey Gaspar, *Limón*, 258.

gradually reducing its birth rate. Such a change was centred in the largest cities of Latin America, especially Buenos Aires and Montevideo, and extended into the rural areas along both banks of the River Plate. The lowering of both the birth and the death rates, though rare and localized, represents the first stage of what would be termed later 'the demographic transition'. In this preliminary phase, however, the birth rate changed less than the death rate. With lower child mortality in particular, and fewer demographic crises from disease and famine, more children survived to maturity, reproduced and accelerated the rate of population growth.

INTERNAL MIGRATION

As foreign and domestic markets increased their demands for goods, agriculture began to require more labour. The arrival of workers from Europe, Asia and the Caribbean, as well as Latin Americans from neighbouring countries, partly helped to fill the gap, as we have seen. But there was also considerable internal migration within certain Latin American countries in the fifty years before 1930 – to the 'frontiers', uninhabited territories under the nominal jurisdiction of the nation, to lands which seemed to offer better opportunities, to small urban centres and to large cities. Attraction or pull factors played a decisive role, but there were, of course, also push factors. In those places where the population was growing at a faster rate than economic activity, an escape valve was in fact opened up. And physical mobility was facilitated by the development of internal communications, especially the railways.

If migrants crossed provincial borders, census reports allow us to reconstruct the volume of such traffic. If no census surveys were taken, or if displacement were seasonal or took place within a small radius, the traces left by migrants are easily lost. Sources available today are only capable of providing a partial view of internal migration, and not all of them have yet been fully explored.

A 'frontier' still existed wherever the Spaniards and Portuguese had failed to penetrate during the colonial period: for example, the Amazon basin, which was shared by Brazil and its neighbours, the far south of the continent, northern Mexico and the tropical coasts. The presence in these areas of a thinly spread Indian population did not stop them from being considered wastelands and therefore the patrimony of the state. National governments drew up various plans for the occupation of these territories. In Argentina, in a few years between 1877 and 1881, the 'campaign of the desert' incorporated nearly 1,400,000 square kilometres, an area half the size of the entire country, into the Republic. The main expansion took place towards the south, through La Pampa and Patagonia, lands which were, for the most part, arid and inclement, and which, soon divided up among a few large landowners, witnessed the arrival of more sheep than men. To the north, the Chaco, which was a less extensive area of tropical forest, was also conquered. Although the newcomers, whether Argentine or foreign, were small in numbers, the demographic growth of the frontier territories was, of course, higher than the already high average growth for the whole country.

In Mexico, the 'march towards the north' was less of a military operation, although force was used to conquer and deport the Yaqui Indians of Sonora, than a slow penetration by excess populations from the centre and south-east. The areas of greatest attraction for these Mexicans were the northern coasts of the Pacific and the Gulf. In 1921, 59 per cent of those registered in the census in northern Baja California, 16 per cent in Sonora and 20 per cent in Nayarit, were born outside the state. In the oil-producing region of Tamaulipas, the figure was 31 per cent. In the northern central area, Coahuila and Chihuahua had populations in which 32 per cent and 13 per cent respectively came from other states.[16] For quite a few migrants, agriculture or stock raising in the north became a transitory activity on a route which would take them further, to California or Texas.

The population of Brazil was concentrated, as it always had been, on a narrow strip along the east coast. The western limits of the country were vague and the subject of controversy with the neighbouring countries. In this vast untamed and empty territory, several frontiers opened up from different sides. The rubber boom attracted Brazilians towards the Amazon. Many of the *seringueiros*, or rubber tappers, were north-easterners who had fled the droughts in Ceará. The population of the Amazon region increased by 65.7 per cent between 1877 and 1890 and by 40 per cent in the last decade of the century. The opulent city of Manaus was the flourishing centre of this boom between 1890 and 1920, but it also had repercussions in the eastern territories of Colombia, Peru and Bolivia, through which the fortune seekers spread.

Coffee cultivation promoted the colonization of the north and west of

16 Moisés González Navarro, *Población y sociedad en México (1900–1970)* (Mexico, 1974), I, 52.

São Paulo towards the end of the nineteenth century. As late as the 1920s, the last pioneers were still advancing, although on a narrower front, namely the Alta Sorocabana. The most significant change was that while the initial penetration had been carried out by immigrants, by 1920 it was the native Brazilians who had taken over. The former foreign colonist either re-migrated to the city, or, having become a smallholder, began to employ day labourers. The latter were drawn increasingly from the other states of Brazil. Coffee also opened up a late southward front, where labour was mainly native Brazilian. At the same time Goiás and Mato Grosso in central Brazil began their process of demographic expansion, also fed by the exodus from the north-east and east.

From Tamaulipas to Maracaibo stretches a long coastal belt which was long considered unhealthy and unsafe and which, apart from some important ports like Veracruz and Cartagena, had remained virtually uninhabited for centuries, despite sporadic attempts to occupy it. Two products, however, were to help shape this frontier: firstly bananas, and later oil. At the end of the nineteenth century, the companies which transported bananas to the United States received generous concessions on the Atlantic coast of Costa Rica. The plantations soon extended south through Bocas de Toro in Panama and Santa Marta in Colombia, and north along the Gulf of Honduras. Oil deposits were also discovered in Tampico in Mexico, in the north of Colombia and in the Gulf of Maracaibo in Venezuela. Permission to extract it was given to North American and British companies, and drilling intensified from the First World War. The banana plantations and oil fields were foreign enclaves contributing little to the economic development of the host nations. Most of the profits left, but the labour remained. The population increased, skewed by age and sex as in all the areas which received immigrants. Foreign workers from the Antilles were preferred on the plantations, while the oil wells made do with the local labour supply. Maracaibo's pull, for example, was felt throughout the western llanos of Venezuela and as far afield as the Andes.

The frontier was an area of land there to be grabbed, but in Argentina, Mexico, Central America and elsewhere, the land to be occupied had often already been grabbed. A handful of individuals or companies, local and foreign, had obtained title to the land, thanks to their influence in government. They were able to frustrate independent attempts at settlement on a small scale which would have laid the foundations for stable family life. Instead, the population drawn to the frontier was largely male and highly mobile, which did not favour reproduction. Frontier regions depended for a long time on arrivals from outside.

Lands which had long since been populated also attracted migrants as soon as their productive capacity intensified, or when, in response to market demands, new crops were introduced to replace the old. For example, in Cuba, when the old sugar mills were replaced by giant refineries, new labour opportunities were opened up in the provinces of Oriente and Camagüey. Cubans from the west of the country and foreigners flocked to the area in pursuit of new job opportunities at the beginning of the century. In Argentina, apart from the recently annexed Pampa and Patagonia where the main activity was stock raising, there were two poles of agricultural development. Firstly, cereal cultivation replaced cattle in the belt stretching from the north of the province of Buenos Aires to the central region of the province of Córdoba. Secondly, there were the sugar plantations which extended through Tucumán. Grain and sugar cane required large workforces, especially at harvest time, and attracted rural labourers from various adjacent provinces. Migratory flows varied over time, but two were steady: from the Mesopotamian provinces southward to the estancias of Santa Fe and Buenos Aires; and from the provinces of the north-west to Tucumán. During the period 1895–1914 in which 1,954,000 foreign migrants entered the country, net interprovincial migrations alone, not counting movement within the provinces, numbered 342,000.[17]

An open labour market had already been instituted in Argentina. People moved spontaneously whenever sharp contrasts in opportunities resulted from the unequal development of regions close to each other. There were, however, cases where the workforce was unwilling to enter the market. Even in the north-west of Argentina, there were known cases of compulsory recruitment of workers for the cane harvest. In the Andes, Mexico and Central America, coercion was not unusual. Incentive often alternated with and complemented coercion. Indians, who predominated in these areas, did not always respond to monetary incentives, while the landowners insisted on keeping wages at a low level in order to reduce costs. Recruitment through agents was therefore common practice, as was debt bondage in order to retain workers. The policy of liberal governments whereby land held by communities, as well as public land, was transferred to private ownership, contributed to the

---

[17] Zulma L. Recchini de Lattes and Alfredo E. Lattes, *Migraciones en la Argentina* (Buenos Aires, 1969), 131.

uprooting of rural workers from their villages. It was this type of policy which opened up the coastal lands of El Salvador, Guatemala and Chiapas in Mexico to coffee cultivation and northern Peru to sugar cane. Migration responding to this type of inducement was frequently no more than seasonal. Yet in the general coming and going, workers occasionally elected to settle on the hacienda or plantation, or in some nearby village, and the population of the area therefore increased.

If demographic growth coincided with the blocking of access to land by the landowners, then the only solution, for the most part, was to migrate. When agriculture entered a new capitalist phase in the central valley of Chile, the owners of *fundos* became more reluctant than before to rent out plots of land, while at the same time demographic growth exceeded the demand for labour. As a result, the excess rural population found itself obliged to look elsewhere for work. Mining in the Norte Grande absorbed some 150,000 migrants between 1885 and 1915. The southern frontier, and beyond that Patagonia, offered a second escape route. However, neither was enough. There was a massive floating population which drifted from place to place and from job to job. For some time, railway construction offered employment, which in one way was certainly compatible with the type of labour they were used to in their villages or *fundos*. At harvest time, work on the railways came to a halt. Finally, this mass of people ended up in the cities; women, especially, found work there in domestic service.

In the central highlands of Costa Rica, the small coffee plantations began to fall into the hands of large enterprises during this period. Many landowners thus lost their independent means of survival. Some opted to become colonists, while others tried other jobs. They made for Alajuela and Guanacaste in the north-west and Punta Arenas in the south, rather than for the Atlantic coast where the banana plantations were situated. As a result of their initiative coffee and other commercial crops spread to those areas.

In Uruguay, the countryside was also unable to absorb excess population because of the nature of its principal economic activity, large-scale cattle raising. Although Uruguay grew cereals like Argentina, it only did so on the coast, along the estuary of the River Plate. The interior remained essentially pastoral. Cows and sheep needed few hands to look after them. As a result, people went to the smaller urban centres which were multiplying and expanding while providing services to the pastoral economy.

These towns, which were part rural and part urban because of the role they played, also grew in the cattle raising area of Argentina. In the pampas, agglomerations of between 2,000 and 10,000 inhabitants increased in number from 27 in 1869 to 225 in 1914, and in the whole of the country, from 48 to 283. The population of these small towns grew from 197,000 to 1,160,000, an increase of 4 per cent per annum, which was higher than the population growth rate for the whole country (3.4 per cent per annum) over the same period. In contrast, in Mexico in 1900, there were 395 towns of between 2,500 and 5,000 inhabitants and 121 towns of between 5,000 and 10,000 inhabitants with a total population of 2,164,000. Ten years later, their number was almost the same and their population had fallen to 2,132,000. In 1930, there were 388 towns in the first category and 136 in the second, only a few more than in 1900, while their population stood at 2,138,000, that is, 26,000 less than in 1900. The stability of these towns may be attributed to the failure of the agrarian policies of the Porfiriato, to the retention of rural workers on the land as a result of the Revolution and to the existence of a viable alternative, namely migration.

Throughout Latin America the larger towns and cities expanded even more rapidly than the small towns both in absolute numbers and as a percentage of total population. Their growth was fed, in some countries, as we have seen, by constant streams of immigrants from Europe and, everywhere, by internal migrants from the countryside and the small towns.[18]

CONCLUSION

The outstanding features of the population of Latin America during the period 1850–1930 were its substantial growth, higher than any other region in the world at that time with the exception of the United States, and its high degree of physical mobility. At the same time its life patterns experienced only slight change.

With regard to birth and death rates, Latin America would appear to have been going through the last stage of a demographic regime of the old type. Death peaks seemed doomed to disappear, although the death rate remained high. The birth rate remained equally high, or actually grew. In some areas, however, both death and birth rates decreased,

[18] On the growth of the Latin American cities in this period, see Scobie, *CHLA* IV, Ch. 7.

anticipating the coming demographic transition. This transformation began in relatively sparsely populated areas like the River Plate and, above all, in the cities. However, Latin America, it should not be forgotten, was largely rural at this time. Whatever their ultimate significance these changes were modest and local. Further proof that the demographic patterns were still rather traditional was the fact that the population of Latin America was quite young. The age pyramid was wide at the base and narrowed considerably at the top. The elderly were few in number.

Within this rather stable society in demographic terms there was considerable movement of population. Europeans, Asians and British West Indians entered as immigrants, and, wherever they settled, they contributed to the increase of the population in various regions and countries. There was also a substantial redistribution of people within the area, even across political boundaries. The advance of the frontier, which had been halted for a century since the end of the colonial period, was renewed. In some areas along the Atlantic seaboard, this advance meant the reoccupation of lands which had been depopulated since the sixteenth century. Men made especially for those areas which prospered through international trade. Finally, the urban population increased more rapidly than the population as a whole. With regard to migration within Latin America, it could also be said that, generally speaking, the population came down from the sierra to the coast. The highlands no longer held their former advantage. The population movement was also centrifugal, from the heart of the Andes and Central Mexico towards the far north and far south of the continent, and more especially to the eastern seaboard, where the most economically dynamic regions and most prosperous cities were situated. This redistribution of the population not only facilitated economic growth, it also reinforced social stability since demographic pressure was released and demographic catastrophes were avoided.

5

RURAL SPANISH AMERICA, 1870–1930

INTRODUCTION

Any attempt to treat the rural history of such a large and varied area as that embraced by the term Spanish America must first make clear the conceptual difficulties and the limitations imposed by uneven research.[1] One approach has been to divide the entire area by elevation into lowland and highland or by zones of plantations and haciendas. This permits a broad and useful distinction between the sugar-producing, former slave regions such as the Antilles and the classic hacienda-dominated landscape of central Mexico or the Ecuadorian highlands. But the usefulness of this scheme disintegrates as one attempts to squeeze additional regions into it. The Cuautla depression in the Mexican state of Morelos, or Salta in Argentina, for example, both had many of the features of plantation life, such as capital intensive sugar *centrales* and a modern national market, but their labour force was drawn mainly from the smallholder Indian peasantry.

Another typology can be drawn along vegetative lines, that is, to examine rural society in terms of the crop it produces. To the extent that coffee or tobacco or sugar do in fact produce certain common or general requirements this scheme is useful, but only up to a certain point. The coffee plantations of Cundinamarca led to a very different society from that found among the independent smallholder coffee growers of Caldas or Costa Rica. And while it is true that the classic hacienda built on the

---

[1] The emphasis of this chapter is on the 'traditional' core zones of Mesoamerica (Mexico and Central America) and the Andean highlands (Colombia, Ecuador, Peru, Bolivia and Chile). On the plantation economies and societies of the Spanish Caribbean, especially Cuba, see Moreno Fraginals, *CHLA* IV, chapter 6. On the areas of new settlement in the nineteenth century, especially Argentina and Uruguay, see Cortés Conde, Gallo, Rock and Oddone, *CHLA* V, chapters 9–13.

153

The agrarian landscape of Latin America, 1870–1930

high culture remnants of Mesoamerica and the Andean highlands shared several features, there are wide ethnic and cultural differences among both landowners and village workers.

The more serious difficulty in any of these organizational schemes or typologies is the temptation to consider any one sector of rural society in isolation; to make false dichotomies between modern and traditional, or between hacienda and community. To do so ignores the fact that certainly by the period 1870–1930, and in many places much earlier, the fundamental feature of rural society was its inter-dependence with other zones or markets; the articulation of its various modes of production. And it is not just that different sectors within a country were linked into one system but also that these in turn were often influenced or even created by external demand. And finally, even this more comprehensive picture may be interpreted in very different ways. Some see the benefits of modernization spreading out from the modern enclaves which introduced new techniques and organization; others condemn this very process as one that underdeveloped, or at the very least, locked the poor and powerless into an unsatisfactory existence.

But if we are faced with a bewildering variety of rural environments in Spanish America, and for the most part a mosaic of unconnected research, a degree of unity may be found in the experience the entire region underwent after 1870; for, as Henri Favre points out, Spanish America is a particularly rich field for the study of the many responses which colonial and seigneurial societies can make to capitalism. 'Response' may strike some as an excessively academic term, for the sixty-year cycle of economic expansion left in its wake the destruction of the last remnants of native people from Araucanía to the Yaqui river and the virtual enslavement of thousands more from Yucatán to the Amazon. The penetration of capitalism also brought higher wages for those workers who would submit to its discipline, coercion and dispossession for those who would not, and often, 'long-lasting adjustments by which two social formations came to articulate and consolidate themselves over a period of time . . . thereby helping to perpetuate the local colonial system in which they [the peasant population] remain as firmly embedded as ever'.[2] Another concern here is the degree to which the change over the period 1870 to 1930 can be

<hr/>

[2] Henri Favre, 'The dynamics of Indian peasant society and migration to coastal plantations in Central Peru' in Kenneth Duncan and Ian Rutledge (eds.), *Land and labour in Latin America* (Cambridge, 1977), 253–67.

explained as a function of objective economic forces – population and the rise of the market particularly – and how much to extra-economic coercion on the part of landowners assisted by the liberal state; or, to put this in a slightly different way, should emphasis be placed on a reified world system or on internal political dynamics, and particularly on intra-class conflict, as the motor of change?

To understand why one thing happens here and another there is no easy matter especially since in the absence of written evidence, motive must often be inferred from action or resistance. Beyond that, there is the usual difficulty in trying to decide how much of the picture we have reflects reality or the ideological distortions ground into our spectacles. But the growing volume of recent research, especially that based on estate records and local archives, makes it possible to present in this chapter a general review of the changes which occurred in the social landscape of rural Spanish America between 1870 and 1930 as well as an outline of some of the theoretical issues in dispute.

RURAL SPANISH AMERICA *c.* 1870

It may be useful to begin by pointing out the main patterns in rural Spanish America as they took shape around 1870. We shall look at three types of rural environment in the older zones of settlement, for the most part in the higher elevations of Mesoamerica and the central Andes, where an insular agrarian society was occupied with subsistence or the production of food crops for local markets. In all of these zones, large private estates (haciendas), peasant village communities, and independent family farms were interrelated in a variety of ways.

A fairly small but economically important number of rural people were small and medium-sized farmers, such as those in the Sierra Alta de Hidalgo or the Bajío in Mexico, in Central Costa Rica, Antioquía, Colombia, and in several other pockets scattered about Spanish America. The coffee zone of Caldas in Colombia had only twenty-eight units of over sixty hectares, the rest were held by yeoman farmers. In the area surrounding Huancayo, Peru, for another example, perhaps less than 2 per cent of the rural population worked for the larger estates, the majority were independent small farmers. Loja and Carchi in Ecuador, the immediate environs of Arequipa, Peru, and the department of San Felipe in north-central Chile were all examples of zones where ordinary independent farmers were common. In a land generally dominated by the large estate, the widespread existence of family farmers is important to notice.

There are historical and racial explanations for their presence. The independent family farm seems to have appeared when population or overseas immigrants brought about frontier settlement into a region where there had been no sedentary native farmers (or where they had been eradicated), where the land had not been previously granted in large units and where, although a market existed, it still was not strong enough to promote economies of scale. Settlement patterns in eighteenth-century Bajío and Antioquia a century later were both products of migration, mainly by *mestizo* migrants. In other cases, local urban markets for horticultural produce or the accidental fragmentation of a large estate led to the proliferation of small farmers. Unlike those areas where the hacienda provided the link between city and country, these zones were by 1870 already quite urbanized, employed family or wage labour and meshed smoothly with the full emergence of capitalist agriculture in the following decades.

In the core areas of Spanish America where in the sixteenth century European agrarian forms were imposed upon a sedentary and dense Indian population – central Mexico, the Guatemala highlands and much of the Andean highlands – is found the type of rural environment most characteristic of Spanish America. The fundamental elements were large private estates, known generally as haciendas, and communities of smallholders.

The conflict between the original prehispanic village, usually organized in some communal form, and the private estate brought by European settlement is one of the main themes in Spanish American history. During the course of three centuries haciendas managed to establish a claim to much fertile and well-watered land and in some cases, vividly and admiringly described by travellers, they were large and imposing baronial spreads, virtually dominating entire regions. Fanny Calderón, for example, was impressed by the cultivated owner of San Bartolo in Michoacán who was 'the monarch of all he surveys', a king among his farm servants and Indian workmen.[3] Despite the abundance of similar description elsewhere, one must be careful not to mistake the exception for the rule for, in the 1860s, the much more typical hacienda was an exceedingly rustic, ill-defined and unmeasured spread populated

[3] Fanny Calderón de la Barca, *Life in Mexico*, ed. and annotated by Howard T. and Marion Hall Fisher (Garden City, New York, 1966), 561.

with scrawny livestock and an overabundance of resident workers. Haciendas co-existed and overlapped with villages and squatter settlements with whom they carried on a running squabble, now and then erupting into violence, over boundaries and water rights.

But if the rural estate was a rustic and backward place, it was an integral part of the national economy. Long ignored, the hacienda has been the subject of research in recent years. The picture emerging is that of an agrarian organization that faced in two directions: forward toward the market economy of local towns and cities; backward toward a workforce still often attracted and regulated with pre-capitalist relations. Landowners sold their produce to local towns and mines for money and they bought in return equipment, rudimentary manufactures, goods and food that they did not themselves produce, such as the odd furnishing or bit of luxury clothing from abroad. There is no doubt that landowning did confer prestige and the estate did have its personal rewards and recreational value, but its main business was making money. For the ordinary hacienda in the nineteenth century, self-sufficiency, never completely possible, was as much convenience as principle. It made sense to have one's own masons, smiths and leatherworkers, given the minuscule cost of resident labour and the absence of nearby suppliers.

There was an open and active land market. Haciendas changed hands with surprising frequency, and there was a continual process of subdivision and amalgamation. So much so that it is rarely possible to trace the history of a single estate back over two or three generations. In all of these senses – economic function and sentimental value – recent research has weakened the conventional picture of an autarkic 'feudal' estate and established the pattern that, even in the remote corners of Ecuador or Zacatecas, the hacienda was profit-oriented and actively – if imperfectly and inefficiently – engaged in a market economy.

In this core-area rural landscape, interrelated with, and inevitably opposed to, the large estate, stood a wide variety of peasant communities. Many of these traced their descent back to pre-hispanic roots; others to the mission towns and Spanish settlement policy of the sixteenth century. Into these communities, in degree varying with proximity to roads, cities and mines, clerical energy and native resistance, were introduced, along with European and Asian plants and animals, four enduring cultural imports: Christianity, Castilian forms of town government, the Spanish language and *compadrazgo*, the Mediterranean system of co-parenthood.

Despite the tendency to prefix the label 'indigenous' or 'Indian', by the 1870s one is really talking about a hybrid peasant community based on the legal possession of land, the cultivation mainly of native plants, the production and sale of hand made goods and a large degree of political autonomy. After three centuries of conflict, accommodation and, ultimately, co-existence with the private estate during Spanish colonial rule, the communities had held their own. In Bolivia, for example, they held at least half of all agricultural land into the 1860s; and even in Chalco, Valley of Mexico, an area of intense hacienda–community competition, the villages had abundant lands up to mid-nineteenth century. The community, in Eric Wolf's words, 'supported in its autonomy by a grant of land, charged with the autonomous enforcement of social control, constituted a small, closely defended island securing the social and cultural homogeneity of its members within, struggling to maintain its integrity in the face of attacks from without'.[4]

Much of the history of Spanish America since 1870 can be written in terms of the effort to disestablish these twin foundations of hacienda and community. In this period, the community's turn came first as the champions of liberal capitalist development sought to separate the *communards* from their means of subsistence while transforming personal into contractual relations. During this same time the large estate itself was reshaped to the new economic opportunities through gradual subdivision and modernization. But this pace was judged insufficiently rapid by a burgeoning urban population and, after 1930, the hacienda as well has come under assault.

The third general kind of rural landscape was that dominated by the large estate where neither yeoman farmers nor peasant community offered political opposition, nor competition over resources. Areas as widely separated as the Mexican north and central Chile were similar in this respect. In both of these cases European settlement had swept aside a shallow-rooted native population and, with the nearly complete control of land, encouraged the few survivors to settle within the confines of the hacienda itself as sharecroppers or service tenants. Some of these estates were huge and grew even larger in the course of the nineteenth century. Recent research on Zacatecas describes the hacienda 'del Maguey', an estate of 416 square miles, but only eighth in size in that state. Others

[4] Eric Wolf, 'Levels of communal relations', vol. 6 of *Handbook of Middle American Indians*, cited in Benjamin Orlove and Glen Custred, *Land and power in Latin America: agrarian economy and social processes in the Andes* (New York and London, 1980), 19.

contained 1,000 to 3,000 square miles and the Sánchez Navarro holdings in Coahuila encompassed some 25,000 square miles in the 1840s. Essentially a livestock estate, del Maguey employed on the average 260 permanent workers and let pasture and small arable plots to another 100 renters. Haciendas in central Chile were similarly organized but smaller, and because of better soil and irrigation had a much denser permanent population. As time went on, squatter settlements grew up in the ignored interstices of the countryside; or, in other cases, dependent villages were formed on the estate itself. From these and sometimes from migratory workers the estate could count on a ready supply of casual workers when the market justified shifts or increase in production. Squatter and dependent villages as well as the clusters of service tenants around the hacienda house were, of course, very different from the ancient communities of central Mexico or the central Andes. Where no village focus existed, the rural population turned around the hacienda which formed the social, economic and often the spiritual centre of the countryside. Many haciendas had their own chapels and several had a resident priest. Towns were scarce, no peasant culture and little peasant revolt developed; the hacienda was the link between city and country and effectively dominated the mass of rural inhabitants.

It would be easy to overstate the traditional features of agrarian society and it would be foolish to suggest a rural idyll, for if people worked little, the rewards and comfort of their life were likewise scant. But still, before the 1870s in these interior, isolated regions, we are dealing with a way of life whose economic rhythms were gentle, where work turned around the seasons and climate and the larger world scarcely intruded. Although Spanish America as a whole had been drawn into the Atlantic economy as early as the sixteenth century, large areas of the countryside were only slightly touched by this contact. A place such as Sicuani a few miles above Cuzco, or the haciendas hidden away in the intermontane valleys of the central Andes, were in fact little changed from the seventeenth century. If we look beyond the fields immediately surrounding the cities or the odd mining town, the picture of rural isolation drawn in vivid detail by Luís González holds true for great stretches of Spanish America well into the 1860s. In San José de Gracia (west central Mexico), time is marked off by the seasons and the church calendar, no one reads, there is no school, jail or judge. Few villagers venture more than a day's ride from home and the local tranquillity is disturbed only by the arrival twice a year of a string of mules and their driver come for hides, cheese, wax, a bit of mezcal. Salt, a few tin pans, are left in exchange for a jumble of coins reverently sorted from a clay pot.[5]

AGRARIAN CLASS STRUCTURE AND ECONOMIC GROWTH AFTER 1870

A general interpretation of change in traditional or insular Spanish American rural society after 1870 must include a number of elements. In the first place there is no doubting the importance of the growth of trade arising from urbanization and the demand for agricultural produce generated by a variety of export enclaves from copper mines to banana plantations. The demand for greater output presented landowners with new opportunities for gain but also with stiffer competition as better roads and railroads penetrated the interior zones. Secondly, the interpretation must consider population, or, more specifically, the number of actual or potential rural workers. Studies of European rural systems have long seen demography as a key variable in the transition to agrarian capitalism. Population increase is associated with rising prices, greater estate profits and lower incomes for the rural mass and a reversal of these in times of population decline. But although it is arguable that progress toward agrarian capitalism in the later nineteenth century in Spanish America is in many ways analogous to a much earlier transition in Europe, the change here took place in a very different context. Once again we must remind ourselves of the disjointed or accidental development of Spanish America brought about not so much by organic growth as by external influence. Thus, although the forces of change after 1870 in Spanish America fell upon a rural working people using many features of seventeenth-century technology and with an outlook to match, these same Spanish American peasants had before them a widening urban frontier and, often, steam locomotion to carry them to the cities. One manifestation of the paradox of population growth in Spanish America is the perennial lament by landowners of the 'scarcity of hands' at a time of steadily increasing population. The third element is the role of the state in providing the political and judicial framework within which agrarian change occurred and in conditioning the course of development.

Although it is true that the market, demography and the role of the state are all key elements in the analysis of agrarian society, neither can be

[5] Luis González, *Pueblo en vila, Microhistoria de San José de Gracia* (Mexico, 1968), 100–13.

dealt with in isolation; it is obvious that they are intimately related and interdependent. But, more importantly, neither the impersonal nor objective forces of the market and population provide an adequate explanatory model of Spanish American change between 1870 and 1930. In the first place this is because there are really several histories rather than one history of this period and it is exceedingly difficult to give a single explanation of agrarian change. Moreover a supply–demand market mechanism is not adequate, nor even by itself appropriate, to the discussion of agrarian change where men and land are not yet commodities. What an examination of the market and population does achieve is to focus attention upon the class structure of rural Spanish America, and the ways in which a complete range of economic and extra-economic mechanisms were employed by landowners to extract a surplus from rural workers. It is to the discussion of the various labour systems, their relationship with each other and to the land, that we now turn.

Systems of rural labour

By 1870 two main categories of rural people worked on the Spanish American estate. The first were permanent residents, a group that included administrators, field bosses, clerks and artisans along with a number of service tenants described by the terms *peón acasillado* in Mexico, *concertado*, *huasipunguero*, *colono* and *yanacona* in the Andes and *inquilino* in Chile. Permanent residents were often sharecroppers or sub-renters as well although these could come forward from amongst industrious smallholders or other landowners. Seasonal workers drawn from the resident families themselves, from nearby communities when these were present and from squatter or migrant groups when they were not, were the second main component of estate labour.

The transfer of surplus from the permanent residents assumed a variety of forms and, of course, varied with the nature of production and the intentions of the estate. In exchange for a small subsistence plot on the estate, a daily ration in maize or wheat flour and grazing privileges for a certain number of animals, the service tenantry was required to work on the estate. The labour service could be ordinary work throughout the year with extra duties and extra hands from the tenant's household required at harvest or during the annual slaughter.

In some cases a wage was also paid, or, rather, one often sees a wage expressed in monetary terms in hacienda registers, but more often than not this was a wage on account not in cash. In 1870 and into the twentieth century, the ordinary estate worker rarely saw or handled money. Rudimentary trade items such as thread, dye, knives, or imported cloth, were funnelled through the hacienda store, their value simply marked against the worker's account. In some cases the estate issued its own currency in the form of tokens. A principal aim of the estate was to sell its own produce for money on the market but at the same time to pay out as little as possible in cash. To the extent that the estate's own produce – maize and, above all, alcoholic drink – was exchanged for labour, the goal was obviously attained. In any case the store aimed to make a profit, although the recent research in estate records shows that the rates were not as exorbitant as is often believed.

Exchange among hacienda workers and among the isolated villagers far from the market sources of towns or mines generally took the form of barter. They saved the rare coin for commerce with the ambulatory merchant or the local priest. Clerical services usually required cash although these, too, were often paid by the estate against the promise of future labour from the new parent or newlywed. Those villagers or estate workers who managed to produce the odd speciality such as honey or wax or pottery exchanged these for tin pots, a knife, a fancy kerchief. In San José de Gracia, an ordinary village in Michoacán, money served the local *rancheros* three purposes: a means to buy tiny plots of land; display as 'jingling coin' in their pockets at dances and weddings; and for burial in the backyard.

The other main group of hacienda workers were seasonal labourers hired by the day or week during times of peak labour need. They were normally recruited from nearby villages, squatter settlements, from migrants, or from independent families seeking to supplement their income. The seasonality of labour was an important feature of estate agriculture; it varied of course with the level of technology and the nature of activity.

From the landowner's point of view, the ideal situation was to have available for specific periods of the year a large number of reliable men and women who would work at short notice for low pay during precisely the days required and then remove themselves from the estate without demanding off-season sustenance or welfare. From the landowner's point of view, slavery was objectionable, although in some regions where no one else was available to work absolutely necessary. From the same point of view a village community was an ideal source for seasonal labour as long as villagers did not insist upon tending or harvesting their own crops when the estate called upon them. When land was abundant and underused, before railroads or markets imposed stricter timetables, and before the opportunities for profit were so clear, haciendas tolerated and indeed encouraged the settlement of a surplus under-employed population on the estate. But by the 1870s, the permanent resident population was being reduced in most places and seasonal workers put more and more on a cash basis.

The wage of seasonal workers was calculated and often paid in money, but here, too, something less than a fully-fledged labour market existed. From the scanty data and incomplete series now available it would seem that in the 1870s both employer and worker were just in the process of learning the rules of the wage labour game. The point of departure for all daily wage offers around mid-century seems to have been two *reales* or twenty-five cents of the peso or its equivalent. Obviously, children were paid less, as were women for the kind of hard labour where their output was judged to be less; but for the ordinary male adult, two *reales*, a customary wage during the previous two centuries, was the base line offer. This amount landowners from Mexico to Chile were prepared to offer, sometimes adding or deducting a food ration depending on the nature of the task at hand.

During times of peak labour needs, wages were often paid in a form that to many rural people was more attractive than money. In Ecuador and many sections of the Peruvian highlands down into the 1920s, and even among the rural squatter settlements of mid-nineteenth-century Chile, haciendas provided huge fiestas of food and drink as incentive and reward for tasks that required a large number of workers for a short but specific time.

The underlying assumption in fiesta as well as wage labour was that a man would not work unless driven by hunger, that the quality of work was the same regardless of the wage and that once the immediate need was satisfied the worker would shirk or leave the job. Hence the need on the one hand for supervision by the hacienda staff and a large pool of unemployed people on the other.

Population growth had begun everywhere in the eighteenth century; it advanced unevenly in the first half of the nineteenth as cholera, smallpox and whooping cough continued to take their toll, and then became general from 1870 on. Thus, a large pool of potential day labourers not only existed but was steadily increasing. The demographic dimension is obviously important in understanding forms of rural labour and the static and even falling real wages during a period – post 1870 – of higher agricultural output; but absolute population density is not in itself a sufficient explanation, although it does shift the advantage to those who control land. Once again the fuller explanation lies in the rural people's relationship with the land and each other.

The greatest number of seasonal workers were recruited from among nearby communities of smallholders or independent farmers. They had their own planting and harvesting schedules which naturally coincided with those of the estate. And as long as peasants had their own land they naturally gave second priority to the estate's call. This situation can be seen clearly in new research dealing with the earlier nineteenth century on the Chalco area in the Valley of Mexico where landowners pleaded and cajoled but could do little to extract workers from a landholding village peasantry.

Later in the century as the market grew but before the massive assault on village land, the paradox was everywhere; people thick on the ground yet the landowners constantly lamenting the *escasez de brazos* (shortage of hands). From the landowner's point of view there existed a shortage of hands whenever workers did not appear on the day required, at the wage offered and work at the pace demanded. As railroads and wholesale buyers created delivery schedules, landowners were less willing to tolerate a conflict between their own and the peasants' planting and harvesting schedules, less tolerant of absenteeism and shirkers but were still very reluctant to pay a wage sufficient to attract a steady work force. Under the circumstances, the landowners' own racial views and newly acquired liberal ideology ran together with the new opportunities for profit to justify a solution, as we shall see below.

Population was no less abundant in those regions such as central Chile or the Mexican north where ancient village communities did not exist and where the increase took the form of squatter settlements, sometimes on the estate and at other times in the interstices between estates, and, inevitably, of out-migration. Thousands of peons migrated from central Chile to the nitrate fields and railroad construction projects after 1870, while, with little technological improvement, agricultural output steadily increased and wages scarcely increased. To the extent, however, that construction projects in the cities, or other countries, offered competition in the form of higher wages, landowners were also forced here to seek a solution if dependent workers and low wages were to be maintained.

Liberal development: attitudes and policy

Along with the penetration of railroads into Spanish America and the growth of a larger world and domestic demand for its produce there occurred, among the landowners and entrepreneurs who stood to benefit, a gradual shift in attitude. Many elements of this were present from the late eighteenth century but it now hardened into orthodoxy: the theretofore protected peasantry should become free workers. To accomplish this the archaic colonial tribute which for centuries had been used to exact labour services from the Indian peasantry (the landowner normally paid the Indians' tax and then demanded labour in recompense) was finally abolished over the protests of a minority of recalcitrant *hacendados* in Peru in 1854, Ecuador in 1857 and Bolivia in 1882. Peasant communities likewise came under attack on the grounds that they stifled initiative and impeded social integration while the liberal insistence on tariff reduction meant that village artisans would be forced either to compete with cheap imports or enter the labour market. The Church, seen as the purveyor of backward ideas and a sponge for capital, was now, in the 1870s, progressively removed from the economic sphere.

That this entire bundle of classic liberal attitudes was not completely or quickly translated into successful policy is explained as much by the liberals' deep-running contempt for their own lower classes, and their consequent ambivalence about the chances for success, as by political opposition. For after 1870, the propertied classes, and especially the *agricultores progresistas*, were dominant in national government. This was true until the 1910 Revolution in Mexico and until the advent of mass urban politics after 1920 in Peru and Chile. There was also the stubborn reality of an enormously varied Spanish America. In a number of special regions such as Yucatán, the Amazon basin, or the Valle Nacional in south-east Mexico where labour was scarce and profits high, the state was prepared to support planters with force and supply them with convict labour conscripts and forced immigration: all considered necessary given the reluctance of men to work under the harsh conditions of these zones.

Elite opinion in the later nineteenth century, however, generally turned against peonage and the use of labour contractors – the system of *enganche* – except where such devices were deemed absolutely indispensable to form a disciplined work force. 'Free labour produces more', discovered a delegate to an 1896 Agricultural Congress in Chiapas (Mexico) while others, worried about the negative image projected to countries from whom capital might be obtained, reminded the Congress that the labour system in Chiapas was an embarrassment to the 'civilized world'. While these attitudes were increasingly common among the men who ran Spanish America at this time, they co-existed uneasily with the parallel opinion that the rural lower classes, product of Indian fatalism and Black sloth, were incurably lazy, would work properly only under the prod and might not be susceptible to progress.

Thus, relations between landowner and peasant remained stubbornly constant despite the wrenching change demanded by the onrush of agrarian capitalism. The years between 1870 and 1930 do not reveal a linear transition to wage labour and the triumph of a full capitalist mode of production, but rather a discontinuous, pragmatic advance and retreat, compulsion and resistance, that depended ultimately upon the strength of the new forces of production, the political power of individual *hacendados* or the landowning class, and peasant resistance. Let us look first at changes among the workers resident on the landed estate, those that some observers have called 'the internal peasantry.'[6]

In the first place there is some evidence of a change from shares of produce to money rents. This shifted the responsibility for marketing to the sharecropper and was only possible under special conditions such as found in the Mexican Bajío, where, in fact, such a trend is found much earlier. More common was renegotiation of share tenancy with landowners attempting to gain a larger percentage of flocks or crops. At the same time landowners everywhere began to increase the labour obligation on that sector of the rural lower class with precarious tenure and much to lose, the service tenantry. *Inquilinos* in Chile were now after 1870 required to provide two and even three day labourers from their households to whom the estate then paid the standard wage. By stepping up labour demands on the residents, the landowners thus attempted to make labour brokers out of the service tenantry and to put the responsibility for compliance upon them, an arrangement often filled with uncertainty and interminable haggling. At the same time many

---

6 Rafael Baraona, 'Una tipología de las haciendas en la sierra ecuatoriana', in Oscar Delgado (ed.), *Reformas agrarias en América Latina* (Mexico, 1965), 688–96.

estates here took on additional service tenants but gave them sharply reduced perquisites. Such a practice was reasonable where estates had an abundance of land, especially irrigated land, to attract and support tenants, and nearby villages were not available to provide a ready and reliable source of workers. But new research has shown that the great livestock haciendas of Puno in southern Peru also held fast to their *colonos* (service tenants), were, moreover, reluctant to reduce the flocks they customarily pastured on hacienda land and continued to remunerate the *colonos* in pasture rights and food and goods from the estate store instead of cash wages. The rural population resident on haciendas in Azángaro province (Puno) in fact increased from 23 to 36 per cent between the two censuses of 1876 and 1940.

In other regions new market opportunities encouraged landowners to bring more land under cultivation or fence off pasturage, and in those cases it made little sense to settle additional year-round, space-occupying residents. In San Luis Potosí during the last third of the nineteenth century, where the process has been described in detail by Jan Bazant, landowners abolished the special low maize prices and gradually reduced the number of tenants, while hiring more day labourers. The same pattern holds for the Tlaxcala-Puebla zone. As late as the mid-nineteenth century haciendas were willing to tolerate and maintain a large number of underemployed residents and hangers-on whom they had inherited from the colonial centuries. This practice probably reduced the number of unemployed and vagrants who might otherwise have been on the move, spared the need for a kind of American poor law and diminished the potentially large social problem in the countryside. But by the 1870s and thereafter, modernizing landowners generally began to expel residents, or, if new ones were taken on, they were given reduced land rights and rations. There was also a tendency to re-establish the legal boundaries of estates which in a more casual era had been neglected or informally marked. In some cases an excess rural population was found to have formed squatter settlements within what was held to be hacienda boundaries. Now the estates attempted to evict those they could and restrict to a fixed area those they could not.

This was not always easy. The records of some Peruvian livestock haciendas reveal the tenacity with which residents resisted expulsion for themselves or their flocks. The newspaper advertisement offering an hacienda for sale 'together with its peons', once cited as evidence of feudal inhumanity is now often interpreted to show just how difficult it was to separate tenants from rights and security they held to be customary. It also shows the limits of landlord authority even in those regions believed to be most dominated by landowners. To push too hard ran the risk that dispossessed tenants would return to invade or infiltrate hacienda land or steal animals.

At the same time that excess tenants were expelled the ones that remained – those judged most loyal and industrious – were a privileged group in the countryside. They frequently received the benefits of an often benign paternalism which could take the form of medical care, gifts at the ceremonies of birth and marriage which punctuated rural life, and guarantees against famine and military conscription. The price paid for this security was the acceptance of discipline and heavier labour service.

The occupation of land by European settlers and their creole and *mestizo* descendants is, of course, a long process beginning in the sixteenth and seventeenth centuries. Private and clerical estates proliferated and grew in size through grants from the crown, purchase, frontier settlement and the steady usurpation of indigenous holdings. By mid-nineteenth century, although there are few reliable overall figures on distribution, it is clear that the estate had come a long way in the occupation of land.

In central Chile where indigenous holdings were not deeply rooted, some 90 per cent of all land was already within the boundaries of large estates (200 hectares and up). In the Mexican near north, in San Luis Potosí, large haciendas held some 25,000 to 30,000 hectares and the size increased with aridity and distance from Mexico City. But here the few Indian villages formed after the conquest by migrant groups from the south also had abundant lands and in other cases, at the time ignored but later to be called illegal, squatter settlements took place on the estates themselves. In the core areas of Mesoamerica and the Andean region, expansion of private estates had been slowed by the tenacious resistance of Indian communities and protection offered them by the crown. This together with scant market opportunities and consequently diminished interest on the part of *hacendados* to acquire more land, meant that by the 1860s villages still held as much as two-thirds of all land in Bolivia and perhaps half in central Mexico and the Andes.

Of the many profound changes which took place in rural Spanish America after 1870, the assault on communal villages and the absorption of their land by the large estates has drawn most attention. Liberal legislation and its interpretation in the later nineteenth century enabled villages to sell their property and private landowners to acquire it. In Mexico, the Lerdo Law and its amplification in the 1857 Constitution, the 1861 destruction of the Indian *resguardos* in Colombia and similar laws throughout the hemisphere during the nineteenth century, aimed to convert smallholding communities into yeomen farmers to create, in short, a true market for land and labour. In fact a liberal offensive was mounted on three fronts. Workers were better organized on the estate and in some cases improvements in farming techniques were made to reduce the number of workers needed; attempts were made to define boundaries, expel illegal squatters and enforce anti-vagrancy laws; and, most importantly, to take over village lands.

The appropriation of village land has been followed most closely in Mexico. In the most extreme examples such as in Morelos where cane planters managed to obliterate completely a few villages or extend the hacienda boundaries to the very edge of the village gates, a smallholder peasantry had been by 1910 almost completely converted into a proletarianized work force. But Morelos, with its hard-driving planters and a resolutely supportive state, was still an exception in the kinds of traditional zones we are concerned with here. Elsewhere the process did not carry that far. In Bolivia perhaps a third of all land was transferred to private holding in the decades after 1870, leaving roughly a third in the hands of villages. A similar pattern has been described in the Cauca valley of Colombia, Guatemala and the Peruvian highlands.

Neither the effect, nor the aim, of this process was, as is often supposed, the abolition of village lands. Where there was no institutional receptacle to hold a pool of casual labour, and towns, mines or construction projects offered real competition, it is true that estates settled additional tenants through the offer of irrigated land. This was the case in central Chile and the Mexican far north where the U.S.A. offered better paid employment.

But in the core areas where a true village peasantry had existed 'from time immemorial' and people were strongly inclined to remain close to the land, the effect of the takeover of village land was not to obliterate totally the village and transfer its people to the estates. Rather, villages were preserved but reduced to such a low resource level that employment on the estate was necessary for survival. By 1910 only 45 per cent of the core area Mexican rural population lived on haciendas; in Peru by 1940 only 20 per cent. The rest were relegated to a sharply reduced area of inferior land, often arid or on steep hillsides, where they made up an impoverished mass that could be drawn upon by the ordinary haciendas of Mexico or highland Peru for casual labour, and also, in time, by the new enclaves of fully capitalist agriculture in the tropical elevations, by railroad contractors, miners and urban employers.

Another element in peasant income was cottage industry. The tariff, a main source of state finance, had up to the middle of the nineteenth century given some protection to local spinners and weavers, to hat and sandal makers and other kinds of coarse production. Probably more important was the protection provided by high freight costs in isolated regions. The liberal goal of unregulated flows of imports was never completely achieved, but reductions of tariffs and the penetration of railroads enabled imports to compete with and then eliminate local producers. In Santander, Colombia, long a thriving centre of artisan production, women hatters, candlemakers and weavers were put out of work after the 1870s. In Chile, spinners and weavers disappeared under the competition of Lancashire cottons. By the early twentieth century, the enthusiastic reports on opportunities in trade and business written up by the commercial emissaries of the U.S.A. and Great Britain show the extent of the market and the contempt for local manufactures.

The effect in the core can be seen in the wages paid to day labourers. Rates in San Luis Potosí and Puebla stayed for long at the seventeenth-century rate of two *reales* and even dropped. Around Arequipa and in central Chile the nominal wage rose but the information now available indicates that the real wage rate generally dropped after the 1870s in the more insular zones. The growth in agricultural output at roughly the same technological level then, did not have the effect that one might anticipate in a true market model. In part this is explained by higher labour productivity brought about by the imposition of better organization, greater discipline, longer hours, more days and weeks worked during the year. But the success landowners had in keeping the wage rate low and extracting a surplus that underlay their dominance of social and political life in the later nineteenth century was due to their ability to limit the options available to the growing number of the rural lower class. This was done essentially through the control of land and water. So successful was this strategy that extra-economic coercion was rarely needed. But the armed force of the state was usually available, in the wings as it were, in case of conflict.

A central issue in the study of rural history has been the question of extra-economic coercion. In Spanish America it has long been assumed that the device of debt-peonage provided landowners with the mechanism of worker control long after the formal institutions of slavery, *encomienda* and *corvée* labour were abolished. Such an informed observer as Frank Tannenbaum, writing in the 1920s, argued that the greater part of resident workers were 'kept upon the hacienda by a system of debt'.[7] This opinion was shared by a great many writers especially in Mexico and Peru in the 1930s, so that the belief in widespread peonage became an accepted truth in textbooks and standard interpretations. This notion was reinforced by the theoretical requirements in the mode of production controversy that emerged around the work of Andre Gunder Frank in the 1960s; for in the challenge to Frank's argument that the Latin American countryside was really capitalist (and in fact had been so since the sixteenth century) his critics took pains to show that capitalist expansion into Latin America had actually increased servile exactions on the peasantry with debt peonage serving as a principal instrument in the process.

A great deal of new research that reaches into a more fundamental level of evidence such as estate records and local archives has since been carried out. This shows that debt in many cases should really be understood as credit, i.e., a benefit extended to the most reliable and stable members of the rural work force. Other students of the subject found that workers demanded pay in advance of work and that, although this may show up in the account books as debt, it did not necessarily mean that the worker could be held to his task because of it. The new work then, questioned the vocabulary previously used, opened new categories for study and suggested that the ways things actually worked on the ground were not as they seemed to a different generation of observers.

The implication of the new research was that the market and population were the key elements in a model of agrarian change that would best fit the period 1870–1930: villagers and hacienda residents alike were freer than previously supposed to seek employment and landowners competed for their services; emphasis was shifted away from class structure. But if peonage was less common and debt carried less coercion it does not follow that we are in the presence in 1870 or even in 1930 of a society where men and work were freely bid for and exchanged. Enrique Semo reminds us that the landowner exercised control over the worker because he paid the priest who performed religious services; maintained the school that provided the minimum education to the sons

<hr />

[7] Frank Tannenbaum, *The Mexican agrarian revolution* (Washington, 1930), 110.

of chosen workers; he controlled or influenced the forces of law and order; he was the only one who could provide medical attention; was the exclusive importer of local and overseas merchandise; he could invade the lands of rebellious communities and carry through long and costly legal suits; he had influence with local and at times national officials. In the end, he had the power of punishment over those who offended him by tossing them in the hacienda jail, and even of death.[8]

This analysis can undoubtedly be applied to many zones of Spanish America in 1870 and even in 1930. By this last date Mexico, of course, was undergoing an agrarian revolution which had begun to dismantle the *ancien régime* hacienda and bring the state as mediator into landowner–peasant relations. Elsewhere the mounting demographic tide was eliminating most of the need for overt 'seigneurial domination', as landowners could pick and choose from the lengthening line of unorganized rural people rattling the hacienda gate in search of work.

Resistance and revolts

The history of rural Spanish America shows a great many examples of conflict and violence. For the nineteenth century, and especially after the 1870s, it is necessary to distinguish first of all between the regions we have so far examined and the areas where newer forms of agrarian capitalism emerged. In the modern enclave sector, which is described more fully later on, workers brought together in large plantations had by World War I organized into unions and a bit later into political parties to fight for better working conditions and higher pay. In the Huara valley of central Peru, for example, anarchist ideas spread from the port of Huacho to rural workers where in 1918 several strikers were shot by troops. On the north coast workers in the cane fields and mills formed unions, many of which were integrated into Alianza Popular Revolucionaria Americana (APRA). In Colombia the first rural unions were formed in 1917 and the following year strikes were called on the United Fruit Company plantation in Santa Marta and around coffee plantations on the lower Bogotá river. All of these movements had their ideologies and organization and often aimed at real changes in the political and economic systems. Occasionally in the more remote regions, however, there were stirrings of larger issues. On 1 May 1931,

[8] Enrique Semo, 'Comentarios', in *El trabajo y los trabajadores en la historia de México* (Mexico, 1979), 395.

for example, Colombian Indians occupied the small town of Coyaima, raised the red flag and established a soviet.

In the interior and more traditional zones resistance and revolt were usually in response to the expansion of haciendas into village lands, or the efforts at reform of estates which aimed to proletarianize the internal peasantry and often took the form of localized caste war. In this sense they were 'archaic' social movements insomuch as they reflect a process of adaptation by pre-political people to penetration of agrarian capitalism, who remained by and large uncomprehending victims of modernization. Eric Wolf explained peasant revolt as a reaction to impoverishment, but also to fairly rapid changes in the quality of personal relationships which occurred as village life or the hacienda communities were shattered while alternative institutions had not yet developed. This is perhaps a roundabout way of saying something quite simple as John Womack has done in his study of one of the most important of all peasant movements in Spanish America. The people of Morelos wanted to be left alone to farm their land as they always had. When it became clear that the voracious land-grabbing sugar haciendas would not permit this – and did not need to employ very many of them either – the revolution broke out. The conditions which led to the Zapata revolution explain to a greater or lesser extent most peasant revolts in our period. They have their roots in the property relation between landowner and worker which became increasingly one of conflict after 1870.

To give this element primacy does not mean that identical results were produced everywhere since circumstance varied a great deal. A necessary feature was a community focus for resistance and action. Casting a broad look over Spanish America as a whole, one finds very few revolts, if any, in those regions such as central Chile or the Mexican north during the Porfiriato where the hacienda dominated the rural landscape, itself forming a community with its rows of workers' dwellings and its own chapel and patron saint. Mayan workers on Yucatán henequen (or sisal) plantations barely stirred in the early years of the Mexican Revolution, and although the rancheros of Pisaflores were avid supporters of the rebel cause those of Los Altos of Jalisco were not.

Apart from the classic case of the Morelos revolt in 1910–19, similar revolts took place throughout the Andean region where haciendas and communities co-existed. Perhaps the most important in terms of size and violence took place in the Bolivian Altiplano in 1899 when Pablo Zárate, a community leader, later known as 'El temible Willka' led a movement which aimed to restore to the Indians the land usurped by *hacendados*. In Cerro de Pasco, Huanta, Tocroyoc and Molloccahua, in highland Peru, to list a few examples where studies exist, we have evidence of conflict generated essentially by economic development. All of these were put down by force – local police or the national army together with local landowners – and in the case of Tocroyoc, the body of the leader was left exposed for several months on the roof of a local church.

The role of the liberal state

The history of agrarian society in eastern and western Europe shows that in the late medieval and early modern period the common interests of landlords and the state in the exploitation of the peasantry generated different attitudes toward it. The state competed with landowners over peasant surplus and was often concerned to preserve the peasant class as an economic and military base. This could to some extent be applied to the Spanish American colonial period when the crown and church exercised a certain paternal custody over the indigenous population. Royal courts occasionally ruled against the colonial elite; alliances were occasionally struck between crown and peasant. And, of course, the urban middle class in modern European democracies was forced early in the nineteenth century to seek political support among farmers and peasants.

By the 1870s in Spanish America, the liberal state had settled into place following the political uncertainties of the independence era. With exceedingly few exceptions, from then until the Revolution in Mexico (1910) and the emergence of mass political parties in the 1920s and 1930s (and later in some countries), political power was essentially identical with class power, that is, it was interrelated and interwoven with the landowning class. The fact that intra-class conflict occasionally arose between older hidebound *hacendados* and modern commercial owners or between a mining or nascent industrial sector and agrarian interests, such as in Chile and Colombia in the 1890s, does not detract from their position against the rural lower class. The role of the liberal state in conditioning the development of agrarian capitalism was at times – such as in the transfer of church and village lands to the private sector – decisive; and at others, such as the enforcement of anti-vagrancy laws or extension of courts and order to remote areas, ineffective due to the sheer incapacity of the civil administration. Because of this, although the state was undoubtedly the arm of the dominant class, it was generally a weak arm and social relations in the countryside depended to a good degree on accommodation and compromise. Thus, the effective control of the landowners over rural workers especially in the remote regions was limited. This statement would not be true in the exceptional cases of highland Guatemala or Yucatán or the Amazon where the state judged the export of coffee, henequen and rubber of such great importance that full force was applied. But when the mayordomo of a Chilean hacienda in 1895 points out that he must make the workers understand 'with good and prudent instructions' and put up with all manner of 'impertinences', one hears the more common voice of daily reality.[9]

The union of landowners and the state can be seen in rural taxes. Where state and landowners often competed for peasant revenues in Europe, in Spanish America landowners were often permitted to collect peasant tax for the state. This practice, commonplace in the colonial era, permitted landowners to extract labour services from rural workers whose taxes they paid, and the early nineteenth-century republican governments had no hesitation in handing over this instrument of labour exaction to *hacendados*. By the time the *tributo* was abolished, taxes on the peasantry were not worth fighting over. In Peru the head tax, imposed on Indian households since the sixteenth century and carried into the early republic was abolished in 1854, in Ecuador in 1857. In Chile the state contemplated a tax on smallholders but they dropped the plan when the projected cost of collection would clearly exceed the revenue generated by impoverished minifundia. Only properties of a fairly good size were liable, the rest of the rural lower class paid a stamp tax and a series of small municipal taxes. The tithe rarely applied to peasant output and in any case was made voluntary by most republican governments in the 1830s and 1840s.

As Spanish America became more fully integrated into the world market after 1870, more convenient sources of revenue than peasant taxes appeared (the principal one was customs revenue) and the abundance of these undoubtedly reduced interest in the peasantry as a source of state income and enabled the landowner-dominated governments to eliminate or reduce their own burdens.

If little state revenue was generated in the rural areas, the services provided by the state were correspondingly scant. By the 1870s, only a

---

[9] Rafael Herrera, 'Memoria sobre la hacienda "Las Condes" en 1895', introduction by Gonzalo Izquierdo, *Boletín de la Academia Chilena de la Historia*, 79 (1968), 202–3.

handful of rural gendarmerie were stationed in most rural zones, their rustic *caseta* often on hacienda property itself. Porfirian Mexico was precocious in its concern for rural police – the *rurales* were reorganized and strengthened in the 1880s. In Peru no significant improvement came until 1920 with Leguía's Guardia Civil and in Chile with the development of the Carabineros at about the same time. And the armies, of course, after the war of the Pacific (1879–83), occupied themselves essentially with internal enemies. The army was used not just to put down rural revolt; but recruitment served as a net to gather up malcontents and troublemakers. Nothing was more onerous nor feared by the young peasantry of Morelos than army recruitment.

The organization of justice was likewise intimately related with the propertied class. Chile, spared much of the post-independence turmoil, had by the 1840s already installed a fairly effective fiscal administration and provincial judgeships. But in the more remote areas of rural Mexico there was no judge or public jail until well into the second half of the nineteenth century, while at the same time on the Peruvian north coast the landowning Aspíllaga family exercised a *de facto* seigneurial jurisdiction in the absence of a civil judge. Thus, when an hacienda overseer was chopped to death with a machete, the estate tried and executed the presumed culprit, a Chinese worker. Not until the 1890s did the state effectively bring Cayaltí and other north coast plantations under its judicial umbrella.

Even in the 1920s when landowner hegemony in the rural zones was breaking down, the partnership of state and landowners can be seen in the implementation of forced road construction in Guatemala and Peru. *Conscripción Vial*, a road building act promulgated in Peru in 1920, required adult males between the ages of eighteen and sixty to work six to twelve days each year without pay to build and maintain roads. In the rural zones, local landowners often controlled the provincial Board and used state-mandated labour to build roads linking their estates with market towns.

Undoubtedly the most important assistance the state offered the landowning class was the transfer of ecclesiastical property into private hands. In addition to vast stretches of vacant lands acquired by individuals through survey contracts or reclamation, the sale of millions of acres of church land led to enormous growth and consolidation of the larger estates which came by the end of the century to exercise a far greater rural hegemony than during the feudal colonial centuries.

Actually, the take-over of church property goes back to the 1760s, when the foremost ecclesiastical landowners, the Jesuits, were expelled and their property sold at public auction. Throughout the nineteenth century but especially after the liberal legislation of the mid-century, millions of acres of church land passed into private hands. This made little difference in terms of production or technology because much of the land had previously been rented from the Church and operated by private landowners before the forced sales, but the sudden availability of large amounts of land brought prices down and enabled merchants and urban professionals to enter the ranks of landowners, thereby broadening the social base of landownership, keeping alive the social values of landownership and in general enormously strengthening the private landowner sector.

Apart from transferring church land into the private sector, the liberal state also undertook to relieve landowners of the ancient burdens of clerical debt. Over the previous centuries, hardly a single landowner, especially in the heavily clerical core areas of Mexico and Peru, failed to institute a chantry or pious fund which obligated the estate to pay annuities, which, if not always honoured especially in the early nineteenth century, normally meant that a large share of estate income was siphoned off through this vast network of encumbrances and liens. In the 1850s and 1860s nearly all of the Spanish American republics carried out policies which enabled landowners in the subsequent decades to get out from under the weight of clerical obligations. In Colombia in 1851, a law made it possible for owners to redeem the total capital value of a clerical lien by paying one-half its amount to the state in devalued bonds. The government then agreed to pay the obligations to the Church. By 1863 new legislation made it easier still for the *hacendados*. Chantries and liens could be redeemed by paying as little as one-tenth of their value in bonds of the public debt. In Peru laws similar to those in Colombia were passed in 1850 and 1864 and in Chile in 1865. Between 1865 and 1900 in this last country, the treasury received some $3.5 million in redemptions which meant that landowners were freed of over $17 million at least in encumbrances. In Mexico, although the Reform laws of 1859 did not deal explicitly with chantries and pious works, later legislation permitted landowners to pay off their debts, in effect, to clear their mortgages, by paying only a fraction of their value, often as little as 15 per cent. The Church, and ultimately the popular classes that depended on clerical social services, were the victims of liberal policy while the landowning class enjoyed a massive capital gain and reduced overhead costs.

THE MODERN ENCLAVE SECTOR

Up to now we have been concerned with what may be called for convenience the traditional or insular hacienda-village community society of Mesoamerica and the Andean highlands, and the changes brought about by liberal policies during a period of growth in both internal markets and population. On the outskirts of this older society, generally in the lower and medium elevations, very different agricultural enterprises now appeared, brought into existence by the enormous demand in the North Atlantic countries for tropical foods and fibres. Coffee plantations spread rapidly and although Brazil supplied 70 per cent of the world market by 1900, the crop also transformed the zones of medium elevation in a vast arc from Venezuela through Colombia, Central America and Mexico. World sugar production at the same time grew enormously, although the price, beaten down by the international competition of beet sugar, dropped from 25 shillings a hundred-weight in 1880 to less than half that by 1900. The result, in the sugar cane zones of tropical America, was huge corporate investment, often by foreigners, in more efficient, large-scale *centrales* that appeared in the Caribbean and Brazil, the Peruvian north coast, and in smaller pockets of production in Colombia, Salta and Tucumán, Argentina, Morelos and the Veracruz coast.

Added to these two basic exports were bananas on the littoral of Central America and Ecuador; rubber which made up 25 per cent of Brazil's exports by 1910; and henequen produced by thousands of peons in Yucatán to permit labour savings in the grain harvests of the United States and Europe. This latter product increased from around 11,000 tons in 1877 to 129,000 by 1910 and accounted for 15 per cent of Mexican exports; cotton and wool were shipped from Peru; cacao from Venezuela and Central America, and grain from central Chile and the newly conquered lands of Araucanía.

The new agrarian industries moved at a different rhythm. Workers were required on schedule and expected to work steadily, not in short bursts followed by 'drunken sprees', nor could they be permitted to return to village and family to tend their own land. The new industries, their own schedules set by a world market, wanted labour when they wanted it, not at the convenience of the workers. This new market, impelled by European demand and a revolution in transport which enabled these distant corners to compete on a global scale, fell with a rush upon a rural population which, if numerous and certainly accustomed to arduous work, was not prepared for the discipline now expected. For a rural people accustomed to working when climate permitted and nature demanded, the stopwatch, clocks and bells, were now installed. In 1916 a worker on the Cerro de Pasco railways was fined and mistreated by his foreman for having been one minute late.

As in most pre-capitalist agriculture, rural people, in E. P. Thompson's phrase, were essentially 'task oriented'.[10] This means that men and women worked long and hard hours when the harvest was on, during the annual slaughter or shearing, but that during much of the year the usual routine of fence repairs, ditch cleaning, was undemanding. Hacienda accounts show that few men worked more than three to four days a week; many less than fifteen days of the month. The rest of the time work dragged on at a very low level and had, in Luis González's view, as much moral as economic value. To the smallholder of San José de Gracia, joy and work were not in conflict, indeed they were mutually dependent. For that reason it was incomprehensible to the local rancheros that anyone would want to be an *absentee* landowner. When it came to sloth (*ociosidad*) only men could permit themselves this vice: women worked all day long in household chores.

There are a number of places where new research makes it possible to follow the impact of this new kind of labour demand in some detail. Sugar cane had been raised on the Peruvian north coast since the sixteenth century and until 1850 the work force there was black slaves. In the initial stage after abolition, planters hired some free blacks, recruited from among the independent smallholders on the coast, attempted to attract workers from the largely *mestizo* population in the Cajamarca sierra, but ended by importing some 88,000 male (and 170 female) Chinese in the years before 1874. The need to seek workers 7,000 miles across the Pacific and pay for their recruitment and passage is eloquent proof of the difficulty in acquiring local workers. Although many planters believed that Peruvians, especially the *serranos*, were better workers when they worked, they were also considered unreliable and inconstant. In order to get labour when they wanted it, the plantations employed coolie workers, bound as they were by indentured contracts.

The War of the Pacific (1879–84) wrecked the north coast sugar economy, but its recovery was brought about by investment from Germans and Americans as well as local capitalists. To be able to

[10] E. P. Thompson, 'Time, work-discipline, and industrial capitalism', in *Essays in Social History*, ed. M. W. Flinn and T. C. Smout (London, 1974), 42.

compete in the global market, the new planters in Peru went in for economies of scale and they were particularly intent upon keeping labour costs low. Out of a coastal population of freed blacks, Chinese who stayed on after their indentured contracts ended and the local smallholder population, the planters attempted to recruit a work force. But this was unsatisfactory on several counts. The local population often had an alternative income in the form of land, fishing, or artisan manufacture; the Chinese, once compulsion had ended, tended to move from plantation work into petty commerce and trade.

Under these circumstances, efforts were made to recruit seasonal workers from the *mestizo* highlands around Cajamarca and La Libertad. This was a zone of large estates – the Pelayo-Puga families owned some 300,000 hectares, for example – and smallholder communities where the large majority of people lived. The 1876 census found the population to be on the whole made up of white and *mestizo* peasants. Mere announcements in newspapers or in posters tacked to village walls were not sufficient, and, as labour demand increased, coastal plantations turned to a system of much earlier origins, *enganche*, or labour contracting, in order to obtain schedules of workers. The typical labour contractor was a man with a foot in the social world of both coast and sierra. Socially and culturally akin to the planter class, he was often a merchant or landowner in the sierra, a person with local contacts and influence. To these men the plantation advanced sums of cash stipulating their labour requirements. The contractor or his employees then endeavoured to make young sierra males sign labour contracts by advancing them a certain portion of an agreed-upon salary in the form of salary or goods. Such immediate and visible payment was necessary; few sierra peons would be brought into the labour market with the distant and abstract promise of wages once work was completed. Unlike modern workers, they required payment in advance. The contractor then provided transportation to the coast and was responsible to the plantation that labour be performed for pre-paid salary. Peons worked in the common tasks of weeding or cane cutting until the salary advance had been paid off. For his role in recruiting, transporting and supervising this heterogeneous and undisciplined labour force, the contractor got about 20 per cent of the total wage bill.

It is easy to imagine the abuses that such a system permitted. Peons inexperienced in the ways of sharp contractors were sometimes encouraged through drink or signed while actually drunk; and once on the coast, they could easily accrue more debts for food or goods dispensed at the plantation store thus prolonging the time needed to pay off the original advance. The injustice and abuse of *enganche* have been abundantly recorded, and many observers have insisted that this was a cruel and brutal, often forced system of labour. It is also true that peons voluntarily signed on year after year, while others stayed on the coast and requested that further wage advances be paid to their sierra families. From a few hundreds the seasonal flow of contracted workers rose to several thousands. The sugar industry on the north coast alone employed some 20,000 men in 1912 (only 3 per cent of the total work force in 1912 was female) and 30,000 a decade later.

Once broken to the task of capitalist agriculture and given a taste of its rewards, sierra peons in increasing numbers stayed on the coast. Some found permanent work in the mills, others crowded into the new towns and squatter settlements; by the 1940s, we are talking not about a migratory pre-capitalist work force, but a true rural proletariat, formed into unions and political parties, its links to the land cut, its acceptance of rural industrial discipline more or less complete.

The same kind of linkage between modern plantation and peasant zones took place in a number of other regions, but at times with strikingly different results. In the sugar zone of Salta and Tucumán in northern Argentina labour contractors recruited workers in Catamarca and the Jujuy highlands. There is some evidence that planters bought out *hacendados* as a means of acquiring workers in the mills. German merchants, who acquired some 60 per cent of all Guatemalan coffee land around the turn of the century had on their side an especially enthusiastic rural gendarmerie which came down hard against 'vagrancy', while Costa Ricans seem to have made an easier transition to United Fruit Company's plantation system. In another case, Henri Favre shows how a traditional Indian peasantry around Huancavelica in 1880 chose, without the need for wage advances or labour contractors, to work for wages in coastal cotton plantations and then return with their earnings to preserve an ancient way of life rather than become proletarianized.

Different in kind from traditional hacienda labour, which only became more productive through an intensification of existing practice, the new agrarian enterprises keyed to the export market, required a very different kind of discipline and constancy in their work forces. In neither case was extra-economic coercion very important. For the interior regions, the reduction of village lands together with population increase permitted *hacendados* to extract a greater surplus from workers; in the modern sector plantation owners and their agents adjusted the form of economic incentive to appeal to a pre-capitalist peasantry and formed in the course of one generation a wage-earning rural proletariat. Of course, the formation of a rural proletariat also took place within a context of population increase, and the appearance and attractiveness in the countryside of an entire range of clothing and merchandise that only money could buy and the increasing intolerance of sloth and idleness, now called vagrancy, on the part of the liberal state. To comprehend fully why one man stayed on his tiny plot in the shadow of the hacienda and another chose to cut sugar cane on a coastal plantation would require a study of the options open, and, above all, of how people perceived their options. Until those mentalities are uncovered we can only infer motive from observed action. The historical actors themselves do not speak except with their feet.

THE PERIPHERY

In those regions peripheral to the main centres of Spanish America such as the Amazon headwaters, Chilean Araucanía, Yucatán or the Far Northwest of Mexico, there were whole peoples who had not yet, in 1870, been effectively brought into the national economy or even 'pacified'; people who had been bypassed by European occupation, who had resisted, or whose land or resources were not considered valuable enough to warrant the effort needed to expel them. In these areas, the onset of liberal capitalism spelt their doom.

In the northern Mexican state of Sonora, the Yaqui nation which had held out against Spanish occupation, had been sheltered by Jesuit missions and resisted national governments in the first two-thirds of the nineteenth century were now brought under heavy pressure by the Porfirio Díaz regime, which saw the Yaqui and Apache as its main obstacles to progress. The aim of the Díaz regime, in Porfirio's own words, was to put every Yaqui behind a plough, or, as a leading *científico* put it, to convert the Indian into a social asset, into a colonist on the newly irrigated land. North Americans and Mexicans invested in large irrigation works – one company, the joint Mexican-North American Sonora and Sinaloa Irrigation Company, was granted 547,000 acres in the Yaqui Valley. The owners hoped that the 30,000 or so Yaquis would be content, after being shown the benefits of new tools, stock, clothing and irrigation, to settle as colonists on their ancestral land. Mining and the arrival of the railroad in the 1880s intensified the pressure, and the Yaqui and Maya were driven into open resistance in the years 1875–86. Although that movement was crushed by federal troops, the Yaqui continued a guerrilla resistance for the next 25 to 30 years. At the turn of the century, the aims of the Sonoran government to pacify the Yaqui and the labour needs of Yucatán *hacendados* coincided (indeed, there was at least one Porfirian general responsible for suppressing the Yaqui who also owned large henequen plantations in Yucatán). The solution to both was massive deportation of Yaqui males to the harshly driven henequen plantations of Yucatán. Although opposed to some extent by local landowners or developers who held that Yaqui deportation deprived themselves of workers, deportation continued down to the eve of the 1910 Revolution, involving at least 3,000 and perhaps as many as 15,000 out of a total Yaqui population of 30,000. In the Mexican south-east, henequen and sugar cultivation led to a sharp demand for labour. Some new machinery was employed in the elaboration of raw materials, but little for planting or harvesting because it was still possible, even in a labour scarce area, to find men whose aggregate costs were cheaper than machinery. Pressure was brought to bear on resident workers by reducing their perquisites and stepping up labour requirements, and the isolated and defenceless Maya from Yucatán and Quintana Roo were pressed into service; but the southern planter still had to turn to outside sources. Chinese and Korean indentured workers were introduced, and even one attempt was made to bring in Italian workers; but the Asians could not withstand the conditions and Europeans were too expensive. Given this, the landowners turned to deported Yaquis, convict labour, political dissenters, and vagrants and the unemployed, who were considered criminal only by the standards of the Porfiriato.

In southern Chile, the Araucanians who had resisted the Incas, Spaniards and Chileans for over four hundred years could not withstand the railroad and repeating rifles brought by those who saw in the fertile lands of Cautín the opportunity for profits in the international grain trade. In a few years, beginning in the 1880s, the Araucanians were confined to reservations or a restricted service tenantry on the newly formed *fundos* in this region. In the Putumayo district of the Amazon headwaters, driven on by the double stimuli of 'terror and alcohol', latex gatherers were recruited from the tropical tribes or imported from the Caribbean and Barbados. Rubber workers drawn from the drought-ridden Brazilian north-east produced more than 25 per cent of that country's exports by 1910.

CONCLUSION

During the sixty years following 1870, the rural people of Spanish America probably underwent a greater change than at any previous time in their history except for the conquest of America itself. The engine of change after 1870 was not the sudden intrusion of *conquistador* and pestilence but rather the inexorable growth of the market and population. These two forces, economic and demographic, formed the general context within which agrarian society was formed. But it was the social relations of rural workers between themselves and with the propertied class, and, behind this, the way people perceived their life, which help explain the variety of response to the onrush of liberal capitalism.

None of this, of course, can be seen in isolation. While it is apparent that the main impulse to economic activity came from abroad, it should also be made clear that change in rural Spanish America was mediated through, and ultimately controlled from, the cities. From the sixteenth century, Spanish American cities of European foundation – Guadalajara, Puebla, San José, Medellín, Arequipa, Santiago, etc. – were artificial creations, points for the distribution and collection of goods and produce, nuclei of residence of the rural elite, centres of European culture and loci of political power. During the last third of the nineteenth century, the pattern of railroad construction, the creation and professionalization of centralized armies, the further consolidation of central political administration, and the rise of banks and credit agencies, assured urban hegemony over the countryside.

Such a view does not conflict with the earlier explanation of the landowner's role in extracting rural surplus. Landowners in this period lived in the city and formed part of the urban elite. Although at times themselves dependent upon merchants and bankers, more often their interests were interwoven and they themselves were interrelated with the local and foreign commercial and financial elite. Throughout most of our period, landowners had a dominant influence in politics and, even after the early appearance of industry and an urban service sector, they were able to strike political alliances with the proletariat and urban middle classes to ensure that an unorganized and powerless countryside would shoulder the main burden of capitalist development.

The instruments of control were in the end political and military. Thus, in Chile, rural workers were not permitted to organize legally until 1931, and then, when a measure of peasant militancy arose in the 1930s, urban sectors – industrialists and the proletariat together – acquiesced in the landowners' demand for peasant submission in return for the control of agricultural prices in the city. In Bolivia after 1880, an urban elite used the army to crush the occasional violent outbreak of localized caste war and to exclude completely the indigenous peasant from politics. In Colombia in the 1920s, a number of labour strikes among coffee and banana workers were put down by army troops. Finally, even in Mexico, often held as the one country in Latin America to undergo a modern peasant revolution, it has become increasingly clear that, as early as 1929 when the Cristero insurrection was crushed by the federal army, here too the peasantry has been submerged by an urban-based, authoritarian state.

6

PLANTATION ECONOMIES AND SOCIETIES IN THE SPANISH CARIBBEAN, 1860–1930[1]

AN OVERVIEW

During the eighteenth and the first half of the nineteenth centuries the patterns of sugar production and the sugar trade in the Caribbean changed very little, and what changes there were were either geographical (shifts in production from one island to another) or determined by limited technological innovation. From the 1860s to the 1890s the centuries-old structure of the sugar industry was shattered, to be replaced by completely new forms of production and commerce and by a new form of the end-product itself, a sugar produced to different standards and even shipped in different packaging. The successive developments that occurred in the sugar world during the thirty years from around 1860 affected sugar producers, merchants and consumers; they modified human and labour relations and they altered age-old habits of consumption. This great transformation was at once the cause and the

---

[1] A plantation is an organized unit of production, producing one single raw material of agricultural origin intended for export (or, at least, for shipping out of the region) and thus controlled by a foreign (or outside) market, even though the plantation is itself owned by a person or group native to the region; the plantation must be established in a country or a region possessing a dependent colonial or neo-colonial economic structure; its efficiency must be based on economy of scale, exploiting large tracts of fertile land (and thus relying more on natural conditions than on technical or technological factors); and, finally, it must principally use unskilled mass manual labour in the shape of slaves, peons, indentured servants or contract labourers, or a combination of the various forms of exploited agrarian proletariat. Moreover, for a unit of production to be considered a plantation (as distinct from, say, a farm, a ranch or a hacienda), it must possess each and every one of these characteristics. From the decline of coffee as an important factor in the Cuban economy in the 1840s the only plantations in Cuba were sugar plantations. In Puerto Rico, with the abolition of slavery in the 1870s, the coffee and sugar plantations became haciendas; the plantation system was restored with the U.S. occupation of the island, but then only for sugar. In the Dominican Republic sugar plantations alone existed during this period. The following discussion, therefore, is limited almost exclusively to sugar: for the countries and dates under study (Cuba, Puerto Rico and the Dominican Republic, c. 1860 to c. 1930), 'plantations' and 'sugar plantations' are virtually synonymous.

consequence of other economic, social and political factors, and was at the same time connected by innumerable links to other world events such as the crisis of Spanish colonialism, the emergence of the United States as a world power, the rapid developments in science and technology, the universal increase in population and new systems of communications.

A series of radical innovations occurred at every stage of the sugar-making process, causing the old manual machines (run by unskilled workers) to be abandoned and replaced by relatively sophisticated machinery which required skilled operators and efficient technical supervision. The installation of this new machinery required an extremely large economic investment and the scrapping of existing production lines and even of most of the buildings constructed under the previous system. Consequently, the new enterprise cannot be considered an old mill that had been modernized (as was the case with the introduction of the first steam engines into the sugar mills); rather, what we have here is the elimination of the old sugar mill, which was demolished, and in its place – or elsewhere – the erection of new buildings, housing new machinery run by new types of workers. The only things which remained of the old sugar mill complex were, in general, certain buildings for social use, the communications infrastructure and the cane fields, which in any case supplied only a small part of the new production centre's needs: for, obviously, to be profitable the new industrial plant had to process much greater quantities of cane than the old sugar mill. The new industrial plantation (the *central*, or centralized factory, as it came to be known from the end of the nineteenth century on) replaced one or more of the old sugar mills (*ingenios*) and sought additional fertile low priced land.

Here we have both a quantitative and a qualitative change. From the point of view of quantity, the new *central* differed from the old *ingenio* both in grinding capacity and in a higher rate of extraction of sugar from the cane it ground. For example, the so-called 'modern' mechanized sugarmills of 1860 ground, on an average, the cane from 30 to 50 *caballerías*[2] (roughly 425–500 hectares, or about 1,050–1,250 acres) of land; the *central* of 1890 could handle the production of 100–120 *caballerías*, and

---

[2] The following equivalents are used in this chapter:

1 Caballería (Cuba)	= 13.42 hectares =	33.162 acres
1 Caballería (Puerto Rico)	= 78.58 hectares =	194.178 acres
1 Caballería (Dominican Republic)	= 75.45 hectares =	186.444 acres
1 short ton = 2000 lb avoirdupois	= 0.907 metric ton	
1 long ton = 2240 lb avoirdupois	= 1.016 metric ton	

In this chapter a ton means a metric ton of 1,000 kilograms.

centrales which could grind the cane from up to 150 or 200 *caballerías* were not uncommon. But production increased at an even greater rate than milling capacity, because the new factories could extract almost twice the amount of sugar from the same amount of cane as did the old mills.

This increase in production capacity brought about a speeding-up in the process of consolidation. In Cuba, for example, in 1860 there were 1,318 sugar mills producing some 515,000 metric tons of sugar; by 1895 the number of mills had decreased to 250 while production was up to almost one million tons. In Puerto Rico, where a similar process began somewhat later, there were 550 mills in 1870 producing about 100,000 tons of sugar, the highest figure achieved here in the nineteenth century; by 1910, fifteen *centrales* were producing 233,000 tons. In turn this brought about the emergence of the sugar latifundia in Cuba, Puerto Rico and the Dominican Republic (a century and a half later than the corresponding process in British West Indian islands like Barbados). Socially, the consolidation process undermined the old class of slave-owning planters (except in the Dominican Republic where such a class did not exist), who were replaced by a new type of industrial entrepreneur. In Cuba, by 1895 only 17 per cent of the owners of *centrales* came from the old plantation-owning families. The 'industrial revolution' in the sugar industry also made it necessary to transform labour relations. There occurred the final crisis of the slave system upon which the old *ingenio* had been based, and slavery was abolished in Puerto Rico in 1873 and in Cuba in 1880–6.

This Caribbean industrial revolution was not, however, accompanied by a complementary agrarian revolution. On the contrary, the agricultural side of the sugar industry (planting, cultivation and harvesting) retained its traditional backwardness, which had originated in slave-owning cultural patterns, even under a new legal regime. Thus, there arose a technological gap between the industrial sector and its agricultural base. In contrast to the modernity of the *central*, the agricultural sector retained its traditional obsolete ways: within a few years the law of diminishing returns (which applies where, as in this case, no efforts were made to improve crop yields by modern methods of cultivation) made its appearance, marked by the trend towards smaller cane yields.

The first response to this situation, aggravated by other social and legal factors, was the creation of an administrative separation between the manufacture of sugar (the industrial sector) and the supply of raw material, cane (the agricultural sector). The relationship between these two sectors was to be a permanent source of conflict from the end of the nineteenth century. The old creole sugar oligarchy of Cuba and Puerto Rico, for the most part forced out of the manufacturing side of the industry, in many cases stayed on as *colonos*, owners of cane plantations, and were in constant conflict with the new industrial barons, the *hacendados*, owners of the *centrales*.

As a result of the industrialization process, the productivity of the industrial worker in the *central* rose steeply; but the productivity of the agricultural worker, especially that of the cane-cutter, remained the same, since the methods of cultivation and harvesting had not evolved. Moreover in order to take advantage of the enormous capacities of the new industrial installations, the *zafras*, or sugar crops, became bigger and bigger, but carried out in shorter periods, generally starting in January and ending in April. This, in turn, created two problems of far-reaching magnitude: one having to do with labour, the other with the amortization and optimal utilization of the expensive new industrial equipment.

With respect to labour, the amount of cane required by the modern industry made it necessary to employ hundreds of thousands of agricultural workers (cane-cutters) simultaneously for a period of three to four months out of the year. Thus, there arose, in all its tragic dimensions, the problem of seasonal employment during four months of the year, which for the majority of the labourers meant seasonal unemployment for eight months of the year. This situation had not made itself felt previously, because with unskilled slave labour (which in any case had to be supported all year round), with rudimentary manufacturing equipment, small daily millings and long harvest seasons, there was almost always work for all hands. But the modern plantation required, for its optimal running, the existence of an army of unemployed workers, ideally located off the *central* but subjected to economic pressure which forced them to sell their services cheaply, and with a minimum of social benefits, as cane-cutters. These workers made up a migratory mass, and their migration could be either internal (from one part of the country to another), or external (from one country to another). A mixture of both kinds of migration became the normal pattern.

The other problem created by the installation of modern industrial equipment was the need to find additional sources of income, not necessarily connected with the sugar industry, which would help to amortize the enormous economic investment. Certain dual-purpose equipment (railways, power plants, foundries, etc.), as well as some specific services, became 'independent' enterprises, with an autonomous economic existence. Thus, we find that in typical *centrales*, the cane-hauling railway also offered passenger services, the power plant provided electricity for the *central*'s facilities as well as for nearby settlements which would pay for it, and the foundry made items ranging from park benches to manhole covers for the municipality – and all at high prices, because the *central* enjoyed a monopoly of these services in its region, besides having decisive economic and political influence. The typical Cuban *central* of the 1890s controlled the general store, the hotel, houses and barracks, either permanent or temporary, the barber's shop, the butcher's, the drugstore, and sometimes even the gaming house and the brothel. And partly for its own financial benefit and partly in order to tighten its overall grasp on all the surrounding region, the *centrales* even issued their own private coinage, in the form of tokens. Thus Cuba, Puerto Rico and Santo Domingo reproduced, under conditions of colonialism and underdevelopment, one of the most typical aspects of the English Industrial Revolution.[3]

There were two ways in which the sugar token was employed. One was for the *central* to pay its workers in tokens. These tokens were 'legal tender' in all the shops and facilities around the mill, and could be redeemed there, though at a discount, which was the equivalent of a wage reduction. The other system was for the *central* to pay monthly wages in official currency; but since workers had to pay for their daily needs from their first day on the job, the store owner would advance them small loans in tokens, which could be spent only in his store or in the establishments of other members of the group. The store owner would notify the management of the *central* of the advances made to each worker, and the totals would be automatically docked from his wages at the end of the month. In cases of illness or when the worker was laid off, the mill would immediately notify the shopowners to withhold credit. There exist payrolls for Cuban and Puerto Rican mills showing how at the end of the month many workers received only 10 per cent of their wages in cash, the balance having been 'advanced'.[4]

[3] Manuel Moreno Fraginals, *El token azucarero Cubano* (Havana, 1975), 13–16.
[4] In the 1880s, the Santa Lucía sugar mill in Gibara, Cuba, operated as subsidiaries 5 general stores, 7 grocery stores, 1 shoe shop, 3 barber shops, 1 distillery, 1 drugstore, 9 bars, 1 school, 1 confectioner's, 2 canteens, 3 blacksmiths', 3 bakeries, 3 clothing stores, 2 tailor shops and 1 saddlery. All of these establishments accepted payments in the nickel tokens issued by the *central*. What made this particular case somewhat unusual was that the official Cuban paper currency, issued by the Bank of Spain, was not accepted by these places: it had to be exchanged for Santa Lucía company tokens – at more than 10% off face value. See *Boletín Comercial* (Havana), 14 July 1886, 2.

There was during this period one further extremely important change that has been little noted: the end-product, the sugar produced by the new-style industry, was as different from the previous product as the *central* was different from the *ingenio*. Indeed, it is enough to glance at any Market Report of the 1860s to see that it does not give the prices for sugar (in the singular) but for sugars (in the plural). Until the 1860s the Havana market played a key role in fixing world sugar prices, and the Colleges of Brokers of Havana and Puerto Rico quoted prices for 14 different types of sugar daily. The Dutch Standard ('Tipo Holandés' in Spanish-speaking countries) which was accepted world-wide as the most suitable set of standards for trading in sugar, listed 21 different grades, based on colour, where grade 1 was practically *massecuite* and grade 21 was powdered white sugar. This plethora of grades of sugar was the logical consequence of sugar being manufactured with primitive equipment, set up in different ways in hundreds of small factories throughout the Caribbean: mills in which the quality of sugar depended on natural factors (the degree of ripeness of the cane) or on the purity of the cane juice obtained by manual operations, or on the intensity of the fire which heated the boilers (a fire fed by slaves who might throw on more wood or less wood), and, in the final event, on the know-how of a *maestro* (generally illiterate) who was guided only by his senses (smell, taste, touch, hearing), by his long experience and by orally transmitted tradition.

On the other hand, the industrial processes of the sugar-mills of the nineties were standard, supervised by technically trained professionals, who were aided by internationally adopted analytical methods, carried out in modern laboratory equipment. Thanks to these controls, by the end of the century all the Caribbean mills were producing centrifugal sugar Pol 95°. In the early years of the twentieth century a sugar purity of Pol 96° became the standard. The different types of sugar produced in the pre-industrialized stage required at least three types of packing: the box, the hogshead and the bag. This latter was little used in the 1860s (only 4 per cent of total New York market sales). By 1890 the situation had changed completely; the United States imported more than 95 per cent of its sugar in bags; by the beginning of this century the box and the *bocoy*, the hogshead, were virtually museum pieces.

One type of sugar, one type of packaging: these factors influenced the transformation of the sugar trade. The Pol 96° sugar of the new industrial period, as we have seen, was a standardized product, whose origin (cane or beet) or the region it came from (Cuba, Puerto Rico, Java, Australia, Mauritius, Brazil) were impossible to determine. It was also a long-lasting product; packed in bags it could be stacked and stored cheaply. In contrast, the muscovados of the sixties differed widely in quality, spoiled easily and the hogsheads in which they were shipped could only be stacked three high without those on the bottom bursting. There were other essential differences: the hogshead was expensive, the bag was cheap; the hogshead was heavy (10 to 14 per cent of the weight of the sugar it contained), the bag light (less than 1 per cent); the hogshead was hard to handle and raised shipping costs enormously, the bag was easy to handle.

All these factors brought about a new commercial practice: the storing of large surpluses from successive sugar crops. As the new-type centrifugal sugar came more and more to be packed in bags it became feasible to store it indefinitely. This was the beginning of a new dimension of the problem of 'initial' stocks (those visibly on hand in warehouses at the beginning of the sugar year) as a factor affecting sugar prices. It is important to note that sugar traders had always taken initial stocks into account in fixing their prices, so it was not in itself a new phenomenon: what changed was its magnitude. Before 1860, stocks on hand rarely were as much as 10 per cent of the estimated annual consumption; by the 1890s it was common for them to run over 30 per cent of estimated consumption, and the trend was constantly upwards.[5] The bigger the stocks sugar importers had in their warehouses, the more pressure they could bring to bear on the producers to lower their prices.

All these new conditions (uniform product, packing in bags, world-wide standards, large on-hand stocks) inevitably led to what can be called the Revolution of the Sugar Trade. This commercial revolution was in part the result of the factors detailed above, but it was also caused by other features of the world's economy in the last third of the nineteenth century. There were several significant dates in the 1860s and 1870s. For example, historians point to 1871 as the year in which the tonnage carried by sailing ships, subject to the whims of the winds, was first surpassed by that shipped in steamers – fast, punctual and with low freight rates. A

---

[5] In general, sugar statistics for the nineteenth century present a confused picture. The first regular series of 'Initial & Final Stocks' reports for European markets began to be published in Caesar Czarnikow's famous *Weekly Price Current* in 1872, although sporadic reports had previously seen print. Almost at the same time other listings began to appear in F. O. Licht's *Monthly Report on Sugar* and in Willett and Hamlen's *New York Statistical Sugar Trade Journal*. The figures appearing in these publications sometimes differed by up to 80%.

steamer could carry five times the cargo of a sailing ship of the same displacement. In addition, the opening of the Suez Canal had eliminated sailing ships from the regular Europe–Far East runs. In general, it may be reckoned that freight rates between America and Europe fell, on average, by 25 per cent between 1860 and 1880, while those between Europe and the Far Eastern sugar colonies (India, Java, Mauritius, Philippines) fell by 63 per cent. As a result, these eastern colonies were finally able to breach the wall that had been built around them by high freight rates and had limited their development. At the same time, sugar from Hawaii began to reach California.

So far, these new factors had affected only those countries that produced cane sugar. But, simultaneously, the last decades of the century saw a tremendous boom in beet sugar. In 1860, the 352,000 tons of beet sugar produced made up 20 per cent of total world sugar production. By 1890, however, beet sugar production was up to 3.7 million tons, for a total of 59 per cent of the world's production. From being a net importer of sugar, continental Europe had become an exporter. And, logically, what resulted was not by any means 'fair competition': an immensely intricate protectionist system, complemented by a system of subsidy and direct aid (the so-called Sugar Bounties), brought beet sugar prices below any possible competition, and drove Cuban, Puerto Rican and Dominican sugar off the European markets. In 1870 Cuba exported to Europe (excluding the Spanish home market) some 260,000 tons of sugar amounting to 37 per cent of total exports. In 1880 the figure had fallen to 50,000 tons, some 8.54 per cent; and in 1890 exports to Europe were a mere 4,702 tons or 0.72 per cent of total Cuban sugar exports.

The three Spanish-speaking countries (of which two were still colonies) had only one customer left for their sugar: the United States. Java increased its sugar production thanks to the protected Dutch market; India and Mauritius benefited, to a certain degree, from English protectionism, as did Reunion (formerly Bourbon Island) from French policy. Cuba and Puerto Rico (and the Philippines), on the other hand, never had a protected market: of all the colonial countries of Europe, Spain had the lowest sugar consumption *per capita*, and, besides, its poor commercial and maritime development did not allow it to become a re-exporter of its colonies' raw materials. Santo Domingo's sugar was also in the hands of its almost exclusive customer: the United States.

By 1890, the commercial sugar world had acquired the same characteristics it was to keep until 1960. In the first place were the

European beet-sugar producers, highly developed and defended by protectionist barriers. In the second place were those colonial countries that produced cane sugar for the protected markets offered by their mother countries (the French and British colonies, the Dutch East Indies and Hawaii). In the third place were those colonies – Cuba, Puerto Rico, Philippines – and independent countries like Brazil and Santo Domingo, which had no protected markets to which to sell their sugar. The difference between total European sugar consumption and the supply of local beet sugar plus the cane sugar from protected colonies made up the prize that Cuba, Puerto Rico, Santo Domingo and Brazil, principally, competed for. This minimal breach in the protectionist barrier, irregular, unstable and residual, was to receive, in the twentieth century, the imposing name of the 'free market'.

At the end of the nineteenth century the European market for sugar imports was characterized by its lack of elasticity: it may be said without exaggeration that it was only to a very limited degree (in the above mentioned 'free' or residual market) that free competition or the interplay of supply and demand existed. The American market possessed characteristics of a free market in that its local producers, although benefiting from protectionism, supplied a minimal percentage of the country's needs. Cuba was its principal supplier: in the 1860s Cuban sugar exports to the United States covered more than 60 per cent of that country's consumption and the trend was a rising one. The balance was supplied mainly by Puerto Rico and Brazil and, to a lesser degree, Santo Domingo. Cuba and Puerto Rico, however, were colonial countries and the Dominican Republic, though an independent country, must be considered a colony from an economic point of view. They were poor, tied to a single major crop and a single major export to a single major market. They completely lacked the means of economic self-defence, nor did they have at this time the remotest chance of forming a producers' pool to safeguard the prices of their raw materials.[6]

With the cane sugar-producing countries virtually defenceless, the

---

[6] It was in the critical years of the 1930s, when sugar prices frequently fell to below the cost of production, that the first international conferences were held to limit production and fix export quotas. The International Sugar Agreement, signed at the London Conference of 5 April–6 May 1937, was the first to include both importing and exporting countries, the former undertaking to reserve for the latter certain fixed proportions of their imports. However, it was not until the discussions preceding the International Sugar Agreement of 1968 that the developing sugar-producing countries were able to make some of their fundamental interests prevail.

sugar trade was rapidly dominated by powerful international trade interests which drove out even the local traders, who became simple intermediaries for the great international firms. There was a corresponding shift in the location of the price-setting markets: in 1884, for example, the Hamburg price was more important, played a more decisive part in commercial decisions, than the Havana quotations. There was, moreover, another fundamental development that marked the coming of a new age to the sugar trade. Until the 1860s, sugar prices were fixed in the market. And the concept of the *market* was a strictly physical one: it referred to the geographical, urban, districts where warehouses were located and where the traders carried out their operations. In London it was Mincing Lane; in New York, lower Wall Street; in Le Havre, the great square where the Exchange Building stands today; in Havana, the dock area near the College of Brokers, where the principal trading firms – Drake y Hermanos, Samá y Cía., Ajuria y Hermanos, and others – were located. And what was meant by 'market prices' were the highs and lows of the day's most important sales, that is, the maximum and minimum spot prices paid for sugar for immediate ('fast' or 'prompt') delivery. Payment for purchases was generally made on delivery. (Although it was also customary to ship sugar on consignment to European or U.S. markets to be sold through agents there, again for immediate delivery.)

In this world of commerce, physical and tangible, the parameters to be fixed were equally objective and concrete, requiring the trader's personal attention in the solving of specific problems rather than the theoretical analysis of market conditions and trends. The trader's calculations were done with elementary arithmetic – hence the figure of the rich but illiterate sugar merchant. Just as the old slave-operated sugar factories were swept away by modern industry, this type of trading (and consequently, this type of trader) would be replaced by new firms, using new methods, in the last thirty years of the nineteenth century. There was a simple physical reality: the old trading organizations could no longer cope with the multiple factors that now went into the making of a sugar sales agreement, or the dealing in futures on the exchanges of New York, Paris, London or Hamburg.

In brief, then, the modern sugar industry of the late nineteenth century, an intricate economic complex with an enormous volume of production that had to meet international standards of quality, came into being in a world that since the 1860s was being constantly shaken by new developments: the rise of monopolistic world capitalism, the ever-

increasing speed of transport, the radically new techniques for handling information. The application of mathematics to business (especially
sampling surveys, the concept of indexes, the improvement of economic
statistics); modern data processing (the decimal classification system,
other coding and retrieval systems, punched cards); new methods of
transmitting information (the telegraph, telegraphic codes, the telephone, the Atlantic cable, the stock ticker); the concept of marketing,
new methods for evaluating the efficacy of management and for
manipulating public opinion; the use of sociological and anthropological
studies to help the incipient international trusts achieve economic
domination – all of this can be found in the large-scale sugar speculation of
the last years of the nineteenth century.

In this sense, the sugar trade led the field in international business. For
example, the German firm, F. O. Licht, founded in 1861, was the first
firm of sugar brokers to apply successfully, and on a large scale, the use of
sampling to predict world sugar production. Licht's figures, published
in the famous *Monthly Report on Sugar* from 1868, were a fundamental tool
of the big sugar speculators. C. Czarnikow Ltd, of London, did work
similar to Licht, but concentrated on the Caribbean. In 1897 this firm
opened a branch office in New York which was to play a decisive role in
the sugar trade of Cuba, Puerto Rico and Santo Domingo: merging with
the New York-based Cuban broker Manuel Rionda in 1909 as the
Czarnikow–Rionda Company, within a few years they had so dominated
the market that they could act as sole brokers for the Cuban crops of the
war years (1914–18) and for some 80 per cent of both Puerto Rican and
Dominican crops of the same period.[7] These and similar firms functioned
simultaneously as market researchers, trade publishers and brokers, and
acted as agents for certain powerful sugar interests, although this last was
done more or less discreetly: for example, Willet & Hallen (later Willet &
Grey Inc.) acted covertly for the American Sugar Refining Co., at the
time one of the world's largest trusts.

In the last thirty years of the nineteenth century, the world sugar
market fell into the hands of a small group of refiners and bankers, who
used the most up-to-date 'big business' methods to win control of the

[7] For a general description of the firm of F. O. Licht, see the *Jubiläumausgabe* published in 1961 on
the occasion of the company's centennial. A contemporary account of the sampling methods used
by F. O. Licht may be found in *L'Economist Français*, section on 'Sucres', 13 September 1890, 340.
For information on the Czarnikow firm, see Hurford Janes and H. J. Sayers, *The Story of
Czarnikow* (London, 1963). The archives of the Czarnikow–Rionda Company may be consulted
at the Center for Latin American Studies, University of Florida, Gainesville, Florida.

producers of raw sugar and eliminate the old traders. In this struggle, which cannot be fully described here,[8] the key strategy was to create a price-fixing mechanism which, while appearing to observe the rules of supply and demand, would make it possible to take over the market. Here the commodity exchanges played a fundamental role, opening a new era in the trade of colonial products. For the Caribbean, especially Cuba, Puerto Rico and Santo Domingo, the London Sugar Exchange and New York Produce Exchange (which later became the famous New York Coffee and Sugar Exchange) were especially significant.

These exchanges, in theory at least, were of ancient origin: some scholars claim that they were the direct descendants of the medieval bourses. But whatever the kinship, the similarity was only skin-deep. Commodity exchanges, prior to this commercial revolution, had been organizations made up jointly of buyers and sellers, a kind of organized market where the forces of supply and demand would meet to carry out commercial transactions. But the new exchanges were marked by an essential difference: the products were not really sold directly, and the transactions carried out were exclusively speculative. Briefly stated, commodity operations consisted of signing sales contracts in which one party undertook to supply a certain amount of sugar on a certain date: that is, a sale was made at the price of the day for future delivery. When the date of delivery arrived, no sugar was delivered, but the price of the sugar in the contract was then re-calculated on the basis of the price in effect on the delivery date, and the difference between the two prices was paid by one party to the other in cash, less a commission paid to the exchange for its services. As there were many such operations daily, the exchange provided the means for settling the transaction: i.e., it acted as a clearing house. Sugar actually changed hands in less than 1 per cent of the deals. Thus, the exchange did not replace the physical market in which real sugar was bought and sold: it simply dominated it, imposing prices and terms. It is clear why London's authoritative *Economic Journal* described the Produce Clearing House in the 1890s as '. . . a gambling table, a Monte Carlo in Mincing Lane'.[9]

As already mentioned, however, the exchanges were not only places in

[8] For a detailed study of the rise of the Sugar Trust in the United States, and the methods it employed, see Alfred S. Eichner, *The emergence of oligopoly. Sugar refining as a case study* (Baltimore, 1969) and Jack Simpson Mullins, 'The Sugar Trust: Henry O. Havemeyer and the American Sugar Refining Company', unpublished Ph.D. dissertation, University of South Carolina, 1964.
[9] See A. Ellis 'Does speculation raise prices?', *The Economic Journal*, 1 (1891), 197.

which to gamble in commodity prices, but were also invented by economically dominant groups for the sole purpose of broadening and consolidating their control of the market. In 1897, appearing before a United States Senate hearing that was investigating the great sugar trust scandal, Theodore Havemeyer, president of the American Sugar Refining Co., stated that he regularly used the Stock Exchange to bribe government officials and the Commodities Exchange to impose the prices he wanted on the raw sugars of Cuba, Santo Domingo and Puerto Rico.[10]

As might be expected, the activities of the commodity exchanges were unregulated in the last decade of the nineteenth century. Operations were carried out, daily, which today could not even be attempted. It must be remembered, however, that data gathering and handling were new phenomena at that time, and that there were no regulations affecting relations between different exchanges, so it was possible (thanks to the international telegraph, which was itself poorly regulated and, further-more, controlled by a group of speculators) to take advantage of the five-hour time difference between England and America's East Coast to learn London's closing prices before the New York Exchange opened. In general, it may be said that in the United States (at the time practically the only market for Cuban, Puerto Rican and Dominican sugar) sales of sugar futures lacked any regulatory legislation until the incredible speculation of 1920–1 led to the controversial Futures Trading Act of 24 August 1921. The Act was declared unconstitutional shortly afterwards, though finally passed again, with minor changes, on 21 September 1922.

GROWTH OF SUGAR PRODUCTION, *c.* 1860–*c.* 1900

Throughout the nineteenth century, Cuba's sugar production increased steadily, year by year, until 1875, when the slave plantations, which for some time had been showing clear signs of crisis, started on the downward path to their final disintegration with the end of slavery in the 1880s. Plotted on a graph, the fortunes of the sugar industry would show marked fluctuations, especially for the period between 1876 and 1880, reflecting the transition from the old *ingenio* to the modern *central*. By the 1890s, however, Cuba had regained its position as the world's largest sugar producer, with five successive crops of just over or under a million

[10] See Mullins, 'The Sugar Trust', chapter VII.

tons, only to fall into the great slump brought about by the War of Independence (1895–8).

Puerto Rico, on the other hand, maintained its steady upward economic trend only until the 1850s, when a series of ups and downs started which reflected the instability of its slave-based production. In 1873 slavery was abolished during a period of ample harvests. Abolition in Puerto Rico, however, was not accompanied by a general process of modernization, and production fell sharply in the 1890s.

Diverse factors contributed to the dissimilar development of these two colonies which had the same mother country and therefore the same form of government, as well as sharing the same climate and geographical region.

In the first place, the two islands had a different historical background. From the sixteenth to the eighteenth centuries and on into the first two decades of the nineteenth, Cuba was a centre for the defence of the Spanish empire, the main maritime base for both naval and mercantile fleets and an important productive region. These factors allowed an oligarchy to grow up which came to wield an almost unique political power, and which from the beginning accumulated large capital sums derived from services such as trade, shipbuilding, construction of fortifications, etc. This capital was subsequently invested in agro-industrial resources: tobacco, coffee and sugar. The Cuban oligarchy was able to take advantage of favourable conditions for foreign trade created by the 1791 revolution in Haiti, which had been up till then the largest sugar producer in the world. Cuba emerged as the possessor of an important sugar complex which was by 1840 producing more than the whole of the British West Indies together.

In Cuba, unlike in the French or English West Indian colonies, the sugar-mills were financed by native investments, and with very few exceptions they never belonged to absentee owners. On the contrary, their owners lived in Cuba and, as a general rule, at the beginning of each sugar harvest they would move into their *ingenios* to watch over and manage their interests directly. Like modern entrepreneurs, they kept abreast of world technological developments, and incorporated with little delay those items of equipment and technological advances which could improve the capacity or the profitability of the Cuban sugar industry.

As far back of 1796 these native businessmen had carried out the first experiments in adapting the steam engine to the cane mill; in 1837 they inaugurated the world's first railway devoted to hauling sugar and molasses from the mills to the ports (and, indeed, the first railway of any kind in Latin America); in 1842 they started using vacuum pans for obtaining sugar; in 1844 (the same year as in the United States) they put up the first telegraph wires; in 1849 they installed sugar centrifuges. Cuba, a colonial possession, outpaced all other Latin American countries in technological developments during the nineteenth century. Under the twofold influence of legislative privileges and a dynamic class of entrepreneurs, and helped by extraordinarily favourable natural conditions (highly fertile lands, ideal weather, large forestry resources, etc.), Cuba was understandably the world's largest sugar producer from 1840 to 1883. Puerto Rico, which did not share these characteristics, was a much smaller producer.

However, in the 1860s both Cuban and Puerto Rican plantations began to show the first symptoms of crisis. The crisis was a structural one, provoked by the steadily decreasing profitability of slave-based labour and by the difficulties resulting from the adoption of the new technologies.[11]

Thus, there began a period of instability in which the principal problem faced by the producers – and therefore by officialdom – was to find a solution to the transition from slavery to wage labour. The aim of the producers was to obtain from Spain an abolition law which would indemnify them so they could recoup the capital they had invested in slaves in order to re-invest in modern equipment. They also hoped for related legislation which would provide a cheap and constant supply of 'free' labourers, that is to say, semi-enslaved, obliged to work 12–14 hours a day for starvation wages and then to be laid off at the end of the harvest.

It is a fact that in Cuba in 1863 over 95 per cent of all sugar properties were mortgaged. Economic studies of the period showed that the 300 million pesos invested in sugar bore 200 million pesos in mortgages, i.e., two-thirds of the sugar industry was in the hands of merchants who, in Cuba and Puerto Rico, carried out the functions of bankers.[12]

In the 1860s, this critical situation on the two islands was abruptly alleviated by a series of favourable external events, which did not so

---

[11] The conclusions here on the profitability of slavery to the slaveowner are based on an econometric analysis of Cuban sugar mill book-keeping records. See Manuel Moreno Fraginals, *El ingenio* (Havana, 1977), vol. II, chapter 1. For further discussion of the Cuban sugar industry in the period before 1870, see Thomas, *CHLA* III. ch. 7.

[12] Raúl Cepero Bonilla, *Azúcar y abolición* (Havana, 1971), 39ff.

much solve the inherent structural difficulties (for the slave plantation had exhausted all possibility of internal reform), as extend the system's lease on life. For years the Civil War in the United States and the Franco-Prussian War in Europe created the classical wartime effect of upsetting market conditions, increasing demand and forcing up prices. In Cuba itself, the Ten Years' War (1868–78), the first large-scale struggle for independence, also heightened the panic in the sugar trade and extended favourable market conditions. There were almost ten years of good harvests and high prices (even though most of these, in Cuba, coincided with the Ten Years' War) which allowed Cuban sugar producers to pay off a great part of their mortgages and their Puerto Rican counterparts to begin the mechanization of their sugar mills, which had, in general, lagged behind Cuba in this respect. But this period was an exception to the trend, and once it had passed the crisis again made itself felt more strongly than ever.

In Puerto Rico, the disintegration of the old-style sugar plantations was extremely rapid. In 1870 there were 550 mills with a total output of 96,000 tons; by 1880 this had fallen to 325, producing 50,000 tons. Because techniques were so backward, the crisis in production was matched by a crisis in quality, and many United States importers refused to buy the Puerto Rican raw sugars that were being rejected by refiners. But there was an even more significant reason for the island's crisis: the basic problem was that there was no physical and economic infrastructure on which to base industrialization. Without investment capital or an adequate railway system and without concerted action by the producers, what few efforts were made were individual and for the most part limited to the purchase of machines (which were not always efficiently installed) and to the construction of a few *centrales* which, until the end of the century, alternated between good and bad years, and generally ended heavily in debt. To cite but one example: Central San Vicente, in Vega Baja, founded by Leonardo Igaravidez, marquis of Cabo Caribe, had by 1873 taken over the larger surrounding plantations to ensure a supply of cane for its mill and was employing several hundred cane-cutters. But by 1879 its debts had risen to over a million pesos (1 peso = 1 dollar), an incredible amount for that time. Besides the San Vicente, there were in 1880 four other *centrales*: the Luisa, the San Francisco, the Coloso and the Canovanas. Throughout the nineteenth century their histories were, from the economic point of view, similar.

Another key factor limiting the development of Puerto Rico's sugar industry was the failure to effect a successful transition from slavery to free labour. It is usually said that slavery was abolished in Puerto Rico in 1873, but this is true only in the legal sense. In fact, the institution of slavery had for a long time been in a state of collapse, and by the 1870s the island lacked a labour force which could be subjected to the conditions that the plantation-owners considered necessary. Unlike Cuba, there was no significant influx of migrant labour into Puerto Rico. Very few coolies came from China; efforts to set up a system of migrant workers from Spain (colourfully known at the time as *golondrinas*, or swallows) met with no success; and the experiment of importing labourers from the British West Indies ended with a handful of groups who settled on off-shore Vieques and on the sugar mills of Ponce, Humacao, Loiza and Carolina.[13]

The Cuban case was different. The great sugar boom took place in regions that had had easy access to ports which, by mid-century, were already served by an excellent rail network. In general, this railway system, originally designed to carry hogsheads and boxes of sugar, turned out to be exceptionally useful for carrying cane from the fields to the mills. As far as the labour force was concerned, 1847 saw the beginning of an impressive immigration of coolies that probably reached 150,000 by the end of the century. Another source of labour had an unusual origin. The Spanish regular army being needed at home for the Carlist Wars, garrisons in Cuba were manned chiefly by *quintos*, or conscripts from Spain. A series of Cuban regulations – which were, of course, considered thoroughly illegal in Spain – gave the draftee the choice of serving out his full term as a soldier or of signing on as a hand in a sugar mill. As the Cuban Ten Years' War was being fought at the time, not unnaturally many *quintos* became cane-cutters. And in the 1880s, the owners of the new *centrales* were able to set up an efficient flow of migrant workers, who would arrive at the beginning of January and leave at the end of April. These workers came from the Canary Islands and from the Spanish provinces of Galicia and Asturias, where living standards were extremely low, and there was over-population and high unemployment.

Having large sums of capital available, many Spanish merchants and some families belonging to the old *criollo* (Cuban-born) oligarchy

[13] On the Puerto Rican sugar industry, see Andrés Antonio Ramos Matttei, 'The influence of mechanisation in the system of sugar production in Puerto Rico, 1873–1898', unpublished Ph.D. thesis, University of London, 1977, and *La hacienda azucarera, su crecimiento y crisis en Puerto Rico (siglo XIX)* (San Juan, 1981). Also José Curet, *De la esclavitud a la abolición* (San Juan, 1979).

invested in *centrales*, especially from the 1880s on. In this respect it is useful to point out that from an economic point of view, Cuba's bloody Ten Years' War of Independence turned out to be profitable for the modernized sugar industry. The war, which was fought mainly at the eastern end of the island, destroyed over a hundred old sugar mills, all of which were technologically backward and scarcely productive. The western part of the country where the new 'giant' mills were located, and which produced 80 per cent of Cuban sugar, did not suffer the ravages of the war.[14]

Moreover, the Banco Colonial and the Banco Español de la Isla de Cuba, both controlled by the big Spanish merchants and by some members of the Cuban oligarchy as well, had been charged with the financing of the war by the Spanish government, and this turned out to be an enormously profitable deal. Cuban–Spanish shipping and railway companies handled the transportation of troops and war supplies. With a military colonial administration, and under psychological 'state-of-war' pressures, shady business deals of all types were made, and illicit enrichment became the norm. It is evident that at the end of the war these groups would have the necessary liquid capital to invest in the great 'new' (i.e., radically modernized) sugar industry.

There were still other factors. With a sugar-oriented background, political experience, well organized and united by long-time common interests, local producers were well aware of the needs of the times and began to create a group of institutions to steer the new industry. In this way there came into being the Asociación de Hacendados de la Isla de Cuba in 1879 for the purpose of co-ordinating the actions of the principal minds (and largest investors of capital) in the sugar world. From its beginnings, the Association guided the activities of the producers, promoted projects for bringing in migrant workers, founded agricultural and industrial training schools, sponsored research, set up direct communications with the sugar exchanges in New York and London, published a widely-read magazine, and formed a powerful lobby to defend the industry's interests. During this period there arose many similar but local associations of *colonos* or cane planters.

[14] Only two sugar censuses were carried out in Cuba during the nineteenth century. These may be found in the following: Carlos Rebello, *Estados azucareros relativos a la producción azucarera de la Isla de Cuba* (Havana, 1860: no publisher's imprint appears in the book, which, moreover, was actually printed in New York); *Noticias de las fincas azucareras en producción que existían en toda la Isla de Cuba al comenzar el presupuesto de 1877–1878*, a report published in *La Revista Económica* (Havana), January 1877, 6off.

Finally, two further important points need to be made. The first concerns the abolition of slavery. Slavery was abolished in Cuba in 1880 (seven years later than in Puerto Rico). Abolition did not, however, mean that a mass of people, chattels subjected to their masters' every whim, suddenly found themselves free and in full possession of civil rights and responsibilities. Had this been the case, the abolition of slavery would have brought about the total collapse of the sugar industry, for as late as 1877 (the last year for which reliable statistics on Cuban slavery are available) more than 70 per cent of sugar production was based on slave labour. That this did not occur was due to the simple fact that the Law of Abolition was merely the *de jure* recognition of a situation characterized by the *de facto* disintegration of the slave system.

As a matter of fact, as far back the 1860s, and much more so the 1870s, the term 'slavery' covered a wide range of means of exploiting labour. To begin with, there was the 'pure' slave, physically forced to work in the sugar mill. Next to him was the hired slave. The latter was subject to totally different conditions from the former: physical punishments were banned, and he received part of the money paid for his hire. Then there was the *jornalero*, or wage-earner, a variant of the above, the slave who personally signed on at a sugar mill for a certain figure, and who periodically handed part of his wages to his nominal owner as payment for the status of a semi-freedman with the right to sell his services freely. There was also the wage-earning slave (a very common feature of the time) whose wages were generally 50–70 per cent of those of a freeman. Many slaves, of all types, enjoyed the usufruct of small plots of land where they grew produce and raised animals, selling part to the *ingenio*. With them worked free blacks and whites, Chinese and contract labourers from Yucatán (virtual slaves themselves) and, at times, convicts with which the state provided the mills and who were paid a small wage. This anomalous situation in the labour supply acted as a brake on capitalistic industrial development: the Law of Abolition was a way to rationalize the confused labour system productively.

All of this leads us to a conclusion: the essence of the changes arising in the production of Cuban sugar from the 1880s was much more economic and social than technical. This does not mean that there were no significant improvements in equipment and processes: there were, as we have seen. What we affirm is that the complete renovation of the process of production was not merely a question of installing modern industrial equipment (that had already begun in numerous Cuban sugar mills since the middle of the century); it also implied a renovation at the social and institutional level that simply could not be carried out by slave-owners. The more reactionary among these retained and exploited their slaves as long as they could: clinging to a past that was doomed to disappear, they held on to their slaves because they considered them part of their investment. Perhaps, for them, there was no alternative.

The other key point to be mentioned here is the process of consolidation in Cuba. Industrialization, as we have seen, led to the early disappearance of the less efficient units. In Matanzas, Cuba's most important sugar region, there were 517 mills in 1877, producing some 350,000 tons; by 1895 the number of mills was down to 99, but production, at 600,000 tons, had almost doubled.[15] However, during these final decades of the nineteenth century, the concentration of production in fewer but larger mills did not find a counterpart in landownership. Possibly, the liens and other obligations of landownership (especially the unredeemable and indivisible type of *censo*, or living pledge) conspired against all efforts to bring about a consolidation of lands which would complement industrial concentration. This led to a broad discrepancy between agriculture and industry and in part explains the backwardness of cane planting in a period of industrial and technological advance.

From the point of view of direct ownership, either of land or of mills, there are few signs of the presence of United States capital in the Cuban sugar industry of the nineteenth century. There were, of course, individual American millowners, just as there were French, Canadians and Germans. The figures of the U.S. forces, who occupied the island in 1898, show that at the time, 93.5 per cent of the sugar-mills belonged to Cubans and Spaniards; only the remaining 6.5 per cent belonged to foreigners, including, of course, U.S. citizens. It should be pointed out, moreover, that many of the mills then listed as 'American' really belonged to native Cubans and Spaniards who had only recently acquired U.S. citizenship.

So far we have mainly discussed the behaviour of those internal factors that shaped the development of the Cuban sugar industry during the last decades of the nineteenth century. But external factors also played a decisive role in the process. Thus, the statement that the U.S. had only a

---

[15] For 1877, see note 14. Data for 1895 are from *La relación de los ingenios de las provincias y datos relativos a los mismos*, Matanzas, 23 September 1895 (a register compiled by order of the provincial authorities). The manuscript is in the Archivo Histórico of Matanzas.

limited presence in the Cuban sugar industry refers exclusively to the ownership of sugar mills. But from the point of view of international trade, the United States had long exercised hegemony. By the 1870s the 'golden age of competition' had come to an end in the United States, at least where sugar was concerned; there existed an oligopolistic structure. The Sugar Trust was legally established in August 1887 with the incorporation of the American Sugar Refining Company and the agreement of twenty-one refining companies in seven U.S. cities to become members in October. It had in practice come into being a decade before.[16] The U.S. Sugar Act of 1871 was the first legislative tool of neo-colonial domination forged in the United States, under pressure from the East Coast refiners, for the specific purpose of dominating Cuba, Puerto Rico and Santo Domingo economically. By the 1880s, the three islands were selling virtually all their sugar to the United States, dealing with one sole firm in the market, the American Sugar Refining Co.; their sugar was shipped in U.S. vessels; the sugar prices were fixed by the New York Produce Exchange; island planters and millowners got their market prices and production estimates from Willet & Grey, in news items reported by Associated Press and carried by Western Union. Without direct investment in lands or mills the economic annexation of the three islands was under way: physical annexation by forcible means would come a few years later.

In 1895 Cuban sugar development suffered an abrupt interruption. On 24 February, in the middle of the harvest season, a new war of independence broke out, one that, unlike the Ten Years' War, was fought over the entire island. The magnitude of the operations may be gathered from a few figures: Spain moved in 400,000 soldiers, the largest army ever to cross the Atlantic until the days of World War II. This represented one Spanish soldier for every three inhabitants of the island. During the War of Independence (1895–8) hundreds of thousands of hectares of cane-fields were repeatedly set on fire (cane is an easy crop to burn). An unknown number of sugar-mills was also destroyed. Unfortunately, quantitative documentation that would allow an exact appreciation of war damage inflicted on the sugar industry is lacking.

Traditional Cuban historiography, influenced by the interests of the sugar magnates, created the myth of the total destruction of the sugar industry during the war. As there were no censuses of sugar plantations

---

[16] Mullins, 'The Sugar Trust', 32–3.

taken during the period, the theory of total ruin still prevails among many modern historians. But painstaking qualitative studies, which have analysed thousands of dispersed sources, would seem to prove that while an enormous drop was evident in cane production (the result of repeated burnings), the industrial sector, on the other hand, received much less damage. Of the 50 largest *centrales* in production in 1895, only 7 were destroyed during the war, 4 received some damage, and 39 remained standing, ready to start a new grinding season. It is probable that the effective overall loss suffered by the industry was at most between 20 and 25 per cent of installed productive capacity. To start up the industry anew required an extensive programme of cane planting at a time when farm labourers had been widely dispersed (since the war had completely changed the pattern of settlements in many areas). This explains the drop in production in the war and immediate post-war years. It also explains why, within three years of the end of the war, sugar production reached almost a million tons, which was about the total installed capacity in 1895.

The sugar industry of Santo Domingo in the late nineteenth century was heavily influenced by the Ten Years' War in Cuba, which led large numbers of Cubans to emigrate to Santo Domingo, among them many small capitalists, mill-owners from eastern Cuba. Santo Domingo offered them refuge: a country where their own language was spoken, with similar physical and social conditions to those in Cuba, with relative political stability and where foreign capital investments in agro-industrial business were encouraged and protected. Among the facilities offered investors were exemptions on import and export duties, and even grants of state-owned lands for building sugar mills. Natural conditions (climate, soil fertility, natural irrigation, etc.) were similarly suitable for the development of the sugar industry.

It was under these conditions that the first phase of Santo Domingo's modern sugar industry began, dominated by Cuban entrepreneurs, although there were some other nationalities. The original, generally modest, capital investments were made by these businessmen personally and/or by their Dominican associates; later investments were made by local businessmen and moneylenders, or by foreign machinery manufacturers who would offer credit, taking mortgages on the budding industries as security. Land was very cheap, and the original government grants were soon extended by purchases and leases. From a technological point of view, though innovative by the standards of existing local mills, these new plants were modelled on the mills of eastern Cuba, that is, they were *ingenios* which did not incorporate the most up-to-date industrial equipment. Obviously, this type of enterprise could only succeed thanks to official support and to the exceptional conditions of the sugar market in the 1870s. By 1882 there were 21 sugar-mills in Santo Domingo, but once their original success was over, all rapidly faced crisis. In 1884, when sugar prices fell to the lowest levels ever recorded, many of the original entrepreneurs were squeezed out and there was a concentration of ownership. One single financier managed to gain control of over ten mills after 1884. Some fourteen mills went bankrupt and closed down, either temporarily or permanently, between 1884 and 1900.

Another consequence of the depression was a growing effort on the part of the surviving mills to incorporate modern technology in an attempt to reduce costs of production, and so there appeared on the Santo Domingo sugar scene the first *centrales* on the Cuban model – and with them the same problems described above: the *central* required larger sugar cane fields and a more rapid flow of cane to the mill. Railways offered the structural conditions for latifundia, but, as in Cuba, industrial consolidation outpaced the concentration of land. The new, large *centrales* found themselves obliged to set up the so called *colonato* (independent cane growers) system, thereby separating the agricultural from the industrial sector. The largest *central* in Santo Domingo in the nineteenth century was the Central Consuelo, in San Pedro de Macorís, founded by the Cuban partnership of Padró, Solaún y Cía. In the 1890s, under the management of a new partner, the American William L. Bass, the *central* became a 'small republic', to quote the press of the day: this may be taken to mean that it had acquired the characteristics of an economic giant that socially and politically dominated the region.

The sugar industry of Santo Domingo in the nineteenth century was very small in comparison with that of Cuba and even with that of Puerto Rico. During the critical decade of the 1880s total production never rose above 20,000 tons annually. However, with the start of the Cuban War of Independence in 1895, there was a temporary shortage of sugar and a corresponding increase in world prices. The Dominican mills increased their production, but the installed capacity did not allow for harvests of more than 50,000 tons; Cuba, during these war years, was producing over 250,000 tons.

GROWTH OF SUGAR PRODUCTION, *c.* 1900–1930

In 1900 the total sugar production of Cuba, Puerto Rico and the Dominican Republic was 430,000 tons, or approximately 4 per cent of world production. During the next twenty years, the Cuban sugar industry grew at annual rate of 14.2 per cent, the Puerto Rican at 14.3 per cent and the Dominican at 8.2 per cent, so that by 1920 the three countries accounted for a joint 4,533,119 tons, or 29.3 per cent of total world sugar production although it must be acknowledged that the figures for 1920 were somewhat distorted by the crisis in the European sugar industry caused by the First World War. In all three cases, the growth process had one common feature: the boost received from the respective United States military interventions. The U.S. army, it will be remembered, occupied Cuba and Puerto Rico in 1898, and Puerto Rico was subsequently annexed. Military intervention in Cuba lasted until 1902, and a further intervention took place in 1906–8. In the Dominican Republic the process was different: nominally independent since 1844, the convulsed affairs of the country led to a 1905 convention authorizing the United States to collect and administer the country's customs duties. In 1915, faced by the possible election of a government inimical to its interests, the U.S. intervened militarily and its forces occupied the country until 1924.

In each case, those American corporations interested in the sugar business obtained from the occupation authorities the material facilities and the legal framework to make their investments a worthwhile venture. The calculations of the American sugar companies, as can be seen from their prospectuses and advertisements in the early 1900s, were based on simple premises: first, the United States constituted a constantly-growing market for sugar, due both to its extraordinary population growth (absolute increase) and to the ever-larger *per capita* consumption (relative increase); secondly, the very fact of U.S. intervention (i.e., armed occupation) or outright annexation guaranteed the permanence of the internal juridical status and socio-political conditions favourable to U.S. investments; thirdly, externally, the relations between these countries and the United States were similarly fixed, thus providing for stable market conditions; fourthly, due to their natural conditions (rainfall, temperature, soil, etc.) the three countries were ideal sugar producers, and this was enhanced by their geographical proximity to the mainland; all three were key points in the

United States policy of a Caribbean-Central American sphere of interest; fifthly, under these conditions, investments in the sugar trade were among the surest and most profitable in the world; sixthly, no changes were foreseen in these conditions even in the long term.

It must be remembered that the United States had an excellent sugar technology of its own, besides the factories capable of making the entire range of sugar-manufacturing machinery as well as every kind of equipment for the cultivation and haulage of the cane. Even better, the entire industrial complex could be shipped, erected, started up, operated and managed by Americans either by themselves or with the aid of native staff technically and culturally trained by them.

The Achilles' heel of such investments was the cane itself, which had necessarily to be planted, tilled and harvested in these countries by native labour, or by labourers imported from nearby islands. The large machines, their installation, the enormous complex of buildings, transport, power, telephone and telegraph, repair shops, etc., implied an extremely large capital investment to be amortized over a long period, whose profitability depended on the absolute certainty of a steady supply of cane at a determined cost and in the required quantity, quality and delivery periods. In these respects cane is an infinitely more sensitive product than sugar-beet. While beet can be harvested and stored for later processing, cane must be cut in the exact amounts to be milled within twenty-four hours: it cannot be stored.

For these and other reasons the agricultural side of the industry (which, as has been seen, is basically manual, involving as many as 300,000 workers in Cuba alone during the 1920s) had to match the industrial side in precision and rhythm. But, to complicate matters, at the end of the sugar harvest, whose average length was four months, more than half of the agricultural workers were immediately laid off; subsequent layoffs were gradual, but only 10 per cent of the workers had year-round employment.

Given these conditions, from its inception the modern sugar industry faced two fundamental problems: an assured supply of cane and a sufficient labour force for each harvest. The labour system will be discussed below. Regarding the cultivation of cane, three separate stages in the history of Cuba and Puerto Rico, though not of the Dominican Republic, may be described. During the first stage, corresponding to the primitive, slave-based systems of sugar production (remnants of which lasted into the 1880s) the sugar-mill, or *ingenio*, was basically an agricultural enterprise, since the two main components of its assets, or capital, were its lands and its slaves (i.e., agricultural workers). In such an enterprise, where slaves had to be maintained all year round, they naturally had to be worked all year round, planting and tilling the cane during the off-season. Thus the mill-owner grew the cane that his mill ground.

In the second, post-abolition, stage, which may be called transitional, there occurred the division, described above, into separate industrial and agricultural sectors. This so-called 'division of labour' stage took place during the period of development of the large industrial centres (*centrales*) in those areas where the canefields belonging to the old slave-worked *ingenios* already existed. The characteristic feature of this stage of development was that the large *central* processed not only cane fom its own lands, which was never enough, but also had to meet its needs by buying additional quantities of cane from the surrounding *colonias* or cane-growing properties.

The establishment of a pattern of purchases of cane from outside growers by the new industrial centres marked the emergence of an extraordinarily important socio-economic stratum in the modern history of the Spanish-speaking Caribbean. These cane-growers, called *colonos*, were as a rule former owners of *ingenios* (or their heirs). They possessed a reasonable cultural level, political experience and a sense of group, if not class, identity. By the 1880s they had begun to organize into associations for the defence of their common interests. Thus, as soon as the economic separation between the industrial and the agricultural sectors of the sugar industry became an accomplished fact, there was an open clash between the interests of the two sectors; and it may be said that, at least at the end of the nineteenth and the beginning of the twentieth centuries, the *colonos* had the upper hand.

This was the situation faced by the large corporate investors when United States capital began to penetrate the Caribbean sugar industry. It was natural for these corporations to be unwilling to assume the risk of allowing a native group, well organized and with a nationalist political orientation, to control the supply of cane. The logical solution, then, in the case of Cuba and the Dominican Republic, was for them to set up their new *centrales* in sparsely populated regions where, moreover, land was very cheap, and to make the *centrales* responsible for the cultivation of their own cane, either directly or through intermediaries selected by them. In Puerto Rico, a very small island (8,896 sq. km) which had been the site of an extensive slave-worked sugar industry during the nineteenth century, there was no unpopulated virgin land suitable for cane cultivation, and there the situation was different: to establish economic control by forcing the existing cane-growers to sell their properties to the new companies. There is one further, equally important, consideration. The United States had developed an impressive degree of mechanization in the cultivation of certain crops. It was thus logical that the new corporate investors should envisage for their new cane lands in eastern Cuba, where the labour force was very small, a similar process of mechanization for the cultivation of cane in order to obtain the marginal profits of a scale economy. But large-scale agricultural mechanization implies large tracts of land, and thus there arose in Cuba the sugar latifundia, the result of economic realities and not simply of a voracious greed for land, as the political literature of the time put it. In the event, the mechanization of agriculture did not come about, partly because the infrastructural conditions of Cuba and the Dominican Republic (the cultural level, the availability of mechanical facilities, knowledge of soil conditions, necessary varieties of cane, etc.) were insufficient to permit it; and partly because of the low level of development of suitable machinery for planting, cultivating and cutting cane.

But a third solution was found for Cuba, one economically satisfactory for the American sugar companies but of disastrous social and political consequences for the country: extensive agriculture. Noël Deerr, one of the most distinguished British experts on sugar cane in the twentieth century, visited Cuba before the First World War and rapidly grasped the reason behind the apparent contradiction whereby the world's largest and most economical producer of sugar was 'the most poorly farmed of all countries in which cane is produced'.[17] Where land is abundant and labour scarce, the logic of economics leads to a greater use of land. Obviously, with these methods, yields per area will be low, but the cost of the cane will be less than that obtained by applying more (and high-priced) labour to the same area to obtain higher yields.

For all these reasons, the cane latifundia of Camagüey and Oriente provinces reached virtually aberrant sizes, if we consider Cuba's total area of about 111,000 sq. km. In 1900, for example, two *ingenios* in Camagüey, both belonging to old provincial families, produced a total of

---

[17] Noël Deerr, Memorandum, *Condiciones de la industria azucarera en Cuba* (Havana, 1913).

21,700 tons of sugar from some 4,000 hectares of land. In 1925, there were 26 *centrales*, all foreign-owned: only the two old mills were still in Cuban hands. These 26 new mills owned or controlled approximately one million hectares and their total production for the year was 1,402,175 tons. In Oriente, similarly, just three of the new mills built in the first two decades of this century (the Chaparra, the Delicias and the Mercedita, all belonging to the Cuban American Sugar Co.) eventually owned about 180,000 hectares between them.

The Joint Resolution of 1 May 1900 which institutionalized the United States colonial government in Puerto Rico, provided that '. . . every corporation hereafter authorized to engage in agriculture shall by its charter be restricted to the ownership and control of land not exceeding 500 acres'. This law has been the object of numerous interpretations, but one thing is certain: it was a dead letter from its promulgation.[18] The process by which land ownership became concentrated in the hands of the sugar companies in fact took place relatively more rapidly in Puerto Rico than in Cuba. In 1899, the total amount of land given over to sugar cane was 29,197 hectares; by 1909 it had jumped to 58,857 hectares; and by 1919 it had reached 92,197. In 1919 it has been estimated that Puerto Rico imported 60 per cent of the agricultural produce it consumed: the proletarization of the peasant, the changing of the small farmer into an agricultural worker, had been completed, and the patriarchal hacienda system had disappeared.

From 1915 complaints against the cane latifundia were increasingly frequent. Perhaps this was the reason that the '500-acre Law', as it was called, was incorporated into the provisions of the island's Organic Act of 1917; but the island legislature passed no laws that would make it mandatory for the limitation to be observed. Nonetheless, the law existed, and the sugar companies protected themselves in case it were ever to be applied. Thus, for example, in 1917 the Central Aguirre Sugar Co. 'sold' all its lands and made over all its rights in the sugar acreage it controlled (5,558 wholly-owned hectares, 3,211 hectares in leasehold) to Luce and Co.; in that same year, the South Porto Rico Sugar Co. did the same to Russell and Co. Needless to say, both Luce and Russell were subsidiaries of the two sugar companies. In 1936, the four largest American sugar companies operating in Puerto Rico owned 29,646 hectares and controlled another 20,902 hectares: a total of 50,584

[18] Arthur D. Gayer, *The sugar economy in Puerto Rico* (New York, 1938), 97.

hectares, or more than 10 per cent of the total improved land in Puerto Rico.[19]

Sugar production in the Dominican Republic had been growing slowly but steadily since the beginning of the century (53,000 tons in 1900; 126,058 tons in 1915). La Romana (still the largest sugar mill in the country) was founded in 1911 and other mills like Consuelo, bought by the Bartram interests, Santa Fe, Quisqueyn and San Isidro (also Bartram) were corporately owned by 1916. Nevertheless, production received a further boost during the American occupation (1916–24). The occupation witnessed the starting up of the Barahona and Las Pajas y Boca Chica sugar mills. The history of land acquisition by the American sugar corporations is full of accusations of fraud, extortions and other illegalities. The application of the Land Registration Law of 1900, which was followed by the first land survey in modern Dominican history, brought about the dispossession of many small farmers who had no documentary title to the land their families had lived on for years. The new *centrales* and the expansion of the existing *ingenios* allowed a doubling of production during the occupation years, from 128,000 tons in 1916 to 233,000 tons in 1924. In this same period the ownership of land by the sugar companies tripled: from 56,420 hectares in 1916 to 159,913 in 1924. The process of investment and control by American companies may be seen in the following: in 1900 there were 14 sugar mills in the Dominican Republic, of which none was owned by large American corporations; at the end of the U.S. occupation there were 22 mills, of which 12 were American. Even more significantly, these 12 mills owned 81 per cent of the country's cane lands and represented 82 per cent of the industry's declared capital. And just three of these mills, Romana, Consuelo and Barahona, accounted for almost 50 per cent of the Dominican sugar production.

The enormous expansion of the Cuban sugar industry came to an abrupt halt in 1929 with a harvest of 5,352,585 tons. Just three years later production had fallen by 61 per cent to 2,073,055 tons. The last sugar mill built in Cuba had been the Santa Marta, in Camagüey, in 1929, the co-owner and manager of which was General Mario García Menocal who was president of Cuba 1912–20 and for many years simultaneously general manager of the U.S. corporation, the Cuban American Sugar Co. Fifty years were to pass before construction would start on another Cuban sugar mill.

[19] Ibid., 103–5.

Investments in Cuba's sugar industry had, throughout the twentieth century, been made with just one main market in view: the United States. But it was with this same market in mind that investors had poured their money into the U.S. territories of Puerto Rico, the Philippines and Hawaii, into the Dominican Republic during the occupation and, of course, into the United States itself. The Great Depression of the 1930s would show just how an uncontrolled economy had built up an industry whose productive capacity was almost twice the market's effective demand.

Cuban sugar, moreover, could find no other markets than the United States, for the European beet-sugar industry had long recovered from the crisis it suffered during the First World War, and once again the barriers of protectionism were being raised high. Java, Australia, India and other sugar cane regions had also increased their milling capacities.

For the first time, the Cuban government took concrete measures towards bringing about an agreement to regulate the world sugar market. But, lacking political influence in the international arena, its intervention was finally reduced to accepting the so-called 'Chadbourne Plan' (1930), which, though undoubtedly successful in regulating the American market by adjusting production among the different U.S. corporations with sugar interests (and with sugar mills in Cuba, Puerto Rico, Santo Domingo, the Philippines, Hawaii and in the continental United States), was absolutely ineffective as regards the world market. It was precisely when Cuba's production had reached its lowest point, in 1933–4, that three U.S. territories, Puerto Rico, the Philippines and Hawaii, had their largest harvests ever, each one producing over a million tons. The Dominican Republic was not affected by the Chadbourne Plan's reduction, because its production, though mainly in American hands, was not aimed at the internal U.S. market. In 1912, approximately half of Dominican sugar had been exported to the British market and a large proportion of the remainder to Canada. The U.S. occupation had reversed this: in 1920 some 70 per cent of the Dominican production had been exported to American markets. But when the new U.S. tariffs came into effect in that year, a shift in policy took place, and by 1925 only 2 per cent of the Dominican sugar was exported to the U.S.; the other 98 per cent went to Canada, Holland, France and, above all, England, which was to remain its main customer until the 1960s.

With the Depression, sugar ceased to be the source of the exceedingly high profits it had been for the forty preceding years: King Sugar was no longer king. American capital, therefore, flowed towards other areas of greater profits: Cuba, as the world's largest sugar producer, was logically the worst affected country. The American corporations started selling their Cuban sugar-mills and lands to Cuban interests. This process, seen and idealized by some as a slow 'Cubanization' of the sugar industry, must rather be considered as merely the shedding of decreasingly profitable enterprises into native hands. However, it is also true that another decisive factor was the rising and sometimes aggressive Cuban nationalism, as well as a strong and unified labour movement which put forward a series of demands (including wage increases, an 8-hour day and profit-sharing) and even forcibly occupied several of the largest American-owned sugar mills.

SUGAR AND LABOUR

It is possible to identify certain regular trends in the evolution of plantations. The first to become visible, due to the land/labour ratio, is always the unsatisfied craving of the planters for a large number of cheap and submissive workers. A pamphlet published in London in 1714 observed: '. . . If the colonies are not furnish'd with negroes, they cannot make sugar; and the more and cheaper they have negroes, the more and cheaper they will make sugar'.[20] Such was the philosophy of the eighteenth-century planters, and such also was the philosophy of the twentieth-century planters. The labour requirements of modern plantations in Cuba, Santo Domingo and Puerto Rico had naturally specific characteristics. During the course of the nineteenth century, sugar yields (the amount of sugar extracted from a given weight of cane) rose from about 2.5 per cent in 1800 to 10 per cent in 1900. On the other hand, the productivity of the industrial sugar worker can be calculated as having risen by no less than 1,500 per cent during the same period, as a consequence of the installation of modern machinery and the adoption of sophisticated manufacturing methods. But the average cane-cutter of 1900 used the same tools and methods and had the same low output as his 1800 counterpart. A technological gap had developed between the agricultural sector, which planted, tilled and harvested the cane, and the industrial sector, which turned that cane into sugar.

Now, although the industrial process does not, properly speaking,

[20] (Anon.), *The Present State of the Sugar Plantations Consider'd; but More Especially that of the Island of Barbadoes* (London, 1714), 27.

manufacture sugar so much as extract what is already present in the cane, it is obvious that there is an upper limit to the amount by which yields can increase, a limit set by the total sucrose content of the cane. As industrial yields approached this limit, the relative share of production costs to be charged to the static agricultural sector became larger, reflecting the fact that the cost of cane was closely linked to the price of manual, unskilled labour. Since the planters were unable to bring about an agricultural revolution – at least in the short term – their solution to the problem of increasing cane costs relative to total production costs was to keep agricultural wages, especially those of cane-cutters, to an absolute minimum.

It is in the light of this situation that the constant complaints of modern cane planters about labour shortages must be interpreted. It was not, in general, a question of an absolute shortage, but of a specific shortage, which may be defined as follows: the lack of sufficiently large numbers of unemployed workers who could be forced to migrate to the sugar cane regions to work at cutting cane for three or four months at most and then to leave the area of the sugar mill at the end of the harvest. And all for a minimum wage that barely allowed physical subsistence, the poorest possible food and a hammock in a crude barrack, and with the further disadvantage that in many cases wages were not paid in legal currency but in tokens and vouchers whose circulation was limited to certain of the sugar mill's stores and shops.

In Cuba between 1899 and 1902, immediately after the War of Independence and during the U.S. intervention, certain sugar interests and mining companies repeatedly sought permission from the occupation authorities to import labourers, at the very time that a large army of unemployed workers were roaming the island's cities and countryside. The apparent contradiction serves to underline the sorry conditions obtaining in the agricultural sector of the sugar industry and mining: the native unemployed, badly off as they were, simply refused to work in mines or in the canefields where conditions were even worse.

The Cuban labour market of the time was unbalanced by extra-economic factors which brought about a particularly complex situation. Veterans of the *Ejército Libertador*, the Cuban Army of Liberation, for the most part blacks or mulattos (at least the rank and file), were emerging as a powerful force in the country's social and political life. They represented the most oppressed sectors, doubly exploited as workers and blacks. At the same time, as we have seen, commercial and sugar wealth was again principally in the hands of white Spaniards. The scene was thus set for Cuba's three basic socio-economic conflicts: class (employer–worker), race (white–black), and nationality (Spaniard–Cuban). The presence of a foreign army of occupation and a popular national army which was refusing to turn in its weapons provided an ominous background.

The insistent demand for permission to import foreign workers came principally from American sugar and mining companies operating in Cuba, rather than from the then predominant Spanish interests. In spite of this, these demands met with the refusal of the U.S. occupation authorities to allow any attempt at importing black West Indian workers into Cuba. In line with this policy, both the occupation authorities and the successive republican governments, dependent on the United States, showed great interest in stimulating immigration from Spain. This reciprocal policy of forbidding entry to blacks while encouraging Spanish immigrants (to the point of offering the soldiers of the defeated army of Spain the opportunity of remaining in Cuba) pursued three separate objectives of a social and political nature. First, to 'whiten' the island, to reduce the increasing political influence of the blacks and to try to limit this sector of the population to a mere source of cheap and pliant labour. Secondly, to denationalize Cuba, by a massive introduction of citizens of the very country whose colonial yoke Cuba had just shaken off. And thirdly, to win the backing of Spanish capitalists on the island, who had been unaffected by the war, and who had by this time become wholehearted partisans of United States annexation of Cuba. (In the event, the economic and racial confrontations intensified, but nationalist feelings became stronger and annexation could not be carried out.) United States opposition to the introduction of contract workers (black West Indians and Chinese coolies, principally) had a legal precedent: since the 1880s, entry of these workers into the United States was forbidden by law, and now that Cuba was occupied by the U.S. Army, it was argued that the same legislation held for the island. In spite of every difficulty, however, enough men were found to replant thousands of hectares and to cut the cane for each of the four harvests carried out under U.S. occupation (1899–1902) in so successful a process of recovery that in 1902 Cuba became the world's second sugar producer, with a harvest of 876,000 tons compared to Java's 897,000 tons.

The spectacular growth of the Cuban sugar industry between 1900 and 1925 – production, increasing at an annual rate of about 12 per cent, rose from 300,000 tons to 4.5 million tons – was linked to a simultaneous change in the geographical centre of the industry, which moved, as we have seen, from the densely populated western regions of the island east to sparsely populated Camagüey and northern Oriente. The construction of new sugar mills required not only a very large volume of capital investment but also the employment of thousands of workers to build the mills and install the machinery. In this task Spanish immigrants – officially favoured, as we have seen – played a decisive role. Between 1902 and 1911, Cuba received 322,878 immigrants; of these, 77.26 per cent were Spaniards. At the same time the number of cane-cutters needed to carry out the harvest increased from about 30,000 in 1900 to 315,000 in 1925. The need for cheap labour to work the newly-opened cane lands of Camagüey and Oriente eventually prevailed over the whites-only policy of the U.S. occupation years, and Cuba opened its doors to West Indian immigration.

The regular, legal, importation of contract workers seems to have begun in 1913 when a permit was given to the Nipe Bay Company to bring in a thousand Jamaican labourers. (Before this date a group of five thousand had already entered Cuba, but their entry, which appears in Jamaican emigration figures, is not reported in Cuban records.) Between 1913 and 1929 about 280,000 Haitians and Jamaicans entered Cuba. As this was a seasonal migration, many of these workers returned home at the end of the harvest. But many remained in Cuba, working on cane planting and cultivation and then trying somehow to tide over the gap between the coffee-picking season (September–November) and the sugar harvest (January–May). The overwhelming majority of those who remained in Cuba did so illegally: and their very illegality made them all the more vulnerable to exploitation. Living in the fields, huddled together, these West Indian workers, especially the Haitians, were a picture of the most degrading misery. The 1933 census gave a total of 79,838 Haitians and 40,471 Jamaicans living in Cuba, but the Cuban Immigration Department itself denied the accuracy of these figures and put the total of both nationalities at over 150,000. The sugar plantations finally had more than enough cheap labour, especially for cane-cutting.

The 1929 sugar harvest, like that of 1925, may have required some 315,000 workers: but by 1933, with the onset of the depression, possibly fewer than 100,000 were used. Exact data on unemployment and underemployment are unfortunately lacking. Photographs of the time show long lines of unemployed in front of sugar-mill offices, waiting for the opportunity to obtain a few days' work in the cane fields. Later official figures, corresponding to the recovery and boom years of the Cuban economy during World War II, show 50 per cent of the island's agricultural workers as being employed for only four months of the year.[21] If these are the figures for a period when the economic crisis was supposed to be over, then the figures for 1930–5 must have indeed been staggering.

The original, relatively sparse, population of Cuba, plus the characteristics of the immigration influx, resulted in the displacement of native workers by foreigners who, owing to their total lack of resources, were willing to work for less than the stipulated wages, and who, due to the illegality of their status (as was the case with the majority of the Haitians and Jamaicans who remained in Cuba), were susceptible to economic pressure and would thus accept conditions which would ordinarily be refused by a native worker. In addition, these illegal workers constituted a malleable group that could be used to break strikes, while at the same time, fearful of deportation, they were unwilling to take part in any organized labour movement. These conditions soon created a climate of xenophobia which during the depression led to the passage of the Labour Nationalization Decree of 8 November 1933, popularly known as the '50 per cent Law', whose object was to have a specific number of permanent foreign workers replaced in their jobs by Cubans. The measure was aimed particularly at the Spaniards (who for the most part held year-round jobs). The law did not solve, nor even attempt to face, the problem of unemployment: it merely shifted the burden of joblessness from one part of the population to another. As it applied to permanent (i.e., non-seasonal) jobs, it chiefly affected urban enterprises: shops, stores and small businesses where most of the Spanish immigrants worked.

The other principal legal measure of the depression years, aimed exclusively at the sugar industry, was the Decree of 19 October 1933, which ordered the obligatory repatriation of all foreigners who were unemployed and without means of support. This resulted in the forcible expulsion of Haitians and Jamaicans (principally the former) by the Cuban army in an operation marked by incidents of extreme violence. The actual number of Haitians deported, however, was less than 10,000: the pressure brought to bear by the sugar companies to protect their reserves of unemployed workers stopped the scandalous action.

[21] Julián Alienes Urosa, *Características fundamentales de la economía cubana* (Havana, 1950).

Conditions in the industrial sector of the Cuban sugar industry were completely different. It has already been indicated that cane agriculture, from planting to harvesting, showed the same patterns as those of the preceding centuries, and that the cane-cutter had virtually the same productivity in 1914 as in 1814. But the industrial sector of the industry, the sector that processed this primitively obtained cane, was the most up-to-date, the most technologically advanced and the most productive in the world. A primitive agriculture, with predominantly black labourers, a modern industry with white workers: the lopsided structure of the sugar industry, the cornerstone of Cuba's economy, underlined the dichotomy existing in society.

Industrial work created opportunities for united action on the part of workers which could hardly exist in the agricultural sector. By 1917 the industrial labour movement had advanced to the point where it could call a widespread strike which would affect several mills in the Cienfuegos area, at that time producing somewhat more than 30 per cent of Cuban sugar. The strikers' fundamental demands were for higher wages and an 8-hour work day. (The 8-hour work day was already in effect in many urban centres, but sugar mills still held to their traditional 12-hour work day of two *cuartos*, or 6-hour split shifts). The Cienfuegos strike had profound nation-wide repercussions. Labour unrest and work stoppages in individual mills had been common enough before, but this was the first time an entire important sugar region had been hit by this type of concerted action. Although they did not win all their demands, the workers did get a 10-hour work day, a 10 per cent wage increase and the elimination of payment in tokens or vouchers (although certain mills kept up the custom until the 1930s).[22]

After the end of the 1914–20 sugar boom, and especially after the sharp drop in sugar prices during 1929–33, labour strife increased in the Cuban sugar industry. The unity of the labour movement grew in direct proportion to the worsening of the economic crisis. The Sindicato Nacional de Obreros de la Industria Azucarera (National Union of Sugar Industry Workers, SNOIA) was formed, and held its first convention in December 1932, after a wave of strikes. However, according to the analysis made by the labour leaders themselves, these strikes did not affect Camagüey and Oriente, the two provinces that between them accounted for 56 per cent of all Cuban sugar production; and the great

22 An interesting account of this strike is to be found in John Demoulin, *Azúcar y lucha de clases* (Havana, 1980).

mass of immigrant Haitian and Jamaican workers could not be prevailed upon to join the strikes. Bearing in mind that it was precisely in these two eastern provinces that 90 per cent of these migrants worked, this serves to underline the argument already stressed: the mass of immigrant labour, besides providing plantations with cheap labour, also offered them the additional security that these workers would not join in the growing labour movement.

In 1933–4, with sugar prices at an all-time low, several of the largest *centrales* refused to accept the conditions demanded by the labour movement, threatening to close down and actually interrupting harvest preparations. In a situation marked by extreme tension and possibilities of great violence, the unions occupied twenty of these mills, holding the managers and top staff prisoner and setting up what they themselves called 'soviets'. In September 1934 such a 'soviet' was set up in Central Jaronú, at the time the world's largest sugar mill.[23] The government's reaction was to suspend constitutional guarantees and to establish life sentences, and even the death penalty, for those found guilty of setting fire to cane fields or other acts of sabotage. These repressive measures, on the one hand, and the rise in sugar prices and a definite improvement in working conditions, on the other, solved, or at least defused, the crisis.

In a way Puerto Rico presents a land–labour ratio that is the very antithesis of Cuba. When American troops occupied the two islands in 1898, their population densities were as follows: Cuba, 14.2 inhabitants per sq. km; Puerto Rico, 107.2 inhabitants per sq. km. This great difference in population has been used to explain the different demographic processes observed in the plantations of the two countries. But Malthusian interpretations are generally insufficient: the differences between Cuba and Puerto Rico went deeper than can be explained away by these population figures. In 1898, sugar was Cuba's principal crop; Puerto Rico's was coffee. Coffee required relatively less labour and capital investment than sugar; then, too, on average, coffee haciendas were smaller than sugar plantations. The last thirty years of the nineteenth century had seen a steep growth of coffee production in Puerto Rico and a decline of 40 per cent in the production of sugar, and this economic shift led to the foundation of a number of settlements in the central and western areas of the island – the main coffee regions – and

[23] This was the first time that the word 'soviet' was used in Cuba (and possibly in Latin America) as the name for a local worker–peasant council.

to a seasonal flow of internal migrations of workers who brought in the crop and then, in lesser numbers, went down to the plains to work in the cane harvest. As a result Puerto Rico's coffee growers talked of 'overpopulation' while its sugar producers were complaining of a lack of workers.

In the second half of the nineteenth century the coffee haciendas of Puerto Rico, and many sugar plantations, may be considered as a continuation of the slave plantation. At the same time slavery as a way of production had disintegrated and was finally abolished. The land–labour ratio did not lend itself to semi-slave forms of labour and there was, moreover, a shortage of capital. Under these conditions, the size of the average agricultural unit tended to be small (most were between 40 and 120 hectares), and workers were linked to their haciendas by wage considerations, by crop-sharing agreements, by an arrangement of part payment in cash and part in the use of *conucos*, or plots of land, for their own use, by family ties, or by a combination of these factors.[24] The 1899 census showed that 50 per cent of Puerto Rico's cultivated lands belonged to farms of under 20 hectares. Thus, it could be said that in this sense there was no real labour shortage; the labour force was dispersed and disunited; and there was no mass of agricultural workers available for contract wage relations. Population pressure was eased by migration. As far back as the 1870s groups of Puerto Rican workers began seasonal migrations to the sugar areas of Santo Domingo. In the 1880s the Asociación de Hacendados de la Isla de Cuba managed to divert this migration toward Cuban plantations. And in the early years of the twentieth century, when Puerto Rico had become an American colony, there occurred the unfortunate migrations to take part in the sugar harvests of Hawaii.

The United States' occupation of Puerto Rico in 1898, as we have seen, signalled a complete upheaval in the island's economic and social conditions. The transformation was so sudden that sugar's share of the island's total exports had risen in only three years from 30 per cent to 63 per cent. As a natural result of this shift in the centre of the island's economy, there was an immediate internal migratory movement which was the direct opposite of that of the previous thirty years: the trend of the population shift was away from the mountainous central and western

[24] For a study of haciendas and *conucos* in Venezuela in this period, see Gastón Carvallo and Josefina Ríos de Hernández, *Notas para el estudio del binomio plantación-conuco en la hacienda agrícola venezolana* (Caracas, 1977).

regions, and towards the cane-growing plains, especially in the south coastal region. Some of the latter places more than doubled their populations in a few years. Now that the island's economy responded mainly to the sugar interests, the existing population pressure became a problem of overpopulation, that is to say, a relative overpopulation deliberately created for the purpose of making possible the building of large *centrales*.

The redistribution of agricultural properties, the emergence of sugar latifundia (described in the preceding section) and the need for the maximum exploitation of possible sugar-cane lands, all tended to diminish the imbalance between the amount of land held and the amount actually cultivated, to suppress the acreage given over to *conucos* for subsistence farming, and to incorporate what was left of the old slave mills into the modern plantations. At the same time the coffee haciendas were in decline (in fact a consequence of natural forces), and at such a rate that by 1930 coffee represented a mere 1 per cent of Puerto Rican exports. Their age-old labour relations dissolved, and, with no access to plots of land for subsistence farming, the dispossessed peasantry became simple agricultural workers.

American investors found in Puerto Rico, especially in the sugar cane areas, exactly the opposite conditions to those prevailing in the underpopulated regions of Cuba. As has been seen, the abundance of cheap land in Cuba brought about a tendency toward extensive cultivation, which permitted using lesser amounts of scarce labour and making the most of available investment capital. In Puerto Rico it was land that was scarce, and this determined not only a policy of total land occupation – virtually land-grabbing – but also one of intensive cultivation. This process was carried out on the basis of massive injections of capital – in the form of agricultural machinery, fertilizers, etc. – which resulted in significant increases in yields of cane per area and per man-hour. The increase in productivity per area in turn reduced the number of man-hours per ton of cane grown and cut and per ton of sugar produced.

All of these factors – relative overpopulation, closing of sources of employment, introduction of modern technology – resulted in an unemployment rate which by the middle of the depression reached 37 per cent. This high level of unemployment in turn finally led to the proposing of an official 'solution': the emigration of the surplus population. Under the U.S. occupation of the Dominican Republic during the years 1916 to 1924 there had already emerged the project of 'settling' that country with Puerto Rican workers. The project fell through, though during that period at least one firm, the South Puerto Rico Sugar Company, which owned mills in Puerto Rico and in the Dominican Republic, used the surplus manpower from its Puerto Rican mill in its Dominican mill. During the 1920s there was a certain amount of emigration of Puerto Rican labour to Cuban sugar mills, and a special publicity campaign was even mounted toward this end. The newly formed Cuban workers' organizations attacked this campaign in a historic letter sent to the Spanish–Puerto Rican labour leader Santiago Iglesias.[25] Between 1910 and 1930 the total number of Puerto Rican emigrants was 46,794 persons. Between 1931 and 1934, due to the general conditions of unemployment prevailing in the United States as a result of the depression, there was a net influx of returning Puerto Ricans, but in 1935 the movement was once again emigratory as it has remained until the present.

In Puerto Rico, as in all Caribbean countries where the modern system of sugar plantations was implanted, there occurred the traumatic process of the conversion of large number of peasants and small farmers into agricultural proletarians. As a class, this proletariat channelled its actions chiefly through the Federación Libre de Trabajadores (Free Federation of Workers, FLT) founded at the end of the nineteenth century. In 1915 the Puerto Rican Socialist Party emerged from the FLT to act as its political arm. A statistical correlation has been shown to exist between the number of votes received by the Socialist Party and the incidence of cane cultivation in the different municipalities in the 1920 elections.[26] This correlation indicates a degree of class consciousness becoming evident at the time in a series of workers' actions which were increasingly widespread and radical. During the depression, the labour movement's protests against poor working conditions naturally intensified: in 1931–2 there were 10 strikes involving 3,355 workers; in 1932–3, 14 strikes involving 13,594 workers; and 1933–4 a total of 33,333 workers participated in 18 strikes.[27] The signing of the National Industrial Recovery Act in 1933 – one of the key New Deal measures to cope with the increasing amount of labour unrest in the United States – with its provisions establishing minimum wages, maximum number of work-

[25] First published in the Havana labour newspaper, *Justicia*, 16 Dec. 1922, 1–7.
[26] Angel Quintero-Rivera, *Conflictos de clase y lucha política en Puerto Rico* (San Juan, 1977). See also, Quintero-Rivera, *CHLA* v, ch 6.   [27] Gayer, *Sugar economy in Puerto Rico*, 223.

hours and the recognition of labour unions, etc., led to a wary truce between the workers and the sugar corporations and the following year both sides signed the historic *Convenio General*, the first large-scale agreement to regulate working conditions in the island's sugar industry. Under the terms of the *Convenio*, wages increased from 20 per cent to 69 per cent for different types of work, but the application of the Recovery Act in the United States had resulted in a sharp increase in food prices, and the average Puerto Rican agricultural worker's food bill increased by 58 per cent. On the whole, however, these workers' conditions did improve, especially when the price of sugar rose during the Second World War.

Cuba and Puerto Rico present two Caribbean variants of the same problem of labour in the sugar industry. The Dominican Republic offers in turn a third variant which is at present engaging the attention of social scientists: that of a country with an extremely high unemployment rate, a marked tendency of its population to emigrate in search of work and, at the same time, an influx of foreign labourers to work in the country's sugar mills.

This, of course, has not always been the case. At the end of the nineteenth century the Dominican Republic had a low population density with some 610,000 inhabitants in an area of 48,442 sq. km, or 12.6 inhabitants per sq. km. The agrarian structure was based on small farms, under which the peasants had multiple forms of access to title or ownership of the land.[28] In general, the economic writers of the country at that time referred to a 'natural', 'peasant' (*campesina*) or 'subsistence farming' (*conuquera*) economy, always noting the numerical superiority of small farmers; there was even a tendency to point out the advantages to be derived from agricultural diversification (tobacco, sugar, coffee, cacao, timber, fruits and vegetables, etc.). It was common in the writings of the time to find it stressed that these 'independent' peasants had no need to sell their labour to the incipient sugar corporations, or, if they did hire out, it was not on a regular basis. Understandably, then, from its very

---

[28] Cuba and Puerto Rico each have adequate agricultural statistics for the period under consideration. Until the 1920s, however, the Dominican Republic had no land register which would serve as a basis for analysing land holdings. This explains why all studies up till the present are based on partial investigations which gather data on some specific region or economic activity, but which in general are characterized by lack of precision. At any rate, the very lack of such a land register is by itself indicative of a situation in which land was not a decisive economic factor. From the beginning of the U.S. occupation, however, when the expansion of the cane areas caused property conflicts with small landowners, modern agricultural cadastres became vitally necessary.

beginnings the rebirth of the Dominican sugar industry depended on foreign labour.

At the western end of the island of Hispaniola lies the Republic of Haiti, with its high population pressure and one of the poorest economies in the world. These two factors have made Haiti, throughout the twentieth century, the source of the cheapest manpower in the Americas. Thus the Dominican sugar planters had at their borders the type of labour best suited to their interests. But the Dominican Republic and Haiti were separated by a centuries-long social and political conflict.[29]

Moreover cultural differences initially ruled out any attempt to introduce Haitian workers into the Dominican Republic: the Dominican planters, therefore, sought the labour force they needed for their sugar mills in the British West Indies. Thus, until the beginning of the American occupation in 1916, most foreign sugar workers were from the English-speaking Lesser Antilles. Due to the lack of official records, there are no reliable figures for the total number of these immigrant workers: it was only in the 1920s that official records began to be kept that allow estimates with an adequate range of reliability to be made.[30] However, between 1912 and 1920, an average of some 6,000 immigrant workers yearly is probably close enough.

But with the great industrial expansion brought about by the increasing influx of U.S. capital during the occupation period (1916–24), there began a steadily growing Haitian immigration, both legal and illegal, to make up the army of cheap and submissive workers that all planters sought. The collision between nationalistic cultural values and the economic realities that imposed the importation of a foreign labour force willing to work for wages that were under the subsistence level for a Dominican peasant (and especially from a country that had been regarded as an enemy for years) naturally produced constant and long-lasting internal conflicts.

As happened with the '50 per cent Law' in Cuba, a strong movement arose for 'nationals only' in the sugar mills, and this movement, plus the

---

[29] On relations between the Dominican Republic and Haiti in the period before 1870, see Moya Pons, *CHLA*, III, ch. 6.

[30] See José del Castillo, 'La inmigración de braceros azucareros en la República Dominicana, 1900–1930', *Cuadernos del Centro Dominicano de Investigaciones Antropológicas* (Universidad Autónoma de Santo Domingo), 7 (1978); and Patrick Bryan, 'The transformation of the economy of the Dominican Republic, 1870–1916', unpublished Ph.D. thesis, University of London, 1977.

effects of the world-wide depression and the xenophobia of the Trujillo regime then in power in the Dominican Republic, culminated in the slaughter of more than 12,000 Haitian immigrants in 1937.[31]

In spite of these tensions, the overwhelming majority of the cane-cutters for Dominican sugar harvests continued to be Haitians, as is still true today. An explanation of why this phenomenon has survived in conditions of high unemployment must be sought in a complex of economic and political factors. The first of these has already been stated in the Cuban case: when the rise in the industrial productivity of the sugar business approaches its limit, the reduction in costs is seen to be more and more a matter for the agricultural sector. And since the Dominican planters, like their Cuban counterparts, found it impossible to bring off an agricultural revolution in the short term and were tied to the same primitive cane-growing practices, cutting costs inevitably turns out to be paying agricultural workers the lowest possible wages. And the lowest wages paid in the Americas are those paid in Haiti, ranked by the United Nations as one of the ten poorest nations in the world. The concept of 'minimum wages' is a relative one, and the Haitian minimum is below the Dominican minimum.

Dominican planters have other advantages. The country's labour movement, the weakest in the Spanish-speaking Caribbean, has been unable to bring about any co-ordinated wave of strikes, stoppages or protests to force the sugar companies to raise wages. The movement, moreover, found itself in a situation from which it was not able to find a way out: it was too weak to fight against the importation of Haitian labour, and each wave of incoming foreign workers weakened it further.

The predominance of Haitians in the cane harvest, plus the low wages paid, created in the Dominican agricultural worker a negative reaction to this type of work, and further increased his already existing anti-Haitian prejudices. But the high rate of Dominican emigration, principally to the U.S., has reduced population pressure and thus defused the potentially explosive unemployment situation. A combination of labour relations and migratory phenomena unique in the Caribbean has thus taken shape in the Dominican Republic.

[31] The official explanation of this episode refers to armed incursions of Haitians against the Dominican Republic. Joaquín Balaguer, later president of the Dominican Republic, gave this explanation in a letter of 11 October 1945 to Roberto García Pena, editor of *El Tiempo* of Bogotá, while a government minister in 1945. (Andrés Corten *et al.*, *Azúcar y política en la República Dominicana* (2nd ed. Santo Domingo, 1976), 32.)

CONCLUSION

Thus, in conclusion, an attempt has been made to show that the sugar plantations in the Spanish-speaking Caribbean follow two clearly defined patterns. First, the plantation based on slave labour, which included an *ingenio*, a semi-mechanized mill or one still moved by animal power, producing a very low grade of muscovado sugar. It was characterized by its functional generality, that is, the slaves worked indiscriminately at any task, either in the cane-fields or in the mill itself. Besides slaves, workers might include coolies (contract labour) and a very small number of hired labourers. Secondly, the 'modern' sugar plantation, which produced the cane but did not process it, and was associated with a highly efficient and technically advanced mill, or *central*, producing a standardized raw sugar and presupposing a large capital investment. The 'new model' plantation was exclusively agricultural, the logical consequence of its functional specificity resulting from the division of labour. In this type of plantation, though ostensibly adapted to post-slavery conditions, there still prevailed ways of exploiting the hired labourer either by simple starvation, or else subsistence wages, paid in tokens redeemable only in company stores, etc. From the technological point of view there had been no advance: its agricultural methods and implements were as primitive, and its productivity almost as low, as the old-style plantation. The *central* was not a plantation; from its inception it was the intermediate industrial link between the plantation and the foreign refineries. The *central* supplied the latter with a standardized semi-processed raw material (Pol 96° raw sugar) which they processed into different forms of refined sugar. The *central* and the plantation were not, of course, independent of each other, but were linked by common ownership or contractual bonds, but in either case it was the *central* which dominated the plantation. The great modern *centrales*, with their associated plantations, were extremely profitable concerns, especially for those foreign corporations which started to invest in them in the early years of this century. But due to the seasonal nature of the work they provided, the conflictive labour relations in them, their tendency to create latifundia, their deliberate continuation of primitive forms of extensive cultivation on their associated plantations, the economic and social domination they exercised over their entire zone of operations, etc., the *centrales* created political and labour problems of such magnitude that, inevitably, they came to be rejected by almost all sectors of the population, even when they were the chief source of labour and income for the country in which they were established. The rejection was even more noticeable in times of economic crises because of the open opposition of nationalist movements and labour and peasant organizations who demanded an end to the constant flight of capital, to latifundia and to the power of the foreign corporations. From a purely economic point of view, moreover, the contrast between the backward agricultural sector, the plantation, and the industrial sector, the *central*, created increasing difficulties which ended by destroying the originally high profitability of the investment. The emerging labour movements, as they became more united and stronger, made it difficult to continue the crude forms of labour exploitation: wages had therefore to be raised. To offset the increases, it became necessary to improve the primitive techniques of agriculture by such means as fertilizers, irrigation and mechanization, which only reduced profits even further. Simultaneously with these local factors, other external circumstances were contributing to the disintegration and downfall of the plantation in the Spanish Caribbean: the inflexibility of sugar prices (both on international markets and in the local markets of importing countries), the large amounts of subsidized sugar produced by developed countries (especially in Europe), the trend towards lower per capita consumption of sugar: all these factors affected the world sugar market unfavourably. The peak of the crisis was marked, first, by a reduction in new investment and, eventually, by the transfer of ownership to local groups. By that time, however, other fields were offering better returns on investment than did the sugar industry.

7

THE GROWTH OF LATIN AMERICAN CITIES, 1870–1930

INTRODUCTION

The European or North American who visited Latin America in the years before 1870 invariably came away struck by the diversity of the area – in geography, in people, in environment. Cities there were. Indeed cities had played a dominant role in the development of Spanish America at least, even when they contained only a small percentage of the area's total population. But generally they appeared small, poor and broken down. Far more impressive was the countryside of Latin America – the imposing Andean mountains, the vast Amazonian jungle, the endless grasslands of the llanos or the pampas, the picturesque Indian hamlets, the enormous landed estates. Consequently it was rural Latin America that most vividly emerged from the travel accounts, letters and dispatches of the middle decades of the nineteenth century. Nevertheless, a bird's eye view of the Latin American city in 1870 will set the stage for the dramatic changes that the ensuing decades brought to the area's urban landscape.

Even the largest Latin American cities appeared small, in large measure because of their plaza-orientation. Both the residences of the wealthy and the powerful and the principal urban activities of administration, services and trade were concentrated around the central plaza. Rio de Janeiro, Havana, Mexico City and Buenos Aires all had central districts of only a few hundred blocks. These areas, often extending no more than five or ten blocks from the main plaza, had the appearance of an urbanized zone: substantial housing, paving, sidewalks and street lights. Located in this central district were markets, offices, stores, clubs, theatres, churches and schools to serve the elite. Beyond this core extended the shacks of the poor, the rutted dusty lanes of outlying districts, and an environment that appeared more rural than urban to the casual observer.

In these small urban centres, the homes of families, especially of the upper class, were protected from the city. Hispanic patio architecture prevailed. Behind thick walls, solid wooden doors and grilled windows a self-contained social existence, depending little on the outside world, had developed. Set on elongated urban lots, running back from the street as much as three to four times their twenty- or thirty-yard width, these comfortable residences sheltered patios, wells, gardens, fruit trees, woodsheds, latrines, chickens, ducks, occasionally even some goats, pigs, or horses, along with servants, distant cousins, maiden aunts, or some employees and their families. There was little temptation to display wealth since only family members entered this sanctuary.

The bulk of the urban population – labourers, servants, artisans – lived much more modestly. Their houses, made of the cheapest local materials, such as canes, branches, straw, or stones, were erected on the urban fringes, often as much as a couple of miles from the main plaza. Although their daily diet consisted of no more than one or two items – corn, beans, potatoes or manioc, depending on the zone – and did not include seasonal fruits and vegetables or meat, these lower classes, by living in or moving to the city, had nevertheless escaped much of the exploitation and controls associated with Latin America's rural scene. The demand for their skills and services within the urban money economy even enabled some to improve their economic and social standing.

In this apparently primitive and static urban environment, Europe's industrial revolution had sown the seeds of change. The rising demand from Europe's markets and factories for the wide range of foodstuffs and raw materials which could be produced in Latin America, combined with the new-found capacity of local inhabitants to buy manufactures from abroad, was beginning to stimulate levels of trade unthinkable in the colonial period. And new technology further increased commercial activity. Steam navigation doubled the capacity of ships in the two decades before 1870 and halved the time needed to cross the Atlantic. Not only could far greater quantities be transported for much less, but also, with the added refinements of refrigeration and improved handling in the 1870s, even perishable products would enter world commerce. By mid-century the results were notable. The import of French wines into Buenos Aires rose from 500 barrels a year prior to 1850 to more than 300,000 barrels by the 1870s, while wool exports increased from 7,000 tons to 100,000 tons a year. In Brazil, coffee exports rose from an annual

19,000 tons in the 1820s to 158,000 tons in the 1850s. The foreign trade of Chile trebled in the period between 1845 and 1860. Several coastal cities expanded from fishing or coastal hamlets into major harbours: Tampico in Mexico, Colón in Panama, Barranquilla in Colombia, Bahía Blanca in Argentina.

Railways worked even more important changes. Freight costs dropped to one-twelfth of those charged by oxcarts and mule-trains, while the speed of transportation increased thirty times. Although railways tended to follow the well-worn paths of earlier trade routes, they brought unusual vitality to any centre cast in the role of a hub or terminus. Thus, Valparaíso's surprising doubling of population between 1850 and 1870 probably owed as much to the completion in 1863 of the railway from the Chilean capital as to its privileged location on the Pacific Ocean. Rosario, likewise, nearly doubled in size in the decade following completion in 1870 of the first major railway from this river port into the interior of Argentina. Panama emerged from serious economic prostration once the trans-isthmus railway to Colón had been completed in 1855. The railway link to Rio de Janeiro and to the coast at Santos sparked the beginnings of São Paulo's vertiginous growth after 1870.

The railway and the steamship, by their very nature as greatly improved freight vehicles, thus encouraged concentration of commerce. Rather than disseminating the effects of increased trade, the new transportation technology stimulated growth of the already existing centres. The larger volume of goods transported by individual trains meant that cargoes had to be handled at central locations in order to utilize carrying capacity to the maximum. Shipping companies, because of the still greater volume of freighters and the cost of repeated stops, sought to load and unload at a single emporium in each country. The Pacific Steam Navigation Company made regular calls at Valparaíso, Callao and Guayaquil, while, by the 1860s, British and French lines regularly stopped at the Caribbean ports of Veracruz, Colón, Cartagena, La Guaira and Havana, and at the South Atlantic ports of Rio de Janeiro, Montevideo and Buenos Aires.

Capital cities, possessing facilities for handling the flow of finished imports and raw material exports and containing substantial upper- and middle-class elements to consume European goods, benefited the most. The greatest growth occurred at the coastal capitals: Buenos Aires, Montevideo, Rio de Janeiro, Lima with its adjacent port of Callao, and Caracas with its nearby outlet at La Guaira. But the building of a railway link to the nearest seaport also tended to stimulate the growth of inland capitals as well as their outlets, as in the case of Santiago and Valparaíso, Mexico City and Veracruz, or in Brazil's developing coffee area with the capital of the state of São Paulo and its port at Santos.

By 1870, however, the new technology and increased trade had brought few changes to the quality of urban life, even in the ports and major cities. Ports still gave few signs of frantic activity. The bales of hides or wool, the bags of coffee beans or wheat or coarse sugar, the crates of European finery, foodstuffs and hardware had not yet acquired sufficient volume to produce more than a lethargic movement of stevedores and peons. The arrival of a ship or train might stir a temporary bustle, but tranquillity soon returned.

Except for commerce and business, little drew either the well-to-do out of their homes or the poor from their remote suburbs. Thus, movement on the streets was slight – servants out on errands, an occasional group of women headed for Mass, or a passing carriage or horseman. Streets, rarely wider than the thirty-foot standard established at the time of the Conquest, seemed even narrower and darker, closed in as they were by the solid masonry walls of buildings that rose from the very edge of the sidewalks and overhung by balconies at the second- and third-floor levels. Paving stones had somewhat improved the condition of the streets, but potholes, dust or mud, and refuse abounded. As in the medieval city, many a household, even of the well-to-do, discarded table scraps and rubbish along with the contents of chamber pots into the street. Drains, which at intervals crossed streets in the centre, helped in rainy climates and hilly terrain to flush away some of the accumulating filth, but nothing could disguise their primary function as open sewers. The rural presence seemed everywhere ready to overwhelm the city. Stray animals, pigs and dogs in particular, roamed the streets and with their foraging supplemented the sporadic collection of garbage. Cows, driven from door to door, brought daily milk to wealthy homes. Mules, donkeys and horses likewise carried merchandise and food supplies to individual doorways, while troops of animals on the way to market or carrying merchandise continued to be a common sight in many Latin American cities until the end of the nineteenth century. And all those who could travelled the streets on horseback rather than on foot. Flickering torches or oil lamps had been attached to fronts of some buildings even in the colonial period and were lit for several hours in the evening. But few individuals chose to venture forth at night. In case of need, the wise individual equipped himself with sword or pistol and a lantern and, in the company of a few armed friends or relatives, mounted horses for a night-time trip across town. Security consisted of some night watchmen who called out the hours but hardly served as an effective police force.

During the last decades of the nineteenth century, however, the urban landscape of Latin America was completely transformed by a number of different but interconnected factors: population growth and an acceleration in the pace of urbanization; the more effective integration of the Latin American economies into the world economy as primary producers; the beginnings of industrial growth in some areas; improved transportation and public services; national political integration and administrative centralization; increased social differentiation; and, not least, the gradual move of elite groups away from their traditional locus near the main plaza towards outlying suburbs. Many secondary cities as well as towns and villages often appeared frozen in a past century, but the primary cities of Latin America, at least, changed dramatically in size and structure. And nearly everywhere the capital cities came to possess striking similarities to, and enjoyed many of the amenities of, the major European and North American cities.

URBAN POPULATION AND SIZE OF CITIES

The worldwide expansion of population and concentration of people in cities had acquired new intensity during the nineteenth century. In the industrializing nations of Europe, especially England, the rate of population growth and of urban expansion seemed the most pronounced, but the factors influencing that growth also applied in some fashion to non-industrialized or marginally industrializing areas, including Latin America. The revolutionary changes in agricultural production, the development of mechanization and the use of steam power, the rapid application of technology to transport, particularly the railways and steamships, the accompanying specialization of labour and of commercial and industrial functions, and the measures for sanitation and control of epidemics, especially within the cities, permitted and encouraged an increase and a concentration of population hitherto unthinkable.

All of these factors began to play major roles in Latin America during the final decades of the nineteenth century. Perhaps most dramatic was the decline of the death rate, especially in the largest cities which could afford water and sewer works. Infant mortality from gastroenteritis fell dramatically, above all in the lower classes, while measures to control epidemics such as yellow fever added their impact. Birth rates, meanwhile, showed, with a few exceptions, little tendency to decline, even in the urban environment. At the same time the railway and steamship added powerful incentives and facilities for expanding the increasingly profitable export of agricultural and mineral products and concentrating the necessary processing and merchandising of goods. This transportation revolution stimulated considerable migration to cities and, in a few areas, massive immigration into both city and countryside.

As a result of these factors, the period from 1850 to 1930 marked an upturn in Latin America's total population growth and, after 1900, a more rapid increase than in Europe or North America. The population of Latin America grew from 30.5 million in 1850 to 61.9 million in 1900 and 104.1 million in 1930.[1] Latin America's population, which in absolute figures had fallen behind the rapid surge of the United States and the Canadian growth by the 1880s, finally overtook North America again in the 1950s as the birth rate there slowed. During these years (and as continued by demographic projection to at least the year 2000) Latin America showed relatively little tendency to replicate the European or North American model where lowered birth rates slowed population growth.

Within this overall framework of population expansion, the individual Latin American countries showed wide variations that would in turn affect their degree of urbanization. In all cases, however, rapid increases in total population resulted in high rates of urbanization. Uruguay and Argentina, the two countries with the highest percentage of their populations living in cities by 1930, were those with the highest average annual rate of growth. The sharp rise in the urban populations of Brazil and Cuba in the early twentieth century was likewise related to their increased growth rate. In each of these four cases, improved public health and mass immigration resulting from economic changes fuelled the increase and facilitated the urban explosion. Chile, Colombia and Peru, with lower but regular rates of growth largely untouched by massive immigration, contributed less spectacular urban expansion.

---

[1] See Sánchez-Albornoz, *CHLA* IV, chap. 4, table 1.

Elsewhere, Mexico's population growth and urban development was slowed by the revolutionary years following 1910, while in Venezuela the relatively low rate of population growth brought few changes in the level of urbanization.

Thus, the period 1870–1930 witnessed a wide variety of urban growth patterns in Latin America. Curiously, however, the urban population in Latin America cannot be established with anywhere near the accuracy that exists for total population figures. The statistics in Table 1 provide the best available estimate for Latin America's urban population during these years, but the reader must be aware of the limitations of the data.[2]

The distinction between urban and rural population was never clearly established in contemporary accounts or censuses or in the historical literature. Although students of urbanization today have largely agreed on 20,000 inhabitants as the lower limit for the study of the contem-

---

[2] The following information, taken from the Library of Congress, *General Censuses and Vital Statistics of the Americas* (Washington, D.C., 1943), provides some measure of the problems faced by those seeking to compare urban population data prior to 1940 in different Latin American countries.

Argentina: Good census data with urban centres detailed down to 2,000 inhabitants; widely-spread censuses, 1869, 1895 and 1914.

Bolivia: Only one published census in 1900 based on very incomplete returns.

Brazil: No distinction of urban populations made prior to 1940; all censuses – 1872, 1890, 1900 and 1920 – criticized for serious defects in enumeration.

Chile: Although nineteenth-century distinctions between urban and rural areas defective, advantages in urban populations down to 1,000 inhabitants and in frequency of censuses – 1865, 1875, 1885, 1895, 1907, 1920, 1930.

Colombia: Censuses of 1870, 1912, 1918, 1928 and 1938 all hampered by under-enumeration and lack of accurate distinction between urban and rural populations.

Costa Rica: First adequate census dates from 1927.

Cuba: Limitations of under-enumeration and absence of urban–rural distinctions in Spanish censuses of 1877 and 1887; comprehensive United States census in 1899; subsequent enumerations of 1907, 1919 and 1931 primarily concerned with securing information for electoral allotments.

Dominican Republic: First censuses date from 1920 and 1935.

Ecuador: No census fully carried out or published.

Guatemala: Serious under-enumeration problems and absence of urban–rural distinctions in censuses of 1880, 1893 and 1921.

Haiti: No census carried out or published.

Mexico: First national census dates from 1895; following ones of 1900, 1910 and 1921 criticized for serious defects in enumeration; 1930 contains urban–rural distinction and extensive breakdowns of population.

Paraguay: 1886 census incomplete and 1936 census never published.

Peru: 1876 suffered from serious under-enumeration and absence of urban–rural distinction; no subsequent census until 1940.

Uruguay: Censuses of 1860, 1873 and 1900 provided brief resumés only; 1908 census last taken until 1960s because Uruguayans considered censuses an invasion of privacy.

Venezuela: Serious problems of lack of urban–rural distinction; 1873 and 1881 censuses criticized for serious enumeration defects; subsequent censuses in 1891, 1920, 1926 and 1936 show some improvements.

Table 1. *Population in major types of urban settlement as a percentage of total national population*

(Number of settlements in each category in brackets)

Country	1 Total national population (000s)	2 Primary cities (over 100,000)	3 Secondary cities (20,000 to 99,999)	4 Towns (10,000 to 19,999)	5 Villages (5,000 to 9,999)
Argentina					
1869	1,737	(1) 10.8	(2) 3.8	(5) 3.5	(12) 4.7
1895	3,955	(1) 16.8	(7) 7.4	(8) 2.6	(29) 5.0
1914	7,885	(3) 24.1	(19) 9.4	(26) 4.6	(80) 7.1
Brazil					
1872	10,112	(3) 4.9	(10) 3.6		
1890	14,334	(4) 5.8	(11) 2.8	(19) 2.4	
1940	41,570	(10) 10.7	(31) 4.6		
Chile					
1875	2,076	(1) 6.3	(1) 4.7	(6) 4.2	(14) 4.3
1895	2,696	(2) 14.0	(4) 5.0	(6) 2.8	(22) 5.9
1930	4,287	(2) 20.7	(13) 11.7	(17) 5.6	(22) 3.7
Colombia					
1870	2,951	—	(2) 2.4	(7) 2.7	
1905	4,144	(1) 2.9	(6) 4.8	(5) 1.7	
1928	7,851	(1) 1.8	(15) 6.9		
Cuba					
1877	1,509	(1) 13.2	(3) 7.4		
1899	1,573	(2) 15.0	(5) 10.0	(7) 5.7	
1931[a]	4,962	(2) 12.7	(8) 7.4	(26) 7.4	(28) 2.9
Mexico					
No census data available prior to 1895					
1900	13,607	(2) 3.3	(21) 6.0	(35) 3.4	
1930	16,553	(4) 8.8	(26) 6.8	(51) 4.3	(137) 5.6
Peru					
1876	2,700	(1) 3.7	(2) 2.2	(10) 4.7[b]	
No intervening census data available between 1876 and 1940					
1940	6,208	(1) 8.4	(10) 6.2	(41) 6.0	
Venezuela[c]					
1873	1,725	—	(4) 7.3	(14) 9.5	
1891	2,222	—	(4) 8.5	(23) 14.2	
1926	3,027	(1) 4.5	(11) 12.5	(45) 19.7	

porary city, no such standard numerical distinction was imposed by census takers or analysts in the nineteenth century. The retrospective imposition of a dividing line between what was urban and what was rural must contend with several problems. Depending on the country or the year, cities might be defined as populations whose minimum size ranged from 500 to 2,500 inhabitants, or as heads of municipalities whose populations occasionally numbered only a few hundred inhabitants. Even when standard minima have been established, one must face the frustrating fact that in Latin America the area or boundaries of a municipality vary enormously from country to country. Frequently, then as today, municipalities enclosed sizeable areas of farms and rural settlements and thus could distort the 'urban' population by several hundred per cent. The Brazilian publications, for example, make no attempt to distinguish between urban and rural populations until the 1940 census. In Venezuela, Colombia and Peru no systematic measures exist to separate individuals living along streets of a town or city from those on farms or in rural settlements on the outskirts.

Beyond numerical considerations lie more subjective judgements of function, attitude and way of life that may distinguish an urban from a rural population. For example, village communities often contained several thousand peasants. These settlements, especially characteristic of certain highland and Indian areas of Mexico, Guatemala, Ecuador, Peru, and Bolivia, seemed to possess few, if any, urban elements. At the same time, a railroad depot almost anywhere in Latin America with its few adjoining stores and houses and several hundred inhabitants might claim many more facilities generally associated with a city and represent an urban way of life.

Beyond these difficulties in defining what was urban as opposed to rural lie further distinctions imposed by the size of the urban settlement. Enormous differences exist between the urban centre of several thousand inhabitants and those with more than a million inhabitants. In order to relate these differences to the number of city dwellers in each country and at the same time make some viable definitions of urban

Notes
[a] In 1931 census categories, secondary cities equivalent to 25,000–99,999; towns, 8,000–24,999; and villages, 4,000–7,999.
[b] Estimated data
[c] Data for secondary cities and towns questionable because of possible inclusion of rural populations within urban classifications.

Table 2. *Population of urban centres variously classified as a percentage of total population, 1870–1930*

Country	National classifications (over 2,000)	In centres over 20,000	In centres over 10,000	In centres over 5,000
Argentina				
1869	28.6	13.8	17.3	22.0
1895	37.4	24.2	26.8	31.8
1914	52.7	33.5	38.1	45.2
Brazil				
1872	—	8.5	—	—
1890	—	8.6	11.0	—
1940	22.5	15.3	—	—
Chile				
1875	24.0	11.0	15.2	19.5
1895	32.7	19.0	21.8	27.7
1930	46.1	32.4	38.0	41.7
Colombia				
1870	—	2.4	5.1	—
1905	—	7.7	9.4	—
1928	—	8.7	—	—
Cuba				
1877	—	20.6	—	—
1899	—	25.0	30.7	—
1931	—	20.1	27.5	30.4
Mexico				
1900	—	9.3	12.7	—
1930	37.2	15.6	19.9	25.5
Peru				
1876	—	5.9	10.6	—
1940	26.9	14.6	—	20.6
Venezuela				
1873	—	7.3	16.8	—
1891	—	8.5	22.7	—
1926	—	17.0	36.7	—

(Tables 1 & 2) *Sources:* Richard M. Morse, *Las ciudades latinoamericanas* (2 vols., Mexico, D.F., 1973), II, 62–3, 82–4, 120–1, 144–5, 164, 174–5, 200, 214; Jorge E. Hardoy and María E. Langdon, 'Análisis estadístico preliminar de la urbanización de América Latina entre 1850 y 1930', *Revista Paraguaya de Sociología*, 42–3 (1978), 115–73; Nicolás Sánchez-Albornoz, *The population of Latin America* (Berkeley, Calif., 1974), 178–9; William P. McGreevey, *An economic history of Colombia, 1845–1930* (New York, 1971), 110;

settlements which can be stated in numerical terms, four categories have been established for eight major Latin American countries in Table 1: primary cities with populations over 100,000; secondary cities with 20,000 to 100,000 inhabitants; towns with populations of 10,000 to 20,000; and villages, 5,000 to 10,000 inhabitants. Since data in some of these categories cannot accurately be estimated for several countries, percentages of urban population have been indicated on the basis of three numerical definitions: over 20,000 inhabitants with data available for all countries; over 10,000; and over 5,000 with data available only for Argentina and Chile (see Table 2).

Despite the fragmentary nature of the data, several interesting conclusions emerge from these figures. No matter what definition of urban is adopted, there is a significant increase in the percentage of total population living in cities in all eight countries during the sixty years from 1870 to 1930. Argentina, Chile, Cuba and Venezuela are clearly the most urbanized nations of this group. In three out of four cases the increase in urban population is impressive: the number of Argentines living in centres over 10,000 inhabitants in size increased from 17.3 per cent to 38.1 per cent of the national population; of Chileans from 15.2 per cent to 38.0 per cent; and of Venezuelans from 16.8 per cent to 36.7 per cent. Quite different are the cases of Brazil, Colombia, Mexico and Peru. Instead of one-third or more of the populace living in centres of over 10,000 inhabitants by 1930, the proportion is closer to 15 per cent.

The primary cities, which, except for Brazil, Mexico, and Argentina, never numbered more than two in each country, absorbed a substantial

Sources cont.

Miguel Izard, *Series estadísticas para la historia de Venezuela* (Mérida, 1970), 54–60; Peru, Oficina Nacional de Estadística y Censos, *La población del Perú* (Lima, 1974), 147–8; Argentina, *IV censo general de la nación* (3 vols., Buenos Aires, 1948–52), I, 68, 146–9, 171, 198–9, 226, 246, 263, 284, 307, 331, 355, 372, 397–8, 424, 440, 472, 530, 546; Mariano Felipe Paz Soldán, *Diccionario geográfico-estadístico del Perú* (Lima, 1877), 716–40; Chile, *X censo de la población* (3 vols., Santiago, 1931–5), I, 46–9; Brazil, *Análise de resultados do censo demográfico* (12 vols., Rio de Janeiro, 1944–50), IX, 9; Mexico, *V censo de la población* (8 vols., Mexico, D.F., 1933–5), Table III from each state's statistical section; John Durand and César A. Pelaez, 'Patterns of urbanization in Latin America', *Milbank Memorial Fund Quarterly*, 32/4, part 2 (1965), 166–96; Venezuela, *V censo nacional, 1926* (4 vols., Caracas, 1926).

Without making them responsible for any errors that this data may contain, I express my appreciation for assistance in the search for information to Nicolás Sánchez-Albornoz, John Lombardi, Thomas Davies, Jr, Brian Loveman, Richard M. Morse, Joseph Love and Stuart Schwartz.

proportion of that increase. One can clearly conclude from these figures that the contemporary phenomenon of concentration of growth and resources in major centres had its roots in this period of rapid expansion of both national populations and urban centres. In Argentina and Cuba that concentration in one major city already contributed slightly over 10 per cent of the national population by the 1870s. While that proportion held steady for Cuba's two largest cities in 1931, by 1914 Argentina's three largest cities contributed nearly one-quarter of the national total. Elsewhere the 6.3 per cent of the national total living in Santiago, Chile, in 1875 had risen by 1930 to 20.7 per cent divided between Santiago and Valparaíso. In Peru, Lima claimed 3.7 per cent of the total population in 1876 and 8.4 per cent by 1940. Mexico's 3.3 per cent located in Mexico City and Guadalajara in 1900[3] had increased to 8.8 per cent distributed between Mexico City, Guadalajara, Monterrey and Puebla in 1930. The only exception to this pattern appeared in Colombia where the country's one primary city, Bogotá, declined from 2.9 per cent of the national total in 1905 to 1.8 per cent by 1928.

Contained within the category of primary cities was the related phenomenon of the primate city or single large urban centre that towered over all other populations in the country. In recent years, scholars and analysts have determined that the primate city often dominates and directs the economic and political development of Latin American countries. Migrants have poured into each country's major city, swelling its population to one-fifth, and in some cases one-third, of the national total. Resources in terms of political power, consumer demand and industrial potential are overwhelmingly concentrated at this core.

According to the simplest definition, the tendency toward primacy is indicated by a population more than double that of the second-ranked city within a country. Table 3 ranks in descending order of primacy (as of 1930) the capitals of the eight largest Latin American nations, with populations for the two largest cities in each country for 1870 and 1930. By this definition, the primate city had major importance in Cuba, Mexico, Argentina and Peru in 1870 and in all these countries, plus Chile, in 1930. Brazil showed the least tendency by 1930 toward primacy, although in the Brazilian case one can argue that because of the territorial size of that nation, the largest primary cities – Rio de Janeiro, São Paulo,

---

[3] The first Mexican census dates from 1895, so earlier data remains a matter of conjecture.

Table 3. *Degree of primacy for capitals of major Latin American countries, in 1930 and 1870, determined by ratio of population in largest city to country's second-ranked city, arranged in descending order of primacy as of 1930*

Country	First & second cities	Date of data	1st city (000s)	2nd city (000s)	Ratio
1. Cuba	Havana/Santiago	(1931)	654	102	6.4
	Havana/Santiago	(1875) (1879)	230	45	5.1
2. Mexico	Mexico City/Guadalajara	(1930)	1,049	180	5.8
	Mexico City/Guadalajara	(1877)	230	65	3.5
3. Argentina	Buenos Aires/Rosario	(1932) (1930)	2,178	481	4.5
	Buenos Aires/Córdoba	(1869)*a*	187	29	6.4
4. Peru	Lima/Arequipa	(1931) (1933)	273	66	4.1
	Lima/Arequipa	(1876)	100	29	3.4
5. Chile	Santiago/Valparaíso	(1930)	696	193	3.6
	Santiago/Valparaíso	(1875)	150	98	1.5
6. Colombia	Bogotá/Medellín	(1938)	330	168	2.0
	Bogotá/Medellín	(1870)	41	30	1.4
7. Venezuela	Caracas/Maracaibo	(1936)	203	110	1.8
	Caracas/Valencia	(1873)	49	29	1.7
8. Brazil	Rio de Janeiro/São Paulo	(1940)*b*	1,519	1,258	1.2
	Rio de Janeiro/Salvador	(1872)	275	129	2.1

Source: Jorge E. Hardoy and María Elena Langdon, 'Análisis estadístico preliminar de la urbanización de América Latina entre 1850 y 1930', *Revista Paraguaya de Sociología*, 42–43 (1978), 146–8.

a For this case, data comes from Argentina, IV *censo general de la nación* (3 vols., 1948–52), I, 68 and 198.

b For this case, data comes from Brazil, *Análise de resultados do censo demográfico* (12 vols., 1944–50), IX, 9.

Recife, Salvador and Porto Alegre in 1930 – each functioned as a primate city for its region. Colombia's and Venezuela's capitals clearly fell short of primacy. Among the smaller nations an overwhelming one-third of the population of Uruguay was concentrated in Montevideo; in 1930 no city even reached one-twentieth of its size. At the other extreme, in Ecuador, the highland capital of Quito, with over 100,000 inhabitants by 1930, had virtually the same population as its rival, the tropical seaport of Guayaquil.

A more sophisticated approach expands this simple definition of primacy by examining the rank–size distribution of cities on the assumption that the more this distribution diverges from the lognormal pattern (with the second, third, fourth and etc. cities having half, one-third and one-quarter respectively of the population of the first city) the greater the tendency toward primacy. This shows that the capitals of Mexico, Cuba and Chile had already achieved a significant degree of primacy by 1870; that in Argentina, Brazil and Peru a primate structure developed between 1870 and 1930; while primacy for Venezuela's and Colombia's capitals came only in the 1960s.[4] This approach increases our understanding of the historical origins of primacy in Latin America. Its more sophisticated measurements indicate, for example, that despite the presence of several major primary cities in Brazil, Rio de Janeiro had established its primacy in the course of the early twentieth century.

At the level of secondary cities (20–100,000 inhabitants), growth in terms of both absolute numbers and percentages of national population also occurred, although rarely at the rate of primary cities or primate cities. Argentina's two secondary cities in 1869 together had 3 per cent of the national total; by 1914, this category had increased to 19 cities with 9.4 per cent. In Chile the increase was from one city with 4.7 per cent in 1875 to 13 cities with 11.7 per cent by 1930; in Colombia from two cities with 2.4 per cent in 1870 to 15 cities with 6.9 per cent by 1928; in Mexico from 21 cities with 6 per cent in 1900 to 26 with 6.8 per cent by 1930; in Peru from two cities with 2.2 per cent in 1876 to 10 cities with 6.2 per cent by 1940; and in Venezuela from four cities in 1873 with 7.3 per cent to 11 cities 12.5 per cent by 1926.[5]

At the town level (10–20,000 inhabitants) the growth was generally more modest than for secondary cities. Argentina, Brazil, Chile, Colombia, Mexico and Peru usually recorded between 3 and 5 per cent of the population living in towns. Venezuela provided the only significant departure from this trend with nearly 20 per cent of its population located in towns by 1926. This latter data may be inflated by sizeable rural areas included within town boundaries, but also, since Venezuela did not have as much of its population concentrated in primary and secondary cities, the locus for urban dwellers may well have been skewed in favour of the towns. Cuba also showed some tendency in this direction with 7.4

[4] See William P. McGreevey, 'Un análisis estadístico de hegemonía y lognormalidad en la distribución de tamaños de las ciudades de América Latina', in Richard M. Morse (ed.), *Las ciudades latinoamericanas* (2 vols., Mexico, D.F., 1973), II, 231.

[5] In the case of both Venezuela and Colombia in 1870, the capital cities Caracas and Bogotá, are included within the category of secondary cities.

per cent of the national total in towns in 1931 – the same percentage as recorded for secondary cities.

Generalization at the village level (5–10,000 inhabitants) is only possible for Argentina and Chile and in 1930 for Mexico.[6] In the other countries census takers failed to distinguish contiguous urban-type housing from isolated rural farms or small clusters of housing in the countryside. In Argentina, there appears to have been substantial growth in village settlements, somewhat more than in towns and parallel to that for secondary cities, while in Chile and in Mexico the village pattern more closely resembled that for towns.

These considerations of urban population and size of cities in Latin America point to several conclusions: first, the number of urban inhabitants and the proportion of the national population living in cities increased substantially in the major Latin American countries between 1870 and 1930, a period of rapid increase in total population; secondly, those countries with the greatest increase in total population, often accentuated by massive immigration, were also the ones where urbanization proceeded most rapidly; thirdly, the largest cities tended to grow most rapidly and to absorb an ever larger percentage of total population; fourthly, the extraordinary growth of national capitals confirmed a tendency towards primacy in most of the larger countries as well as in several of the smaller countries; fifthly, while secondary cities, towns and villages also increased in numbers and in percentage of total national population, they gained a far smaller proportion of urban population.

ECONOMIC FUNCTION: COMMERCE, BUREAUCRACY AND
INDUSTRY

The variations in the population and size of Latin American cities resulted in large measure from differences in economic function. Commerce proved to be the dominant factor in all of these urban experiences, with growth or stagnation depending largely on the degree of integration of the city and its region into the international economy dominated by the industrializing nations of Europe and North America. Population expansion and accompanying urban growth occurred during economic booms resulting from rapidly expanding exports of agricultural or mineral products. Lack of urban growth signified isolation

---

[6] In Cuba, although data has been included for 1930 at the village level, the definitions of town and village are different, thus making comparisons impossible.

from world trade or a loss in the value or competitive advantage for the particular raw material being produced.

In order to clarify the discussion of function, Latin American cities can be grouped in four principal categories. The most striking and best-known type was the commercial–bureaucratic city. A second and less common type had a major industrial component as well as commercial and bureaucratic activities and thus resembled more the cities of Western Europe and the United States. A third and specialized type was the commercial–mining city in which the principal activity in addition to trade consisted of extracting and processing a mineral product. The remaining urban centres fell into the commercial category, where the principal function was to serve as a collection and distribution point for the immediate surrounding area or as a centre through which goods were funnelled.

The first type, the commercial–bureaucratic, included all national and provincial or state capitals, and even a number of district or county seats of government. The direct relationship of such commercial and administrative centres to the export-oriented economy can best be seen, however, at the national level, and, for that reason, the following discussion focuses on national capitals. Except for highland Quito in Ecuador, which faced a very different and rival centre of power in the tropical seaport of Guayaquil, or Bogotá in Colombia which had to contend with several other regional centres, the seats of Spanish and Portuguese imperial administration in the eighteenth century and then the capitals of the emerging nations in the nineteenth century combined unusual control of commercial and financial resources within their areas along with their governmental functions.

In several countries this historical commercial and administrative domination was also reflected in the proportion of the national population located in the national capital. Buenos Aires held 20 per cent of Argentina's population by 1930; one-third of all Uruguayans lived in Montevideo; while both Havana, Cuba, and Santiago, Chile, claimed 16 per cent of their national populations by 1930 (see Table 4). Furthermore, between 1870 and 1930, the capital of every country increased its percentage of the national population: La Paz, Bogotá, Santiago, Mexico City and Caracas had doubled that percentage in sixty years, while Rio de Janeiro and San José fell just short of the mark.

The rates of growth, however, varied enormously, and these related closely to each country's involvement in production for export (see Table 5). Buenos Aires' growth ranged between 3 and 6 per cent per

Table 4. *Size of national capitals (in 000s) and percentage of national population located in national capital, 1870 and 1930*

Country	Capital	Capital's population		Percentage of national total	
		1870	1930	1870	1930
Argentina	Buenos Aires	187	2,178	10.8[a]	18.3
Bolivia	La Paz	69	176	3.5	8.2
Brazil	Rio de Janeiro	275	1,701	2.7	5.0
Colombia	Bogotá	41	330	1.4	3.8
Costa Rica	San José	9	51	5.5	10.8
Cuba	Havana	230	654	15.2	16.5
Chile	Santiago	150	696	7.2	16.2
Ecuador	Quito	76	127	7.1	8.2
Guatemala	Guatemala City	50	121	4.6	6.0
Mexico	Mexico City	230	1,049	2.4	6.3
Paraguay	Asunción	25	97	7.6	11.0
Peru	Lima	100	273	3.7	4.8
Uruguay	Montevideo	110	572	25.0	33.0
Venezuela	Caracas	49	203	2.8	6.0

Source: as for Table 3.
[a] 1869 Argentine national census figures substituted for those used by Hardoy and Langdon.

Table 5. *Percentage rate of average annual growth for national capitals, 1870–1930[a]*

Country	City	1870	1880	1890	1900	1910	1920	1930
Argentina	Buenos Aires	3.3	6.0	5.5	4.0	4.9	3.4	1.0
Bolivia	La Paz	0.1	− 5.5	2.1	1.1	3.7	2.4	3.8
Brazil	Rio de Janeiro	2.8	—	3.6	2.8	2.9	2.1	2.4
Chile	Santiago	2.7	2.3	3.1	2.2	—	3.3	3.2
Colombia	Bogotá	2.2	6.3	2.5	− 1.5	2.8	4.2	3.5
Cuba	Havana	1.0	—	0.4	1.8	2.4	4.0	2.9
Mexico	Mexico City	0.6	3.7	0.8	1.1	3.2	3.1	5.2
Peru	Lima	0.8	—	0.3	1.8	—	3.0	3.4
Uruguay	Montevideo	4.7	5.9	6.1	0.8	3.5	1.5	3.7
Venezuela	Caracas	− 0.3	1.7	2.5	0.1	—	2.0	5.1

Source: as for Table 3.
[a] Number of years used for each calculation varies depending on data available.

annum until the very end of the period when it declined, not for economic reasons but because the population of the area of the Federal District was approaching saturation point and growth had begun to spill over into the contiguous urban areas of Greater Buenos Aires. The city benefited from the continued expansion of the Argentine economy along already established lines, maintained in the early twentieth century by increasing exports of chilled meats to supplement the wool, hides and grains, and by rising amounts of foreign investments. Montevideo's rapid growth toward a half-million population likewise responded to the flourishing agricultural export trade funnelled through this port and capital. Elsewhere the growth pattern proved more irregular. Santiago grew at a steady rate of 2 to 3 per cent throughout these years as the alternating cyclical booms in copper and nitrate production received supplementary support from agricultural exports of wheat and wool. A very similar growth rate characterized Rio de Janeiro, where much of the impact of Brazil's coffee boom went instead into the industrial as well as the commercial and bureaucratic growth of the capital of the state of São Paulo. Several other national capitals showed upturns in growth primarily in the twentieth century. Highland La Paz began to expand notably after 1900 on the basis of increasing Bolivian tin exports. Bogotá benefited from a profitable coffee boom after the turn of the century. Havana's growth rate increased substantially on the basis of a rapid increase in the island's sugar production tied to United States' markets and investments. Under the stimulus of Venezuela's rising petroleum production, Caracas achieved a 5 per cent annual growth in the late 1920s. Lima's more modest 3 per cent came from its increased commercial and political domination over Peru's other cities.

The commercial–bureaucratic city, as exemplified by the development of national capitals, showed a consistent tendency to expand on the basis of increasing trade, facilitated by booms in the production of raw material exports and by governmental influence over transportation and financial resources. Even when commercial stimulus slowed, the political centralization exerted by this type of city over its immediate surroundings tended to support continued growth. The most spectacular cases of expansion occurred when the impact of increased trade and of political centralization for an extended area was overwhelmingly concentrated at a single point.

Buenos Aires provides one of the most astounding examples of commercial–bureaucratic growth. Its expansion from a primary city of nearly 200,000 inhabitants in 1870 to a world metropolis of more than 2 million by 1930 was accompanied by a rise in its share of national population from 10 per cent to 20 per cent. Since the late seventeenth century, Buenos Aires had been the largest city in the Río de la Plata, and it had served since 1776 as capital first of the viceroyalty of the Río de la Plata, then of Argentina. Its extraordinary growth in the late nineteenth century resulted directly from the virtual monopoly on handling through its port Argentina's steadily rising exports and the inflow of consumer goods from abroad. By 1890 it had also become the hub of the developing national railway system. As a result, it served as the entrepot of commerce for all Argentina and for much of the trade entering and leaving Bolivia and Paraguay as well. The potential for expanding agricultural production in the fertile pampas region appeared limitless, as did the expansion of markets in Europe for Argentine products. European immigrants – primarily Spaniards and Italians – poured into the coastal area of Argentina in response to the demand for manual labourers. Foreign capital flowed into the country to finance the commercial and transport infrastructure as well as to modernize the city of Buenos Aires. Economic prosperity also strengthened Buenos Aires' position as national capital and furthered the importance of the bureaucratic function. Political centralization gradually erased the local autonomy of the provinces and made Buenos Aires the effective residence for a national elite. Such centralization further enlarged Buenos Aires' share of federal funds, dominance over the transportation network and control over investment possibilities.

Although the second type of Latin American city, the commercial–industrial–bureaucratic city, occurred far less frequently than the commercial–bureaucratic centre, it proved significant because of the presence of the industrial function, only infrequently found as a major component of Latin American urban growth. The more common industrial experience was one in which formerly flourishing artisan or household industries were overwhelmed by cheaper, often superior, foreign manufactures. In these situations, characteristic of most of the larger commercial–bureaucratic cities, industrial output tended to be limited to the initial processing of a raw material for export or the production of bulky or perishable items such as some construction materials, beverages and foodstuffs. The following case studies of cities where industry played a major role in their growth suggest interesting parallels and distinctions from commercial–bureaucratic cities.

The most striking case of this type was that of São Paulo, which got its start on the commercial–bureaucratic impetus of Brazil's coffee boom and its position as capital of the important state of São Paulo. São Paulo's growth rate outdid even that of Buenos Aires: in 1870 it had 30,000 inhabitants; by 1930 it was approaching the one million mark in its rapid rise to overtake Rio de Janeiro.

The coffee boom, which had started in valleys near Rio de Janeiro in the 1830s and 1840s had spread in the next several decades south and west into the state of São Paulo in search of new frontiers suitable for that extensive type of cultivation. In 1870 the area around Rio still yielded ten times more coffee than the state of São Paulo. By 1890 the two areas were on a par, while from 1900 to 1930 São Paulo produced twice as much coffee as Rio. As in Buenos Aires, immigrants – especially Italians after 1890 – and foreign capital quickly responded to the opportunities and made much of this expansion possible.

What proved unique in São Paulo's case, however, was that the high annual population growth rate (1890, 4.2 per cent; 1900, 14.0 per cent; 1910, 4.8 per cent; 1920, 3.6 per cent; 1930, 7.1 per cent) resulted not only from a commercial infrastructure and from strong state government assistance supporting a booming agricultural export commodity but also from substantial export-led industrial growth. Rising income from coffee cultivation as well as from associated activities of drying, bagging and transport created local demands and markets that encouraged local producers to challenge the tendency to import all consumer goods from abroad. The profits made by the coffee barons went, in part at least, into local textile and food-processing industries as well as into construction industries, china and glassware, wood processing and simple chemical industries. A natural alliance, facilitated by intermarriage and common interests, grew up between investors in agriculture and industry in São Paulo and contributed further multiplier effects to the industrialization process in the city. These conditions set the stage for continued industrialization and urban growth that have characterized São Paulo's development since 1930.

Colombia's coffee boom started much later than Brazil's, but its impact from 1900 to 1930 was similarly concentrated in a single area, Antioquia, and especially in the region's major city and capital, Medellín. That city's population of 30,000 in 1870, the same as São Paulo's, nearly doubled by 1900 and doubled again by 1930. By 1920 Antioquia coffee contributed more than one-quarter of the country's total exports. The same local market and multiplier effects that encouraged industrial growth in São Paulo stimulated investments in Medellín's textile factories. Many writers have also suggested that Antioquia's earlier gold-mining boom, lasting until 1850, fostered entrepreneurial abilities in risk-taking and association, and provided capital and technical skills useful for industrialization. Tariff protection by the national government, increased use of hydro-electric power, the influx of foreign capital to help build the transport infrastructure, and the tendency of coffee growers to support local manufacturing, all contributed to a firm base for industrialization in Medellín by 1930.

In Mexico, Monterrey's development came more from transportation facilities and mineral resources than from the stimuli of export agriculture or entrepreneurial heritage. Its rail link with the United States, established via Laredo in 1882, its proximity to coal and iron ore deposits north and west of the city, its connection to the nearby seaport of Tampico and its rail line to Mexico City, and the presence of abundant hydro-electric potential facilitated the formation of metallurgical and industrial enterprises in the 1880s and 1890s heavily financed by United States capital. State and national legislation in the late nineteenth century encouraged such foreign investment, while adjacent grazing and irrigated crop lands afforded a base founded on local workers, consumers and capital. The city's growth closely paralleled that of Medellín – from 29,000 in 1880 to 133,000 by 1930. By the later date, factories producing beer, glassware, pottery, textiles, cement and foodstuffs, as well as smelters, ironworks and foundries, made industry at least as important to Monterrey as its role as capital of the state of Nuevo León or as major commercial entrepot of north-eastern Mexico.

São Paulo, Medellín and Monterrey each present distinct cases of urban growth. They show, however, the common characteristic of major industrial function. Their experience demonstrates that under certain conditions industry could flourish in its own right even within highly export-oriented economies and could become as much a component of urbanization as in Europe or the United States.

The third type of city, commercial-mining, characterized specialized urban centres found in the nitrate deserts of northern Chile, in the oil fields of Venezuela and Mexico, and in the highland regions of central Chile, Peru, Bolivia and Mexico where copper, tin, silver and gold were mined. Also included in this category because of their economic similarity are the rubber-collecting stations and villages of the Amazonian jungle. In all these cases urban growth or decline depended directly on the world demand for the region's product. The commercialization of that product, and in some cases its initial processing or refining, attracted population which provided a labour force which became in turn consumers of urban services and retail outlets. But when world markets no longer demanded that product, or shifted to cheaper or better sources of supply, no other functions could sustain this type of urban centre and it quickly withered or vanished.

In the 1860s and 1870s nitrate deposits in the arid deserts of northern Chile and southern Peru became the world's best source of this essential ingredient for fertilizers and explosives. From 1879 to 1883 Chile waged a war on Peru and Bolivia to ensure complete possession of these resources. Under Chilean sovereignty, mining camps, ranging in size from a few hundred to several thousand inhabitants, housed migrant workers who broke up the hard slabs of nitrate deposits on the desert floor, transported them to vats for dissolving, purifying and drying, and then loaded them on flat cars to be carried to the ports and provincial capitals of Iquique, Arica and Copiapó. These mining camps boomed or collapsed as migrants flooded northward or retreated to traditional agricultural labour and bare subsistence in central Chile as the world market fluctuated. The development of synthetic nitrates, strongly stimulated by the First World War, finally led to the decline of these towns, and by 1930 many had vanished.

Likewise the development of rubber as a material needed by industrial nations fostered the sudden and unlikely blossoming of the Brazilian Amazon region from 1890 to 1920. Numerous little river settlements sprang up which fed the hard balls, coagulated over smoky fires from latex collected from wild trees, into the rapidly expanding commercial-bureaucratic centres of Manaus and Belém. The success of British botanists in transplanting seedlings in the late nineteenth century to plantations in Ceylon, Malaya and India quickly ended the comparative advantage enjoyed by Brazil's wild jungle product. Plantation rubber, far more easily controlled, collected and marketed than wild rubber, and synthetic substitutes, given stimulus by German needs in the First World War, sounded the death knell for many of these riverside villages.

Elsewhere, although the peaks and slumps for tin, copper, silver, gold and other metals, and for petroleum, proved to be less dramatic than those for nitrates and rubber, the same dependence on the world market dominated the life and existence of these camps and villages. Where subsistence or commercial agriculture supported a substantial local population, as was the case in much of highland Peru, Bolivia, Mexico, or in coastal Venezuela and Mexico, these centres could revert to primarily commercial functions. But where urban population depended only on the export of a mineral product, the impact of falling world prices or demand could be disastrous.

The final type of Latin American city, the commercial city, requires little discussion even though numerically it provided the bulk of Latin America's urban experience. The commercial function played a major part in the three previous categories. In the commercial city it served as the only major function. In size these centres ranged from the smallest whistle stop on a railway line, or a rural town on a dirt road, to major ports such as Santos in Brazil, Bahía Blanca and Rosario in Argentina, and Veracruz in Mexico. Also characteristic of this category were the small collection and distribution outposts of agricultural zones, for coffee in Brazil and Colombia, for sugar along Peru's northern coast, for cattle in northern Mexico, inland Venezuela, southern Brazil and central Argentina, for sheep in Uruguay and southern Argentina, or for wheat in central Chile and the Argentine pampas. In these areas, the intersection of several transportation routes often fostered the development of larger towns and cities which provided services and activities that could not be supported in the villages: a range of retail outlets, medical and legal services, banks, secondary schools, newspapers and theatres or cinemas. Ultimately, however, all these commercial centres, even when they served sizeable rural populations, depended for prosperity and growth on the functioning of an urban network dominated from the commercial–bureaucratic cities and in some cases on foreign markets and demand. But that dependency never reached the overwhelming level of the commercial–mining centre.

In terms of economic function, dependency on foreign markets heavily influenced the urban development throughout Latin America. At the level of mining centres and smaller commercial cities, declining world prices or competition from alternative sources could sharply reduce growth or even cause decline in population. Even for larger commercial cities and for many commercial–bureaucratic cities, their growth depended heavily on foreign demand for local products. Furthermore, the benefits of such externally-led growth tended to be skewed in favour of the major commercial–bureaucratic cities or those that possessed an added industrial function. As shown in Table 6, the

Table 6. *Percentage rate of average annual growth of population*[a] *of cities in selected countries*

Country	Period	Overall growth rate	Growth rate in cities over 100,000	Growth rate in cities 20,000– 100,000	Growth rate in settlements less than 20,000, incl. rural
Argentina	1869–1895	3.0	4.2	2.5	2.7
	1895–1914	3.5	4.8	3.9	
Bolivia	1900–1950	1.1	2.9	2.0	0.9
Chile	1907–1920	1.1	2.4	1.9	0.6
	1920–1931	1.4	2.7	2.4	0.9
Cuba	1919–1931	2.6	3.4	2.5	2.4
Peru	1876–1940	1.2	2.1	1.7	1.1

Source: Seminar on Urbanization Problems in Latin America, Santiago de Chile, 1959, *Urbanization in Latin America*, edited by Philip M. Hauser (New York, 1961), 97.
[a] Average rate of increase defined as the total increase over the period divided by mean population (average of initial and last census) and by intercensal period in number of years.

secondary cities of Argentina, Bolivia, Chile, Cuba and Peru grew at significantly slower rates than the primary cities, all commercial–bureaucratic centres. Even slower was the growth of the countryside, in which were included the population of the towns and villages principally dependent on commerce and in some areas on mining.

PHYSICAL CHANGES: PLAZA AND SUBURB

Despite the variation in the size and function of Latin American cities, all shared a common experience in the type of physical expansion brought about by growth. In a few cases, such as in Santiago, Chile, that expansion started as early as the 1850s; in the cities of most of the major countries, it was under way by the end of the nineteenth century (although in Bolivia, Paraguay and Central America it had to wait until well into the twentieth century). In every case this growth pushed outward from the main plaza, the focus for the colonial city, towards adjoining suburbs.

The upper classes largely determined the direction and timing of this outward growth in both primary and secondary cities. Although this upper class move to residences in the suburbs seemed to resemble the earlier flight by elites from the older centres of European and United States cities, the Latin American upper classes retained their attachment to the plaza area, and the result was a totally different urban environment.

Housing and life styles for the upper classes changed substantially in the latter part of the nineteenth century under the impact of rising commercial profits diverted into the cities. The wealthy began to move their homes away from the central plaza, often in search of higher and consequently more pleasant and healthier environments or, more simply, of more space, and these moves determined the direction of urban expansion. In Mexico City wealthy Mexicans increasingly chose sites southwards along the Paseo de la Reforma, begun in 1864, toward Chapultepec Palace; in Guadalajara they spread westwards into newly formed residential suburbs. In São Paulo, the newly enriched coffee barons erected seigneurial homes along the ridge marked by the Avenida Paulista. In Rio de Janeiro they built along the Avenida Rio Branco, which had been carved out of the centre of the old city with a perspective toward the picturesque Sugar Loaf, or southwards along the coast to Catete and Laranjeiras. In Buenos Aires, upper class families started in the 1890s to move north a dozen blocks from the environs of the Plaza de Mayo to occupy mansions in Barrio Norte and, by 1910, along the bank of the estuary to suburbs extending beyond the Federal District. In Montevideo they moved eastwards along the shoreline of the estuary toward Pocitos. In Lima railway connections with the seaport at Callao as well as with nearby Chorillos on the coast to the south initially facilitated the outward spread of the upper class. By 1920 the opening of fashionable Avenida Arequipa speeded that exodus south-westwards toward the Pacific. In Santiago the initial spread away from the immediate environs of the main plaza was accentuated by an eastward move in the 1920s to gain better air and more privacy on gently rising ground toward the Andes. In Bogotá the wealthy remained concentrated around the Plaza de Armas until the 1900s, but, with commercial expansion and the coffee boom, those families started to move to higher land immediately to the north of the central city and in the direction of the village of Chapinero. In Caracas the direction was to the south towards the suburb of El Paraíso and later, by 1930, towards Los Chorros to the east.

The upper classes changed not only the location but also the appearance and structure of their homes. The enclosed patio style had fallen out of favour, to be replaced by French, Italian, British and, by 1930, United States models. The wealthy, especially the *nouveaux riches*, preferred the multi-storied mansions, designed on the drawing boards of Paris or Brussels, which better displayed their status. Grand entrances and sweeping balustrades gave a new sense of space and also advertised to the world the power of their owners. Richly ornate foyers and vestibules hung with heavy draperies and furnished with brocade and satin sofas accentuated the distance travelled from the rustic, almost Spartan, wooden chairs or horsehair couches of the colonial-style drawing room. Two-story chalets or smaller bungalows set back from the street, meanwhile, typified the preferences of growing numbers of professional and managerial groups. In each case, the home had lost much of its aspect of a retreat enclosed and hidden from the world and became an open expression of its inhabitants' prestige and income.

Pastimes requiring more physical space were introduced along with this outward move. Golf, rugby, polo and tennis became popular as sports for the wealthy. The afternoon or evening outing in carriage or automobile gained popularity – to Palermo Park in Buenos Aires, Paseo de la Reforma and Chapultepec Park in Mexico City, Jardím Botánico in Rio de Janeiro, or along the Paseo de Colón in Lima, the Prado in Montevideo and the Alameda in Santiago. A few restaurants, clubs and theatres catering for the well-to-do even began to appear in outlying elite suburbs.

The initial outward move by the wealthy was soon supplemented by pressures from the increasing numbers of inhabitants of all classes. While the well-to-do congregated along certain desirable avenues or in secluded suburbs, urban expansion created many other suburbs, often predominantly middle or working class. For these neighbourhoods, a church, a police station, a public market, a streetcar, train, or bus stop, and a plaza provided a focus. Around this core a number of stores, a branch bank, a few offices of professionals appeared. As in the colonial city, those who were better off built their residences close to this centre in order to be near to transportation and services, while humbler households spread out along back streets. As cities extended outwards, largely in the form of one- and two-story residences, retail outlets – grocery stores, butcher's shops, bakeries, fruit and vegetable stands – accompanied the expansion. In settled areas, stores for the daily purchase of staples, meat, bread and other supplies were never more than two or three blocks distant. Likewise, in this same neighbourhood of a dozen or so blocks, there was usually a dentist, a tailor, a shoemaker, a chemist's shop, a laundress, a blacksmith, a milkman, a furniture maker, a bricklayer, a barber, or almost any skill or trade that might be needed. As a result, even as urban areas ballooned outward, the suburbs and the smaller neighbourhood units proved to be remarkably self-sufficient and self-contained.

At the same time as cities were sprawling outwards, the urban nucleus retained its importance. Latin America's upper and middle classes, even as they moved out to more desirable residential locations, retained their connection with and reliance on the central plaza. The increasing concentration of economic and political resources had gradually led to the formation of a resident elite in the national capital cities, who began to insist on creating modern, open environments of the kind which Georges Haussmann had introduced into Paris and a few other European cities. As the layout of narrow streets and squat, deteriorating houses became more constricting, upper class residents sought a new facade and architecture for their capital cities. This approach in turn was mimicked by elites in all the provincial or state capitals and indeed in any centre that had funds for improvements.

Central to this environmental reconstruction was the concept that the principal plaza itself represented the city – a concept deeply rooted in the origins of these Hispanic centres. In the larger cities, the plaza became the focal point for the building of diagonals and boulevards to open up the narrow streets and to introduce vistas and a sense of space. Around that plaza the principal public buildings – cathedral, executive mansion, legislature, supreme court, ministries – received a major facelift, or more often were completely rebuilt along massive Greco-Roman lines. In smaller centres, the same constellation of Church and State also benefited from improvements: an imposing new municipal building or a costly refurbishing of the local church.

Theatres, clubs and hotels, particularly in the primate cities, added an impressive appearance to the changing facades of the downtown centre. The Palace of Fine Arts in Mexico City, the Municipal Theatres in Rio de Janeiro and Caracas, the Colón Theatre in Buenos Aires, the Politeama in Lima, or the Solís Theatre in Montevideo reflected the desire of the national elites to have a showplace for operatic and dramatic performances and, perhaps more importantly, a place to see and be seen. The imposing foyers, marble balconies, tapestries, velvet upholstery and up-to-date lighting and staging effects often rivalled those of Milan, London or New York and attracted some of the world's best talent from La Scala, Covent Garden and the Metropolitan Opera. Along nearby streets other spots where the elite gathered and were entertained were to be found, and were increasingly frequented by rising members of the middle classes. These theatres, cinemas, restaurants, private clubs and cafés catered to the desires of the rich to have the best and latest from Europe.

Great efforts also went into the beautification of the downtown centres and the main plazas in particular. Statues, trees, gardens, benches and fountains were alternately installed, removed, or upgraded as the local elite strove to create the best possible image. The adjoining streets had been the first to be paved and then to receive the latest technical improvements, be they wood blocks or asphalt coverings. From the centre radiated the lines for horse-drawn and later electric-powered streetcars. Water and sewer connections, the use of oil, then gas and finally electricity for public lighting, the installation of telephones, rubbish collections, the sweeping of streets, the protection provided by police and firemen, all these invariably first occurred in the centre and continued to be better maintained and more modern and efficient in the areas closest to the main plaza.

All these changes led to a substantial reconstruction of the Latin American city. In colonial times and in the nineteenth century wealthy people had invariably lived close to the main plaza where the institutions of power and prestige as well as urban conveniences were located. In this scheme, the lower classes, except for servants living in the homes of the well-to-do, occupied the urban fringes. With the city's population explosion in the late nineteenth century, the residential preferences of the elites, as well as of the newly emerging professional, commercial and industrial middle sectors, began to change. Their demands, more than transportation facilities or industry or urban planning, guided the direction and timing of each city's outward growth. Since the plaza and the central area still retained its attraction for the elite and the middle sectors, that move was toward the nearest available elevated ground affording larger sites, ease of transit to the city's centre, as well as privacy and seclusion. In this fashion the well-to-do, by their choice of new residential areas and by life styles requiring more space and ostentation, began to alter greatly the physical layout of the former plaza-centred city, especially after 1900, to conform more closely to that of the suburb-oriented city of North America and Europe. At the same time, they continued to lavish attention on the central city as their principal focus for work and play, with the result that the area around the main plaza acquired still greater importance and charm even when it was no longer residential.

THE POLITICAL CONSEQUENCES OF URBANIZATION

In general, urban growth has had minimal effect on local municipal government. The traditional weakness and poverty of municipal authority that characterized the colonial era carried over into the nineteenth century and continues to the present day. If cities played a critical role in Spanish and Portuguese control over their American empires it was primarily because they were seats for military and administrative officers appointed and directed from Madrid and Lisbon. Imperial rule allowed no more autonomy at the town or city level than the authority to regulate weights and measures, maintain streets and lighting and supervise night watchmen. The almost total absence of financial resources further ensured that this level of government exercised no effective control or power. Such was the hollowness of power that the imperial authorities even permitted limited local representation through the sale of or election to council seats carrying only honorific value.

The heritage of weak municipal institutions was transferred to the new independent nations. Local chieftains and rural caudillos exercised effective authority, and when they chose to legitimize their rule they used national or provincial, not municipal, political institutions. As cities expanded and problems of public health, sanitation, transportation and security became more pressing, once again it was national and provincial authority, not municipal government, which provided direction, money and solutions. Commercial–bureaucratic cities, with access to the combined wealth and administrative power of the nation or the province, were best able to resolve these problems of growth. And, throughout Latin America, it was the police chief, the garrison commander or other representative of higher authority, not the municipal councillors, who ultimately governed the cities. At the same time political activity during these decades was not generally directed toward seeking solutions to urban problems but was concerned instead with regional and national problems.

From the point of view of the changing power structure at the national level several major adjustments in perceptions and roles resulted from the increasing importance of cities during the period from 1870 to 1930. The first of these, an increasingly urbanized outlook, requires little discussion since it was almost completed by the beginning of the period. In all of the major Latin American countries, the age of the rural caudillos had begun to draw to a close by mid-nineteenth century. In the decades immediately following the removal of imperial controls administered from Madrid and Lisbon, a great deal of authority had devolved on local landowning families, especially those able to muster large, although untrained, military forces from workers on their estates. The powerful rural caudillo landowner had thus become the decisive political force throughout Latin America. Whether countries experienced prolonged periods of anarchy or quickly reached a state of authoritarian order and stability largely depended on how quickly strife between local chieftains yielded a dominant caudillo who was successful in exerting his authority over the others. In that process of establishing national control, however, these rural chieftains could no longer rely solely on irregular military forces composed of peasants. They turned more and more to urban dwellers for financial resources, for expertise and for support. And gradually the rural caudillo himself became a city man, and in that process he eventually lost his power base in the countryside.

A second related development occurred within the upper classes. As population and commerce inflated the size and wealth of cities, the well-to-do and powerful increasingly resided in cities and became more urban in their outlook. They also came to depend more and more on cities and in particular on the national capital. Not all of the upper class lived in the national capital, but they began to form a single national elite which established its principal centre of power and leadership there, and many of its members also lived there, at least some of the time. Even when living in provincial capitals, or in towns, or on country estates, they maintained close contact with events and colleagues in the national capital. This creation of a national elite in turn encouraged the replacement of the individual strong man or caudillo with institutionalized government composed of an all-powerful executive named by elite consensus and a largely advisory legislative branch staffed and controlled by the same elite.

This domination by a national elite eventually provoked a reaction bred in turn by the increasing size, wealth and social differentiation of the major urban centres. The appearance and growth of new groups, such as a more professional military (before, during and after the First World

War), university students (especially with the spread of the University Reform Movement from Córdoba, Argentina, after 1918), organized labour and, above all, the administrative, professional and commercial middle classes broadened the base of those aspiring to participate in government.

The protests and influence of middle-class elements in particular began to introduce changes that significantly altered the degree of political control exercised by national elites in a number of Latin American countries. More broadly based political parties, increasing electoral participation, and political programmes designed to benefit broader sectors of the population, were in the end political consequences of the growth of the major cities.

Political parties had flourished everywhere in Latin America since the early nineteenth century, but only as factions supporting rural caudillos or later as coalitions within the national elite. Leaders might mobilize peons and labourers to vote just as they could mobilize their economic resources or irregular military forces for decisive confrontations. But elections at best presented results predetermined by manoeuvring among these elite groups and thus involved no popular participation in the political process. The growing size of urban populations in the late nineteenth century, especially of middle groups that could not gain access to elite or upper-class status but distinguished themselves in education, income and attitudes from the mass of manual labourers, made continued elite control of politics increasingly difficult. Political leaders emerged among the urban middle classes and formed their own parties or broadened the base of existing political parties. By means of newspapers, public meetings, parades, and demonstrations they rallied increasing numbers of citizens against corruption, for example, or inflation and in favour of more participation in political decisions. Even rebellions involved the participation of substantial civilian elements from the cities, for example in Buenos Aires in 1890, in Lima and in Guayaquil and Quito in 1895, and in Asunción in 1904. And few coups or regimes long survived which did not secure at least the acquiescence of the urban middle classes. Urban middle-class opposition played a part in the fall of Porfirio Díaz in Mexico in 1911 and triggered off a decade of war and rebellion fuelled by tensions and inequities that reached far beyond Mexico's major cities. The urban middle classes were to some extent behind the rise to power of José Batlle y Ordóñez in Uruguay in 1903 and, more temporarily, the administration of Nicolás Piérola from

1895 to 1899 in Peru. In Argentina, as a result of the appeal and power of the Radical Party in the relatively urbanized coastal zone after 1890, the governing elite accepted universal male suffrage in 1912 and four years later surrendered the presidency to the Radical caudillo, Hipólito Yrigoyen. Arturo Alessandri's championing of political and social reforms in his 1920 election in Chile echoed many of these same middle-class attitudes, as did the military interventions in 1924 and 1925. During that same decade, Augusto Leguía's break with Peru's traditional landed elite, his massive expenditures on public works and government bureaucracy, and the resulting surge of new elements into positions of political and economic influence, opened the way for the more radical appeals of the Alianza Popular Revolucionaria Americana (APRA) and its leader, Víctor Raúl Haya de la Torre.

The opening moves in the achievement of broader political participation came largely from white-collar middle classes in the cities. They often recruited students and sections of the military to their reformist programmes, and 'populist' leaders were beginning to make appeals to labour. But their initial success usually came because they seemed so disorganized and at the same time so resembled the national elites in attitudes and background that they aroused few fears and little resistance from these elites. As the political control of the national elites began to weaken, the limited goal of increased participation often blossomed into the desire to replace the national elites in power. In this situation, the middle classes' very lack of unity or purpose, which had served to allay elite fears, eventually proved to be their undoing. In the decades after 1930, this weakness allowed more disciplined elements, such as the military or labour, to seize the initiative.

CONCLUSION

This chapter has summarized a process of rapid urbanization, concentrated especially in the primary and primate cities of Latin America during the late nineteenth and early twentieth centuries. By 1930 what had once been an overwhelmingly rural part of the world boasted metropolises like Buenos Aires, Rio de Janeiro and Mexico City. The proportion of the national population living in urban centres with more than 20,000 inhabitants ranged from one-third in Argentina and Chile to approximately 15 per cent in other major countries. In a few countries, half the population lived in settlements with more than 2,000 inhabitants. Commercial exchange fuelled most of this urban expansion. Increasing exports of raw materials to the industrializing nations of Europe and North America and the return flow of consumer goods, largely responding to new demands from the urban centres, stimulated the growth of processing and mining centres, ports, railway terminals and, above all, national and provincial capitals. As both cities and wealth expanded, the upper classes, especially in the larger urban centres, moved away from their former locus around the main plaza and sought better residential locations on higher ground in the suburbs. The well-to-do, nevertheless, remained closely linked by business, amusement and tradition to the plaza area and consequently expended effort and monies to beautify and modernize their capital cities. The growth of cities, most evident in the national capitals and in a few state or provincial capitals, fostered and facilitated the formation of progressive national elites. But by 1930, these elites, which had for the most part replaced the rural caudillos of the early nineteenth century with institutions of representative government responsive to their domination, found themselves in turn under increasing pressure from new urban groups, especially the middle classes, to share or give up that control. Thus the city in the years from 1870 to 1930 played a critical role in Latin America's economic, social and political development.

8

INDUSTRY IN LATIN AMERICA
BEFORE 1930

INTRODUCTION

The attainment of a modern society founded upon a developed economy has been an enduring objective in Latin America, exercising the minds of *pensadores* and policymakers intermittently since the revolutions for independence at the beginning of the nineteenth century. The promotion of manufacturing activities was regarded as central to the realization of that objective. Various views as to the most appropriate means of stimulating industrial expansion prevailed: options included direct state aid for manufacturing and a more generalized encouragement of economic growth that would promote individual initiative in the industrial sector alongside investment in other activities. Frequent contemporary recourse to the word *industria* (often employed in a context where modern usage would require the expression 'industrialization') is evidence of the importance attached to it and possibly the perception of a failure to develop a manufacturing base – at least during the period before 1930.

It used to be argued by historians of Latin America that industrialization only became feasible after the depression of the 1930s, that is, after a period of profound economic crisis in the central, industrialized capitalist economies. The world economic crisis and associated reduction in international trade had a profound impact upon the foreign trade sector of the republics and undermined a peculiar socio-institutional order committed to a political economy rooted in economic internationalism. Principally associated with authors writing from a dependency perspective, the view was advanced that adverse externally induced dislocation facilitated industrialization in Latin America. The collapse of the import–export complex removed an anti-industry bias in Latin

American societies as the political dominance of a landed and commercial oligarchy was challenged by a rising industrial bourgeoisie and (in a few cases) an incipient urban industrial proletariat.

A not dissimilar chronology had previously been elaborated by structuralists who sought to differentiate between an increase in manufacturing activities (albeit limited in the range of goods produced and restricted geographically) which had occurred in many Latin American countries during phases of export-led growth before 1930 and industrialization *per se*. Indebted to the Economic Commission for Latin America's assessment of the continent's economic problems after the Second World War, structuralists depicted industrialization as a profound secular change involving *inter alia* the relative decline of agriculture, rapid urbanization and the emergence of the industrial sector as the key to self-sustaining economic expansion and argued that industrialization could only proceed in Latin America as the result of direct state action designed to overcome factors – such as an inadequate infrastructure, lack of market integration, deficient demand, irrational factor allocation and scarcities – that inhibited manufacturing.

Thus both *dependentistas* and structuralists were inclined either to ignore or to minimize the full extent of the growth of manufacturing activities before 1930. These approaches also failed to appreciate the originality of measures devised to promote diversification during the nineteenth and early twentieth centuries. As a result of recent research greater caution now exists with regard to the projection of a generalized chronology for the progress of manufacturing: the claims of 1914, the 1880s or even earlier decades are advanced as more pertinent starting-points for the growth of industry than 1930. The monocausal explanation implicit in crude dependency texts has been disputed and the theoretical assumptions which underpin structuralism have been questioned. The debate about the impact of adverse exogenous shocks on the pace of Latin American industrial growth now extends beyond a consideration of the interwar depression to encompass the effects of the First World War (an event subsumed in the original discussion, if usually presented as of great though ephemeral significance) and more specifically the impact of earlier ruptures. Notable amongst these were war-induced shocks of the early national period and late nineteenth-century financial and commercial crises. De-linkage explanations of industrialization carry conviction only if sustainable when other dislocations occurred. Although temporary phenomena, the Baring Crisis of the early

1890s, the 1873 panic and indeed instability in world commercial and financial markets in 1866 may have been of relatively greater significance for individual national economies then at a critical phase of incorporation into the international system than the admittedly devastating crash of 1929. Increased volatility in the foreign trade sector during the years immediately before 1914 or again in the 1920s was less spectacular than the world depression but was of no less importance in contributing to policy reappraisal that favoured the growth of manufacturing.

Other themes that now command consideration are adjustments of tariff regimes, essentially of the bases upon which duties were levied and the application of differential rates to finished items, intermediate inputs and raw materials. Also relevant are the external value of Latin American currencies, rates of domestic inflation and international price movements. All relate to the controversy about effective protection. Credit and monetary policy also feature in the discussion. In addition, the revitalized study of artisan, *obraje* and cottage industrial production during the late colonial and early national periods is of significance. Did such 'proto-industrial' activities constitute a base from which the modern factory system emerged? Related to the achievements and durability of 'colonial' manufacturing is a concern for the origins of social actors intimately involved in the process of industrial growth. Who were the industrialists? What was their relationship with the dominant elite: did their appearance constitute a threat to the *status quo*? Indeed, were industrialists a distinct or homogeneous group? Similar questions arise with respect to industrial labour. To what extent may the emergence of an industrial proletariat be observed prior to 1930? Central to recent revisionism is the political economy of industrial growth, the formulation of policy, the role of policymaking agents and institutions and a definition of industrialisation. It is the lack of such a definition which has, above all, bedevilled the study of the subject since the 1960s.

A CHRONOLOGY OF INDUSTRIAL CHANGE

The elaboration of a generalized framework for pre-1930 industry is not easy but several sub-periods can be identified. While every period may not be sharply demarcated for each Latin American economy, the specific characteristics of various phases, and processes associated with transitions from one phase to another, have a wide – if not a continental –

aspect. Precise dating is not possible for all economies, and the exact duration of phases often defies definition: the magnitude of change differs between countries (small shifts in one area may have assumed a large dimension elsewhere). But three distinct periods can be observed: (i), the decades immediately following independence, years of sharp readjustment for various expressions of colonial manufacturing that also witnessed attempts to establish modern industry; (ii), the classic age of export-led expansion from *c.* 1870 to the First World War associated with institutional modernisation, the development of an infrastructure and demand expansion that created a market for consumer and capital goods; (iii), the period from the First World War to the World Depression which was marked by changes in both the scale of manufacturing and the composition of industrial output. For some Latin American economies this third phase began around the turn of the century. Other Latin American economies had not reached the end of the second phase before the inter-war depression.

Narrative accounts of industry before 1850 permit some generalizations, most of which point to crises and contractions in the volume of domestic production. Another feature of this period is both the diversity of modes of production and the survival of various pre-independence processes and units. Plurality of structures in the industrial sector was to be an enduring characteristic. For the early nineteenth century, however, the principal issues were the impact of, and responses to, the threat of sustained upheaval consequent upon the struggles for independence. The implications for national industry of a liberalization of external trade were also critical.

Various forms of manufacturing existed at the beginning of the national period. At one extreme were self-sufficient Indian communities that barely participated in the market economy, and large estates like the sugar producers of north-east Brazil or the natural dye growers of Mesoamerica which, although raising primary commodities for the international market, supplied most of their own essential needs. Tropical and sub-tropical export agricultural production often relied upon one or another form of forced labour and met the demands of armies of negro slaves or semi-servile Indians for food staples and basic household wares from estate-based rudimentary workshops. Occasionally rural industrial units realized a surplus for sale in the towns, and there were examples of communal Indian cottage production for local or national markets, usually supplied at annual fairs. Nevertheless, for the continent as a whole, manufacturing was an urban phenomenon, though one that assumed many forms in provincial and national capitals. At the apex of the 'colonial' industrial structure was the *obraje*. The *obrajes* had a long history dating from at least the seventeenth century in the principal countries of Spanish America. *Obraje* production was both urban and factory-based and was also almost invariably large in scale. Major concerns employed hundreds of workers who often resided in the factory complex. They were also characterized by the use of servile labour, either conscripted in the countryside or purchased in local slave markets. In some centres there was, by the end of the colonial period, an increasing tendency, both in the *obrajes* and small sweat shops, to employ wage labour, principally drawn from the free coloured population or newly arrived immigrants.

Large-scale *obrajes* existed alongside smaller units of production – modest workshops and prosperous artisan-dominated enterprises – in virtually all urban centres. By the beginning of the nineteenth century there was, however, in more advanced areas of the continent, such as Mexico, a tendency for large enterprises to move away from the cities. In part the trend favouring re-location of factories was occasioned by a desire to escape from excessive guild and municipal regulation. During the late eighteenth century this process may also have been accelerated by a determination to escape the attention of colonial administrators. For, had later Bourbon ordinances against manufacturing been rigorously applied, the Spanish colonies would have possessed at independence few establishments other than the most basic export-processing plants. Similar proscriptions against industry existed in Brazil. But a more pressing reason making for the re-siting of large workshops could have been the need for closer access to raw material supply or fast-running rivers to propel water-driven machinery – factors that imply both quantitative and qualitative changes in late-colonial manufacturing.

Diversity in the scale of early national industry was mirrored by variety in the range of items turned out for local, national and occasionally extranational regional markets. The principal industrial product – if by industry is meant a process that was factory-based and utilized techniques that were not too distant from those employed in other industrializing economies – was textiles, mainly woollens though cotton goods were of growing importance by the 1850s. Mexican mills were particularly prosperous in the early nineteenth century. Brazilian cotton textile production was established in the north-east by the 1840s.

Elsewhere in pastoral economies, as in the Río de la Plata, leather was cured and worked into a range of products – shoes, aprons, trousers, bridles, harnesses, straps, bags, pails – to serve consumer and industrial needs. There was also cart-making which served the domestic end of the pastoral export complex. Other animal products, such as grease and tallow, were rendered for the home market to produce soap and candles. Indeed, a multiplicity of rural products, from dried or cured meats, to flour and bread, and to beer, wines and cheap spirits, were everywhere elaborated for domestic consumption. Tableware and pottery, porcelain and glass, and building bricks were also fired for home use. In mineral-producing economies, foreign travellers often remarked upon the degree of production for local needs, pointing to the robust condition of Mexican metal working during the early national period. By the middle of the nineteenth century, copper and silver production in Chile was dominated by local capital, and the mining industry served as a vehicle for the diffusion of primitive smelting and working techniques to other branches of metal manufacture. Here, as in Mexico, iron foundries attempted to supply regional and limited national demand.

Yet, in virtually all cases, production for the domestic market was overwhelmingly carried out in small establishments employing a traditional and an obsolescent technology. Moreover, during the second quarter of the nineteenth century, the zones served by local industry became increasingly regional in focus as national markets fragmented, weakened by the twin evils of civil strife and foreign competition. A contraction in market horizons reinforced the primitive features and stagnating prospects of Latin American industry. But the once widely held view that independence resulted in the adoption of policies of free trade which ruined national industry can no longer be sustained. As the example of Buenos Aires reveals, some coastal regions were flooded with foreign manufactures. Products were dumped in the nearest urban centres capable of cash purchases when foreign merchants' exaggerated expectations of market potential failed to materialize, undermining local industries. Elsewhere the position is less clear cut. Although the struggles for independence destroyed industrial plant, decimated the workforce, dislocated production and disrupted traditional trade routes (as did later civil wars and the subsequent drawing of national boundaries), the consequences were not wholly negative. Cottage industry located in the Argentinian north-west is a case in point. Before independence the area had supplied the burgeoning littoral market and also the mining zone of Upper Peru. Free trade brought the loss of the Buenos Aires market and early royalist victories in Upper Peru and Chile closed markets on the far side of the royalist–insurgent frontier. Later Argentine producers were to be even more effectively excluded from these markets with the independence of Bolivia and a rising tide of protectionism in Chile. Yet the disintegration of Argentina into a loose confederation of provinces offered some solace to regional manufacturers in the west and north-west as potent forces of localism were reinforced by the fiscal policies of impecunious provincial administrations that subjected inter-provincial commerce to a plethora of duties. Geography, reinforced by fiscal policy, also accorded Andean and Mexican industries a degree of natural protection from the ravages of foreign competition until the coming of the railways in the last quarter of the century. But regional markets were rarely sufficiently dynamic to sustain, let alone revitalize, local industry.

If the long-term prospects for traditional, colonial industries were bleak, those for specific lines of export production were apparently more positive, even in the period to 1850. The processing of pastoral products for both continental and world markets was possibly the most rapidly expanding area of industry during this period. During the 1820s and 1830s the Buenos Aires *saladeros* enjoyed virtually unrestricted access to American markets for dried and salt meat. By the 1840s other suppliers entered the trade. Circumventing *rosista* restrictions *entrerriano* producers established a presence in the market and output recovered in Uruguay. Later, by the 1850s and 1860s, in Buenos Aires wool-washing and ovine tallow-rendering would be added to the list of units processing for overseas markets. The early national period was less kind to other export industries. Precious metal production, for so long the colonial staple, was seriously affected by the independence wars, and did not fully recover until the 1850s or even later. Gold mining in Colombia, being based upon small-scale panning for alluvial deposits was less disrupted and remained highly profitable. But placer 'extraction' can hardly be compared with operations which had evolved in areas of underground mining in Peru and Mexico. Only in Chile during the middle third of the nineteenth century was there a sustained increase in metal production, especially in the copper industry which expanded to supply the domestic, British and Asian markets.

The scale of operations in export-processing, like that of domestically orientated firms, varied. Although dependent on rudimentary labour-intensive techniques and functioning only during the season from November to March, Buenos Aires *saladeros* and *graserías* like those operated by the Anchorena were large establishments, employing several hundred workers and tied up huge sums of capital. Between the 1840s and 1880s the typical salting plant was transformed into a substantial factory style establishment. These enterprises were massive vertically integrated concerns involved in cattle raising, meat and by-product processing and wholesale operations.[1] New handling techniques were applied to accelerate carcass preparation, maximize the use of by-products and generally raise efficiency through the reduction of waste. These changes, accompanied by the introduction of steam vats, larger cauldrons and the sheer scale of operations increased the costs of entry into the industry and fostered consolidation. At the other extreme were West Coast copper producers. By mid-century Chile was well established as the world's largest copper exporter: 'Chile bars' were a recognized market leader, establishing the international reference price for copper. But the industry was dominated by national capital located in small and medium-scale firms, employing traditional technology.[2]

These were the 'industries' of the early national period. Of greatest interest to students of the subject is the production of secondary items for domestic consumption. Yet even at this early date, in economies where the subsistence, non-money sector was large, export extractive and processing industries probably made a larger contribution to a quantifiable gross domestic product. The range of goods produced for the home market, the variety of items processed for export, and widely differing techniques and scales of production indicate both diversity within the sector and preclude an easy categorization of industrial activities. Various 'definitions' of manufacturing compete for acceptance. One emphasises factory production (which often functioned in conjunction with putting-out cottage operations), the use of mechanical power, the modernity of production techniques and a capacity to generate or absorb innovation. A second approach would stress also the scale of operations and capital requirements. But this is a contentious point and may under-appreciate processes of metamorphosis whereby primitive establishments evolved into 'modern' manufacturing units. By these latter

---

[1] Province de Buénos-Ayres, Ministère de Gouvernement, Bureau de Statistique Générale, *Annuaire Statistique de la province de Buénos-Ayres, 1882* (Buenos Aires 1883) 371; J. C. Brown, *A socioeconomic history of Argentina, 1776–1860* (Cambridge 1979), 111–12.

[2] M. J. Mamalakis, *The growth and structure of the Chilean economy: from independence to Allende* (New Haven, 1976) 40; A. Pinto S.C., *Chile: un caso de desarrollo frustrado* (Santiago, 1962), 15.

standards, many craft and home industry lines of production would be dismissed as, possibly, would the output of some artisan enterprises. A third definition draws a distinction between the production, on the one hand, of finished manufactures and, on the other, the elaboration and refining of raw materials. This definition would result in the exclusion of most export-processing industries.

Definitions are less problematical during the second major period of Latin America's industrial expansion. Although artisan and craft production survived in many areas (emphasizing the fragmented nature of the industrial sector), profound changes resulted from the continent's progressive and more complete insertion into the world economy after the 1870s. Associated *inter alia* with Latin America's integration in the international economy was the modernization of the infrastructure. Port construction and the building of railway lines, especially in the Southern Cone countries of Argentina, Chile and Uruguay, and in parts of Brazil, exposed domestic producers to the rigours of foreign competition. A growing volume of imports and the monetization of the economy virtually eradicated what remained of colonial-style industrial production. Elsewhere incomplete or regionally biased patterns of railway construction undermined, if they did not totally demolish, craft, artisan and other traditional manufacturing processes. Similar factors also occasioned the thorough transformation of several lines of export processing. Nowhere was the change more complete than in the case of the Chilean copper industry after the 1880s. Local capital proved incapable or unwilling to shift from a form of production based on the rudimentary exploitation of high grade ores employing simple techniques to one founded on a sophisticated use of capital-intensive technology and large-scale production necessary to extract copper from poor ores. The result was a rapid growth in the size of the firm and the denationalization of the industry – a tendency that mirrored an earlier development in West Coast nitrate extraction and presaged similar trends first in non-ferrous metal production in the Andes and Mexico and subsequently in oil.

Corresponding trends can be observed in other branches of export production. Accelerating world demand, coupled with innovations in refining, compelled sugar cane production to become a more complex and integrated process, partly in response to the threat of protected domestic beet production in European markets. In the Caribbean, changes in the scale and in the organization of production were associated with the establishment of a dominant position by US corporate capital. In Mexico, and more especially Peru, domestic capital prevailed, absorbing and sustaining technological innovation in refining and the organization of cane growing.[3] New technology and an increasingly discriminating foreign market also promoted the denationalization of the River Plate pastoral processing industry.[4] Both in Argentina and Uruguay, though only to a lesser extent in Brazil, the transition from low grade dried and salt beef production to modern meat packing resulting in the early penetration and ultimate hegemony of foreign capital. An Argentine meat freezing plant had been established in the 1880s with anglo-*criollo* capital though traditional *saladeros* continued to dominate processed meat exports until the end of the nineteenth century when the value of frozen mutton exports exceeded that of jerked beef. But the appearance of the US meat packers in 1907, by which time frozen beef represented one-half of the value of total meat exports, marked the end of the dominance of English capital and also the large presence of domestic finance. British participation in the industry was only safeguarded by the First World War and the critical importance of the British market for chilled beef exports during the inter-war decades.

Thus, the combination of a growth in world demand for Latin American exports and accelerated technological change had profound consequences for several export industries. More sophisticated extractive or processing techniques transformed the scale and nature of production. The result was often a loss of national control. Equally significant was the type of plant that emerged. By 1914 Chilean copper mines at El Teniente and Chuquicamata were on the way to becoming, respectively, the largest open-cast and underground workings in the world. The Armour and Swift meat packing plants at Buenos Aires in the 1920s bore comparison with the Chicago operations of those firms. In short, by the eve of the First World War Latin American capital-intensive export processing plants were equal in scale and structure to similar extractive and processing establishments located anywhere else in the world.

Large-scale modern units were not, however, exclusive to the export

[3] See B. Albert and A. Greaver (eds.), *Crisis and change in the international sugar economy, 1860–1914* (London, 1985), I, 165–6, 200–1.
[4] S. G. Hanson, *Argentine meat and the British market: chapters in the history of the Argentine meat industry* (Palo Alto, 1938), 53–4, 143, 144–85; J. Fuchs *La penetración de los trusts yanquis en la Argentina* (Buenos Aires, 1958), 193–7.

sector. By the early twentieth century some capital-intensive factories were producing for the domestic market. Technical change in brewing which required large sums of capital was rapidly absorbed in several countries during the 1900s and 1910s. Breweries at Quilmes and Lomas de Zamora near Buenos Aires were reputedly amongst the largest establishment in the world producing light beers while the Antártica brewery in São Paulo was already established as one of the largest corporated undertakings in Brazil.[5] Equally sophisticated and profitable were modern flour mills, as the British financed Rio de Janeiro Flour Mills and Granaries Company revealed.[6] Similar examples could be cited for other economies where large concentrated urban markets had emerged by 1914. By this date major cities were endowed with extensive automated plant producing a range of foods and beverages. Satisfying other basic consumer demands and employing mass production techniques were branches of Alpargatas S.A. in Argentina and Brazil which manufactured cheap rope sandals and shoes for the lower end of the market.[7] Textile manufacturing was also well advanced in Mexico and Brazil on the eve of the First World War, many mills employing large numbers of workers who tended up-to-date spinning and weaving equipment. These factories like their counterparts in the export sector were physically large, dominated the districts within which they were located and employed some of the most modern processes then known. Nevertheless, these firms were atypical, in the majority of cases labour-intensive workshops employing small groups of workers were the norm. The *Yearbook* for 1882 produced by the Buenos Aires provincial government indicated that the average number of workers employed in industrial establishments was six, ranging from one hand employed in the province's single listed distillery to an average of 145 in the *saladeros*. The Third National Census, taken in 1914, demonstrates that small rather than large units remained the dominant feature of most branches of industry.[8] Well into the twentieth century, Chilean industrial firms outside the mining sector were recorded to be 'large' if employing more than five workers – a yardstick which indicates the endurance of

[5] Cervecería Bieckert S. A., *Centenario 1860–1960* (Buenos Aires, 1960); *La Epoca* 31 de Agosto de 1918; J. Padilla, *Datos estadísticos referente a la industria cervecería* (Buenos Aires, 1917).

[6] R. Graham, *Britain and the onset of modernization in Brazil, 1850–1914* (Cambridge, 1968), 146–9, and 'A British industry in Brazil; Rio Flour Mills, 1886–1920', *Business History*, 7/1 (1966) 13–38.

[7] Graham, *Britain*, 144–5.

[8] Province de Buénos-Ayres, *Annuaire Statistique*, 371; República Argentina, *Tercero Censo Nacional, 1914* (Buenos Aires, 1916), VII, 26–34.

sweatshops rather than the emergence of modern factories. In 1914, establishments employing less than five workers still accounted for more than one half of Chile's domestically produced manufactures.[9] Small units also characterized Peruvian industries established after the war of the Pacific, notably foodstuffs, leather working, tobacco and furniture making. The only exception being cotton textiles: Peru's mills, like those in Mexico and Brazil, were sizeable and provided about 50 per cent of home consumption by 1908.[10]

This feature has long been recognised as a strategic weakness in the evolution of Latin America's industries. The adoption of modern capitalist techniques of manufacturing by some firms did not result in the speedy (or even slow) transformation of whole industries. Archaic processes and units existed alongside modern. Industries remained fragmented, the diversity of techniques employed and plurality of organizational structure inhibiting integration at industry level and frustrating spin-offs and transfers between sectors. The compartmentalization of manufacturing and the isolation of individual firms within industries forestalled industry-deepening backward-and-forward linkage effects whereby specialist suppliers of intermediate goods emerged in response to the growth of production of finished manufactures. Unlike Japan, few Latin American economies were able to establish a symbiotic relationship between large-scale capital-intensive plant and small workshops (or cottage industry).

Traditionally the duality of Latin America's industry has been stressed for the sub-period between the late nineteenth and early twentieth centuries. Large-scale high technology units engaged in the processing of minerals and some agricultural products characterized the export sector. Manufacturing for home consumption was undertaken in small, primitive, labour-intensive workshops which supplied principally foodstuffs, beverages, clothing and footwear to the lower end of the market. In three respects this highly dichotomized image may be challenged. First, as has been argued, capital intensive units were to be observed in a few lines of domestic non-durables production. Secondly, local manufacturers supplied a wider range of items than previously identified. Production of industrial oils, mining machinery and paper was an

---

[9] J. G. Palma, 'External disequilibrium and internal industrialization: Chile, 1914–1935', in C. Abel and C. M. Lewis (eds.), *Latin America, economic imperialism and the state: the political economy of the external connection from independence to the present* (London, 1985).

[10] R. Thorp and G. Bertram, *Peru 1890–1977: growth and policy in an open economy* (London, 1978), 120.

established feature of Chilean industry by 1914.[11] A large mix of metal products for use in the home and industry was already being manufactured in the Argentine by the 1880s using imported bar iron. Between 1895 and 1914 the number of workers employed in Argentinian metallurgical industries grew from 6,000 to over 14,600, some employed in large factories like the Vasena Foundry.[12] Similarly, in Brazil, metal working was well established by the 1890s, a number of companies originating in the third quarter of the century. Here and elsewhere there was also domestic production of chemicals (pharmaceuticals and industrial raw materials). Thirdly, a few economies possessed another area of heavy industry, i.e., that represented by the workshops and repairshops of large public utility companies, especially the railways. By the early years of the twentieth century all the principal Latin American railways operated extensive maintenance depots, some of which had already begun to manufacture rolling stock and even locomotives.[13] According to any definition these were major industrial complexes catering for the needs of the home market. Occasionally the scale of operations of these establishments was matched only by that of arms factories and government run arsenals and dockyards.

What of the final phase from the First World War to the World Depression? As indicated above, it is impossible to construct a general, continental framework. In a few cases the First World War may have occasioned a shift from industrial growth to industrialization. Elsewhere, the early decades of the twentieth century saw a process of continued if uneven expansion in manufacturing output with qualitative developments – principally in terms of the organization of production – confined to sub-sectoral levels. And in some economies the pace of industrial change slackened during the 1910s and 1920s. In Brazil the War is often depicted as accelerating a transformation to industrialization, stimulating resource allocation, policy formulation and institutional consolidation in favour of manufacturing. It is also confidently argued that Chile industrialized between 1914 and 1936, or rather that

[11] H. W. Kirsch, *Industrial development in a traditional society: the conflict of entrepreneurship and modernization in Chile* (Gainesville, 1977), 25–45; O. Muñoz, *Crecimiento industrial de Chile, 1914–1965* (Santiago, 1968), 53, 55–6.

[12] R. Cortés Conde and E. Gallo, *La formación de la Argentina moderna* (Buenos Aires, 1967), 77–8; V. Vázquez-Presedo, *El caso Argentino: migración de factores, comercio exterior y desarrollo, 1875–1914* (Buenos Aires, 1971), 223–4; *La Epoca*, 10 September 1918; *Anuario La Razón*, 4 (1920), 158.

[13] C. M. Lewis, 'Railways and industrialization; Argentina and Brazil, 1870–1929', in Abel and Lewis, *Latin America*; Kirsch, *Industrial development*, 12, 32–3.

industry assumed the role of lead sector during this period. But there is disagreement as to whether this process represented an inevitable progress from the nitrate age or contrasts with a weakening commitment to manufacturing during the first decades of the century. The Argentine experience is usually presented as one of sustained, if cyclical and sub-sectorally specific, industrial expansion from the 1890s to the 1920s. However, this chronology has been challenged, particularly for the years 1914–33 which have been projected as a period of missed opportunities, an era when the potential for industrialization was not realized.[14] Peru's manufacturing sector, on the other hand, witnessed secular decline. Following years of flourishing industrial activity between 1891 and 1908 the next twenty years was a period of relapse. Sluggish domestic demand, the negative consequences of exchange stabilization and reduced protection for local manufacturers saw a decline in the momentum of industrial activity and imports displacing domestically produced goods in the home market.[15]

In Argentina, the ratios of agriculture and livestock output to manufactured output had shifted from 2.1 : 1 in 1900 to 1.3 : 1 in 1929, confirming that while the index of agricultural production had risen from 29 to 117, the index for manufacturing had increased at a much faster rate from 9 to 46 (1950 = 100).[16] These trends indicate a major restructuring of the economy, notwithstanding the small base from which manufacturing expanded or the continuing bias towards food processing in the industrial sector. However, the bias should not be exaggerated because although the output of food and beverages increased by a factor of 3.5, and of clothing by 3.6, chemical production grew by a factor of 6.1, and metals, machinery and vehicles by 25.6. The late 1920s also witnessed remarkable industrial activity in Mexico, partly evidencing recovery from the effects of the Revolution but also representing an advance upon Porfirian achievements. Manufacturing output, which had grown by an average of 3.1 per cent per annum during the period 1901–1910, registered a decline of 0.9 per cent per annum from 1911 to 1921 and then expanded at an average annual rate of 3.8 per cent between 1922 and 1935.[17] Both in Mexico and Brazil, qualitative changes in manufacturing were reflected in an increased use of electricity (only

[14] G. Di Tella and M. Zymelman, *Las etapas del desarrollo económica argentino* (Buenos Aires, 1967).
[15] Thorp and Bertram, *Peru 1890–1977*, 112, 118–31.
[16] C. F. Díaz Alejandro, *Essays on the economic history of the Argentine Republic* (New Haven, 1970), 418, 420, 433–4, 449.   [17] L. Solís, *La economía mexicana* (Mexico, 1970), Table III:1.

partly explained by a switch from earlier forms of power generation such as steam), particularly cheap hydro-electricity. There was, too, an increase in the size of the firm. For Brazil there is disagreement whether by this time manufacturing was on the threshold of becoming the lead sector in the economy. What is not in doubt is the erratic but nonetheless dramatic expansion in industrial output between 1914 and 1929. Perhaps the most significant feature of the final years of this period were two inter-related developments in the areas of transport equipment, chemicals and electrical goods. Influenced by the greater availability of electrical power and the expansion of domestic demand, the first was the accelerated increase in productive capacity, the second the penetration of these sub-sectors by trans-national corporate capital. Four key trends are observable with respect to Chilean industry between 1914 and 1929, a period of sustained if variable expansion. There was a change in the scale of production in favour of larger firms; local manufacturers increased their share of the domestic market by approximately 50 per cent; there was a relative decline in the profile of current consumption goods (such as foodstuffs and textiles) in total domestic manufactured output and an increase in the share of consumer durables, intermediate products and capital goods (like paper, chemicals, machinery and transport equipment); manufacturing increased its relative participation in Gross National Product (in part the result of the crisis in nitrate production).[18] Furthermore, the 1920s witnessed a steady increase, possibly for the first time in the modern period, in the output of and investment in Colombian industry.

Intra-sectoral diversification – identified with an expansion of consumer durables production (featuring both the manufacture of household articles and motor vehicle assembly), a broadening mix of intermediate products including chemicals, and some capital goods – was a generalized process that took place in most of the larger economies and several of the more advanced second-order states, like Chile and Uruguay, between the 1900s and 1929. In these economies factory production finally displaced the artisan. The consolidation of industries after 1930 is testimony to the scope of the pre-crash manufacturing base. Obviously the magnitude of early twentieth-century industrial change is easily exaggerated. A growth in manufactured output and installed industrial capacity must be set against the continued dominance of the

---

[18] Palma, 'External disequilibrium'.

foreign trade sector. Agriculture and mining often remained the focus of activity even if industry may be projected as a dynamic – possibly the most dynamic – sector. Against complacent accounts depicting an inexorable progress to an industrial society in Argentina, Brazil and particularly Chile must be set more cautious interpretations which stress that the limits of fragmented (albeit diverse) industrial expansion induced by export-led growth had been reached by the 1920s. Possibly the Latin American economies had already exhausted their capacity to realize an increased flow of exports by means of an extensive use of natural resources. Post-1914 instability in North Atlantic financial and commodity markets indicated the limited benefits likely to accrue from continued integration into a world economy founded upon the international division of labour. The easy phase of industrial expansion rooted in the processing of rural products, the refining of minerals and the manufacturing of basic consumer goods was drawing to a close in the larger economies. Deepening the industrial base and indeed the continued growth of manufactured output required a fundamental restructuring of the social order that would permit the formulation of policies congruent with the needs of the industrial sector. Peru's case of stalled industrial growth was a warning to others even if resulting from a particular combination of circumstances. Colombia presents a different example of the limits to industrial growth: by the 1920s only 3 per cent of the active labour force was employed in manufacturing, most in small shops that were little different from artisan forms of production.[19] In this context the impact of the First World War was critical. The War revealed strategic deficiencies in the Latin American economies and emphasised the dangers of an over-dependence upon the external sector. With respect to domestic manufacturing, the War promoted more efficient use of installed capacity while post-1919 readjustments strengthened the position of large-scale firms in most industries.

EXPORT-LED INDUSTRIALIZATION AND EXOGENOUS SHOCKS

Many of the conditions essential for the growth of industry emerged during cycles of export-led growth. The expansion of the foreign trade sector facilitated the consolidation of a money economy between the 1870s and 1920s, and encouraged stable, occasionally semi-represent-

---

[19] W. P. McGreevey, *An economic history of Colombia, 1845–1930* (Cambridge, 1971), 213.

ative, political systems. Well before the end of the nineteenth century most Latin American polities had successfully resolved problems associated with the destabilizing centrifugal forces of localism and regionalism that had crystallized during the revolutions for independence. Effective insertion within the world economy, based upon international exchange and upon a rational use of the continent's natural resources concentrated in the supply of those commodities where the countries of the region enjoyed the greatest comparative advantage, resulted, *inter alia*, in the modernization of transport and communications that, for some, generated order and progress. Railway construction and the laying of telegraph lines (and indeed the professionalization of the armed forces) produced political stability and an environment conducive to general economic expansion that yielded the particular social, legal and institutional context within which manufacturing for domestic consumption expanded. Primary export production was associated with increased domestic profits, an influx of foreign capital and with a rise in consumer demand occasioned by population growth, fuelled by immigration, and the consolidation of a wage economy.

This model of industrial development stresses the diffusion of finance and expertise from the foreign trade sector to domestic manufacture. Before the turn of the century, when North American and European manufacturers began to despatch their agents to the continent, the Latin American trades were dominated by commercial houses representing many firms and dealing in a diversity of products. They acted as consignees, linking producers with consumers (of exports) and manufacturers with customers (for industrial imports). Dealing in a heterogeneous mix of goods and often operating in volatile foreign exchange markets, the houses also performed rudimentary banking service and initiated railway projects. Given an access to export sector profits and an intimate knowledge of market conditions, merchant houses were well placed to respond to changes in the exchange rate or marginal modifications in tariff regimes that tipped the balance towards domestic manufacture and against importation, particularly for bulky products of prime necessity where unit profits were low and home production might be favoured by cheap raw material supply or attract state subsidies. Moreover, merchant houses, manifestations of commercial capital in a period of accelerated transition to industrial and possibly finance capitalism, were squeezed by the continuing industrial transformation of the North Atlantic economies. New manufacturing processes and

sophisticated industrial products in an increasingly competitive environment required careful marketing or after-sales services which the
import–export houses could not provide. The houses were also
pressurized by other tendencies, notably declining profit margins that
encouraged overseas industrial firms to internalize all aspects of
production and commercialization and to seek direct representation in
Latin American markets or to forge close links between production and
finance. This trend was especially pronounced in the more dynamic
capitalist economies. The kind of institutionalization of industry and
banking that occurred in Germany was particularly dangerous for
traditional mercantile firms in regions such as Latin America because
various overseas banks were already well established in the republics.
One option available to the houses was to convert to manufacturing. It
was seized with alacrity by West Coast houses such as Graham Rowe,
Duncan Fox and Balfour Williamson who moved into sugar refining,
cotton textiles and milling respectively.

Immigrants constituted another strand of industrial entrepreneurship
as indicated below. During periods of immigration, penny capitalists
launched a range of ventures, though many may have differed little in
character from artisan sweatshops. Occasionally individuals might
found clans, like the Matarazzos of São Paulo or the Di Tellas of Buenos
Aires, and industrial empires. These, and some of their lesser imitators,
gained not only financial success but also social acceptance and entered
the ranks of the oligarchy: examples of social upward mobility which
demonstrate that in some countries dominant elites may not have been as
closed as sometimes portrayed. The Chilean and Colombian elites in
particular displayed a capacity to absorb aspiring immigrant talent.

In the case of Brazil, Warren Dean has argued that national capital
originally concentrated in the export sector was central to the expansion
of manufacturing.[20] *Fazendeiros*, independently and in association with
foreigners, were involved in a mix of activities, manufacturing and
otherwise, that were not always ancillary to coffee. Just as coffee
generated the growth in incomes which underwrote the expansion of
demand for manufacturers so coffee profits funded industrial firms
established by members of the national elite. This hypothesis carries
conviction. And the centre of the debate has moved beyond direct
discussion of industrialization. Monetization of the economy was

[20] W. Dean, *The industrialization of São Paulo, 1880–1945* (Austin, 1969).

essential for the development of a market but the nature, and changes in the composition, of aggregate demand were of great significance for the consumption of manufactures. Rising real wages permitted that growth in discretionary incomes upon which a more diversified demand for manufactures, embracing not only basic goods but also consumer durables, was founded. In Brazil state policy may have been more responsive to the demands of industry than had been argued hitherto. Thus, the presentation of the history of Brazilian industrialization, that depicts manufacturing as opposed to agriculture, is no longer tenable. Industrialists recognized a community of interest with the coffee sector, realizing that coffee earning generated the foreign exchange required to import industrial equipment and raw materials besides determining the general level of activity in the economy. Paulista *fazendeiros* were rational capitalists, diversifying interests and allocating capital so as to maximize profits, and they also exhibited a preference for corporate and institutional patterns of investment. Instability in the coffee sector occasioned a pragmatic approach to land ownership and promoted a move away from coffee into domestic staples and manufacturing.

Can an approach based largely upon the experience of São Paulo be generalized to include other parts of Brazil, other coffee-producing areas or even other primary export economies? The example of Mexico indicates the limits to export-induced industrial growth. As elsewhere, Mexico experienced, if belatedly, infrastructural modernization and while the volume of railway construction was lower and more regionally concentrated than, for example, in the Southern Cone, the greater part of the rail network was located (with the exception of Northern mining districts) in areas of greatest population density. Mexico enjoyed not only a substantial degree of export diversification but also a mining sector from which transfers of technology to domestic-orientated metal working was possible. And as indicated above, at independence the country possessed the largest, most developed and diversified manufacturing base in Latin America. It was hardly surprising, then, that manufacturing was apparently well established by 1911. Metal working was probably more advanced than in any of the South American states and the textile industry was second only to that of Brazil's. But the pace of industrial expansion was faltering on the eve of the Revolution.

Symptoms of pre-Revolutionary crises in manufacturing were manifold. Increased instability was associated with the general cyclicality of the world economy during the years immediately prior to the First

World War, exacerbated by the peculiar problems of the silver mining sector and Mexico's attempts to come to terms with the Gold Standard. Within manufacturing the intensity of the crisis was revealed by bankruptcies and heightened tensions between labour and capital which took the form of strikes, lock-outs and a rising tide of repression in response to increased labour militancy. Central to the problems of domestic manufacturing was the failure of export growth to promote a dynamic expansion of the home market. In the face of depressed domestic demand, high duties on imported goods and the increased incidence of effective protection resulting from currency depreciation were of little consequence. Between the end of the nineteenth century and 1911 real wages in Mexico fell by about a half although there were sharp regional differences. This index of misery was partly explained by the capital intensive form of much activity in the export sector. More particularly it was due to the nature of the Porfirian model which facilitated foreign penetration and exceptionally skewed patterns of wealth distribution. The result was a seepage of resources from Mexico and extremely limited domestic income spin-offs. Inter-related with these problems was the increased cost of subsistence (which squeezed disposable incomes in the money economy), the result of a contraction in the supply of basic food staples as fertile land was switched to export production. Wages were also compressed by population growth and the large size of the subsistence sector – a reserve army of labour – which further depressed the wage rates of urban workers. In these circumstances manufacturing in Mexico, which had displayed several positive traits (namely a preference for limited liability, a capacity to apply new technology and remarkable product diversity) had probably stagnated by the early twentieth century. Global output and sectoral rates of growth for industry peaked by 1907 and declined thereafter. The Revolution was required to effect a productivity-raising change of gear in manufacturing and initiate a further round of accumulation and investment.

Yet, if the principal weakness of export-led growth in Mexico was a failure to generate an increased demand for wage goods through greater employment or rising real incomes in an economy with a large indigenous population, these conditions were not mirrored in the other larger economies. In Brazil and the River Plate Republics markets expanded either as the result of the monetization of the rural economy or because of real increases in wages, but not more equitable patterns of income distribution. Before 1914, employment in the export and public sectors stimulated the growth of home demand in Chile. European emigration to these republics and the movement of people across national frontiers and provincial boundaries indicate a response to differing wage levels and at least a perception that conditions were better in some areas than others. Qualitative changes, in addition to mere expansion, of aggregate demand may be observed in Argentina between the 1890s and 1914.[21] A breakdown of data on the increased volume of consumption of manufactures reveals a rising trend of domestic supply reflected in the diversification of imports. Various changes in the structure of Argentine import schedules during the period before the First World War corroborate the extent of industrial diversification. Not only do imports of basic consumer goods reveal a steady relative decline after the 1880s, but imports of capital goods and intermediate products registered a shift towards industrial machinery (away from transport equipment) and supplies of fuel and industrial materials. Less pronounced for the other republics, similar trends were nevertheless in train elsewhere and would become more obvious during the latter part of the 1920s.

The evidence of increased manufacturing activity during the phase of export-led growth emphasises the implausibility of an analysis that advocates remarkable expansion from scratch in 1929 to a position of – in several cases – domestic market dominance at high levels of consumption by 1939. If domestic manufactured output grew rapidly during the early 1930s it was due to a full-time working of previously installed under-utilized capacity. The situation could hardly have been otherwise given the logic of a necessity to import manufacturing equipment in a pre-industrial economy. Thus the de-linkage aspect of the adverse exogenous shocks theory has been attacked from all sides, notably for a failure to differentiate adequately between the consequences of war and depression and, indeed, between the precise effects of the First and Second World Wars. World conflicts tended to produce buoyant markets and high prices for Latin American exports. Supply side problems, as belligerent economies restructured production to wartime needs, restricted access to imports. Depressions, on the other hand were characterized by weak export prices and a drift towards bilateralism in international trade that narrowed market opportunities. Undifferenti-

[21] Díaz Alejandro, *Economic history of Argentine Republic*, 40–44; Vázquez-Presedo, *El caso argentino*, 135–7; R. Cortés Conde, *El progreso argentino, 1880–1914* (Buenos Aires, 1979), 211–40.

ated accounts of the impact of the world wars must also be regarded with suspicion. During the First World War Latin America's commercial isolation was less pronounced: a rapid growth of imports from Japan and the United States partly filled the gap created by shortfalls in supplies from the European powers. Exponents of the theory have also been castigated for exaggerating the size of the foreign trade sector and lack of specificity in the focus of overseas commercial relations. Most recently the thesis has been criticized for failing to identify pressures emanating from the central economies during periods of shock and crisis which enhanced rather than weakened the external connection. Examples of this process are the exercising of monopoly buying powers by the Allies during wartime or the imposition of bilateral trade and clearing arrangements upon the Latin American countries such as the Anglo-Argentine Roca–Runciman Pact of 1933. Many of these issues lie outside the scope of this chapter but indicate the weight of opinion against the interpretation.

CRISIS, WAR AND MANUFACTURING

Paradoxically the obloquy heaped upon original crude expositions of the adverse shocks school of Latin American industrialization has revitalized the debate, resulting in a projection of the analysis backwards into the nineteenth century. If the original proposition that the World Depression precipitated an industrial breakthrough is no longer tenable, earlier periods of instability in the external sector may have yielded more positive benefits for manufacturing. Nineteenth-century commercial and financial panics and the impact of the First World War, a major rupture, may be depicted not so much as forerunners of 1929 style de-linkage but as direct stimulants to entrepreneurial initiative or policy reformulation.

Hitherto, destabilizing externally-induced cyclical crises were addressed in terms of the denationalization of key sectors of the economy. The 1890s in particular witnessed large-scale transfers of national enterprise to foreigners. In Peru and Argentina there was a massive liquidation of state holdings in public utilities which were sold to foreign consortia. Here and elsewhere a national presence in the manufacturing sector faded during the last decades of the nineteenth century as local capitalists were bought out by companies registered overseas. Foreign firms, enjoying the advantage of large-scale operations and falling international freights aggressively penetrated Latin American markets thereby thwarting the formation of an authentic national capitalism. More nuanced interpretations now prevail. From the 1880s onwards foreign interests certainly bought out financially embarrassed national capital in Argentina and the West Coast republics in fields such as milling, wine making, sugar refining and cotton textiles. But these external interests were often already established in the economies, commercializing exports and advancing finance to an incipient industrial sector. Direct investment in manufacturing by such groups is now presented as leading to an infusion of more dynamic managerial and productive techniques. Similarly the consequences of the First World War now assume a positive aspect. Previously it was argued that hostilities in Europe occasioned an essentially ephemeral increase in manufactured output from labour intensive sweatshops unable to compete with foreign suppliers when normal external commercial relations were re-established after 1918. Weak, under-capitalized firms failed to secure effective support from government. They could not challenge vested interests enjoying direct access to the state apparatus such as export sector groups who regarded any hint of protectionism as anathema and likely to provoke an adverse reaction in overseas markets. Also of importance were the attitudes of organized urban labour employed in export sector-related activities. Workers, with first hand experience of war-induced inflation, were fully aware of the impact of tariff increases upon their standard of living. Less dichotomized interpretations dispute such crude rebuttals of the shocks thesis of industrialization and stress instead that war produced a favourable environment for investment in manufacturing and, revealing structural deficiencies in the Latin American economies, accelerated the evolution of a new political economy.

Three areas in particular illustrate the degree to which instability in the external sector may have promoted manufacturing, and indicate also a continued need for caution when approaching this subject. Mexico provides a classic example of the impact of war upon foreign trade activities during the early decades of the nineteenth century. Equally crucial is the Argentine case which demonstrates the effects of adverse shocks upon an economy during the opening stages of effective incorporation within the world economy. Chile, and also Brazil, are increasingly presented as near textbook case studies of the dynamic consequence for industry resulting from the First World War.

Mexico has been singled out for special attention.[22] Late colonial Mexico possessed the most elaborate manufacturing sector in Spanish America, possibly in the whole of the Americas. The country experienced several extensive periods of de-linkage between the 1770s and 1850s. As contemporaries observed, Mexican manufacturing and craft production prospered during periods of European warfare when the colony/republic was at peace. Equally, disruptions to transatlantic trade emanating from the centre, for example the 1825 crash in London, encouraged increased industrial activity. When war in Europe disrupted communications with Spain and privateering threatened a lucrative contraband trade, imports fell away and exports (principally of silver bullion) accumulated in Mexico. The retention of silver increased the stock of currency and capital and, coupled with reduced imports, produced inflation and induced in entrepreneurs expectations of higher profits from domestic production and exchange. The increased stock of currency in circulation expanded the scope of the money economy and yielded higher wages and salaries for Mexico's expanding population. Buoyant markets and increased demand for domestic manufactures attracted the attention of merchants accumulating capital that could not be employed in overseas trade. This positive scenario, which accurately depicts events during the late 1770s, the mid 1790s, the turn of the century and the late 1800s, undoubtedly stimulated various lines of production. During these years secondary production, especially of textiles, expanded enormously. And, until trade with neutrals became fully operational, Mexican industry supplied Spanish garrison towns in the Caribbean and Central America with coarse cloth, flour, sugar and occasionally salt pork. Although largely confined to the home market by the 1820s, various branches of industry continued to prosper. A converse pattern emerged during periods of stability in transatlantic commerce. Silver bullion and coin flowed abroad, decapitalizing home-based manufacture and financing imports. Merchants turned from production to commerce and Mexican industry which had exuded an air of activity and prosperity during periods of de-linkage lapsed into lethargy. Only in the 1830s was there a conscious attempt to manipulate the external connection so as better to serve domestic requirements with an application of selective import tariffs, official finance for industry

---

[22] C. Cardoso (ed.), *México en el siglo XIX (1821–1910)* (Mexico, 1980); R. Potash, *El Banco de Avío de México: el fomento de la industria, 1821–1846* (Mexico, 1959); G. P. C. Thompson, 'Protectionism and industrialization in Mexico, 1821–1854; the case of Puebla', in Abel and Lewis, *Latin America*.

and the introduction of a base-metal currency that, lacking intrinsic value, would both augment the monetary base and insulate domestic money supply against drainage overseas. Even if applied consistently and with greater continuity, it is doubtful, however, if such institutionalized de-linkage would have stimulated self-sustaining industrial expansion.

The lessons that emerge from the experience of Mexico during these years are not so much the absolute necessity of policy continuity, vital though this might be, but rather the structuralist proposition, confirmed by the case of Paraguay before the 1865 war, that it was impossible to promote an enduring industry by government fiat unless widespread modification to the economic substructure could be concurrently implemented. Mexico failed to industrialize during the period not because the country lacked a manufacturing tradition (which was clearly not the case) nor because of political instability and the debilitating effects of a rising flood of imports (significant though these factors may have been). De-linkage failed to occasion self sustaining industrial growth because of inadequate communications which in the post-colonial period had strengthened the powerful regionalist tendencies that confined industrial progress to a provincial level. And, of paramount importance, was the mercantile character of enterprise before the 1840s. When merchants had invested in textile manufacturing during the exogenous shocks of the pre-1830s period, they did so in putting-out operations not in factory-based production. Dealing in raw materials, yarn and cloth spread their risks by shifting any losses onto cottage spinners, artisan weavers or retailers. Mercantile practices characterized these operations involving limited investment in fixed plant, ensured liquidity and helped to secure the dominance of merchant interests in the chain of activities from raw material supply to final product.

Other examples of sudden ruptures in external economic relations corroborate the conclusion that exogenous shocks were not by themselves sufficient to promote industrial expansion. Argentine perceptions of industry during the wool cycle, 1840–80, were more narrowly drawn than Mexican during the first part of the nineteenth century. Observing the misery and the social disturbances provoked by contracting world demand for, and decline in the price of, wool, commentators remarked upon the shortcomings of a system whereby Argentina exported fleeces in a near raw state and imported finished textiles. Both at the time of the 1866 panic and 1873 depression projects were formulated to encourage a larger domestic participation in the process of transforming wool into cloth.[23] Yet there were limits to these and other sensible schemes to promote manufacturing upon a broader front. Local markets were small. The total population of Argentina when the first national census was held in 1869 was less than two million. Pastoral interests in Buenos Aires, the core of the protectionist movement during the crises of the 1860 and 1870s, realized that the home market could absorb only a small proportion of the annual wool clip. Their commitment to protectionism was transient, an immediate response at the moment of crisis. When foreign demand recovered, their attachment to protection faded. By the time the Baring Crisis administered another, more substantial, shock to the system, *bonarense* ranchers were even more firmly wedded to internationalism and were, moreover, able to diversify into a wider mix of rural products, thus offsetting contraction in one activity by expansion in another. Other groups in the protectionist lobby during the 1860s, 1870s and 1880s were more anxious to secure major and lasting changes to the external tariff regime, but lacked the political influence of land owners.

Argentine industrialists consistently advocated the advantages of protectionism throughout the third quarter of the nineteenth century and beyond. The Industrial Association presented its membership as a veritable product of exogenous shock, threatened by an ascendant policy of free trade.[24] Although industry and projects to support manufacturing enjoyed something of a vogue during the 1870s, their contribution to the national economy was limited. Still dominant in Buenos Aires surveys of the sector, though now of declining significance as pastoral activities moved away from dried meat and hide production to wool and later prime cattle, were the *saladeros*. Milling was the second most important activity followed by a host of lesser trades directly related to the pastoral economy, tanning, cheese manufacture, soap and candle making. While these activities were principally conducted in large or medium size establishments, there were a multiplicity of other trades undertaken mainly, though not exclusively, in small sweat shops, for example household metalware, ceramics, papermaking and cabinet making.[25] While the limited size of the workforce employed in some of these units

[23] J. C. Chiaramonte, *Nacionalismo y liberalismo: economicos en Argentina, 1860–1880* (Buenos Aires, 1971).

[24] *Ibid.*, 205; J. C. Nicolau, *Industria argentina y aduana, 1835–54* (Buenos Aires, 1975).

[25] Province de Buénos-Ayres, *Annuaire Statistique*, 371.

may have indicated a precocious application of new technology, the majority were unmechanized and short of capital. They catered for the bottom end of the market hardly affected by export boom or exogenous shock. Their response to external crisis and a decline in imports was likely to be an augmentation of price rather than increased output. Only those firms with access to capital were able to take advantage of the 1876 tariff revision and import machinery to meet home demand which was in any case faltering as the result of declining export sector incomes.

Exogenous shocks would have little impact upon the long term course of Argentine industry while the domestic market remained small and fragmented. For dominant sectors of Argentine society the debate about protectionism was essentially a case of short-term nationalist posturing, to be discarded when buoyancy returned to the external sector. Pastoral interests had learnt early in the wool cycle that there was little advantage to be had even from investment in rudimentary processing activities when tariffs in overseas markets could be modified to discriminate against semi-finished Argentine exports or when foreign customers were so dismissive of the country's capacity to refine or clean raw commodities that they refused to pay the premium attached to semi-finished items. Indeed, during the period many Latin American commodities were exported in a crude or semi-finished state, other examples being blister copper from Peru, Bolivian tin *barilla*, and *granulada* sugar. Perhaps there was little to gain from additional investment in processing and refining at a time of rapid technological change that made for a high risk of obsolescence.

Elsewhere, however, exogenous shocks may have resulted in a spurt to industrialization. The Chilean response to the crisis of 1873 undoubtedly stimulated manufacturing in the long run. An unwillingness to reduce the scale of public sector activities when the foreign trade sector (and consequently government revenues) faltered necessitated a recourse to an expansionist monetary policy and increased tariffs in an attempt to recoup state finances. And the evidence for the First World War as a stimulant to Chilean industrialization is pressing. But domestic manufacturing did not expand as a result of the war *per se*. Rather growth was occasioned by profound changes in the external sector resulting from the war. Between 1914 and 1918 industry in Chile behaved much as in other countries in Latin America where export prices soared as a consequence of wartime demand.

Natural nitrates were an essential ingredient in the manufacture of explosives. The loss of markets in the countries of Central Europe were more than compensated for by increased demand from the Allies, sustained by the requirements of the munitions industry and farmers in Britain and the United States seeking to raise crop yields. But the war also encouraged the development of the synthetic nitrate industry. Technically feasible before 1914, the scale of European – particularly German – investment in synthetic nitrates was such as dramatically to reduce production costs to levels well below those of the Chilean industry. Chilean *oficinas* were notorious for ossified inefficient production techniques. The natural nitrate industry was doomed, chances of recovery inhibited by the large stocks of nitrates held abroad in consuming centres, gross ineptitude on the part of the companies and acrimonious relations between foreign-owned nitrate *oficinas* and the Chilean state. Responding to this negative situation in the external sector, the government applied measures designed to stimulate production for the home market, building upon an already established interventionist tradition and benefiting from the scale of the pre-1914 industry. Tariffs were revised principally to defend domestic manufacture and levels of effective protection increased by currency devaluation. Credit facilities were extended and the state assumed a major profile in the capital market. Some attempt was made to control inflation and there was a sustained shift in demand from imports to items of domestic manufacture. As a result, while domestic manufacturing grew at a rate four times faster than that of a buoyant export sector during the war, industrial output increased at an even faster rate relative to export production between 1919 and 1929 when the foreign sector was depressed. Before 1930 manufacturing was well established as the most dynamic sector of the Chilean economy largely as a consequence of a policy response to external disequilibrium (founded upon historic precedents) rather than as a function of adverse crisis as such.

The Chilean experience was clearly exceptional. But it is increasingly recognized that in a number of respects the First World War stimulated manufacturing both directly and indirectly. The most obvious immediate impact of the outbreak of hostilities in Europe was dislocation in the foreign trade sector: shortages of shipping disrupted flows of exports and imports. However, by 1915/16 most Latin American exports had recovered and production, especially of strategic raw materials and essential foodstuffs, was running at levels well above those prevailing in 1914. Buoyant export incomes produced once again positive market conditions for domestic industry. Continuing scarcity of imports, on the other hand, also tended to enhance the presence of local suppliers in home markets and occasionally neighbouring overseas markets. Distorted patterns of transatlantic commerce and a far from total disruption of imports effected further restructurings of import schedules that gave heightened prominence to intermediate products and some capital goods – a tendency that, coupled with the rising price of imported consumer goods, additionally encouraged domestic manufacture.

It is hardly surprising that Latin American industry responded to such a fortunate configuration of domestic demand and foreign supply by expanding output. Increased production was to be observed in most lines of established manufacture, but especially in non-durables and industrial goods like textile equipment, lathes, boilers, motors and compressors. Rising indices of secondary production were achieved as the result of a more effective utilization of installed capacity, usually by the introduction of a second or even a third shift. Occasionally firms that had previously specialized in the repair of imported machinery and equipment were encouraged to begin manufacturing – a leap forward that required little extra capital or expertise. This tendency was most pronounced in Brazil, Chile and Peru.

Throughout the continent, but especially in Brazil, the First World War increased industrial entrepreneurs' perceptions of home market potential and stimulated new investment. By 1917, notably in those economies that already possessed diversified, if small, manufacturing sectors many businessmen were committed to extensive programmes of capital expenditure. While investment decisions were taken before the end of the War, rarely could projects be completed before 1918 as the paradoxical growth in Brazilian manufacturing capacity during the post-war slump demonstrates. These programmes were testimony to the high level of profits – from which new investment was financed – between 1915 and the end of the War and also to the confidence of industrial investors. That these programmes were initiated during the period of hostilities in Europe indicates in addition the advanced condition of the construction industry and the availability of capital inputs. Sometimes firms embarked upon over-ambitious investment schemes and, like the Vasena foundry in Buenos Aires, were caught by a post-war contraction in demand and a rising tide of imports partly explained by domestic currency appreciation. But other firms survived until renewed expansion in the export sector during the mid 1920s improved prospects for home production when order returned to world currency markets.

Instability in Latin American money markets and illiquidity amongst the banks was another pressing problem during the early years of the War, though one that was less easily resolved. Tightness in financial markets as European bankers called in loans and reduced overseas commitments was rapidly transmitted from the foreign trade sector to other areas of the Latin American economies. In a number of countries government responded to the clamour of elite groups for credit accommodation and the violent protests of the urban unemployed by easing fiscal burdens and pursuing expansionist monetary policies. Elsewhere, repression, appeals to patriotism and the imposition of orthodox palliatives was the norm. Wartime lessons of the opportunities for pragmatic Keynesianism were not easily learnt and usually only imperfectly digested. If Brazil was prepared to resort to Chilean-style loose money policies at various times during the 1920s, Argentina was not. Thus in a few countries the legacy of the War was policy pragmatism and the imprinting upon the bureaucratic mind of memories of programmes suited to the requirements of industry. More usually the siren call of economic orthodoxy was too strong to be resisted, at least during the 1920s.

Most significant was the nature of the adverse exogenous shock rather than de-linkage *per se*. Equally, the phasing of export boom and shock have a bearing on the issue. External crises were unlikely to foster the growth of manufacturing in an economy devoid of industrial capacity or structures capable of sustaining dynamic factory based production. The critical factor was often policy response, i.e. whether or not appropriate measures were devised either to protect fledgling industries established during cycles of export expansion (not so much from foreign competition in the first instance as from a collapse of domestic purchasing power) or to sustain a comprehensive programme of industrialization. De-linkage could enhance the use of installed manufacturing capacity but only rarely was the consequence increased investment in industry. Only in those areas where manufacturers were confident that the domestic market could be secured against foreign competition during the post-crisis period was there a sustained flow of investments into the sector.

THE SEARCH FOR AN EXPEDIENT POLICY

Since independence, and for much of the period studied, the debate about an appropriate milieu in which industry might prosper was premised almost exclusively upon the reshaping of commercial codes and tariff protection. Broader state action is now stressed. Discussion has moved outwards to embrace subjects such as exchange depreciation, labour policy, credit management and more general aspects of government intervention in the economy, for example, social reforms and welfare legislation. The tariffs issue has also become more complex. To what extent were these measures effectively implemented? And were they explicitly applied to stimulate industry?

Throughout the nineteenth century taxes upon foreign trade constituted the principal source of government revenue. Duties on overseas trade financed the day-to-day operations of the state. Customs receipts provided the state with access to gold based foreign currencies and, when expenditure beyond the capacity of current income was required, could be mortgaged in order to secure loans abroad. Taxing foreign trade was a comparatively cost-effective means of providing revenue. Tariffs on overseas commerce raised more revenue than would probably have been generated from excise duties, required a smaller establishment than that needed to implement a multiplicity of inland and direct taxes – a process necessitating a degree of technical proficiency beyond the competence of state bureaucracies. Taxing the foreign trade sector also avoided the political complications inherent in any form of direct taxation that would inevitably fall upon dominant strata in Latin American societies. In as much as tariffs were applied mainly to imports and represented a tax upon consumption, the burden of revenue provision fell disproportionately upon poorer members of the community while export interests receiving an income in gold or gold-based foreign currencies were insulated from domestic inflation implicit in the tax and revenue structure.

Dependence upon import duties, it has been argued, committed Latin American governments to a political economy founded upon free trade and struck from their hands the most effective means of stimulating industry. The view that revenue and protective duties are incompatible may be disputed. Brazilian tariffs were raised in 1844 following the expiry of the unequal trade treaties with Britain, maximizing government revenue and providing a modicum of protection for domestic manufacturing. Though liberalized in 1853, Brazil's tariff code was subsequently repeatedly revised during the Empire. Later the decentralized administrative structure established after 1889, which transferred much of the responsibility for fiscal policy determination to the states, may also have made the political system more responsive to demands for protection emanating from lobbies in those areas where manufacturing was developing. By the mid-1870s duties upon imported textiles which ranged from 50 per cent to 80 per cent were considered to confer a clear advantage upon local industry.[26] Whether tariff revisions were intended to stimulate manufacturing remains a subject of debate. Before the end of the century revenue considerations were uppermost in determining big tariff increases, even in the most advanced areas where precocious industrial growth could be observed. Short-lived tariff reforms may also be presented as cheap political measures, expedient devices to consolidate support for a regime threatened at home or subject to foreign pressure. Protective measures adopted in Argentina in 1835 were introduced at a critical moment for the Rosas regime. The 1835 tariff and further increases in import duties in 1837 were popular with rural and urban interests in the provinces and amongst domestic workers in the city of Buenos Aires whose livelihoods were threatened not only by imports from Britain but also by local factory based production.[27] Foreign observers admitted that the measures might stimulate agriculture and industry. Yet these revisions were introduced when trade was already slack as a result of the 1836/7 panic in London and due to a deterioration in Argentina's relations with foreign powers. Rosas' intervention in Uruguay and a chill in Franco-Argentine contacts, originating in 1834, by 1837 resulted in the declaration of a French blockade of the River Plate. Was the much vaunted Brazilian tariff revision of 1844 similarly little more than political posturing, a negotiating ploy designed to strengthen the government's hand in dealing with Britain at a time of renewed pressure against the transatlantic slave trade? Causality, chronology and effect may be disputed but the conjecture admits speculation.

A dynamic model of tariff revision has, however, been elaborated for Brazil which may have a wider application. Accepting the revenue function of import tariffs, the analysis itemizes forces necessitating an expansion of the fiscal base which could only be met by tariff increases. Pressures for modernization – improvement of infrastructure and state subsidies for productive enterprizes – emanated from various quarters and were regarded as a means of consolidating the influence of central

[26] *Parliamentary Papers* (hereafter *P.P.*), 1876, LXXV, 36.
[27] Nicolau, *Industria argentina*; Chiaramonte, *Nacionalismo*, 13, 15, 21–2; M. Burgin, *Economic aspects of Argentine federalism, 1820–1852* (Cambridge, Mass., 1946), 237–45; H. S. Ferns, *Britain and Argentina in the nineteenth century* (Oxford, 1960), 251–2.

government. Domestic instability or foreign adventures also necessitated extra expenditure. Exogenous shocks produced a shortfall in
revenue as overseas trade contracted, compelling a search for new sources
of funds. Given increased demands upon the fiscal resources of the state
and limited possibilities for borrowing at home or abroad, notably during
periods of financial instability, there was an inexorable tendency to
modify import duties. Revenue raising tariff increases inevitably altered
differentials between import prices and domestic production costs. Local
manufacturing responded by consolidating its share of the home market
or commenced new lines of production. These moves enhanced the size
of the pro-industry lobby which became more effectively organized,
pressing for the retention of measures initially introduced as temporary
fiscal expedients. During subsequent periods of growth, newly enlarged
manufacturing interests solidified, and were more effectively placed to
take advantage of the next revenue-inspired increase in duties, pressing
for tariff re-classification or across-the-board surcharges. This model of
industrial expansion and consolidation acknowledging the fiscal impera-
tive and classifying demands upon the resources of the state offers an
explanation for the cyclical nature of tariff revisions. It may also account
for a tendency deplored by importers, i.e. the implementation of repeated
tariff adjustments within a short space of time. The desire to maximize
revenue often provoked repeated small downward revisions (and
occasionally further increases) after large hikes. This explanation offers a
more convincing explanation for 'instability' in tariff regimes than those
which stress ideological considerations – the product of a confrontation
between advocates of free trade and proponents of neo-mercantilist
philosophies of *fomento*.

Importers were certainly not alone in protesting against successive
changes in rates of duty or the reclassification of customs schedules.
Manufacturers voiced similar complaints. However, if the former were
exercised by non-tariff barriers to the flow of trade, such as bureaucratic
inefficiency or, worse, official bloodymindedness and bribery in the
customs house, the latter were concerned about undiscriminating duties
which reduced the effectiveness of tariff protection. Consequently when
searching for evidence of a pro-industry bias in tariff revisions, special
attention must be paid to the categorization of imports and the
application of differential duties on finished products, raw materials and
machinery. In Chile after a trend towards increasing specificity in tariff
legislation as revealed in the 1851 General Ordinance and to a lesser

extent in the new Act of 1864, there was a far-reaching revision of duties during the late 1870s, a period of acute financial crisis. Fiscal considerations occasioned a 10 per cent tariff surcharge in 1877, preceding a thorough restructuring the following year. The 1878 Ordinance which raised the general level of duties to 35 per cent can be presented as a response to both fiscal objectives and protectionist sentiments. The number of items imported free of duty was expanded dramatically and included virtually all industrial raw materials and inputs. The discriminatory nature of the new law is seen in a narrowing of the rubric by which the duty on machinery imports might be waived. 15 per cent tariffs would now apply on imports of vehicles, engines and hardware as these items were produced domestically. Consumer goods industries such as food processing, textiles and footwear, paper making and cabinet making particularly benefited from the 1878 Act as did those capital goods industries, notably metal working, whose imports of intermediate products – pig iron, steel, zinc, bolts etc – entered duty free. The 1878 law, which remained in force until 1884, fostered manufacturing. Although the intentions underlying the law were fiscal, its structure was a pragmatic response to domestic manufacture, a sector whose representations to government could not by that time be totally ignored. Chile was undoubtedly an exceptional case in that during the last third of the nineteenth century import duties provided a diminishing proportion of state revenue. In 1860 customs receipts (mainly import duties) accounted for over 60 per cent of total government revenue. By 1878 the figure was 44 per cent. After the War of the Pacific taxes on nitrate exports represented the principal source of government income. Whereas export taxes yielded only 3 per cent of exchequer receipts in 1875, by 1920 they produced 71 per cent.[28] Import tariffs were accordingly liberated from an exclusively fiscal function and became available as an instrument of development policy. There is some discussion about whether rising nitrate revenues had a wholly beneficial effect upon tariff policy. If protectionism now became a viable policy option, there is no agreement that the option was effectively exercised. Did the prosperity of the nitrate age deflect state and entrepreneurial attention away from manufacturing?[29]

[28] L. Ortega, 'Economic policy and growth in Chile from independence to the War of the Pacific', in Abel and Lewis, *Latin America*; Mamalakis, *Chilean economy*, 20.
[29] For differing assessments, see Mamalakis, *Chilean economy*, Palma, 'External disequilibrium', Ortega, 'Economic policy in Chile', and Kirsch, *Industrial development*.

There was a distinct pro-industry drift in Brazilian tariff policy after the 1880s. Taxes upon imports accounted for approximately 60 per cent of Brazilian central government revenue between the middle of the nineteenth century and the First World War with duties on cotton textiles accounting for a large share of this revenue.[30] Despite the fiscal bias of the tariff, the cotton textile industry developed apace. Similar tendencies may be observed for other industries, for example, shoe manufacturing where home production virtually accounted for the totality of domestic consumption in 1914. There are several explanations for this paradox. First, tariff codes became more sophisticated and discriminatory with the passage of time. Relatively small adjustments to levels of duty and the reclassification of imports reconciled the demands of an increasingly articulate industrial lobby and the government's need for revenue. Secondly, the general fall in the nominal price of imports for much of the later part of the nineteenth century actually increased the clamour of infant industry for protection and extended the scope for revenue raising. With a fall in the price of imports, increased duties were required in order to maintain the price of foreign goods in the market place. Few impecunious administrations could fail to respond to this situation which also permitted greater flexibility in the use of the duty free list. Machinery and necessary inputs could be placed on the free list without jeopardizing revenue. Moreover import duties began to bite with greater force towards the end of the nineteenth century as various governments began to insist that obligations at the Customs House be met in gold rather than in paper currency. The Argentine tariff regulation of 1890, introduced in the midst of the Baring Crisis, reduced duties on productive machinery and equipment to 10 per cent and 5 per cent while placing some items on the free list. But rates on various finished manufactures and foodstuffs that competed with domestic production were raised to 60 per cent. All duties were payable only in gold, a sharp reversal of the situation that prevailed in the 1880s.[31] Brazil also raised the gold quota (the proportion of duty to be paid in gold) repeatedly around and after the turn of the century.[32] Finally a number of republics applied a customs regime that set fixed official gold values for individual items against which prevailing rates of duty were levied. The

[30] F. R. Versiani, *Industrial investment in an 'export' economy: the Brazilian experience before 1914* (University of London, Institute of Latin American Studies Working Paper No. 2, 1979), 20.

[31] Ferns, *Britain and Argentina*, 457.

[32] Versiani, *Industrial investment*; W. Cano, *Raízes de concentração industrial em São Paulo* (São Paulo, 1981), 149–50.

discrepancy between official dockside values and the nominal prices of imports widened after the 1870s, as shipping freights declined and manufacturers' f.o.b. prices fell resulting in an increased incidence of protection.

Consistent protection from the mid-1870s onwards, whether resulting from perspicacious tariff policies or from the vagary of world price movements, was an important element – though not the only factor – contributing to business confidence. Tariffs facilitated the growth of infant industries. As customs codes evolved, becoming more discriminatory, backward linkage effects fostered a deepening of the industrial process as entrepreneurs vertically integrated distinct stages of the manufacturing process or new suppliers emerged, stimulated by a demand for industrial inputs. A good example is provided by the Brazilian footwear industry: the industry grew during the nineteenth century under the protective umbrella of a tariff regime that levied high duties on finished imports. By 1907 domestic output accounted for 96 per cent of total consumption. Until the turn of the century the industry was heavily dependent on imported inputs – of machinery and raw materials. Because of unreliability of supply and the variable quality of domestically tanned leather, Brazilian shoe manufacturers imported most of their requirements from the United States. Thread was also imported. Given domestic resource availability, the industry switched to local leather suppliers during the First World War. But as early as 1908 Brazilian shoes were being manufactured on equipment made in the country by a U.S. conglomerate, the United Shoe Manufacturing Company. The U.S.M. Co. provided a comprehensive service to shoe producers, leasing machines and offering maintenance contracts to leasees. The U.S. firm also trained operatives, supplied parts and gave advice on installation. At this stage it was claimed that the industry no longer required protection.[33]

In Brazil lessons derived from tariff experimentation with respect to the shoe industry, and more particularly with cotton textile production, may have served as a model for tariff changes that had a broader impact during the 1920s. Experience with cotton goods demonstrated the need for precise adjustments of duties not merely with regard to imports of machinery and directly competitive finished items but more especially with respect to various intermediate inputs – threads, yarns, bleaches and

---

[33] W. Suzigan, 'Investment in the manufacturing industry in Brazil, 1869–1939' (unpublished Ph.D. thesis, University of London, 1984), 152, 154–5, 156, 157–8.

dyes – if domestic production was to cater for more than the bottom end of the home market. Without such attention to detail there was little prospect of rapid diversification and the emergence of local sources of supply, in short a deepening of the industrial base. By the 1920s Brazilian and Mexican customs codes had probably achieved a suitable degree of sophistication. Elsewhere tariff regimes were cruder, less attuned to the evolving requirements of domestic manufacturers.[34]

Protection was clearly important for the emergence and consolidation of industrial production. But the issue can be exaggerated: excessive claims on behalf of protectionism project an uncritical acceptance of a traditionalist view that stresses the dominance of *laissez faire* philosophies in Latin America. It is facile to present tariff reform as a crucial, but unrealized, alternative to outmoded liberal strategies; to depict individual revisions of customs regimes as isolated examples, indicating a positive development strategy which was unfortunately not adopted due to a widespread commitment to free trade. Policy pragmatism rather than an intransigent adherence to liberal principles may account for a cautious approach to the tariff. Some industries did not require protection; expansion occurred when government was indifferent to the requirements of the sector or the impact of tariffs was at best neutral. The 1864 customs ordinance, which reputedly inaugurated an era of doctrinaire liberalism in Chile, did not prevent the founding of new factories. On the contrary, industrialists responded positively to the boom conditions in 1865–73, a period decisive for the consolidation of national industry. Brazilian hat makers did not require protection in the 1860s though favoured by government subsidies and licensed to import raw materials free of duty. By 1888 mills in Rio Grande do Sul were using local wool to produce coarse saddle blankets and flannels that undercut imports. The industry did not need protection and firms declared high dividends.[35]

A marginal, often isolated element of the economy manufacturing was, especially before the last quarter of the nineteenth century, susceptible to changes in national and international economic environments. Factory production utilizing complex plant (requiring access to foreign technology, possibly imported inputs and relatively large

[34] F. R. Versiani, 'Before the depression: Brazilian industry in the 1920s', in R. Thorp (ed.), *Latin America in the 1930s: the role of the periphery in world crisis* (London, 1984); Suzigan, 'Investment in Brazil', *passim*.; R. Miller, 'Latin American manufacturing and the First World War', *World Development*, 9/8 (1981).   [35] P.P., 1889 LXXVII, 446.

amounts of investment in capital hungry economies) was particularly exposed. Industrialists, unlike pastoralists, could not retreat into subsistence. As late as the 1860s and 1870s when links with the world economy had not fully crystallized and techniques of production remained rudimentary, *estancieros* ranching on a large scale could suspend processing operations, stockpile non-perishable commodities and allow herds and flocks to multiply when conditions were adverse, re-entering the market when economic or political situations improved. This option was not available to manufacturers dependent upon a complex nexus of commercial and financial services. Like other modern activities, industry was a beneficiary of the process of state building that occurred during the phase of outward orientated expansion. Increased political stability, new legal frameworks for the incorporation of firms, professionalization of administration, improved communication, rising aggregate demand and greater capital availability influenced the environment within which business decisions about investment and production were taken. There were also aspects of public policy that had a direct impact upon manufacturing.

From the late 1880s until 1930 expenditure upon development projects (public works and education) in Chile grew at an average rate of 4.0 per cent per annum, accounting for approximately 30 per cent of all monies allocated by the state. Large sums were also devoted to administration. Before 1910 railway construction absorbed the largest share of public works expenditure, to be superseded thereafter by roads and port improvement. Education and the provision of adequate schooling was an unending topic of debate during the period. The impact of infrastructural modernization outside the central valleys has been questioned, as has the quality of educational services. What is not in doubt is that an integrated market was consolidated in central Chile and that these labour intensive activities had a high domestic multiplier effect in an economy where the home market was corralled behind a thicket of protective duties and non-tariff barriers. Equally, state expenditure upon public works had a direct and positive impact upon heavy industry notwithstanding some backsliding in the 1890s. Given that for most of the period the principal export industry was dominated by foreign capital, and in as much as the greater part of government income was derived from export taxes, public policy ensured a transfer of resources from the external sector to the domestic economy and facilitated national capital formation.[36] Moreover, the interventionist practices evolved during the nitrate era would later be translated into mechanisms of demand management designed to orientate internal purchasing power towards the home market.

Banking and currency management is another area of obvious importance. Approaches to the role and policy of banks reflect the diversity of opinion present in the wider debate about economic policy. If a concern for stability in the sector set the parameters within which contemporary discussion occurred there was less agreement as to whether banks should perform a neutral or development function. It was recognized that banks might serve as agents of government intervention. Yet the potential for state activity was limited by the large presence of foreign banks in most countries and the late appearance of national entities in many others. Foreign institutions were also inclined to crowd out domestic firms and could constrain the activities of official banks, being regarded as less prone to failure or subject to overt political manipulation. Non-institutional forms of finance were, of course, available to industrialists who in other circumstances were dependent upon profits to fund expansion. Immigrant entrepreneurs could raise loans in their respective communities and some manufacturers had access to export sector earnings. But such opportunities were not widespread. Most would-be industrialists clamoured for institutional accommodation.

Exacerbated by external crises, shortages of working capital and investment finance were problems common to most Latin American economies during the period studied, fostered in part by institutional inadequacy and instability. Equally important was the focus of banking activities upon the external sector and adverse balances of trade that occasioned an export of specie. Several banks were founded in Brazil during the early 1850s, a period of general liquidity following the end of the transatlantic slave trade that witnessed the establishment of many commercial and industrial firms. But Brazil continued to experience acute illiquidity in the banking sector. With the 1866 crisis the state was compelled to act and various proposals were discussed in order to meet the growing needs of the expanding coffee economy and short-term exigencies of the Paraguayan War. Yet few fundamental reforms were

[36] Mamalakis, *Chilean economy*, 73–4.

introduced. Company law, ordered by the commercial code of 1860 that had been introduced in the aftermath of the 1858 crash, was restrictive in the extreme. Council of State authorization was required before any firm, in the banking sector or elsewhere, could operate under a regime of limited liability. The 1860 code which remained in force for more than twenty years, proved impervious to all attempts to liberalize banking legislation. Only during the 1880s did the number of banks increase. Few houses, with some notable exceptions, provided adequate accommo-dation for local industry. Greater flexibility came with the establishment of the Old Republic, assisted by loose monetary policies and an expan-sion of state credit especially during the early 1890s, during the First World War and intermittently during the second coffee valorization programme.

Banking practice in Argentina was possibly even more restrictive, despite a brief period of experiment. Modelled on U.S. legislation, the 1887 National Guaranteed Banks Law was an attempt to instil both order and flexibility into the system which would thus become more attuned to domestic requirements. Coupled with projects for currency reform, the new law was also designed to facilitate government regulation. This aspect of the 1887 reform has been projected as an attempt to control foreign banks and place credit at the disposal of national industry. If these were indeed the objectives, the policy was unsuccessful. The Baring Crisis not only carried away many state banks but also revealed the speculative (and illegal) practices adopted by the guaranteed banks. Engendered by a highly critical appraisal of the conduct of the guaranteed bank, an extremely orthodox banking code evolved sub-sequently. By the turn of the century Argentina possessed one of the most restrictive banking sectors in Latin America with excessive liquidity requirements. Whatever had been the intentions of the guaranteed banking legislation, the reaction against the 1887 Act was to prevent the emergence of public service or development banking for several decades. Complaints from industrialists about the rigidity of banking practices continued during the early decades of the twentieth century and reached a crescendo in the 1920s when it was claimed that the Banco de la Nación's refusal to rediscount suffocated the Buenos Aires money market.

The contrast with Chile is marked. Coins – gold, silver and copper – alone had constituted legal tender in Chile until 1860. The monetary system was wholly inadequate particularly with the increased level of economic activity that occurred from mid-century onwards. The first bank of issue was established at Valparaíso in 1848. Despite official opposition, and in the face of the hostility of vested business interests, four further banks commenced operations between 1854 and 1860. The *ad hoc* arrangements that had applied previously were regularized by legislation in July 1860 that formally conferred the right of note issue on these banks. The 1860 law was an extremely liberal piece of legislation, it established no minimum capital requirement for the incorporation of banks of issue, did not oblige the banks to hold metallic reserves, nor provide for any form of government inspection. The result was a dramatic increase in the number of banks and in the volume of notes in circulation.[37] Banking legislation was but one facet of the assumption of a more active stance by the Chilean state. Government mortgage banks were created and the state was itself a major customer. There was a rapid increase in the domestic and foreign debt and the state pursued a generally expansionist monetary policy in order to finance the growth of the public sector. Given an unwillingness or an inability to increase the tax base, borrowing and printing money were the only methods by which increased government expenditure on administration and social overhead projects could be sustained until nitrate revenues came on stream. This trend was not without its costs, as the crisis of the 1870s revealed. Yet the system was also responsible for remarkable domestic diversification. The role of the state and its capacity for effective macro-economic management were further enhanced by ownership of railways in central and southern Chile, the formation of state-run manufacturing establishments and the creation, during the 1920s, of a host of credit agencies. The efficiency of these bodies and the efficacy of policy may be questioned. What is not in doubt is the scale of official intervention in the economy and the government's ability to initiate counter-cyclical measures.

While the Chilean state was exceptional in the scale of its activities, the actions and some of the programmes of administrations in Santiago conformed to a continental pattern. Increased instability in the export sector compelled government to project a more responsive image. Public policy was usually ameliorative, occasionally reformist; rarely was the explicit promotion of industrial expansion the objective of policy notwithstanding contemporary rhetoric. Chile presents a precocious example because instability occurred at a critical conjuncture. The

[37] Ortega, 'Economic policy in Chile'.

impact of the onset of the 'Great Depression' of 1873 was probably no more acute in Chile than in other Latin American countries. The principal difference lay in the early consolidation of central government authority and the ability of interests which had crystallized during export booms based on cereals and copper to elicit positive responses from the state. Interventionist arrangements secured at this point solidified during the nitrate age. Responses to export-sector instability around the turn of the century may be observed in Brazil, Mexico and elsewhere. *Batllismo* in Uruguay, and possibly programmes applied in the Argentine during the period following Radical electoral victories, can be presented as examples of reformist distributionism occasioned by the increased complexity of social structures. Interventionist policies, however, drew upon honoured precedents.

Throughout the nineteenth century the granting of subsidies and waiver of import duties remained amongst the most preferred means of stimulating desirable economic activities. State aid in the form of guaranteed rates of profits on capital invested in officially approved projects was widespread. Profit guarantees were a common form of promoting railway schemes, especially on the east coast, and continued to be employed in one form or another by Brazil until well into the twentieth century. Although they were the principal beneficiaries, railway companies were not the only recipients of guarantees. Even more important for manufacturing were subsidies and bounties. Central and provincial/state governments in Brazil were the main exponents of a regime of grants in aid of industry. Initially devised to assist railway companies and river and coastal steamer lines, starter grants and annual subsidies were later applied to firms engaged in manufacturing. In capital scarce economies such tangible assistance was crucial. Grants and bounties had a greater impact during the 1860s, 1870s and 1880s than the conferment of temporary monopolies, freedom from taxation or promises of government orders. And export expansion inducing a growth in state revenues more or less commensurate with developmentalist aspirations imparted greater effectiveness to such programmes.

Access to revenue was only part of the process. As indicated above, greater competence in those areas where government arrangements had consolidated by the end of the nineteenth century permitted a harmonization and more effective implementation of policy. In Mexico much emphasis is placed upon changes in the commercial code and arrangements relating to incorporation. Increased bureaucratic competence had, by 1900, fostered in some countries institutional innovation congruent with policy requirements. The sophistication of various government apparatuses is revealed in responses to exchange rate movements. Changes in the external value of a currency had, amongst other things, an impact upon domestic incomes, directly affected the price of imports (not least of inputs required by manufacturers) and influenced rates of domestic inflation and the incidence of tariff protection. Manufacturers were acutely aware of the relationship between exchange rates and the tariff in determining levels of protection. Industrialists knew that while tariff protection offered safeguards against a fall in the price of imported manufactures or a rise in domestic production costs, the exchange rate influenced both. It is argued that there was a bias in Argentine exchange policy in favour of a relatively depreciated exchange rate. In 1864, early in the 1880s and again in 1899 fixed parities were resorted to in order to prevent the appreciation of the *peso*. Other things being equal, currency depreciation unless accompanied by an exponential increase in domestic inflation gave added bite to protective duties. There was a tendency for industrial investment in Brazil to grow at a faster rate during periods of exchange depreciation (and currency or credit expansion) than at times of relative stability in exchange markets. The steady depreciation of the Chilean *peso* following the decision to abandon convertibility in 1878 is likewise argued to have been an effective device for internalizing demand and, as it was accompanied by loose monetary policies, promoting domestic manufacture. Similar trends have been observed for Peru and Mexico when those countries' currencies were based on a silver standard. Local production of silver ensured both an expanding monetary base and a fall in the external value of the *sol* and *peso* which secured domestic producers against the general decline in import prices. Conversely, Peru's accession to the Gold Standard in 1897 set the process into reverse. In Argentina and Brazil, manufacturers viewed with unease occasional appreciations in the external values respectively of the *peso* and *milreis* during the 1920s, tendencies that it was feared might induce a flood of 'cheap' imports. The result was often a campaign for tariff protection such as that mounted by the Argentine Industrial Union between 1922 and 1924.

Policy changes, especially sharp adjustments to import duties following currency appreciation have provoked a debate about the political strength of industrial entrepreneurs and their access to government.

Similar questions are raised by easy money regimes and a willingness by various groups in several countries to tolerate extended periods of currency depreciation. Were such programmes a conscious response to demands by manufacturers? Or were these policies required by other groups and merely of incidental benefit to industry? In contrast, it may be asked whether changes in money supply and the exchange rate should be dignified with the title of 'policy'. No more complex explanation may be required than inexorable pressures upon the state to spend, and the hidden hand of the market. *Empleomanía* rather than a desire to foster development or improve policy efficiency could account for the establishment of regulatory agencies, government banks and the like. Job creation not policy implementation was the objective and the simple achievement of bureaucratization.

THE INDUSTRIAL COMMUNITY AND THE DOMINANT OLIGARCHY

The social origin of industrial entrepreneurs and other beneficiaries of the process of an expansion in manufacturing activities is central to the process of industrial growth before 1930 for these origins in part explain the relationship between industrialists and the state and attitudes to the role of labour in the expansion of the sector. Traditionally Latin American manufacturers have been categorised as artisans, penny capitalists, businessmen with a broad spread of activities. Less simple than it at first appears, this typology incorporates two inter-related criteria that identify the classic dichotomies which divided the community of would-be industrialists, i.e. differences in the size of firms and techniques of production. Some enterprises were large and employed advanced technology. Others, if smaller in scale, also operated with modern technology. These units contrasted with craft shops that used techniques traditional to the artisan and journeyman and also with cottage manufacturing. The high degree of social heterogeneity implicit in this typology was characteristic of many early industrialist organizations which drew a membership from the ranks of the landed oligarchy, merchant community and others of more modest means.

Additional potential compartmentalization resulted from the role played by immigrants. A classic case is Argentina. In 1914 two-thirds of the owners of industrial establishments were foreign-born. Immigrants were preponderant in almost every branch of manufacturing, with the major exception of textiles. The contrast with ranching was marked: almost three-quarters of estate owners or managers were native born. In 1935 industry remained the preserve of foreigners, with more than 60 per cent of industrial entrepreneurs born outside Argentina. The figure had been over 80 per cent in 1895.[38] Natives maintained a strong presence only in handicraft activities, processes closely linked to agriculture and in establishments located outside the federal capital. The preponderance of immigrants dates from the early national period. As a country of mass immigration, Argentina was exceptional only in the degree of migrant preponderance. Qualitative material stresses the role of immigrants in Chile's industrial expansion and accessible evidence sustains similar conclusions for Peru. Immigrants were also responsible for the foundation of most modern industries in Uruguay and by 1908 owned over 60 per cent of Montevideo's manufacturing establishments. It was certainly the case that foreign – notably Italian – banks were well disposed to lend to their own nationals seeking finance for industrial enterprizes, and immigrant penny capitalists borrowed from more established members of their communities. Impressionistic evidence and quantitative data caution against a facile extension of this generalization to Brazil where immigrant entrepreneurs projected a dynamic image in manufacturing, but where national initiative must not be underestimated.

If the prominence of immigrant entrepreneurs signalled the compartmentalization of the sector, further fissiparous tendencies resulted from the growing presence of transnationals and continued regional fragmentation. However, the significance of the former should not be exaggerated and that of the latter may not be generalized. As indicated above, corporate capital was dominant in many export processing activities by the turn of the century. Technological advances and financial considerations induced in the metropolitan economies structural changes in the organization of production which associated with falling world freight rates encouraged expansion overseas. There was already a conglomerate presence in manufacturing for the domestic market before 1914, the scale and range of which increased during the post-war decade. British and U.S.-based transnational corporations commenced operations in Argentina during the long boom of 1908–12. By 1930 U.S. motor manufacturers had virtually ceased exporting finished vehicles to Argentina (the largest market in South America) and were assembling in

[38] Díaz Alejandro, *Essays on the economic history of the Argentine Republic*, 215.

the country. A similar trend occurred in Brazil. Major U.S. manufacturers who produced shoe-making and textile machines locally before 1914 were joined during the 1920s by Ford, General Motors, International Harvester and so forth who set up branch factories to manufacture or assemble motor vehicles, electrical appliances, agricultural equipment and various other machines. By 1929 branch factories operated by transnational corporations accounted for 17 per cent of the capital and approximately 14 per cent of the number of units amongst São Paulo's 79 largest manufacturing firms.[39] Notwithstanding the rapid growth of paulista industry during the first three decades of the twentieth century, by 1930 manufacturing in Brazil was still regionally dispersed, major foci being São Paulo and the city of Rio de Janeiro with an important concentration of capacity in the far south. In Mexico, the growing significance of Mexico City as a centre for manufacturing, partly accelerated by the Revolution, disguised the absolute decline of historic locations such as Puebla and León and the increased isolation of border complexes like Monterrey.

From these accounts a view of industry emerges that projects the fragmentation of the sector and the weakness of industrial capital. These features, it was asserted, explained a lack of coherence in manufacturing 'strategy', a distance from political power and a marginalized role in national economies wedded to export activities. And artisan production remained a prominent feature of the sector in several countries for much of the nineteenth century. The survival of an artisan presence amongst manufacturers clearly undermined the social status of industrial entrepreneurs in countries dominated by landed elites with aristocratic pretensions. Little kudos attached to small-scale industrial activities in societies that vaunted extensive land holdings or involvement in transatlantic commerce and which, imbued with exclusive Hispanic cultural mores, valued employment in the service of the state or the liberal professions. In practical terms, the survival of a class of artisans precluded the formation of a concensus amongst the industrial community on critical aspects of policy. While all might agree in broad terms about the desirability of tariff protection, specific measures commanded less general support. As is evidenced by the experience of textile production in Mexico and Argentina during the second quarter of the nineteenth century, sharp conflicts were provoked by the debate over

[39] Cano, *São Paulo*, 224.

duties. Petty artisans and those engaged in cottage production favoured the exclusion of finished items and virtually all articles connected with garment production. Factory owners, on the other hand, lobbied for prohibitive duties to be applied to finished items but favoured the duty free import of machinery thereby ensuring a clash with cottage workers. Weavers might seek a reduction in duties on yarn imports; spinners, on the contrary, did not. Factories without access to secure raw material supplies encouraged unrestricted imports; estate owners who integrated raw material production with manufacturing were less inclined to this view. The conflicts were endless, but the most significant clash was that between factory and non-factory producers. The late survival of artisan units, and consequent fragmentation of the sector, undoubtedly inhibited the projection of a more dynamic, coherent image by manufacturing in many areas. Though far from the most important factor discouraging industrial growth, the negative significance of the late survival of the artisan has been underestimated in revisionist accounts anxious to present artisan production as a springboard for fully-fledged factory industry. There are few examples of such a successful transformation.

Equally the deadhand of the artisan should not be exaggerated. By the latter part of the nineteenth century, largely under the influence of immigration, domestic production was being displaced by factory work, even if the scale of production remained small. During the 1880s Montevideo manufacturing was already losing its craft character. Although data is inconclusive, there was a shift towards mechanical power at the end of the century. As late as 1889 more than one-third of the energy requirements of 'industry' was provided by traditional means. By 1908 not only had industrial energy consumption increased almost threefold but, at least in Montevideo, power was provided exclusively by mechanical means – three-quarters by steam and one-quarter by electricity. The shift to mechanical power can be interpreted as representing a change in favour of modern factory-based manufacturing. There was a parallel increase in the scale of production and a diversification in manufacturing activities. Before the end of the century less than 5 per cent of the total number of firms employed almost 60 per cent of the labour force; in 1913 14 establishments, some 0.5 per cent of the total number of industrial enterprises accounted for over 26 per cent of the work force. With the expansion of Uruguay's industrial base came import diversification. During the 1880s non-durable consumer goods – foodstuffs, beverages and textiles – dominated the import schedules. By the quinquennium 1896–1900 the participation of these items in imports was only 56 per cent with machinery and intermediate products already representing 17 per cent. In 1906–1910 the respective figures were 46 per cent and 25 per cent. The restructuring of imports was a function of the expansion of domestic factory production.[40] Similar developments are reported for Chile, increased energy consumption and recourse to mechanical power signalling the demise of artisan production and a consolidation of the modern factory. As indicated above, the larger economies participated in this trend.

If the collapse of the artisan class was associated with an enlarged immigrant presence and the emergence of an industrial 'complex' with more recognizably modern patina, the result was not necessarily an upgrading of the social prestige associated with manufacturing activities. Industrial entrepreneurs suffered severe disabilities. Like many immigrants they were not citizens, retaining the nationality of their country of origin, and they lacked a political base. In a sector still characterized at the turn of the century by small to medium scale operations, manufacturers were not always able to rise above their socially-inferior penny-capitalist origins. Industrialists also existed in a sphere distinct from that of other middle class groups. The expansion of export activities and of the urban economy had, by the turn of the century, produced in Argentina the largest, most articulate middle class in Latin America. Education reforms and the growth of the public sector largely financed by taxes upon foreign trade had widened employment opportunities for professional groups and the political class. The ranks of the middle classes were further swelled by openings in commerce, finance and public utility companies, all of which required lawyers, accountants, engineers, administrators and clerks. The class composition of Argentine society shifted dramatically between 1870 and 1930. But the bulk of the burgeoning middle sectors shared few common aspirations with manufacturing. Lawyers, state functionaries and professional politicians constituted a dependent middle class associated with export sector interests. Overawed by elite mores and values, the aspirations and achievements of the Argentine middle classes were absorbed within a tertiary sector, and a culture that was indifferent to, if not actually anti, industry. Most professionals were appalled by campaigns for tariff 'reform' that threatened middle class patterns of consumption. In this

[40] J. P. Barran and B. Nahum, *Batlle, los estancieros y el imperio británico: el Uruguay del novecientos* (Montevideo, 1979), 202–4.

they shared a common perspective with segments of urban labour.

Argentina's class structure and social formation isolated and emasculated industrial entrepreneurs who were politically marginalized. Striking exceptions, such as the Di Tellas and Frazers, immigrants who founded major industrial complexes, or the Bunges and Borns who moved from commerce and finance into manufacturing and joined the ranks of the oligarchy, or the Anchorena, a traditional landed family who developed industrial interests, were inclined to be dismissed precisely as not representing a general process. This thesis of ineffective political representation and an exclusion of manufacturers from the state apparatus permeated an earlier view which assumed a continent-wide dimension. Analyses that stress the inadequacy of policy are clearly indebted to this tradition. The compartmentalization of industry, its separation from the dominant activities of mining and agriculture, also made for capital scarcity. Organized by a socially distinct group, manufacturing could not benefit from a direct transfer of export activity profits. Indirectly, these interpretations sustain the proposition that, before 1930, the sector was weak, fragmented, isolated and of little consequence.

That these assessments were so long sustained, indicates both the sparse nature of available material and the parameters within which the discussion has taken place heretofore. For, as the few studies that have been undertaken reveal, there is a need for industrial biographies and general investigation into the social background of manufacturers. The work that has been completed in this field suggests a different situation. Writing on Brazil challenges orthodoxy and suggests both the transmission of modernizing influences to the national elite by foreigners and the emergence of a dynamic domestic capitalism. 'Heroic' Brazilian industrialists were imbued with Anglo-Saxon perspectives of economic expansion, exhibited a zeal for manufacturing activities and manifested a preference for corporate practices.[41] But did a few 'heroic' modernizers constitute a general process? That they did is indicated by the close proximity of manufacturing, agricultural and commercial interests in Brazil during the coffee cycle. Class-sector solidarity rather than antagonism appeared to prevail, and resulted in the formation of an authentic national capitalism. A growth of *fazendeiro* interest in manufacturing paralleled general structural changes in the economy.

---

[41] Graham, *Britain and onset of modernisation, passim.*

While coffee profits flowed directly into manufacturing, other channels also existed to facilitate a transfer of funds to the sector: banks were founded by coffee growers as a mechanism to facilitate investment outside agriculture.[42]

The dissemination of capitalist practices within the paulista coffee area is now well established, a process that is conveniently dated from the beginnings of the transition from slave to free labour which commences in the early 1870s. At this juncture there was a surge of interest in commercial and industrial enterprise that compelled recourse to formalized devices in order to raise finance. Limited liability and the institutionalization of the savings-investment nexus were substituted for archaic, personal forms of procuring funds. The capitalist and precocious nature of nineteenth century industry in Chile is also recognized. And, if the role of immigrant entrepreneurs is acknowledged, emphasis is placed upon endogenous participation in secondary activities and the absorption of aspiring immigrant talent by the elite. Diverging from earlier interpretations, some new studies present the upper echelons of Chilean society as accessible to socially mobile migrants. An acceptance that Chile was a less rigidly stratified, more accommodating, society than previously depicted admits the possibility that industrialists may have exerted influence within – certainly upon – the state apparatus. The speedy domesticization of immigrant enterprise, not least during the First World War, may be similarly explained. Mexico offers only limited corroboration of this hypothesis. Immigrants dominated key sectors of manufacturing such as textiles while domestic entrepreneurial initiative was manifest elsewhere. Manufacturers in Mexico, however, appear to have enjoyed less direct contact with the dominant oligarchy or the state than their counterparts in other countries, at least for the period before 1930.

Evidence of enhanced social status and rising political influence may be provided by the growth in the membership of industrialists' associations before and after the turn of the century and the increased confidence with which industrial clubs and associations represented sectional interests before the state. The establishment of these organizations, and the increase in membership, at least indicates a perception of

---

[42] Cano, *São Paulo*, 129; E. W. Ridings, 'Class sector unity in an export economy: the case of nineteenth century Brazil', *Hispanic American Historical Review*, 58/3 (1978); Z. M. Cardoso de Mello, 'São Paulo 1845–1895: metamorfoses da riqueza. Contribução ao estudo da passagem da economía mercantil escravista à economía exportadora capitalista' (unpublished Ph.D. thesis, University of São Paulo, 1981).

the need to create pressure groups to defend manufacturing and cultivate local opinion in favour of industry. Before the First World War bodies such as the Sociedad Nacional de Industrias in Peru or the Unión Industrial Argentina were recognized channels for the articulation of the grievances of manufacturers. During the 1920s the Unión Industrial Argentina and Brazil's Associação Industrial organized industrial expositions and mounted sophisticated campaigns in favour of tariff reform which stressed national security and job creation, playing upon deficiencies in these economies revealed by the First World War and responding to fears that protection would have an adverse effect upon the cost of living. Even if lobbying rarely achieved the desired objective, by the 1920s industrial associations in Argentina, Brazil, Chile and Peru claimed to command the attention of the presidency.

While the discussion about industry before 1930 has provoked new interest in the social origin of industrialists, the position of dominant domestic groups and the role of the state, it has also invigorated the debate about the role of labour. This theme is part of a larger reconsideration of labour which is resulting in a less dichotomized view of social structures. Analyses of economic activity based on supply factors had not neglected labour, rather the focus was limited. Industry, it was alleged, depended upon a suitable political framework and required access to a specific mix of factors. Labour was one of these factors. If industry presupposed entrepreneurs, it presupposed also industrial workers. But urban workers are to be viewed less as a factor of production than as a market or a class. Scholars have been as assiduous in their search for a proletariat as for a modernizing cadre of industrial capitalists. The identification of a process of industrialization (as distinct from an expansion of the manufacturing base) prior to 1930 needs to discover a class of urban industrial workers, a further token of structural transformation. This task is not easy.

As the case of Mexico reveals, groups of waged industrial workers – factory-based, dependent on machines and the sale of their labour in the market – are not difficult to discover, even during the early national period. It is known that in those countries where slavery survived after independence, there were cases of slaves being employed in factories. This situation has been depicted as a phase in the emergence of a proletariat. Similar claims are made for the contracting of rural labour in Brazil, Peru and elsewhere. Undoubtedly of intrinsic significance, such groups constitute isolated examples and rarely illustrate a general process. Trade union activity may provide a more appropriate litmus test of class identity and class cohesion. Observed social discontent – both urban and rural – increased repression and heightened elite fears of unrest, point to a growing articulation of grievances by labour which assumed a degree of effective organization. By 1914 trade unions were no longer ephemeral organizations – *ad hoc* groupings formed to address a specific issue or confront a given problem which disbanded when the issue was resolved, or more probably when violently suppressed. Like their peers in other sectors, manufacturers regarded industrial relations as a police matter and often called upon the coercive power of the state to resolve labour disputes. Yet a national labour organization existed in Chile before the First World War and in Argentina and Uruguay by the 1920s. Mexican urban workers were also organizing by the beginning of the twentieth century. In Brazil the alacrity with which the state moved to co-opt or placate urban labour after 1930 indicates that the sector was both large and identifiable at this stage. But industrial workers did not constitute the core of these movements. Typically workers in the export sector, for example Chile's nitrate unions, were the prime movers in the struggle to organize labour. Elsewhere utility workers, like Argentina's railway union, or white collar groups like Uruguay's bank workers, were to the fore.

Before 1914 groups of industrialists may be clearly identified in several Latin American countries. Modern scholarship presents these groups as more homogeneous than has previously been allowed. Manufacturers, or so it is now argued, were not necessarily marginalized. But the thrust of revisionist writing, with its emphasis on perceptions of dominant class integrity and a proximation of interests, hardly permits the portrayal of heroic industrial entrepreneurs as agents of profound social change even if they represented an identifiable component in a process of economic diversification. Similarly, urban labour – and some elements of the rural workforce – may have been relatively effectively organized by the 1920s. Indeed urban labour, whether by conscious action or the vicarious consequence of economic growth, had prior to the First World War secured in some countries an increase in welfare (and possibly a larger relative participation in national income). Labour's ability to command a share in the gains of productivity resulting from the expansion of manufacturing and thereby enlarge the market for secondary products is recognized. Elements of the labour force may have become more articulate during this period, but in most societies the organized sector was overshadowed by workers employed in activities that precluded effective unionization. And if a city-based proletariat was to be observed in the more urbanized economies of the southern cone, it was hardly an industrial proletariat.

INDUSTRY OR INDUSTRIALIZATION?

While the nature of the subject precludes facile generalization, it cannot be doubted that the decades before the inter-war depression witnessed a growth of industry in all countries. Contemporary accounts, produced by the 1900s, both observed an expansion of industrial production and advocated policies to promote manufacturing. Industrial censuses undertaken before the 1930s, usually incomplete and often premised upon questionable assumptions, also record the scale of industrial activities. Innovative trends in production and organization confirm that in several areas the origins of modern industry can be traced to the 1880s, notably in Chile and Brazil. Qualitative changes in domestic manufacturing may also be observed in Argentina and Mexico: in specific sectors there was a rising participation of local supply in national consumption of finished products. Before the First World War manufacturing activities had also expanded in Peru and Colombia. A notable exception to the continent-wide process of export induced industrial growth was Cuba where increases in aggregate demand and infrastructural modernization facilitated market consolidation and a rising demand for manufactures supplied by imports. Whether the origins of modern manufacturing can be pushed back beyond the 1870s is debatable. Equally contentious is the ability of 'colonial' style domestic and sweat-shop manufacturing of the early national period to transform itself into modern industry. Cottage, *obraje* and artisan units reveal several proto-industrial characteristics. Yet the restructuring of industry that occurred during the middle third of the nineteenth century was associated with the consolidation of an immigrant presence and a vigorous penetration of manufacturing by export sector groups – both national and foreign. The basic problem for 'colonial' forms of industry was less the shift to mechanical means of production, than the emphasis upon task specialization and the novel forms of organizational arrangements implicit in the modern factory.

Can a process of industrialization be observed before 1930, given that the greater part of the discussion is cast in terms of a *growth* of industry?

For Chile it has been confidently, if not undisputedly, asserted that industrialization indeed occurred, assisted by the emergence of pragmatic industry-stimulating programmes during the late nineteenth century and conscious demand management by the second or third decade of the twentieth. Greater caution prevails in the case of Brazil. The course of modern industry in Brazil can be charted from the 1880s; there was also a process of sectoral deepening – the manufacture of a wide range of items beyond non-durable consumer goods to include capital equipment. Manufacturing was clearly well established by 1930, domestic production dominated the national market in several lines and in some areas, particularly São Paulo, the sector was effectively integrated into the regional economy. Few writers, however, interpret these advances as industrialization, though most would accept that the observed phases of industrial deepening and diversification represented an important stage in the process leading to industrialization. Elsewhere it would be inappropriate to use the term 'industrialization' in its modern context. By the early 1920s Argentina possessed the largest, most sophisticated and dynamic market in Latin America: the participation of manufacturing in Gross Domestic Product was almost twice as great as in any other country. At this stage the rate of growth of secondary output was also faster than that of primary production. Yet the process of industry deepening had not progressed as far in Argentina as in Chile or Brazil. Colombia, during the 1920s, was perhaps experiencing its first sustained phase of manufacturing growth though from a very low base. For different reasons the progress of industrial growth faltered in Mexico and Peru during the inter-war period.

Although disagreement and uncertainty remain regarding the general theme, consensus prevails with respect to important matters of detail. No longer can 1930 be presented as the point of departure for modern manufacturing in Latin America. While there were clearly defined limits to the process of export-led industrial expansion, modern manufacturing in Latin America dates from the phase of export-led growth, as is confirmed by the differing national chronologies of *desarrollo hacia afuera*. The adverse exogenous shock in 1930 did not initiate manufacturing, though the events of the 1930s may have triggered industrial deepening, a process made possible by the already advanced level of secondary activities in some countries. In specific cases the First World War may have constituted a more profound stimulant to manufacturing than has previously been realized, either because the disruption resulting was relatively more profound in 1914 than in 1930 or because *ad hoc* measures devised to combat war-induced problems and post-war difficulties served as a model for programmes later applied during the 1930s.

Similarly the controversy about industry has resolved misconceptions in other fields. Discussion about government policy refutes simplistic assertions that the continent was, during the nineteenth century, an area of dogmatic doctrinaire *laissez-faire*. Regimes variously sought to open their economies to external influences during the century or so after independence: states and regions were drawn, or propelled, into an expanding world capitalist system. Yet despite the prevalence of ideologies associated with the classical economists or concepts of society founded upon precepts elaborated by Spencer and Comte, the countries of Latin America cannot be depicted as near text book case studies in economic liberalism. There can be little doubt about the intensity of the debate that raged during the nineteenth century, or the widespread absorption of the rhetoric of liberalism into official publications and the public utterances of statesmen. Rarely, however, were liberal sentiments translated into practice. Whether due to the strength of inherited Iberian mercantilist traditions, or pressing immediate fiscal and political considerations, government policy was pragmatic and interventionist. Work on the sources of industrial capital which emphasizes the presence of domestic finance in the sector sustains the hypothesis of policy pragmatism and explains the drift in government action with respect to manufacturing during the period studied.

However, if there is agreement that official action stimulated industry, controversy remains regarding the most appropriate mechanisms employed. Indirect actions of the state which resulted in general improvements in the economic environment may have been more significant than specific measures applied piecemeal to promote individual industries or firms. Tariff protection attracts widespread attention: import duties performed a crucial role for industry. But there were examples of manufacturing activity that developed without protection or under neutral fiscal tariff regimes. Exchange rate policy complemented the tariff and could offset reductions in real rates of protection resulting from a divergence in official valuations, upon which rates of duty applied, and dockside prices. Exchange rates were certainly more amenable to adjustment than tariff regimes, the reformulation of which required extensive consultation and possibly a re-negotiation of commercial treaties with foreign powers. Administrations in Santiago and

Rio de Janeiro which applied lax currency policies must have been aware of the consequences of their action: exporters certainly knew that, all other things being equal, a dramatic increase in exports resulted in exchange valorization.

Nevertheless the mechanics of tariff and exchange policy, which may only have been imperfectly comprehended by ill-trained bureaucracies, were probably of less moment than larger changes in the economy. Institutional reforms that facilitated the incorporation of industrial enterprises were of significance as was legislation to stimulate banking, the provision of incentives and subsidies for manufacturing and a general professionalization of services provided by the state, from education to administration. The modernization of infrastructure was crucial: the expansion of railways and the telegraph integrated and homogenized national (or regional) markets. The growth of services provided by these and other utilities lowered entry costs into an industry and enabled firms to operate on a smaller capital base. Port improvements reduced the cost of imports of intermediate products, capital goods and fuel. In many countries the expansion of utility services meant the growth of the public sector. Income growth – whether resulting from an enlargement of the public sector, conscious demand management or vicariously from an increased scale of export activities – was possibly the single most important factor responsible for the development of domestic manufacture.

Before 1930 the process of industrial expansion in the major Latin American economies was manifestly cyclical. It was also incomplete. Based upon the experience of the more advanced economies, a tentative model of industry may be advanced. Periods of export expansion created an environment conducive to the growth of manufacturing. In spite of seepages, exports generated an increase in domestic profits and incomes. Government revenue, and the scale of public activities, grew. In all save mineral exporting economies, the demand for labour increased with the growth of exports: the expansion of the wage sector implied a monetization of the economy and an enlargement of the market. Crisis in the external sector obviously reversed income growth and undermined resources available for industry. However external disequilibrium, while certainly curtailing government revenue, probably enhanced the importance of, and demands made upon, the public sector. Political expediency compelled a search for remedies to the fiscal crisis that precluded an excessive reliance upon policies based solely on retrenchment (though this was often attempted). The result was normally an increase in tariff duties which either served to broaden the scope for domestic manufacturing or deepened the industrial base. Crisis also produced qualitative changes within the industrial sector, undermining weaker units (starved of capital or devoid of essential imports) thereby creating more space in a contracting market for successful (often larger) firms. Recovery and renewed growth in the export sector favoured the consolidation of surviving firms that were required to expand capacity (or accept a reduction in market share) as domestic demand grew, sheltered behind tariff barriers. Thus another cycle was established, an alternating round of growth in manufacturing output and investment in productive capacity. Dynamic opportunities in manufacturing attracted the attention of native capitalists, immigrants and foreign capital. As the sector grew, industrialists – who were by now well connected with the state, or integrated into national elites – were able to command the attention of government and, with other interests, press for direct measures to sustain and promote domestic manufacture.

9

THE URBAN WORKING CLASS AND EARLY LATIN AMERICAN LABOUR MOVEMENTS, 1880–1930

During the period from 1880 to 1930, although the population of the region remained overwhelmingly rural, urban workers became a significant force in the national life of most Latin American countries. The specific form of Latin America's incorporation in the world economy, however, meant that the urban labour movements which emerged in the region were different in important respects from those of Europe or North America.

THE ECONOMY, THE BOURGEOISIE AND THE STATE

Most Latin American countries served in the international economic order as exporters of primary products and importers of manufactured goods; until well into the twentieth century industry played a relatively minor role in the economies of the region. Not only were most Latin American economies fundamentally dependent on decisions made elsewhere and subject to the sometimes violent fluctuations of the world market, but the labour force was often highly segmented. Those employed in the export sector sometimes lived in considerable isolation from other workers, although they generally had the advantage of relatively greater bargaining power. When the carpenters or even textile workers went on strike in Buenos Aires or São Paulo or Santiago the effects might be serious, but were scarcely comparable to the repercussions of a disruption in the export economy. If the railway workers failed to bring Argentine wheat or Brazilian coffee or Chilean nitrate to the ports, and if these commodities were not quickly loaded onto the ships which were to take them to European or North American markets, serious crisis almost immediately threatened the respective national economies.

The strategic place which miners and transport workers occupied in the export economy meant that they were often subject to the full force of state control, but their bargaining power sometimes allowed them to secure significant economic gains and occasionally even political gains. The nitrate miners of northern Chile, for example, managed to create – despite immense obstacles – the unity and militant practice which often characterize rather isolated mining communities. In Chile the miners' political and economic organizations, rather than those of the craftsmen in the small workshops of Santiago, ultimately came to shape the later labour movement. Railway workers in almost every country were among the first and most effectively organized, although their strong bargaining position in some cases separated them from the bulk of the working class and turned their unions toward reformism. Stevedores and dockers in the port of Santos, the 'Brazilian Barcelona' as admiring militants termed it, remained among the most combative and cohesive members of the Brazilian labour movement throughout a large part of the twentieth century; the port workers in Rio de Janeiro, on the other hand, became a bastion of reformism.

Workers outside the export sector were generally to be found scattered in quite small-scale enterprises. These characteristically provided goods and services which could not be supplied readily – if at all – from abroad. The early labour movement in most cities, for example, typically included printers and construction workers of various kinds, as well as bakers and others employed in food processing. Workers in the clothing trades, particularly tailors and the makers of shoes and hats, also appeared prominently, as did certain other craft workers such as those involving metalworking, glass-making and furniture manufacture.

Workers in these trades were not necessarily independent artisans in the strict sense of skilled small producers who owned their own means of production. These cases still existed to be sure, and such artisans could at times exert considerable political influence. Since mechanization proceeded rather slowly, many crafts survived until quite late; in Mexico some 41,000 handloom weavers were still at work in 1895, although the development of the textile industry left only 12,000 by 1910. Nevertheless the craftsmen in the construction trades and small workshops of Latin American cities by the turn of the century, though sometimes highly skilled, were generally wage workers obliged to sell their labour power in the market.

The size of this sector is not easy to specify. Craftsmen formed a substantial category in Mexico, where one interpretation of the 1910 census gives the very considerable figure of 873,436 'artisans and workers', who represented nearly 16 per cent of the economically active population.[1] The urban trades attained significant proportions almost everywhere in Latin America in the late nineteenth century, but, given the relatively high capacity to import of many of the economies, this sector was generally not as developed as in most European cities of comparable size. Moreover, the less than decisive position of many such trades in the economy limited workers' political and economic power. Nevertheless, despite dispersal, heterogeneous working conditions and the often paternalistic atmosphere of the small workshops, craftsmen in many cases succeeded in forming quite militant organizations. They frequently managed to exploit whatever advantages their skills gave them in the labour market, and in general played a highly important role in most Latin American labour movements until well after 1930. The political practice of the urban craftsmen was by no means uniform. While some movements, particularly in the nineteenth century, represented essentially the objectives of small producers, on the whole wage workers' strategies and tactics prevailed.

The industrial proletariat, in the sense of workers in large and mechanized factories, had only begun to appear in significant numbers in the early twentieth century and nowhere occupied a central place in any national economy before 1930. Textile factories represented overwhelmingly the largest modern enterprises; in some countries they were virtually the only ones. Most other industrial activities remained closely tied to the export sector, as was the case of Argentine meat-packing plants and flour mills.

Census figures on the numbers of workers in factories are not strictly comparable, and categories leave room for considerable ambiguity. The Mexican census of 1910, which reported a national population of 15.1 million, classified 58,838 as industrial workers, compared with 45,806 in 1895. Many of the largest and most modern factories in Mexico were the textile plants located in mill towns in the states of Puebla and Veracruz. The Brazilian industrial census of 1920 located 275,512 factory workers in a country of 30 million inhabitants. Although the Brazilian census excluded many small workshops, the results still showed an average of 21 workers per plant. About half the total lived in the city of Rio de Janeiro

---

[1] 'Industrial workers' are excluded from this figure. Ciro F. S. Cardoso, Francisco G. Hermosillo, Salvador Hernández, *De la dictadura porfirista a los tiempos libertarios* (*La clase obrera en la historia de México*, ed. Pablo González Casanova, vol. III, Mexico, 1980), 47, 54.

or the state of São Paulo, and some 40 per cent worked in the textile industry. The 1914 Argentine census considered 24,203 'industrial establishments' to have 'the characteristics of true factories'. In a country of 8 million, these employed 242,138 people, including administrative personnel, but many of the establishments were clearly small workshops, as the average number of employees – ten – indicates.[2]

The distinction between factory and workshop remained in fact far from clear. Only in the extreme cases, as between Mexico City artisans and workers in the modern textile factories near Orizaba, do different political practices emerge with some clarity. Elsewhere in Latin America, the small industrial proletariat seems to have played no independent role before 1930. In Brazil, for example, women and children formed a majority of workers in the textile industry and proved difficult to organize. Within the Brazilian labour movement, the practice of workers in textile factories scarcely differed from that of those in smaller enterprises.

The early creation of a substantial industrial reserve army also marked the development of the labour movement from its inception. In the Brazilian case, the large-scale importation of immigrants by the state for work on the São Paulo coffee plantations had the additional effect of flooding the urban labour market and, despite considerable efforts, the labour movement never managed to impede the process. Argentine governments also actively encouraged immigration by recruitment campaigns in Europe and, in certain periods, by paying subsidies to shipping companies in order to reduce the price of passage to Buenos Aires. Although the Argentine policy was also intended primarily to provide cheap labour for agriculture, it likewise served to limit the bargaining power of urban workers. In Mexico, toward the end of the nineteenth century, rapid population growth and the advance of capitalist agriculture had much the same effect of saturating the labour market and keeping wages low. The creation of a large reserve army during the earliest phases of the industrialization process thus made labour organization especially difficult in several of the most important Latin American countries, particularly since the effectiveness of the strike weapon diminishes considerably when strikers can be readily replaced.

[2] Mexico: *ibid.*, 47; Brazil: Directoria Geral de Estatística, *Recenseamento do Brasil realizado em 1 de setembro de 1920*, vol. v, pt. 1, pp. lxxii, lxxvii; Argentina: *Tercer Censo Nacional levantado el 1° de junio de 1914*, VII, 35.

Workers, moreover, faced a highly intransigent bourgeoisie. In part, the owners' unwillingness to compromise resulted from the fact that labour often represented a high proportion of total costs, and from the competitive conditions prevailing in many industries. Thus industrialists in many sectors did not always find it easy to pass higher labour costs along to consumers. Such conditions, typical of the competitive period of early capitalism, were not only frequent in the sectors characterized by the presence of a large number of small firms and a low level of mechanization. Owners of large and modern textile plants in both Brazil and Mexico, for example, also found it difficult to restrict competition. Moreover, the newness of most industry often meant that owners needed the use of considerable overt coercion since they had not yet been able to develop other forms of control – ideological and institutional – over their labour force. The heterogeneous composition of the early bourgeoisie, as well as its recent formation, in some cases made broad co-operation difficult among the various segments. Firms differed considerably in the nationality of their ownership, as well as in size and in the extent of mechanization. Nevertheless, owners in the various sectors generally managed to mobilize the state on their behalf, organize lockouts, co-ordinate strike policy and maintain blacklists of militants with considerable efficiency.

The fact of frequent foreign ownership influenced industrialists' relations with both workers and the state in various ways. Large foreign interests, primarily British and North American, dominated most major activities in the export sector, such as mining, meat-packing and railways. Nationalist resentment toward foreign owners and managers in many cases, as among Mexican and Chilean miners, served as an important element in working-class consciousness. Nor was foreign ownership limited to the export sector. Resident French capitalists owned some of the largest and most advanced textile factories in Mexico. In Lima, the two major textile plants were controlled by W. R. Grace and Company. The Spanish merchants who dominated much of the commerce of Cuba often provoked hostility from workers by their discriminatory hiring practices as well as by their credit and pricing policies. Resident foreigners owned most industrial enterprises in São Paulo and Buenos Aires, although this seems to have made little difference to their predominantly immigrant work force.

While the industrial bourgeoisie had nowhere become hegemonic in Latin America before 1930 – the state remained for the most part in the hands of groups quite clearly tied to the export sector and decidedly uninterested in large-scale industrial expansion – it generally managed to secure most of its immediate objectives, not the least of which was ready state repression against workers. The Díaz regime in Mexico (1876–1911), for example, zealously promoted and defended the interests of foreign capital, despite some gestures toward ending discrimination against Mexican workers on the railways. In the labour disputes involving large foreign-owned enterprises which marked the last years of the regime, state repression was notably thorough and violent. The agrarian groups which dominated the state in Argentina, while generally solicitous of the fundamental interests of large foreign capital in the export sector, showed considerably less concern on behalf of immigrant industrialists. Although the Argentine state rigorously maintained order and became quite brutal at times in repressing anarchists and others, working-class organizations secured a certain space in which to operate, in part because industrial workers did not appear directly to threaten agrarian interests. The Brazilian case differed somewhat, since many important planters – particularly following the coffee crisis of the late 1890s – had become involved in industrial and commercial activities. They formed a cohesive bloc with immigrant industrialists, and the state embarked on a policy of quite comprehensive repression against the working class.

In theory, state policy was liberal in a nineteenth-century sense almost everywhere. In practice, the state intervened in a number of areas. The manipulation of the labour market which several governments, most notably that of Brazil, carried out by means of their immigration policies represented one of the less violent but highly effective forms of such intervention. Monetary policy also served as an important instrument for industrial interests, as in Argentina where depreciating paper currency operated in effect for many years to lower real wages. In general, however, the main role of the state in the struggles between capital and labour was to coerce the latter. The level of violence in such repression could be very high indeed. During the first decade of the century, for example, the Chilean government carried out a series of extraordinary massacres against workers, killing several hundred people in the course of strikes and demonstrations in Valparaíso (1903), Santiago (1905) and Antofagasta (1906). In 1907, troops murdered well over a thousand defenceless men, women and children in Iquique by opening fire on nitrate workers and their families who had come to appeal for higher wages and better working conditions. The Díaz government in Mexico acted with comparable brutality. The number of workers massacred during the Río Blanco textile strike of 1907, for example, will never be known, but most estimates run to over one hundred killed. At one point, and apparently on Díaz's instructions, a firing squad publicly executed six workers at Río Blanco in order to force others back to work.

Less murderous though still violent forms of repression also occurred regularly, in particular those aimed at weakening or destroying working-class organizations. Virtually all the Latin American governments, at one time or another, closed union headquarters, ransacked newspaper offices, prohibited or disrupted demonstrations and meetings, and ordered the beating and imprisonment of labour leaders. The frequent use of police spies and *agents provocateurs* within the labour movement served as additional weapons. Most regimes also zealously protected strike-breakers, and sometimes even provided them from the armed forces and elsewhere as well as arresting and intimidating strikers on a large scale. The ferocity of state repression even shocked foreign police agents, not normally suspected of excessive sympathy toward the labour movement; an Italian agent in São Paulo, for example, thought that in the characteristically violent Brazilian strikes 'provocative action, with some exceptions, comes more from the police than from the strikers'.[3]

On the pretext that 'foreign agitators' lay behind growing labour unrest, the governments of Argentina, Brazil, Chile, Cuba and Uruguay all enacted laws providing for the summary expulsion of foreign-born militants. In Argentina, by 1916 some 383 individuals had been expelled under the 1902 Law of Residence. A comparable Brazilian law of 1907 led to at least 550 deportations by 1921. Both states applied such measures particularly to leading militants, with damaging results at times for the labour movement, to say nothing of the intimidating effects which the threat of expulsion had on working classes heavily composed of foreign immigrants. Moreover, several governments regularly sent labour militants to internal detention camps, in many cases virtually a death sentence. The Díaz regime became particularly notorious for interning workers at camps in Campeche, Quintana Roo, and Yucatán on account of their labour activity. Prisoners hardly fared better at the Brazilian regime's infamous Clevelândia camp in the Amazon, where a number of

[3] Rome, Archivio Centrale dello Stato, Direzione Generale Pubblica Sicurezza, Ufficio Riservato (1879–1912), busta 13, fascicolo 41, sottofascicolo 13, Cesare Alliata-Bronner to Luigi Bruno, 30 June 1909.

well-known labour leaders died in the 1920s. Argentinian governments used Ushuaia, in Tierra del Fuego, to similar effect.

In the period before the First World War most governments also attempted other means of controlling the working class, besides direct repression. Díaz in Mexico and Hermes da Fonseca (1910–14) in Brazil, for example, sought to create or encourage compliant trade union organizations, although results remained rather mixed. Social legislation, however, hardly existed before 1917, except for occasional limited measures dealing with Sunday rest, hours of work, accidents and the regulation of work by women and children. Much of this legislation was restricted to specific categories of workers, generally state employees, or to certain geographical areas such as national capitals. Compliance in any case appears to have been sporadic at best. The governor of São Paulo remarked during the 1917 general strike, in response to a journalist's question, that he could not quite recall whether there was child labour legislation on the books in that state. The one early exception occurred in Uruguay where during the two presidential terms of José Batlle y Ordóñez (1903–7 and 1911–15) several measures were passed creating the continent's first ministry of labour and assuring the right to strike, the eight-hour day, minimum wages, old-age pensions and accident compensation. Elsewhere, however, in a famous Brazilian phrase of the period, the social question remained 'one for the police'. Although some regimes, including that of Díaz, occasionally attempted to arbitrate specific disputes, for the most part only after 1917 and particularly after 1930 did the state in Latin America undertake more comprehensive policies for regulating relations between capital and labour, and among capitalists themselves.

THE COMPOSITION AND CONDITION OF THE WORKING CLASS

The ethnic composition of the early working class varied considerably from one country to another and even from city to city. In Buenos Aires, Montevideo and São Paulo, European immigrants long formed a majority among workers. Most were Italians and Spaniards, joined in São Paulo by a large contingent of Portuguese. Foreigners in Rio de Janeiro and Santos, particularly immigrants from Portugal, represented a very significant, though less overwhelming, element in the labour force. Elsewhere, European immigration took place on a much smaller scale, although Spaniards, for example, played a far from negligible role in the working classes of Cuba and Chile. In several Latin American cities, notably Rio de Janeiro and Havana, African-born former slaves and their descendants also formed a substantial part of the working class. Even in such countries as Mexico, where foreign immigration remained slight, the experience of internal migrants was by no means totally different from that of the men and women who crossed the Atlantic to other parts of Latin America.

The immigrant composition of the working class in Argentina, Uruguay and southern Brazil prior to the First World War brought a number of ultimately rather ambiguous consequences. Some immigrants had clearly acquired a certain political experience before arrival, and a handful of leaders had even played significant roles in the labour movements of their native countries. However, few militants appear to have regarded the immigrants' general level of political experience as high. In fact, many complained bitterly about the absence of revolutionary traditions among the immigrants and their lack of familiarity with political issues or working-class organization. Nor does the proportion of skilled workers or of those with prior industrial experience appear to have been great, which is hardly surprising in an immigration stimulated and organized to serve the needs of export agriculture. Moreover, many observers argued that immigrant workers generally sought only immediate economic gains and an early return to their homelands. Their individual projects of upward mobility thus represented an obstacle to the development of broader forms of organization. Nor did such immigrants easily lend themselves to political strategies which depended on large-scale electoral participation by workers.

Ethnic diversity also complicated co-operation among workers, and employers were often quick to exploit such difficulties. Animosities not only existed among the various national groups and between foreigners and the native-born but divisive regional antagonisms – particularly among the Italians – also served to hinder collaboration on many occasions. Such ethnic hostilities troubled the labour movement for decades in the form of strikes lost and organizations weakened or destroyed on account of prejudices and cultural differences among workers.

In part, however, many of the problems which have been attributed to the presence of large numbers of immigrants resulted primarily from the recent formation of the working class. Workers everywhere have encountered enormous difficulties in establishing organizations and collective forms of action, particularly in the early phases of industrialization and even under political and economic conditions less unfavourable than those prevailing in most of Latin America. Ethnic hostilities and individual projects of mobility contributed to the difficulties encountered by the labour movements in the areas of heavy European immigration, but they did not cause them. Moreover, similar attitudes and consequences surfaced in other parts of Latin America among internal migrants. While the lack of a common culture and history posed serious initial obstacles for some Latin American working classes, the accompanying lack of customary historical sanctions for containing workers within the prevailing social order also made resistance and class autonomy less difficult. Immigrants had escaped to some extent from the influence of the local priests, landowners and police in their countries of origin; the re-establishment of similar patterns of control in the New World was neither rapid nor complete.

The immigrant origins of the early working class in several Latin American countries, however, left its members especially vulnerable to certain forms of repression. The nationalist campaigns mounted in Brazil, Uruguay and Argentina against so-called foreign subversion, especially after 1917, weakened the labour movement in all three countries. Such organizations as the Nationalist League in Brazil and the Patriotic League in Argentina enjoyed considerable success in dividing the working class, isolating many of its most combative elements and generally helping to create a climate favourable to deportations and other forms of repression. The effect of nationalism differed considerably in Mexico. There a relatively small number of foreign workers, primarily from the United States, monopolized most of the better-paying positions on the railways and in many of the larger mining firms. Moreover, foremen and other supervisory personnel in the modern textile factories were quite often foreigners, enjoying what appeared to most Mexican workers to be very high salaries and other privileges. The Díaz regime, heavily compromised by its associations with foreign interests, unwittingly provided some of its opponents with a powerful weapon in the form of nationalist resentments. The bitterness generated by the relatively privileged position of foreign workers and supervisors thus served greatly to unify much of the working class on the basis of nationalism against what appeared to be a common enemy.

In most Latin American cities, the general level of public services, never high, lagged far behind the rapid growth of population from the late nineteenth century onward. The early working classes encountered quite severe problems of overcrowding, contaminated water supplies and inadequate sanitation, which made urban living conditions scarcely superior to those prevailing in the rural areas of southern Europe or Latin America from which most of the workers had recently come.

A very large part of the working classes lived in the grim slum dwellings known variously as *cortiços* (literally 'beehives') in São Paulo, *conventillos* in Buenos Aires and Montevideo, *mesones* in Mexico City. Severely overcrowded and unhealthy as these buildings were, rent for them still absorbed a substantial part of most workers' incomes. In Buenos Aires probably as much as a third of the working class lived in such single-room tenements at the end of the nineteenth century and the beginning of the twentieth. Conditions were hardly better in cities which grew more slowly; in the province of Lima in 1920, 42 per cent of the families occupied single-room lodgings.

Urban living conditions contributed to alarming public health problems in many cities. In the 1904–12 period the death rate in Mexico City (42.3 per 1,000 inhabitants), though lower than in the 1890s, still compared unfavourably to those of Cairo (40.1) and Madras (39.5). Epidemic diseases were common, and prevailing sanitary conditions helped spread a wide variety of serious illnesses.

The densely crowded and homogeneously working-class neighbourhoods of many cities did help to foster certain forms of political and social solidarity. Various districts, such as Brás in São Paulo or La Boca and Barracas in Buenos Aires, became well known as strongholds of political militancy and a somewhat autonomous working-class culture. With the development of tramways, working-class neighbourhoods did become more dispersed, although living conditions on the whole do not appear to have improved very substantially before 1930.

Workers in mining areas and mill towns suffered some special forms of exploitation. When company housing was available, owners could use the threat of the immediate expulsion of troublesome workers and their families as a powerful means of intimidation. Such housing could also serve as a pretext for even closer control over workers' lives. In the 1906 Puebla textile strike, one of the workers' major demands called for the elimination of provisions prohibiting those living in company housing from receiving visitors without permission, and grievances of this sort were by no means unknown elsewhere.

Company stores, especially notorious in Mexico and the Chilean nitrate zone, created particular anger. Firms used such stores as an additional means of control through debt and as a way of further reducing their costs. By paying in scrip redeemable only at these outlets, which often charged exorbitant prices, the owners in effect lowered workers' wages and increased their own profits. The resentments which this highly visible mechanism of exploitation generated could assume quite violent forms. One of the first acts of workers in the Río Blanco strike of 1907 was to set fire to the company store, soon followed by the burning of similar stores at other textile mills in the area.

Working conditions in most countries varied considerably from one sector to another, although skilled workers fared substantially better than unskilled factory hands. Nevertheless, few serious observers ever attempted to describe conditions for the bulk of the Latin American working class in the early twentieth century as much better than miserable. Since trade unions remained generally weak or non-existent, and the labour market imposed few restraints, owners for the most part managed to establish quite coercive work regimes.

In most factories an atmosphere of arbitrary authority and personal abuse prevailed; observers often drew analogies with prisons or slavery. Owners used draconian internal regulations to discipline the labour force and control the work process as completely as possible. These regulations specified high and much resented fines, even in cases of trivial offences, and sometimes fees for such matters as the use of lavatories. The arbitrary application of fines easily absorbed a substantial part of many workers' pay. A number of factories also charged employees for the replacement of broken or worn-out parts as well as for defective materials. Workdays, in addition, could be extremely long. In Mexican industry before 1910 they ranged from twelve to sixteen hours for a six-day work-week. Moreover, owners and supervisors often submitted workers – particularly women and children – to various forms of physical, sometimes sexual, abuse. Workers also complained of the late or irregular payment of wages, the arbitrary manipulation of wage scales and various petty extortions by foremen and others. The widespread use of piece-rates and speed-ups served to maintain a high intensity of work. Since owners tended to ignore even minimal safety precautions, serious accidents occurred with notorious frequency, and any compensation for injuries was quite rare. Respiratory illnesses became common in textile factories, and the risk of occupational diseases also presented a serious hazard in mining and many other industries.

Data on wages and the cost of living are difficult to interpret but there is little indication of any widespread rise in living standards before the First World War. In Mexico, real minimum wages in industry rose briefly in the late 1890s and then declined slowly during the first decade of the twentieth century. While wages were higher in Argentina, data indicate that the average unskilled worker received roughly the same real wages in 1914 as in 1890.

The irregularity of employment, however, means that wage rates provide an incomplete picture of the standard of living. The quite violent fluctuations in the world market for Latin American exports regularly resulted in large-scale unemployment. The number of workers in the Chilean nitrate industry, for example, fell from some 57,000 in 1918 to less than half that number in 1920. Employment then fluctuated sharply throughout the following decade until the nitrate industry finally collapsed in the early 1930s. Even in Argentina, where re-emigration in periods of economic crisis served to transfer to Spain or Italy many of those thrown out of work, unemployment could reach severe proportions. Figures are sporadic, but between a fourth and a fifth of the wage workers in Buenos Aires were estimated to be unemployed at several points in the 1900–14 period. Even in relatively favourable conjunctures, or in economies subject to somewhat less drastic fluctuations, the threat of unemployment remained severe throughout Latin America. Workers almost everywhere complained bitterly about the frequency of arbitrary dismissals, which were often a reprisal for even slight resistance to factory abuses. The high turnover of workers during favourable periods, however, may well have served in part as a means of protest when collective forms appeared impractical.

THE LABOUR MOVEMENT BEFORE THE FIRST WORLD WAR

The first collective attempts by artisans and others to protect themselves from the effects of their living and working conditions took the form of mutual aid societies. Such organizations, which often included both the owners of workshops as well as their employees, emerged in most of the larger Latin American countries by the middle of the nineteenth century. In exchange for regular payments, mutual aid societies usually attempted to provide benefits in cases of accident, sickness or death and sometimes to furnish a few other services.

Such institutions became especially numerous in the highly developed artisan economy of Mexico where, in the 1860s and 1870s, they formed part of a labour movement without parallel in size or scope elsewhere in Latin America. During this period in Mexico City and several other urban centres, the divisions between the numerous small owner-producers on the one hand and wage workers on the other, remained sufficiently obscure to permit the emergence of a number of common organizations. Workers and their bosses could still unite to defend the interests of their trade, and the possibility of an employee's becoming the owner of a workshop did not appear wholly unrealistic.

The movement which arose in this milieu in Mexico represented essentially the interests of independent artisans and small entrepreneurs. Some notion of uniting direct producers with the means of production generally lay behind the egalitarian and liberal political ideas and strategies of the movement. Anarchists of various kinds, such as the Greek-born schoolteacher Plotino Rhodakanaty and his circle, also exercised considerable influence at certain periods. In particular, the anarchists led a continuing attack against any form of collaboration with the state. However, in the political system of the Restored Republic (1867–76) and the early years of the Díaz regime, the support of artisans and their followers became rather valuable to various political figures. The benefits of such collaboration attracted a substantial part of the movement, despite the opposition of anarchists and others.

The *Gran Círculo de Obreros* began to operate in 1870 in Mexico as a national co-ordinating body among various existing organizations, largely mutual aid societies. It published a newspaper, *El Socialista*, and by 1875 had twenty-eight affiliates in the capital and several states. Anarchists initially dominated the *Gran Círculo* but lost out by 1872, and the organization began to receive a subsidy from the government. Disputes over the question of electoral participation and divergences among various political factions eventually divided and weakened the *Gran Círculo*, which virtually ceased to function by the end of the decade. The organization did manage to hold a national Workers' Congress in 1876, and at a second congress in 1879 a successor body was formed which eventually became an instrument of the Díaz regime.

Strikes, which grew in number during the 1870s, further divided the movement. There are accounts of at least twenty-one such work stoppages in Mexico between 1872 and 1880, several led by certain mutual aid societies composed primarily of wage workers, which were beginning to take on at least sporadically some of the tasks associated at a later period with trade unions. In a number of the disputes the *Gran Círculo* sought to mediate between strikers and their employers. Such a position reflected the essential contradiction of a movement attempting to unite wage workers and independent artisans. Since many of the latter were themselves employers, they regarded the spread of the strike tactic with understandable uneasiness.

As Mexico became increasingly integrated in the world economy during the 1880s, the early labour movement disintegrated, unable any longer to conciliate the contradictory interests of small owners and wage workers. Those artisans who managed to survive the advance of capitalism often reached a *modus vivendi* with the Díaz regime, which in any case had little further use for the political participation of subaltern groups. The dictatorship then turned its substantial powers of repression against the relatively isolated wage workers with devastating effect. Despite the considerable achievements of the first labour movement, its growth was specific to a particular moment of transition in the Mexican economy and political system; it left few direct heirs.

Elsewhere in Latin America, independent artisans and wage workers were considerably less numerous in the mid-nineteenth century than in Mexico, and mutual aid societies remained for some time almost the only form of labour organization. The members of a few such institutions used them on some occasions to mount strikes, as was the case of the Rio de Janeiro typesetters as early as 1858. However, the clear emergence of organizations going beyond strictly mutualist functions, usually known as 'resistance societies' in the terminology of the period, dates in most countries from their increasing incorporation in the world economy and the growth of wage labour in the 1880s or even later. (Slavery in Brazil, it is worth recalling, ended only in 1888.) National organizations and workers' congresses on the scale of those which appeared for a time in Mexico in the 1870s are elsewhere generally a phenomenon of the twentieth century.

Most of the varieties of utopian socialism found supporters in one part of Latin America or another from the 1840s onward, and European followers of Fourier or others founded several experimental colonies. Such currents, however, seem to have had little influence among the local artisans and workers of what was in any case generally still a very small working class.

Militants in several countries, including Mexico, Chile and Brazil, established contacts, sometimes rather fleeting, with the First International. In Argentina and Uruguay, however, affiliated organizations began to operate by the early 1870s. Refugee *communards* in Buenos Aires helped to found a French section of the International in 1872, which was joined shortly thereafter by Italian and Spanish sections. In 1873 the groups together numbered some 250 members, but soon split into divergent Marxist and Bakuninist factions. The organizations suffered a certain amount of persecution and seem to have disappeared by the early 1880s.

The labour movements which began to emerge in various Latin American countries toward the end of the nineteenth century clearly drew on the experiences of workers elsewhere in the world. The incorporation of knowledge and doctrines from abroad, as modified and developed in Latin American practice, was, however, a complex and varied process and resulted in the formation of a number of different political groupings.

Anarchists exercised at least some influence almost everywhere in Latin America, although they differed considerably among themselves as to strategy and tactics. Many anarchists, for example, remained highly sceptical of the effectiveness of trade unions, which they regarded as inherently reformist. Such anarchists worked instead through small affinity groups in order to win over workers and others on behalf of a revolution that would destroy the state and bring about a new society, the general features of which provoked some dispute. Other anarchists, while sharing doubts as to the revolutionary potential of trade unions, joined such organizations nevertheless, arguing that they provided a useful place for propaganda, and that their struggles could sometimes be influenced in revolutionary directions.

The current broadly known as anarcho-syndicalism played an even larger role in most of Latin America. This doctrine began to spread widely in various parts of the world at the end of the nineteenth century in reaction to what its supporters regarded as the increasingly reformist character of socialist movements, and the ineffectiveness of previous anarchist methods. While the utopia of small producers which is prominent in much anarchist thought clearly appealed to many independent artisans and similar social groups, anarcho-syndicalism represented an adaptation of certain anarchist principles to the conditions of industrial capitalism. Whatever its strategic weaknesses – and they proved to be immense – anarcho-syndicalist in Latin America was fundamentally both a proletarian and a revolutionary doctrine.

While different organizations varied considerably as to their adaptation and incorporation of anarcho-syndicalist tenets, the notion of 'direct action' generally occupied a central place. By this militants meant that workers should rely on strikes, sabotage, boycotts and similar weapons, rather than seeking gains through the institutions of the bourgeois state, among which they included all political parties. Anarcho-syndicalists maintained, for example, that electoral participation by workers simply strengthened the capitalist order. Their objective, they insisted, was to destroy the state, not to take control of it. To this end they emphasized the trade union as both the main instrument for present struggle and the nucleus of a new society.

Anarcho-syndicalists diverged considerably among themselves on several questions regarding the form of trade union organization. For example, many defended what were in effect unions limited to minorities of militants, and criticized others who sought to enrol as many workers as possible in a given category regardless of consciousness or convictions. Somewhat similarly, many anarcho-syndicalists warned against the dangers of establishing types of union structures which might weaken revolutionary militancy. They attempted instead to create organizations which dispensed with what they regarded as bureaucratic and potentially reformist features such as paid officials, a permanent staff and strike funds. In theory, many anarcho-syndicalists tended to favour the organization of unions on an industrial rather than craft basis, the latter being the usual anarchist preference. Such unions were to unite in local federations in order to counteract corporativist tendencies and to co-ordinate actions over a given geographical area. These federations would then form part of provincial and national organizations. In practice, repression and internal divisions remained so severe in most of Latin America that the rather hybrid anarcho-syndicalist organizations which managed to survive generally corresponded only in part to such principles.

Anarcho-syndicalists expected to destroy the existing order by means of a revolutionary general strike. In some formulations this took on the aspect of a mass armed rising, although in others it was envisaged as a relatively peaceful phenomenon, so widespread as to be invulnerable to state repression. However, strikes for limited economic objectives posed a strategic question of some complexity. Although anarcho-syndicalists usually insisted that such struggles could not secure significant economic improvements for workers, in practice they tended to support strikes of this sort in the name of 'revolutionary gymnastics'. They argued that while any economic gains would soon be lost, workers in the course of such struggles could come to understand their power and develop their spirit of solidarity and militancy.

While a very large number of trade unions, and several national federations, affirmed anarchist or anarcho-syndicalist positions, the question of the real influence of such doctrines remains difficult to evaluate. The distance could often be considerable between programmatic declarations, using the concepts and language common to revolutionaries in much of the world before 1917, and the actual practice of workers. Militants clearly recognized that membership in a union adhering to 'direct action' did not necessarily mean that workers intended to carry out the letter of anarcho-syndicalist theory. Moreover, the unionized represented a quite small percentage of the working class throughout Latin America.

The history of the labour movement during this period in most countries provides frequent instances of ostensibly anarcho-syndicalist unions dealing directly with the state, for example, or of strikes calling for state intervention. On the other hand, cases of exemplary anarcho-syndicalist actions also abound, and in some general strikes as well as on other occasions, anarcho-syndicalists clearly mobilized considerable parts of the working class. Moreover, the substantial anarchist and anarcho-syndicalist publishing activities, including daily newspapers, as well as their extensive cultural programmes could not have been sustained under the circumstances without broad working-class support. While the intricacies of anarcho-syndicalist doctrine may not have meant a great deal to many workers, various elements of its theory and style almost certainly did express important aspects of working-class consciousness and significantly influenced practice.

Anarcho-syndicalism by no means represented the only tendency in the early labour movement, and in some cases the revolutionary and anarchist aspects of the doctrine became very diluted indeed. A distinct syndicalist current emerged most clearly in Argentina, although somewhat similar movements could be found in Rio de Janeiro and elsewhere. While influenced by some elements of anarcho-syndicalism, particularly its *ouvrieriste* ethos and the primacy it assigned to the union, syndicalists devoted a considerable amount of their attention and energies to the securing of immediate economic gains. Although they did not necessarily abandon explicitly the notion of a revolutionary general strike, syndicalists in practice tended to concentrate on piecemeal improvements. Moreover, they proved quite willing to negotiate and even collaborate with the state when they thought such tactics would serve their interests.

With some exceptions, socialism made relatively few advances in Latin America. The size and composition of the working classes, as well as the nature of the state, made most countries decidedly unpromising terrain for social democratic strategies based on electoral participation by workers. The Argentine party, by far the most significant, from its founding in 1896 pursued a policy of very moderate parliamentary reformism, and after the party's first years its links with trade unions became rather tenuous. Following the 1912 changes in Argentine voting procedure, the party enjoyed some electoral success, although its influence with the bulk of the working class remained far from decisive. The Chilean *Partido Obrero Socialista* (POS), founded in 1912 by the veteran militant Luis Emilio Recabarren, took a less reformist line. The POS secured a significant working-class following particularly in the north, although its electoral successes remained slight. Chilean socialists also played a decisive role in the shift of the FOCH, one of the country's main labour federations, to an anti-capitalist direction from 1919 onward.

A number of trade unions in various countries also claimed to be independent of any political doctrine. Some, termed 'yellow unions' by their enemies, were openly conservative in practice and often operated under Church or company auspices. Especially after the promulgation of *Rerum Novarum* in 1891, the Catholic Church made considerable efforts to counteract the growth of revolutionary or even reformist movements among workers. The real influence of these policies, however, and of conservative currents in general within the working class, remains unclear.

The workers who organized the resistance societies which began to appear toward the end of the nineteenth century were generally skilled craftsmen. The unionization of their trades and, soon, of less skilled sectors tended to proceed in irregular bursts of activity, coinciding generally with favourable moments in the economic cycle. During phases of expansion in the economy, with unemployment relatively low, workers could often succeed in forming unions and carrying out strikes for material improvements. In the ensuing downturn, frequently combined with the effects of severe repression against the labour movement, many of the economic and organizational gains would be lost. However, collective experience grew, additional goals and tactics developed, and successive organizing waves tended to spread to new areas and new categories of workers. By 1920, few urban sectors in the larger countries remained untouched.

The predominant working-class organizational form in most countries continued to be the local craft union, although industrial unions appeared more frequently with the passage of time. Few organizations of either type, however, managed to enrol more than a small percentage of workers in national terms from a given category, and both the labour market and state policy in most parts of Latin America ensured that unions remained rather fragile. Membership fluctuated sharply, and organizations appeared and disappeared with some frequency. In several countries, however, most notably Argentina, it proved possible to maintain quite important national, provincial and local trade union federations. Moreover, the capacity of unions to mobilize workers often extended far beyond the relatively small contingents of formal dues-paying members.

Attempts to establish organizational forms other than trade unions met with less success. In São Paulo, neighbourhood leagues composed of workers from all trades developed significantly in 1917 and 1919, but largely disappeared under the intense repression directed against the working class following the general strikes of those years. With the partial exception of Argentina and Uruguay, the role of political parties in the labour movement remained slight until after 1917.

Strikes proved to be the workers' strongest weapon against their employers and the state. Early strike movements, in particular, tended to be rather defensive in their demands, as workers sought to prevent reductions in wages or increases in their workday. Such movements at times also included protests against specific work rules, irregular payment, abuses by foremen and related matters. These early strikes, characteristically limited to a relatively small number of workers, often broke out spontaneously and under rather unfavourable circumstances. In later years, while defensive stoppages never disappeared, strikes tended to become broader and better organized. Increasingly, demands came to include such questions as reductions in hours, increases in real wages and union recognition. Strikes in solidarity with other workers also grew in size and frequency in most countries.

Even apparently mild strike demands often provoked extremely harsh and violent repression; mass dismissals of strikers also became almost routine in some countries. Under the circumstances, even the strongest labour movements faced enormous difficulties in actually winning strikes. Statistics on the subject are sparse, but workers in Buenos Aires, for example, during the 1907–13 period reportedly emerged victorious in 30 per cent of 1,081 strikes, with partial gains achieved in another 10 per cent.

City-wide or regional general strikes broke out on a number of occasions and closed down Buenos Aires, Rio de Janeiro, São Paulo and several other cities for considerable periods as early as the first decade of the twentieth century. Some of the general strikes were planned as such, although many took place more or less spontaneously when movements spread beyond an initial category of strikers, often to protest against acts of repression or to take advantage of what appeared to be favourable conditions for more widespread gains. While the general strikes of the period mobilized vast numbers of people, tangible results of the tactic almost always proved very slight or short-lived.

Besides strikes, workers also used boycotts, slow-downs and occasionally sabotage. Movements of consumers mobilized substantial parts of the population, including elements of the middle class on some occasions. Campaigns to lower the cost of living met with little concrete success; one in Santiago in 1905 led to a large-scale massacre of demonstrators. Rent strikes in several countries resulted in some temporary gains. Over 100,000 people joined the largest such movement, in Buenos Aires in 1907, although repression and the underlying shortage of housing sent rents spiralling upward again shortly thereafter.

Specific national histories present considerable variation in the use and results of different tactics and organizational forms during the last two decades of the nineteenth century and more especially, the first decade of the twentieth century. The labour movements of Argentina, Chile, Brazil and Mexico merit separate treatment. In Central America and much of the northern part of South America, working class organizations before the First World War remained generally weak and fragmented.

The strongest labour movement emerged in Argentina, where the first major wave of activity took place in the late 1880s. Economic expansion and falling real wages during that decade helped to provoke both a number of strikes (at least fifteen in 1889) and the formation of various trade unions. Anarchists played an active role in several of the new organizations. In fact, the Italian anarchist Errico Malatesta, exiled in Argentina between 1885 and 1889, wrote the statutes for the bakery workers and several other Buenos Aires unions. Socialists exercised significant influence in the labour movement at this period, and other currents also appeared. *La Fraternidad*, for example, founded by railway drivers and firemen in 1887, sought from the beginning to concentrate on securing immediate economic improvements for its members. The union, influenced by the example of the railway brotherhoods of the United States, proved over the following decades to be a powerful and militant, though decidedly unrevolutionary, element in the Argentine labour movement. These doctrinal divisions among workers contributed to the failure of two attempts at forming a union confederation in the late 1880s, and the severe economic crisis of 1890 in Argentina led to the collapse of many of the recently founded unions. However, some recovery took place in the mid-1890s, and by 1896 at least 26 unions were functioning in Buenos Aires. Strikes also resumed on a broad scale.

During the first decade of the twentieth century workers in Argentina brought about an extraordinary explosion of labour activity. Not only were many sectors unionized for the first time, but strikes grew in frequency and size. According to government figures, for example, in 1907 there were 231 work stoppages in the city of Buenos Aires which involved some 75,000 strikers. In response to labour activity, the government resorted to state of siege decrees on four occasions between 1902 and 1910 as well as enacting two major repressive measures: the Law of Residence (1902) and the Law of Social Defence (1910).

Despite severe state repression and serious divisions within the labour movement, workers carried out a remarkable series of general strikes in Buenos Aires, Rosario and other cities. Some, such as the 1902 general strike in the capital, began as limited disputes over working conditions but soon spread beyond the initial group of strikers and paralysed entire cities. In both 1904 and 1907 workers in Buenos Aires carried out general strikes in solidarity with their colleagues in Rosario. In 1909, in protest against the massacre of demonstrators by the police during a May Day celebration, workers called an impressive week-long stoppage in Buenos Aires which secured several concessions from the government. The last of the pre-war general strikes took place in 1910 during the observations of the centenary of Argentine independence and met with especially severe repression.

After several unsuccessful attempts during the 1890s to form a national labour confederation, the *Federación Obrera Argentina* (FOA) finally emerged in 1901, representing some 27 unions in the capital and interior. Differences among militants over the strategy and tactics of the new organization, however, proved to be insuperable. The socialists and many other non-anarchists left the FOA in 1902 and formed a separate organization, the *Unión General del Trabajo* (UGT), in the following year. In 1903, the FOA reportedly represented some 33,000 affiliated members, and the UGT 7,400.

While the FOA (which became the *Federación Obrera Regional Argentina* or FORA in 1904) increasingly came under anarchist influence, a distinct syndicalist current began to emerge within the UGT. The syndicalists, dissatisfied with both the moderation of the socialists and with what they considered the inefficacy of anarchist methods, formed a new organization, the *Confederación Obrera Regional Argentina* (CORA) in 1909. The syndicalists, who proved to be particularly strong among port workers and in other key sectors of the export economy, gained considerable influence as their policy of militant though limited strikes for immediate economic gains met with some success.

Following the failure of several earlier merger attempts, the FORA and the CORA managed to unite in 1914. However, at the ninth congress of the FORA in the following year, the syndicalists took over the newly unified organization. The anarchists then withdrew and formed what became known as the FORA V, adhering to the anarchist declarations of the FORA's fifth congress in 1905. The syndicalist organization was referred to as the FORA IX, from its origins in the ninth congress of 1915. The syndicalists continued to attract adherents and during the Yrigoyen government (1916–22) began to engage in some tacit collaboration with the state. In practice, this meant that the government, in exchange for electoral support for the Radical Party, withheld the police from strikes under certain conditions and occasionally mediated labour disputes. By 1918, the FORA IX claimed 80,000 members in Buenos Aires, which would have represented between a fourth and a fifth of the workers in the city.

While the internal divisions, particularly between anarchists and syndicalists, weakened the Argentinian labour movement, it remained by far the strongest in Latin America and exercised considerable influence on the movements in Uruguay, Chile, Peru and elsewhere. Not only did the Buenos Aires anarchist daily *La Protesta* and other publications circulate far beyond Argentina, but the example of the FORA served as a point of reference during the early years of the century for militants throughout the continent.

A notable phase of labour movement expansion took place in Chile during the first years of the twentieth century. Resistance societies appeared in a number of trades in Santiago and Valparaíso, as well as among port workers. The relative success of direct action tactics in the Valparaíso maritime strike of 1903, despite extraordinary repression which led to some 100 deaths, served to strengthen the already considerable influence of anarchists and anarcho-syndicalists in the new unions. The expansion reached a peak between 1905 and 1907, when scores of new resistance societies sprang up and at least 65 strikes took place in Santiago and Valparaíso.

In the mining areas of Northern Chile, where the class structure seemed especially transparent, a distinctive form of organization, the *mancomunales*, emerged during the same period. Such associations, a combination of mutual aid society and trade union, were formed on a territorial rather than craft basis. Composed primarily of nitrate miners and transport workers, the *mancomunales* joined together the skilled and unskilled in what proved to be quite cohesive and militant organizations. Nevertheless, under the combined effects of heavy repression and severe economic crisis, both the resistance societies and the *mancomunales* virtually ceased operations in Chile after 1907, to revive only toward the end of the First World War.

In Brazil, while there had been occasional strikes and some trade union activity earlier, during the 1890s the labour movement began to grow on a considerably larger scale. In Rio de Janeiro a burst of labour activity at the beginning of the century led to the country's first city-wide general strike in 1903. This movement had begun as a stoppage by textile workers seeking a pay increase and a shorter workday, but the strike then spread to other trades. The strikers, who numbered some 40,000 at the height of the movement, virtually paralysed the city for 20 days, and ultimately secured some gains.

The first São Paulo general strike broke out in 1906 when employees of the Paulista railway stopped work, primarily on account of what they considered abuses by management. Workers in other sectors soon joined, in part as a protest against repression, and the state eventually suppressed the strike with notable brutality. In 1907, skilled workers in various São Paulo trades took advantage of an expanding economy and organized a successful general strike in which many secured an eight-hour day. However, in the following economic downturn, owners were able to increase the workday once again, and most of the newly formed unions disappeared. The Brazilian labour movement, despite something of a revival in 1912–13, only began to expand significantly once again in 1917.

Nevertheless, workers had achieved some organizational gains which were far from negligible. The first Brazilian workers' congress met in 1906, with 28 organizations from various parts of the country represented. The resolutions took an anarcho-syndicalist position, and the delegates voted to form a national organization, the *Confederação Operária Brasileira* (COB) which began to function in 1908. The COB facilitated the exchange of information on a national basis and provided some co-ordination of activities, although its existence always remained rather precarious. At a second workers' congress in 1913, attended by representatives of 59 organizations, the delegates reaffirmed the anarcho-syndicalist positions of the earlier meeting.

In Mexico, despite the severe repression directed against the working classes by the Díaz regime, at least 250 strikes took place between 1876 and 1910. Working-class organizations of some types managed to exist, notably among railway workers, but the government generally suppressed those which demonstrated significant militancy or even went much beyond mutualist functions. State violence was mitigated at times by paternalistic gestures, attempts at co-option, and the regime's *ad hoc* arbitration of some disputes.

The Díaz government, however, could be implacable in attacking its enemies and undertook a particularly uncompromising campaign of repression against militants associated with Ricardo Flores Magón. This group, which began to publish the newspaper *Regeneración* in 1900 and eventually formed the *Partido Liberal Mexicano* (PLM), suffered such persecution that most of its leaders ended up in exile in the United States. Although arrests and harassment continued there, the exiles managed to establish contact with various working-class groups in Mexico. The PLM included a wide variety of opponents of Díaz, and its official programme of 1906 took a rather liberal and reformist position. Ricardo Flores Magón, however, and some of his colleagues had been considerably influenced by anarchist theories and practice, although this became widely apparent in their writings and actions only after 1910.

While the real influence of the PLM among Mexican workers remains a matter of dispute, militants with ties to the organization did play important roles in the two most significant labour conflicts of the late Díaz period. The first of these broke out at a large American-owned copper mine at Cananea in the state of Sonora. Mexican workers there had become embittered by various forms of discrimination against them, particularly in regard to wages, since they were paid substantially less than foreigners. In 1906, influenced to some extent by PLM organizers, workers declared a strike for higher pay and a shorter workday. When the company rejected the demands, violence broke out in which at least eighteen Mexicans were killed and many wounded. The company, in order to control the situation, made use of some 275 armed men from across the border in Arizona. The Cananea strike became a major public issue, and the killing of Mexicans by foreigners served to discredit the regime even among some of its conservative supporters.

Later in the same year, textile workers in Puebla went on strike against the imposition of severe new factory regulations. The strike led eventually to a national lock-out by textile owners, and Díaz himself finally arbitrated the dispute. However, many workers rejected the arbitration settlement, and some of these staged a virtual revolt at the Río Blanco textile factory near Orizaba on 7 January 1907. Organizers sympathetic to the PLM had been active in the Orizaba area during the previous year, although by the time of the uprising most had been jailed or forced to leave the region. The regime, as we have seen, suppressed the Río Blanco insurrection with great violence.

The events at Río Blanco shook the Díaz government in several ways. The factory, like much of the modern textile industry, was French-owned, and the regime had once again massacred Mexicans to protect foreign interests. Moreover, the government's somewhat half-hearted attempts to counter growing worker militancy by the encouragement of tame union leadership became increasingly implausible. While the regime largely succeeded after 1906–7 in isolating the more militant elements of the PLM from the working class by means of increased persecution, labour unrest continued on a sizeable scale through the fall of Díaz in 1911. Although industrial workers as a group did not play a decisive role in Díaz's overthrow, their disaffection contributed to the weaknesses of a regime already well-supplied with them.

MEXICO AND THE ORIGINS OF STATE-CONTROLLED UNIONISM

The history of the Mexican labour movement between 1910 and 1930 differs in certain respects from that of movements elsewhere in Latin America. During the lengthy civil war which erupted in Mexico in 1910, urban workers became a political force of considerable importance. Although far from unified, the labour movement represented both a potential ally for the contending factions and a threat to those attempting to hold power. The eventual outcome – a labour movement closely tied to the state apparatus – foreshadowed arrangements to be found after 1930 in several other Latin American countries.

During the short-lived government of Francisco Madero, which replaced that of Díaz in 1911, persecution of the PLM and other groups continued, but extensive trade union organizing and strike activity also took place. In 1912, workers in Mexico City established the *Casa del Obrero Mundial* as a centre for labour movement activity in the capital. Support for the Casa came primarily from craftsmen, skilled workers and those in the service sectors; ties with industrial workers remained much weaker. The Casa included representatives of a number of different currents, although anarchist and anarcho-syndicalist influence appears to have been widespread, particularly during the organization's early years.

The Casa, as well as the working class of Mexico City in general, suffered considerably from the vicissitudes of the military struggle. Many militants came to abandon their earlier opposition to political participation, and in February 1915 the Casa accepted a pact with the Constitutionalist faction led by Venustiano Carranza and Álvaro Obregón. Under the terms of the agreement, the Casa supplied several contingents of soldiers, known as the 'Red Battalions', for use against the peasant armies of Zapata and Villa. In return, the Constitutionalists allowed members of the Casa to organize trade unions within the parts of Mexico under their control and promised not only measures to improve the conditions of workers but also support for their 'just demands' in conflicts with their employers.

Although many workers opposed the pact as a violation of anarcho-syndicalist principles, and others regarded it as at best a short-term tactical manoeuvre, the accord represented a first major step on the part of a significant sector of the working class toward collaboration with the new regime then emerging from the military upheavals. Moreover, the Constitutionalists' anti-clericalism, nationalism and advocacy of a strong central state coincided with the views of a substantial part of the Casa's membership. While the military role played by the Red Battalions proved to be minor, their collaboration served as an important source of legitimacy for the Constitutionalists at a crucial period by giving support to the notion that Carranza headed a broad multi-class coalition. The Casa also took advantage of the opportunities the Constitutionalist military commanders provided them and established a large number of new unions which spread the organization's influence far beyond its initial base in the capital.

By 1916, however, the Constitutionalists had largely eliminated serious military threats from rival factions and, faced with troublesome strike activity, moved to restrict the power of the labour movement. Carranza disbanded the Red Battalions in January and shortly thereafter began the harassment and arrest of various members of the Casa. In the midst of severe inflation, the economic conditions of the working classes deteriorated sharply and unrest came to a head by July 1916. At this point, the Casa called a general strike in the capital demanding that wages be paid in gold or its equivalent in the rapidly depreciating paper currency issued by the Constitutionalists. Carranza considered the strike, which was widely observed, a direct threat to his regime and managed to crush it through the use of extensive violence, martial law and the threat of the death penalty. The severe defeat which the failure of the 1916 general strike represented for the advocates of direct action, along with continuing repression by the Carranza government, served to strengthen substantially those currents within the labour movement inclined to seek better conditions through political bargaining and collaboration with the state.

At the Constitutional Convention of 1917 the delegates rejected Carranza's conservative proposal on labour matters and adopted instead, in Article 123, a number of measures dealing with workers and their organizations. Among its various provisions, the new Constitution specified the eight-hour day, set limits on work by women and children, posed some restrictions on the employers' right to dismiss workers and endorsed the principles of a minimum wage, profit sharing and indemnification for accidents. Article 123 also eliminated company stores and debt peonage. Moreover, it declared that unions and even strikes would be legal under certain rather ambiguous conditions and outlined a system of arbitration and conciliation to resolve struggles between workers and their employers. The state, by deciding on the legality of unions and strikes, as well as regulating the settlement of disputes, assumed broad new powers. In fact, the labour provisions of the 1917 Constitution were only partially implemented until the 1930s or even later. (Measures for profit sharing, for example, date from the 1960s.) Considerable regional variation also existed within Mexico, as some state governments attempted to enforce elements of Article 123, while others did not.

The labour provisions of the Constitution of 1917 generally served to secure certain minimum material conditions for workers at the same time that they eliminated or restricted any autonomous means (such as independent trade unions) by which workers could express their political and economic will. Article 123 and similar measures sought to guarantee class collaboration and successful capital accumulation through the creation of a strong state apparatus which would attempt to suppress class struggle by mediating between capital and labour. A similar political and economic project appeared later in a number of other Latin American countries.

The *Confederación Regional Obrera Mexicana* (CROM), the first effective national trade union confederation in Mexico, emerged from a congress held at Saltillo in 1918 under the auspices of the governor of Coahuila. The new organization, which proved to be an important element in state control of the labour movement during the 1920s, remained from the beginning under the direction of a small group of labour leaders headed by Luis N. Morones. Several had been active in the *Casa del Obrero Mundial*, but by 1918 had embarked on a policy of political negotiation and mild reformism. In 1919 Morones and his colleagues formed a political party, the *Partido Laborista Mexicano* to support the presidential candidacy of General Obregón. During the latter's term in office (1920–4), the CROM grew considerably and secured material improvements for many of its members. Along with the *Partido Laborista*, it represented one of the more powerful elements in the Obregón government. In practice, the CROM began to function as a virtual arm of the state and served to maintain order, restrict unauthorized strikes and weaken or destroy rival labour organizations.

The CROM's growing influence did not go unchallenged. In 1921, a large number of anarcho-syndicalists, Communists (see below) and others opposed to the policies of the CROM formed the *Confederación General del Trabajo* (CGT). At its founding, the CGT was thought to represent a sizeable contingent of some 12,000 to 15,000 workers throughout the country. (Comparisons are of questionable usefulness, especially since the CROM's membership figures were notoriously inflated, but in 1921 the CROM claimed 150,000 members, over 40 per cent of whom were listed as belonging to its affiliated peasant organizations.) The communists soon left the CGT, whose declarations by 1922 generally took anarcho-syndicalist positions, favouring direct action and opposing political involvement. During strikes led by the CGT in the textile industry and other sectors, the struggles with the CROM were often at least as intense and violent as those with the employers.

The techniques used by the CROM against other unions included the supplying of strike-breakers to firms during labour disputes and the creation of rival affiliates which enjoyed the support of the state and even of employers. The CROM also maintained its own armed squads to attack its enemies and was widely believed to have been responsible for more than one political assassination. Since the CROM could count on the assistance of the police as well as of other parts of the state apparatus, its methods – which could also include a variety of benefits for those willing to collaborate – proved highly effective in weakening rival organizations.

The CROM attained its greatest power during the presidency of Plutarco Elías Calles (1924–8). The organization had strengthened its position within the regime shortly beforehand, in the course of the De La Huerta revolt of 1923–4, when the CROM furnished the government with decisive assistance in the form of troops and other support. During Calles's electoral campaign, the CROM had gone so far as to declare him its honorary president. Upon assuming office, Calles named Morones to be Secretary of Industry, Commerce and Labour; several figures from the CROM and its Partido Laborista occupied other positions of importance in the government and congress. The organization's already notorious opportunism, corruption and gangsterism grew even more marked, while it issued declarations calling for the 'harmonious consolidation of labour and capital', and the creation of 'a spirit of confidence for industrialists and foreign capitalists'. Its systematic anti-communism and cordial links with the American Federation of Labor served as further indications of the CROM's support for continued capitalist development. In 1928, the organization claimed the highly unlikely figure of two million members.

In the complex manoeuvring to select Calles's successor, however, Morones and his circle seriously miscalculated. They had hoped for a time to impose Morones himself as president and opposed until almost the last moment the re-election of Obregón, despite the latter's wide support among the membership. The accumulated discontent of much of the rank and file, and even some leaders, over the CROM's compromises, alliances and limitations came to a head with the murder of Obregón in July 1928. Although nothing was ever proved, many believed that Morones himself probably had a hand in the assassination.

Internally divided and deprived of most state support during the interim government of Emilio Portes Gil, the CROM lost a great deal of strength after 1928. Not only was the executive now hostile to Morones and his circle, but the regime gradually embarked on new policies for dealing with the labour question, exemplified by the creation of a new government party in 1929 and the adoption of the rather corporatist Federal Labour Law of 1931. Under the new law a number of functions left to the CROM before 1928 were henceforth to be performed directly by the state apparatus, which began to control the registration of unions and the character of labour contracts, as well as determining the course of strikes and imposing obligatory arbitration.

POST-WAR LABOUR UNREST, 1917–20

Throughout much of Latin America outside Mexico the years between 1917 and 1920 had witnessed an unprecedented explosion of labour activity. Vast general strikes erupted in many of the major cities, and workers in many areas and trades began for the first time to form unions, carry out strikes and take other actions. The dramatic events of these years helped shape to an important extent the course of subsequent struggles. The labour movement, the industrialists and the state all began to reformulate their strategies in the light of their experiences in 1917–20, when the class struggle reached a new level of intensity.

The great strikes and mobilizations stemmed in part from the hardships which the First World War had caused for the Latin American working classes. The disruption of international trade and the consequent economic dislocations in countries highly dependent on foreign commerce led initially to substantial unemployment and sharply rising living costs. The specific impact of the war on the working classes varied somewhat from one area to another according to such matters as the importance in the local economy of imported food and raw materials, or the extent to which increased agricultural exports reduced the production of foodstuffs for local consumption. In general, the interruption in the importation of manufactured goods served as a stimulus to industry in Latin America, and production by the latter years of the war had increased significantly in many areas. While industrialists exploited the advantages of monopoly, wages continued to lag far behind the rising cost of living. However, the irregular economic expansion which was under way in some countries by about 1917 provided conditions more favourable for labour action than had existed since before the beginning of the war.

The impact of the Russian Revolution also played a role in the events of 1917–20 in Latin America. Although information from Russia remained scarce and distorted, the very fact of the revolution served as an enormous inspiration to militants and thoroughly alarmed most ruling groups. News of Díaz's overthrow and the subsequent struggles in Mexico had provoked similar effects. Accounts of revolutionary outbreaks in Germany, Hungary, Italy and elsewhere filled the labour press from 1918 onward. Even though the Latin American general strikes of the period were far from insurrectionary, they took place in an atmosphere fired by the prospects of world revolution and by the fear of it.

The São Paulo general strike, which broke out in July 1917, began as a work stoppage for higher wages at a large textile factory. In the midst of the prevailing economic hardship, the movement spread to other firms. When police killed a demonstrator, the passage of his funeral procession through the city served to set off a largely spontaneous general strike. Some 45,000 people stopped work, the civil authorities virtually lost control of São Paulo for several days, and various incidents raised the possibility that the police and troops could not necessarily be counted upon to shoot strikers. Some looting took place, particularly in the sacking of bakeries, warehouses and at least one large mill whose owners were accused of withholding flour from the market.

Workers organized a *Comitê de Defesa Proletária* (CDP), composed largely of anarcho-syndicalists, which formulated an extensive list of rather moderate demands. Several of the items called for state action in such matters as the lowering of rents and food prices, which served to maintain some middle class support for the movement, but were hardly consistent with anarcho-syndicalist doctrine. The CDP negotiated with the governor through a committee of journalists (so as not to appear to be dealing directly with the state) and eventually secured a general 20 per cent wage increase as well as promises – quickly forgotten – that the government would undertake a series of other reforms. The 20 per cent increase, though imperfectly observed, represented a major victory for the strikers and was followed by an extensive wave of labour organizing.

The strike also spread to the interior of the state of São Paulo, and helped to touch off a general strike later in July in Rio de Janeiro. Workers in Rio won some gains and embarked on widespread unionization drives in various sectors. Not only had the Brazilian state been caught somewhat unawares by the scope of the July strikes, but the subsequent large-scale expansion of union activity seriously alarmed industrialists and their allies.

In September 1917, with the repressive apparatus reinforced, the state began to close unions and mounted an extensive campaign of arrests and deportations. Police activities continued during 1918 under the cover of a state of siege and, when a new wave of strikes erupted in various parts of Brazil in the following year, the labour movement met with increasingly effective persecution.

Although workers managed to carry out partially successful general strikes in São Paulo and several other cities during 1919, the results of large-scale repression became increasingly apparent. Not only had the labour movement lost many of its most able militants through deportation but growing internal divisions over strategy and tactics left the movement in considerable disarray. The activities of right-wing vigilante groups and intensified campaigns against alleged foreign conspiracies served further to weaken and isolate workers and their organizations. The failure of attempted general strikes in 1920, in the midst of a worsening economic situation, marked the end of the great explosive period in early Brazilian labour history.

Even larger mobilizations took place in Argentina between 1917 and 1921. In each of those years more than 100,000 workers participated in strikes in the city of Buenos Aires alone. During 1919, the peak year, 308,967 workers carried out 367 strikes there.

The largest and most violent upheaval, known as the *Semana Trágica* (Tragic Week), occurred in January 1919. During the course of a strike by metal workers at a factory in Buenos Aires, clashes broke out between pickets and police which resulted in the death of four workers. Violence then spread through the city, and at the funeral of the slain workers the police opened fire on the crowd and left some twenty dead. Workers responded with a massive general strike, the first in Buenos Aires since 1910. The army, police and vigilante groups battled with workers in the streets, killing at least 200 according to some accounts. The major union federations supported the general strike, but it had effectively been in force before their declarations. There is, in fact, little indication of planning or co-ordination by working-class organizations in the *Semana Trágica*, despite groundless rumours of a Bolshevik plot which served as one of the pretexts for a virtual pogrom against the Jewish working-class community of Buenos Aires. The syndicalists eventually negotiated an end to the general strike on the basis of the freeing of all those imprisoned and the granting of most of the metal workers' original demands. The anarchists opposed the settlement, but proved unable to sustain the strike.

Right-wing 'patriotic' groups, which had been active in repression against the labour movement, emerged much strengthened from the events of 1919. Along with their military and civilian allies, they helped to restrict Yrigoyen's attempts to establish closer ties with the syndicalists. In 1921, under increasing conservative pressure, the government moved openly against the syndicalists during a strike by port workers, and an attempted general strike called by the syndicalists proved abortive. The severe internal divisions of the Argentine labour movement persisted, and the depression of the early 1920s weakened the movement as a whole.

In Chile, at least 229 strikes took place in Santiago and Valparaíso between 1917 and 1921, 92 of them occurring in 1919. Mobilizations against the cost of living drew large crowds, perhaps as many as 100,000 in Santiago in 1919. Port and packing plant workers staged a brief insurrection at Puerto Natales in 1919 and took over the town until the army crushed them.

The state directed some of its fiercest repressions against the anarcho-syndicalists, particularly the Chilean affiliate of the Industrial Workers of the World (IWW), which had met with considerable success organizing port workers in Valparaíso. The state also carried out a substantial massacre of nitrate workers at San Gregorio in 1921. The depression which began in Chile at the end of 1920 greatly strengthened the position of the employers. In 1921 they staged an effective series of lockouts and managed to reverse many of the gains which workers had won in the strikes of 1917–19. Nevertheless, the employers' victory proved far from decisive. Although many organizations were weakened and some even disappeared, the labour movement as a whole had gained considerable strength in Chile and withstood the attempts to destroy it with much more success than had been the case in the repression and economic crisis following the expansion of 1905–7.

Working class mobilization also occurred during 1917–20 on a large scale in several countries in which the labour movement had been rather limited before the war. In Cuba, workers in the ports, railways and in construction, as well as those in several other trades, carried out important work stoppages during 1918 and 1919. A strike wave involving considerable violence swept Colombia between 1918 and 1920. Port workers in Barranquilla and Cartagena, as well as railway workers in Santa Marta, struck in 1918 with some success. A series of stoppages in Bogotá during 1919 culminated in a generalized strike in

November. Strikes by miners and port workers broke out in Ecuador. In Peru, Lima workers staged a remarkably successful general strike in January 1919, in which many secured an eight-hour day. In May, however, another general strike in Lima and Callao was defeated at the cost of perhaps one hundred dead.

LABOUR MOVEMENTS IN THE 1920S AND THE EMERGENCE OF COMMUNIST PARTIES

The post-war depression, which struck most Latin American countries by 1920 or 1921, helped bring the cycle of labour movement expansion to a halt. However, the unprecedented size and intensity of working-class mobilization during the years 1917–20 led to significant changes in the characteristics of the struggle between capital and labour during the 1920s. In many countries, the state and ruling groups had been shaken, at least momentarily, by the scope of working class unrest. In the aftermath, they strengthened the repressive apparatus. Repression became even better organized and more thorough, with the use of such measures as more effective black lists, although savage physical violence also continued to be employed against workers. At La Coruña in 1925, to cite an extreme case, the Chilean authorities massacred several hundred nitrate workers as a result of a labour dispute. At the same time other ways of controlling the working class began to be explored. Institutional innovations usually included at least some partial social reforms, coupled with attempts to establish new modes of state domination over labour organizations. Most such projects were consolidated only after 1930, but their roots lay to a large extent in the events of 1917–20.

Attempts to create or encourage unions which would carry out state objectives began to appear in several countries during the 1920s, although none enjoyed the success of the CROM in Mexico. Regimes as diverse as those of Yrigoyen in Argentina (1916–22, 1928–30), Bernardes in Brazil (1922–6) and Ibáñez in Chile (1927–31) all sought at one point or another to co-opt unions for electoral or other purposes. The Chilean labour code, for example, first adopted in 1924 but only implemented from 1927, foreshadowed a strategy followed in various other parts of Latin America after 1930. The Chilean code authorized the existence of trade unions but severely restricted their autonomy and effectiveness. Industry-wide union federations were prohibited and state control both over strike procedures and the legal recognition of unions, as well as their finances and elections, was established. Attempts before 1930 to adopt comprehensive labour codes failed in both Brazil and Argentina, in part on account of conservative opposition, but also, in the case of Argentina, because the labour movement effectively mobilized to oppose such a measure.

Most governments adopted or extended various forms of social legislation during the 1920s, as they sought to lessen unrest by workers and, in some cases, respond to electoral pressures. Employers often opposed the adoption of social legislation, although many specific provisions actually served to restrict competition among firms and otherwise facilitate capital accumulation. The more common measures included limitations on the length of the working day, regulation of work by women and children and provisions for compensation in case of accidents. Some countries also adopted regulations governing factory conditions, pensions and holidays. While often quite limited in application and erratically enforced, the social legislation of the period partially mitigated some of the worst abuses by employers.

A significant part of the labour movement also reformulated its strategy and tactics in the course of the 1920s. Although the gains which workers had won previously by no means disappeared entirely in the frequent defeats and severe repression of the early 1920s, dissatisfaction with existing labour movement strategies, especially the general strike, became widespread. Many militants regarded the tangible results of the struggles of 1917–20 as slight, especially in view of the size of the mobilizations and the costs the movement had paid. And most anarcho-syndicalist movements entered a period of serious crisis. Reformist and collaborationist currents gained strength in several countries, partly, as we have seen, as a result of state policies which increasingly encouraged such movements for political purposes. Political participation and negotiation appeared to offer new and attractive possibilities. At the same time, Leninist parties also emerged to compete with the tendencies which had prevailed in the Latin American labour movements before 1917.

The immense prestige of the Russian Revolution served to inspire militants throughout the continent. The early Communist parties, however, suffered severely from factional disputes and the effects of persecution. With the partial exception of Chile, parties remained relatively small and their influence on the labour movement slight until at least the latter part of the decade. They did succeed, nevertheless, in several cases during the 1920s in establishing unions among previously unorganized groups, the most notable examples being peasants in parts of Mexico, Peru and Chile, and white-collar workers in Argentina and Chile.

In contrast to Socialists and anarcho-syndicalists, the Communists sought to combine – under party leadership – strategies aimed both at electoral participation and union organization (including attention to immediate economic gains). The Communists also emphasized imperialism as a principal obstacle against which the working classes should fight. Their analysis held that the labour movement could take advantage of rivalries between sectors of the local and international bourgeoisies through temporary alliances which would advance the long-range revolutionary movement. Communists thus at times supported nationalist governments that attempted to curb foreign penetration of local economies. The anarcho-syndicalists, in constrast, saw little to distinguish local from foreign capital and regarded nationalism as nothing more than an ideology of the bourgeoisie.

The strategies of the Communist parties varied somewhat from one country to another, particularly in the early years, but were generally informed by a series of notions about the feudal nature of Latin American societies, the necessary progression of the region through a series of historical stages (in particular that of the bourgeois revolution), and the temporarily progressive character of the national bourgeoisie. Such analyses led to strategies aimed at hastening bourgeois revolution and national industrialization.

The Communist International directed relatively little attention to Latin America, with the exception of Mexico, before the late 1920s. After 1928, however, the Comintern entered what is known as its 'third period' (which lasted until the adoption of Popular Front tactics in 1935), and made considerable effort to secure adherence to its new and intransigent line of 'class against class'. This policy opposed among other things the collaboration of Communists with Socialists and other non-Communists; its adoption in Latin America, for example, helped bring to an end a moderately promising electoral front in Brazil – the *Bloco Operário e Camponês* (see below) – and led in a number of countries to the departure of Communists from existing labour organizations, with the subsequent creation of separate Communist-led unions and federations. In 1929, at a congress in Montevideo, the Communists organized the *Confederación Sindical Latino-Americana*, which was intended as a continent-wide union confederation. Shortly thereafter, the Latin American Communist parties held their first joint meetings in Buenos Aires, attended by delegates from fourteen countries, at which they reviewed the role of the parties throughout the region and sought to bring practice into accord with the policy of the 'third period'.

The first Latin American Communist party had emerged in Mexico in 1919 from within a small Socialist group. The Indian nationalist, M. N. Roy, organized the new party with the encouragement of the Bolshevik Michael Borodin, then in Mexico primarily it seems on a trade mission. The party led a precarious existence during its first years, in part because of fluctuating leadership not always familiar with Mexican conditions. The first secretary general, José Allen, turned out to be an agent of United States Military Intelligence. Roy himself, who had fled from the United States when that country entered World War I, left Mexico for the second congress of the Comintern in 1920 and never returned. A number of other foreign militants played important roles at various times in the early years of the party: the Japanese Sen Katayama, the Swiss Alfred Stirner (Edgar Woog), several Communists from the United States and elsewhere.

After the Communists' departure from the anarcho-syndicalist CGT in 1921 (see above), they experienced difficulty in maintaining effective ties with the labour movement, although they had more success in organizing peasants, especially in the state of Veracruz. During the mid-1920s, Bertram Wolfe, a member of the Communist Party of the United States, directed a reorganization of the Mexican party aimed at eliminating reputed anarchist tendencies which had troubled the Comintern for some time. By 1926–7 the party exercised considerable influence among railway workers and some miners. The Communists' trade union strategy in general had been to work through the CROM, but with that organization in disarray after 1928, and in accord with the Comintern's policy of the 'third period', the party established a separate organization under its direction. The *Confederación Sindical Unitaria de México*, as the new confederation was known, became for a time in the early 1930s an important force in the labour movement.

The divisions which had long troubled the Argentine labour movement persisted through the 1920s. The syndicalist FORA IX remained the strongest of the national trade union confederations; one of its major affiliates virtually controlled the ports. In 1922, the FORA IX, incorporating the Communists, changed its name to the *Unión Sindical*

Argentina (USA). The smaller FORA V continued to represent an important anarchist current within the labour movement. Several independent groups also existed, notably those of the railway workers, who provided the basis for another national organization, the *Confederación Obrera Argentina* (COA), founded in 1926. The syndicalists and independents, seeking concrete benefits for their members, engaged in various forms of political bargaining with the state. The Radical party governments of the 1920s often proved receptive, since they hoped to secure working-class votes, and in any case appeared more tractable than the employers.

At the end of the decade the Argentine labour movement remained divided into three national confederations (the USA, the FORA, and the COA), several independent groupings, and a new Communist trade union organization, the *Comité de Unidad Sindical Clasista*. Shortly thereafter, however, the major confederations – except the anarchist FORA – joined together to form the *Confederación General de Trabajo* (CGT). The military group which seized power in 1930 followed a policy of considerable hostility toward the labour movement and, although a part of the CGT was disposed to collaborate with the new regime, the possibilities of accommodation proved slight. Faced with rising unemployment and state repression, the Argentine labour movement – despite notable struggles by meat-packing and petroleum workers among others – suffered serious setbacks in the early 1930s, reversing many of its gains over the previous decade.

The group which came to form the Communist party in Argentina emerged from a split which had taken place among the Socialists in 1917 over the question of participation in the First World War. Socialists favouring neutrality eventually formed a separate *Partido Socialista Internacional* (PSI) in 1918 which, in the following year, voted to join the Communist International. The PSI formally became the Communist party in December 1920. The Socialists, at their convention in 1921, rejected (by a vote of 5,000 to 3,600) a proposal that they should adhere to the Comintern. Many of their members, however, left the party to join the Communists, who elected candidates to local office in several cities during the 1920s. Factional disputes within the new party from both Left and Right proved bitter; only in the latter part of the decade did the group led by Victorio Codovilla and supported by the Comintern manage to impose its control.

In Chile the labour movement managed to withstand state repression and the severe post-war depression. The *Partido Obrero Socialista* (POS) decided to seek admission to the Comintern in December 1920 and formally became the Communist party in January 1922. The organization maintained considerable autonomy from the directives of the Comintern until the late 1920s. In the presidential elections of 1925, the Communists strongly supported a coalition candidate who received over 28 per cent of the vote. Communists also represented an important element in the trade union movement: the FOCH, the confederation which dominated the nitrate and coal mining zones, voted to affiliate with the Comintern's union organization in December 1921. Anarcho-syndicalists, including the Chilean affiliate of the IWW, continued to lead the major unions of Santiago and Valparaíso, among them the maritime and construction workers. However, after 1927 harsh repression by the government of Carlos Ibáñez seriously weakened the parties and unions of the Left.

In Brazil the harassment, arrests and expulsions which took place as a result of the strikes of 1917–20 had decimated the labour movement, and repression continued throughout the decade, facilitated by the state of siege in force between 1922 and 1926. Yellow and reformist unions, encouraged to some extent by the state, continued to influence a sizeable part of the working class, especially in Rio de Janeiro and several northern cities. The labour movement split further as many anarcho-syndicalist militants rejected much of the movement's earlier strategy and, influenced by the success of the Bolsheviks, came to support the notion of a disciplined vanguard party which rejected neither political participation nor strikes for short-term economic objectives. While anarcho-syndicalism remained an important current in the labour movement, and in São Paulo the predominant one, its position in most cities declined decisively, weakened by repression and defections.

No significant Socialist party emerged in Brazil, and former anarcho-syndicalists founded the Communist party in 1922. The new organization gradually established itself in several Rio de Janeiro unions and in 1926 organized an electoral front, which later became known as the *Bloco Operário e Camponês* (BOC). In 1927 the BOC campaigned on behalf of a successful non-Communist parliamentary candidate and in the following year elected two party members to the Rio de Janeiro city council. The party suffered serious defections in the late 1920s, both from Trotskyists and from members opposed to the policies of the 'third period'. Nevertheless, it continued to occupy an important position in the labour movement and in 1929 created a short-lived national trade union confederation, the *Confederação Geral do Trabalho*.

The Communist party had maintained contacts with Luís Carlos Prestes, the young military officer whose exploits in leading the 'Prestes Column' through the backlands of Brazil between 1924 and 1927 had captured the imagination of a large part of the population. The political positions which Prestes took during the 1920s, however, proved to be rather far from those of the Communists, and relations remained inconclusive until the following decade, when Prestes finally entered the party that he was to lead for over forty years.

CONCLUSION

The small urban working class of the late nineteenth century had, by 1930, undergone substantial changes. While the Latin American economies, as producers of primary products, remained fundamentally tied to Europe and North America, industry in the larger countries had grown significantly. Workers almost everywhere had created institutions to defend themselves, acquired experience and in some cases managed to improve their living and working conditions. Their struggles had led to a sizeable body of social legislation and a growing role for the state in labour matters – ambiguous legacies, as it turned out, which also served as instruments for containing the working class within the prevailing order. Labour movements formed in the course of the struggles over the preceding decades represented in most countries a force capable of influencing the direction of national life. The doctrines of the pre-1930 movements, however, generally lost ground to the populist, nationalist and statist movements which dominated politics in much of Latin America in the decades after 1930. Yet populism itself was a reaction to class struggle and to the real and potential mobilization of the working class. Its roots can be seen clearly in the events and policies of the earlier years.

10

POLITICAL AND SOCIAL IDEAS IN
LATIN AMERICA, 1870–1930

THE LIBERAL HERITAGE IN AN ERA OF IDEOLOGICAL
CONSENSUS

Political and social ideas in Latin America have been affected by two obvious though frequently unappreciated facts that distinguish the region from other parts of the 'non-Western', 'developing', or 'third' world with which it has often been compared. First, the culture of Latin America's governing and intellectual elites is integrally Western, that is, it has emerged within the broader confines of Western European culture, modified of course by the special characteristics Spain and Portugal imparted to their former colonies. Second, the nations of Latin America, with the exception of Cuba, gained their political independence at the beginning of the nineteenth century.

It is now common to refer to nineteenth-century Latin America as 'neo-colonial', which suggests a situation of economic and cultural dependence for nations that were politically independent. The implication is that independence was formal and superficial and that dependence was the deeper and more significant experience of the region. It is clear that the elites of ninteenth-century Latin America were tied to, even dependent on, Europe, and that their economic interests within the international capitalist system formed part of that tie. It is also clear that the bond with Europe was strengthened after 1870, with the burgeoning of the Latin American export economies. Less clear is that the circumstance of early political independence can be regarded as a superficial element in Latin American culture. On the contrary, the ideologies, political programmes and social theories of the nineteenth century, while intellectually 'European', were nonetheless distinctive and authentically 'Latin American', in part because they emerged in

367

politically independent nations. To dismiss or downgrade these political and social ideas as 'imitative' or 'derivative', or as mere rationalisations for the economic interests of a dependent governing class, is to make insignificant what was regarded then as of great significance, and to distort our understanding of Latin American history.

Thus, we begin this chapter with a discussion of liberalism, which in the newly independent nations formed the basis of programmes and theories for the establishment and consolidation of governments and the reorganization of societies. The distinctive experience of liberalism in Latin America derived from the fact that liberal ideas were applied in countries which were highly stratified, socially and racially, and economically underdeveloped, and in which the tradition of centralized state authority ran deep. In short, they were applied in an environment which was resistant and hostile, and which in some cases engendered a strong opposing ideology of conservatism. The years from the 1820s till about 1870, in contrast to the era that followed, were ones of ideological conflict and political confusion. They were also years in which the classic doctrines of liberalism underwent severe modification within this unique environment, a modification which followed changes within European thought itself.[1]

As perceived by the contemporary elites of Latin America, the two decades following 1870 represented the fulfilment of liberalism. With the victory of the liberal forces over the empire of Maximilian in Mexico in 1867 and the abdication of Pedro II in Brazil in 1889, the remnants of the Old World monarchical system had succumbed to the New World system of republican, constitutional and representative institutions. The earlier American phenomenon of 'barbarous' regional caudillos finally yielded to a 'civilized' and uniform regime of law, most dramatically in Argentina but also in other nations. The liberal struggle to establish the secular state had been won, the result in Mexico of civil war and imposition of the Laws of Reform, and of more moderately enacted legislation in Argentina, Brazil and Chile. The obscurantist restraints of colonial society had given way to modern secular standards in education and in civil organization. 'Spiritual emancipation', the dream of early nineteenth-century liberals, was now a reality. Guided by the principles of free individual enterprise, the Latin American nations had entered the economic system of the civilized world. The resulting commercial prosperity and the growth of sophisticated, cosmopolitan, urban centres

---

[1] See Safford, *CHLA* III, Chapter 9.

were for contemporaries only further signs that the liberal age had arrived.

What appeared the fulfilment of liberalism was in fact its transformation from an ideology in conflict with the inherited colonial order of institutions and social patterns into a unifying myth. In comparison with the first half-century following independence, the years after 1870 were years of political consensus. The classic liberal doctrines based on the autonomous individual gave way to theories construing the individual as an integral part of the social organism, conditioned by time and place and ever-changing as society itself changed. A theoretical conflict existed between classic or doctrinaire liberalism and the new concepts (often referred to loosely as 'positivism'), but it was a conflict that could be submerged in an era of consensus. However transformed, liberalism provided an almost universal heritage for the governing elites of the post-1870 years. Let us first, therefore, examine the principal elements of that heritage.

Republicanism and the American 'spirit'

Spanish American liberals of the mid-century decades were ambivalent toward Europe. Most shared the view of the Argentine, Juan Bautista Alberdi (1810–84) that their civilization was European and that 'our Revolution' in its ideas was no more than a phase of the great French Revolution. And yet, the New World held out hopes for human progress under free institutions, hopes which were continually being frustrated in the Old World. In short, there was a distinctive American 'spirit' separating the two worlds, at the heart of which was republicanism. Except in Brazil, political independence in the Western Hemisphere had entailed the rejection of monarchy, and Spanish American intellectuals throughout the century were sensitive to threats of monarchical restoration on their continent and to the ebb and flow of the republican ideal in Europe. This ideal was at its low point in the fifties and sixties, following the failure of the French and Italian republics in 1848 and the creation of the empire of Napoleon III. The brief presence of Maximilian of Habsburg on a Mexican throne from 1864 to 1867 and the even briefer belligerence of monarchical Spain on the South American west coast in 1865–6 inspired an eloquent expression of Americanism, particularly by the Chileans José Victorino Lastarria (1817–88) and Francisco Bilbao (1823–65).

Both Lastarria and Bilbao had published notorious essays in the 1840s attacking the spiritual and social legacy of Spain in America. Lastarria excoriated the persisting feudal mentality and extolled utilitarian values that were consonant with the republican institutions Chile had adopted. Bilbao was more radical, calling for the 'de-hispanicizing', even the 'de-catholicizing', of Chile. Forced into exile, Bilbao spent the momentous years 1845 to 1850 in France, exposed to the growing republican movement, to the controversy over the role of the Church in education and, ultimately, to the Revolution of 1848 and its aftermath. He developed personal friendships with the liberal giants of the era, Felicité de Lammenais, Jules Michelet and Edgar Quinet. Quinet, himself an exile from Napoleon III's France, took a great interest in the young Chilean during the subsequent decade and encouraged the republicanism and the anti-Catholic mystical rationalism (tinged with freemasonry) which pervaded Bilbao's *América en peligro* (1862) and *El evangélico americano* (1864).

A year later, Bilbao died aged forty-two in Buenos Aires where he had published these tracts. His youth, his radical free-thinking views, and perhaps his unique cosmopolitanism, gave his writings wide currency among later generations. Bilbao's more moderate former teacher, Lastarria, struck similar themes and added others in *La América* (1865). For instance, he defended the 'liberal system' of republican North and South America against the 'ridiculous' recent notion that there existed a Latin race in Europe and America which shared a common destiny. For Lastarria, 'Latin' America was a Napoleonic idea designed to restore 'absolutism' in the New World.

The republican ideal was dramatically vindicated with the withdrawal of French troops from Mexico and the collapse of the Second Empire. The summary trial and execution of Maximilian and two Mexican Conservative generals in June 1867 was followed on 15 July by the declaration of Mexico's second independence by Benito Juárez, the embattled republican leader and hero of America. The Mexican victory evoked great enthusiasm among European republicans, thus removing much of the ambivalence Latin Americans had earlier expressed toward Europe. A principal agent of this new rapprochement of liberal Europe and America was the Spanish orator, republican propagandist, prolific publicist and statesman, Emilio Castelar. Though Castelar is today almost totally forgotten, his fame in Spanish America from 1870 to 1900 cannot be overestimated. He was the great Hispanic orator in an age of eloquence, and his verbose and elegant style was widely imitated in chamber and lecture hall. Since his employment as a politician after 1867 was sporadic, Castelar turned to journalism for a living, and for twenty-five years his fortnightly commentaries on Spanish and European politics filled newspapers (often the entire front page) in Buenos Aires, Lima, Mexico City and even New York.

As a pan-hispanist Castelar had reacted sharply to Bilbao's message of *desespañolización*. But the mood had now changed. Present at a Paris restaurant on 4 July 1867 when Domingo F. Sarmiento (1811–88) announced his candidacy for president of the Argentine Republic, Castelar toasted American democracy and the melding of the souls of Spain and America, as liberty triumphed on both continents. Sarmiento responded in kind with a tribute to Castelar's liberalism. The latter's prestige in America was further enhanced when he became president of the First Spanish Republic in September 1873. Castelar's policy of strong central government in the face of regional rebellions on the Left and the Right struck a responsive chord among those Latin American political leaders seeking a 'conservative-liberalism' in the years of consensus after 1870.

If the American spirit meant the advance of republican values and institutions, it also signified the plague of 'barbarous' caudillos who rose to power in the post-independence decades and whose power was sustained by charisma, by popular following, or by regional interests. In 1845 Sarmiento had evoked, even romanticized, the telluric force of the gaucho chieftain in his famous *Facundo: civilización i barbarie*. But Sarmiento was ambivalent toward this emanation of Americanism, for he also identified the march of civilization with the ascendancy of Buenos Aires, the city that faced outward toward Europe. After the gaucho tyrant, Juan Manuel de Rosas, had mastered Buenos Aires and triumphed over the provincial Facundo Quiroga, then 'the tyrant himself was superfluous' and fell in 1852 to the advance of liberal institutions.[2] Sarmiento was at heart a Buenos Aires centralist, an *unitario*, and it was fitting that he should as president of the Republic (1868–74) relentlessly pursue the last of the regional caudillos, Ricardo López Jordan of Entre Rios. 'Every caudillo carries my mark', announced Sarmiento proudly in the Senate.

Sarmiento's contemporaries in Mexico, Benito Juárez and Sebastián Lerdo de Tejada, also intervened vigorously in the provinces, following

---

[2] D. F. Sarmiento, *Facundo*, ed. Alberto Palcos (Buenos Aires, 1961), 265.

ten years of open civil conflict (1857–67), which had seen the strengthening of regional power centres such as Guerrero, San Luis Potosí and Yucatán. The government campaign to reduce provincial chieftains reached a climax in 1873 with the defeat and execution of Manuel Lozada, the long-time popular rebel and proto-agrarian reformer in the remote Sierra de Álica of Jalisco. Spanish American liberal governments after 1870 had no tolerance for 'Americanism' that took the form of regional and social challenges to central authority; and by 1880 Presidents Julio A. Roca of Argentina and Porfirio Díaz of Mexico could confidently proclaim the reign of 'peace and administration'.

The American spirit and its association with republicanism had by this time also made inroads in Brazil, the one Latin American nation to retain monarchical institutions. It was enunciated unequivocally in the Republican Manifesto of 1870, issued by a group of disaffected Liberal Party politicians and intellectuals. The Manifesto, which spawned a number of republican clubs and newspapers, grew from the internal political criticism, factional contention and call for reforms which accompanied the War with Paraguay (1865–70). Since the war allied Brazil with the republics of Argentina and Uruguay, it did much to make liberals aware of the ideological isolation of the Brazilian empire. This isolation was an important theme of the Manifesto. The restoration of the Republic in Mexico and the collapse of the European regime promoting monarchy in America clearly had an effect on Brazilians; the Manifesto, dated 3 December, was published only three months after the fall of Napoleon III. 'We are Americans', asserted the document. 'Our monarchical form of government is in its essence and practice contrary and hostile to the rights and interests of the American States.'

It should be noted, however, that in contrast with Spanish America, the most distinctive feature of the Brazilian republican movement, reiterated in the Manifesto, was its irrevocable tie to federalism. A republic had always meant the overthrow of an oppressively centralized monarchy and the establishment of provincial autonomy. In Spanish America, federalist challenges had to be made against already established centralist republics, not against monarchies. Despite this peculiarity, the growing republican cause in Brazil did much to enhance the sense of American solidarity among post-1870 liberals throughout the continent.

The decline of classic constitutionalism

A significant element of Latin America's liberal heritage was an enthusiasm for constitutional arrangements. Political independence had been achieved in the heyday of western constitutionalism, the governing conviction of which was that a rationally conceived and written code of laws could effectively distribute political power and thus guarantee individual liberty, the mainspring of social harmony and progress. Constitutional liberals characteristically sought to limit authority by establishing legal barriers against the 'despotism' they associated with the colonial regime. In doing this they were guided by two variants of Enlightenment political philosophy, the natural rights of man and utilitarianism, variants which were theoretically in conflict but which had a common emphasis on the autonomous individual. The classic constitutional doctrines, though still persisting in some quarters in Latin America, had been seriously eroded as early as the 1830s and were in full decline by the 1870s.

The Argentine writers of the Asociación de Mayo and those of the Generation of 1842 in Chile derived their principal intellectual orientation from the broad European attack on the validity of the doctrines of natural rights and utility, doctrines now judged to be abstract, legalistic and of questionable universal application. Sarmiento acknowledged the new direction taken by the 'social sciences' in France after 1830. 'We then began', he wrote in 1845, 'to learn something of national inclinations, customs, and races, and of historical antecedents', and to abandon Bentham, Rousseau and Constant for the historians, Thierry, Michelet and Guizot, for Sismondi, and ultimately for Tocqueville.[3] Esteban Echeverría (1805–51), in his *Dogma socialista* (1839), was drawn to the precepts of Mazzini's Young Europe movement and the socialist 'religion of humanity' of Leroux; Alberdi, in his seminal essay, *Fragmento preliminar al estudio del derecho* (1837), cited Lerminier, the French popularizer of Savigny's comparative and historical approach to law. Law should be considered, said Alberdi, not as a 'collection of written documents', but as 'a living and continually progressing element of society'.[4]

[3] Sarmiento, *Facundo*, 118.
[4] J. B. Alberdi, 'Fragmento', *Obras completas* (Buenos Aires, 1886), I, 105.

In Chile Lastarria also mentioned Lerminier, but drew particularly from Quinet's introduction to his translation of Herder's philosophy of history. The laws of human progress and decadence can be found only in history, wrote Lastarria, not in nature.[5] *Sociabilidad*, as in Bilbao's *Sociabilidad chilena* (1844), became the key word of the day. Liberal reformers and constitution makers must be guided by the peculiarities of a country's historically conditioned social relations, not by abstract principles. In Mexico, this erosion of classic liberal doctrines appeared prior to the *Reforma* only in the essays of Mariano Otero, a minor figure. The Mexicans, by comparison with the Argentine and Chilean liberals, were peculiarly resistant before 1870 to new ideas from Europe.

The new orientation in Latin American social and legal thought was clearly reflected in the Argentine Constitution of 1853. Despite the acknowledged influence of the North American model on the document's form, much of its spirit was drawn from Alberdi's *Bases* (1852), written for the constitution makers from his exile in Chile. Applying the themes of his *Fragmento* of 1837, Alberdi called for originality in the Constitution; it should reflect the real conditions of the people. The legalistic spirit of the Constitution of 1826 must be abandoned as out of harmony with the 'modern necessities of Argentine progress'.[6] Liberty is still the principal constitutional objective, but the new era demands more practicality and less theory. Constitution makers should be versed in economics, not just in 'moral science'.[7] The Constitution of the newly consolidated Argentine nation must guarantee the expansion of commerce, the rise of a spirit of industry, the free pursuit of wealth, the entry of foreign capital and, most of all, immigration. These priorities were taken up and made specific in articles 25 and 67 of the document that emerged from the Convention at Santa Fe. Thus, the cult of material progress that engulfed the governing and intellectual elite between 1870 and 1914 was in harmony with the pragmatic spirit of the Constitution.

The precepts of the changing philosophy of law also worked to resolve the major constitutional issue of nineteenth-century Argentina: territorial organization. The Asociación de Mayo writers had sought to surmount the sterile conflict between federalists and *unitarios*. The ideals of the Buenos Aires *unitario* tradition and the interests of the provinces

---

[5] J. V. Lastarria, 'Investigaciones sobre la influencia social de la conquista i del sistema de los españoles en Chile' (1844), *Obras completas*, VII (Santiago, 1909), 25.

[6] J. B. Alberdi, *Bases y puntos de partida para la organización política de la república argentina* (Buenos Aires, 1953), 14.   [7] *Ibid.*, 23.

must be reconciled. In practice this reconciliation meant the adoption of the federal form of organization in 1853, along with a renewed commitment to make the city a federal district and thus the capital of the Republic. The opposition to federalization came principally from the province of Buenos Aires, which had monopolized the economic benefits of independence for half a century. When the Federal District was finally created in 1880, Alberdi saw the 'despotic power of evolution' and the 'natural progress of civilization' at work.[8] For him, the Colony had finally given way to the Republic. But the realization of the *unitario* dream also solidified the effective dominance of the city of Buenos Aires over the provinces. The theoretical federalism of the Constitution gave way to the realities of centralization.

In surveying the constitutions of the hemisphere in 1852, Alberdi singled out the Chilean code of 1833 (along with that of the United States) as a model of originality. One of the principal authors of this admirable document was Mariano Egaña, an aristocrat and frank political conservative, who had spent the years 1824–9 in Europe and had absorbed the ideas of Edmund Burke and the French traditionalists, Bonald and De Maistre. The final version of the Constitution modified some of Egaña's extreme proposals, such as an indefinitely re-electable president and an hereditary senate. Moreover, a reference was inserted to popular sovereignty. Yet the president still emerged as a monarch in republican dress, in concert with, but superior to, an oligarchic senate. Provision was made for the re-establishment of Church privileges and the entail of landed properties, both of which had been circumscribed in the Constitution of 1828. That a political liberal like Alberdi would praise this conservative document can be understood in part by the breadth of the reaction in European thought against the philosophy of natural rights and against the radical egalitarianism of the French Revolution. This change in philosophic premises could inspire both political liberals and conservatives. Alberdi's praise can also be understood as recognition of the prestige enjoyed by Chile's constitutional stability. The 'peace of Chile' seemed an enviable model for Argentina after a generation of civil war.

The Constitution of 1833 did engender much controversy in mid-century Chile, but it gradually diminished and yielded to consensus after 1891. Varied critics, including Lastarria, the historian Benjamín Vicuña

---

[8] J. B. Alberdi, *La república argentina consolidada en 1880* (Buenos Aires, 1881), xiii.

Mackenna, and a future president, Federico Errázuriz, agreed that the document embodied a 'colonial reaction', guided by the authoritarian minister, Diego Portales, against the liberal spirit of the Revolution for Independence.[9] Their model was the Constitution of 1828, which could have implemented 'the great principle of social regeneration' and 'the democratic representative Republic'. However, since both critics and upholders of the Constitution of 1833 rejected the 'mechanistic' for the 'organic' view of society,[10] and since both adopted the historical philosophy of law, their positions were destined to merge. Moreover, both groups were part of the same narrow elite that showed pride in the country's peaceful economic growth and its victories in the War of the Pacific (1879–83). The Liberals could take satisfaction in the reforms of 1871–4, in particular the limitation of the presidency to one term. As one commentator in 1887 put it, 'the sickly and feeble plant of 1833' had 'grown into a gigantic fifty-year-old tree'.[11] With the shift of power from president to legislature following the Revolution of 1891, a benign Whig Interpretation emerged. The conservative Constitution was viewed by such liberal historians as Diego Barros Arana and Luis Galdames as an integral element in Chile's unique record of prosperity and peaceful evolution.

In Mexico, the liberal constitutionalist impulse was stronger and more persistent than in Argentina and Chile. The Constituent Congress of 1856–7 reacted sharply against the last government of Antonio López de Santa Anna (1853–5), whom it branded a conservative centralist dictator. The document that emerged from the Congress not only reaffirmed federalism, but also established a parliamentary regime based on a single-chamber legislature and a limited executive. Though the Constitution of 1857 served as the standard for the liberal and republican cause in the subsequent decade, it reigned only briefly, a few months in 1857 and from 1861 to 1863. Juárez was accorded formal dictatorial powers in 1864 to lead the struggle against Maximilian and the French. When the government's call for elections (*convocatoria*) came in August 1867, it included a series of 'reforms', particularly a presidential veto and the

[9] J. V. Lastarria, 'Don Diego Portales. Juicio histórico' (1861), *Obras*, IX, 203; B. Vicuña Mackenna, *Dom Diego Portales* (Santiago, 1937), 135–7 (1st edn 1883); F. Errázuriz, *Chile bajo el imperio de la constitución de 1828* (Santiago, 1861).

[10] The terms and phrases are Lastarria's, in 'Constitución de Chile comentada' (1856), *Obras*, I, 193–6, 202–5.

[11] Cited in Simon Collier, 'Historiography of the "Portalian" period (1830–1891) in Chile', *Hispanic American Historical Review*, 57 (1977), 666.

addition of a senate, designed to restore 'constitutional balance'. The phrase was that of Lerdo de Tejada, Juárez's chief minister and wartime deputy, who probably inspired the reforms. Their submission to a plebiscite, as proposed by the government, aroused strong opposition from defenders of the Constitution who regarded the procedure as arbitrary. For the next decade insurrection against the governments of Juárez and Lerdo could be mounted in the name of the Constitution, culminating in the successful rebellion of Porfirio Díaz in 1876.

Because it had been the banner of national defence against foreign intervention, the Mexican Constitution of 1857 acquired an aura of sanctity that was unique in Latin America. Yet by 1880 the defence of the pure Constitution had been decisively undermined. The influence of the historical school of law, through Edouard Laboulaye, a French adherent of Savigny, was apparent in the successful official campaign to reinstitute a senate. The Mexican Senate, like the Chilean Senate from 1833 to 1871, was designed to be not only a buttress against excessive democracy, but also an agent of centralization. Thus Porfirio Díaz, once in power, retained the Senate (adopted in 1874), despite the cry of his extreme constitutionalist followers to abolish it. A campaign further to reform the Constitution in the direction of 'stronger' government was launched by a self-styled new generation of intellectuals from 1878–80. Led by Justo Sierra (1848–1912), they combined the historical philosophy of law with new 'scientific' doctrines to provide significant support for an authoritarian regime that was to last thirty-five years. Though by no means dead, doctrinaire (or classic) constitutionalism in Mexico gave way to the imperatives of a new era of economic progress and political stability.

The supremacy of the secular state

The distinguishing element of the classic liberal programme in Latin America which set liberals apart from conservatives was the ideal of the secular state.[12] The objectives of secularization and reform were theoretically in conflict with those of constitutional liberalism, since they entailed a strengthening rather than a weakening of governmental authority. Yet the decline of classic constitutionalism by the 1870s made this traditional conflict less apparent, and for intellectual and govern-

---

[12] See Lynch, *CHLA* IV, Chapter 12.

mental elites the triumph of liberalism became synonymous with the advance of the *estado laico*.

A modern secular state was made up of free individuals, equal before the law and unrestrained in pursuit of their enlightened self-interest. They were first and foremost citizens whose primary loyalty was to the nation and not to the Church or to other corporate remnants of colonial society. As citizens they had a civil status that must be regulated and administered by the state. Vital statistics, fiscal processes, judicial procedure, education, even the calendar and births, marriages and deaths must be removed from Church control. Ecclesiastical wealth, whether in tithe income, real estate, or in mortgages, must pass from the 'dead hand' of the Church and be made a stimulus to individual enterprise. These objectives of secularization were enunciated by liberal writers and policy makers of the post-independence decades, for example the early reform governments of Bernardino Rivadavia in Buenos Aires (1822–3) and of Valentín Gómez Farías in Mexico (1833–4). Sarmiento's depiction of the colonial mentality of Córdoba in contrast with modern and liberal Buenos Aires, José María Luis Mora's (1794–1850) analysis of the corporate spirit in Mexico, and Lastarria and Bilbao's call for spiritual emancipation in Chile were classic early expressions of what came to be generalized assumptions in the period after 1870.

The liberal programme of secularization and anti-corporate reform was most clearly formulated in Mexico, where it engendered an opposing conservative ideology in the 1830s and 1840s, the creation of a conservative party in 1849 and a liberal–conservative civil war from 1854 to 1867. The liberal programme grew more radical as conservative opposition mounted. The moderate Ley Lerdo of 1856, forcing the Church to sell its real estate to tenants, was superseded by outright nationalization of all non-essential Church property in 1859. Freedom of worship, voted down as a constitutional article in 1856, was decreed by the Juárez government in December 1860, a year after another decree separating Church and state. These were essentially war measures, along with the secularization of cemeteries, marriage, vital statistics, and hospitals and the suppression of nunneries. Collectively known as 'La Reforma', the laws were incorporated into the Constitution in 1873, becoming a permanent part of the heroic liberal heritage.

Secularization in Argentina, Brazil and Chile came later and more gradually, but perhaps more decisively, than in Mexico. Following fifty years of relative peace, during which the Catholic Church enjoyed official status, the years 1870 to 1890 were marked by continual Church–state contention, national debates in the legislatures and the press, and successful passage of the standard reform measures. The pattern and timing of this activity ran parallel to the experience of European Catholic nations such as France, Germany and Italy, where the spirit of secular liberalism was sharpened by the intransigence of Pope Pius IX (1846–78) toward the modern world. After the publication of the Syllabus of Errors in 1864 and the pronouncement of Papal Infallibility in 1870, ultramontanism took on new life among national clergies; and Church–state confrontation was inevitable in Argentina, Chile and Brazil, as it was in Europe.

In each of the three countries the latent conflict was activated by an incident that touched on a characteristic issue. In Chile, the issue was Church control of cemeteries, brought into the open in 1871 when the bishop of Concepción refused public burial to Manuel Zañartu, a prominent army officer who had lived openly with a mistress for many years. In Brazil, the overt issue was the status of freemasonry, which had made broad inroads into imperial circles and had been tolerated by the ecclesiastical hierarchy, though now condemned by the pope. Beneath the masonic issue was another of greater political import, the close identification of the Brazilian Church with the Empire. Both issues were made public in 1872 when the bishop of Rio de Janeiro suspended a priest for preaching in a masonic lodge. There followed a vigorous anti-masonic campaign by Bishops Vital of Pernambuco and Macedo Costa of Pará. In Argentina, the confrontation came a decade later over the limits of state-controlled education, which had advanced rapidly since 1870. In 1884 the interim bishop of Córdoba forbade Catholic parents to send their daughters to a local public normal school whose directors were Protestant, an incident that led ultimately to a sixteen-year break in relations between the Argentine government and the papacy.

The bases of the secular state were laid down more peacefully and more decisively in Argentina, Brazil and Chile than in Mexico because reformers faced less resistance. Church establishments were weaker. Populations were sparser and lacked the reservoir of religious intensity of Mexican rural villages. Outside influences, both intellectual and social, were more prevalent. For example, it was the presence of an influential Protestant merchant community in Valparaíso that forced virtual abandonment of official intolerance in 1865 through a law 'interpreting' Article 5 of the Chilean Constitution. Toleration was scarcely an issue in Argentina and Brazil. One of the compelling arguments used in Argentina for instituting civil marriage and a civil register in 1884 was the inadequacy of the Church bureaucracy to contend with the influx of immigrants. In all three countries, the principal objectives of secularization could be achieved without an attack on Church property, the basis of bitter conflict in Mexico. In Chile and Argentina they could be achieved without a legal separation of Church and state. Separation did come ultimately in Chile in 1925, but never in Argentina, possibly the most secularized country in all Latin America. In Brazil, the separation of Church and state, along with other measures of liberal reform, was subsumed in the republican movement, given added intellectual support by positivism and decisively instituted within a year of the fall of the empire in 1889.

By 1890, then, the liberals, or *laicistas* as they were called in Argentina, had prevailed. The papacy, the national hierarchies and their conservative lay supporters temporarily acquiesced in the broad advance of the secular state. The passing of Church-related issues was further testimony that political consensus had been achieved among Latin American elites.

The vanishing ideal of a rural bourgeois society

One of the anomalies of the liberal legacy was the juxtaposition of political centralism and socio-economic individualism. While liberal constitutionalist opposition to centralized state authority weakened, the adherence to *laissez-faire* economics remained strong. At the heart of a liberal society was the enlightened individual, juridically equal to others and free to pursue his own interest. This interest was based on property, the right to which was regarded an extension of the individual's right to life itself. Thus, the sanctity of private property was upheld by both the doctrines of natural rights and of utility and became a virtually unquestioned liberal assumption.

In Latin America, as in other agricultural societies, liberals had placed their greatest hopes for social harmony and economic progress on the small property holder. The transformation of liberalism after 1870 from a reformist ideology to a unifying myth can be seen in part as the inadequacy of the ideal of the small property holder in countries made up of latifundia owners and dependent rural peoples, whether slaves, peons, hereditary tenants, or communal Indian villagers. In an era marked by the resurgence of export economies, the elites could and did conveniently hold to the formalities of liberal social philosophy while neglecting its earlier spirit.

The efforts of reformers were undercut by the limitations of liberal theory as well as by the realities of Latin American society. Liberals drew a distinction between corporate or legally entailed property and individual property. The former, a creation of society, could be restricted by lawmakers; the latter, predating society, could not. Influenced by the eighteenth-century 'Economists', especially Gaspar Melchor de Jovellanos, whose *Informe de ley agraria* (1795) was revered throughout the Hispanic world, liberals saw the central problem of society as removal of colonial legal and juridical privileges. These they regarded as obstacles to the realization of a 'natural' economic order. Though liberals frequently idealized the rural bourgeois of post-revolutionary France or the yeoman farmer of pre-Civil War United States, their theory provided no basis on which to resist the undue accumulation of land by individuals.

In Mexico, the main target of socio-economic reform from the 1830s through the 1850s was entailed ecclesiastical property, while in Chile it was the uniquely strong entailed estates of laymen, the *mayorazgos*, legally abolished in 1852. 'Privileged' Indian communal property also came under attack in Mexico and was left vulnerable to encroachment in the Constitution of 1857. Pre-1870 liberals, following Jovellanos, lamented excessive private holdings, particularly those that were uncultivated. However, their successors, such as the Generation of 1880 in Argentina or the Porfirian elite in Mexico, acquiesced in, and indeed often benefited personally from, the rapid accumulation of private holdings which accompanied the expansion of commercial agriculture.

Thus, the liberal vision of a rural bourgeois society, permeated by the work ethic, faded after 1870. Not only did the efforts to put entailed property into circulation prove ineffective, but so did the cherished plans for colonization by European farmers. To be sure, Alberdi's dictum of 1852, 'to govern is to populate', inspired numerous Argentine colonization efforts, beginning with the prosperous Swiss settlements introduced by the government of Justo José de Urquiza in Santa Fe. In Chile, farming communities totalling some 3,000 people were established in the southern Llanquihue region, to the accompaniment of notable colonization essays by Vicente Pérez Rosales (1854) and Benjamín Vicuña Mackenna (1865).

Enthusiasm for colonization also ran strong in Mexico, though the loss of Texas and the War with the United States turned its focus away from the frontier to 'the already populated part of the Republic'. In 1849 Mora urged 'the fusion of all races and colors' as a means of curbing future Indian rebellions like those just experienced in Yucatán and the Huasteca.[13] Colonization ideas persisted in Mexico throughout the century but led to even fewer tangible results than in South America. In Argentina, the aging Sarmiento still envisioned a society transformed by European farmers when he uttered his famous plea in 1883: 'Let us be [like the] United States.'[14]

The small property holder was also idealized by the leaders of the Brazilian movement to abolish slavery. André Rebouças, in his *Agricultura nacional* (1883), saw 'rural democracy' resulting from 'the emancipation of the slave and his regeneration through landownership'.[15] Both Rebouças, from a poor mulatto background, and Joaquim Nabuco (1849–1910), from an aristocratic landowning family in Pernambuco, saw the economic and moral progress of the country held back by a decadent latifundia society resting on slavery. In his tract *Abolicionismo* (1883), Nabuco demonstrated the baneful influence of slavery on all aspects of Brazilian life. It made 'the air itself servile', he said. The revival of agriculture held a central place in his vision of a free Brazil. Was this revival to come through land reform that would accompany emancipation, producing a new class of small landed proprietors, in part former slaves, in part European colonists, in part former owners? Or was the progress of agriculture to depend on the efforts of the existing landed class, once freed from the corruption imposed by slavery? Nabuco was ambivalent on this point prior to 1888. After emancipation and the downfall of the monarchy, he came increasingly, like many latter-day Spanish American liberals, to accept the rural status quo.

THE ASCENDANCY OF POSITIVISM

The political consensus of the late nineteenth century was upheld by a set of philosophic and social ideas that proclaimed the triumph of science

[13] Phrases from Mora's letter to Mexican foreign relations ministry (31 July 1849), Luis Chávez Orozco (ed.), *La gestión diplomática del Doctor Mora*, Achivo histórico diplomático mexicano, 35 (Mexico, 1931), 151–2.

[14] '*Seamos Estados Unidos*', the final sentence of the 1915 edition of *Conflicto y armonías de las razas en América*. The rendering of the sentence here is prompted by its context.

[15] Cited in Richard Graham, 'Landowners and the overthrow of the empire', *Luso-Brazilian Review*, 1 (1970), 48.

in Latin America. This set of ideas is commonly referred to as positivism, though there is no accepted definition of the term. In its philosophic sense, Positivism is a theory of knowledge in which the scientific method represents man's only means of knowing. The elements of this method are, first, an emphasis on observation and experiment, with a consequent rejection of all *a priori* knowledge, and, secondly, a search for the laws of phenomena, or the relations between them. We can know only phenomena, or 'facts', and their laws, but not their essential nature or ultimate causes. This theory of knowledge was not new in the nineteenth century, only its systematic formulation and the term positivism itself, both of which were the creation of Auguste Comte in his *Cours de philosophie positive* (1830–42). As a set of social ideas positivism shared the contemporary view that society was a developing organism and not a collection of individuals, and that the only proper way of studying society was through history. These characteristics of Comte's philosophy were, as John Stuart Mill put it in 1865, 'the general property of the age', which explains why the term has been subject to such widespread use and imprecise definition.[16]

If one considers positivism as the philosophic system of Auguste Comte, its original constructs were the Classification of the Sciences and the Law of the Three Stages. Comte presented 'positive philosophy' as the interrelation of the various 'sciences of observation', regarding them as 'being subjected to a common method and as forming different parts of a general plan of investigation'.[17] This interrelation is hierarchical in form. In studying and classifying the sciences (or even a given science) one must move from the simpler, more general, more abstract and more independent to the more complex and interrelated. For example, one progresses from celestial to terrestrial physics (from astronomy to mechanics to chemistry), or from physics to physiology, and finally to social physics or sociology, the least perfected and most complicated of the sciences. This procedure is natural because in each of its conceptions the human mind passes successively through three stages, the theological (imaginary [*fictif*]), the metaphysical (abstract) and the scientific (positive). By extension, society itself also passes through these stages. The main problem Comte saw in the contemporary state of knowledge was that the theological and metaphysical methods, having largely

---

[16] J. S. Mill, *Auguste Comte and positivism* (Ann Arbor, 1961), 8.
[17] A. Comte, *Cours de philosophie positive* (Paris, 1830–42), I, xiv.

disappeared in dealing with natural phenomena, 'are still, on the contrary, exclusively used . . . in all that concerns social phenomena'.[18]

Education of a new elite

In Latin America Comtean philosophy had its principal direct influence on the efforts to refashion higher education to meet the imperatives of the new era. Progressive modern economies and stable effective governments demanded a leadership imbued with a systematic mastery of modern science. The traditional universities, academies and professional institutes were deemed inadequate for the task. And yet in this age of consensus there was little disposition to abolish or even to renovate existing institutions, except in the unique circumstances of Mexico. Instead, new entities were created, centres of scientific preparation which ultimately came to influence the established schools.

In Mexico, the formal university structure was a casualty of the mid-century Reforma; and the focus of educational renewal became the Escuela Nacional Preparatoria, founded with the restoration of the Republic in 1867.[19] It was inspired by Gabino Barreda (1818–81), a professor of medicine who had attended Comte's lectures from 1848 to 1851 and who brought positivism to President Juárez's educational reform commission. The new school, which Barreda directed until 1878, replaced the ancient and esteemed Colegio de San Ildefonso and assumed the latter's role as the principal educator of Mexico's intellectual and governmental elite.

The agency for positivist education in Argentina was the Escuela Normal de Paraná, created in 1870 by President Sarmiento. The school far exceeded its intended role as the model provincial institution for teacher training. Taught by inspired pedagogue-philosophers such as José María Torres, Pedro Scalabrini and J. Alfredo Ferreyra, an unusual proportion of its graduates became national leaders. The Brazilian counterpart to these institutions was the Escola Militar, made a distinct entity in 1874. The positivist (and republican) orientation of the school was provided by Benjamin Constant (1836–91), its professor of mathematics who later served as Minister of Education in the first government of the Republic. The Chilean analogue, the Instituto

---

18 *Ibid.*, 12.

19 The demise of the Real y Pontificia Universidad de Mexico, closed and reopened several times after 1834, finally came with the decree by Maximilian of 30 November 1865. This decree confirmed earlier liberal measures of 1857 and 1861. The present-day university, founded in 1910, was first proposed by Justo Sierra in 1881.

Pedagógico of the University of Chile, was not established until 1889. Positivist educational philosophy was welcomed by the liberals Lastarria and Barros Arana as early as 1868, but its chief promoter was the latter's student, Valentín Letelier (1852–1919). Letelier began his reform campaign in 1879, and after an educational mission to Germany from 1882 to 1886, returned to found the Instituto and to become Chile's major intellectual and educational leader for the next thirty years.

Much of the study of Latin American positivism has been focused on the efforts to establish the Religion of Humanity and the Positivist Church, obsessions of Auguste Comte's 'second career' after 1848. Comte's French followers divided between religious or Orthodox Positivists, under the leadership of Pierre Lafitte, and philosophical or Heterodox Positivists, who, following Emile Littré, rejected Comte's religious schemes. While Heterodox Positivism was by its nature diffuse and difficult to identify as such, Orthodox Positivism was put forth by a small, coherent and clearly identifiable group of 'true' disciples of Comte, men like the Lagarrigue brothers, Jorge and Juan Enrique, in Chile, Miguel Lemos and Raimundo Teixeira Mendes in Brazil, and, somewhat later, Agustín Aragón in Mexico. Thus Orthodox Positivism, as a new religion, a new Church and as an elaborate cult, enjoyed much notoriety, but its impact on social and political thought was slight. As an educational philosophy in Latin America, positivism was clearly heterodox, and leaders like Barreda, Constant and Letelier shunned the Religion of Humanity.

Positivist influence can be discerned in three general characteristics of educational theory of the era: first, an emphasis on 'encyclopedic' learning of subjects placed in an ordered hierarchy; secondly, a growing bias toward scientific and practical as opposed to humanistic studies; and thirdly, an adherence to secularism and state control. Positivist educators believed that a uniform curriculum based upon systematic study of the sciences would encourage mental and social order and correct the anarchical influence of 'the disintegrating doctrines of the eighteenth century'.[20] In Comte's prescription for a 'universal education', one would study the several sciences in the order of their complexity and emerge with a sense of their interrelation.[21] Mathematics was the foundation, as Constant impressed upon generations of students at the

[20] The phrase is Barreda's in 'De la educación moral' (1863), *Opúsculos, discusiones, y discursos* (Mexico, 1877), 117.
[21] See Paul Arbousse-Bastide, *La doctrine de l'éducation universelle dans la philosophie d'Auguste Comte* (Paris, 1957).

Escola Militar; sociology was the capstone. The science of society could lead one to an understanding of the laws of development, a new way of studying history to replace what Letelier condemned as a mindless chronicle of names and events.[22]

The traditional humanistic and idealist orientation of higher education persisted but some positivist innovations did make headway by 1900. In Chile there was a successful campaign by Letelier and others to eliminate required Latin from the curriculum, an effort similar to one at the Paraná Normal School. In Mexico, controversy raged beginning in 1880 over the choice of logic texts for the National Preparatory School. The positivists finally prevailed, but not until the curricular reform of 1896, followed by the publication in 1903 of *Nueva Sistema de lógica* by Porfirio Parra, which marked the apogee of Positivist educational thought in Mexico. A new enthusiasm for specialized technical and utilitarian studies, despite apparent conflict with the Comtean predilection for encyclopedic learning, became a permanent legacy of the age of positivism. Nonetheless, positivist-inspired pedagogy in Latin America retained the highly systematized and even authoritarian character of the master's thought, which may have inhibited free and original scientific inquiry.

Despite Auguste Comte's increasing sympathy after 1848 for the Catholic Church and despite his call for the disestablishment of schools from the state, positivist-inspired higher education did not depart from the traditional liberal goals of secularization and state control. Positivist doctrine could be variously interpreted to fit local conditions. In Mexico, reconciliation seemed to be its emphasis, beginning with Barreda's dramatic *Oración cívica* of 1867. In the aftermath of the Reforma, anticlericalism was muted, whereas it was more overtly expressed by positivist educators in Argentina, Brazil and Chile, men such as Luis Pereira Barreto, Constant and Letelier. The difference was more apparent than real, however. Heterodox positivists throughout Latin America, like the Frenchmen Littré and Jules Ferry, disregarded the idiosyncratic religious and social views of Comte's later years.

---

[22] V. Letelier, 'El nuevo plan de estudios secundarios i la filosofía positiva' (1879), *La lucha por la cultura* (Santiago, 1895), 301. The positivist bias toward scientific education was actually a distortion of the pedagogical theories of Auguste Comte. He had intended that the sciences should not be introduced until the age of fifteen; before then instruction was to be in the arts and languages under maternal direction at home. But positivism had little impact on primary education and thus the balance in Comte's pedagogy was ignored.

'Scientific politics' and authoritarianism

Though positivism was not explicitly a theory of politics, its precepts provided important assumptions for Latin America's governing elite. A concept of 'scientific politics' was formally expressed in Mexico and Chile, less formally so in Argentina and Brazil. The concept entailed a conviction that the methods of science could be applied to national problems. Politics was seen as an 'experimental science', based on facts. Statesmen should no longer be guided by abstract theories and legal formulas which had led only to revolutions and disorder. The new guides must be observation, patient investigation and experience. New value must be placed on the economic, the concrete and the practical.

Despite their hostility to political abstractions, which they judged the hallmark of the 'metaphysical' mentality, the advocates of scientific politics had a reverence for theory. Theory was the starting point for a science of society and served to co-ordinate observed facts. In the positive stage, Comte had said, the human mind is no longer concerned with the origin and destiny of the universe or with the search for essences, but instead works to 'discover by a nice combination of reason and observation, the effective laws [of phenomena]'.[23] Such laws were the increasingly scientific character of the human mind and thus of society (Comte's three stages), the 'fundamental notion of progress', and the historical relativity of institutions.

A tenet of scientific politics at its origin was that society should be administered, not governed, by elected representatives. The idea was first expressed by Comte's predecessor and early collaborator, Henri de Saint-Simon, who, like Comte, sought a principle of order for a Europe disorganized by the 'metaphysicians and legists' and by the dogmas of the French Revolution. The new society would be industrial in character and Saint-Simon argued that *les industriels*, practical men of affairs who knew finance and who could prepare budgets, should be the new administrators. Comte also looked to the intervention of an elite, *savants* who saw the relation between scientific and political analysis and could thus provide the leadership for social regeneration. These ideas in their modified Latin American form strengthened a leaning toward technocracy which went back at least to the eighteenth-century Bourbons.

Scientific politics stood in an ambivalent relation to political liberalism

[23] Comte, *Cours*, I, 3.

in Latin America, now transformed from an ideology into a myth. Its precepts were in large part a repudiation of classic liberal principles; indeed in Comte's formulation one might read 'liberal' for 'metaphysical' as the second stage of history. By 1870 the classic liberal faith in constitutional arrangements had already been eroded by the influx of social and historical theories akin to positivism. The authoritarian and technocratic strain of scientific politics added further to this erosion. Yet the advocates of scientific politics regarded themselves as liberals, or occasionally as 'new liberals' or 'conservative-liberals'. The confusion and reconciliation of theoretically contradictory terms was a characteristic of this era of consensus.

In Mexico the concept of scientific politics was elaborated by Justo Sierra and his collaborators in their newspaper *La Libertad* (1878–84). Guided by science, they said, the nation's leaders must repudiate a half-century of revolutions and anarchy, reconcile conflicting parties and strengthen government to meet the needs of the industrial age. Gabino Barreda had sounded this note briefly a decade earlier, interpreting Mexican history in Comtean terms. 'All the elements of social reconstruction are now assembled', said Barreda, 'all the obstacles overcome'. Independence has been vindicated, the Laws of Reform and the Constitution reign supreme; henceforth, our motto will be Liberty, Order and Progress.[24] But Barreda made it clear that Liberty was an accomplishment of the past, Order and Progress the task for the future. In his famous debate with José María Vigil, Sierra blamed disorder on the 'old' liberals of the Reforma. He compared them with the 'men of '93' in France, who believed that society could and should be moulded to conform with the rights of man, by violence and revolution if necessary.[25] Telésforo García (1844–1918), a Spanish-born entrepreneur and colleague of Sierra, summed up the themes of the debate in his widely read pamphlet, *Política científica y política metafísica* (1887).[26]

The most dramatic feature of scientific politics was *La Libertad's* frank appeal for authoritarian government. Especially notorious was the outburst of Francisco G. Cosmes (1850–1907). Society now rejects 'rights' for 'bread . . . security, order, and peace', asserted Cosmes.

[24] Barreda, 'Oración cívica' (1867), *Opúsculos*, 105.
[25] *La Libertad*, 30 August 1878 (also J. Sierra, *Obras completas* [Mexico, 1948], IV, 158). Vigil's articles appeared in *El Monitor Republicano*.
[26] The pamphlet, first published in 1881 under another title, was a reprint of a series of articles in *La Libertad*, beginning 12 Oct. 1880. Though prompted by the educational debate of 1880, it also treated general political issues.

Rights have only produced distress. 'Now let us try a little tyranny, but honourable tyranny, and see what results it brings.'[27] Sierra's language was more muted, but his points were similar. *La Libertad* began to call itself a 'conservative-liberal newspaper'; it extolled contemporary European 'conservative republicans' Jules Simon and Emilio Castelar; it ran essays by Littré. It called for constitutional reforms, particularly a lengthened presidential term and a suspensive veto, 'to strengthen the administrative power'. The objective was a 'practical' constitution, not one that was 'utopian' and conducive to extra-legal dictatorship. Constitutional reform to strengthen government was an idea introduced by Juárez and Lerdo in 1867, as we have seen; in 1878 it was given added force by arguments from science. These arguments, along with the others constituting scientific politics, became quasi-official assumptions of the Díaz regime by the late 1880s.

As a new departure in political thought, the concept of scientific politics in Chile was less definite than in Mexico. Chile had no Reforma or French Intervention, no engrossing mid-century civil war to direct political ideas. Thus, the openness of Chilean intellectuals to changing currents of European thought was greater than in Mexico, and the grafting of new ideas onto old ones came more naturally and imperceptibly. The difference between Chile and Mexico was epitomized by the intellectual career of José Victorino Lastarria. This liberal leader of the Generation of 1842 is also credited with introducing Comtean positivism in 1868 and with first applying it to politics in his *Lecciones de política positiva* (1875). Therefore, scientific politics in Chile was not the dramatic statement of a post-civil war generation, and its relation to the liberal heritage was even more ambiguous than in Mexico.[28]

Though Lastarria's *Lecciones* was a lengthy treatise intended to establish the bases for a science of politics, it contained much that was reminiscent of his earlier writings. His critique of *a priori* knowledge, his depiction of the individual as moulded by society and of law as a reflection of historical circumstances were not new. Moreover, he maintained his faith in individual liberty, despite the anti-individualistic bias of positivism, and concluded that liberty was destined to increase with the progress of society. Lastarria was more Comtean when he

---

27 *La Libertad*, 4 Sept. 1878.
28 Lastarria's 'discovery' of positivism in 1868 might be compared with Gabino Barreda's first presentation of it in 1867. They were both of the 'older' generation, only one year apart in age. Barreda, however, was not politically oriented, either before or after 1867.

compared the Latin American nations to those in Europe that had received the 'French impulse'. They were in a 'painful and anarchical transition' between metaphysical and positive ideas because of the lingering tendency to impose 'revolutionary' doctrines of rights and equality on societies not prepared to incorporate them. A thorough anglophile, Lastarria extolled the 'positive spirit' of English origin now in practice in North America.[29] He saw this spirit manifest in *semecracia* (self-government), which for Lastarria had the status of a social law, guiding his long campaign to gain for municipalities the autonomy denied them in the centralist Constitution of 1833.

Lastarria's thought and practice (for example, as Minister of the Interior in 1876–7) revealed the traditional tension within political liberalism between the limitation and the strengthening of state authority. Lastarria could be both an advocate of municipal freedom and an anticlerical reformer. Though his adoption of scientific politics reinforced his sympathy for strong reformist government, his *Lecciones* did not contain the frank apology for authoritarianism present in *La Libertad*. On a theoretical level he was more explicit about the limits of state power than either the Mexicans in 1878 or his younger colleague and fellow advocate of scientific politics, Valentín Letelier.

Social evolution was Letelier's supreme law. For him the science of politics demonstrated 'how society is subject to continuous changes that preserve or advance it, when reform rather than resistance is legitimate, and what the norm is that must serve to guide all statesmen, be they conservatives or liberals'. For example, the 'scientific statesman' (as opposed to a mere empiricist) would respond differently to a riot of fanatics opposing freedom of thought than to a riot of workers seeking higher wages. The first involves intolerance, a dying tendency in society, whereas the second involves the pretensions of newly articulate classes. One belongs to the past, the other to the future.[30] Letelier looked upon liberty and authority as relative principles, not the absolutes that had dominated politics since the days of Portales. In addressing a convention of the Radical Party in 1889, he told his colleagues that though liberty was at this stage of history the 'organic principle' of our 'scientific philosophy' and though specific freedoms must be upheld, we should not hesitate to promote state authority over education, child labour,

[29] Lastarria, 'Lecciones', *Obras*, ii, 54–9.
[30] V. Letelier, *De la ciencia política en Chile* (Santiago, 1886), iii, 83–4.

prostitution, social insurance and Church property. The end of politics is not to advance abstractions like liberty and authority, but to 'satisfy social needs in order to secure the improvement of mankind and the development of society'.[31] Letelier revealed clear admiration for 'responsible' authoritarianism and frequently cited Bismarck as a model. Also, it should be noted that his chair at the University was in the law and theory of administration.

The breach in the liberal establishment

Just as the fulfilment of liberalism seemed a reality and political consensus achieved, there occurred a significant breach in the liberal establishment of Latin America's four major nations: Argentina, Brazil, Chile and Mexico. The infusion of scientific concepts had enhanced the political consensus; yet the theoretical conflict that existed between classic liberalism and scientific politics was bound to emerge. Such a conflict can be discerned in the political events of 1889–93, which afford suggestive parallels in the four countries. The turbulent events of these years were closely related to economic and financial dislocations, and indeed these dislocations now provide the standard point of departure for interpreting them. The political turbulence, however, may also be examined as a significant moment in Latin American thought.

In 1895 Joaquim Nabuco published an essay on José Balmaceda, the Chilean president who was overthrown by a parliamentary and naval revolt in 1891, in which he implicitly compared the upheaval in Chile with contemporary events in Brazil.[32] Throughout 1890 and 1891 both countries experienced a mounting conflict between executive and congress. In Brazil, following the establishment of the Republic on 15 November 1889, two military presidents, Manoel Deodoro da Fonseca and Floriano Peixoto, clashed with the Constitutional Congress of 1890–1 and with its successor. Deodoro's resignation in favour of Floriano came three weeks after he had dissolved Congress on 3 November 1891. In 1894, after a civil war, the military finally withdrew from power and Prudente José de Morais e Barros, the leader of the senate, was elected

---

[31] V. Letelier, 'Ellos i nosotros o sea los liberales i los autoritarios', *Lucha*, 11, 30–1.

[32] J. Nabuco, *Balmaceda* (Santiago, 1914), 7. The work first appeared as a series of newspaper articles (January–March 1895), designed as a critique of the laudatory account by Julio Bañados Espinosa, *Balmaceda, su gobierno y la revolución de 1891* (Paris, 1894). The first Spanish edition was published the same year in Valparaíso.

Brazil's first civilian president. In Chile, the parliament condemned Balmaceda for 'electoral intervention', particularly for the threat that he would impose a favourite as his successor and for decreeing a budget without its approval. The president closed the parliament twice during 1890 and reshuffled his cabinet several times to no avail. Civil war began early in 1891, ending with Balmaceda's resignation followed by his suicide on 19 September.

Argentina's dramatic events of 1890 ('El Noventa') also involved a challenge to presidential power, but one that emanated from beyond the legislature. On 26 July a 'revolution' broke out in downtown Buenos Aires and a momentary 'provisional government' was established under Leandro Alem, who had been a founder the year before of the Unión Cívica de la Juventud, a political club 'to co-operate in the re-establishment of constitutional practices in the country and to combat the existing order of things'. The existing order of things was the presidency of Miguel Juárez Celman. The revolt was suppressed but Juárez Celman was in turn forced by Congress to resign on 6 August in favour of his vice-president, Carlos Pellegrini. In Mexico, the events were less dramatic and well known. Instead of open conflict between branches of government, they consisted of a debate within the Chamber of Deputies (and the press) on an obscure constitutional amendment. The debate broadened to include the limits of presidential authority and reached a climax in November and December of 1893. It was preceded by a thinly disguised challenge to Porfirio Díaz in Justo Sierra's *Manifiesto* of the National Liberal Union, issued on 23 April 1892, overtly to promote the President's third re-election. The unsuccessful challenge to Díaz came from the *científicos*, a small group close to the government.

In all four countries the conflict entailed resistance to authoritarian leadership in the name of constitutional principles. Moreover, with the partial exception of Argentina, the resistance came from within the governing elite, even from some who were ministers. Since the assumptions of scientific politics and the dictates of historic constitution-alism had become intertwined, the challengers did not reject the principle of strong authority, despite open political conflict. From ambivalence in 1889, Letelier in Chile turned against Balmaceda in 1890, was briefly imprisoned and then championed the triumphant 'Revolution'. Its object, he said, was not to implant a parliamentary oligarchy, but rather to restore constitutional liberties *and* 'administration', of which the latter had become mixed with 'politics' under the personal tyranny of Balmaceda.[33]

In Brazil, the positivist ideas that permeated the founding of the Republic tended to sharpen the conflict between authoritarianism and constitutionalism. Orthodox Positivists, like Lemos and Teixeira Mendes, expressing Comte's disdain for constitutional liberties, called for a 'republican dictatorship', just as Comte had welcomed Louis Napoleon's coup in 1851.[34] The heterodox Benjamin Constant, however, clashed with Deodoro before he died in 1891. Another opponent of the Provisional President was his Minister of Finance, Rui Barbosa (1849–1923), author of the draft constitution for the Republic. Barbosa's attack against Floriano was even sharper, both at home and as an exile in *Cartas de Inglaterra* (1896). The conflict in Brazil was complicated by the fact that it came in the wake of Pedro II's overthrow. Constitutionalist enthusiasm was exaggerated, as was a vain effort at political reconciliation, judging from the diverse makeup of the first republican ministries. Moreover, as Deodoro and Floriano became more 'dictatorial', nostalgia set in for the supposed constitutional balance achieved under the empire. It was this nostalgia that inspired Nabuco's massive biography of his father, a Liberal Party leader, and his essay on Chile. Both Brazil and Chile, he wrote, 'had [before 1889] the same continuity of order, parliamentary government, civil liberty, [and] administrative purity'. Only a 'Liberal League' of enlightened men could now save Latin America from further chaos.[35]

Letelier's ambivalence toward statism can be compared with that of Sierra in Mexico. In the main, Sierra's programme of 1892 seemed to epitomize the socially conservative, technocratic and economically oriented principles of scientific politics. However, he ended the *Manifiesto* by asserting that if 'effective peace has been acquired [since 1867] by the *strengthening of authority*, definitive peace will be acquired by its *assimilation with liberty*'.[36] He then proposed several constitutional reforms, particularly one to make judges irremovable, that is, appointed by the president

---

[33] V. Letelier, *La tiranía y la revolución, o sea relaciones de la administración con la política estudiadas a la luz de los últimos acontecimientos* (Santiago, 1891). This was the initial lecture of Letelier's course in administrative law for 1891.

[34] The Chilean positivist, Juan Enrique Lagarrigue, likewise supported Balmaceda. His brother Jorge, while in France, had addressed a pamphlet in 1888 to another would-be republican dictator, Boulanger.   [35] Nabuco, *Balmaceda*, 14, 219.

[36] *El Siglo XIX*, 26 April 1892. Italics added.

for life, rather than democratically elected and thus subject to popular whim or presidential manipulation. In the 1893 debate on the measure, Sierra supported it with the arguments from 'science' he had used to support strong government in 1878. In the face of the dictatorial power acquired by Díaz in the intervening years, Sierra had turned constitution-alist in hopes of limiting that power. He was opposed in this complex three-sided debate by both the defenders of the President and by the 'jacobins', defenders of the 'pure' or 'democratic' Constitution. These opponents labelled Sierra and his group *científicos*, a label they accepted with pride.[37]

The conflict in Argentina was similar to that in the other countries, but it also had unique national features. Scientific politics was not formally articulated, as in Chile and in Mexico, though many of its assumptions, stemming back to Alberdi and Sarmiento, became articles of faith among the liberal establishment.[38] The transition from liberal to positivist ideas was even more imperceptible than in Chile and the entanglement of the two by the 1880s even more complete. The practice, if not the theory, of authoritarian government took hold with the presidencies of Roca and Juárez Celman, enhanced by secularization policies, by the new economic and political centrality of the city of Buenos Aires and by the merging of the old parties into the single Partido Autonomista Nacional (PAN). The president became *jefe único del partido único*, branded the *unicato* by opponents.

The focus of resistance in 1889–90 was not Congress, as in Brazil or Chile, nor a definable inner circle like the Mexican *científicos*. The Unión Cívica included Alem, Aristóbulo del Valle and Bernardo de Yrigoyen, old Buenos Aires Autonomistas who resented the new centralism of the former provincials, Roca and Juárez Celman. Thus, they implicitly kept alive Argentina's peculiar constitutional question. The Unión Cívica also drew in former president Bartolomé Mitre, a principled old liberal who disliked the regime's corruption. The vague rhetoric of the Civic Union movement was constitutionalist, but it also had democratic overtones not present elsewhere.

[37] The phrase *los científicos* probably first appeared in an editorial in *El Siglo XIX* on 25 November 1893.

[38] Because of the early questioning of doctrinaire liberalism by Sarmiento and Alberdi, and because of the obsession with material progress and utilitarian values among the elite after 1870, there has been a tendency among Argentinians to regard positivism as of 'autochthonous origin', e.g. Alejandro Korn, 'Filosofía argentina' (1927), *Obras*, III (Buenos Aires, 1940), 261.

The sealing of the breach was the work of Carlos Pellegrini (1846–1906), whose career and ideas epitomized the merging in practice of constitutionalism and scientific politics. A respected jurist and legislator, he was also a partisan of professionalism and administration; he became an expert in finance and as president (1890–2) established the Banco de la Nación in 1891. Pellegrini had been an uneasy participant in the *unicato*, an old porteño friend of Alem and del Valle who stayed in touch with them even during El Noventa. Yet he was a part of Buenos Aires high society and had been a founder of the Jockey Club in 1881. His prime concern was governmental continuity, which led him in 1892 to short-circuit the Civic Union by successfully proposing Luis Saenz Peña, the father of its candidate, Roque, as PAN candidate for president. Roque Saenz Peña withdrew from the race.

Political peace was quickly restored in all four countries, facilitated by a fundamental agreement on economic and social values. The PAN remained in power in Argentina until 1916, Díaz in Mexico until 1911. The Chilean parliament continued supreme until 1924. The constitutional 'balance' established in Brazil by 1894 prevailed until 1930. A mood of reconciliation took hold in the aftermath of conflict. In Chile, the punitive measures enacted against adherents of Balmaceda were never put into effect. A general amnesty was declared in August 1894, and by 1895 Balmacedistas were returning to office. The Mexican *científicos* were co-opted by the Díaz regime. Justo Sierra was elevated to the Supreme Court in 1894, an appointment that must have seemed almost insulting to the defender of judicial independence. José Yves Limantour, the most famous *científico*, served as Díaz's finance minister until 1911.[39] In Argentina, the Mitre branch of the Civic Union movement became thoroughly reconciled with the governing PAN; in fact, its would-be candidate of 1892. Roque Sáenz Peña, was elected president in 1910.

The conflict nonetheless left significant legacies. Though the authoritarian impulse in scientific politics was temporarily thwarted (except in Mexico) by a resurgent 'constitutionalist' oligarchy, presidential power acquired new arms for future battles. One position in the Mexican debate was a defence of strong government on proto-populist grounds, the argument that Díaz was dedicated to attacking servitude in the countryside and the tyranny of the upper classes, both of which would

---

[39] Limantour was one of the original eleven signatories of the Liberal Union Manifesto of April 1892. He was appointed minister in March 1893 and thus did not participate in the debate.

only be strengthened by irremovable judges.[40] An interpretation of Balmaceda as a strong popular and nationalist leader, if not present in 1891, developed soon thereafter and had great impact on twentieth-century politics in Chile. Democratic ideas also appeared, most significantly in Argentina where the Unión Cívica split in 1892, producing the Radical party. The third group in the Mexican debate, the jacobins or doctrinaire constitutionalists, were ineffective in 1893, but did provide a precedent for the underground liberal clubs of 1900–6 and ultimately for the revolutionary movement of 1910. The term jacobin also appeared in Brazil, though its democratic import was questionable.[41] The breach in the liberal establishment was sealed and political unity restored, but the new ideas suggested that the consensus would not endure without future challenges.

Social evolution, race and nationality

After maturing for several decades, by the turn of the century positivism as a set of social ideas was in full flower in Latin America. There was little dissent among the elites from the conviction that society was an organism analogous to nature, subject to change over time. Among the numerous theorists of social evolution, it was Herbert Spencer who was most often cited by Latin Americans. He became the symbol of the age, though his actual influence was perhaps less than that of Auguste Comte, the other 'twin pillar' of positivism. Despite the appeal of Spencer's Law of Evolution and of his systematic use of biology as a model for social theory, his assumptions about socio-political organization were less congenial to Iberian traditions than were those of Comte. Spencer adhered to *laissez faire* and utilitarianism throughout his life, as manifested in his first work, *Social statics* (1850), and in one of his last, *The man versus the state* (1884). His envisioned Industrial Society, the culmination of human evolution, was individualistic, liberal and stateless (an idealized nineteenth-century England), though he saw these characteristics as the product of habit and instinct after centuries of natural adaptation and not as the product of man's rational choice.[42] Comte's

---

[40] The position was argued in *El Siglo XIX*, principally by Francisco Cosmes, who split from his former colleague Sierra in a series of articles dated 14–30 December 1893. The irremovability measure passed the Chamber of Deputies but never left committee in the Senate.

[41] The Jacobin Club of Rio and a jacobin press supported Floriano in 1893, espousing an extreme republican (anti-monarchist) and xenophobic (anti-Portuguese) position.

[42] J. W. Burrow, *Evolution and society. A study in Victorian social theory* (Cambridge, 1968), 222–3.

ideal was a hierarchically organized and non-competitive collectivism in which state and society were one.

Despite their limited impact on political programmes, Spencer's ideas (more than Comte's) were an important component of the intense intellectual concern with Latin American society between 1890 and 1914. Spencer's evolutionary system was based on the development of particular societies, and his volumes were filled with a vast array of comparative data on specific customs, beliefs, rituals and ethnic characteristics. Thus, in a general way Spencer helped Latin Americans focus their attention on the peculiarities of their own society within the universal scheme. His thought had an anthropological dimension that was lacking in Comte. Comte's system posited the progress of humanity (in an almost eighteenth-century sense) as the progress of the European white race.[43] His analogy for society in the Law of the Three Stages was the human mind, whereas Spencer's analogy in the Law of Evolution was all of nature.

One element of Spencer's evolutionary system, though not the major one, was race, which came to be a central preoccupation of Latin American social thought. Modern European racism seems to have sprung from at least two sources, both of which were relevant to Latin American theorizing but were difficult to separate by the 1890s. The first was the quest for national origins and peculiarities, as reflected in Romantic historiography, literature and philology. A 'race' was simply a nationality or a people developing over time, distinct from others by language, religion or geography. It was primarily a European grouping or its antecedent, for example the 'Aryan race' of Central Asia. In Latin America we encounter this sense of race occasionally before 1870, for example in Sarmiento's *Facundo*. The notorious racist views of the Frenchman, Count Arthur de Gobineau sprang partly from this source, fortified by an aristocratic revulsion for democracy, incipient mass society and the mixing of peoples.[44] Still another and more influential exponent of the historical sense of race was Hippolyte Taine, whose

---

[43] John C. Greene, 'Biology and social theory in the nineteenth century: Auguste Comte and Herbert Spencer', Marshall Clagett (ed.), *Critical problems in the history of science* (Madison, 1959), 427.

[44] Michael D. Biddiss, 'Gobineau and the origins of European racism', *Race*, 7 (1966), 255–70. Gobineau's major work was *Essai sur l'inégalité des races humaines* (1853–5). I use the term 'racism' to refer to theories that attributed social change, psychology, and behaviour exclusively to race, however defined. Thus, a theory could be racist without necessarily assuming the innate and permanent inferiority of non-whites, though most did include that assumption.

famous introduction to his history of English literature (1864) was widely read in Latin America.

A second source of nineteenth-century racism was empirical and anthropological, that is, the changing European attitudes toward primitive dark-skinned peoples which came from increased contact. Enlightenment ideals of the Noble Savage and of a universally attainable Civilization gave way to scientific evidence of the actual degradation of remote primitive peoples and to the resulting notion that only certain 'races', that is, human groups distinct from others by permanent inherited physical differences, were capable of becoming civilized.[45] A parallel idea in the development of the discipline of physical anthropology was 'polygenism', the initial creation of separate races, as opposed to the traditional 'monogenism' of biblical Creation or the scientific monogenism of Charles Darwin's *Origin of Species* (1859) and *The Descent of Man* (1871). The racism inherent in polygenism proved compatible in practice if not in theory with social Darwinism, the survival of peoples (or races) best able to adapt in the struggle of life. Thus, the Latin American preoccupation with race was further strengthened by the Darwinist aspect of Spencer's thought and that of other influential evolutionary theorists such as Ludwig Gumplowicz and Ernst Haeckel.

The burgeoning science of psychology provided another dimension to nineteenth-century race consciousness, and much of Latin American racist thought took the form of an inquiry into social psychology. Taine was probably the initial inspiration for this genre, though by 1900 Latin Americans were more directly guided by Gustave Le Bon, 'the supreme scientific vulgarizer of his generation' and the most frequently read of European racial theorists.[46] Taine argued in 1864 that the historian as scientist must seek the 'elemental moral state', or 'psychology', of a people which lies beneath the surface of observable human artifacts, literary creations, or political documents. The visible or external man in history reveals an invisible or internal man. This psychology is produced by the action of three 'primordial forces', *le race, le milieu, et le moment*.[47] In

[45] George W. Stocking, Jr., *Race, culture, and evolution. Essays in the history of anthropology* (New York, 1968), 13–41.

[46] Robert A. Nye, *The origins of crowd psychology: Gustave Le Bon and the crisis of mass democracy in the Third Republic* (London, 1975), 3.

[47] H. A. Taine, *Histoire de la littérature anglaise* (6th edn, Paris, 1924), I, xxii–iii. Latin American *pensadores* were probably attracted to Taine in part because he seemed a perfect combination of the man of science and the man of letters. His *Histoire* was followed by *Sur l'intelligence* (1870), a key work in the development of scientific psychology.

Taine's historical scheme, race (defined as 'innate or hereditary tendencies' normally tied to 'marked differences in temperament and body structure') was only one determining element. However, it became predominant in Le Bon's *Lois psychologiques de l'évolution des peuples* (1894), in which the historical and the anthropological notions of race converged and became joined with numerous other themes of nine-teenth-century social science.

'Race is the key, then climate, followed by history. All are complemen-tary, but blood, the psychological heritage, is the mainspring of events. . . .' So wrote the Argentinian Carlos O. Bunge (1875–1918) in his *Nuestra América* (1903), a model Le Bonian essay that was heralded throughout Spanish America.[48] Le Bon emphasized the 'soul' of a race or people, which he equated with its 'mental constitution', or the moral and intellectual characteristics which determine its evolution. He saw these characteristics as virtually unalterable, constantly being reproduced by heredity. 'It is by its dead [and not by its living] that a race is founded' was his famous phrase.[49] He went on to classify and rank races psychologi-cally, stressing that character was more critical than intelligence. Of his four categories, the only 'superior' races were the Indo-European, with the Anglo-Saxon sub-race clearly above the Latin. Character is derived from ideas that penetrate the racial soul and become permanent uncon-scious sentiments, such as Anglo-Saxon individualism, liberty and sense of duty as opposed to the Latin pursuit of equality and dependence on the state. He offered the Americas as proof of his psychological laws. The progress and stability of the North versus the 'sanguinary anarchy' and 'absolute autocracy' of the South were for him clearly the result of differences in European racial character.[50] Moreover, South America was only one instance of the Latin decadence that Le Bon saw as universal.

Le Bon's early career was in medicine and his approach to social science was diagnostic, a characteristic that also permeated Latin American thought. Numerous intellectuals saw themselves as 'diagnos-ticians of a sick continent'.[51] Their pessimism was derived not only from the Le Bonian conclusion that the Latin race was degenerate but also

[48] C. O. Bunge, *Nuestra América* (Barcelona, 1903), 20. The second edition (1905) was subtitled *Ensayo de psicología social*.
[49] G. Le Bon, *Lois psychologiques de l'évolution des peuples* (3rd edn, Paris, 1898), 13.
[50] *Ibid.*, 111–16.
[51] The phrase is from chap. 2 of Martin S. Stabb, *In quest of identity* (Chapel Hill, N.C., 1967).

from the prevailing scientific strictures on racial mixture. Le Bon did recognize that the formation of new races, as in Europe, could come only from intermarriage. Mixture initially destroys the soul of the races and leads to a 'period of intestine struggles and vicissitudes', out of which gradually emerges a new psychological species. The result can be positive, wrote Le Bon, given certain conditions: races that interbreed must not be too unequal in numbers; their characters must not be too dissimilar; they must be subject to identical environmental conditions. While generally present in Europe and North America, these conditions have been clearly absent in Latin America, and the result is psychological instability.[52] The outlook was gloomy indeed for a continent that was both Latin and *mestizo*.

There was a cosmopolitan and hemispheric cast to the expressions of racial pessimism in Latin America. Three examples will suffice: Bunge's *Nuestra América* (1903); *Pueblo enfermo* (1909) by the Bolivian, Alcides Arguedas (1878–1946); and *Les démocraties latines de l'Amérique* (1912) by the Peruvian, Francisco García Calderón (1883–1953). All three works were first published in Europe and included laudatory introductions by distinguished European intellectuals.[53] Arguedas and García Calderón spent large portions of their lives in France; the latter actually wrote several of his works in French. Two of the essays surveyed all of Latin America, and the nationality of the authors is not obvious; the third, *Pueblo enfermo*, though an intensely Bolivian work, was intended (and often taken) to apply to Latin America generally.[54] All three works revealed in exaggerated form the tendency in Latin American thought to adopt European theories that were injurious to regional or national pride. Self-depreciation reached its peak in the age of positivism.

Hispanic America, wrote Bunge, is a racial 'Tower of Babel'. Unlike the Yankees, Spaniards in America are not a pure race, but 'mestizo-ized, indian-ized, and mulatto-ized Europeans'. Each racial stock has its own inherited psychological traits, and the 'national psychology' of each republic varies according to its peculiar racial amalgam. However, three fundamental characteristics constitute the 'spirit of the race': arrogance

---

[52] Le Bon, *Lois psychologiques*, 43–50. Countries in which the proportion of half-breeds is too large, he said, 'are solely for this reason given over to perpetual anarchy, unless they are ruled with an iron hand'. He cited Brazil as an example and quoted (p. 45) from Louis Agassiz.

[53] The first two were published in Barcelona, the third in Paris. The introductions were by Rafael Altamira, Ramiro de Maeztú and Raymond Poincaré, respectively.

[54] See author's *advertencia* to second edition (1910), including comments by José E. Rodó (p. 8). The subtitle of the first two editions was *Contribución a la psicología de los pueblos hispano americanos*.

(of Spanish origin, traced back to the Visigoths), sadness (of Indian origin), and laziness. Scientifically analysed, arrogance and laziness are from the same root. 'In animals arrogance is the preservation instinct of the defenceless, in men, of the lazy.' Laziness, *la pereza criolla*, was for Bunge a 'parent quality' and to it he attributed the lack of imagination among the elite, the proclivity towards *caciquismo* in politics and, most of all, the disdain for work. 'Work is progress', asserted Bunge, 'laziness is decadence'.[55] The unrelieved pessimism of Bunge's racial characterology gave way to ambivalence in García Calderón. The decade between the publication of the two volumes saw the effects of a growing philosophic reaction against positivism and a new appreciation of the Latin spirit. Though García Calderón, as we shall see, was a leading spokesman for this new idealism, much of *Les démocraties latines* followed Bunge and Le Bon. For García, race was the 'key to the incurable disorder that divides [Latin] America'. He envisioned the 'brilliant and lazy' creole as the true American of the future, yet he seemed to preclude unity because of the absence of Le Bon's conditions for constructive miscegenation.[56]

Self-depreciation probably reached its extreme with Arguedas, and yet his *Pueblo enfermo* was more than facile racial theorizing in the manner of Bunge or García Calderón. It was also an evocative, though depressing, portrait of the regional cultures of Bolivia, which displayed another tendency of positivist sociology, the impulse toward factual description. For Arguedas, regional psychology seemed to be determined more by geography than by race. He depicted the character of the Aymara as harsh like his habitat, the *altiplano*, just as the 'dreamy, timid, and profoundly moral' Quechua reflected the 'mediterranean' environment of the Cochabamba valley.[57] However, when Arguedas moved from region to nation, from Indian to *mestizo* (*cholo*), race became the major determinant of character. He showed some sympathy for the abject, undernourished and exploited Indian, but only disdain for the *cholo*.[58]

---

55 Bunge, *Nuestra América*, 77. The second half of the essay was a more specific racial interpretation of politics, to be considered below.

56 F. García Calderón, *Les démocraties latines*, 337. Le Bon was the editor of the series in which García Calderón's volume was published.

57 A. Arguedas, *Pueblo enfermo* (1909), 38, 79. It is significant that in discussing regional psychology *per se*, Arguedas referred to Taine (p. 68).

58 Arguedas also wrote a proto-indianist novel, *Wata Wara* (1904), and a later version, *Raza de bronce* (1919). See Martin, *CHLA* IV, chapter 11. It should be noted that his antipathy toward the *mestizo* was more pronounced in the much-altered third edition of *Pueblo enfermo* (1937), where, for example, *psicología de la raza mestiza* was expanded and made a separate chapter. His change in attitude might have reflected his own frustrating experience in politics, which he (an aristocrat) claimed was dominated by *cholos*.

Though he attributed the numerous defects in national psychology – deception, passion for hollow oratory, lack of enterprise, intellectual sterility and so on – to the heavy infusion of Indian blood,[59] he did not identify these defects as Indian characteristics *per se*. Thus Arguedas's sociology revealed a tension between racial and environmental determinism, which was even more pronounced with other positivists for whom nationality was a major concern.

Though the racial pessimists did not emphasize remedies for Spanish America's social predicament, they did tend to perpetuate the traditional liberal panacea – European immigration. Bunge urged Europeanization 'through work'. García Calderón pointed to Basques and particularly Italians who were already transforming Argentina. Arguedas concluded that the profound defects in Bolivia's national character could only be altered by radical methods, like grafting in horticulture, and he proposed 'selected' immigration.[60]

The dictates of racial determinism were particularly agonizing for Brazilians, since Brazil had a population that by 1890 was approximately 15 per cent black and 40 per cent *mestizo* or mulatto. Many Brazilian writers, for example Silvio Romero and Raimundo Nina Rodrigues, accepted the indictment of miscegenation in evolutionary thought and endured the harsh social judgements of learned visitors like Gobineau and the American naturalist, Louis Agassiz. Yet by 1900 there was a growing tendency among other social theorists to counter extreme racial pessimism by rationalizing Brazil's multiracial society. They began to express the conviction that miscegenation and European immigration were leading inevitably to 'whitening' and thus to progress.

One such optimist was a young journalist, military engineer and ardent republican, Euclides da Cunha (1866–1909), whose bland positivism of the early 1890s was put to the test by a supposed pro-monarchist and religious rebellion of *sertanejos* (backlanders) at Canudos in Bahia. Sent by his newspaper, *O Estado de São Paulo* in 1897, Da Cunha witnessed the fierce resistance of the racially mixed rebels, and then their annihilation by overwhelming numbers of government troops supported by modern artillery. His journalistic assignment turned into *Os sertões* (1902), a massive narrative of the conflict, preceded by a full-dress scientific treatise on the 'sub-races' of the backlands and their successful

---

[59] Arguedas began his chapter '*el carácter nacional*' (pp. 91–2) by referring to Bunge.
[60] Bunge, *Nuestra América*, 98; García Calderón, *Les démocraties latines*, 339–40; Arguedas, *Pueblo enfermo*, 244.

interaction with a hostile, drought-ridden environment. Da Cunha's account revealed a profound contradiction between an acceptance of racism and social Darwinism and the empirical realization that the adaptive backlanders might be 'the very core of our nationality, the bedrock of our race'.[61] He theorized that the *mestizo* was psychologically unstable and degenerate, regressing always toward the primitive race, a 'victim of the fatality of biologic laws'. Canudos was the 'first assault' in a long struggle, 'the inevitable crushing of the weak races by the strong', a process (citing the Polish sociologist Gumplowicz) Da Cunha equated with the march of civilization. Yet he also spoke of the *sertanejo* as an 'ethnic subcategory already formed, an historic subrace of the future'. Being isolated from the coast for three centuries, it had been spared the exigencies of the struggle for racial existence and therefore could freely adapt to the environment. Thus Da Cunha distinguished between the 'rachitic' *mestizo* of the coast and the 'strong' *mestizo* of the backlands.[62] He seemed to surmount theory, however, in describing the sheer courage, heroism and serenity of the last defenders of Canudos, 'beings on the lowest rung of our racial ladder'.[63] Without abandoning the scientific racism of his day, Euclides da Cunha introduced a new question into social thought, the ethnic or racial basis of national identity.

The question raised by Da Cunha was pursued intensely in late nineteenth-century Mexico, partly because of unique features of its recent history. The two great national movements, the Revolution for Independence and the Reforma, involved mass participation and social conflict; and many patriotic heroes, including Morelos and Juárez, were *mestizos* or Indians. Prior to the Reforma, the intellectual elite had tried to ignore the Indian and had espoused a creole sense of nationality. In an unusual mid-century essay, the scholar Francisco Pimentel (1832–93) had drawn a bleak picture of the degradation of the Indians, but his remedies were still those of the creole liberals: immigration, the whitening of the population and the elimination of the word race, 'in fact as well as in law'.[64] After 1870, the influx of evolutionary thought

---

61 E. Da Cunha, *Rebellion in the backlands* [trans. of *Os sertões*] (Chicago, 1944), 464; also author's note (from 1905 edn) on p. 481, where he explained the bedrock simile.

62 Da Cunha, *Rebellion*, 84–9, xxix. Gumplowicz was an extreme social Darwinist who saw racial struggle as 'the motive force of history'.

63 *Ibid.*, 440–1, including his moving portrait of a Negro captive who, as he approached his execution, became transformed from 'the wizened appearance of a sickly orangutan' to a 'statuesque masterpiece' of an ancient 'Titan'.

64 F. Pimentel, 'Memoria sobre las causas que han originado la situación actual de la raza indígena de México y medios de remediarla' (1864), *Obras completas*, III (Mexico, 1903), 148.

brought a new consciousness of race, but the conclusions were generally optimistic. For example, the theme of Justo Sierra's histories was the growth of the Mexican nation as an 'autonomous personality,' one element of which was racial mixture. We Mexicans, he asserted, are the offspring of two races, born of the Conquest, products of Spain and of the land of the aborigines. 'This fact rules our whole history, to it we owe our soul.'[65] Specifically refuting Le Bon's theories on the debilitating effect of miscegenation, Sierra demonstrated that the *mestizo* population had tripled in the nineteenth century and was the 'dynamic [political] factor in our history'.[66] Though he occasionally advocated immigration along with education as a social remedy, his ideal was not racial whitening. For him, national identity resided in the *mestizo*.

Another positive appreciation of racial mixture in Mexican society appeared in an austere study of 'Mexican sociology' by Andrés Molina Enríquez (1866–1940), a provincial judge who was outside Porfirian elite circles. Published in 1909 on the eve of Mexico's social upheaval, *Los grandes problemas nacionales* emphasized the problem of land and its maldistribution, thus making the work a famous (but little-read) precursor of revolution. Molina was an environmental determinist, citing Haeckel's theory of the unity of organic and inorganic matter. The selection and adaptation of organisms are the result of a struggle between the internal forces derived from 'vital combustion' and the external forces of nature. A race is simply a group of people who (through this process) adapt to similar environmental conditions and thus 'have acquired a uniformity of organization, indicated by a certain uniformity of type'. Though Molina went on to classify Mexican races scientifically, he admitted that any such classification was defective – largely because of the facts of Mexican history. His portrait of the *mestizo* was not always flattering, but on the whole, he accepted miscegenation as an inevitable and positive force. For example, he saw the greatest benefit of the 'republican form' to be civil equality, 'which has greatly favoured the contact, mixture and confusion of the races, leading to the formation of one single race'.[67]

[65] J. Sierra, 'Evolución política del pueblo mexicano', *Obras*, XII, 56 (1st edn 1900–2). It should be noted that *mestizo* for Sierra meant only Indian-white mixture, whereas for Da Cunha in Brazil it meant black-white or Indian-black-white.

[66] Sierra, 'México social y político. Apuntes para un libro' (1889), *Obras*, IX, 128–31. He cited a Le Bon article published the previous year in the *Revue scientifique*.

[67] A. Molina Enríquez, *Grandes problemas*, 34–7. Molina also classified property from an evolutionary perspective, Indian communal property being a lower form than European individual titled property. His views influenced two post-1910 assumptions, (1) that all property was evolving toward the higher form and (2) that practicality dictated the temporary acceptance and legalization of communal holdings.

In the absence of a large Indian or Negro population, the principal issue in Argentine social thought was not the effect of racial mixture on national identity, as it was in Bolivia, Mexico, or even Brazil. After the military conquest of the 'desert' (i.e., the Indian frontier) in 1879, Argentina's Indians became regionally isolated in the south and the north-west and were largely ignored by intellectuals and policy makers of the positivist era. The focus of social thought was rather the impact of the flood of European immigrants on a sparse creole population. The statistics themselves were dramatic. By 1914 about 2,400,000 immigrants, three quarters of them Spanish and Italian, had settled permanently in Argentina and 30 per cent of the total population was foreign-born. The concentration was most dense in the littoral provinces, and especially the Federal District. The 'new' Argentina, like Uruguay and southern Brazil, was ethnically a southern European province. Though rural colonization by Europeans had long been advocated by the elites throughout Latin America, the Argentine response to the reality of an urban immigrant tide was, at best, mixed.

Concern with the character of the new society appeared as part of a remarkable scientific and cultural efflorescence between 1900 and 1915 which has remained unrivalled in modern Latin America. Positivist thought seemed to find its ideal milieu in *belle-époque* Argentina, nourished by the fabulous prosperity of the export economy, by the burgeoning of Buenos Aires as a sophisticated world metropolis and by a continuing consensus among the governing class. The cultural pretensions of the porteño elite found rich expression in the monumental Teatro Colón, planned in the late 1880s and finally completed in 1908. The establishment of the Universidad Nacional de La Plata in 1905, especially its Facultad de Ciencias Jurídicas y Sociales, was symptomatic of the special place occupied by social science in intellectual life. A series of important journals, beginning with the *Revista de derecho, historia y letras* (1898) and ending with the *Revista de filosofía* (1915), recalled the *Revue des deux mondes* and other major French intellectual journals of the late nineteenth century. The list of significant scientists, social theorists and their works is long and impressive.

The 'archetypal savant' of the positivist age in Argentina was Florentino Ameghino (1854–1911), a geo-palaeontologist whose prodigious research on the antiquity of man in the Río de la Plata region gained him world renown. In his famous declaration, *Mi credo* (1906), he espoused an absolute faith in science and in man's perfectibility; the pursuit of truth, he said, will become the 'religion of the future'. José

Ingenieros called him a 'modern saint'. Ameghino's scientism was extreme, but it nonetheless inspired many who pursued the application of science to society.[68] Another star in the positivist constellation was José María Ramos Mejía (1849–1914), a pioneer in medicine (especially in psychiatry), who established a national tradition of medical engagement in social questions. His *Estudios clínicos sobre las enfermedades nerviosas y mentales* (1893) was followed by *Las multitudes argentinas* (1899), an application of Le Bon's crowd psychology, and by its sequel, *Rosas y su tiempo* (1907), which depicted the caudillo as an emanation of the masses.[69] Scientific rigour in legal and historical studies was championed by Juan Agustín García (1862–1923) in his *Introducción al estudio de las ciencias sociales argentinas* (1899). He applied his precepts in *La ciudad indiana* (1900), a lasting study that emphasized economic interests and social structures in the development of colonial institutions.

We have noted the extreme sensitivity of Argentine social thought to varied and changing European ideas. Another characteristic in the positivist era was an almost exaggerated effort to establish an 'Argentine' sociology, built upon the ideas of the nineteenth-century *pensadores*. This paradox, that is, the dual Argentine tendency toward cosmopolitanism and cultural nationalism, was epitomized in the work of the most eminent of Argentine positivists, José Ingenieros (1877–1925). Besides his preoccupation with Argentine society, Ingenieros aspired (at least until 1915) to be a 'man of science', and he gained widespread European recognition as a psychologist, criminologist and psychopathologist. After 1915 he turned to philosophy and ethics. His works were a veritable encyclopedia of continental writers and their ideas. He was as well-travelled as any of his contemporaries. Nonetheless, he presented his studies of Argentina's sociological evolution as built upon premises of Echeverría, Sarmiento and Alberdi, and he wrote substantial essays on their thought.[70] He also edited an important series of Argentine classics entitled 'La cultura argentina', in which he included Sarmiento's unfinished *Conflicto y armonías*, forgotten since its appearance in 1883. In his *Sociología argentina* (1913), Ingenieros tried to combine 'biologi-

---

[68] F. Ameghino's works and correspondence were published in 24 folio volumes (La Plata, 1913–36). 'Mi credo' appeared in vol. xv, 687–719, the eulogy by Ingenieros in 1, 33–5. See also the oration by Ricardo Rojas, *Obras* (Buenos Aires, 1922), ii, (*Los arquetipos*), 197–237 ('Ameghino, el sabio').

[69] See J. Ingenieros, 'La personalidad intelectual de José M. Ramos Mejía', *Revista de filosofía*, 2 (1915), 103–58. Ingenieros received his psychiatric training under Ramos Mejía.

[70] First published in 1915–16, these essays were included by Ingenieros in the 1918 edition of *Sociología argentina*, reprinted as vol. viii of *Obras completas* (Buenos Aires, 1957), 214–304.

cal' and 'economic' sociology, that is, Spencerian social Darwinism and economic determinism (*economismo histórico*), especially as espoused by the Italian theorist, Achille Loria. Though Loria had rejected social Darwinism as elitist and *laissez faire*, Ingenieros was too eclectic to be troubled by such contradictions.[71] He depicted Argentine history as a struggle for existence among social aggregates, yet also as an economically determined evolution from indigenous barbarism to Spanish feudal dominion to an agrarian-pastoral (*agropecuario*) capitalism, and finally toward a 'progressive socialization of the great collective functions in the hands of the state'. Argentina shared this inevitable transition from capitalism to socialism with other nations of the white race. Ingenieros was a pioneer socialist and was active politically until 1903; however, he gradually moved away from his socialist-inspired interpretation of Argentine society.[72]

Ingenieros viewed the recent European influx positively, perhaps in part because his own parents had been Italian immigrants. For Sarmiento in 1883, the great national evils had been the Spanish heritage and *mestizaje*, his remedies public education and immigration. Ingenieros perpetuated this view, asserting in his *Formación de una raza argentina* (1915) that while the first (colonial) immigration had been sterile, the second was consolidating a nationality. In the temperate zones, he wrote, there has been a 'progressive substitution of the aboriginal races of colour by white immigrant races, engendering new societies to replace the native ones'. The process was simply a struggle for life between species in a given environment, the most adaptable ones surviving. When species mixed, the strain 'better adapted to the dual physical-social environment' prevailed. He defined race as 'a homogeneous society of shared customs and ideals', a concept that was more historical than anthropological. Ingenieros portrayed the Argentines as a race of 'working and educated men' which now commanded the respect of

---

[71] See A. Loria, *Contemporary social problems* (London, 1910), 104, 118 (1st edn 1894). Though Ingenieros frequently cited Loria, it is significant that he apparently ignored Loria's major theme, the effect of free land in history, especially in colonial areas. Loria's theory was important for Frederick Jackson Turner. See Lee Benson, 'Achille Loria's influence on American economic thought: including his contributions to the frontier hypothesis', *Turner and Beard* (New York, 1960), 2–40.

[72] The phrase 'progressive socialization . . .', which appeared in the preface of the 1913 Madrid edition of *Sociología argentina* (p. 8), was omitted in the 1918 edition. The writings of Ingenieros present a bibliographical challenge because of his passion for publication and thus his tendency to reproduce earlier writings (with small revisions) in later publications. His *Sociología* went through many transformations, but the principal arguments first appeared in essays dating from 1898 to 1910.

Europe. An Argentine tradition does exist, he affirmed. It was born with nationhood itself and it was nourished by the ideals of 'our *pensadores*'. It is a tradition that points to the future, not to the past.[73]

By 1915, few major intellectuals shared the positive view of immigration held by Ingenieros. Instead, they sympathized with the growing xenophobia that was in part an elite reaction to hordes of European peasants and labourers, some of whom prospered in urban commerce and in the trades and professions. Immigrants became the scapegoat for urban social problems, and psychologists of the day identified immigrants as more prone to crime than lower class creoles. Since socialism and particularly anarchism grew along with immigration, the labour unrest of the 1900–10 decade was blamed on foreign extremists. The first immigrant restriction law was passed in 1902 following a crippling general strike, another in 1910 after a bomb explosion in the Teatro Colón. One deputy attributed the crime to 'a dastardly, ignominious, foreign mind'. Among the supporters of the 1910 Social Defence Law were Ramos Mejía, whose hostility to immigration had appeared as early as 1899 in his *Las multitudes argentinas*, and Bunge, whose assessment of the benefits of immigration had changed sharply in the years since *Nuestra América*.

'Cosmopolitanism' came to be used in a new way, no longer referring to elite European cultural influences, but rather to the materialism and political radicalism of recent immigrants; and the response was nationalistic. Ricardo Rojas (1882–1957), in his *La restauración nacionalista* (1909), became the advocate of a new education in Argentine history and values as a way to lead future generations away from an 'ignoble materialism which has come to confuse for them progress with civilization'.[74] His contemporary, Manuel Gálvez (1882–1963) evoked the traditions of the creole provinces in *El diario de Gabriel Quiroga* (1910) and of Spain in *El solar de la raza* (1913). Though Gálvez's conclusions later turned extreme, at this stage they were still balanced. 'Modern Argentina', he wrote, '[though] constructed on a base of immigration, or cosmopolitanism, can and must preserve a foundation of *argentinidad*'.[75] Rojas and Gálvez both emphasized the revival of humanistic and spiritual values, and their resistance to immigrant

[73] 'Formación' first appeared in Ingenieros' major journal *Revista de filosofía*, 2 (1915), 464–83, and then in the 1918 edition of *Sociología*.

[74] R. Rojas, *La restauración nacionalista. Informe sobre educación* (Buenos Aires, 1909), 64.

[75] M. Gálvez, *El solar de la raza* (5th edn, Madrid, 1920), 17–18n.

influence drew from a new idealist challenge to positivism, to be considered below.

Immigration was not a major issue in Chilean social thought, principally because the influx of foreigners was small, generally middle class and mostly into the sparsely settled north rather than the central valley. The response of the elite (for example, Letelier) was generally benign, but one significant exception was Nicolás Palacios (1854–1911). His immensely popular *Raza chilena* (1904) espoused a biological racism in the manner of Le Bon (whom he quoted constantly) and drew from it unique conclusions on the role of racial mixture in nationality. The true Chilean race is *mestizo*, he said, combining the superior qualities of the Spanish *conquistadores* (traced to 'Gothic' origins in Scandinavia) and the fiercely independent Araucanian Indians. The recent entry of inferior 'Latin races' is harmful, and immigration (particularly Italian) should be curtailed. The peculiar version of racial nationalism Palacios espoused has had lasting influence in Chile.

Social determinism and caudillo government

The racial and environmental determinism inherent in social thought from 1890 to 1914 sharpened and solidified a diagnosis of Latin American politics which had been developing since at least the 1840s. The early faith in the efficacy of constitutional arrangements had faded as law came to be regarded as a product of history and not as an emanation of reason. With the influx of Comtean positivism liberal doctrines and constitutional formulas were branded 'metaphysical'. After 1870 consensus-minded elites sought a remedy for disorder in scientific politics, a programme that would respond to social realities, strengthen government (often through constitutional reform), and ensure economic progress. Programmatic scientific politics and diagnostic social thought were not in conflict. They were merely variants within nineteenth-century positivism, the first derived principally from Comte, the second derived more from Darwin and Spencer. Whereas the latter tended to be more pessimistic and self-denigrating than the former, they both produced stereotypes about Latin American political behaviour which are still popularly accepted, particularly among foreigners.

Carlos O. Bunge argued that a nation's form of government must be construed as an 'organic' outgrowth of its racial and psychological heritage and not as an 'independent abstraction'. Arguedas quoted approvingly Le Bon's assertion that 'political institutions . . . are the expression of the stage of civilization of a people and they evolve with it'. If a country is organically monarchical or republican, wrote Bunge, 'its workshops, its laboratories, its arts, and its books are monarchized or republicanized'. In Latin America, where the regime of *caciques* is organic, all of life is 'caciquized'.[76] Independence was seen by the pessimists as premature, in part the product of exotic ideas, in part the personal creation of *caciques* or caudillos. Lacking any organic principle of institutional balance, the result was alternation between anarchy and despotism, the two sides of what Bunge called the 'American disease'. The caudillo was thus a natural phenomenon. For García Calderón, the great caudillos, such as Rosas, Portales and Díaz, were those who by 'interpreting the inner voices of [their] race' could impose political unity and advance material progress. Bunge, echoing a widely held view, referred to Porfirio Díaz as 'the progressive cacique', one of the great statesmen of the century. 'He governs Mexico as Mexico must be governed.'[77]

The growing acceptance of the caudillo as a socially determined and natural political phenomenon appeared not only in popular essays but also in more elaborate histories. The most notable case was that of Juan Manuel de Rosas, whose federalist regime from 1831 to 1852 was substantially reinterpreted in works by Adolfo Saldías (1850–1914), the brothers José María and Francisco Ramos Mejía (1847–93) and by Ernesto Quesada (1858–1934). These authors purported to examine Rosas and federalism scientifically and thus to surmount the partisan passions that had led to a quasi-official *unitario* condemnation of the 'tyrant' in the years since 1852. José María Ramos Mejía claimed to be guided only by 'cold curiosity'; his approach would be that of 'an entomologist studying a new insect'. Saldías envisioned himself doing an 'autopsy' of the 'social body' in order to discover the 'nature of the foetus, which is Rosas'.[78] The revision of the Rosas era was also a more specific product of Argentine politics, particularly the mounting provincial opposition to the *unicato* and the democratic impulse in the

[76] Bunge, *Nuestra América*, 158; Arguedas, *Pueblo enfermo*, 207.

[77] Another important example of this interpretation was *La anarquía argentina y el caudillismo. Estudio psicológico de los orígenes argentinas* (Buenos Aires, 1904) by the physician turned social essayist, Lucas Ayarragaray (1861–1944). Though Bunge regarded *caudillismo* as a 'deformd' *caciquismo*, other writers, including Ayarragaray, did not distinguish between the two.

[78] José María Ramos Mejía, *Rosas y su tiempo* (3rd edn, Buenos Aires, 1927), I, xxxiii (1st edn 1907); A. Saldías, *Historia de la confederación argentina. Rozas y su época* (Buenos Aires, 1951), III, 497 (first published 1881–7).

Unión Cívica. In *El federalismo argentino* (1889) Francisco Ramos Mejía viewed that phenomenon as a natural legacy from the colonial past, not as an artificial implant of the era of independence. Saldías sought to understand why the masses had supported Rosas and thus to discover the course they had followed since Rosas's day. He concluded that the dictator was the 'incarnation of the sentiments, ideas and aspirations of the Argentine countryside'.[79]

The most significant and influential work of the revisionist movement was Quesada's lucid essay, *Rosas y su tiempo* (1898), the synthesis of his numerous monographs published after 1893. Quesada had studied in Germany and brought to his subject the standards and premises of German historical scholarship. For Quesada Rosas was simply a product of his times, 'no more, no less'; his 'tyranny' was no worse than the tyranny of numerous *unitario* chieftains. Since the Argentine masses lacked 'political education', liberal institutions could not function; the result was anarchy and petty dictatorship. Rosas provided the 'autocratic' leadership the masses demanded. His federalism was not localist; on the contrary, it brought unity and order out of chaos. By 1852, said Quesada, 'his historic mission had ended'.[80] Though Quesada avoided the overt psychological and racial theorizing of many of his contemporaries, his scholarship had the effect of reinforcing intellectual acceptance of caudillo leadership.[81]

As we have noted, a hostility toward classical liberal and democratic doctrines permeated deterministic social thought. By 1890 the label 'jacobin' was increasingly applied to those who believed that society could be transformed by the imposition of rational principles, replacing the comparable term 'metaphysical' of the 1870s. The new label was inspired by Hippolyte Taine's trenchant indictment of the jacobin mentality, first published in 1881 and subsequently popularized by Le Bon and others. For Taine jacobin 'psychology' was the bane of French politics from the Revolution of 1789 to the Commune of 1871. Its indestructible roots, he wrote, are 'exaggerated pride' and 'dogmatic reasoning', which exist beneath the surface of society. When social bonds dissolve (as in France in 1790), jacobins spring up 'like mushrooms in

[79] Saldías, *Historia*, III, 487. Both Saldías and Francisco Ramos Mejía were active in the Unión Cívica, and Saldías expanded and reissued his work in 1892.

[80] E. Quesada, *Rosas y su tiempo* (Buenos Aires, 1923), 63. Cf. Sarmiento's interpretation of Rosas, cited by Quesada.

[81] Quesada made an intriguing comparison (*ibid.*, 149–53) between Rosas and Portales, citing the conservative Chilean historians Ramón Sotomayor y Valdes and Carlos Walker Martínez.

rotting compost'. Their principles, such as the rights of man, the social contract and equality, are the simplistic axioms of 'political geometry', espoused by the young and the unsuccessful and then imposed on a complex society by 'the philosophe legislator'. But, added Taine decisively, they are imposed in vain, because society 'is not the product of logic, but of history'.[82] Taine's diagnosis of French politics struck a responsive chord in Latin American sociologists, and it was universally cited in their writings.

The half-century long attack upon classical liberalism reached a climax in two works which represented the subtle but significant variants within positivist thought. The first, *La constitución y la dictadura* (1912), by the Mexican jurist Emilio Rabasa (1856–1930), marked the culmination of scientific politics, as enunciated by *La Libertad* in 1878 and reiterated by the *científicos* of 1893. Rabasa's work was a measured analysis of the defects of the Constitution of 1857. 'We have placed our hope on the written law and it has shown its incurable weakness', he wrote. The jacobin legislators of 1856 severely restricted presidential authority in defiance of 'sociological laws'. The inevitable result, according to Rabasa, was the two dictatorships of Benito Juárez and Porfirio Díaz, which enjoyed popular sanction because they served 'to satisfy the needs of national development'. Rabasa's work has been attacked as an apology for Díaz in the wake of his overthrow in 1911.[83] Yet Rabasa maintained his faith in historic constitutionalism, the buttress of an enlightened oligarchy. 'The dictators have completed their task', he concluded. 'The constitutional stage must follow.' Rabasa's goal, like that of Sierra, was to bring the written and the real constitutions into harmony, to solidify the reign of political institutions and liberties in concert with strong and effective central administration.[84] It was an optimistic goal shared by the liberal establishment throughout Latin America.

The second work, *Caesarismo democrático* (1919), by the Venezuelan, Laureano Vallenilla Lanz (1870–1936), perpetuated the pessimistic

[82] H. Taine, 'Psychologie du jacobin', *Revue des deux mondes*, 44 (1881), 536–59, republished the same year in *Les origines de la France contemporaine* (*La révolution*, II ['La Conquête jacobine'], 3–39). In Latin America, see, eg. J. E. Rodó, *Liberalismo y jacobinismo* (Montevideo, 1906), 72–8. Rodó emphasized jacobin 'intolerance'.

[83] Most recently by Daniel Cosío Villegas (1898–1976), in *La constitución de 1857 y sus críticos* (Mexico, 1957). Cosío's passionate defence of the Constitution was directed against both Sierra and Rabasa, but particularly against the great influence Rabasa's work had in re-establishing an authoritarian presidency in the Constitution of 1917.

[84] Cf. E. Rabasa, *La constitución y la dictadura* (3rd edn, Mexico, 1956), 244–6, and Sierra, 'Evolución política', 395–6 (written in 1900).

diagnosis of politics in the tradition of Bunge, Arguedas, García Calderón and the Rosas revisionists. Vallenilla's focus was the civil strife unleashed by the Venezuelan revolution for independence, which he characterized (borrowing from Taine) as 'a state of spontaneous anarchy'. He identified in this anarchy an 'egalitarian and levelling democracy', which, as a natural American phenomenon, brought with it the necessity for strong government. Vallenilla excoriated the 'abstract principles of jacobinism' inherent in unworkable written constitutions and asserted that Venezuela could only be ruled effectively by a caesar who responded to 'the psychology of our popular masses', the mixed race of the interior plains (*llanos*). The two caesars Vallenilla singled out were the *llanero* chieftain José Antonio Paez, who exerted 'a personal power that was the concrete expression of the political instincts of our positive constitution', and Simón Bolívar. The latter's 'brilliant intuition as a sociologist' led him naturally to the concept of dictator for life, the 'Bolivian principle (*ley Boliviana*)'.[85] Vallenilla could thus present the great Bolívar as a forerunner of the contemporary dictator, Juan Vicente Gómez (1908–35), whom Vallenilla served as minister and as editor of the official newspaper.

The late positivist interpretation of politics, as represented by both Rabasa and Vallenilla Lanz, was based on a conviction that the Latin American nations, following the dictates of history, race and social psychology, were unable to realize liberal and democratic principles as practised in the 'advanced' countries of Europe and particularly in the United States. Latin American positivists recognized that their society had unique features, but the limitations of evolutionary theory forced them to view that society as inferior on a unilinear scale of civilization. While Rabasa clung to the hope that an enlightened governing class and a strong central administration could bring stability and progress, Vallenilla saw the only solution in a charismatic leader who could respond to the instincts of the unruly masses. While Rabasa maintained a modicum of faith in liberal institutions, Vallenilla despaired of them altogether. The influence of both positivist conclusions, the one drawn from programmatic scientific politics and the other from diagnostic

---

[85] L. Vallenilla Lanz, *Caesarismo democrático: estudio sobre las bases sociológicas de la constitución efectiva de Venezuela* (2nd edn, Caracas, 1929), 281, 214. The book was made up of several studies originally published as early as 1911. Though Vallenilla acknowledged the uniqueness of Venezuelan society, he clearly meant his argument to apply to Latin America as a whole; see his references to Arguedas, Bunge and García Calderón (pp. 229–35).

social determinism, persisted, but not without facing a fundamental challenge to the intellectual assumptions on which they were based.

THE NEW IDEALISM, SOCIAL RADICALISM, AND THE PERSISTENCE OF THE AUTHORITARIAN TRADITION

In 1900, an Uruguayan litterateur, José E. Rodó (1871–1917) published a short essay which had an immense influence on Spanish American intellectuals for two decades and which has retained a symbolic importance to our day. Rodó's *Ariel*, dedicated to 'the youth of America', became the clarion call for a revival of idealism. By evoking a Latin American 'spirit' and identifying it with a revised sense of race, the essay inspired a reaffirmation of the humanistic values in Latin American culture and a resistance to the tide of pessimism in social thought. Moreover, *Ariel* included an indictment of the utilitarianism and democratic mediocrity of the United States, thus providing intellectuals with an easy basis for differentiating and defending 'their' America. They responded quickly to Rodó's appeal to reject the 'mania for the north (*nordomanía*)' that had prevailed, he said, since Alberdi's day, and to abandon 'the vision of a voluntarily delatinized America'. The 'mighty confederation', Rodó added, 'is realizing over us a kind of moral conquest'. Though he did not refer specifically to the Spanish American War, Rodó's essay was clearly a response to the shock produced by Spain's disastrous defeat in 1898. In short, 'from the moment of its appearance', it has been said, *Ariel* became 'the very symbol of Latinamericanism, defined for the first time'.[86]

The appeal of *Ariel* was in its timing and perhaps also in its elevated and abstract tone. For it lacked literary originality, philosophic depth and specific social or political analysis. Rodó's view of North American culture, though containing insights, was secondhand, based on *Del Plata al Níagra* (1897) by Paul Groussac and on a tendentious use of French travellers' accounts. Rodó drew his symbolism explicitly from Shakespeare's *Tempest*, though he modelled the essay itself more on Ernest Renan's philosophic drama, *Caliban, suite de 'la Tempête'* (1878). *Ariel* took the form of a year-end lecture by a venerated teacher ('Próspero') to a group of students, delivered beside a cherished statue of 'Ariel', symbol of spirituality, grace and intelligence. The antithesis of Ariel was

---

[86] A. Zum Felde, *Índice crítico de la literatura hispanoamericana: los ensayistas* (Mexico, 1954), 292.

'Caliban', symbol of materialism, 'sensuality and torpor'. In Renan's play, Caliban prevailed over Ariel and Prospero resigned himself to the victory. Rodó would not accept such a conclusion and began where Renan left off.

Though Rodó was heralded as the prophet of a new idealism, much of *Ariel* was cast in a positivist mould. In fact, the same was true of the writings of those intellectuals he directly inspired, often known as *arielistas*. Rodó's 'transitional' quality reflected one version of the continuing interaction between empiricism (positivism) and idealism (spiritualism) in nineteenth-century French thought. Auguste Comte and Victor Cousin (and some of their followers) promoted the notion of two sharply antagonistic philosophies, but they exaggerated the differences, which were based in part on a personal and academic rivalry. The thought of Renan and Taine, two of Rodó's mentors who are generally regarded as positivists, was in constant tension between science and metaphysics. Renan was plagued throughout his life by religious longings, Taine by the urge to abstract causes or essences in experience and thus to surmount the limitations of the positivist method.[87]

Rodó's principal intellectual guide in *Ariel* was probably Alfred Fouillée, whose prolific writings were specifically directed toward reconciling the values of philosophical idealism, especially liberty and free will, with the determinism of science.[88] Fouillée's central concept, the 'thought force' (*idée-force*), was an attempt to apply the scientific notion of force to mental states. Force is a fact of consciousness; conversely, every idea is a force that can be realized in action. Fouillée's influence was most apparent in Rodó's optimistic (and often overlooked) vision of an ultimate reconciliation between North American and Latin American values. 'All history', Rodó said, 'clearly shows a reciprocal influence between the progress of utilitarian activity and the ideal', and he pointed to Renaissance Italy as an example. Though he saw present evidence lacking, Rodó was confident that 'the work of North American positivism will in the end serve the cause of Ariel'. The energy of the United States will be transformed into higher values.

---

[87] W. H. Simon, 'The "Two Cultures" in nineteenth-century France: Victor Cousin and Auguste Comte', *Journal of the History of Ideas*, 26 (1965), 45–58; D. G. Charlton, *Positivist thought in France during the Second Empire, 1852–1870* (Oxford, 1959). Charlton characterizes Renan and Taine, along with Comte himself, as 'false friends of positivism', that is, of positivism as a theory of knowledge.

[88] The principal relevant work of A. Fouillée was *L'idée moderne du droit en Allemagne, en Angleterre, et en France* (1878); also *Le mouvement idéaliste et la réaction contre la science positive* (1896).

Rodó asserted in *Ariel* that 'we Latin Americans have an inheritance of race, a great ethnic tradition to maintain'; a decade later he went on to identify 'the idea and sentiment of race' with 'the communal sense of ancestry (*la comunidad del origen, de la casta, del abolengo histórico*)'.[89] Rodó was departing from anthropological or scientific racism and instead was reviving the historical conception of race. Did his 'inheritance of race' refer to national traditions or to the Hispanic past? Did it include indigenous and black culture? Or, was the inheritance more broadly 'Latin', a product of the humanistic and aesthetic ideals of Greco-Roman and Christian civilization? The message of *Ariel* was ambiguous in the extreme and thus became a point of departure for diverse tendencies in twentieth-century thought. Also unclear were the social and political implications of Rodó's appeal to America's youth. The tone of the essay was primarily elitist; it evoked aestheticism, a 'well-employed leisure', and 'Renan's wisdom of the aristocrat' against the tyranny of the mass. Rodó was clearly disturbed by the effects of urban immigration. Yet he recognized democracy (along with science) as one of 'the two props upon which our civilization rests' and agreed with Fouillée (against Renan) that the law of natural selection works in society toward the softening of hierarchies and the broadening of liberty.[90]

The new continent-wide idealism took nationally diverse forms, as exemplified by its experience in Argentina, Peru and Mexico. Argentine intellectual life from 1900 to 1920 was not only rich but remarkably complex. Though these years were the apogee of positivism, they were also marked by growing intellectual dissent, fed by changing European ideas, by political questions raised in the aftermath of El Noventa, and by a national soul-searching prompted by the influx of immigrants. Rodó's voice from across the Río de la Plata helped give focus to these varied national concerns. One early dissenter from positivism was the French-born historian and critic Paul Groussac (1848–1929). As a life-long disciple of Taine and Renan, he combined 'scientific' erudition with a strong critique of utilitarianism, both in North American and in Argentine society. Alarmed by immigrant values, he warned that 'material preoccupations may gradually dislodge pure aspirations from

---

[89] J. E. Rodó, 'Rumbos nuevos', *El mirador de Próspero* (Montevideo, 1958 [1st edn 1913]), 26 (commentary on *Idola Fori* [1910] by the Columbian *arielista* Carlos Arturo Torres), Rodó also praised (p. 30) Rojas's *La restauración nacionalista* (1909) as promoting the new 'consciousness of race'.

[90] Rodó, *Ariel*, 6–7, 64–6. Rodó dismissed Nietzsche's 'anti-egalitarianism' as the product of 'an abominable, reactionary mentality'.

the Argentine soul, without which national prosperity is built on sand'.[91] The centennial of independence in 1910 abetted these sentiments and brought forth the essays by Gálvez, as we have noted, and also Rojas's *Blasón de plata* (1912).[92] The latter was followed by *La Argentinidad* (1916) and finally by *Eurindia* (1924), both of which sought Argentine cultural identity in a lyrical but ill-defined interplay between (European) 'exoticism' and 'Indianism'. However, the new idealism in Argentina had more than literary manifestations; it also took the form of significant political and educational departures, to be considered below.

Nowhere did Rodó's message have a more overt effect than in Peru, where a remarkable '*arielista* generation' or '*generación de novecientos*' emerged from the University of San Marcos in 1905. Its leaders were Victor Andrés Belaunde (1883–1966) and José de la Riva-Agüero (1885–1944), as well as Francisco García Calderón (see above). As students they first absorbed the dominant positivism of San Marcos, but soon embraced Rodó (our 'veritable spiritual director', said Belaunde) and also the idealism of Émile Boutroux and Henri Bergson, as taught to them by the philosophical dissenter, Alejandro Deústua. All three were aristocrats, Riva-Agüero from one of the great families of Lima, Belaunde from provincial Arequipa, where he nostalgically recalled the existence of a dignified 'democracy of gentlefolk (*hidalgos*)'.[93] The elder Francisco García Calderón (also born in Arequipa) was a respected jurist and provisional president of the Republic in 1879.

The lives and thought of the three ultimately took quite different courses, but all began by seeking national renovation in a strong constitutional presidency, supported by a progressive and enlightened oligarchy. This ideal of scientific politics seemed to them embodied in the Civilista Party of Presidents Nicolás Piérola (1895–9) and José Pardo (1904–8). However, the *arielistas*' ambivalence towards rapid economic development and the materialism of the new 'plutocracy' of their day led them to advocate ethical and spiritual values and a tutelary political role

---

[91] P. Groussac, passage (1906?) quoted by A. Korn, *Influencias filosóficas en la evolución nacional* (Buenos Aires, 1936), 205. Groussac was defending the teaching of Latin in a report on secondary education.

[92] The *arielista* emphasis on race as ancestry was further evident in Rojas's subtitle: *Meditaciones y evocaciones . . . sobre el abolengo de los argentinos*.

[93] V. A. Belaunde, *La realidad nacional* (Paris, 1931), 189–90; *Arequipa de mi infancia* (1960), as quoted in F. Bourricaud, *Power and society in contemporary Peru* (New York, 1970), 54–6. The family estates and brandy enterprise were ruined by the railroad, and Belaunde's father became a wool merchant.

for intellectuals.[94] García Calderón published *Le Pérou contemporaine* (1907), an ambitious (and unappreciated) sociological study. Riva-Agüero and Belaunde founded the ill-fated National Democratic (Futurista) Party in 1915 and then turned conservative and Catholic. Belaunde clung to traditional constitutionalism, and despite persecution and exile, pursued a distinguished career as law professor, founder of the Catholic University (1917), and finally as President of the United Nations General Assembly (1959). Riva-Agüero's idealism drew him to the colonial and Hispanic past; and beginning with *Perú en la historia* (1910), he became its leading interpreter and apologist. In politics he was increasingly isolated and in the 1930s even advocated Italian fascism.

At the age of twenty-three, García Calderón, along with his three brothers, left Peru for a diplomatic sinecure in Paris, not to return for forty years. He made an impressive debut as a protégé of Boutroux in French literary and philosophical circles, and until the end of World War I was a leading apostle of Americanism and of solidarity among the Latin races. Besides his numerous books and essays, García Calderón founded *La Revista de América* (1912–14), which he said 'belonged to the intellectual elite from across the sea'.[95] Though his goal was the autonomy of American thought and letters, first, he wrote, we must absorb 'our [Latin] inheritance'. 'Imitation will prepare the way for invention'; and perhaps, he implied, Latin leadership will eventually pass to America. Even the eminent Poincaré was impressed and recommended García Calderón's *Les démocraties latines* (1912)' to all Frenchmen concerned for the future of the Latin spirit'.[96] Yet García Calderón's Americanism, as we have seen, also had its pessimistic side, rooted in Le Bonian scientific racism; as such, it emphasized social disorganization and dictatorship stemming from the 'depressing' Iberian and Indian racial heritage. García Calderón surmounted this pessimism as his interests moved from sociology to letters, from Indian and *mestizo* Peru to the cosmopolitan Latin elite. By 1916 he could note the 'declining

---

[94] See F. García Calderón, 'La nueva generación intelectual del Perú' (1905), *Hombres e ideas de nuestro tiempo* (Valencia, 1907), 206–7, an explicit yet ambivalent expression of scientific politics.

[95] *Revista de América* (Paris), 1 (June 1912), 2; also *Creación de un continente* (Paris, 1913), a full exposition of Americanism. Contributors to the 20 issues of the *Revista* included Arguedas (Bolivia), Ingenieros and Gálvez (Argentina), Enrique Pérez (Colombia), Manoel Oliveira Lima and José Verissimo (Brazil), Alfonso Reyes (Mexico) and Ventura García Calderón, Francisco's brother.

[96] R. Poincaré, preface to *Les démocraties latines*, 1. García Calderón said Poincaré submitted the preface in Dec. 1911, just before becoming President of the Council and Minister of Foreign Affairs.

prestige of the biological notion of race', yet the persistence of 'the idea of race as a synthesis of the diverse elements of a defined civilization'.[97] In 1912 he still adhered to both concepts. So the elitist pan-Latin and pan-American ideal, as espoused by García Calderón, enjoyed its brief, significant moment, soon to be overwhelmed by world war and social revolution.

In Mexico, the main forum for the new idealism was the Ateneo de la Juventud, organized in 1909 as a study and lecture society by a philosophically minded group of young intellectuals. The principals of the Ateneo were Antonio Caso (1883–1946), José Vasconcelos (1882–1959) and Pedro Henríquez Ureña (1884–1946), who between 1910 and 1925 were to lead a profound cultural renovation in Mexican life. Henríquez Ureña, a native Dominican who settled in Mexico in 1906, was the catalyst of the group, giving it a cosmopolitan and Americanist orientation.[98] The Ateneo critique was directed at the positivist curriculum of the Escuela Nacional Preparatoria (ENP), long fixed by the Díaz regime. Yet the rebellious 'new generation' found implicit encouragement from the ever-flexible Justo Sierra, Minister of Public Instruction since 1905. In 1908 Sierra spoke in defence of Gabino Barreda, founder of the ENP, against attacks by 'intransigent' Catholics. Most of his oration upheld the school's state-controlled curriculum and Barreda's work as 'consummator (*completador*) of the Reforma, the Juárez of mental emancipation'. However, Sierra's 'let us doubt' passages acknowledged changing conceptions in many scientific areas. Continual questioning of orthodoxies (whether scholastic or positivistic, he implied) was in the spirit of Barreda. Going a step further in 1910, Sierra announced that the new National University's Escuela de Altos Estudios would emphasize philosophy, the (metaphysical) 'why' of the universe, not just the (positivistic) 'how'. Moreover, he added (paraphrasing Fouillée), ideas must be turned into action; 'only thus can they be called forces.'[99]

[97] F. García Calderón, 'El panamericanismo: su pasado y su porvenir', *La revue hispanique*, 37 (June 1916), 1.

[98] From 1907 to 1911 Henríquez Ureña edited the important *Revista moderna* (Mexico), in which he included seven contributions by his friend García Calderón and an annotated Spanish version of the latter's 'Les courants philosophiques dans l'Amérique latine' in Nov. 1908, a month after its appearance in France. He also commented on Rodó's writings and in Aug. 1910 delivered an Ateneo lecture on Rodó.

[99] J. Sierra, 'Homenaje al maestro Gabino Barreda en el Teatro Abreu' (22 Mar. 1908), *Obras*, v, 387–96; 'Discurso en el acto de inauguración de la Universidad nacional de México' (22 Sept. 1910), *ibid.*, 448–62.

The Ateneístas ranged widely in their intellectual effort to break from positivism. In Kant and Schopenhauer they found the impetus to philosophic contemplation and aesthetic experience. Nietzsche inspired individual rebellion against slavish adherence to any doctrine. Like their mentor Sierra, they were attracted to the pragmatism and instrumentalism of James and to his assertion that 'the immediate experience of life resolves the problems that are most troubling to pure thought.'[100] Like Rodó and Groussac they also turned to the classics. Alfonso Reyes (1889–1959), a younger Ateneísta, called for a restoration of Latin, the key to literature, both of which had been 'erased' by the positivists as a sequel to the 'liberal reaction' against the Church.[101]

The Ateneístas and their *arielista* contemporaries were most directly guided by what Vasconcelos called the 'new French philosophy' of Boutroux and particularly of his student Bergson.[102] Boutroux emphasized contingency in the evolutionary process, thus undermining determinism. Bergson's distinction between precisely measured scientific time as space and 'real' time as experienced continuity or duration was for the Americans a liberating concept. Time as duration is perpetual movement, inherent in life itself, and it can only be sensed internally through 'intellectual sympathy' or 'intuition'. Intuition in turn is the basis of a 'vital impetus (*élan vital*)' in all of nature, a creative force that guides humanity to surmount all obstacles, 'perhaps even death'. García Calderón called Bergsonism 'the philosophy of young races' because it affirmed moral freedom and the value of struggle.[103] While accepting evolutionary theory, Bergson gave it a new and optimistic interpretation, which had great appeal to the new idealists of America.

Dramatic events in Mexico determined the ideas and careers of the Ateneo leaders, even though they may also be seen as part of a Spanish American intellectual cohort with common concerns and even some personal ties.[104] Two months after the pompous Centennial festivities of

[100] Passage quoted by Sierra, *ibid.*, 461.
[101] A. Reyes, 'Nosotros,' *Revista de América*, 20 (1914), 111. Reyes left Mexico in 1913 after the death of his father Bernardo, former war minister and state governor.
[102] J. Vasconcelos, 'Don Gabino Barreda y las ideas contemporáneas' (12 Sept. 1910), *Conferencias del Ateneo de la Juventud* (2nd edn, Mexico, 1962), 111.
[103] F. García Calderón, 'La crisis del Bergsonismo' (1912–13), *Ideas e impresiones* (Madrid, 1919), 237, a lucid and discerning essay. The 'crisis' was Bergson's immense popularity after publication of *L'evolution créatrice* (1907), in the face of hostility by professional philosophers, especially Julien Benda. The *Revista de América* also carried articles on Bergson.
[104] It should be noted that Rojas, Gálvez, Belaunde, García Calderón, Caso, Vasconcelos and Henríquez Ureña were all born between 1882 and 1884.

September 1910, occasion of the Ateneo lectures and the inauguration of the University, the country was engulfed in revolution. By June 1911 Porfirio Díaz had resigned, Francisco I. Madero was triumphantly proclaimed president, and popular rebellions dominated the regions. Among the Ateneístas, Henríquez Ureña and Reyes left Mexico, the former to return in the early 1920s, the latter not permanently until 1938. The apolitical Caso remained. During the chaotic years 1913–16, with the University in disarray, he was virtually the only major teacher of the new student generation, but he successfully managed to instil in it the humanistic and moral values of the Ateneo. Vasconcelos became a committed revolutionary with Madero and in the Convention of 1914–15 and then began his wanderings abroad as a new Ulysses. In Lima he compared the Latin American nations to the dispersed Greeks, in search of a Minerva to 'shape the soul of the great race of the future'. Our America, he told the Peruvians, 'is the creation of *mestizos*, of two or three races by blood and of all cultures by spirit'.[105] Vasconcelos was joining the Mexicanism of Sierra, *mestizaje* as the base of nationality, with the cosmopolitan Americanism of Rodó and García Calderón. He developed the theme more fully in the 1920s, thus bringing revolutionary Mexico into ideological contact with a new wave of social consciousness in Peru (see below).

The new idealism made some headway in Brazil between 1900 and 1915, but essentially the country followed political and intellectual rhythms distinct from those of Spanish America. The political system of the Old Republic (1889–1930) to a large extent inhibited the kind of democratic impulse we will encounter in Argentina, Mexico and Chile. After 1898 the 'politics of governors' prevailed, in which presidential elections were determined by agreement of São Paulo and Minas Gerais and, failing that, by intervention of a broker like the outlying Rio Grande do Sul. Between elections, local bossism (*coronelismo*) and a constitutionally sanctioned regional autonomy held sway. The ideal of effective liberal institutions on the national level was kept alive by an older group of former monarchists and 'historic' republicans, notably Joaquim Nabuco and Rui Barbosa. But its demise came in 1910 with Barbosa's presidential campaign, which failed despite the fact that he was idolized for his learning, his prolific writing and florid oratory, and for his juridical leadership at The Hague in 1907.

---

[105] J. Vasconcelos, 'El movimiento intelectual contemporáneo de México' (1916), *Conferencias*, 120.

Among younger intellectuals, there was by 1910 a growing dichotomy between the cosmopolitan majority and a nationalist minority, represented by two contemporaries, Manoel Oliveira Lima (1865–1928) and Alberto Torres (1865–1917). From an old Pernambuco family and educated in Portugal, Oliveira Lima was a distinguished historian and Brazil's leading diplomat from 1892 to 1913. He was the 'civilized' face to the world of a race-conscious Brazil. He upheld an optimistic version of the whitening ideal of racial progress and an Americanism based on the equality of North and South; he also made overtures to the ideal of Latin solidarity.[106]

While Oliveira Lima served as an 'intellectual ambassador' abroad, Torres was a successful legislator, minister, governor and supreme court justice at home. He resigned in 1909, disillusioned with the political system, and in 1914 published his collected articles as *O problema nacional* and *A organização nacional brasileiro*. Torres was an idealist, probably touched by Bergson, but always self-consciously autochthonous in his analysis. He went further than Euclides da Cunha in repudiating scientific racism; for him, race was not relevant to national progress. He sought an organic society based on the 'value of man', and he spoke of an awakening 'primitive instinct'. The Brazilian elite, he argued, was alienated from reality by its fondness for verbal culture, European ideas and unworkable institutional formulas. Instead, he advocated a 'Brazilian solution', namely, increased central authority and the creation of a 'Coordinating Power', including a National Council of life-time appointees to set policy goals and resolve regional antagonisms. Though unappreciated in his own lifetime, Torres became an apostle for a 'spiritualist and nationalist' generation of the 1920s and 1930s in search of new political solutions.

The democratic and constitutional impulse in Spanish America

The decade 1910–20 saw an intense but brief surge of liberal democracy in Spanish America. In Argentina it grew from the crisis of the early 1890s and was embodied in the Radical Party (UCR) under the leadership

---

[106] M. Oliveira Lima, 'A América para a humanidade', *Revista de América*, 9–10 (1913), 181–90, 257–75, an article that won the praise of the considerably younger editor, García Calderón. It was a Portuguese version of the final lecture given in the fall of 1912 on his multi-university U.S. tour: *The evolution of Brazil compared with that of Spanish and Anglo-Saxon America* (Stanford, 1914), 112–29.

of Hipólito Yrigoyen. The Radicals developed strong middle-class support, urban and rural, but abstained from elections. Abstention was interpreted by the oligarchy as preparation for revolution, and the response was a movement within the governing PAN after 1900 to broaden the suffrage (and thus support for the PAN) through electoral reform. Carlos Pellegrini stated that the movement's objective was 'the restoration of representative government', which 'will allow us to organize ourselves to fight for our interests'.[107] An early reform measure in 1904, initiated by Minister of the Interior Joaquín V. González (1863–1923), was followed by the Sáenz Peña Law of 1912. The latter established compulsory voting for native-born Argentinians and the Incomplete List, by which representation from any jurisdiction would be divided two to one between the political parties running first and second. The modern party system had become a reality, but contrary to President Saenz Peña's expectations, Yrigoyen won the election of 1916. Once in power, the Radicals differed little from the 'enlightened' wing of the PAN. Radicalism was mainly political, rhetorically identifying itself with the national community while ignoring the immigrant masses and upholding the economic interests of the landholding elite.

Political democracy was reinforced by philosophical idealism and by the search for *argentinidad*, the roots and essence of national culture. One aspect of this search was a reaffirmation of the liberal tradition, the democratic, constitutional, secular and cosmopolitan ideas and programmes of Mariano Moreno (1810–13), Rivadavia, and the *pensadores* of the Asociación de Mayo. The liberal interpretation had a *unitario* and porteño bias, and it repudiated the Rosas revisionists, who had provided a rationale for charismatic authoritarian government. One lofty and discursive exposition of liberalism was *El juicio del siglo: cien años de historia argentina* (1910) by Joaquín González, who concluded that Argentina was 'a state worthy of exaltation as home and shrine of the qualities and ideals that most honour the human soul'.[108] More cogent were the essays of Alejandro Korn (1860–1936) on the development of Argentine philosophy, which were infused with a new appreciation of the metaphysics of Kant, and which ended with a trenchant critique of the narrow positivism of the Generation of 1880. Korn said the latter pursued an 'exclusively economic ideal', thus subverting the liberal principles of

---

[107] Letter to Miguel Cané (24 Mar. 1905), quoted in David Rock, *Politics in Argentina, 1890–1930; the rise and fall of radicalism* (Cambridge, 1975), 34. Pellegrini died a year later.

[108] J. González, 'Juicio', *Obras completas*, XXI (Buenos Aires, 1936), 216.

Alberdi.[109] The most influential interpreter of Argentine liberalism during this decade was Ingenieros, in his essays on the *pensadores* (see above), in his proposal for a 'new idealism founded in experience', and finally in *La evolución de las ideas argentinas* (1918), presented as a 'breviary of civic morality'. This detailed work portrayed Argentine history as the conflict between authoritarianism and liberty, 'two incompatible political philosophies' emanating from the 'Old Regime' and from the 'Revolution'. The Argentine experience, he implied, paralleled that of France.[110]

Liberal democracy in Argentine politics and the new idealism in thought converged in the movement for university reform, which began in Córdoba in March 1918, spread throughout the nation and had strong international repercussions. Its principal objectives, though often inconsistent, were student participation in university government, curricular reform to incorporate modern scientific and humanistic ideas, and reorientation of the university toward social change. The movement was student led, and though it engaged in confrontation politics and aggressive nation-wide organization (the Federación Universitaria Argentina), it won the support of the Yrigoyen government and of major intellectuals, such as González, Korn and Ingenieros. Persistent student rallies, protests and strikes at Córdoba first brought sympathetic government intervention, then a compromise effort to placate faculty conservatives and finally (after students had occupied university buildings), presidential accession to the reformers' demands in October 1918. The process was repeated, with less turmoil, at the Universities of Buenos Aires and La Plata. The Argentine student federation soon established contacts abroad; by 1920 similar reformist organizations had sprung up in Chile and Peru. In 1921 an International Student Congress met in Mexico City.

The ideology of university reform incorporated many of the ambiguities of the new idealism. One theme, articulated by the movement's major theorist, Ingenieros, and by the student manifestos, was instrumentalist and democratic. The university should become 'an instrument of social action', whose mission was to transform the ideals of the 'higher culture' into 'scientific disciplines' in the service of society.

---

[109] A. Korn published three essays between 1912 and 1914; he wrote the fourth (on positivism) in 1919. The four became the chapters of *Influencias filosóficas en la evolución nacional* (Buenos Aires, 1936).

[110] J. Ingenieros, 'Para una filosofía', *Revista de filosofía*, 1 (1915), 5; *Evolución de las ideas argentinas* (Buenos Aires, 1918), 1, author's preface.

The first Córdoba manifesto used the term 'scientific liberalism'. The reforms called for open admissions and outreach; 'popular universities' sprang up in Argentina and spread to Peru.[111] For the students Córdoba symbolized, as it had for Sarmiento in 1845, the jesuitical bastion of the 'colonial mentality'; the 'university as cloister' must give way to the 'university as laboratory'.[112]

The second reform theme was humanistic and elitist. The growth of professional and technical education, said Ingenieros, has killed the old university; what remains is a 'simple administrative mechanism (*engranaje*), a parasite of the specialized faculties'. The faculties can form the professionals, he continued; but the university of the future, with philosophy at its centre, must form men. Korn also argued this point vigorously at Buenos Aires, where he became dean in October 1918. There was an '*arielista* hue' to the Córdoba manifestos, an emphasis on the 'heroic destiny of youth'.[113] In the 'future university republic', announced the militant Cordobeses, the only professors will be 'the true builders of souls, the creators of truth, beauty and the good'. Favourite student reading was *El hombre mediocre* (1913) by Ingenieros (an analogue to Rodó's *Ariel*), which called on youth to be 'forgers of ideals' and which advocated an 'aristocracy of merit' to counteract social mediocrity. This theme had also been struck by José Ortega y Gasset during his influential visit to Argentina in 1916.[114] The inner contradictions of the Córdoba movement, the conflict between democracy and elitism, between social reform and humanism, were not confined to Argentina; they also appeared in Mexico and Peru.

Whereas the vehicle for democracy in Argentina was legislative initiative, electoral politics and university reform within a flexible and 'maturing' party system, in Mexico its vehicle was revolution against an ossified dictatorship. In Argentina the liberal oligarchy came out of the crisis of 1889–92 strengthened at the expense of the executive, and it

---

[111] An analogous Universidad Popular Mexicana had been founded in 1913 by Ateneo leaders.

[112] J. Ingenieros, 'La filosofía científica en la organización de las universidades', *Revista de filosofía*, 3 (1916), 285–306, revised (and made more emphatic) as *La universidad del porvenir* (1920). The two principal Córdoba manifestos (31 Mar. and 21 June 1918) are in Gabriel del Mazo (ed.), *La reforma universitaria* (3rd edn, Lima, 1967), I, 1–8.

[113] F. Bourricaud, 'The adventures of Ariel', *Daedalus*, 101 (1972), 124. The different history and character of the several universities, e.g., ancient Córdoba and twentieth-century La Plata, must have contributed to the ambiguity in reformist ideology.

[114] A section of *El hombre mediocre* had appeared as 'Los forjadores de ideales' in F. García Calderón's *Revista de América*, I (1912), 105–19, 243–67. The book went through four editions by 1918. For J. Ortega's reflections, see 'Impresiones de un viajero' (1916), *Obras completas*, VIII (Madrid, 1962), 361–71.

made concessions to democracy; in Mexico the *científicos* failed to limit the power of Porfirio Díaz. Moreover, the democratic arguments present in the debate of 1892–3 were suppressed. Democracy re-emerged after 1900 and culminated in Madero's abortive electoral challenge to Díaz in 1910 and then in his successful open rebellion. The movement drew inspiration from Mexico's liberal heritage of popular struggle against native conservatives, the Church and the French during the Reforma era; its symbol was Benito Juárez and its banner the Constitution of 1857. Madero's programme, 'effective suffrage and no re-election', like that of Yrigoyen, was narrowly political. Nonetheless, his fervent idealism galvanized wide support (including that of intellectuals like Vasconcelos), and his assassination in 1913 made him a martyr to democracy for contending revolutionary factions. The triumphant faction, the Constitutionalists under Venustiano Carranza, preserved Madero's restricted political focus without his degree of democratic idealism. The Constitution of 1917, except for its significant social articles not favoured by Carranza, reaffirmed the liberal formalities of 1857. Even the latter were modified, however, by a strengthened six-year presidency of positivist inspiration.[115] What emerged after 1917 was a broadly based but quasi-authoritarian revolutionary state, dedicated to the restructuring of society and to national development. Liberal democracy, after its brief resurgence, became a will-of-the-wisp in twentieth-century Mexico.

Chile also experienced a democratic and constitutional movement but it took place within a singular intellectual environment. There were few traces of *arielismo* or of French idealism in Chilean philosophy and letters between 1905 and 1920. One possible explanation was the strength of German influence in higher education and culture, beginning with Letelier's mission to Germany, which resulted in the establishment of the Instituto Pedagógico in 1889 (see above). For two decades the Instituto was staffed largely with German professors, whom Letelier and others deemed best able to guide Chilean education toward scientific ends.[116] The Instituto not only trained teachers but also, like the earlier Escuela Normal de Paraná in Argentina, the nation's intellectual and governmental elite. One Instituto product was Enrique Molina (1871–

---

[115] See discussion on Rabasa above.

[116] There was some opposition to the German professors, notably a series of articles on 'the German bewitchment' by Eduardo de la Barra in 1899. Letelier was rector of the university from 1906 to 1913.

1964), the leading philosopher and educator of his generation. Molina remained attached to positivism and resistant to Bergson even longer than did Ingenieros.[117] *Arielismo* may also have been inhibited by the racial nationalism of Nicolás Palacios, which construed Chile's European roots to be Teutonic and not Latin. Palacios won high praise from Armando Donoso (1886–1946), the country's major literary critic and essayist of what elsewhere was the *arielista* generation. Donoso, who had studied with Molina and then in Germany, rejected Rodó's cosmopolitan Americanism, welcomed the replacement of French cultural influence by German, and urged younger writers to pursue national themes.[118] In short, exaltation of the 'Latin spirit' had little attraction for Chilean intellectuals.

Political democracy grew out of the multiparty parliamentary system that was dominated for the thirty years after Balmaceda by an extraordinarily narrow oligarchy from the central valley. The democratic instrument was the Liberal Alliance, a coalition of younger dissidents from the Radical, Liberal and Democratic Parties, who were sensitive to the social dislocations brought by rapid urbanization and by periodic recessions in the nitrate industry. In 1915 the Alianza placed Arturo Alessandri, a successful lawyer from northern Tarapacá, in the Senate. Alessandri then led the Alianza to congressional victory in 1918 and to the presidency in 1920. The victory constituted a 'revolt of the electorate', to use the standard phrase, but it was a middle-class electorate; because of literacy qualifications only 8 per cent of the population voted.

Nonetheless, Alessandri developed a mass following. His triumph 'stupefied the rich and powerful classes', in part because it introduced a new political style, even more dramatically than had Yrigoyen's triumph in Argentina.[119] Politics were forced out of the gentleman's club and into the street; Alianza parades, slogans and inflammatory harangues replaced dignified discourse and bargaining among intimates. For genteel central-valley politicians Alessandri was an arriviste outsider, a power-seeking Italian adventurer.[120] As president he faced a hostile

---

117 Molina recalled his 'unjustified' opposition to Bergson, despite encouragement in 1912 from Bergson's German enthusiast Georg Simmel, in 'La filosofía en Chile en la primera mitad del siglo xx, *Atenea*, 315–16 (1951), 246–7.

118 A. Donoso, *Los nuevos. La Joven literatura chilena* (Valencia, 1912), xi–xxiii.

119 The phrase is from Ricardo Donoso, *Alessandri: agitador y demoledor* (Mexico, 1952), I, 243.

120 Ricardo Donoso (b. 1896), brother of Armando and a graduate of the Instituto Pedagógico, perpetuated this anti-Latin characterization: *ibid.*, 7–10. Alessandri was descended from an Italian 'puppeteer' who settled in Chile in the early 1820s.

senate, but with military support he finally prevailed to institute a new constitution in 1925. The document abolished the parliamentary system in favour of a six-year directly elected president who could control his cabinet. It also separated Church and state, no longer a controversial issue, and advanced the concept of the social function of property. The surge of democracy in Chile broke the political monopoly of the old oligarchy, but it also fortified central state authority, as it did in Argentina and Mexico.

Socialism, the agrarian movement and indigenismo

Accompanying the democratic impulse was another and more fundamental challenge to the political and social consensus reestablished in the 1890s – socialism and agrarian radicalism. Though these ideologies made little headway during the nineteenth century, after 1900 their appearance was sudden and forceful in several countries, sparked by the quickened pace of socio-economic change – expansion of export economies and their integration into the international capitalist system, modest growth of industry and of an urban work force, and in some regions massive immigration. By 1920 the most significant of these radical departures were socialism in Argentina and Chile, indigenous agrarianism in Mexico and a unique ideology in Peru which included elements of both.

Socialist leadership and ideology differed sharply in Argentina and Chile as a result of the dissimilar conditions in which they developed.[121] Luis E. Recabarren (1876–1924), founder of the Partido Obrero Socialista (POS) in 1912 and the soul of Chilean socialism, was a poor, self-taught typographer, devoted by trade to instructing his fellows. Though he became progressively more radical, his programme remained consistent. Private property should be abolished or made collective or communal. The proletarian struggle should simultaneously pursue two ends, economic gains through union organization and political power.[122] He was personally engaged in both and by the early 1920s not only led the Chilean Communist Party affiliated to the Third International and the Federación Obrera de Chile (FOCH) but also was elected a deputy from the nitrate region. Recabarren never became cosmopolitan, despite his

---

[121] See Hall and Spalding, *CHLA* IV, chap. 9.

[122] The most elaborate exposition of Recabarren's ideas was in a series of articles published in *El despertar de los trabajadores* of Iquique (Oct.–Nov. 1912): 'El socialismo ¿Qué es y cómo se realizará?', *El pensamiento de Luis Emilio Recabarren* (Santiago, 1971), I, 7–96.

travels and associations in Argentina, Spain and Russia, but remained a morally austere and ascetic figure who ultimately took his own life.

In contrast to Recabarren, Juan B. Justo (1865–1928), co-founder, with José Ingenieros, of the Argentine Socialist Party in 1894, was a surgeon of middle-class background who was drawn to socialism by his clinical contact with human suffering. He came to Marx late, only after a thorough preparation in positivism. Like Ingenieros, he adhered to biological evolution and, like the professors of Paraná, he saw 'socialist' implications in Comte.[123] He entered politics through the Unión Cívica and was, again like Ingenieros, guided by the national liberal tradition. Korn said of Justo that he was the first to go beyond 'Alberdian ideology'; by adding the idea of social justice, he renewed 'the content of Argentine thought'.[124] Justo was committed to achieving socialism through non-violent parliamentary means, much in the manner of Jean Jaurès, the French leader who lectured in Buenos Aires in 1909 at Justo's invitation. By 1920 socialism had a solid though minor place in the intellectual and political establishment. Justo and Alfredo L. Palacios (1880–1965) had pushed piecemeal social legislation through congress, but the Party's programme remained moderate.[125] It approached workers as consumers, not as producers; it adhered to free trade; it made no distinction between foreign and native capital; it hesitated on the abolition of private property.[126] Since the Party never asserted effective control over workers, who were mostly non-voting foreigners, both socialism and the labour movement floundered in the years following 1920.

We have already seen that ideas in Mexico cannot be separated from the country's unique experience of social upheaval and extended civil conflict. Such is the case with socialism, which appeared in its anarchist form by 1910, but which was always less significant than the more indigenous agrarian ideology that became the radical centre of the Revolution. The leader of anarchism was Ricardo Flores Magón (1874–1922), founder of the newspaper *Regeneración* (1900) and of the Partido Liberal Mexicano (PLM) (1905). Hounded by Mexican and American

---

123 Justo's major work was *Teoría y práctica de la historia* (1909).

124 See Korn's eulogy at Justo's death in 1928: *Obras completas* (Buenos Aires, 1949), 506–7. Korn was a socialist sympathizer from about 1915 but did not join the Party until 1931.

125 The flamboyant and cosmopolitan Palacios was a Socialist deputy from 1904–8 and 1912–15, a law professor and dean at La Plata, a leading spokesman for university reform and a prolific publicist.

126 See Justo's debate on property (1908–9) with the Italian sociologist, Enrico Ferri: *Obras*, VI (Buenos Aires, 1947), 236–49. Ferri called Argentine socialism an 'artificial flower'.

authorities and encouraged by the IWW, the Flores Magón group moved from popular democracy to anarchism and broke with Madero's anti-re-electionist campaign of 1908–10. In 1906, the social content of the PLM programme was limited to the eight-hour day, a one-peso minimum wage, and the distribution of undeveloped land. By 1911 the programme's central provision was the abolition of the 'principle of property', from which spring the institutions of Church and state. Workers, continued the PLM manifesto, must 'take into their own hands the land and the machinery of production' so they can 'regulate the production of wealth for their own needs'.[127] The PLM receded after 1911. Flores Magón remained in exile and finally died in a Kansas prison. However, several of his early adherents joined the agrarian and urban labour movements of the revolutionary decade, bringing anarchist ideas with them.

One such movement was led by Emiliano Zapata in Morelos. Through a decade of rebellion against Mexico City and a dogged adherence to their Plan of Ayala (November 1911), the Zapatistas more than any other faction influenced the direction of national agrarian reform. The Plan of Ayala was indigenous in that it sprang from the consensus of Zapatista peasant chiefs, was phrased inelegantly by a 'country intellectual' (Otilio Montãno) and made the Juárez nationalization decrees a precedent (article 9). Yet the Plan's anarchist images and its call for immediate takeover of property for the common welfare (article 6) were derived from the widely disseminated PLM manifesto of September.[128] The Zapatista programme within Morelos became increasingly anti-statist, anti-liberal and collectivist from 1914 to 1917, abetted by Antonio Díaz Soto y Gama, an ex-PLM intellectual. Article 27 of the Constitution of 1917, primarily the creation of Andrés Molina Enríquez, legalized the agrarian community (*ejido*) and made its lands inalienable. But the article also recognized the 'small [individual] property', reflecting the liberal assumptions of the constitution-makers and the ambivalence of Molina Enríquez on the place of communal property in the scheme of evolution. The reconciliation of the Zapatistas with the government of Álvaro Obregón in 1920 gave radical agrarian-

---

127 The complete text of the programme, issued at Saint Louis on 1 July 1906, can be found in Arnaldo Córdoba, *La ideología de la revolución mexicana* (Mexico, 1973), 405–21; the manifesto issued at Los Angeles on 23 Sept. 1911 is in Juan Gómez Quiñones, *Sembradores. Ricardo Flores Magón and El Partido Liberal Mexicano* (Los Angeles, 1973), 120–5.

128 For the text and a definitive analysis of the Plan of Ayala see John Womack, Jr., *Zapata and the Mexican Revolution* (New York, 1969), 393–403.

ism an official status, but also provided the basis for its co-optation.

The most distinctive formulation of radical ideology prior to 1930 was in Peru, the other major 'Indian country' of Latin America. However, Peru did not experience revolution; thus radical ideas never achieved the official recognition (nor underwent the consequent modification) they did in Mexico. In Peru the new radicalism flowered in the 1920s, reflecting the late but dramatic development of export capitalism there. The new ideas, especially as expressed by José Carlos Mariátegui (1894–1930) and Víctor Raúl Haya de la Torre (1895–1979), were distinctive in that they were derived from both Marxism and from literary and philosophical idealism. Moreover, the university reform movement in Peru was a catalyst for radicalism, a function it did not serve elsewhere. Still another feature distinctive to Peru was the inspiration provided by Manuel González Prada (1848–1918), the unique iconoclast of Latin America's positivist era. The Mexican rebels looked back to Juárez and the *reformistas*, the Argentine socialists to Echeverría and Alberdi, and Recabarren in Chile (less so) to Francisco Bilbao. None of these precursors, however, were so radical or so immediate as González Prada.

Descended from a pious, aristocratic family, González Prada had rejected traditional Peruvian society and its values on a deeply personal as well as a political and literary level. He was an atheist as a result of personal experience – he had fled a Catholic seminary as an adolescent and his older sister died apparently from excessive religious fasting and penitence (from 'fanaticism', he said) – and fiercely anticlerical, partly under the influence of the ideas of Bilbao. His anticlericalism, however, became part of a broader indictment of a Peruvian elite that lacked national coherence or patriotism during the War with Chile, that ignored its depressed Indian population and that welcomed foreign economic exploitation. Through his speeches and essays from the late eighties – many of them published in *Páginas libres* (1894) and *Horas de lucha* (1908) – González Prada became the inspiration for a radical intellectual tradition in Peru as he moved from radical liberalism to libertarian anarchism and socialism in the years before his death in 1918. Some commentators emphasize to the point of exaggeration a direct link between the ideas of González Prada and those of Haya and Mariátegui.[129]

The critical year for Peruvian radicalism was 1919. In January, Haya de la Torre, a leader of the Peruvian Student Federation (FEP),

[129] See Martin, *CHLA*, IV, chapter 11.

successfully turned the focus of the reform movement in San Marcos toward support for a general strike by textile workers for the eight-hour day. Out of this worker-student alliance came the Popular Universities (1921), and three years later the Alianza Popular Revolucionaria Americana (APRA), founded by Haya in Mexico City.[130] In July 1919 a coup by Augusto B. Leguía ended twenty-five years of rule by the Civilista oligarchy and initiated a decade of dictatorship devoted to economic modernization. In October Leguía sent Mariátegui, a journalist who sympathized with the strikers, into European exile, where for three years he was immersed in the intellectual and ideological ferment of post-war France, Italy and Germany. He returned determined to implant socialism in Peru. Though Mariátegui and Haya crossed paths for only a few months before Haya himself was exiled (1923–31), the two co-operated until 1927, when they split over whether APRA should become a party or remain an alliance. The split pointed up a fundamental difference between Haya, who was primarily a political organizer during the 1920s, and Mariátegui, who was primarily an ideologue.[131]

Mariátegui's writings from 1923 to 1930 combined an acute Marxist analysis of Peruvian history and culture with a religious vision of national regeneration through socialism. His major work established the complex coexistence of three economic stages, the indigenous or communal, the feudal or colonial, and the bourgeois or capitalist. With political independence, 'a feudal economy gradually became a bourgeois economy, but without losing its colonial character within the world picture'. The term 'colonial', as used by Mariátegui, meant both economically dependent on foreign capital and culturally dependent on traditional Hispanic values ('the spirit of the fief' as opposed to 'the spirit of the town').[132] He identified the oppressed class as the Indian rather than as the proletarian or worker, abstractly construed, and he saw the redemption of the Indian as the key to national revival. He rejected traditional 'westernizing' approaches to the 'Indian problem'. All such reform efforts, he said, have been and will continue to be subverted by

[130] González Prada had called for a worker-student alliance in 1905: 'El intelectual y el obrero', *Anarquía* (4th edn, Lima, 1948), 49–56. His name was attached to the Popular Universities in 1922.

[131] Ironically, Haya regarded himself primarily a theorist and Mariátegui helped organize the Peruvian Socialist Party (PSP) in 1928 and the General Confederation of Peruvian Workers (CGTP) in 1929.

[132] J. C. Mariátegui, *Siete ensayos de interpretación de la realidad peruana* (Lima, 1928); quotes from English edition (Austin, 1971), 6, 21. All of Mariátegui's longer works were compilations of previously published short articles and speeches. Those making up the *Siete ensayos* appeared mostly in 1925–6.

gamonalismo, the pervasive system of local control imposed by the large landed estate, until the phenomenon itself is rooted out. 'The soul of the Indian' can only be raised up 'by the myth, the idea of the socialist revolution'. He must seek regeneration by looking to his past, to 'the highly developed and harmonious communistic system' of the Incas. 'The Indian proletariat awaits its Lenin.'[133]

Whereas Justo came to socialism from medical science, Recabarren from union organizing, and Flores Magón from law, Mariátegui came to it from avant-garde literature and art. Before becoming 'radicalized' in 1919, he was a dandyish columnist.[134] In Europe he was struck particularly by the ideas of Henri Barbusse, the novelist, and of Georges Sorel, the theorist of syndicalism. Barbusse had just founded the International of Thought and the *Clarté* movement out of disillusionment with the War, which he regarded as the product of a dehumanizing and decadent bourgeois civilization. 'Politics is today the only great creative activity', wrote Mariátegui interpreting Barbusse. Intellectuals and artists must lead the poor to revolution, 'to the conquest of beauty, art, and thought' as well as to 'the conquest of bread'. Sorel made Mariátegui appreciate 'the religious, mystical and metaphysical character' of socialism and how man can be driven by 'myths', whether religious or revolutionary.[135] Sorel in turn idolized Bergson, whom he said demonstrated 'the illusion of scientific truths' as propagated by the positivists.[136] In a sense, Mariátegui was carrying to extreme anti-positivist conclusions the idealism that so affected the Peruvian *arielista* generation of 1905. He was drawn to Barbusse and Sorel just as García Calderón had been drawn to Boutroux and Bergson.[137] Thus Mariátegui

---

[133] Prologue to the militant *indigenista* Daniel Valcarcel's *Tempestad en los Andes* (1925), inserted as a note in *Siete ensayos* (Eng. edn, 29). Mariátegui quoted the Lenin phrase from Valcarcel.

[134] Mariátegui's heirs omitted his pre-1919 'stone-age' writings from his *Obras completas* (1959) as adding 'nothing to his work as guide and precursor of social consciousness in Peru' (Preface to each vol.). Yet it should be noted that Mariátegui's attachment to European literature persisted throughout his life, as revealed for example in the contents of *Amauta* (1926–30), his overtly *indigenista* journal.

[135] J. C. Mariátegui, *La escena contemporánea* (Lima, 1925), 201–2 (on Barbusse); 'El hombre y el mito' (1925), in *El alma matinal* (Lima, 1950), 28–9 (on Sorel). Mariátegui knew Barbusse personally and the latter paid him lavish tribute at his death. He was introduced to Sorel's thought in Italy.

[136] G. Sorel, *Reflections on violence* (Glencoe, 1950), 162 (1st edn, 1908).

[137] Mariátegui and other radicals of the 'Generation of 1919' repudiated the *arielistas* (or *futuristas*) and embraced instead González Prada, despite his atheistic anticlericalism: Mariátegui, *Siete ensayos* (Eng. edn), 184–5, 221–5; Luis Alberto Sánchez (b. 1900), *¿Tuvimos maestros en nuestra América? Balance y liquidación del novecientos* (2nd edn, Buenos Aires, 1955), 10–21. (The answer, of course, was 'no'.)

has been correctly called a 'radical humanist' as well as a socialist and an indigenous nationalist.

Mariátegui's vision of national regeneration was an extreme formulation of *indigenismo* (or *indianismo*), which was widespread in Mexico and Peru by 1920. As the origin of nationality, the Aztec and Inca civilizations must be better understood; and such understanding must be tied to redemption of the present-day Indian majority. *Indigenismo* became 'official' in Leguía's Peru as well as in Obregón's Mexico, though the constitutionally proclaimed protection of the Peruvian Indian was undermined by the regime's pursuit of road building and commercialization in the highlands. In Mexico, one product of rural upheaval was the government's Department of Anthropology (1917), directed by Manuel Gamio (1883–1960), a professional who put into practice the new theories of the relativity of culture and its separation from race. The 'forging of a nationality', he argued, must begin with scientific study of Mexico's diverse Indian groups, a new appreciation of native art and literature, and a reversal of the 'fatal foreignist orientation' of the nineteenth century. In his model project at the pyramid site of Teotihuacán, he tried to integrate archaeology with education of the local populace, always with an eye to the revival and preservation of native arts and culture.[138] His efforts, along with mural art and rural education on a national scale, were promoted by José Vasconcelos, who, as Obregón's Minister of Education (1921–4), was the great 'cultural caudillo' of the new Mexico.

Vasconcelos, however, was not an *indigenista* – beyond his sympathy for agrarianism and his conviction that the Indian must be truly incorporated into Mexican society. For Vasconcelos, nationality, whether Mexican or Ibero-American in the broader sense, resided in racial and cultural *mestizaje*. Whereas Mariátegui rejected past and present efforts to westernize the Indian, Vasconcelos maintained that 'the Indian's only door to the future is that of modern culture, his only road the one opened up by Latin Civilization.'[139] The educational programme of Vasconcelos included the wide distribution of European classics. He regarded the rural teachers of the 1920s as twentieth-century Franciscan

---

[138] M. Gamio studied at Columbia University under Franz Boas, receiving the Ph.D. in 1921. For his ideas, see *Forjando patria* (Mexico, 1916) and the introduction to his massive *La población del valle de Teotihuacán*, 2 vols. in 3 (Mexico, 1922).

[139] J. Vasconcelos, *La raza cósmica. Misión de la raza iberoamericana* (Paris, 1925), 13. Cf. Belaunde's critique of Mariátegui's *indigenismo*: while Mariátegui regards it as 'a supreme and ultimate value', I regard it 'as a step to something higher, *la peruanidad integral*'. See *La realidad nacional*, 198.

friars. Though he tolerated Gamio's 'integral' approach to rural education, he did not believe Indians should be taught first in their native languages. Yet the ideas of both Vasconcelos and his contemporary Gamio, different as they were, retained the optimistic assumptions of evolutionary theory, in contrast to Mariátegui's radical and existential notion of Indian regeneration. 'In history', wrote Vasconcelos, 'there is no turning back because all is transformation and novelty'. Expanding on his address of 1916 to the Peruvians, he envisioned America as the cradle of a 'cosmic race'. The influence of Vasconcelos was apparent in the concept of Indo-America, central to Haya de la Torre's APRA. In fact, it may be that much of Haya's pragmatic *indigenismo* and agrarianism bore a Mexican stamp.

The emergence of corporatism

We conclude this chapter with a consideration of authoritarian or corporatist political ideas in the years prior to 1930. The term 'corporatism' has been used primarily as an analytical construct, 'a scholar's tool' for elucidating the distinctive structure of contemporary (post-1930) Latin American polities. As such, corporatism is differentiated from 'pluralism' and is defined as a system of interest representation by hierarchically organized and non-competitive groups, recognized and regulated (if not created) by the state. Corporatism as a formal ideology, distinguished from corporatism as a system, has not been common in Latin America. Nonetheless, a variety of corporatist assumptions began to appear with some frequency in the thought and policy of the 1920s.

Corporatism was a response to, and yet often intertwined with, both liberal democracy and socialism; thus it appeared largely in political contexts we have already examined. Though contemporary European models were important, emerging corporatism drew even more from the positivist heritage, both scientific politics and deterministic social thought. Like positivism, corporatism was based on a hostility to the role of ideas in political organization, even though its advocates often regarded themselves as idealists. In a few cases corporatist formulations explicitly evoked precedents from the Spanish colonial system. Some prominent corporatist movements of the 1920s, for example in Mexico and Peru (APRA), were populist in orientation, that is, devoted to social reform and to mass participation. The social implications of others, such as in Brazil and Chile, were ambiguous. The least overt corporatist movement of the 1920s, in Argentina, was socially repressive.

In Mexico article 27 (property) and article 123 (labour) of the Constitution of 1917 gave legal recognition to agrarian and labour demands, but they also provided a basis for control, for bringing these militant groups into the revolutionary state. The constitutional rationale was provided by Andrés Molina Enríquez, responding in 1922 to two charges, that article 27 was 'radically communistic' and that the Constitution gave excessive power to the executive. Though Molina acknowledged that the 'spirit' of the Constitution was 'collectivist' as opposed to the 'individualist' spirit of 1857, he claimed this change merely reflected the Comtean concept (unknown in 1857) that societies were 'living organisms'. Moreover, the principle that property is vested originally in the nation, which in turn can grant property to individuals, is not new but merely a modern reaffirmation of the rights of the Spanish crown. As for executive authority, Molina maintained that the weakness of agrarian communities and of workers vis-à-vis landowners and industrialists made it 'indispensable that official action be exerted in their favour in order to balance the forces of the two sides' and to promote justice, as did the tribunals of the colonial era.[140]

Revolutionary governments were ambivalent toward urban labour. A Department of Labour was created in 1912 to mediate industrial conflicts and to encourage and guide workers' organizations. Over Carranza's objections, Department leaders tolerated the anarcho-syndicalist Casa del Obrero Mundial (House of the World Worker) and even persuaded the Casa to send 'Red Battalions' to fight the Villistas and Zapatistas in 1915. The Department also promoted organizations of textile workers, explicitly termed 'clusters (*agrupaciones*) of resistance' and not 'unions (*sindicatos*)', whose elected governing boards would represent labour interests before the government. According to a 1915 Department memo, the *agrupación* policy could 'put an end to the power of independent labor groups and their ability to conspire against legal authorities'.[141] Following a general strike in 1916, Carranza abolished the Casa, the most prominent independent group, and then sponsored a

---

140 A. Molina Enríquez, 'El artículo 27 de la constitución federal', *Boletín de la Secretaría de Gobernación*, 1 (1922), 1–12. He said workers and peasants were like 'minors'. Cf. argument by Cosmes (1893) above, note 40.

141 Cited in Ramón E. Ruíz, *Labor and the ambivalent revolutionaries: Mexico, 1911–1923* (Baltimore, 1976), 57. A new Ministry of Industry, Commerce, and Labour was created in 1916 under Plutarco Elías Calles, who later became the patron of CROM and as president (1924–8) the chief architect of the PRN, founded in 1929.

broad Regional Confederation of Mexican Labour (CROM) in 1918. The CROM, clearly under government tutelage from the start, claimed 300,000 members by 1920. The logic of policy toward peasants and workers led ultimately to their incorporation into the National Revolutionary Party (PRN) as two of three functional 'sectors'.

It should be added, incidentally, that one group clearly not incorporated was the Church, which strongly resisted the severe limitation of its educational role and property rights in the anticlerical articles 3 and 130 of the Constitution. The intense Church–state conflict of the late 1920s, which included a massive rebellion of religious peasants (*cristeros*) in the west, was a phenomenon unique to Mexico, a reenactment of the Reforma of the mid-nineteenth century.

'The Mexican Revolution is our revolution,' wrote the Peruvian exile Haya de la Torre in 1928. The early ideology of APRA may be construed in part as Haya's doctrinal elaboration of assumptions imbedded in what he called Mexico's 'spontaneous movement'. Haya envisioned the formation of an 'anti-imperialist state', an alliance of all those exploited by foreign capitalism, particularly North American. Because of a basically feudal structure, imperialism in Latin America, contrary to Lenin's theory, is the first, not the last, stage of capitalism. The anti-imperialist state will emerge from a single party (APRA), organized 'scientifically', not as a 'bourgeois [liberal] democracy' but as a 'functional or economic democracy', in which classes will be 'represented according to their role in production'.[142] The key problem for Haya was the role of the national bourgeoisie, which he at times interpreted as among the exploited and at other times as tied to imperialism. As an ideologist and organizer out of power, challenged by doctrinaire socialists, Haya was obliged to confront the theoretical problem of the middle classes, one that could be conveniently ignored in Mexico. Haya disguised the confusion by presenting Aprismo as an autochthonous doctrine, free of 'mental colonialism' and 'Europeanism'.[143]

Corporatist themes were particularly apparent in the political ideas of the 1920s in Brazil. The strength and longevity of the Old Republic had the anomalous dual effect of inhibiting liberal democracy and socialism

[142] V. R. Haya de la Torre, *El antimperialismo y el APRA* (2nd edn, Santiago, 1936), 82, 149 (written in 1928, though not published till 1935). Haya's concept of the multi-class party was an expansion of his earlier alliance of workers and students.

[143] See passage from Haya (1928), cited by Bourricaud, *Power and Society*, 156. Haya was clearly referring to Mariátegui, who replied that APRA seemed too much like Italian fascism.

and yet inviting criticism of the republican system. Though positivism persisted in education and in social thought, it led increasingly to a 'sociological' emphasis that challenged intellectual cosmopolitanism and sought institutions in tune with Brazil's society and traditions. The combination of cultural nationalism, sociology and political criticism came forth in a powerful call for a 'new work of construction' by a dozen prominent intellectuals, writing in 1924 as 'the generation born with the Republic' who were overt admirers of Alberto Torres.[144] The most influential statement was by Francisco José Oliveira Vianna (1885–1951), a law professor and widely read social analyst, who attacked in familiar positivist terms the 'idealism' of the Constitution of 1890. He then went on to lament the absence of a 'regime of public opinion', or the kind of 'sentiment of collective interest' which is deep in 'genuine races' like the English. The heart of Brazil's constitution must be economic and social, not political. It must be responsive to land reforms in a country where 90 per cent of the people are rural dependants; to 'institutions of social solidarity', such as an efficient judiciary and strong municipal magistrates to restrain the will of local bosses; and to the diffusion of a 'corporative spirit'. The key to reform and to 'the architecture of the new political system', implied Oliveira Vianna prophetically, was a strong national administration that would interact closely with the interests of groups.[145]

Corporatist ideas in Chile were remarkably varied: like Mexico they appeared in state labour policy, like Brazil in a major historical critique of political liberalism, like Argentina in admiration expressed for European fascism by elements of the military and the Church hierarchy. The labour code of 1924 recognized workers' organizations but subjected them to close government regulation. Passed suddenly and unanimously in 1924 under military pressure, the code was an amalgam of diverse projects that had divided Congress during the Alessandri administration. A major source of inspiration was German state socialism (or 'professorial socialism') of the Bismarck era, imbibed by Valentín Letelier and by Manuel Rivas Vicuña, an important Liberal intellectual and politician who was close to Alessandri. As early as 1906 Letelier had persuaded the

---

[144] Preface to *A margem da historia da república* (Rio de Janeiro, 1924). The collaborative work, delayed in publication, was prompted by the centennial of independence, as was the outpouring of cultural self-examination in the notorious 'Week of Modern Art' in São Paulo (1922). See Martin, *CHLA* IV, chap. 11.

[145] Oliveira Vianna, 'O idealismo da constituição', *ibid.*, 137–60. Oliveira Vianna was a student of Silvio Romero and clung to much of scientific racism.

majority of a Radical Party congress that legislation on social welfare and the organization of work was necessary 'to forestall the expansion of revolutionary (*de combate*) socialism'.[146]

Another response to the social and political turmoil of the twenties was *La fronda aristocrática* (1928) by Alberto Edwards Vives (1874–1932). Edwards attacked the fallacies of liberal ideals, as did Oliveira Vianna, but also the aristocracy, which he said reverted to its natural factious tendency with the breakdown of the Portalian system (1831–91). That system was based on strong central authority which restrained the aristocracy, on a sense of hierarchy and social discipline, and on moral and spiritual force, now undermined by bourgeois materialism. In short, it was a political regime 'in form', a phrase Edwards borrowed from Oswald Spengler. Such regimes depend for their existence on 'living organic elements', not on written constitutions. 'Liberty and organic are incompatible terms.'[147] Edwards predicted the decline of Chilean civilization unless some new Portales emerged. The book was an implicit apology for Carlos Ibañez del Campo, Chile's military president (1927–31), whose authoritarian policies were widely supported until the economic collapse of 1929. Edwards was briefly a minister under Ibañez.

Whereas corporatism in Mexico and Chile before 1930 was manifest in official policy, particularly towards labour, in Argentina it was confined primarily to movements of the dissident Right. After 1910, the creole elite increasingly branded working-class groups and ideologies as 'foreign', and there was little effort by Radical Party governments (1916–30) to patronize, co-opt, or regulate labour. Instead, ad hoc organizations condoned by the government sprang up, particularly during the general strike of January 1919, to defend property and wantonly to attack working-class neighbourhoods, in what became known as the 'tragic week (*semana trágica*)'. The most prominent of these groups was the Liga Patriótica Argentina, which followed up paramilitary repression with an ill-defined programme of 'practical humanitarianism' to achieve class harmony. Educational and welfare programmes for workers were instituted and there was even some discussion of

---

[146] Quoted in Luis Galdames, *Valentín Letelier y su obra* (Santiago, 1937), 378. On professorial socialism (or 'socialism of the chair'), including its concept of the state as an organ of moral solidarity, see Charles Gide and Charles Rist, *A history of economic doctrines* (2nd Eng. edn, London, 1948), 436–46.

[147] A. Edwards Vives, *La fronda aristocrática en Chile* (6th edn, Santiago, 1966), 272. Edwards's work also showed traces of the racial nationalism of Palacios. Both he and Palacios had a strong influence on the conservative historian, Francisco A. Encina.

organizing all productive members of society into functional corporations. However, the premise underlying the League's programme was
'seeing the world as it is', in other words, acceptance of a natural
hierarchy of intelligence, culture and wealth.[148]

After 1923 the relatively benign League gave way to virulent
'nationalist', anti-liberal and anti-semitic groups, which recruited major
intellectuals and reached a crescendo in the years 1927–30. One such
intellectual was the poet Leopoldo Lugones (1874–1939), who turned
from anarchism to fascism, lecturing on Mussolini in 1923, extolling
military virtues in his 'hour of the sword' speech in Peru in 1924 and
attacking electoral politics and liberal democracy in *La organización de la
paz* (1925). Another recruit was Manuel Gálvez, whose suspicion of
'cosmopolitanism' in 1910 became by 1929 an appeal to authority,
hierarchy and Catholic 'spirituality'. He even advocated 'a new
revolution, founded on principles opposite to those which animated the
French Revolution and its derivatives socialism and bolshevism'.[149] Both
Gálvez and Lugones were associated with the bimonthly *La Nueva
República* (1927–31), which called for a functional democracy based on
the 'vital forces of society', and which supported the brief corporate state
experiment of General José F. Uriburu in 1930. Whereas the Liga
Patriótica had made some attempt to broaden its base to include workers
and lower middle class elements, the new nationalism was militantly
elitist, presaging a basic conflict within future authoritarian movements
in Argentina.

The emergence of corporatism in the 1920s revealed the persistence of an
authoritarian tradition in politics, fortified in the late nineteenth century
by the scientific argument for strong government and by the positivist
emphasis on social hierarchy and organic evolution. That political
tradition was challenged, first by the constitutionalist movement of
1889–93, then by the democratic impulse of 1910–20 and finally by
socialism and indigenous radicalism. However, the ideological consensus achieved by the governing and intellectual elite by the late 1880s was
strong enough to withstand these challenges. In fact, this consensus was
reinforced by the heritage of liberalism, with its dominant emphasis on

[148] The long-time leader of the Liga was Manuel Carlés (1872–1946), a former teacher and
conservative deputy.
[149] Gálvez, discussing 'dictatorships' in the Catholic journal *Criterio*, June 13, 1929, as quoted in
Sandra F. McGee, 'Social origins of counterrevolution in Argentina, 1900–1932', unpublished
Ph.D. thesis, University of Florida, 1979, 257.

the strong secular state in combination with economic individualism. The liberal ideal of constitutional limitations on central authority was gradually eroded by the social, historical and racial theories which culminated in turn-of-the-century positivism. The consensus among the elite could also survive the idealist attack on the philosophic assumptions of positivism, in part because of the political and social ambiguities of the new idealism itself. Though authoritarianism may well have been the prevailing tendency of the years 1870 to 1930, this fact should not obscure our appreciation of the richness and diversity of the political and social ideas of the era.

11

THE LITERATURE, MUSIC AND ART OF
LATIN AMERICA, 1870–1930

INTRODUCTION

By the time the great romantic writer Domingo Faustino Sarmiento (1811–88) became president of Argentina in 1868 irresistible changes were sweeping over Latin America which were reflected in each of the arts, though above all in literature.[1] Most works produced at that time still seem romantic to modern eyes, but perceptible differences were emerging, how much or how soon depending largely on the city or region in which they originated. Some of the changes arose from purely internal factors, but the period around 1870 also saw the beginning of the intensification of the international division of labour and the more complete integration of the Latin American economies, including many regions of the interior, into the world economic system. The population of Latin America doubled during the second half of the nineteenth century, and the process of urbanization quickened: by 1900 Buenos Aires had one million inhabitants, Rio de Janeiro three-quarters of a million, Mexico City more than half a million, and a number of other cities, including São Paulo – which in 1850 had only 15,000 – were over a quarter of a million in size. By 1930 in some of the fastest growing cities 30 to 50 per cent of the population were European immigrants, mostly Italian and Spanish, or children of European immigrants. If the period 1830–70 had been mainly one of introspection and internal frustration, particularly in Spanish America, the period from 1870–1914 saw the continent looking outwards again, though an extra dimension of disillusionment, for peoples already sobered by decades of internal strife,

---

[1] This chapter is effectively a continuation of Martin, *The literature, music and art of Latin America from Independence to c. 1870, CHLA* III, chap. 18. The reader is referred to that work as background to the present chapter.

443

was added when Latin American nations began to wage large-scale wars on one another, as in the Paraguayan War (1864–70) and the War of the Pacific (1879–83). Most men began to see things more clearly in this new age of bourgeois 'realism', though others among them – those, ironically, who would call themselves 'modernists' – soon decided that they would rather not see anything at all, and tried to retreat into fantasy and evasion.

The relation of Latin American culture to European models has always involved the complexity of response to be found in any colonial or neo-colonial relationship with the metropolitan centres. A review of the relation during the period 1870–1930 reveals the most varied hybridizations and disjunctures, fusions and fissures, and the most elementary questions of form and content become problematical in such a context. These overlap in any case with such enduring themes in the history of aesthetic philosophy as the relation of mind to emotion, which in the nineteenth-century practice of artistic expression was juxtaposed as the antagonism, firstly of neo-classicism, then of realism, to romanticism. On the whole Latin American artists have tended to opt for passion, spontaneity and intuition, which explains the continuing influence of nineteenth-century romanticism and the special importance of surrealism in the twentieth century. Moreover, in Latin American art as a whole the search for knowledge and self-knowledge – whether undertaken by the mind, the emotions or the senses – characteristic of all Western art since the Renaissance, when European explorers 'discovered' Latin America, has been combined in that region since the early nineteenth century, as in other ex-colonial territories, with the quest for national and continental identity and self-expression.

This chapter will trace the path taken by Latin American writers and artists, architects and musicians, through the labyrinth of Latin American culture from the 1870s to the 1930s. It will treat not just literature but all the arts, and will compare and contrast the cultural experience of both Spanish America and Brazil. This requires a carefully planned approach and implies a complex architectural structure built on solid foundations and then tracked cinematographically from one part of the edifice to another until the picture is complete. In the arts the period 1870–1930, probably the most decisive in the continent's history, falls conveniently into two phases, 1870 to 1900 and 1900 to 1930, though the period 1900–14 is as much a transition as a part of the second era, due to Latin America's neo-colonial destiny as a late developer in the field of cultural activity. At the same time the arts themselves may be conceived, during both these phases, as advancing simultaneously on two fronts – whose paths unite only in the most outstanding cases in the early part of the period, but with increasing frequency after 1920 – namely, those of nativism and cosmopolitanism broadly understood. The generalized divorce in European art after romanticism, between 'realism' and what may loosely be termed 'impressionism', or between objective and subjective approaches to experience, seen most vividly in Latin America in the literary divide between *naturalismo* and *modernismo* from the 1870s to 1914, was prolonged in the continent after the First World War in the contrast between *regionalismo* and *vanguardismo* (or *modernismo*, confusingly, in Brazil). The greatest artists, on the whole, are those who manage to resolve, or rise above, the dilemmas posed by such radical alternatives.

Our broad strategy, then, is to treat the arts as ultimately indivisible, examining each of the major art forms in turn and within them outlining notable trends and illustrating these by reference to leading artists and their works; and to treat Latin America as a cultural unity (however contradictory at any given moment), whilst nonetheless giving full and proper regard to national and regional variations. Since positivism was the unifying ideology of the age,[2] we begin with its most direct reflection in artistic expression, the realist–naturalist narrative, accompanied by a brief survey of Latin American theatre in this same era. There follows an exploration of the contrasting cosmopolitan movements – especially fertile in poetry – known as *modernismo* in Spanish America and *parnasianismo-simbolismo* in Brazil. Music and painting, usually ignored in histories of this kind, are then briefly reviewed, bringing to an end the first phase of the period and the first half of the chapter. Once the scene has been set for the early 1900s, architecture is treated both retrospectively and prospectively, looking back at the nineteenth-century experience and revealing how, with the rise of the great cities and mass culture, Latin American architecture suddenly zoomed up to date and came to symbolize the continent's coming of age at the height of modernity. The chapter then doubles back upon itself by immediately picking up the story in painting and music and following the trends up to the end of the 1920s, thereby setting the stage for the completion of developments in narrative and poetry, so dependent during this period on the discoveries

---

[2] See Hale, *CHLA* IV, chap. 10.

in music, the plastic arts and architecture. The story of the 1920s is viewed primarily in terms of the continuation of realist forms through regionalism, together with the rise of a new revolutionary aesthetic advanced by young avant-garde groups from the new generation born with the century, and ends appropriately with a review of the early decades of the most modern and visual of all the arts, the cinema.

THE LATE NINETEENTH CENTURY

The novel

So strong was the influence of positivism in the last decades of the nineteenth century that literature was either against it, as in the case of modernism, or went over to it wholesale, as in the case of naturalism. Whilst romanticism would remain a permanent feature of the Latin American self-image, because of its identification with independence, its ingredients would now be variously adapted, condensed or re-interpreted; and although both naturalism in fiction and the theatre, and modernism in poetry, would each retain certain continuities with the preceding movement, their divergences from it are more striking. In Europe the realism of Balzac and Stendhal preceded the naturalism of Zola and Maupassant; but Latin America had produced no Balzacs between 1830 and 1860, since the conditions which had produced him were entirely absent. Most Latin American novelists of realist persuasion thereafter relapsed into an anachronistic romantic version on the model of Scott, or degenerated into the less subtle naturalist mode. Realism, after all, is a historical product of the European bourgeoisie after the formation of nation states. It requires sociological complexity, psychological subtlety and a sure grasp of historical process; whereas all the vulgar naturalist has to do is swear by science, concentrate on the sordid and the shocking, and ensure that his characters are determined by the iron laws of heredity and environment. What could have been more suitable as a form for containing the contradictions of a historical moment in which the mainly white elites chose to blame the cultural backwardness of their respective nations on the supposed biological inferiority of the races with whom they were unfortunate enough to share their nationality? Contrary to first appearances, however, naturalism was in many respects an optimistic movement. Its desire to shock, which in the hands of superficial or conservative writers was merely a romantic throwback to the melodramatic or the gothic, was meant to galvanize, not dismay; and its interest in the sordid was really a desire to undermine the residual ideology of precisely those remaining romantics who still believed in some immanent realm of spirituality, or the catholics who continued to imagine that truth was metaphysical. For the naturalist, man lived in an entirely material world, and was an animal: when that was understood, progress was possible.

Given the relatively fluent assimilation of influences from Europe in the nineteenth century, and the close relation between Brazilian and French literature throughout the period, it is not surprising that naturalism flourished more vigorously in Brazil than elsewhere. And it was the north-east particularly which produced the outstanding natural-ist writers between 1870 and 1920, just as it would produce the regionalist movement in the 1920s. Part of this regional–naturalist impulse stemmed from the harsh realities of slavery and its abolition and the transition from *engenho* to *usina*. This was hardly an equivalent process to the conflicts between capital and labour which had helped to focus naturalism in Europe, but it was certainly more perceptibly dramatic than most contemporary labour conflicts in Spanish America, and it also involved the racial question. The Negro had been virtually invisible in romantic fiction: only one novel, *A escrava Isaura* (1875), by Bernardo Joaquim da Silva Guimarães (1825–84), stood up at all for the blacks in the way that Castro Alves (1847–71) had in poetry.[3] A transitional figure, Guimarães was one of the first to treat seriously the folklore of the interior, in this case Minas Gerais, and he dealt also with banditry, the *sertão* and contemporary social themes (as, for example, in *O seminarista*, (1872)). Unfortunately, although bohemian and scandalous in real life, his literary style was colourless.

The true precursor of the naturalist school was the north-eastern polemicist Franklin da Silveira Távora (1842–88), author of an early historical novel, *Os índios do Jaguaribe* (1861), followed by more sociologically informed works such as *Um casamento no arrabalde* (1869), *O cabeleira* (1876) and *O matuto* (1878). The first systematic employer of history and folklore – as against mere romance and local colour – in Brazilian fiction, Távora is so concerned with his documentary materials emphasizing the relation between character and environment, that his personages are frequently overwhelmed and denied the gift of life. A

[3] See Martin, *CHLA* iii, chap. 18.

liberal humanitarian and militant republican, he is especially remembered for his vitriolic attacks upon José de Alencar's patrician detachment from reality.[4] As a northerner, he resented Alencar's efforts to move the centre of literary gravity to the south at a time when coffee was beginning to alter the hegemonic pattern of the national economy. Like Argentine defenders of the *pampas* and later advocates of the Venezuelan *llanos* or the Peruvian *sierras* in symbolic fiction, Távora, the authentic precursor of the 1926 regionalist movement, believed that the soul of Brazil lay in the north-east, whilst the south was the port of entry for alien cosmopolitan influences.

The first unmistakably naturalist novelist, and the first Brazilian to live by pen alone, was Aluísio de Azevedo (1857–1913), who had read both Zola and Eça de Queirós. His literary stance is more conscious and uncompromising than that of any Spanish American novelist of the age. His first novel, *Uma lágrima de mulher* (1880), was still lingeringly romantic, but Azevedo developed astonishingly quickly – suggesting that programmatic naturalism is the inverse of an exalted but disappointed romanticism – and *O mulato* (1881) created a sensation, although a mild one as things turned out compared with the scandal provoked by *O homen* (1887), a case study of female sexual hysteria. Other important works were *Casa de pensão* (1884) and *O cortiço* (1890), an urban naturalistic classic. The very titles of these works reveal a more theoretical, almost sociological dimension to the movement in Brazil. Azevedo's books caused bitter controversy, provoking the same uproar in church and landowning circles as Clorinda Matto de Turner (see below) would elicit in conservative Peru at the end of the 1880s. Despite this, or because of it, Azevedo enjoyed great popular success.

Azevedo was by no means alone. Some critics assert that *O coronel sangrado* (1877) by Herculano Marcos Inglês de Sousa (1853–1918) is the first true naturalist novel in Brazil. Better known today is *O missionário* in which a priest falls in love with an Indian girl in the Amazon wilderness, a favourite naturalist motif. Most Zolaesque of all was Júlio César Ribeiro (1845–1890), a writer involved in all the great issues of his time, who achieved great success with *A carne* (1888), although to the modern reader only the scenes of sex and sadism seem convincingly achieved. Similar was Adolfo Ferreira Caminha (1867–97), as famous for his scandalous relationship with a married woman as for his novels, *A*

---

[4] *Ibid.*

normalista (1893), about small-town prejudice, and *Bom crioulo* (1895), about homosexuality in the navy, both denounced as immoral by the authorities. The response was another, equally scabrous work, *Tentação* (1896).

The cultivation of style seemed inappropriate to those naturalists attempting to change the way polite Brazilian society liked to view itself; yet in France the confluence of naturalist prose and parnassian poetry in Flaubert, Gautier and Maupassant had initiated a line which would eventually lead to Proust, Joyce, Virginia Woolf and the *nouveau roman*. Brazil produced two novelists closer to that model than to Zola. The first, Raul d'Avila Pompéia (1863–95), author of *Uma tragédia no Amazonas* (1880), is best known for *O Ateneu* (1888), a satirical recreation of his adolescent boarding-school experiences. Sometimes compared to Dickens, both for his subject matter and a certain eccentricity of perspective, he is normally considered a symbolist, for the glowing stylishness of writing which hovers between realism and impressionism whilst showing rare psychological insight. The other writer is for some the greatest of all Latin American novelists, Joaquim Maria Machado de Assis (1839–1908), the 'myopic, epileptic quadroon', who came to be considered the 'quintessential Brazilian'.[5] Born in poverty, later a typesetter and proofreader, then a journalist and critic, it was he who founded the Brazilian Academy in 1897. Devoted to his country yet intensely critical, he longed for full social acceptance and bitterly resented his treatment as a mulatto. His novels share with Pompéia's a command of the inner life: framed by social structures, but more psychological than sociological in emphasis. Aesthetically a parnassian, philosophically a determinist, Machado gave an oblique but accurate portrait of Brazil under the Second Empire. The first great novel, after his early poetic phase, was *Memórias póstumas de Brás Cubas* (1881), which begins with the death of its protagonist (recalling Sterne) and concludes: 'I had no progeny, I transmitted to no one the legacy of our misery.' Two other masterpieces of parody are *Quincas Borba* (1891) and *Dom Casmurro* (1899), both marked by precision, a finely balanced irony, sceptical humour and pervasive melancholy. The style is subtle, ingenious, sardonic, profoundly self-conscious; but also socially acute, even worldly-wise, recreating a world view circumscribed by all the determinants known to learned men at the time; also aware, finally, that

[5] See M. Seymour-Smith, *Guide to modern world literature* (4 vols., London, 1975), III, 152.

the imagination itself and its creations have their own relative autonomy, making this the first genuinely self-referential fiction in Latin America (though there were incipient signs in Lizardi's *El periquillo sarniento* at the beginning of the century) and anticipating twentieth-century developments. Machado also wrote poetry, drama, criticism and much journalism, contriving always to distance the immediate and the dramatic through the formal perfection of art. He was *sui generis*, a writer like Swift, Sterne, Kafka or Borges. Samuel Putnam declared in 1948 that no United States novelist – even Henry James – could compare with Machado, whilst William Grossman called him 'the most completely disenchanted writer in Occidental literature'.[6]

No republic in Spanish America can match the richness of Brazilian naturalism, but there too it soon predominated. A typical precursor was the Uruguayan Eduardo Acevedo Díaz (1851–1921), whose historical novels were radically different in focus from anything produced by romanticism. The best known Uruguayan naturalist, influenced by Azevedo, was the prolific Javier de Viana (1868–1926), noted for brutal short stories of life in the rural sector, like *Campo* (1896), or melodramatic novels after the manner of the polemical Spaniard Blasco Ibáñez (1867–1928), like *Gaucha* (1899). Carlos Reyles (1868–1938) wrote *Beba* (1894) and *El terruño* (1916), before turning to the more impressionist *El embrujo de Sevilla* (1922) and his masterpiece *El gaucho Florido* (1932). A wealthy landowner, Reyles combined imperious authoritarianism with a curiously sensitive aestheticism, revealing how close modernism and naturalism really were, as two sides of the same coin.

Nowhere in Latin America is the dialectic between city and country more complex, dramatic and continuous in this period than in Argentina, where the important 1880 generation of 'gentleman writers' carried Sarmiento's message forward after two decades in which the spectre of barbarism, in the shape of Indians, gauchos and general social anarchy, appeared to have been banished. The vivid documentary classic, *Una excursión a los indios ranqueles* (1870), by Lucio Mansilla (1831–1913), gives a remarkably humane soldier's view of the frontier between European civilization and the nomadic Indians a decade before Roca's notorious expedition, whilst Eduardo Gutiérrez (1851–89) produced in *Juan Moreira* (1879) a novel about the legendary gaucho bandit which, although rudimentary in technique, provided the first sign that the

[6] Samuel Putnam, *Marvelous journey: a survey of four centuries of Brazilian writing* (New York, 1948), 48; Grossman quoted in Seymour-Smith, *Guide to modern world literature* III, 152.

gaucho, after the age of Martín Fierro, was on his way to the cities. These works preceded those of the 1880 generation proper, men of leisure with time to enjoy the benefits worked for by others like Sarmiento who, as he remarked without bitterness near the end of his life, had struggled 'so that everyone might take part in life's banquet, which I could but do on the sly'.[7] The result was a naturalism without militancy, as revealed in *La gran aldea* (1884) by Lucio V. López (1848–94), which surveys the transformation of Buenos Aires in the first tide of immigration. As in *Juvenilia* (1884) by Miguel Cané (1851–1905), childhood reminiscences which can be read in revealing conjunction with Sarmiento's *Recuerdos de provincia*, we can sense the growing awareness of a newly cosmopolitan elite, in the era of the Grand Tour, bent on mythologizing its own past formation and securing its claim to the present and the future. Having defined themselves in opposition to the Indian and the gaucho, they would now define themselves in opposition to the waves of immigrants flooding into their republic. The Argentine version, then, would be a somewhat selective brand of naturalism.

Some immigrants were acceptable. Eduardo Wilde (1844–1913), son of an English aristocrat, typified the newly mobile Buenos Aires elite, and Paul Groussac (1848–1929), the half-French author of *Fruto vedado* (1884), semi-autobiographical reminiscences, became director of the National Library from 1885–1929. Even the fiction of the more tempestuous Eugenio Cambaceres (1843–88), arguably Spanish America's first genuine naturalist, contained numerous autobiographical elements, albeit less fondly and self-indulgently recalled. Cambaceres's works are written with the furious bitterness of the recent convert from romanticism: *Música sentimental* (1884), on the relationship between Buenos Aires and Paris; *Sin rumbo* (1885), on the relation between Buenos Aires and the provinces, with the most shocking scenes of sex and violence seen in Argentine literature up to that time; and *En la sangre* (1887), a thesis novel on heredity, environment and the dangers of immigration. Later works about changing Buenos Aires were *La Bolsa* (1891) by 'Julián Martel' (José Miró, 1867–96), dramatizing the rampant materialism of the era, and the stories of 'Fray Mocho' (José S. Alvárez, 1858–1903), a journalist on Mitre's *La Nación* whose books, like *Memorias de un vigilante* (1897), revealed a shabbier, more violent city than that of the literary gentlemen, and anticipated the tango era.

[7] See P. Henríquez Ureña, *Las corrientes literarias en la América hispánica* (Mexico, 1949), 140.

Chile's Alberto Blest Gana (1830–1920), persistently underestimated, is perhaps the nearest any nineteenth-century Latin American comes to emulating a Balzac or Galdós. His novels combine facets of the romantic historical novel, comedy of manners and naturalist slice of life, fused by a dominant realist intention. The best is *Martín Rivas* (1862), set in the Santiago he knew, though his most popular work was *Durante la reconquista* (1897), about the independence era. Similar in style though even less well known was the Bolivian Nataniel Aguirre (1843–88), whose *Juan de la Rosa* (1885) also recreated the independence struggles. Its genuinely popular Americanist standpoint makes it one of the most readable novels of the liberal era.

After Peru's shattering defeat in the War of the Pacific, two militant women novelists emerged, Mercedes Cabello de Carbonera (1845–1909), whose virulent assaults on corruption and social decay in *El conspirador* (1892), *Blanca Sol* (1889) and *Las consecuencias* (1889), provoked a counter-attack by the literary acolytes of the Lima oligarchy which eventually drove her into the municipal asylum; and Clorinda Matto de Turner (1854–1909), generally considered the first Latin American novelist to have produced a true indigenist novel, *Aves sin nido* (1889). Dedicated to González Prada (see below), the work caused scandal and led to excommunication and voluntary exile. She had followed Ricardo Palma, the creator of *Tradiciones peruanas*[8] with a series of *Tradiciones cuzqueñas* (1884–6), and her novel was tinged with romantic melodramatic hues, though genuinely anticlerical and anti-oligarchical. She directed a newspaper, *El Perú Ilustrado* (1892–5), a tribunal for social criticism, and produced another naturalist novel, *Herencia* (1893), on immigration and heredity. Interestingly, one of the first Bolivian indigenists was also a woman, Lindaura Anzoátegui de Campero (1846–98), indicating an intuitive empathy between different oppressed social groups. When so many naturalist novels were set in brothels, it is refreshing to find women looking elsewhere with critical insight and purpose.

The outstanding Colombian novelist of the era was Tomás Carrasquilla (1858–1940), an early *criollista* – not merely a costumbrist, since his grasp of folklore, social types and dialogue was always profoundly contextualized. His particular variant of naturalism, from *Frutos de mi tierra* (1896) to *La marquesa de Yolombó* (1926), anticipated the regionalist mode of the 1920s which he lived to see. With greater mastery

---

[8] See Martin, *CHLA* III, chap. 18.

of technique to match his observation and linguistic virtuosity, he would have become one of the major realists. By contrast José María Vargas Vila (1860–1933) cunningly used stock naturalist themes with a voluptuous late romantic, almost modernist style, to produce works of decadent allure and great popular appeal, including generous doses of anarchism and anti-imperialism, to produce a heady brew with titles like *Aura o las violetas* (1886) and *Flor de fango* (1895), works which allowed him, exceptionally, to live off their amoral earnings.

In Mexico nineteenth-century fiction had been curiously retarded, with a continuity of rather episodic, costumbrist narratives, provincial rather than regionalist. The effect of the war with the United States and the French invasion was to prolong romantic style and subject matter until well after the era of Ignacio Altamirano.[9] José López Portillo (1850–1923), with *La parcela* (1898), anticipated the fiction produced during the revolutionary period, turning to the rural sector in search of a nationalist literature. Other novelists of the time were Rafael Delgado (1853–1914), best known for *La calandria* (1891), and Emilio Rabasa (1856–1930), who, in *La bola* (1887), pointed the way to a genuinely modern critical realist perspective. Federico Gamboa (1864–1939) was Zola's most direct disciple in Spanish America: the protagonists of *Del natural* (1888) and *Suprema ley* (1896) were syphilis and alcohol (modernist works of the period were more likely to feature tuberculosis and opium), with humans mere incidentals acting according to thesis and therefore to type, exemplifying the subordination of character to theme which defines Latin American fiction to this day. *Metamórfosis* (1899) was about a nun who, abducted from the convent, gives herself up to lust; and *Santa* (1903), a name as well known now in Mexico as Zola's *Nana*, was another laboratory demonstration concerning the tragic life of a country girl who, seduced by a soldier, becomes a Mexico City prostitute.

The theatre

The theatre was stagnating in most Latin American countries in the last decades of the century. During the post-independence period, although the quality of writing and performance had not been high, a dramatized sense of history itself had given impetus to the form. Thereafter most writers, responding to public demand, would become

---

[9] *Ibid.*

known first for their novels or poetry and only then feel secure in turning to the stage. Few of these works of secondary enthusiasm have survived; yet playwrights who were not already novelists found it difficult to get plays performed, since theatre owners preferred to play safe. Thus foreign plays, operas, actors and singers predominated. Sarah Bernhardt and the great soprano Adelina Patti, for example, made well publicised visits to cities like Rio de Janeiro, Buenos Aires and Mexico City.

At the same time, other entertainments developed to compete with the theatre. In the 1870s the *can-can* reached Latin America, to the disgust of many and delight of more, and could be guaranteed to fill theatres when more sober fare was flagging. French comic opera was introduced during the same decade, and Bizet's *Carmen*, 'the Spanish cigarette girl who speaks French and dances Cuban', became the rage. Not to be outdone by Gallic invaders, the Spanish *género chico*, in particular the *zarzuela*, likewise grew more popular at the expense of local theatrical activity; it was at the same time more easily Americanized, particularly in Mexico, where by the end of the century titles like *Viva México* were becoming common. The first truly Mexican *zarzuela*, *Una fiesta en Santa Anita* (1886) by Juan de Dios Peza (1852–1910) and Luis Alcaraz, caused a popular sensation. In the great capitals the *café dansant* and the nocturnal restaurant, frequented by dandies, bohemians and intellectuals, and deplored by the *gente decente*, became fashionable. By the early 1880s most people of moderate income had queued to hear the first phonographs in local theatres. In the 1890s American *vaudeville* reached Latin America, and in the same decade the first cinematographs arrived and developed with astonishing rapidity, auguring badly for the theatre's potential growth in countries where a national tradition had never really been established.

Thus, in most Latin American countries drama, which had never scaled the aesthetic heights, entered upon relative popular decline. Naturalist theatre, however, slowly gained momentum. In Mexico Ibsen's *Ghosts* arrived only in 1896, and went unappreciated, but already in 1894 the stolid Federico Gamboa had tried to emulate his achievement. It was Gamboa who in 1905 produced *La venganza de la gleba*, the first mexican drama to condemn the feudal system of land tenure, though characterized more by 'Victorian' sentimentality than by any revolutionary impulse. So dire was the general situation in Mexico that in 1906 Justo Sierra, education minister at the time, launched a drama competition to save the nation from the stranglehold of the music-hall. Sixty plays were entered; all have been forgotten. The situation was similar in most of the other major Spanish American republics, and in Brazil.

All this makes the astonishing theatrical renaissance of the River Plate region at the very high-point of *modernismo* all the more remarkable. This can be explained not only by the rapid growth of Buenos Aires and Montevideo, but also by the particular nature of the transition between country and city and the need for a unifying national mythology at a time of great internal change and heavy immigration. An Uruguayan impresario, José Podestá (1857–1937), began to combine performances in his circus in Buenos Aires with pantomimes and dramas using gaucho themes and trick riding, not unlike William Cody's Wild West circus in the United States. Podestá's first show in 1884 was based on Gutiérrez' *Juan Moreira*, mimed at first and then, in 1886, recited. His family formed travelling companies which toured Argentina and Uruguay, finally moving in 1901 from the suburbs to Buenos Aires, when gaucho themes began to be supplanted by other dramas which attracted a broadly based audience. More ambitious writers now emerged to fill the gap between this popular native theatre inspired by rural themes and the classical European theatre performed by foreign companies in the elegant zones of the city. In 1902 Martiniano Leguizamón (1858–1935), with *Calandria*, and Martín Coronado (1850–1919), with the Ibsenesque *La piedra del escándalo*, achieved overnight acclaim. An important stimulus to serious theatre was the critic Juan Pablo Echagüe (1877–1950), whose erudite commentaries were collected in *Puntos de vista* (1905) and *Teatro argentino* (1917). But the key figure of the era was the Uruguayan Florencio Sánchez (1875–1910), who produced a score of dramas, *sainetes* and comedies during a brief career, showing most clearly how quickly Argentine theatre moved from the melodramatic, mythologized deeds of gaucho outlaws to the real conflicts of ownership and exploitation in the rural sector at the time. His best known works, informed by anarchist and socialist thought, and his intimate acquaintance with suburban down-at-heel Buenos Aires and the outlying rural districts, were *M'hijo el dotor* (1903), *La gringa* (1904), the sombre masterpiece *Barranca abajo* (1905), and *Los muertos* (1905), a naturalist thesis drama written in two days about alcoholism, which, with tuberculosis and poverty, was what sent the great playwright to an early grave.

Poetry

In both Spanish America and Brazil during the late nineteenth century, we see one of those moments where form and content move into sharp contradiction, with prose, under the influence of Positivism, moving firmly in the direction of naturalism and poetry moving in the direction of *modernismo*, broadly speaking an amalgam of the European literary movements then in vogue and corresponding thereby to the moment of impressionism. In Brazil poets merely emulated the French movements – parnassianism (Leconte de Lisle, Gautier) and symbolism (Mallarmé, Verlaine) – and used the same names. It would be difficult to demonstrate a significant process of Brazilianization. Yet it was only in Brazil, as we have seen, that a Pompéia or Machado could unite the formal exquisiteness of parnassian poetry with the social relevance of naturalist fiction to produce the narrative masterpieces of the era. No Spanish American novelist came close to this achievement, in view of the more radical separation of poetry (including 'poetic' short prose) and narrative.

It is sometimes tempting to conclude that the Brazilians were right: Parnassianism possibly would have been the best name for that movement which swept the entire continent from 1870 to almost 1920, and Modernism would have been better reserved – as in Brazil – for the avant-garde currents after the First World War. (This would also have been less confusing to European and North American critics.) At first sight, indeed, there seems nothing in the least 'modern' in those rather ethereal would-be aristocrats, literary poseurs who sang of swans and princesses and seemed to long for ancient regimes. Yet the cries of 'Art for Art's sake' (Darío always wrote the word Art with a capital letter) were really more desperate than defiant, for most of these young poets were journalists and stood in quite a different relation to the literary mode of production than might be guessed from their published poems. Moreover, on closer examination *modernismo* was less apolitical than some critical mythologies suggest. In contrast to the romantic period, politics was expelled from the poetry itself. But most of the *modernista* poets maintained close relationships with leading *pensadores*; many were anarchists or socialists; almost all were nationalists and anti-imperialists.

The 'modernism' or modernity claimed was to be understood above all as a *modernisation of poetry*. This is more significant than the uninitiated might suppose, since the pompous sterility and oratorical arthritis of

Spanish poetry a century ago is difficult now to recapture. Latin American poetry was not truly modern by the end of modernism, but was fully ready to become so. The range of formal and thematic innovations of the movement was extraordinary. The subject matter of poetry, though extremely limited in tone and mood, ranged far and wide in time and space. Latin American themes, considered essential throughout the romantic period, now lay neglected by most poets. Latin America, after all, was not modern, and viewed from Parnassus or Olympus was hardly a suitable subject for aesthetic exploration. The poets would only return to it when they themselves had become modernised.

Much critical time and space has been occupied in debating when Spanish American modernism began – no one disputes that it was Rubén Darío who made it visible with the publication of *Azul* in 1888 – and who were its pathfinders and pioneers. One poet universally considered a 'precursor', even though he outlived Darío, was Manuel González Prada (1848–1918). His earliest works showed a precision and artistry quite foreign to poetry in Spanish at that time, Bécquer excepted, with an astonishing variety of experimental forms and metres. Like his contemporary Martí, González Prada saw literature generally as a high civic calling, but considered poetry pure and autonomous. Such a stance, which would seem astonishing today in a man of his orientation, only underlines the reversion at that time to the classical distinction imposed between poetry and prose. González Prada never troubled to diffuse his poetry, however, and had only limited influence outside Peru.[10]

Another important 'precursor' of *modernismo* was the Cuban José Martí (1853–95). As a poet, he stands as one of the greatest of all time in Spanish, for his remarkable combination of simplicity, ingenuity and vigour, appearing classical even when his verse was in reality intricate and innovative. In prose, he was, along with Juan Montalvo (Ecuador, 1832–89)[11] – best remembered for his famous boast, 'My pen has killed him', when the dictator García Moreno was assassinated in 1875 – one of the great stylists of the period. As the supreme journalist of the era, Martí had the ability to coin phrases which have become part of Spanish American culture. Exiled at sixteen, after a year in prison, Martí devoted

[10] See Hale, *CHLA* IV, chap. 10.
[11] Juan Montalvo's best-known articles were collected in *El Cosmopolita* (1866) and *El Regenerador* (1872). *Capítulos que se le olvidaron a Cervantes* followed in 1873. In 1883 he began to publish his *Siete Tratados*, and in 1886, exiled in Panama, he published the famous *Las Catilinarias* followed by four series of essays under the title *El Espectador* (Paris, 1886–9).

his entire adult life to the Cuban revolutionary cause; when unable to return to Cuba, he contributed to the literary and civic culture of every country he visited (notably Mexico and Guatemala), and spent fourteen years in the United States. In this respect his career was similar to his Puerto Rican contemporary, Eugenio María de Hostos (1839–1903), who also devoted his life to the struggle against Spanish colonialism and who, like Darío, travelled the entire Latin American region, campaigning, writing and teaching wherever he went. Martí wrote the first modernist novel, *Amistad funesta* (1885), and his children's stories, *La edad de oro* (1889), have become classics of the genre. Much of his poetry, such as *Versos libres* (*c.* 1883) and *Flores del destierro*, was published posthumously. Collections which appeared during his lifetime were *Ismaelillo* (1882), delightful miniature masterpieces inspired by his absent baby son; and *Versos sencillos* (1891), as diaphanous and direct as the poet's own existence. He was killed in 1895 leading a military expedition against the Spaniards in Cuba. His example as man of action and man of letters, poet and patriot, is one whose impact on Latin American history could scarcely be exaggerated.

Because Martí and González Prada were greater as men than other modernists, critics have been tempted to see them, in their courage, their heroic individualism and political constancy, as romantic writers; but it is a distortion of the movement to seek to remove from it all whose life or work contained political content, or to assume that those who died young (Silva, Casal – see below) or gloriously (Martí) were really late romantics. On the contrary, what gave the movement its unifying force and differentiated it from contemporary Brazilian developments was precisely the fact that *modernismo* was not only a Spanish American version of parnassian–symbolist formal refinement, but a retarded assimilation of the full philosophical weight of romanticism, whose impact (due to the emphasis on political and historical currents) had been incomplete in Spanish America, together with an incorporation of the second, decadent phase of European romanticism: the 'romantic agony'. The genius of Darío, to whom we shall shortly be turning, is that only in his poetry and his person did all three phases – an accumulation of the entire European poetic experience of the nineteenth century – reach true harmony. Thus *modernismo* was not a school but a broad historical movement which influenced all important poets in the region after 1888; and which can be divided into two periods, before and after Darío's *Prosas profanas* in 1896, at which point a shift takes place from the north of the continent, where it first gained momentum, to the south. Many poets may have seemed, or may actually have been, tormented romantic personalities, or even men of action (Díaz Mirón, Gómez Carrillo, Chocano – see below), but their means of expression had changed irremediably.

Martí and González Prada, then, were part of the modernist tide, but both swept beyond its more limited, merely ornamental positions. One who was a *modernista* pure and simple, before Darío, was Manuel Gutiérrez Nájera (1859–95), founder of the celebrated *Revista Azul* (1894–6) in Mexico City. Curiously, he was from a humble background, but became the most aristocratic of the new writers (his pseudonym was 'El duque Job'); moreover, almost uniquely, he never left his native city, but acted and wrote, with extraordinary intuition, as if he were the best travelled and most experienced of writers. His early models were romantic (Musset, Bécquer), but already refined by his own sense of style; as each new poet – Leconte de Lisle, Verlaine, Baudelaire, Poe – became fashionable, Gutiérrez Nájera absorbed them and dosed them into his own frivolous, sophisticated but remarkably accomplished and musical poetry and newspaper pieces. One of his poems, the charming 'La duquesa Job', is a modernist classic. This writer of innately likeable poetry was as delicate as his verse, and died at the age of thirty-six. As though to demonstrate how different modernist poets can be, his Mexican contemporary, Salvador Díaz Mirón (1853–1928), has been called 'un montonero de las letras'.[12] Twice imprisoned for shooting enemies dead in gun battles, exiled by Porfirio Díaz, his life was of a turbulence only equalled by Martí and Chocano (see below). His famous verse, 'Some feathers cross the swamp/ and bear no stain: such is my plumage', shows not only his provocative temperament, but his insistence – for the phrase also has a literary connotation – that the new poetry need not avoid all serious or substantive content to be 'pure' and beautiful. Only González Prada equalled his determination both to innovate and to avoid all frivolity, and careful readers can trace the path by which American romanticism – Díaz Mirón's first heroes were Byron and Hugo – becomes transformed from an oratorical, essentially external impulse into a more contained, because more carefully internalized, perspective; from his first collection of *Poesías* (1886) to *Lascas* (1901).

More like Gutiérrez Nájera was the Cuban Julián del Casal (1863–93).

[12] L. A. Sánchez, *Historia comparada de las literaturas americanas* (4 vols., Buenos Aires, 1976), III, 111.

Dogged by ill-health, personal misfortune and the island's tragedy, his profoundly anguished version of *mal-de-siècle* decadence nourished a longing to escape to Europe ('Mine is the city's impure love/ and to this sun forever up above/ I much prefer the gaslight's flickering glow'). Neurotic, pessimistic, melancholy, he was influenced by Gautier, Baudelaire and his half-French compatriot, José María de Heredia (1842–95), a leading parnassian whose *Les Trophées* appeared in the year of Casal's death. Similar, but even more authentically tragic, was the life and death of the Colombian José Asunción Silva (1865–96), whose biography is worthy of a Keats or Shelley half a century before him. Like his friend Jorge Isaacs[13] and Casal, Silva suffered the collapse of his family's fortune; his sister Elvira, for whom he felt an obsessive love, died aged twenty-one (Isaacs wrote a famous elegy); he lost most of his writings in a shipwreck; suffered, perhaps more than any of his contemporaries, the despair of romanticism's collision with positivism and materialism; and finally shot himself. Profoundly influenced by Poe, Bécquer and Baudelaire, his *Nocturno* ('Una noche,/ una noche toda llena de murmullos . . .') is among the most famous of Spanish American poems, and his novel, *De sobremesa*, is one of the most characteristic prose works produced by the *fin-de-siècle* mentality. Silva was tortured by the narrow provincial environment of Bogotá, and typifies the sense of marginality and alienation behind much modernist poetry. Positivism denied the artist's right to a central position, denied even that art was important; saw it, rather, like everything else, in instrumental terms, as entertainment, ornamental, decorative, diversionary; whereupon most poets, themselves dimly hankering after a pre-capitalist system of patronage, confirmed the perceptions of the positivists by retreating into a poetry that seemed largely intranscendent, evasive and – at first sight – irrelevant to Latin America's real needs.

The man who moulded the entire modernist movement – and gave it its name – was Rubén Darío (1867–1916), the child prodigy from a small town in Nicaragua who became the most influential poet in the Spanish language since Góngora. Critics now commonly deny his poetry's aesthetic quality, but nothing can shake his place in history, for as Pedro Henríquez Ureña correctly stated, 'Faced with any poem written in Spanish, one can state precisely whether it was written before or after Darío.'[14] He escaped for a long time from the tragic sense of life which

---

[13] See Martin, *CHLA* III, chap. 18.
[14] Henríquez Ureña, *Corrientes literarias*, 173.

carried Casal and Silva to early graves, but he too, in the end, succumbed to the same anguish ('Not knowing where we are going/ nor whence we have come . . .') and the same undermining of his own health. Darío's exemplary trajectory ('Strong with Hugo and ambiguous with Verlaine'), viewed entire, confirms that beneath the opulent surface modernism was indeed a simultaneous assimilation of the still unabsorbed aspects of European romanticism ('Who that is, is not a romantic?') and of parnassianism–symbolism, all within Latin America's invariable tendency to the baroque. It brought poetry in Spanish to formal perfection for the first time since Quevedo and Góngora at precisely the moment when all conventions of metre and verse, like all other artistic conventions, were about to be exploded: that is, just in time, for there was no inevitability about this. Yet Darío's gesture was still more expansive. It was also a celebration, an assimilation of the whole European tradition going back to the Renaissance, which Spain had largely denied or rejected, including romanticism itself, which Spain had been unable fully to absorb and which Spanish America had partly denied. Modernism is to be understood, then, not as 'French poetry written in Spanish', as some have averred, but as a profound rejection of the still living Spanish medieval tradition, a liberation both symbolic in general terms and concrete in the special cases of Puerto Rico and Cuba. At the same time, since Latin American romanticism had, for obvious reasons, largely excluded the classical, biblical and medieval motifs so characteristic of European romanticism, *modernismo* now incorporated these whilst purging them of any possible Hispanic content: that is, Spain now became one more cosmopolitan option among others, a normalization of cultural relations that said much for the sophistication of that poetic generation. In throwing off once and for all the Spanish cultural heritage – indeed, in reversing the process by beginning to influence the mother country – they paved the way for the full literary modernization of the continent, visible immediately in the 1920s with the emergence of poets like Huidobro, Vallejo and Neruda, and narrators like Asturias, Carpentier and Borges. North American poetry also now exerted some influence through two seminal figures: Poe and Whitman. As for France, it lured Latin Americans not only for the obvious positive reasons – the Enlightenment, the Revolution, the continuous ability to produce artistic schools with precise philosophies and practices – but also for equally obvious negative ones: it was Latin, but not Spanish or Portuguese; and it was modern, but not Anglo-Saxon.

Darío was not only the greatest *modernista* poet in terms of fluency, flexibility and musicality, he not only synthesized the movement as a whole within his eclectic, morally opaque but aesthetically diaphanous poetry; he was also the most travelled of the leading poets and indeed, most strikingly, he travelled throughout Latin America. It was in Chile that he published *Abrojos* (1887) and *Azul* (1888), and in Argentina, *Los raros* and *Prosas profanas* (1896); but everywhere he enthused poets young and old, inspiring clubs and associations, and writing innumerable articles for newspapers in each country he visited. In Europe he spent long periods of residence both in Paris, home of the new, and Spain, home of the old, where *Cantos de vida y esperanza* was published in 1905. Exoticist, taking in all the romantic places which, in that newly mobile age, he had seen or dreamed of seeing; nostalgic for past ages of which aristocratically inclined Americans wished to consider themselves heirs, particularly Greece and Rome; cosmopolitan in his desire, shared by the entire generation of elite groups of the region, to transform Latin America into a 'universal' culture, centred on Paris but inspired by Versailles (itself, as heir to classical antiquity, the inspiration for the new monumental city centres of Buenos Aires and Porfirian Mexico); frivolously aesthetic, finally, with a New World hedonism and an innocent eroticism in the midst of the knowing *belle époque*, Darío encapsulates the movement and unifies it. Poets after the Great War would find in socialism a new substitute for religion; Darío claimed to live for art, but art failed to comfort him in his middle years, and sexual distraction merely underlined the transience of life. The poetry of his last years ceased to be merely pictorial or musical composition, however exquisite and compelling, and searched anew for meaning; in the words of Anderson Imbert, 'he poeticized, with incomparable elegance, the joy of living and the terror of dying.'[15] But he was never capable of very precise thinking, confining himself in the vaguest – symbolist, impressionistic – terms to what Sánchez calls his 'movement of enthusiasm towards freedom and beauty'. His contribution to the cosmopolitan element within modern Spanish American culture is as great as Martí's contribution to its specifically Americanist side: Martí universalized all things American; Darío Americanized all things universal. Between them they effectively systematize the movement and the era. Only Darío could unify it, however, partly because of his virtuosity, partly because of

[15] E. Anderson Imbert, *Historia de la literatura hispanoamericana* (2 vols., Mexico, 3rd edn., 1966), I, 407.

his very eclecticism, his refusal to accept any ideological centre except that of Art itself.

As we have noted, the impetus for modernism came from the north of Latin America – Mexico, Central America, the Caribbean and Colombia. In Argentina it came late and would perhaps not have become as important or taken the form it did had Darío not stayed there after 1890 and exerted his powerful influence through Mitre's *La Nación*. Two names above all stand out: Julio Herrera y Reissig (Uruguay, 1875–1910), another short-lived poet, elitist and escapist, the most baroque and Gongorist, but, for a minority of critics, the most innately talented of all; and Leopoldo Lugones (1874–1938), one of the most influential writers in all Argentine literature, whose prose poems *Las montañas de oro* (1897) really initiated Argentine modernism. His prestige was secured in 1905 by *Los crepúsculos del jardín* and the prose epic, *La guerra gaucha*. *El payador*, his study of gaucho troubadours, appeared in 1916. Its nostalgic romantic perspective revealed his increasingly nationalist position, and in 1924, having begun as an anarchist and atheist, then become a socialist, he identified himself with fascism and catholicism. Embittered at his ensuing rejection by the younger generation, he eventually committed suicide. He has since been recognized as a fundamental figure both in Argentine literature and in modernist poetry generally, symbolizing, as Luis Alberto Sánchez has said, 'the almost arrogant will to triumph characteristic of the Argentines of his generation'.[16]

Similar to Lugones in many respects was the Peruvian poet José Santos Chocano (1875–1934), the great hothead of Spanish American poetry, who at his height was conceded the title 'poet of America', which Rodó (see below) had felt should be denied to Darío. Frequently imprisoned, married three times but never divorced, enemy and friend of dictators, briefly secretary to Pancho Villa, sentenced to death in 1920 in Guatemala, he became a fascist in 1925, murdered the young Peruvian intellectual Edwin Elmore, and was himself murdered by a schizophrenic on a tram in Santiago de Chile. He was perhaps the least modernist of the poets of his era. Dante, Byron, Hugo and Whitman were his models, the American landscape and its inhabitants, both human and animal, his themes, from *Alma América* (1906) and ¡*Fiat Lux*! (1908). He initiated a movement called *mundonovismo* ('I am the singer of America,

16 Sánchez, *Literaturas americanas*, III, 191.

autochthonous and wild . . .'), and was the first major poet to treat positively the themes of *indigenismo* and *mestizaje*. Yet his literary persona was egocentric and grandiloquent, his poetry essentially demagogic, Hispanic and oratorical (his public declamations were celebrated throughout the region). His achievement was to carry some of the great uncompleted themes of romanticism forward to the 1920s, where they fused with the new regional, telluric and criollist movements.

Other important modernists were Darío's lifelong friend, Francisco Gavidia (El Salvador, 1863–1950), Aquileo J. Echevarría (Costa Rica, 1866–1909), Darío Herrera (Panama, 1870–1914), Ricardo Miró (Panama, 1883–1940), Fabio Fiallo (Santo Domingo, 1866–1942), Luis Llorens Torres (Puerto Rico, 1878–1944), the Mexicans Manuel José Othón (1858–1906), Francisco A. de Icaza (1863–1925), Luis G. Urbina (1869–1934), Efrén Rebolledo Hidalgo (1877–1929) and José Juan Tablada (1871–1945), the Venezuelans Rufino Blanco Fombona (1874–1944), well known also as a novelist and historian, and his sworn enemy, Andrés Mata (1870–1931); the Colombian Guillermo Valencia (1873–1943), author of *Ritos* (1899), a wealthy poet who was perhaps the most 'classical' of the modernists; José María Eguren (Peru, 1874–1942), whose very personal vision carried him beyond the movement's typical banalities; Ricardo Jaimes Freyre (1868–1933), a Bolivian who spent many years in Argentina, politically radical yet author of *Castalia bárbara* (1899), suffused by strange nordic myths; and his compatriot Franz Tamayo (1879–1956).

The movement was waning before Darío died in 1916. In 1911 Enrique González Martínez (1871–1952) travelled from the provinces to Mexico City with his poems, *Los senderos ocultos*, including one which began: 'Wring the swan's neck, his plumage deceives/ though he lends his white note to the fountain's blue,/ he parades his pale beauty, but has no clue/ to the voice of the earth, or the spirit it breathes'. Since the swan was one of Darío's most characteristic images, it was clear that the Mexican was proposing an end to modernism. It is, however, arguable that the Darío of *Cantos de vida y esperanza* had already initiated precisely the kind of shift from formal complexity to bare simplicity demanded by González Martínez. Such a shift, needless to say, would not have succeeded without the sureness of touch and technique which modernism had already effected. Just as Lugones, after *Lunario sentimental* (1909), had changed the direction of Argentine poetry (anticipating Arrieta, Carriego, Fernández Moreno, Banchs, Capdevila, Méndez, the early

Borges), so González Martínez, conservative by nature, prepared the way for a line of Mexican poets – López Velarde, Pellicer, Torres Bodet, Villaurrutia – who would undertake the poeticization of everyday life. Much of the force behind the new direction came from a regionalist impulse, and thus anticipated developments in fiction after 1918. Amado Nervo (Mexico, 1870–1919), the most popular modernist of all after Darío – especially, thanks to his trite mysticism, with middle class women readers – though one who has worn least well, took the path towards greater simplicity. His success was itself a sign that modernism's ability to stimulate individualized responses in its audience or changes in poetic form was effectively extinguished. The title of his best-known collection, *La amada inmóvil* (posth., 1920), is eloquent in this regard.

The increasingly complex division of labour and pressures of big-city life, the expansion of travel and the new social and geographical mobility, the growth of newspapers and shortage of space within them, all conspired to encourage writing that was brief and to the point, fresh and immediate in its impact. The bourgeoisies in power had created the great Latin American newspapers in the late nineteenth century, such as *La Nación* in Buenos Aires, *La Epoca* in Santiago (its owner, MacClure, was Darío's *Rey burgués*) or *La Opinión Nacional* in Caracas, satisfying the demand of their newly rich readers for news of the elegant social and cultural milieux of Europe during the *belle époque*. All these circumstances taken together encouraged specific developments in modernist literary production: brief lyric poetry (and very little narrative verse), including the *hai-kai*; prose poems; short stories, sometimes less than a column in length (Ricardo Palma in Peru was the precursor of this art form, though the great age of the Latin American short story did not begin until the 1920s); and, most characteristic of all, the *crónica*.

The *crónica* was a curious mixture of genres: word poem, art reportage, interview converted into narrative, imaginative or literary essay, life of a writer, review of a book, exhibition, musical performance or literary evening, autobiographical note, disguised brief narrative or travel tale, and so on. Darío was one of the innovators, but the acknowledged master of this *pot-pourri*, halfway between literature and journalism, the eternity of Art and the fugacity of Life, was the Guatemalan Enrique Gómez Carrillo (1873–1927), who saw a vision of the future when, as a young man, having served the wife of the French ambassador to Guatemala in the lingerie store where he worked, he embarked on a brief passionate affair with her. The rest of his life was a succession of such *frissons*, all grist to his literary mill, until he married Spain's most popular singer and film star of the day, Raquel Meller, and, it was rumoured, had a passionate affair with Mata Hari before betraying her to the French authorities. A brilliant manipulator of newspaper owners and politicians (he represented Estrada Cabrera's dictatorship in Europe for many years), Gómez Carrillo spent all his adult life in Paris, wrote never a word about Guatemala, but travelled the length and breadth of the old world in search of 'sensations' for his readers: 'What I seek in a travel book is not the soul of the countries which interest me. I look for something more frivolous, more subtle, more picturesque, more poetic and more positive: sensations . . . Nature is sensitive and changeable like a women . . . The pleasure of travel is in the journey itself . . .'[17] Nothing shows more clearly than the *crónica*, as practised by Gómez Carrillo, how much modernism was in reality a tacit celebration of the insertion of Latin America, the historically invisible continent, into the international economic and cultural networks, by those who nonetheless adopted the world-weary pose of the spiritual aristocrat in an age of merchants. It was a genre virtually unknown before the 1870s and effectively dead by 1930. No modernist was more eagerly read than Gómez Carrillo, purveyor of mildly intoxicating, titillating but stylish literary gossip, and none more quickly forgotten.

Yet perhaps we should pause a while with Gómez Carrillo in the Paris of the *belle époque*, cultural capital of Latin America and mecca for those with social or aesthetic aspirations. Many wealthy families spent their winters there, or moved the whole household for years at a time. Paris, after all, was the home of Art, and if one could 'conquer' her one could return to one's native land with the laurel – nay, the certificate – of success. Numerous short-lived reviews were published there by figures like Ventura García Calderón (Peru, 1887–1959), Gonzalo Zaldumbide (Ecuador, 1884–1962), Hugo Barbagelata (Uruguay, b. 1887) the ubiquitous Venezuelan Alberto Zérega Fombona, Isidro Fabela (Mexico, 1882–1964), and Alberto Ghiraldo (Argentina, 1874–1947), author of the essay *Yanquilandia barbara*. Like Gómez Carrillo, many of these writers came to seem more important than they really were because Paris gave them prestige and material access to its publicity outlets. Most of them thought of Paris and Europe as autumnal, but were less keenly

17 *La psicología del viaje* (1919), quoted by M. Henríquez Ureña, *Breve historia del modernismo* (Mexico, 1954), 395–6.

aware that they too were autumnal: they had prepared Latin American culture for modernity, but were not themselves modern. After the First World War, the dilettantes from the ruling class had to make way for a new generation of artists from the petty bourgeoisie, although it was the former who continued to provide the social connections and to finance the magazines.

As usual, what had happened swiftly and violently, convulsively and unevenly, in Spanish American modernism, happened more organically – more closely following European models – in Brazil. After the gradual dissipation of romanticism, literary activity there continued to be organized under the same labels as in France, so that Parnassianism and Symbolism, names which have little resonance in Spanish American literature, are the generic terms applied to developments in the last thirty years of the nineteenth century and the first twenty years of the twentieth. Most critics are agreed that naturalism and parnassianism were at bottom different expressions of the same scientific spirit of anti-romantic revolt. The phenomenon was visible as early as the late 1860s in poetry such as Machado's *Crisálidas* and *Falenas*. He and Luís Guimarães (1845–98) were precursors of a new spirit – methodical, correct, restrained. The polemic which heralded the style began in 1878 in the *Diário do Rio de Janeiro*, and was later known as 'The Battle of Parnassus'. The highpoint was Machado's famous article, 'The new generation', in the *Revista Brasileira* in 1879. At this time no one yet spoke of parnassianism, however – the term was not adopted until 1886 – but of such positivist values as realism, social relevance and the scientific spirit. Although such themes may surprise the modern reader – certainly the reader familiar with Spanish American poetry of Darío's era – the movement was opposed to the unrestrained individualism and subjectivism of the romantics, which is why Machado's own prose works may plausibly be included within a so-called parnassian–realist ambit.

Erico Veríssimo said that parnassian verses 'have the cool and reposeful beauty of the Greek temple',[18] as befits the spiritual counterparts of Leconte de Lisle, Gautier, Proudhon and Heredia. Early exponents were Raimundo Correia (1859–1911), philosophical and pessimistic ('All is pain . . .'), and Alberto de Oliveira (1859–1937), a brilliant, dispassionate technician, encoder of intricate literary riddles,

---

[18] E. Veríssimo, *Brazilian literature: an outline* (New York, 1945), 76.

once called the prince of Brazilian poets. Both, however, indulged in poetic licence, forsook grammatical exactitude and resorted to Gallicisms. This was viewed with disfavour from the lofty heights of Parnassus – for poetry in Brazil had not escaped from the academicism constricting all the arts at the time – which opposed all looseness of metre, vagueness and sentimentality. The movement really reached maturity with Olavo Bilac (1865–1918) whose *Poesias* appeared in 1888, the year of Darío's *Azul*. Popular, sensual and fluent, Bilac was also a literary craftsman able to turn his two great loves – the Brazilian landscape and Brazilian women – into finely chiselled images ('Turn, perfect, uplift and polish/ your phrase; and at the last/ set the rhyme on each golden verse/ like a ruby'). Bilac remains the most readable of the parnassians, because in him alone the ideal was combined with the real. In the end, though, the movement was reduced to art for art's sake and effectively died of the cold.

Parnassianism had no sooner been identified and named than symbolism arrived to replace it. In one sense, it was a resurgence of romanticism, in its vagueness and sensuousness, its suggestiveness and musicality, and languid decadence. Perhaps best understood as the literary equivalent of impressionism, its purpose, according to Ronald de Carvalho, was 'to evoke intuitively, through the spontaneous rhythm of words, what the older poetic schools had sought to suggest through an exact representation of things'.[19] Erico Veríssimo declared that 'it had few followers in my country, where colour shades and mists are rare . . . We have few cases of introversion in our literature'.[20] But this was an overstatement. For example, one of its adherents, João da Cruz e Sousa (1861–98), whose *Broquéis* (1893) signals its advent, must be counted among the great poets of Brazil. Known as the 'Black Swan' of Brazilian symbolism, he was born into slavery of two Negro parents, and his life was marked by conflict, resentment and despair. His poetry is by turns bitter, sceptical and melancholy, with a decadent satanic note that many have considered Baudelairian. At the same time he was a vigorous abolitionist jornalist, though he never found the sort of appointment for which his talents fitted him and spent much of his life as a railway clerk, before dying of tuberculosis. His best known books are *Tropos e fantasias* (1885), *Broquéis*, *Faróis* (1900), and *Ultimos sonetos* (1905), all marked, like his brilliant prose poems, by a sonorous musicality. Other important

[19] R. de Carvalho, *Pequena história da literatura brasileira* (Rio de Janeiro, 7th edn, 1944), 348.
[20] E. Veríssimo, *op. cit.*, 81–2.

symbolists were the mystical Alphonsus de Guimaraens (1870–1921), from Minas Gerais, the main theme of whose wilfully archaic poetry is chaste, virginal love; and Augusto dos Anjos (1884–1914), whose work is imbued with his readings in science and philosophy, a despairing view of the human spirit wracked in a mechanistic, deterministic universe. His best-known poems have titles like 'Hymn to pain' or 'The obsession with blood', communicating a naturalistic horror at existence, an almost cosmic pessimism.

Music

Literature was undoubtedly the dominant mode of cultural expression in nineteenth-century Latin America, circumscribing the form and inter-pretation of all the other arts. This merely reinforced the academicism which characterized the century, all the more inevitably in a continent of young nations which had rejected the Iberian heritage with its irrational baroque artistic forms and set themselves the project of constituting new political and cultural systems as a means of integrating Latin America within the wider European order of which they felt destined to be part. Nowhere was literature's influence more evident than in music, which by 1870 was developing rapidly, with numerous theatres and conservatories in most major capitals.

Melesio Morales (1838–1908) guided musical endeavour in Mexico after the national conservatory was instituted in 1866. Of his eight operas, one, *Ildegonda*, was premiered in Italy – the ultimate accolade – in 1868, and he composed a celebrated programme piece, *La locomotiva*, for the opening of the Mexico City–Puebla railway in 1869. When Cenobio Paniagua (1822–82) had staged his pioneering opera *Catalina de Guisa* (composed 1845) at the National Theatre in 1858, some critics sourly noted that its only Mexican feature was its composer; in 1871 Aniceto Ortega (1823–75) produced a one-act opera, *Guatimotzín*, on the last days of the Aztecs, with Cuauhtémoc as tenor and Cortés as bass, starring the renowned Mexican soprano Angela Peralta (1845–83). The Cuban Laureano Fuentes Matons (1825–98) composed the equally indianist *La hija de Jefté* (1875), and Gaspar Villate (1851–91), one of the great propagators of the *danza habanera*, had three operas performed in Europe between 1871 and 1888. The first opera in Venezuela was *Virginia* (1873) by José Angel Montero (1839–81); in Colombia, *Ester* (1874), by José María Ponce de León (1846–82). The romantic titles tell all. The first

'Peruvian' opera, *Atahualpa*, was composed by the Italian Carlo Enrique Pasta (1855–98) and performed in Lima in 1877. Francisco A. Hargreaves' *La gatta bianca*, premiered in Italy in 1875, is generally considered the first Argentine opera. It was in Brazil, however, that the most significant developments took place, culminating in the work of Antônio Carlos Gomes, who, already under the spell of Verdi, lived in Italy from 1864. *Il Guarany*, based on Alencar's novel, triumphed at La Scala in 1870 and was staged in Rio to celebrate the emperor's birthday. Here was an American theme, the noble savage, treated in the most sumptuously lyrical manner in the home of opera. It remains in the international repertory to this day. In 1880 Gomes was persuaded to write on the more dangerous contemporary theme of slavery, but the librettist transformed Negroes magically into Indians when the opera, *Lo schiavo* (which includes the well-known 'Dance of the Tamoios'), appeared in 1889. Gomes has been rejected by nationalist critics, but there are undoubtedly some national and even popular elements embedded in his works.

The style and conventions of European opera were extremely resistant to change. Latin American composers could do little other than join the current, with mere gestures in the direction of national expression. Although increasingly vigorous attempts were made between 1850 and 1880 to master the form and produce Latin American versions, physical and cultural limitations tended to concentrate effort elsewhere. The romantic era was the heyday of the piano virtuoso, the solo song, and the symphonic poem, each ideally suited to Latin American conditions, and musicians like the Venezuelan pianist, composer and singer Teresa Carreño (1853–1917), the Cuban violinist José White (1836–1918) and the Mexican soprano Angela Peralta, achieved international recognition. Thus the era of musical nationalism, the second phase of romantic influence, began timidly in the 1870s, gathered pace by the end of the century and reached its peak in the 1920s. It incorporated both a regional, or nativist, and a national dimension in its essentially emotional expressiveness, multiplying the variety of rhythmic, melodic and harmonic phraseology available (though few Latin Americans saw its more radical possibilities at first) and preparing the way for the musical avant-garde of the 1920s.

Gottschalk's triumphant tour of Latin America in 1869 had made national themes and styles more acceptable, as long as they remained at a superficial level of picturesqueness and local colour. Composers increasingly adopted the European example of Glinka or Borodin,

Albéniz or Granados, Smetana or Dvorak, by incorporating popular national songs and dances, incidentally producing such Americanized European forms as the 'tropical waltz' or 'Paraguayan polka'. Not until the 1920s would Latin American composers definitively master the art of recreating national style from within, at precisely the moment when the international avant-garde was rejecting even the most sophisticated musical nationalism. In Brazil *A sertaneja* (1869) by Brasílio Itiberê da Cunha (1846–1913) was one early localist expression, but it was the famous piano piece *Tango brasileiro* (1890) by Alexandre Levy (1864–92) that first gave the nativist current positive panache. His *Suite brésilienne* (1890) later became part of Brazil's popular repertory, particularly its last movement, 'Samba', inspired not by personal experience but by a description in Ribeiro's novel *A carne* two years before. Hargreaves (1849–1900) was the first Argentine composer to draw regularly on folk music, beginning with the piano polka *El pampero*, also stylizing typical rural forms (*cielito, gato, estilo, décima*) in his *Aires nacionales* (1880). The Colombian José María Ponce de León, who had studied under Gounod in Paris, composed early nativist works such as *La hermosa sabana* and *Sinfonía sobre temas colombianos* (1881), with romantic adaptations of folk dances like the *bambuco, pasillo* and *torbellino*.

In Cuba, with perhaps the richest musical heritage in Latin America, Nicolás Ruiz Espadero (1832–90) produced a work for piano, *Canto del guajiro*, subtitled 'Typical Cuban scene', which illustrates perfectly how romantic rhetoric could smother rhythmic spontaneity. More convincing precursors of 1920s Afro-Cubanism were Manuel Saumell (1817–70), the 'father of the *contradanza*', and Ignacio Cervantes (1847–1905), 'Cuba's Glinka', who studied at the Paris Conservatoire and whose exquisite *Danzas cubanas* (1871–95) were Cuba's most important contribution to nineteenth-century art music. Signposts along Mexico's route to national expression were *Jarabe nacional* (1860) by Tomás León (1826–93) and *Ecos de México* (1880) by Julio Ituarte (1845–1905). The leading piano composer was the Otomí Indian, Juventino Rosas (1868–94), a member of Angela Peralta's touring company and author of the French-style waltz series, *Sobre las olas*, so popular that it was frequently attributed to Strauss. The piano virtuoso Ricardo Castro (1864–1907) achieved the ultimate ambition when *Légende de Rudel* (1906) was performed and applauded in Europe. The price was an essentially mimetic art, even though Castro was also producing arrangements of regional dances like the *jarabe* and the *danza mexicana*.

The father of musical nationalism in Brazil was Alberto Nepomuceno

(1864–1920), who was taught by Grieg how to compose music which was at once national and universal. In 1887 he composed *Dança de negros*, and in 1897 *Série brasileira*, the first orchestral suite based on Brazilian vernacular themes, using a wide range of forms and rhythms, and still popular today. Argentina's central figure was the prolific Alberto Williams (1862–1952), who studied at the Paris Conservatoire in 1882 under César Franck, eventually composing more than a hundred substantial works, including nine symphonies. In 1889 he toured Buenos Aires province to 'saturate myself in the music of my homeland', thereafter writing 'not mere transcriptions, but artistic music with native atmosphere, colour and essence'.[21] The first result was the elegiac *El rancho abandonado* (1890); but when *Aires de la pampa* appeared in 1893 Williams had evolved to writing his own *milongas, gatos, cielitos* and *sambas*. Although he strikes the modern ear as both incorrigibly academic and profusely sentimental, like his contemporary, Arturo Berutti (1862–1938), composer of the *Sinfonía argentina* (1890) and the operas *Pampa* (1897) and *Yupanki* (1899), Williams made an outstanding contribution to regional and national musical integration, especially during the decisive period 1890–1910. Modern critics, however, favour the less ambitious *criollista* Julián Aguirre (1869–1924), a friend of Albéniz, whose piano adaptations, *Huella* and *Gato*, remain in the international repertoire. Another prolific composer was the director of the Colombian national conservatory from 1910 to 1935, Guillermo Uribe Holguín (1880–1971), whose three hundred *Trozos en el sentimiento popular* for piano, based on folk dances, form an enduring legacy.

The most prominent figure in Mexico during this period was Manuel Ponce (1882–1948), universally known as the composer of the irresistible middlebrow hit, *Estrellita* (1914). After working in Paris and Berlin, he carefully studied and re-elaborated Mexico's *corridos, sones, jarabes* and *huapangos*. The results are often compared unfavourably with the later works of Chávez: critics consider Ponce 'folkloric', confined to quoting Indian or *mestizo* materials rather than using them as structural principles. Nevertheless, his works continue to be played world-wide as no other Mexican composer's are, and his mainly anonymous role as creator of many of Segovia's guitar pieces has recently come to light. Like Nepomuceno, Uribe Holguín and Williams, Ponce provided the

[21] See G. Béhague, *Music in Latin America: an introduction* (New Jersey, 1979), 108–10. Béhague's work is indispensable, and has been drawn upon extensively in the preparation of this section.

essential bridge for nativism to cross from romanticism to the avant-garde.

Painting

Even more than music, nineteenth-century painting was in the grip of academicism and social convention. Open-air painting was unknown in Latin America well into the century, and impressionism arrived after its end, more than two decades later than its literary equivalent, *modernismo*, and almost half a century after its European model. Although the delay was understandable, the failure to assimilate impressionism was particularly unfortunate, since European painting in the last third of the century was in the vanguard of changes in artistic perception. Given the specificity of the plastic arts, there was no repertory of popular styles to quote from as in music; and if in the first phase of nineteenth-century painting the depiction of native themes was learned from European travellers in search of the picturesque, in the second, after 1870, Latin American visitors to Europe invariably returned to their homelands with the latest version of academic painting, blind to the new visions of Monet, Renoir, Manet, Pisarro or Cézanne, men who really had put the stifling influence of academic neo-classicism behind them. When impressionism did arrive, early in the new century, the results were timid and its very lateness permitted its conversion, despite general public hostility, into a new academicism. As with music, it was not until the 1920s that Latin American painters finally – and all the more suddenly – joined the international avant-garde.

In Brazil continuity of monarchy and empire encouraged a wilfully grandiose style, midway between the classical and the romantic, based on the French school of battle painting, whilst landscape, as Fernando de Azevedo has written, was generally 'no more than a background of hills, a corner of woods or a curve in the river, as accessories to a bit of sacred, classical or national history'.[22] The two great exponents and most popular painters of the era were Vítor Meireles (1832–1903) and his friend Pedro Américo (1843–1905). Both had spent significant periods in Paris in the 1850s and 1860s. Meireles's *Primeira missa no Brasil* (1861) was the first Brazilian painting exhibited at the Paris Salon, whilst his two best-known works were the *Batalha dos Guararapes* (1869) and *Batalha*

[22] F. de Azevedo, *Brazilian culture* (New York, 1950), 294.

naval do Riachuelo (1872). Two of his disciples, both born in Portugal, produced typical late-romantic works: Augusto Rodrigues Duarte (1848–88), with *Exéquias de Atalá*, following Chateaubriand, and José Maria de Madeiros (1849–1926), with *Iracema*, inspired by Alencar's novel. Pedro Américo's Italian-style nude, *A carioca* (1864), was one of his first successful canvases, but he is most remembered for the *Batalha do Avaí* (1877), exhibited in Florence in the presence of the Brazilian emperor himself, and the massive *Independência ou morte!* (1886). Rodolfo Amoêdo (1857–1941) also studied in Paris, where he did his best work, moving from biblical canvases and romantic works like the nude *Marabá* (1883), or the celebrated *O último tamoio* (1883), to the Manet-like *Más notícias* (1888) in the age of naturalism. José Ferraz de Almeida Júnior (1850–99), by contrast, was the first genuinely nationalist Brazilian painter in both form and subject matter, and for many the greatest Brazilian painter of the century. He had travelled to Paris at the height of the impressionist controversy, but his depictions of rural São Paulo, like *O derrubador brasileiro*, *Caboclo no descanso*, *Caipiras negaceando* and *Picando fumo*, were neither documentary nor merely picturesque, revealing rather 'a mind unequivocally Brazilian, unconsciously barbarous and fertile – a necessary consequence of a young land, which no foreign artist could translate'.[23] After these painters a decline set in. Typical of the ensuing transitional period was a decadent romantic current, often masquerading as a timid impressionism or Art Nouveau, exemplified in the work of Antônio Parreiras (1864–1937), a painter of historical canvases like *A conquista do Amazonas* or of 'Parisian' nudes lascivious in intent but uninspiring in effect, like his late *Flor do mal* (1922). Eliseu Visconti (b. 1864), superficial in conceptualization but perhaps most accomplished of all in purely pictorial terms, experimented successively with all the modes of the era, from academicism (*Maternidade*) to the almost pre-Raphaelite *Dança das Oréadas* (1900), and thence to *modernismo*.

In the River Plate republics, as in Brazil, a radical gulf opened between the objective and subjective approaches to painting (naturalism and impressionism), which would characterize all the arts henceforth. The Uruguayan Juan Manuel Blanes (1830–1901) effectively combined both approaches, albeit within an ultimately costumbrist perspective, successfully applying the formal lessons of European masters to American subjects. His gauchesque and rural paintings, like *La cautiva* or *Las boleadoras*, historical paintings like the *Juramento de los 33 Orientales*, battle scenes like the *Batalla de Sarandí* or the famous humanitarian canvas *El ultimo paraguayo*, and social works like *Dos caminos* and *Fiebre amarilla* (1870), made him a key influence in the River Plate region, a symphonist of light who ranks with Prilidiano Pueyrredón,[24] Almeida Júnior or José María Velasco (see below) as one of the unequivocally great Latin American artists of the nineteenth century. Patronage and taste, however, were in the hands of a small minority, whose predominantly academic orientation could be tyrannical. In 1887 the painter Eduardo Sívori (1847–1918), who had previously concentrated mainly on traditional subjects like *Tormenta en la pampa* or *A la querencia*, presented a canvas, *El despertar de la sirvienta*, which was deemed too 'pornographic' for exhibition in Buenos Aires, despite a successful Paris showing, partly because it was an uncompromising naturalistic nude in the manner of Courbet, but also – no doubt – because of the unmistakably critical social thesis it conveyed. Even more challenging canvases, in an Argentina where urban problems were rapidly replacing gaucho themes, were *La sopa de los pobres* (1883) by Reinaldo Giudici (1853–1921), *Sin pan y sin trabajo* (1894) by the socialist painter Ernesto de la Cárcova (1866–1927), and *La hora del reposo* (1903) by Pío Collivadino (1869–1945), all of which treated urban labour themes with incipient social realism. And even these painters of naturalist works, whether bourgeois or socialist in intention, found public acceptance more easily than those who took the impressionist route. The naturalists were at least narrative painters, and this the critics – invariably literary in orientation – could understand. Martín A. Malharro (1865–1911) renounced romanticism after a visit to Europe and produced works like *En plena naturaleza* or *Las parvas*, saturated with colour and its vibrations. Although his whole purpose, ironically, was to make people begin to *see*, his first exhibition in 1902 was savagely ridiculed and he died a virtual outcast; whereas Fernando Fader (1882–1935), effectively a naturalist like his German mentor Von Zugel, by merely enlivening his painting with an attenuated impressionist veneer, gained immediate critical acceptance in 1905 and became a lasting influence through the Grupo Nexus, such that his brand of 'impressionism' was almost the status quo by 1914. Critics interpreted as impressionist what was in fact, in Fader's essentially *criollista* recreations of the landscapes of rural Córdoba – like *Aclarando en la higuera*, *En el*

---

[24] See Martin, *CHLA* III, chap. 18.

potrero or *Tarde de otoño* – a characteristically metaphysical interpretation of Argentina's solitude and silence.

By far the greatest Mexican painter of the late nineteenth century was José María Velasco (1840–1912), who ran the gamut from romanticism through realism to the edge of impressionism, which he first viewed only in 1889. His best-known series of works were eight canvases on the theme of *El Valle de México* (1894–1905), including the magnificent *Valle de México visto desde el cerro de Guadalupe* (1894) and the famous railway painting *El Citlaltépetl* (1897). Velasco effected a synthesis of emotion, aesthetic impulse and visual mastery to achieve, like Almeida Júnior and Blanes, an almost impossible individuality in that century of servile academic mimeticism disguised as lofty universality. Their historical achievement is that of Nepomuceno, Williams and Ponce in music, pioneers in an inevitably arid landscape.

THE EARLY TWENTIETH CENTURY

The period after the turn of the century was one of great ideological, cultural and artistic confusion in Latin America. Economic and social changes moved faster than thinkers and artists could follow. In Spanish America José Enrique Rodó (1871–1917) inaugurated the century with his epoch-making essay *Ariel* (1900), at the zenith of *modernismo*, two years after the defeat of Spain in Cuba, and at the very moment when the United States had begun its irresistible rise, first to hemispheric and then to world supremacy. Despite his claims to social relevance (his classic essay had concluded that the innately elitist Darío was 'not the poet of America'), Rodó is really to the essay what Darío is to poetry: elegant, superficially assured and, ultimately, aestheticist. His assault on the cultural barbarism of the North American Caliban typifies Latin American thought at the time, in its incorrigible voluntarism and idealism. After the First World War, the Mexican and Russian revolutions, and the 1918 Córdoba student revolt, such spiritual anti-imperialism would be supplanted by a keener perception of social and economic struggle, and art would take on a class character. Although *Ariel* is routinely considered the start of a twentieth-century debate, it is better understood as a last despairing attempt, in the face of modernity, to recuperate the neo-classical project of the emancipation era, now buried in an incoherent jumble of contradictory philosophies and styles. Nevertheless, Rodó's serene prose, with the clarity of line of a Greek temple, did lay the foundation for the debate to follow and re-established the dignity of art after its devaluation by Positivist philosophy.[25]

Architecture

If architecture best exemplifies the rather abstract and ultimately academic direction of nineteenth-century culture, it can equally dramatize the confusing scene at the beginning of the twentieth century. Although colonial styles were largely discontinued, the absence of experienced architects, craftsmen and material resources meant that the neo-classical architecture which predominated before 1870 was generally mediocre, despite the grandiose dreams of statesmen. Even in Brazil, where conditions were most favourable, the lack of coherent planning meant that 'the best buildings were still the oldest',[26] and cities took on their rather shapeless contemporary appearance. Buenos Aires grew more consistently than most on neo-classical lines, and in the two decades before the war underwent a building boom which produced its present image as the most nineteenth-century great city in Latin America. Most others remained largely colonial in layout, though the Haussmann pattern was imposed where feasible (the Paseo de la Reforma in Mexico, the Alameda in Santiago, Rio Branco and Beira Mar avenues in Rio). The national oligarchies erected imposing buildings and monuments in the last years of the century to give that sense of balance, measure and stability which Positivism required, symbolizing generalized prosperity and an officially ordained culture.

And so the *belle époque* dawned, an age of great government edifices, legislative palaces, grand theatres, huge private residences, at the very moment when neo-classicism finally faltered in the face of a chaotic romantic revivalism involving neo-colonial and neo-indigenist elements, Art Nouveau and other early harbingers of 'Modernism'. All planning disappeared and architects began an indiscriminate imitation of new foreign styles and historical models. The only major exception was Havana, which added a relatively coherent neo-classicism on Spanish lines to the basic colonial pattern, virtually excluding French or Anglo-Saxon inputs. Elsewhere a forest of diverse transplanted forms grew up in city centres, vitiating the effect of remaining colonial buildings, but accurately reflecting the eclecticism of Latin American culture generally

[25] See Hale, *CHLA* iv, chap. 10.
[26] Azevedo, *op. cit.*, 309.

at this time. Among the more distinguished constructions, the Teatro Colón in Buenos Aires was planned by Víctor Meano and built in 1908 by Julio Dormal (1846–1924) and the Palacio San Martín by Alejandro Christopherson (1846–1946), whilst the notoriously multi-styled Palacio de Bellas Artes (1903–34) was begun in Mexico City by Adamo Boari. The Brazilian critic Monteiro Lobato called the triumph of flamboyant bad taste the 'architectural carnival'.

Modern architecture reached Latin America in the 1920s through functionalism which, if nothing else, wiped the architectural slate clean; but it was yet another artificial imposition, a product of northern developed societies imported into tropical and mainly agricultural republics. The dominance of the international monopolist bourgeoisie was communicated to Latin Americans in the very industrialization of the construction materials, steel and concrete, in a new capitalist style which was simple, flexible and rapid. Unlike Europe and North America, where the movement also corresponded to the growth of middle-class suburbs, it was required in Latin America to solve the housing problems of the emergent working masses, whilst the middle classes themselves not infrequently returned to colonial styles, albeit 'functionalized', which many architects thought better adapted to Latin American climates and societies.[27]

The Mexican movement began with José Villagrán García (b. 1901), who had graduated, like so many of his muralist contemporaries, from the Academia San Carlos. Seizing upon the most dehumanized of Le Corbusier's theories ('a house is a machine for living in'), he advocated a technologically advanced, socially oriented architecture. As architect to the Public Health Department, he built the Institute of Hygiene and Sanatorium of Huipulco (1925) and the Sanitary Farm at Tacuba (1926), later becoming director of the new National School of Architecture in 1932. Juan O'Gorman (b. 1905), a protégé, was also a painter and sculptor, ideally qualified to effect the integration of visual and spatial arts sought by the ideologues of the soon-to-be institutionalized revolution, who argued that such integration characterized both pre-Columbian and baroque techniques. Yet O'Gorman's militant functionalism (from which he recanted only much later, eventually participating in the construction of the integrationist University City) asserted that aesthetics were irrelevant: architecture should be strictly utilitarian, a

[27] See R. Vargas Salguero and R. López Rangel, 'La crisis actual de la arquitectura latinoamericana', in R. Segre (ed.), *América Latina en su arquitectura* (Mexico–Paris, 1975), 186–203.

mere branch of engineering, with maximum return from minimum expenditure. He built the first functionalist schools and private houses, including one for Diego Rivera, organizing the School of Construction after 1932.

In reality the expansion of capitalism in Mexico required that great public works be executed as rapidly as possible, but with a subtle mass manipulation involving mystical exaltation of the Indian peasant and urban proletarian. Most architects, painters, sculptors and musicians of the 1920s avant-garde, however lucid and well-intentioned, had been completely absorbed by the state by 1930. The Argentine case was quite different. There the French fine art tradition was at its strongest, and the vogue of the *hotel particulier* as urban mansion was the ideal of wealthy Argentines. The conservative bureaucracy did little to encourage the emergence of a modern architecture: during the first phase of the modern movement in the 1920s and 1930s, pioneers such as León Durge, Prebisch and Vilar received little of the state support enjoyed by their contemporaries in Mexico and Brazil, and private commissions remained the rule until Perón's day.

In Brazil, as in Mexico, functionalism swept aside traditionalist debris and cleared the ground for new concepts. After the 1922 Semana de Arte Moderna, Gregori Warchavchik (1896–1972) launched his *Manifesto da Arquitetura Funcional* (1925), clearly influenced by Le Corbusier (who visited Brazil in 1929, and again, most decisively, in 1936: his example eventually led to the construction of Brasília). In Brazil, however, the modern movement took on grandiose overtones from the start, perhaps because there was no need, as in Mexico, to conceal the potential role of private capital as partner to the state. Brazil's new architecture was presented as an overtly multi-class movement, combining nationalism and populism with Le Corbusier's elegant European aesthetics and fantasies. The results were frequently dazzling, especially in the 1930s, and Brazil, where almost any dream could apparently come true, leaped to the forefront of contemporary architecture in its first decade in the international fray. Lúcio Costa (b. 1902), director of the National School of Fine Art, worked closely with Warchavchik, influencing the generation of the great Oscar Niemeyer (b. 1902).

Countries like Venezuela or Colombia, which in the nineteenth century had been too anarchic or too impoverished for major public works, hurtled straight from colonial to modern architecture with little difficulty, since the new movement of Gropius, Le Corbusier and Mies

Van der Rohe represented such a complete break with the past. In the late 1920s, as trans-national oil companies began to exploit new finds, Carlos Raúl Villanueva (b. 1901) returned to Venezuela from Paris to a post at the ministry of public works. Over twenty years, through a brilliant combination of traditional and modern methods in construction and design, he expanded his range and eventually built the new Central University, bringing himself and Venezuelan architecture world renown.

Painting

The 1920s, then, was the decade when Latin American architecture, painting and music finally began to come into parallel focus with international developments, and a few leading exponents in each field attained international reputations. Yet the situation in the plastic arts at the turn of the century had been particularly unsatisfactory, as we have seen. Latin American versions of impressionism were timid and tentative, resulting in an unscientific, merely instinctual movement disconnected from its social and economic base. Nevertheless, although long since outmoded in Europe, impressionism had determined all the new ways of seeing reality and understanding art, giving artists licence to experiment and paving the way for the avant-garde explosion after 1910 and its crystallization in the 1920s, when Latin America itself made the first great landfall in its voyage of self-discovery.

In Mexico the celebrated 'Dr Atl' (Gerardo Murillo, 1875–1964) linked the great engraver José Guadalupe Posada (1851–1913), a key figure in the dialectic between popular and national culture, to the generation of world-famous muralists whom Murillo himself taught at the Academia San Carlos. Dr Atl really belonged to the previous era – his favourite subject was Mexico's topography, typified in his *La mañana en el Valle* – but his dramatic approach to techniques and applications of colour had lasting impact. Atl was a militant in all things, anarchist and socialist by turns, and after founding the Artistic Centre in 1910, encouraged young artists like Orozco and Siqueiros to paint murals on its walls. Although developments were interrupted by the Revolution (whose most important visual chronicler was Francisco Goitia, with paintings like *El ahorcado*, 1916), minister of education Vasconcelos gave renewed momentum to the movement after 1921, unleashing a vast programme of cultural renovation – with the explicit purpose of reconciling fine art with popular arts and crafts – launched by the 1921 exhibition for which Atl wrote the guide.

The best-known painter of the movement was Diego Rivera (1886–1957). During his crucial years in Europe (1907–21), he absorbed a succession of influences (Picasso, Gris, Modigliani, in Paris; Zuloaga and Sorolla, in Madrid) finally moulded into definitive synthesis by the Revolution itself. After eighty Cubist canvases like *El despertador* (1914), or *Paisaje de Piquey* (1918), had built him a solid reputation, a visit to Siena in 1920 helped forge a controversial synthesis of Renaissance fresco techniques (long admired by his early tutor, Atl), pre-Columbian integrated art, the styles and images of Mexican contemporary popular culture (mediated principally through Posada), and Soviet-style social realism. He concluded that avant-garde postures and socialist commitment were incompatible, renounced the easel and became a muralist. After studying his country in depth, he painted the results on the walls of the Ministry of Education (1923–8), the Chapingo Agricultural School (1923–7, see especially *La tierra liberada*), and the National Palace (1930–5). Rivera's trajectory is a paradigm, comparable with Pablo Neruda's journey to his later *Canto general*: documentary (*La molendera*, 1926), illustrative, replete with stock images, propaganda, folklorism (*Retrato de niña*, 1928) and hyperbole, but undeniably grandiose. The sometimes despised muralism of Rivera and Siqueiros foreshadowed Picasso's *Guernica* and much other political painting this century, not to mention North American action painting (following the uproar, both political and aesthetic, provoked by Rivera's visit to the U.S. in the 1930s) and pop art generally. No debate on the possibilities of a Third World art can ignore them.

David Alfaro Siqueiros (1896–1974) studied with Atl and Orozco at the Academy, followed by five years as a young revolutionary soldier which moulded his world view definitively. Like Rivera and Frida Kahlo, he became a communist. In Barcelona in 1921 he issued his famous Manifesto to the Plastic Artists of America, calling for 'a public art, a monumental and heroic art, a human art . . . pre-Columbian in inspiration and workerist in orientation'. In 1922 he was a founder member of the union of artists and technicians, whose purpose, declared their equally famous manifesto, was 'to liquidate the decadence of modern art . . . socialize artistic expression, and destroy bourgeois individualism'. The union's principal organ was the now legendary magazine, *El Machete*. Siqueiros never ceased to be involved in

controversy (the plot to assassinate Trotsky, for example), though he did
return to easel painting and achieved wide popularity with the Mexican
public, beginning with pictures like *Madre campesina* (1929), *La niña
muerta* (1931) and *Zapata* (1931).

Most critics now consider José Clemente Orozco (1883–1949) the
greatest of the big three Mexican muralists, perhaps because he was least
circumscribed by political considerations. The 1922–3 murals at the
National Preparatory School, a composite masterpiece, show none of
Rivera's penchant for rhetoric or decoration, whilst the vibrant
coloration of pictures like *La trinchera* (1922–3), *Soldaderas* (1922–7) and
Zapatistas (1931), or stark expressionism of *Prometeo* (1930) and *Cristo
destruye la cruz* (1934) is well known, perfect in their fusion of concept and
plasticity within a broadly political conception which is more
Americanist than narrowly Mexican. From his earliest works, which
exude loathing for Porfirian Mexico, Orozco communicates a longing
for the identity, however tortured, of artistic form and spiritual content
in a world of materialist determination.

Rufino Tamayo (b. 1899) was the first great artist to emerge from the
shadow of the muralists. Deeply rooted in the indigenism that
underpinned the muralist movement, he too underwent an early political
phase, but later insisted that art is primarily plastic and poetic and can
have 'no political or ideological manifestations'. Influenced by Picasso
and Braque in the 1920s, he was always able to instil a sense of some
personal mythology into his use of such models, as witness his *Retrato
fotográfico* (1928) or *La niña bonita* (1932). Despite rejecting documentary
realism and narrowly referential art, he has searched for forms which can
communicate his specifically Mexican experience whilst engaging
simultaneously with universal currents. Even before this, the Guatemalan Carlos Mérida (b. 1891) became perhaps the first to move entirely
beyond mere folklore in Latin American nativist art. Influenced by
Picasso's blue period during an early visit to Paris (1910–14), Mérida
returned home to search for some Americanist synthesis of folklore,
archaeology and modern plastic concepts. *Imágenes de Guatemala* (1914–
27) conveys his evolution from stylized figuration to semi-abstraction,
whilst remaining faithful throughout to the undulating spirit of his
Mayan inspiration. Although in Mexico from 1919, he abandoned all
romantic, picturesque or anecdotal approaches before the muralist
movement had even begun, and began to treat native motifs with the
same autonomy that Braque and Picasso had applied to their neo-

primitivist work. (Among indigenist writers, his fellow Guatemalan, Miguel Angel Asturias, was influenced by this ultimately more fertile approach in his *Leyendas de Guatemala* of 1930, whilst others would travel Rivera's documentary road.) In 1927 Mérida returned to Paris to work on surrealist and musical analogies, moving now from quasi-geometrical indigenous stylizations, like *Perfiles* (1928), to almost complete abstraction by the time of *Máscaras* (1932). His achievement is comparable to that of Tamayo or Torres García (see below) in painting, Chávez or Villa-Lobos in music, Vallejo or Neruda in poetry.

In the Caribbean area modern Cuban art was taken out of provincialism and plunged into the Parisian cross-currents of the 1920s by Amelia Peláez (1897–1968), whilst retaining, for example in paintings like *Mujer* (1928) or her numerous *Naturalezas muertas* composed of blue tropical fruits, a distinctive *criollo* identity. Cuba's best-known painter abroad was Wilfredo Lam (b. 1902), whose celebrated *La jungla* came later (1943), but typified his fetishistic tropical exuberance, out of Matisse by way of Picasso, a close personal friend. Haitian art only really entered the modern period after 1930, but was influenced by the Afro-Caribbean movements initiated earlier in Cuba and Puerto Rico. Further south, one of the great painters of tropical America was the eccentric Venezuelan recluse, Armando Reverón (1889–1954), virtually ignored until after his death, who became deranged and withdrew to Macuto with his wife, his mistress and the rag dolls filled with sawdust which he used as models. His first outstanding works were *Las mujeres en la cueva* (1919), *Los cocoteros* (1920), *Figura bajo un uvero* (1920) and *Juanita junto a la tripoide* (1921). He painted numerous outstanding nudes and unforgettably vibrant coastal landscapes. After returning to Venezuela in 1921 following a tour of Europe, he became increasingly preoccupied with light – passing through blue, sepia and white periods – until it became an almost literally blinding obsession. Examples of his most characteristic mode are *Fiesta en Caraballeda* (1924), *El árbol* (1926) and *Macuto en oro* (1931). Although consumed by the local, he was in no sense a provincial or costumbrist artist.

In the Andean region nativism swept all before it, although it proved a pale reflection of the Mexican example. Peruvian art in general was bitterly divided between the reactionary Hispanicizing current represented in literature by Palma and Riva Agüero, and the new indigenism advocated by González Prada, Valcárcel, Mariátegui and Haya de la Torre (see below). Mariátegui, whose review *Amauta* was in the political if not the artistic vanguard, declared that futurism, dadaism, cubism and the rest were 'mere pirouettes of the decadent bourgeoisie', quite alien to Peru and its contemporary needs. Unfortunately, Peruvian painting after Pancho Fierro (1803–79) had been grimly academic and derivative, and there was no tradition of simple painterly proficiency on which to build. The new movement was led by José Sabogal (1888–1956) from Cajabamba, initially a painter of undistinguished landscapes lying somewhere between the academic and picturesque. A European visit in 1919 introduced him to Zuloaga, the Spanish master who combined local colour with technical virtuosity; then in Mexico in 1922, he was dazzled by the muralist synthesis of nativism and nationalism, and returned to Peru a militant indigenist and doctrinaire aesthetic nationalist. Although his own painting was a rather crude grafting of Mexican social realism on to Spanish *costumbrismo* (and thereby reminiscent of the 1930s fiction produced by his compatriot Ciro Alegría), Sabogal led the indigenist movement for the next thirty years and there is no denying his lasting impact on the national perception of native arts and crafts. His doctrine can be summed up in his phrase, 'Art is the translation of man and nature'. Unfortunately the translator frequently remains outside the world he is trying to convey. Not until Fernando de Szyszlo (b. 1925) would Peruvian art find a means of representing the pre-Columbian world without mere figuration or socio-economic reflectionism. In Ecuador and Bolivia, meanwhile, movements like Peruvian indigenism have sprung up only since the 1930s. Today the cry is for an 'Indian' – rather than indianist or indigenist – art.

In the southern cone such nativist movements as have existed tend to be labelled *criollista*, and it can fairly be said that even vernacular culture tends to become Europeanized. The Uruguayan lawyer Pedro Figari (1861–1938), a genuinely American artist and undisputed classic, only took up painting seriously after the age of sixty. He moved first to Buenos Aires (1921), then to Paris (1925–34), passing determinedly through the modern kaleidoscope to find the style *he* needed, which crystallized in a uniquely personal post-impressionist mode reminiscent of Bonnard. With his historical canvases like the *Grito de Asencio* or *Asesinato de Quiroga*, and his familiar *criollista* titles like *El gato*, *La doma*, *Potros en la pampa*, *Candombé*, *El Circo*, *No te vayas mi viejo*, *Recordando al finado*, and *Don Segundo Sombra*, Figari's River Plate landscapes, historical recreations and domestic scenes, filtered through his subjective vision and artistically recast, made him Uruguay's best loved painter.

The most influential is Joaquín Torres García (1874–1949), who returned with his family to their native Catalonia in 1891, where he was influenced successively by Gaudí, Toulouse-Lautrec and Picasso. He gradually evolved into an idiosyncratic theorist of Latin American art who, after gravitating to abstract thinkers like Mondrian and Kandinsky in Paris, sought in his own artistic trajectory, through cubism, fauvism and neo-plasticism, to fuse figuration and abstraction, coming at last to equate classicism, humanism and universalism through a unique personal synthesis. The cubist *Album de Nueva York* (1920), the fauvist *Marina de Villefranche* (1924), and the typically personal *Constructivismo* (1929), give some sense of the stages of this journey towards a geometrical aesthetics. He is best known for works like the latter, with their rectangular divisions of the canvas based on his own mystical humanist philosophy, 'Constructive Universalism' (later summarized in *Metafísica de la prehistoria indoamericana*, 1939, and *Universalismo constructivo*, 1944). Few American artists have matched either his force of vision or theoretical complexity.

Argentine artistic circles in the 1920s were still overwhelmingly influenced by Paris at a time when the French capital, though still a great home of culture, was no longer the home of modernity itself. In Argentine painting, misdirected by Fader's pseudo-impressionism, what could be termed post-impressionist art emerged *after* cubism, causing confusion well into the 1930s. Emilio Pettoruti (1892–1971) had been an early futurist in Italy, but thereafter followed the cubist path of Braque and Picasso, with paintings like *La mesa del estudiante* (1917), *El filósofo* (1918), *Pensierosa* (1920), *Carolita* (1925), or *El quinteto* (1927). He was arguably the first Latin American artist to assimilate European avant-garde models through a personal artistic vision, sense of structure and mastery of colour; but when he returned in 1924 to Buenos Aires, where Figari was all the rage, he was shunned by academicians and social realists alike as 'superficial' and 'decorative'. Yet he was a master of formal rigour, contemptuous of all improvisation in his brilliant reconstructions of planes, and effectively introduced the constructivist method of geometrical abstraction into Latin America, with paintings whose forms construct light rather than reflect it, as exemplified in his controversial classic, *El improvisador* (1937). Pettoruti's only supporters were the young men of the avant-garde Martín Fierro movement. In that seminal year 1924, their review of the same name was launched, the influential society Amigos del Arte was formed, Pettoruti's first exhibition was held, and Xul Solar (1887–1963) returned to Argentina. Solar was typical of the era, a wilfully mysterious world traveller obsessed with spiritualism, mythology and astrology, inventor of personal labyrinths, a Jungian, cubist and surrealist by turns, and a bohemian who hated to sell his paintings. Some assert that he was the first Argentine artist to dispense altogether, in his geometrical yet dynamic works, with Renaissance concepts of space. The 'floating' quality of his paintings, typified in *Figura y serpiente* or *Juzgue* (1923), is most reminiscent of Klee.

The young intellectuals of the always effervescent Buenos Aires art milieu were divided at the time between the notorious Florida and Boedo factions. Florida artists, based in the most elegant zones, were cosmopolitan and experimental, and communicated directly with the European avant-garde, despite the deceptively nationalist name of their magazine, *Martín Fierro*: writers like Oliverio Girondo, Eduardo González Lanuza, Ernesto Palacio, Bernardo Canal Feijóo, Jorge Luis Borges, Leopoldo Marechal, and artists like Pettoruti, Solar, Figari, Gómez Cornet and Raquel Forner. Boedo's style was social realist, international only in its political commitment, with occasional infusions of expressionism to give militancy and dynamism: writers like Leónidas Barletta, Elías Castelnuovo, Alvaro Yunque, Abel Rodríguez, the brothers Enrique and Raúl Tuñón, and artists – especially engravers – like José Arato, Adolfo Bellocq, Guillermo Facio Hebécquer and Abraham Vigo. The division into opposing groups underlined and perpetuated a divorce between political and artistic vanguards which has been particularly bitter and intractable in Argentina. Antonio Berni (b. 1905) was one painter who managed to communicate a socialist ideology through avant-garde techniques, using his experience in Paris in the mid-twenties to develop a 'new realism' tinged both with surrealist and expressionist elements, as in *Desocupados* (1934), *Manifestación* (1934) or *Chacareros* (1935). Berni claimed that no Latin American artist of conscience could choose any subject other than the suffering of colonized peoples: avant-garde formalists were led 'like stupid children' through an 'imaginary, abstract and ornamental world', outside of history, without notion of concrete time and space. However, when the flamboyant Mexican Siqueiros arrived in Buenos Aires in 1933, he and Berni disagreed. Although Berni went in for large canvases, he argued that mural painting was inappropriate in a bourgeois-dominated nation like Argentina, and felt justified when the only walls Siqueiros could find were at a newspaper director's country estate. Although Juan del Prete (b. 1897) introduced fully abstract art in 1926, Argentina only finally developed its own distinctively original movements, in painting as in music, and within a generally cosmopolitan conception of Modernism, in the 1940s, at which point it became the unchallenged leader of the Latin American avant-garde.

Brazil, always similar to other Latin American nations in broad outline but always different in detailed focus, discovered its artistic identity in the 1920s – confirmed historically by the architectural explosion of the 1930s – a complex and colourful tapestry of regionalism, nationalism and cosmopolitanism all under the banner of *modernismo*, launched officially by the 1922 Semana de Arte Moderna in São Paulo. Leading figures were the expressionist painter Lasar Segall (1891–1957), a Lithuanian emigré who worked social themes like *Navio de emigrantes*, *Guerra*, or *Mãe negra* (1930); Anita Malfatti (1896–1964), who, after studying in Paris and meeting Marcel Duchamp in New York, scandalized São Paulo art circles in 1917 with the first avant-garde exhibition in Latin America; and Tarsila do Amaral (1886–1973), whose Paris studio was an avant-garde crossroads in the 1920s. Her neo-primitivist paintings, like *O mamoeiro* (1925) or *Antropofagia* (1928) led Oswald de Andrade to posit first the 'Pau-Brasil' style, then in 1927 the 'Antropofagia' movement, Brazil's version of indigenism based, with typical humour and self-confidence, on a theory of aesthetic cannibalism. By the 1930s Amaral herself had turned to social realism, with paintings like *Morro da favela* or *2a classe* (1933).

The German expressionist mode popularized by Segall was developed by the 'revolutionary romantic' Flávio de Rezende Carvalho (1899–1973), also an outstanding sculptor, celebrated for his semi-abstract portraits, bold and vivid coloration and dynamic composition, combining in a bizarre lyrical representationalism. The outstanding avant-garde painter of the generation, however, was Emiliano di Cavalcanti (1897–1976), who adapted Picasso's neo-classical phase from the olympian to the tropical, as in his 1927 study of a seated nude. Like Toulouse-Lautrec, he concentrated on women – black, in this case – graceful even in oppression, from a lucid social perspective. His remarkable versatility – including brilliantly mobile lithographs and etchings – created an astonishing variety of Brazilian scenes, human and natural, combining vivid colours, flowing forms and great emotional empathy. Yet even he was overshadowed by Cândido Portinari (1903–62), who is to painting what Villa-Lobos is to music, the great vehicle of artistic nationalism during the late 1920s and the 1930s, simplifying and developing the lessons of Mexican muralism after assimilating cubism, expressionism and surrealism, the examples of Braque, Picasso and Rivera. Among his most familiar paintings are *Cabeça de índio, Futebol* (1931–2), *Trabalhador rural* (1934), and *Café* (1935). The only Latin American painter outside Mexico to create a vast national pictorial epic, he eventually painted a set of murals, 'The Epic of Brazil', for Costa and Niemeyer's Ministry of Education building, with a fluent mixture of lyricism, realism and traditionalism. Some critics consider him too 'sociological'; others, the 'most modern of the ancients'; most agree, however, that his grandiose record of Brazilian history and landscape is one of Brazil's most important cultural landmarks.

Sculpture

Modern sculpture was slow to develop in Latin America, perhaps surprisingly in view of the vigorous religious and popular traditions. Most nineteenth-century sculptors were routinely occupied on commissioned busts and small neo-classical statues. One of the few large-scale monuments not imported was Noreña's bronze statue of Cuauhtémoc for Mexico City in 1889. The statue of Sarmiento unveiled in Buenos Aires in 1910, year of the International Exposition, was by Rodin, who, with Bourdelle, was an overwhelming influence on Latin American sculpture during that transitional era. As Argentine prosperity gave scope for increasingly ambitious monumentalism, Rogelio Yrurtia (1879–1950) produced his striking statue of Dorrego and the monument to Rivadavia, and Alfredo Bigatti (1898–1964) and José Fioravanti (1896–1977) subsequently carried out numerous commemorative commissions, including the homage to the national flag in Rosario. Uruguay had a similarly influential monumental sculptor in Bernabé Michelena (b. 1888). In the 1920s Latin American sculpture finally began to make strides similar to, though less dramatic than, those in painting. In Argentina Antonio Sibellino (b. 1891) with his *Composición de formas* (1926), produced what is by general consent the first abstract sculpture by a Latin American; other innovators were the cubist Pablo Curatella Manes (1891–1962) and Sosostris Vitullo (1899–1953). Chile's immensely rich modern developments fall outside our period. Brazilian sculpture had been no more than conventionally respectable in the nineteenth century; but the Italian immigrant Vítor Brecheret (1894–1955), an influential participant in the Modern Art Week, was probably the greatest sculptor since Aleijadinho. Generally, though, it was only after the 1920s indigenist movements, although largely figurative, had indicated the historical potential of the pre-Columbian heritage, that the genre really developed. A key precursor was Ignacio Asúnsolo (1890–1965), a Mexican who effected fusions between European examples like Rodin and Amerindian models. Ten of his monuments stand in Mexico City, devoted mainly to poets and politicians. Even countries with little in the way of pre-Columbian relics took up the theme, sometimes opting for solutions like those of Mérida or Torres García in painting. Eventually sculpture came fully into its own everywhere with the new vogue, essentially Mexican in origin, for integrated architecture, painting and sculpture.

Music

Latin American music between 1900 and 1930 shows clearly how rapidly the arts were moving into mutual focus. In 1906 the Italian composer Chiafarelli remarked that Brazil was still hardly more than 'a musical province of Italy', and even in 1916 Saint-Saëns unambiguously dubbed Buenos Aires 'Conservatoriopolis'; yet the slavishly mimetic or aridly academic traces they detected were clues to the past, not signs to the future. Although romanticism survived, particularly in regional music and urban popular song, it had lost its vitality; but those same popular forms, in their raw state, were becoming increasingly assertive and beginning – thanks, ironically enough, to Bizet – to reach a world audience. Songs like the *habanera*, *Tú* (1894), by the Cuban Eduardo Sánchez de Fuentes (1874–1944), and Ponce's *Estrellita*, swept through Latin America, whilst *habaneras*, *contradanzas* and *tangos* successively reverberated around Europe between 1890 and the 1920s. In art music meanwhile the trend was a refinement of romanticism through the French impressionism of Debussy and Ravel, perhaps the final phase in the organic evolution of European music since the Renaissance.

Carlos Chávez (1899–1978), most probably with Villa-Lobos the greatest name in twentieth-century Latin American music, belonged to that generation which came to prominence after the First World War, when so many artistic problems suddenly became soluble at last. Chávez, indeed, is an exemplary figure in the process of internalizing a chosen past, fusing it with the nationalist demands of the present whilst incorporating international developments. To say that he sought an 'Aztec Renaissance' is to simplify his intentions, which were not to recreate pre-Columbian musical patterns or techniques as such, but to connote them and thus disinter 'one of the deepest layers of the Mexican soul', as he declared in 1928. His modal or pentatonic melodies signified an indigenist commitment but did not reconstruct Indian reality past or present: rather, the process used made the past finally communicate with the present and thus compelled its assimilation. Despite adolescent piano arrangements of revolutionary songs like *Adelita* and *La cucaracha*, Chávez was always wary of popular music, placing his main emphasis on classical Indian forms, and two-thirds of his compositions contained no intrinsically Mexican content. His use of folk or popular materials involved extensive distillation and synthesis, far more than was the case with Copland, Vaughan Williams, Falla or even Villa-Lobos. The most characteristic pieces combine modernist and primitivist elements in a manner reminiscent of the early Stravinsky, as in the youthful ballet *El fuego nuevo* (1921). Later Chávez demanded the incorporation of autochthonous musical instruments, studiously avoided all romantic chords and dispensed with harmony, employing devices such as repetition, parallelism, frequent changes of tempo and rhythm, syncopation, and both pentatonic and diatonic modal melodies. In 1925 he produced another ballet, *Los cuatro soles*, followed by *Seven Pieces for Piano* (1926–30). In 1932 the anti-imperialist ballet *Caballos de vapor (H.P.)* was produced in Philadelphia by Stokowski, with sets by Rivera. This was Chávez's most militant phase, during which he instituted workers' concerts and composed populist works such as *Llamadas: sinfonía proletaria* (1934). Like other indigenists, he saw thematic links between pre-Columbian cultural motifs, contemporary indigenous culture and the march of socialism. In 1935 the *Sinfonía india* was performed, the work with which he is associated internationally.

Just as the 1920s saw the first great formative phase in the development of national art galleries, so it was the era of the symphony orchestra. The contribution of the Mexican national symphony orchestra under Chávez to Mexican musical life was unsurpassed; innumerable nationalist works were premiered in the late 1920s and early 1930s. Chávez's assistant throughout the period was Silvestre Revueltas (1899–1949), an outstanding composer in his own right. Where Chávez was austere, even magisterial, Revueltas was exuberantly populist and drew mainly on contemporary folk and popular music, as well as writing film scores. His first full orchestral piece was *Cuauhnáhuac* (1930), the best-loved perhaps the government-commissioned film piece *Janitzio* (1933). Later came a homage to Lorca and in 1938 *Sensemayá*, a vibrant evocation of Nicolás Guillén's Cuban poetry.

Not everyone in Mexico was engaged in nationalist exploration. Julián Carrillo (1875–1965), although of Indian extraction, was closely associated with the Díaz regime and spent many years in Europe. In 1920 he was appointed director of the national symphony orchestra for the second time, and took part in Vasconcelos's contradictory campaign of Indianist nationalism and – Carrillo's own preference – neo-classical revivalism. Thereafter, with his academic and romantic-impressionist phases behind him, Carrillo launched his celebrated theory of microtones, called 'Sonido 13' (symbolizing, according to Slonimsky, 'the field of sounds smaller than the twelve semitones of the tempered scale'),[28] on which he had been working since 1895, together with a new system of notation for which he became internationally recognized, although the theory was never widely applied. His first exposition of the system was with his own *Preludio a Colón* in 1922.

Such was the vitality of popular music in Cuba and so deadening the Spanish academic heritage, that it was difficult for serious composers to find a stylistic foothold in the recently liberated island before the 1920s. It was the Grupo Minorista of poets, artists and musicians who from 1923 provided the intellectual basis for renovating Cuban musical culture. *Afrocubanismo*, inspired in part by the great folklorist and ethnomusicologist Fernando Ortiz (1881–1969), who was particularly influential as a university teacher in Havana between 1909–18, found its most striking exponent in the mulatto composer Amadeo Roldán (1900–39), composer of the pathbreaking *Obertura sobre temas cubanos* (1925), *Tres pequeños poemas* (1926), and *La rebambaramba* (1928), from a story by Alejo Carpentier, who was not only to become a world-famous novelist but also, like Mário de Andrade in Brazil, a leading authority on national music. Another Carpentier story led to Roldán's second ballet, *El milagro de Anaquillé* (1929), and in 1930 he wrote *Motivos de son*, based on Guillén's poems, perfecting his intricate fusion of native folk elements, including syncopation, with sophisticated cosmopolitan orchestration and a mixture of native and European instruments. The work of Alejandro García Caturla (1906–40) was equally striking. Dazzled in Paris by

---

[28] See N. Slonimsky, *Music of Latin America* (New York, 1945), 229.

Stravinsky, Satie and Milhaud, he maintained his identification with black culture, adapting the *conga*, *son*, *comparsa* and *rumba*; and his *Tres danzas cubanas* (1928) and the suite *Bembé* (1929) reveal sure mastery of both traditions. Like Roldán, he collaborated extensively with Carpentier, for example on *Dos poemas afrocubanos* (1929), or the ritualistic symphonic poem *Yamba-O* (1928–31), and adapted various poems by Nicolás Guillén. Although his basic model was the *son*'s essentially pentatonic melody, he wrote an orchestral piece entitled *La rumba* in 1933.

On the whole Peruvian erudite culture has failed to achieve the artistic miscegenations of other parts of the continent. This is evidently due to a deep-seated reluctance to integrate indigenous culture, but is ironic in view of the extraordinary quality of its pre-Columbian arts and crafts, or its contemporary folk music. Teodoro Valcárcel (1902–42) composed the indigenist pieces *Sacsahuamán* (1928) and *Suite incaica*, but could not get his works satisfactorily orchestrated in his native land, whilst the Bolivian José María Velasco (b. 1899) wrote a ballet *Amerindia* to glorify 'the new Indian of tomorrow' in the early 1930s, but had to wait until 1938 to see it performed in Berlin courtesy of the German ministry of propaganda.

Nativism has been the exception in Chile, but Carlos Isamitt (1887–1974) and Pedro Humberto Allende (1885–1959) pioneered research among the Mapuches. Allende also quoted mainstream *mestizo* folk music in the symphonic suite *Escenas campesinas chilenas* (1914), the tone poem *La voz de las calles* (1920) and the *Tonadas de carácter popular chileno* (1922). Carlos Lavín (1883–1962), another indigenist, composed *Mitos araucanos* and *Lamentaciones huilliches* (1928) for contralto and orchestra, and *Suite andina* (1929) for piano. Quite different in orientation was Domingo Santa Cruz (b. 1899), who composed the neo-classical *Cuatro poemas de Gabriela Mistral* in 1928.

In Argentina and Uruguay the picture was particularly complex after 1918. The nationalist rural-gauchesque tradition remained vigorous beyond 1940, complemented by emerging Andean and *porteño* currents. Italian immigrants were especially influential, and the opening of the Colón in 1908 both confirmed Buenos Aires as a world centre for Italian opera and stimulated a spate of nativist operas in the tradition of Williams and Aguirre (see above). Felipe Boero (1884–1958) wrote numerous operas, such as *El matrero* (1929), clothing folk legends in Italian garb, like Juan Bautista Massa (1885–1938), whose full-blown operatic style culminated in the symphonic poem *La muerte del Inca* (1932). Another Italianizer of Argentine folklore was Constantino Gaito (1878–1945), with *Flor de nieve* (1922), *Ollantay* (1926), and a symphonic poem *El ombú* (1925) evoking that symbol of Argentine solitude.

A more authentic regionalist was Carlos López Buchardo (1881–1948), whose symphonic poem *Escenas argentinas* (1922) was one of the most admired *criollista* works of the period. Floro M. Ugarte (1884–1975) composed *De mi tierra* (1923), a tone poem based on Estanislao del Campo's gauchesque poetry, and Honorio Sicardi (b. 1897) wrote *Tres poemas sobre Martín Fierro*. The most effective *criollista*, however, was Luis Gianneo (1897–1968), a member of the influential Grupo Renovación, who composed *Pampeanas* (1924), *Coplas* (1929), based on popular poetry, and the indigenist symphonic poems *Turay-Turay* (1928) and *El tarco en flor* (1930). Uruguay's most influential nationalist work was *Campo* (1909), by Eduardo Fabini (1882–1950), first performed only in 1922. It was to Uruguay that Francisco Curt Lange (b. 1903) emigrated in 1923, later to become one of the continent's foremost musicologists.

In the River Plate countries, however, there was always a certain suspicion of regionalism, and its exponents themselves not infrequently later renounced their youthful enthusiasms, as Borges did the poetry of his 'fervent youth'. Juan Carlos Paz (1901–72) of the Grupo Renovación was resolutely and irascibly opposed to all nationalist music as one more version of programme composition, like 'literary' references, which he also despised. Paz at first adopted a neo-classical style, but later advocated Schoenberg's serial techniques and the work of other avant-garde composers like Weber, Varèse and Berg. Significantly, it was at precisely the moment, in the late 1920s, when nationalism began to falter and cosmopolitanism again became a virtue, that Argentine music, like its painting, began to come into its own.

The Brazilian panorama was dominated by the giant figure of Heitor Villa-Lobos (1887–1959), 'the Rabelais of Latin American music', incomparably the most popular serious composer to have emerged from the continent. He composed over a thousand works for all media and in all genres, fusing the musical traditions of Portuguese, Negro and Indian into one vast synthesis, embracing every Brazilian region and social stratum past and present. No wonder he boasted: 'I am folklore; my melodies are just as authentic as those which originate in the souls of the people'. Once a popular musician himself, he spent eight years travelling the country, learning its music through intuition whilst repeatedly rejecting academic training. His early works were *Suite dos cânticos sertanejos* (1910), already based on folk sources, *Amazonas* (1917), *Lenda do caboclo* (1920), and *Nonetto* ('A quick impression of all Brazil', 1923). He met Milhaud in Rio in 1916 and was a major participant in the São Paulo Modern Art Week in 1922. In Paris from 1923, his 'primitiveness', exaggerated with the born impresario's instinct for playing to his audience, ensured success. The French composer Florent Schmitt called him 'three-quarters god, with blazing eyes and crocodile teeth'.[29] Villa-Lobos instinctively accommodated – indeed, he anticipated – the vogue for combining formal innovation with primitive content. Far from falling for his own image, he underwent a period of intense creativity. *Rudepoema*, completed in Paris and dedicated to Rubinstein, is one of the most complex piano pieces of the century, yet he was simultaneously composing children's songs and his most important nationalist works, the 16 *Choros*, ranging from relatively abstract pieces to completely programmatic and even onomatopoeic evocations of the Brazilian landscape. The nine *Bachianas brasileiras* (1930–35) adapted baroque counterpoint to Brazilian popular music, including a structural exploration of the *modinha*. In the 1930s, perhaps appropiately, the gargantuan Villa-Lobos became involved in Getúlio Vargas's gigantic education programme, organizing immense musical rallies of up to 40,000 people.

It was difficult to live in Villa-Lobos's shadow, but Oscar Lorenzo Fernândez (1897–1948) wrote a *Canção sertaneja* (1924), an Amerindian tone poem *Imbapara* (1929) and an opera *Malazarte* (1933) to a libretto based on Graça Aranha's drama about the Brazilian folk hero. Fernândez collaborated frequently with Mário de Andrade, whose seminal *Ensaio sôbre a música brasileira* appeared in 1928. It was Andrade who, with Luciano Gallet (1893–1931), pioneered the study of Brazilian folk music. Gallet's *Canções populares brasileiras* appeared in 1924 and the piano piece *Nhô Chico* in 1927. Other associates of Andrade's worthy of mention were Camargo Guarnieri (b. 1907) and Francisco Mignone (b. 1897).

The novel

The first decade of the twentieth century saw the broad cultural movement of which literary modernism and naturalism were at once

[29] Béhague, *Music in Latin America*, 186.

opposing and complementary faces, visibly drained of vitality, at a historical moment when the widespread stability of the later nineteenth century was threatened by diverse factors, not least the gathering impact of immigration and the rise of workers' movements. Once the pace of modernization began to accelerate and true modernity appeared on the horizon, Spanish American *modernismo* was doomed, and would become superseded with astonishing rapidity by the post-war avant-garde; as concepts of class struggle overtook the biological and racial perspectives of social Darwinism, naturalism was bound to re-develop, creating new versions of the 'realist' impulse such as regionalism (including *criollismo*, usually conservative in impulse, and *indigenismo* and *afroamericanismo*, both usually progressive) and the social-realist novel.

Spain's defeat in 1898 had put an end not only to the century but to an old world, though Latin Americans were uncomfortably aware that they were the creatures of that world, and that it had been overcome by other, more technologically and economically advanced Americans; new ideas from Europe, notably Bakunin and Marx, arrived to challenge the old and were diffused by a new generation of thinkers and politicians. Positivism, still advocating orderly progress, after several generations in which revolutionary thought had barely existed in the continent, gave way to more explicitly political ideologies, as early socialist parties formed, followed in the 1920s by communist parties.[30] All the more surprising, then, in retrospect, that Rodó's *Ariel* should so have influenced two generations of artists and politicians (like Batlle in Uruguay and Yrigoyen in Argentina) with its message of truth, beauty and spirituality based on Guyau, Carlyle, Emerson and Renan, but then the new generation, particularly the students, were looking almost desperately for some message of hope at the bleak dawn of the new century. Although the magisterial gravity of Rodó's Graeco-Roman prose seems more than eighty years away from us now, it inspired those who themselves were wishing to become educators, not of children but of the workers and peasants.

The First World War was a watershed. Literary developments evolving gradually to 1914 seemed suddenly complete by 1920. Poetry in particular underwent a revolution in form and function, shifting from ear to eye and breaking free of metre, rhyme and rhetoric to become either hermetically avant-garde or wilfully commonplace and prosaic.

[30] See Hale, *CHLA* IV, chap. 10.

Prose, always weighed down by history itself, was slower to react, but the naturalist novel rapidly became more historical, political and economic, less biological and sociological; or, as in Reyles (see above) or Güiraldes (see below), inched towards the poetic pattern by fusing with the modernist novel. Before 1910 realist novelists, within a world view almost exclusively liberal in contexture, had been able to take up vague abstract commitments to 'civilization', 'progress' or 'justice'; after 1918 such political innocence was lost and writers who were apolitical or wished to conceal their allegiances would have to evade or confuse the issue. Before 1900 the progressive writer was against Spain, then the United States; after 1918 he had to oppose the landowners as well, and possibly even capitalism. The Mexican Revolution, the Russian Revolution, the First World War and the University Reform Movement at Córdoba together launched a complex tidal wave, some of whose impact was immediate, some short and some long-term, but whose effect remains today. In 1900 Latin American intellectuals were still assimilating Darwin, Spencer, Nietzsche and Bakunin; now Marx, Lenin, Trotsky, Freud, Bergson and Einstein arrived in rapid succession, not to mention diversionary eccentrics like Spengler and Keyserling, accelerating the development of realist narrative away from biological determinism to a more overtly political perspective based on a newly emerging class consciousness and the alliance between intellectuals and workers advocated by González Prada (for example, in his speech 'El intelectual y los obreros', 1905).

An early symptom of the change was the Chilean Baldomero Lillo (1867–1923), whose story collections *Sub terra* (1904) and *Sub sole* (1907) have usually been dismissed as late naturalist or regionalist, when he was one of the very first to view the proletariat as workers rather than members of the 'lower reaches' of society. Lillo himself was from a poor southern family, and spent many years as an employee in a mining *pulpería*. *Sub terra*'s mining stories include two, 'La compuerta número 12' and 'El chiflón del diablo', which, in their stark unsentimental realism and apparently spontaneous structural logic, represent early masterpieces of the genre. Lillo's concentration on the worker's own experience of industrial labour signals the transition from mechanistic naturalism to a new version of realism grounded in economics and politics, giving rise to the great age of the Latin American social novel between the wars.

In Bolivia, Alcides Arguedas (1879–1946), despite the pessimistic *Pueblo enfermo* (1909), was the first to point Latin American indigenist fiction in a more sociological direction. *Wata Wara* (1904) is a story of Indian lovers brutally mistreated by a *gamonal*, which, instead of the usual sentimental romanticism or brutal naturalism, examines the real social condition of the Indians and even ends with them exacting just revenge. Virtually ignored, Arguedas re-elaborated the book during a period of fifteen years, giving it a more panoramic perspective and an epic dimension which make its definitive version, *Raza de bronce* (1919), the precursors of all the great indigenist works of the next two decades, and inaugurating the theme of 'beggars on golden stools' in the implicit contrast between the soaring, grandiose landscapes of the Andes and the sordid and unjust condition to which its inhabitants have been reduced.[31]

The third great precursor was the Uruguayan Horacio Quiroga (1878–1937), whose life was marked by repeated tragedy. Poe, Maupassant, Chekhov and Kipling were his principal models, and his stories contain a gallery of horrors almost without parallel in Latin American fiction. His first poems, *Los arrecifes de coral* (1901), were dedicated to the Argentine modernist Lugones, who included Quiroga in an expedition to the forests of Misiones. There the Uruguayan writer was destined to spend most of the rest of his life, far from urban civilization, producing numerous outstanding collections of stories: *Cuentos de amor, de locura y de muerte* (1917), *Cuentos de la selva* (1918), *El salvaje* (1920), *Anaconda* (1921), *El desierto* (1924) and *Los desterrados* (1926). Quiroga is the nearest Latin America comes to a Conrad. His stories deal with ordinary, uneducated men struggling against the two equally barbarous worlds of wild nature and human society, and usually end in horrifying defeat. Critics have not found it easy to categorize Quiroga: some, thinking of Poe, have called him 'gothic'; others, anticipating Arlt, have preferred 'expressionist'. Their difficulty is that while Quiroga undoubtedly synthesizes a number of currents within early twentieth-century fiction, his own bleak, almost hallucinatory vision is entirely unique. He is also, however, the first, and one of the very greatest, of the new wave of regionalist writers who, in the social realist era, became the first generation of Latin American novelists – in the 1920s – to come to international attention.

The historical phenomenon which attracted the world's gaze to the continent was the Mexican Revolution (1910–20). In Mexico itself, where the narrative tradition since Lizardi at the beginning of the

[31] See Hale, *CHLA* IV, chap. 10.

nineteenth century had been consistently worthy and vigorous but
somewhat undistinguished, the Revolution stimulated that well-known
regional sub-genre, the 'novel of the Mexican Revolution'. The label
has perpetuated a misconception that Mariano Azuela (1873–1952) and
Martín Luis Guzmán (1887–1976), for example, were revolutionary
novelists. Azuela was, in fact, profoundly sceptical about the Revolution
and Guzmán took an almost conservative perspective. The crucial point
was that both had lived through the conflict: like Lillo, who knew
everything about the mines, like Arguedas, brought up on a semi-feudal
estate, or Quiroga, who had lived and suffered in the jungle. It would be
misleading to suggest that these literary chroniclers of the Revolution
really did manage to reproduce the lives of their characters across the
abyss of class, race and lived experience, but this was undoubtedly the era
– the only one so far – when middle-class novelists in every country
began to reach out and touch the lives of their hitherto alien and still
largely illiterate compatriots to speak on their behalf. After 1945 the
social-realist current would again return to minority status as novelists
undertook the appraisal of their own class which European fiction had
completed by the First World War, but which only Machado de Assis
had been able to bring to a fine art in Latin America.

Mariano Azuela almost literally leaped at the historical opportunity
afforded by the Revolution. A supporter of Madero, whose ideology he
shared, Azuela's first important work was *Andrés Pérez, maderista* (1911),
which communicates his disenchantment with the early months, when
his own political ambitions were frustrated. His lasting claim on literary
history, however, was *Los de abajo* (1915), written partly in the heat of
battle – Azuela was a doctor in Villa's army – and partly in its
disillusioned aftermath. Effectively Spanish America's first modern
novel, the speed, exhilaration and confusion of its revolutionary content
created a nervous, tersely impressionistic style and a structure which
appears to accelerate the reader, along with the characters, to his
disillusionment and their doom. In its freshness and vivacity, pioneering
approach to popular dialogue and national humour, and frank depiction
of the gulf between those who labour by hand and by brain, the novel
provides an unforgettable, almost cinematographic view of the revolutionary era.

Los de abajo was virtually unread until 1924, and the other so-called
novels of the Revolution appeared between 1926, when Guzmán's *El
águila y la serpiente* appeared, and 1939 – coinciding more closely,

therefore, with the golden age of Mexican cinema which followed the Revolution than with the contemporaneous muralist movement. Guzmán's famous novel is really a documentary dramatizing the novelist's own experiences. He too had been a *maderista* and could not subsequently identify with the positions of Villa (who nevertheless became a lifelong obsession), Carranza, Obregón or Calles. Ideologically sceptical, almost classical in its choice of expression, no artistic work of the era has more lastingly influenced the Revolution's perception by later generations. Guzmán's interest is in 'los de arriba'; the peasant revolutionaries are seen only in the mass, as if across a vast social abyss. Yet we obtain a crystal-clear (one would not wish to say 'true') impression of Guzmán's experiences, artfully composed yet apparently as natural as breathing; and an illuminating if unconscious insight into the relation between the middle-class novelist and his peasant or proletarian characters. His next novel, *La sombra del caudillo* (1929), was a bitter critique of the Calles regime, and, though rarely quoted, one of the continent's most important literary explorations of the authoritarian impulse. A third novelist, Gregorio López y Fuentes (1897–1967), although less talented than Azuela and Guzmán, was an important link between the novel of the Revolution and other genres, with *Campamento* (1931), a brief narrative which develops techniques for conveying mass psychology typical of the era; *Tierra* (1932), on the agrarian struggle launched by Zapata; and *El indio* (1935), condemning the treatment of Indian communities both during and after the conflict.

In general, then, the Revolution produced fiction which, for the first time since Mármol's *Amalia* (1851),[32] saw history not as something in the distant past, like the colonial or independence periods, but as both a reality and a concept which could at once mobilize and fix the perception of social, political and economic events. Henceforth this historical awareness would sharply distinguish social realism from the more complacent *criollista* mode within the general movement of realism. The trend is illustrated by Latin America's most famous jungle novel, *La vorágine* (1924) by the Colombian José Eustasio Rivera (1888–1928), whose reputation is deservedly growing. It concerns a Bogotá poet who elopes with his mistress to the Amazon, and is sucked into a whirlpool of social, economic and natural disaster. The protagonist is a theatrical, anachronistic and essentially romantic personality whose first-person

[32] See Martin, *CHLA* III, chap. 18.

narration reproduces his own temperament. This has induced most critics to conclude that the novel is an unrestrained piece of tropical hyperbole, when in fact it subtly undermines the narrator's moral status and gradually transforms itself into a semi-documentary work exposing the exploitation of the Amazon rubber gatherers during the process of primitive accumulation. Rivera was another writer recasting his own experiences, having worked as a boundary commissioner in the Amazon. His newspaper reports on conditions for workers trapped by the *enganche* system in the almost inaccessible forests, combined with the impact of the novel, helped to change government labour policies.

The last line of *La vorágine*, 'the jungle devoured them', has been used ironically by critics to indicate that this fiction remained inherently deterministic, its characters dwarfed and ultimately obliterated by the vast natural landscapes of these novels. Such criticisms have their justification, but ignore the context in which writers were working. Latin American fiction had not yet explored, still less inhabited those vast open spaces, because they had not yet been fully developed in reality. It was hardly surprising that the continent remained largely a 'novel without novelists', in Luis Alberto Sánchez' phrase.[33] Again, critics have condemned both the collective characterization of this fiction and the apparent passivity of its characters; but here too the uneven nature of Latin American development meant that workers' movements appeared on the scene before Latin American fiction had experienced the 'classical' moment of European bourgeois realism, whilst, on the other side, such was the state of development of the early workers' movements in the 1920s that any triumphalist interpretation of their consciousness and achievements would have involved serious distortion.

One country where nature really had been largely domesticated and where the epic phase was past, was Argentina, whose greatest regional novel of the 1920s was *Don Segundo Sombra* (1926) by Ricardo Güiraldes (1886–1927), a wealthy landowner with an *estancia* in Buenos Aires province and apartments in Paris. His gauchesque masterpiece, published long after the golden age of the gauchos had passed into legend, creates a myth to inspire young Argentines to grow up straight and true. Like Jack Schaeffer's *Shane* (1954), the novel employs the device of viewing the cowboy hero through the eyes of a young person, its

33 It is the title of his influential book, *América, novela sin novelistas* (Santiago de Chile, 1933). Sánchez's perplexities took on a still more metaphysical turn in 1945 when he produced a work entitled *¿Existe América Latina?*.

nostalgic force underlined by the dramatic contrast between its exquisite symbolist-impressionist form and the often brutal, always harsh subject matter. Few novels are more dishonest, however: purporting to exalt the cowboy of the pampas but written by a landowner (whose own father, moreover, employed the man on whom the fictional hero is based); mourning the gaucho's loss of freedom when it was families like the author's who fenced off the open ranges and turned the nomadic gauchos from knights of the prairies into hired hands; providing a disingenuous apology for *machista* values – interpreted inevitably as a continuingly valid code of honour – which ruled not only the pampas but the patriarchal world of the Argentine ruling class; in short, regretfully evoking a world uncomplicated by immigration, proletarian mass movements and industrialization, when landowner and gaucho supposedly shared the same individualist, stoical and epic philosophy of life, and the same love of the land. As Don Segundo rode into a tearful sunset, he eclipsed most other works of the pampas, but there are many more: Lugones's *La guerra gaucha* (1905) and *El payador* (1916); *Los gauchos judíos* (1910), by the Russian immigrant Alberto Gerchunoff (1883–1950); a number of books by Manuel Gálvez (1882–1962), polemical author of the well-known novel *La maestra normal* (1914); *El inglés de los güesos* (1924) and *El romance de un gaucho* (1933), by Benito Lynch (1885–1951); Reyles's *El gaucho Florido* (1932), and *El paisano Aguilar* (1934) by his compatriot Enrique Amorim (1900–60). The essential interpretive work for reading such fictional constructs in the light of River Plate history is the brilliant essay *Radiografía de la pampa* (1933) by the Argentine *pensador* Ezequiel Martínez Estrada (1895–1964).

More deluded than hypocritical was the writer generally considered to be, if not the greatest, then the most important Spanish American regionalist: the Venezuelan Rómulo Gallegos (1883–1969), author of the famous *Doña Bárbara* (1929) and many other novels. Bolívar's fatherland had endured the most unhappy of nineteenth-century experiences of *caudillismo*, prolonged into the contemporary period by the dictatorship of Juan Vicente Gómez (1908–35), apparently justifying Gallegos in resurrecting Sarmiento's opposition between civilization and barbarism in *Facundo*. No writer shows more clearly the achievements and limitations of the period. His identification of the essential themes was matchless in its time, and only Vargas Llosa among later novelists has shown his Conradian breadth of ambition. Unfortunately his ideas and arguments are as interesting outside the novels as within, and few of his characters are blessed with life. Like Rodó, Gallegos, a great educator, repeatedly offered cultural solutions for economic problems, showing no more insight into the psychology of his characters than into national politics. (Like Sarmiento he later became president, but was swiftly deposed.) Simplistic distinctions between civilization and barbarism are unhelpful in the face of capitalism and imperialism, and the delusion reached a climax in *Doña Bárbara* when Gallegos somehow persuaded himself and a generation of readers that his protagonist, the idealistically named Santos Luzardo, is a representative of civilization because he replaces an anarchic, inefficient semi-feudal agriculture with a more organized but equally paternalistic system. Nevertheless, he first gave literary form to myths which others would later elaborate, and no writer more lucidly and ambitiously set out to explore and colonize the natural landscapes of the continent through fiction, thereby undertaking the essential task, as Alejo Carpentier described it, of pointing his finger and naming things, like Adam. Without him the fiction of the 1920s could not have appeared so visibly the foundation of all that has happened since.

Nowhere was the confluence of realism and regionalism more decisively established in the late 1920s than in Ecuador, where the Grupo de Guayaquil in 1931 published a joint collection of stories, *Los que se van*. Those involved were Demetrio Aguilera Malta (1909–81), Joaquín Gallegos Lara (1911–47) and Enrique Gil Gilbert (1912–75), the last two communists, joined by Alfredo Pareja Diezcanseco (b. 1908) and José de la Cuadra (1904–41), one of the great Spanish American short-story writers and author of the novel *Los Sangurimas* (1933). Aguilera Malta, however, became the best known, with *Don Goyo* (1933) and *Canal Zone* (1935). This committed, neo-realist, unusually cohesive group were perhaps the nearest literary parallel to the Mexican muralist movement. Ecuador's best known writer of the century was Jorge Icaza (1906–78), from Quito, whose brutal indigenist novel *Huasipungo* (1934) is the culmination of the social-realist current, appearing, appropriately enough, at the moment when Zdhanov was imposing the official Soviet doctrine of socialist realism in the USSR. It traces the chain of exploitation from Chicago to the Ecuadorean sierras. No novel has been more vituperated – for its crude language and technique, its depiction of Indians reduced by priests and landowners to subhuman status – but no novel has so obstinately refused to be marginalized. After Icaza's definitive treatment, however, the indigenist novel began to lose its vitality, although one acknowledged master of the genre, Ciro Alegría (Peru, 1909–67), did not produce his first novel, *La serpiente de oro*, until 1935, and his world-famous *El mundo es ancho y ajeno* until 1941.

Although most of its development came after the period under consideration, the urban novel began to evolve in Spanish America in the 1920s and to reflect the disorientation of significant sectors of society in the face of rapidly changing circumstances. An early example was *Un perdido* (1917) by the Chilean Eduardo Barrios (1884–1963). *Un perdido* gave a petty-bourgeois gloss to the urban alienation theme dramatized by Cambaceres through the aristocratic protagonist of *Sin rumbo* thirty years before (see above). The outstanding exponent of this line was Roberto Arlt (Argentina, 1900–42), whose *El juguete rabioso* (1926), *Los siete locos* (1929), *Los lanzallamas* (1931) and *El amor brujo* (1932) conveyed a tortured, sordid yet fantastic world of almost expressionist horror, the first reminiscent of Gorky, the later works of Dostoyevsky and Céline, anticipating such typically Argentine novelists as Marechal, Mallea and Sábato. Closely associated with the Boedo social-realists, Arlt's own style burst all limitations; instead of providing typological case studies of workers like, say, Leónidas Barletta (1902–1975) in *Royal Circo* (1927), he used characters like pimps, prostitutes, embezzlers, murderers and lunatics as grotesque metaphors for the impact of capitalism as creator of the urban nightmare. His reputation continues to grow. Together with Barletta, Samuel Eichelbaum (1894–1967), Armando Discépolo (1887–1971), and Francisco Defilippis Novoa (1891–1930), Arlt also contributed to the continuing vigour of Argentine drama in the 1920s.

In Brazil, the century had begun dramatically with *Os sertões* and *Canaã*. Euclides da Cunha (1866–1909), an ex-soldier and engineer from Rio, was sent by a newspaper to cover the campaign against the messianic uprising of *sertanejos* at Canudos in 1896. The result, *Os sertões* (1902), was a powerful synthesis of history, geography and sociology, and a remarkable interpretation of the relation between man and environment in a narration of astonishing force and conviction. Although he too was blinded partly by the racial ideologies of mechanistic Positivism, Da Cunha argued fervently for the development and full integration of the north-east into the national economic, political and educational system, catalysing a process of self-analysis and public debate which came to see the *caboclo*, and in particular the *sertanejo*, as the bedrock of Brazilian national identity. This process led directly both to 1920s *modernismo* and to the regionalist movement launched by Gilberto Freyre after 1926 (see below).[34] José Pereira da Graça Aranha (1868–1931) was himself from the north-east, but set his novel *Canaã* – about the differing attitudes of two German immigrants – in the south, target of most immigration and future economic development. Graça Aranha took a pessimistic view of Brazil's existing racial stock and placed his hopes in the new miscegenation. In general, however, novelists before 1918 were disappointingly unable to produce works relevant to Brazil's national problems. Although both Brazilian romanticism and naturalism had been more complete and more 'European' than their Spanish American equivalents, the late arrival of abolition and the republic meant that a number of historical tasks already completed elsewhere had not yet been carried out by Brazilian artists who were overwhelmingly resident in the coastal strip of an immense country which contained, in the *sertão* or the Amazon, for example, some of the most forbidding territories to be confronted anywhere in the continent. Whilst Brazil had continued its coherent but excessively respectful parnassian and symbolist movements, Spanish America undertook the road to true modernity through the continental movement of *modernismo*; and although Brazil produced more authentic naturalist novels than all the Spanish American republics combined, they remained at the level of socio-biological case studies, distanced from characters conceived as specimens with grave 'character' defects – often racial in origin – rather than products of a specific history and social structure. Euclides da Cunha shattered this illusion, but it took many years for the impact to be reflected adequately in fiction. Henrique Coelho Neto (1864–1934), Brazil's most prolific writer, produced numerous rather ornate stories about the *sertão*; João Simões Lopes Neto (1865–1916), published regionalist works like *Contos gauchescos* (1912) or *Lendas do sul* (1913); and Afonso Arinos (1868–1916), the anachronistic, almost picturesque stories in *Lendas e tradições brasileiras* (1917). More interesting was Afonso Henriques de Lima Barreto (1881–1922), mulatto author of bitter iconoclastic works depicting the frustrated inhabitants of suburban Rio in a style reminiscent of Machado, if less balanced. His best novel was *Triste fim de Policarpo Quaresma* (1915).

The writer who began to tie loose ends and weave a new regional pattern was the turbulent José Bento Monteiro Lobato (1882–1948), later recognized both by Oswald de Andrade, a leader of the 1922 modernist movement, and Gilberto Freyre, founder of the 1926

[34] See Hale, *CHLA* IV, chap. 10.

regionalist movement, as a precursor. Lobato called for a nationalist, quintessentially Brazilian art in all genres, pouring scorn on the mimetic quality of most contemporary works. His first book of short stories, *Urupês* (1918), set in his native São Paulo, not only renovated literary language but revealed a new attitude to the *caboclos* of the interior through the affectionately but critically drawn character 'Jeca Tatu', the indolent and illiterate yokel who was the unknown popular soul of Brazil.

In 1928 three fundamental works appeared. One, Mário de Andrade's *Macunaíma*, a fictional compendium of culture traits reminiscent of Villa-Lobos, properly belongs to our discussion of the avant-garde (see below). The second, *Retrato do Brasil*, by Paulo Prado (1869–1943), typical of that era of soul-searching and national characterology, with its memorable view of the Brazilian people as 'a sad race, the product of the fusion of three sad races', defined the Brazilian as melancholy, sensual and envious, and has been called 'the ugliest portrait Brazil could receive from one of her sons'.[35] The third was the first true regionalist novel of the kind then appearing in Spanish America, *A bagaceira*, by José Américo de Almeida (b. 1887). As ideologically incoherent as Gallegos's Venezuelan classic *Doña Bárbara* (1929), it traces the transition between the patriarchal world of the old sugar plantations and the new capitalist *usinas*, with the same ambivalence as Gilberto Freyre's *Casa grande e senzala* (1933) or Lins do Rêgo's novels (see below).

Almeida's work was prelude to a remarkable flowering of regionalist fiction which, in a characteristic dialectical leap, took the Brazilian version in just a few years to a level of universality well beyond that of the Spanish American novels which had only recently seemed so advanced. The explanation lies not only in the different inner rhythms of Brazil's literary advance, but in the specific nature of the historical conjuncture: the complex yet coherent interrelation between *modernismo* (itself far more Americanized in Brazil: based in São Paulo, not Paris) and regionalism, which, given the nation's vast proportions, contrasted a nativist movement based in the north-east with a vanguard movement based in São Paulo and Rio; and the fact that, starting later than in Mexico or Argentina, it accumulated all the experiences of the 1920s. The early 1930s saw the emergence of a compact group of social-realists, based mainly in the north-east, comparable to but even more accomplished

[35] Quoted by Azevedo, *Brazilian Culture*, 118.

than the Ecuadoreans. The first, *O quinze* (1930), by Rachel de Queirós (b. 1910), daughter of a plantation owner, re-enacted the tragic drought of 1915 and the suffering of the rural poor, particularly the women. In 1931 Jorge Amado (b. 1912), from Bahia, published *O país do carnaval*, an important adolescent expression of that generation's search for national values and personal meaning in a corrupt, superficial and unjust society. Amado, later to become Latin America's best known communist narrator, then wrote two short pamphleteering novels, *Cacau* (1933), about life on the cocoa plantations, and *Suor* (1934), on the condition of the urban poor and the workers' struggle. In 1935 *Jubiabá* appeared, on the culture of the Bahian negroes, and in 1942 his masterpiece, *Terras do sem fim*, a historical reconstruction of the rise and fall of the cacao estates.

José Lins do Rêgo (1901–57), a plantation owner's son from Paraíba, turned his family's history into one of Brazil's great fictional monuments, the 'Sugar-Cane Cycle', with *Menino de engenho* (1932), *Doidinho* (1933), *Bangüê* (1934), *O moleque Ricardo* (1934) and *Usina* (1936). In its passionate complexity, condemning the injustice of the plantation system whilst implicitly lamenting its passing, this is one of the most compelling documents of Brazilian social history, with its characters José Paulino, the old patriarch, Carlos, his grandson (a largely autobiographical depiction), and Ricardo, the black boy who goes to the city to seek his fortune. *Pedra Bonita* (1938) is a novel on a theme similar to *Os sertões*, whilst *Fogo morto* (1943), his masterpiece, returned to the subject matter of his first works.

The other great north-eastern writer of the period was Graciliano Ramos (1892–1953), son of a rural judge, Brazil's finest stylist since Machado de Assis. His pessimistic, heavily ironic yet austere prose created a whole new way of perceiving the world-view of the inhabitants of the north-east, similar to the later Mexican novelist Juan Rulfo. No regional novelist from the continent so perfectly fused the sociological and psychological dimensions as Graciliano Ramos did in *Caetés* (1933), *São Bernardo* (1934), *Angústia* (1936) and *Vidas sêcas* (1938).

Poetry

Graciliano Ramos constrained narrative prose to almost impossible spareness, reflecting the anguish of his inarticulate characters and refusing the reader the satisfactions of wordy 'literariness' to escape from the bleak realities of the subject matter. As usual, poetry had been embarked on this process long before fiction – always concerned more with the world outside than the means of signifying it. The shift to prosaic, everyday language in Latin American poetry, known variously as *sencillismo, prosaísmo, exteriorismo* or *antipoesía*, is often thought to be a quite recent phenomenon; so that when it did emerge – the 1920s, the 1930s or even later – it was a belated reaction against modernism accentuated by and coinciding with a reaction against the new avant-garde. It seems more exact, however, to consider it as an extension and re-emergence of traditional *tono menor* poetry, remembering Bécquer's contribution to modernism itself, José Asunción Silva's deliberately ingenuous childhood reminiscences, Martí's *Versos sencillos*, González Prada's *Baladas peruanas*, or even Amado Nervo's rather flat poetic mode. It follows that this poetic line is part of the regionalist impulse, whereas the avant-garde is a dialectical continuation of the dominant modernist mode. That this dominant current made all others invisible whilst it was in full flood only proves how coherent, all-embracing and historically significant it was. Yet even before González Martínez called on poets to wring the modernist swan's neck, Darío had signalled, as we have seen, his own weariness with *fin-de-siècle* postures when he moved ('Yo soy aquel que ayer no más decía . . .') from his earlier artifice and escapism to the simpler, fresher style which followed *Cantos de vida y esperanza* in 1905. Thus some view *prosaísmo* as an anti-*modernista* reaction, others as a transitional second, or third, phase of modernism itself, whilst ignoring all those poets in the early 1900s whose innovatory, conversational approach makes them precursors of a line of composition which has grown increasingly important, linking inevitably to rural folklore, urban popular music and the political song movements of recent times.

Ramón López Velarde (Zacatecas, 1888–1921) originated this poetic mode in Mexico. Like Lugones, he used a familiarity with European innovations to achieve artful simplicity in poetry about provincial life, the anguish of catholic belief for a man not only sentimental but sensual, family life, love and death. This was a new provincialism: earlier poets had been marooned in their regional world, limited by ignorance of life outside; now some, despite experience of other places, chose to write specifically provincial, even parochial verse, rather as Antonio Machado was doing in Spain at this time. López Velarde's collections were *La sangre devota* (1916) and *Zozobra* (1919), though many poems appeared posthumously, including his affectionate portrait of Mexico, 'Suave patria', completed shortly before his death and now one of the country's best loved poems, which feels as if it had been composed in the mid-morning sunshine on the veranda of a small-town bar.

Even more spontaneously conversational was the Colombian Luis Carlos López (1883–1950), another poet whose reputation is steadily emerging from the shadow of modernism. *De mi villorrio* (1908), *Posturas difíciles* (1909), *Varios a varios* (1910) and *Por el atajo* (1920) collected apparently simple poems about everyday life in Cartagena, based on the ironic counterpointing of dreams and reality, past glories and the humdrum flow of the present. In Argentina Evaristo Carriego (1883–1912) was perhaps the most characteristic serious poet influenced by tango culture in the early age of Argentinian urban folklore, with *Misas herejes* (1908), including the appropriately entitled 'El alma del suburbio', and 'La canción del barrio' (posth., 1913). Similar were Baldomero Fernández Moreno (1886–1950) and the more explicitly political Boedo poets Alvaro Yunque (b. 1889), Gustavo Riccio (1900–27) and César Tiempo (1906–80), who once also wrote under the name Clara Beter to make his poems on themes like prostitution more convincing.

More a social phenomenon themselves than producers of social poetry were the women who came to prominence in the early twentieth century and introduced new concerns into the male-dominated literary world. The first was Delmira Agustini (1886–1914), who conveyed passion, eroticism and every aspect of human love with a frankness and audacity astonishing for the times. Shortly after *Los cálices vacíos* (1913) appeared, she was murdered by her husband, who then killed himself. Hardly less dramatic was the life and work of the Argentine feminist, Alfonsina Storni (1892–1938), whose poetry treats the problems of a woman with normal sexual desires who resents submitting to the social conventions of a masculine world. An actress, teacher and journalist, her poetry in *La inquietud del rosal* (1916) and *Ocre* (1925) makes uncomfortable reading for both women and men. She committed suicide on discovering that she had an incurable disease. By contrast Juana de Ibarbourou (Argentina, b. 1895) married an Uruguayan army captain with whom she lived somewhat aridly until his early death. A very beautiful woman, her poetry was implicitly addressed to men, inviting their desire whilst professing the conventions of decent catholic society. During each phase of her life she wrote fresh, ingenuous poetry that perfectly combined the sensual and spiritual aspects of the Latin wife and mother. Perhaps because no one else had made fine poetry out of satisfaction with her imposed social condition, Ibarbourou became known as 'Juana de América' after 1929.

The other great female poet of the era was Gabriela Mistral (1889–1957), a Chilean teacher who in 1945 became the first Latin American to win the Nobel Prize. Still a young woman when her fiancé committed suicide, Mistral could never bring herself to marry, though she longed to have children. Her earliest works, *Desolación* (1922) and *Ternura* (1924), convey her feelings of frustrated motherhood, and vainly seek consolation in nature and religious contemplation. She later joined the consular service and became a roving cultural ambassador concerned with the care and education of the world's children. A fervent Americanist identified specially with Bolívar and Martí, she considered herself essentially Indian, despite her Basque ancestry, but wrote austere, disenchanted poetry shorn of all rhetoric and irony, coinciding therefore with the simpler, unpretentious current of poetry that has gradually become dominant in Latin America through the work of Vallejo, Bandeira, Parra or Cardenal.

THE 1920S AVANT-GARDE

After modernism, poetry either became simpler, more conversational and even prosaic, or much more playful, yet complex, hermetic and experimental under the impact of the European avant-garde. This parting of the ways was a phenomenon of great historical importance, for whereas previously it was possible to see a divorce between prose and poetry, naturalism and modernism, accentuating a tendency initiated but by no means completed by romanticism, what now emerged was the same bifurcation, not merely between poetry and prose but within each of the two forms of literary expression: prosaic poems and poetic narratives now became regular phenomena. And just as modernism had developed above all in poetry – always more flexible and adaptable – rather than prose, where the *crónica* and occasional short novel were much less successful vehicles, so in the 1920s the avant-garde novel was much slower to develop than avant-garde poetry, which in that era sees a small number of Latin Americans, such as Huidobro, Bandeira, Vallejo, Neruda and Guillén, emerge to international significance; whereas the vanguard novelists and short story writers who were actually products of the same historical transformation, like Asturias, Borges, Carpentier and Marechal, followers conscious or otherwise of Joyce, Proust, Faulkner and Kafka, made no international impact until long after the Second World War. If this is not understood, the 1920s, with their almost vertiginous profusion of writers and movements, corresponding more closely than at any time before or since to parallel developments in the other arts, can mistakenly appear to descend into chaos and incoherence.

To understand the Latin American avant-garde means returning to Paris, where a new generation identified their youth with that of the century, their modernity with the aesthetic revolution in poetry, music and the plastic arts, their revolt with the social revolutions of Mexico and the U.S.S.R. *Modernismo* now seemed crepuscular, autumnal, pseudo-aristocratic, a rhetorical vehicle for old men who had turned their faces against the new era of revolutionary change flowing from New York, Moscow, Berlin, Paris and Mexico. Other old men had led young Europeans in their millions to their deaths in the war, but in the process had destroyed their own patriarchal world. Now, in the age of cinema, radio, recorded music, automobiles, aeroplanes, transatlantic liners, Hollywood and *Proletkult*, came the moment of youth, the young artist as athlete or student revolutionary. For the first time in a century it was young men who were producing the dominant ideas and ideologies.

Evidently *modernismo*, now rejected, had helped prepare the ground in Latin America for the assimilation of these developments. Cosmopolitan and internationalist, it had spawned literary circles, *tertulias* and *veladas* in every major Spanish American city, putting Latin American writers in regular contact for the first time in several generations, establishing cultural networks between each of the American capitals and Paris, capital of them all; it was itself an avant-garde movement in its day, anticipating the world to come; was a poetry of the senses, completing a long process in Western literature which allowed the avant-garde to fuse ideas, emotions and sensations into one artistic construct for the first time; brought all the arts into fruitful communication, thereby allowing clear perception of the specificity of each and hence their possibilities for integration (seen most clearly in Mexico and Brazil); and began the appropriation – rather than mere imitation – of European culture, which *vanguardismo* would complete whilst simultaneously incorporating the very different modes of primitive art and culture and the American way of life. Given developments in travel and communications, even petty-bourgeois intellectuals could dream of following Darío and Gómez Carrillo to Paris, assisted by favourable exchange rates through the 1920s until the slump put an end to the *années folles* and sent them back, poor Cinderellas, from the city of light to the gloom of the authoritarian 1930s.

Mexico in the 1920s became what it has remained, the most representative Spanish American republic, home of cultural nationalism and *Latinoamericanismo*, with a Third World ideological orientation before the concept was invented. Only the Spanish Civil War and Cuban Revolution can compare with the impact of the Mexican Revolution on Hispanic art, culture and thought in the 1920s and since. Before it a group of young intellectuals and artists had founded the *Ateneo de la Juventud* (1909), whose orientation was essentially anti-Positivist, at a moment when Bergson's neo-idealism was sweeping deterministic ideologies away. The movement included many who would play key roles in constructing Mexico's new national culture in the post-revolutionary period: Antonio Caso, Alfonso Reyes, José Vasconcelos, Enrique González Martínez, Martín Luis Guzmán, Diego Rivera, Jesús Silva Herzog and the great Dominican literary historian, Pedro Henríquez Ureña.[36]

During the Revolution writers survived as best they could, as we have seen. Afterwards many young writers succumbed without hesitation to the siren song of the cosmopolitan avant-garde. *Estridentismo*, an aggressive mixture of Spanish *ultraísmo*, Italian futurism and vague revolutionary theory, was led by Manuel Maples Arce (1898–1981), Germán List Arzubide (b. 1898) and the Guatemalan Arqueles Vela (1899–1977), author of *El café de nadie* (1926). A succession of little magazines came and went, most notably *Ulises* (1926–8) and *Contemporáneos* (1928–31), gathering young *vanguardistas* into relatively coherent groups within the general aesthetic and political anarchy of that effervescent time. Writers included Jaime Torres Bodet (1902–74), later a great educationalist, and an important poet and critic; Salvador Novo (1904–74), a talented, whimsical poet best known as a tireless social and literary critic in numerous newspapers and magazines, renovator of the *crónica* and modernizer of Mexican culture through his humorous importation of United States culture; Gilberto Owen Estrada (1905–52), founder of *Ulises*, connoisseur of Joyce, Proust, Eliot, Pound and the other 'sacred monsters' of European Modernism; Jorge Cuesta (1903–42), and two brilliant poets, Xavier Villaurrutia (1903–50) and José Gorostiza (1901–1973); and the editor of *Contemporáneos*, Bernardo Ortiz de Montellano (1899–1949), who saw it as his mission, in the aftermath of the Revolution, to maintain literature's contribution to Mexico's spiritual

---

[36] See Hale, *CHLA* IV, chap. 10.

education and cultural intelligence, producing one of the most sophisticated, witty and innovative magazines of the avant-garde era.

The most influential figure of the period was José Vasconcelos (1882–1959), rector of the National University in 1919, education minister in 1921, promoter of cultural missions and muralism, author of *La raza cósmica* (1925), *Indología* (1926) and *Ulises criollo* (1935); though in the 1930s this champion of *mestizo* culture turned violently to reactionary *Hispanidad*.[37] Meanwhile, *Perfil del hombre y la cultura en Mexico* (1934) by Samuel Ramos (1897–1959), became the point of departure for all later explorations of *Mexicanidad*. In Paris Alfonso Reyes (1889–1959), perhaps Latin America's most complete man of letters, was representing his country, a central figure in the network of relations established between Latin America, French and Spanish intellectuals which was to be so important in the next thirty years. One of the great prose stylists and cultural critics of the century, his own literary creations, though never less than exquisitely tasteful and acutely intelligent, failed to achieve the resonance of his essays. *Visión de Anáhuac* (1917), an evocation of Mexico itself, and *Ifigenia cruel* (1924), are perhaps the most memorable.

Cuba's tragic destiny, which forged a succession of great moralists and patriots culminating in Martí, the 'apostle', and Enrique José Varona (1894–1933), the 'Prospero of America', who exerted an incalculable moral and intellectual influence on Cuban national life and culture over several decades and whose reorganization of Cuban education after 1898 paved the way for the outstanding generation of intellectuals and artists of the 1920s, saw Spanish colonialism give way to the Platt Amendment and the Big Stick. Mexico, Haiti, the Dominican Republic and Nicaragua each received short or long visits from the marines in the first thirty years of the century, and the 1920s saw the whole Caribbean zone subject to the unholy alliance between U.S. capital and local dictatorships, as expounded in Luis Araquistáin's *La agonía antillana* (1928) or the celebrated novel *Generales y doctores* (1920) by the Cuban Carlos Loveira (1882–1928). Cuba in the 1920s underwent feverish political and cultural ferment. Haya de la Torre's arrival in 1923 from Peru inspired Cuban students led by Julio Antonio Mella (1905–29) to found the José Martí Popular University, whilst Mariano Brull (1891–1956) formed the Grupo Minorista of young artists and intellectuals to campaign for a renovation of the national culture. Its principal members were Jorge

[37] See Hale, *CHLA* IV, chap. 10.

Mañach (1898–1961), José Tallet (b. 1893), Juan Marinello (1898–1977), Raimundo Lazo (1904–76), Alejo Carpentier (1904–80), Eugenio Florit (b. 1903), Emilio Ballagas (1908–54) and Rubén Martínez Villena (1899–1934). Their opposition to the Machado dictatorship made them more cohesive than their varied ideologies would normally permit, although Cuba's agonizingly unresolved condition eventually produced violent schisms. Their main organ was the *Revista de Avance* (1927–30), a vanguard review with a continental profile comparable to that of *Repertorio Americano* (1920–58), edited by the Costa Rican Joaquín García Monge (1881–1958). The North American threat provoked a Hispanicist revival in Cuba, where Góngora's rehabilitation was also especially enthusiastic, but *Afrocubanismo* was the guiding thread in 1920s culture, from Fernando Ortiz's pathbreaking ethnological work through Tallet's poem 'La rumba', Ballagas's 'Canción para dormir a un negrito', and culminating in Nicolás Guillén (b. 1902), whose *Motivos de son* (1930), *Sóngoro Cosongo* (1931) and *West Indies Ltd* (1934) were classics of the genre combining black themes and rhythms with a Hispanic tinge reminiscent of Lorca's *Romancero gitano*, and underpinned by a militant anti-imperialism. Carpentier's first notable literary work, *Ecue-Yamba-O* (1933), was also an exploration of black culture. Except for Guillén, most writers of 'black' literature were white men, including the Puerto Rican Luis Palés Matos (1898–1959).

In Peru the intellectual and cultural scene was equally agitated. Here the precursor figures were González Prada, and the ambiguous figure of Abraham Valdelomar (1888–1919), a mulatto, the self-styled 'Conde de Lemos', whose persona was modelled on Wilde and D'Annunzio and who led the young artists and intellectuals grouped round the magazine *Colónida* in 1916 as Peru emerged reluctantly from the *belle époque*. Valdelomar talked openly of homosexuality, cocaine, heroin and revolution, scandalizing the susceptible Lima bourgeoisie but dazzling young provincial intellectuals. The heirs of González Prada were Víctor Raúl Haya de la Torre (1895–1980) and José Carlos Mariátegui (1894–1930), editor of the legendary *Amauta* (1926–30). Having begun as a *colónida*, or literary aesthete, Mariátegui became politically committed during a visit to Europe and in 1923 took over as editor of the journal *Claridad* from Haya who founded the Alianza Popular Revolucionaria Americana (APRA) a year later. In 1928 Mariátegui's *Siete ensayos de interpretación de la realidad peruana* appeared, a landmark in Latin American Marxist thought and a fundamental interpretation of Peruvian history and culture still debated to this day. *Amauta* was close to an *aprista* position at first, evolved towards a communist one thereafter, but always published cultural and political material from a wide range of sources, and remains essential reading on Peru's unresolved debates on national-ism, Americanism, *aprismo*, socialism, communism and indigenism.[38] Most contemporary intellectuals contributed, including Haya and Mariátegui themselves, Luis E. Valcárcel (b. 1893), author of the influential indigenist *Tempestad en los Andes* (1927), Carlos Oquendo de Amat (1909–36), author of *Cinco mētros de poemas* (1929), José Diez Canseco (1904–49), best known for *Estampas mulatas* (1930) and the urban novel *Duque* (1934), Martín Adán (b. 1908), author of the novel *La casa de cartón* (1928), Luis Alberto Sánchez (b. 1900), Peru's outstanding literary historian, and the indigenist painters José Sabogal and Julia Codesido (b. 1892).

Meanwhile in Europe César Vallejo (1892–1938), from the northern sierras, was writing the works which would make him one of the greatest of all twentieth-century poets, testifying to his long march to a communism wracked to the last by the unanswered spiritual questions which his traditional catholic childhood had posed. *Los heraldos negros* (1918), although not free of modernist influence, was already unlike anything written before, and *Trilce* (1922), composed partly in prison, was a unique and almost incredible achievement for one from his background who had never even left Peru. Their combination of surreal imagery, typographical and linguistic innovation, fractured and crippled syntax, disgust with life as it is and longing for future solidarity, place them among the most painful, disorientating and moving of all modern poems. His contribution to subsequent poetry in Latin America is incalculable. He left for Paris in 1923, never to return, visited Russia and Spain during the Civil War. His *Poemas humanos* and great Spanish Civil War poems appeared only after his death. In 1931 he published *El tungsteno*, a socialist realist novel on the ravages of capitalism and imperialism in the mining sierras of Peru.

In Chile the most visible literary and intellectual movements were the Grupo de Montparnasse in the plastic arts, and the literary circle, 'Los Diez'. Pedro Prado (1886–1952), author of the autobiographical novel *Alsino* (1920), provided an old colonial residence in the city centre for the group, with which Eduardo Barrios and Gabriela Mistral were also

[38] See Hale, *CHLA* IV, chap. 10.

associated. The Chilean mainstream, then as now, was realist, in an era which saw the rise of Recabarren and Alessandri, strikes in the dock and nitrate sectors between 1907 and 1918, and the political martyrdom of the poet Domingo Gómez Rojas (1896–1920). 'Los Diez' were in effect attempting to stem the leftist, objectivist tide. Writers like Augusto d'Halmar (1880–1950) and Eduardo Barrios had written early naturalist novels but diverged from the movement when the realist mode became implicitly political, as in the famous novel *El roto* (1920), by Joaquín Edwards Bello (1887–1968), about the Santiago lumpenproletariat.

Chile at this time saw the emergence of a succession of brilliant poets without equal in Spanish America. Vicente Huidobro (1893–1948) was possibly the most important Latin American poet of his era, though critics still disagree both about his excellence and his influence. His doctrine, *Creacionismo*, evolved from his 1914 manifesto, *Non serviam*, which rejected all reflectionist interpretations of art, which should not imitate reality but create it. Like Darío, he travelled from Santiago to Buenos Aires (in 1916), and from there to Paris and Madrid, winning converts and imitators on his way, although his militant insouciance was resented and his influence frequently denied, then and since. He joined Apollinaire's celebrated *Nord-Sud*, working with Reverdy, Tzara and Jacob. Much of his poetry was written in French, including the first important collection *Horizon carré* (1917), immediately remarkable for its bizarre associations, original images and astonishing ability to poeticize modernity and the new, as it were, on the wing. Part of *Altazor, o el viaje en paracaídas* (1931), perhaps his greatest achievement, reads: 'Here lies Altazor, skyhawk struck down by altitude./ Here lies Vicente, antipoet and sorcerer'. The remarkable *Mío Cid Campeador* (1929), half-novel, half whimsical essay, was dedicated to Douglas Fairbanks, and Chaplin was another emblematic figure. Huidobro's influence on the Spanish ultraist movement after 1921 was considerable, and, later, on the Brazilian Concrete Poetry movement of the 1950s. The true nature and extent of his historical influence remains to be clarified.

Another Chilean who came to attention in the 1920s was later to become the best-known Latin American poet of all time, Pablo Neruda (1904–73). His *Veinte poemas de amor* appeared in 1924, as fresh and youthful as the poet himself, and have never lost their popularity. In 1927 he began six years in the Far East, undergoing existential anguish and a persistent nihilism which only the poetic act itself seemed able to assuage. So intuitive was his composition at this time, verging on a native surrealism, that readers felt they were witnessing the evolution of a soul in progress. Contact with Spain after 1933 produced a complete change towards an explicitly political humanist poetry, but we must leave him in Asia during the World Depression, aghast at the spectacle of alienated existence in the dark hours of late European colonialism.

Across the Andes, it is prose writers who have stood out and poetry has traditionally taken second place. Buenos Aires in the 1920s, at the height of its splendour and historical promise, was home to one of the richest artistic experiences of the period, attracting a succession of foreign celebrities such as Ortega y Gasset, Keyserling and Waldo Frank. Argentina was one of the richest nations in the world, and did not feel much like a victim of imperialism; its population was largely European and so, accordingly, was its culture; it appeared to have liquidated the age of caudillos and dictators sixty years before; although always super-ficially turbulent and polemical, its literary development since *Facundo* had been more organic and less convulsive than elsewhere; it had the most vigorous theatre in the continent and a convenient unifying nationalist myth in the gaucho of the pampas. It exercised enormous cultural patronage through great newspapers like *La Nación* and *La Prensa*, enjoyed a range of widely read cultural reviews, like *Nosotros*, and had a flourishing concert, exhibition and opera life. National culture here, it seemed, was not in need of discovery or exploration; as in the United States, the road ahead was clear.

The young vanguard writers collaborated on two now legendary magazines, *Proa* (1922–5) and *Martín Fierro* (1924–7), whose titles condense the two characteristic currents; an avant-garde, futuristic and cosmopolitan form, and a nativist or nationalistic content. Beyond was the overtly committed social realist stance of the Boedo writers. Many writers took up all three postures in turn. A founder of *Proa*, involved in most innovations in those days, after returning from Europe as an ultraist, was Jorge Luis Borges (b. 1899), whose homecoming was similar in its importance to Echeverría's in 1825. Argentina's great man of letters at the time was Lugones, but the young generation considered him an anachronism and carried out the inevitable paricide. A secret mentor of the young iconoclasts was Macedonio Fernández (1874–1952), who wrote little, but smoked, played guitar and philosophized, and, like Xul Solar or the Spaniard Gómez de la Serna, impressed his youthful companions with the example of his lifestyle and mentality. His only significant publication in the 1920s was *No toda es vigilia la de los ojos abiertos* (1928), but as Borges, his direct heir, once said, he was really an 'oral writer' at a time when café life reigned supreme. Borges may have been prompted by Macedonio's bizarre whimsicality and maverick reclusion to retire from his own frenetic activity of the 1920s and become the eccentric of the late 30s and after. Curiously enough, although the literary packaging is experimental, Borges's 1920s works are primarily localist, *Fervor de Buenos Aires* (1923), *Luna de enfrente* (1925) and *Cuaderno de San Martín* (1929). Only later would he repudiate those early works and become the writer of *ficciones* and *inquisiciones* we know today; but even in the 1920s we see the peculiar mix of the fantastic and the real, the geometrical and the deconstructionist, which would make him the most influential Latin American writer of the century. His fake seriousness, his solemn undermining of solemnity and academicism, his rigorous assaults on philosophical rigour, are in reality a Latin American strategem for fending off cultural imperialism, though Borges himself would never agree to see it this way; but he is the cardinal figure for any assessment of the evolution of Latin American literature from a regional–cosmopolitan dichotomy to a persuasive universal identity, without whom no *nueva novela* writers such as García Márquez could have emerged. He was also a vital element in the success of *Sur* (1931–70), the cultural magazine edited by Victoria Ocampo (1890–1979).

Two other writers associated with *Proa* and *Martín Fierro* were Oliverio Girondo (1891–1965), the playful, provocative author of *Veinte poemas para ser leídos en el tranvía* (1922) and *Calcomanías* (1925), ranging from ultraism to surrealism; and Leopoldo Marechal (1900–70), later a catholic and a Peronist and the author of the gargantuan *Adán Buenosayres* (1948), but in the 1920s avant-garde author of *Los aguiluchos* (1922), *Días como flechas* (1926) and *Odas para el hombre y la mujer* (1929).

The apotheosis of Modernism in Brazil did not all come to pass in the seven days of the Semana de Arte Moderna in São Paulo in February 1922, as some histories suggest, but that event did bring into focus a cultural explosion whose range and depth is rivalled only by the contemporary Mexican experience. Its precursors were Da Cunha and Lobato, foreshadowing the new regionalism, and the cosmopolitan Graça Aranha, who returned to Brazil to lend support, resigning from the Academy in a famous gesture in 1924 when it turned its face against the new wave. Whereas Spanish America had already begun to achieve a cultural synthesis – albeit artificial and partly illusory – through its own earlier *modernismo*, Brazil still had that task to undertake. Participants in the great unifying Week were Mário de Andrade (1893–1945), Oswald de Andrade (1890–1954), Ronald de Carvalho (1893–1935), Guilherme de Almeida (1890–1969), Menotti del Picchia (b. 1892), Sérgio Milliet (1898–1966), Raul Bopp (b. 1898), Manuel Bandeira (1886–1968), Ribeyro Couto (1898–1963), the painters Di Cavalcanti, Malfatti, Amaral and Segall, the sculptor Brecheret, the composer Villa-Lobos and many others. It was not accidental that the scene was São Paulo, Brazil's New York in the tropics, the most futuristic city in Latin America: the event set out to explore and synthesize modern art and, simultaneously, to explore and synthesize Brazil.

As in Mexico, it was the plastic arts which opened Brazilian consciousness to the nature and meaning of modernity. Malfatti's famous 1917 exhibition and Brecheret's sculptures took young artists into the world of cubism, futurism and expressionism before they had even heard of Cézanne, and they, like Oswald de Andrade and Manuel Bandeira, who had travelled back from Europe shortly before the war, were viewed with the reverence once accorded to religious pilgrims on their return from some holy shrine. Or so said Mário de Andrade, by 1922 the central figure in the movement, remarkably so since he, unlike the others, had never left Brazil. He perceived with astonishing lucidity what Brazil's cultural condition really was and what had to be done about it. No Latin American thinker of the time was more far-sighted than this remarkable poet, novelist, critic, musicologist, folklorist and professional iconoclast; and no one did more than he to acclimatize humour as an essential ingredient of Latin American artistic culture, even if, as he remarked, it was often like 'dancing on top of a volcano'. Yet although he often conceded that *modernismo* was more a destructive than a constructive movement, he insisted that it was at bottom a spiritual response to the horrors of the Great War which had made him a poet. His first poems, *Há uma gôta de sangue em cada poema* (1917) were followed by *Paulicéia desvairada* (1922), about São Paulo, inspired by Verhaeren's *Villes tentaculaires*. Under the slogan 'no more schools', he set to 'saving Brazil, inventing the world'. His novel *Macunaíma* (1928) was Latin America's first example of what is now called 'magical realism', a mythological narrative, at once epic and humorous, in which the Brazilian culture hero of the title stitches together with his own travels and adventures the disparate pages of Brazil across time and space. The novel, which appeared two years before Asturias' *Leyendas de Guatemala* (1930), and five years before Carpentier's more timid *Ecue-Yamba-O* (1933), is a paradigm in its effort to fuse European avant-garde forms and Latin American primitivist contents, a gesture which only became possible in the 1920s, which presupposes the integration of all the arts and depends, above all, on an educated awareness of the potential for relating universal mythology and anthropology with localist folklore.

The Brazilian 1920s was a great age of manifestos. Mário himself began the trend with his foreword to the first number of *Klaxon*, a modernist magazine which appeared in São Paulo after the 1922 Semana. In 1924 Oswald de Andrade, whose contribution to the movement was hardly less substantial than Mário's issued the *Manifesto Pau-Brasil*, inspired by Tarsila do Amaral's paintings, calling for fresh, spontaneous art 'seen through free eyes', executed with the agility of jungle monkeys and intended, like Brazil-wood itself, for export only. Like Mário, Oswald urged an end to academies and schools, declared the cinema the most relevant of the arts, and asserted that 'the whole of the present is to be found in the newspapers'. In 1928 he published the famous *Manifesto Antropofágico*, inspired by Tarsila's *Abaporu*, and, in addition to the famous 'Tupi or not tupi, that is the question' – a frivolous approach to nativism inconceivable in Mexico or Peru at the time – declared that the new movement would cannibalize European culture and undertake the permanent transformation of 'taboo into totem', revealing how important was Freud's role and that of surrealism in allowing Latin Americans from this time to accept their own native 'barbarism'.

Whilst the two terrible twins (who were not related) were translating Brazilian culture into European and vice versa (the import–export business, as Oswald saw it), other intellectuals were attending to the dialogue between the regions and the Rio–São Paulo axis, at the moment where the regional and the national at last became definitively superimposed. In 1926 Gilberto Freyre announced his historic *Manifesto Regionalista*, and in 1929 the ultra-nationalist *Manifesto Nheengaçu Verde Amarelo* was launched, denoting with its name the colours of the Brazilian flag. Though considering such movements retrograde, Mário de Andrade later confessed that he and the other modernists had, in the last analysis, been 'abstentionist', since politics was the very foundation of modernity. Rather than the first of the new, as they had imagined, they were the last of the old, 'children of a moribund civilization'. Perhaps he was unduly hard on himself: Modernism, truly anti-academicist, had effected the first authentic fusions of Brazilian and European forms and contents, and achieved artistic dialogue between erudite and popular culture, as did Asturias, Borges, Carpentier, Vallejo, Neruda and Guillén in Spanish America. However, the Brazilian movement also strayed closer to mere exoticism than most Spanish American versions, and there are times when Mário and Oswald, Villa-Lobos and Cavalcanti resemble sympathetic and enlightened foreigners gazing at their country.

Nevertheless, the impact on Brazilian poetry and language was remarkable. All literary conventions were abolished: beauty, tranquility and sentiment gave way to dissociation, violence and directness. Most resolutely anti-poetical of all was Oswald de Andrade, whose *Pau-Brasil* (1925) and *Caderno do aluno de poesia Oswald de Andrade* (1927), once routinely dismissed by critics, now appear revolutionary. Manuel Bandeira spent the First World War in Zurich, like Borges, Tzara, Joyce and Lenin, and remains the most generally admired, if not the most typical of the *modernista* poets. His *Carnaval* (1919) foreshadowed its moods and attitudes, both affectionate and ironic, to national culture. He became increasingly realist and anti-poetical by the 1930s. Ronald de Carvalho did not live long enough to become a truly great poet (dying in 1935 aged 42), but was well respected, after his early *Poemas e sonetos* (1919), *Epigramas irônicos e sentimentais* (1922) and *Toda a América* (1926). He was more familiar with Spanish America than any other Brazilian writer of the period. Raul Bopp (b. 1898) was the author of the uncompromisingly primitivist *Cobra Norato* (1931), the result of a visit by the writer, a native of Rio Grande do Sul, to the Amazon jungle. The circle of Brazilian regional culture, already traced by Villa-Lobos in music, was now effectively complete in literature as well, after Mário's cinematographic novel and Bopp's symphonic poem. Brazil, like Latin America as a whole by 1930, was now more inside the twentieth century than outside it. Modernity, for good or ill, had been achieved.

THE EARLY YEARS OF THE CINEMA

The first thirty years of the century coincided with the early years of the cinema and the age of the silent movie. The birth of a new art form gave Latin America the opportunity to get in at the beginning, and the region quite quickly developed thriving national industries and one of the largest audiences in the world. Films by the Lumière brothers had appeared in Mexico City, Havana, Buenos Aires and Rio only months after the first showings in Paris in 1895, the Mexican poet Luis Urbina lamenting, despite his bedazzlement, that the new invention lacked colour and sound. Newsreels, *actualidades*, were inevitably predominant in the first twenty years to 1914, with views of European and South American capitals and state ceremonial occasions typical of the earliest period. Some historical footage from the continent, such as the hazy scenes of the Spanish American War or the arrival of Madero in Mexico City, is familiar to all students of the cinema's pioneering period. One of the earliest examples of all was a film of brief scenes (*vistas*) of Guanabara Bay, shot appropriately from on board the French liner *Brésil* as she steamed into Rio in July 1898. It was France, indeed, which was most closely associated with the early production and distribution in Latin America. The Pathé Company dominated the foreign share of the market up to 1914, with branches in Rio, Mexico City, Buenos Aires and Havana. The First World War, however, paralysed the efforts of European filmmakers. After 1914 the United States came to control some 95 per cent of the Latin American market – with profound long-term consequences for Latin American cultural development.

In the pre-war period the leading republics had each begun to produce the occasional feature picture. The first man in Mexico to make a primitive fiction film was Salvador Toscano Barragán (1872–1947), in 1898, with the first of many film versions of that nineteenth-century romantic staple, *Don Juan Tenorio*. In 1908 Felipe de Jesús Haro produced the first Mexican scripted feature, *El grito de Dolores*; in 1910 a second feature, *El suplicio de Cuauhtémoc*, appeared. In Argentina, too, the first feature film was on a nineteenth-century historical topic, *El fusilamiento de Dorrego* (1908), directed by an Italian, Max Gallo, who had originally gone to Buenos Aires, ironically enough, to stage operas. In 1915 there was violent controversy in the Argentine capital when two films appeared on the Rosas era, one from Hollywood entitled *El capitán Alvarez o bajo la tiranía de Rosas*, which gave the American ambassador at the time a grotesquely distorted leading role, and the other Max Glucksmann's *Mariano Moreno o la Revolución de Mayo*. This juxtaposition gave rise to one of the earliest examples of Latin American protest against the 'Hollywood' version of the history of the southern republics. The titles of both films reveal that the cinema was still very much immersed in the conventions of romantic theatre, a concept of drama which was itself at least seventy years out of date. Needless to say, the temptations of melodrama were accentuated by the absence of language from the movies, but there is little doubt that this technical limitation had stylistic and even thematic implications which encouraged the popularity of exotic themes in general, and in particular those involving 'Latin' passion. Adolfo Urzúa Rozas produced the first feature in Chile: *Manuel Rodríguez* (1910). The first true Brazilian feature film, characteristically, was sociological rather than historical in orientation. *Nhô Anastácio chegou de viagem* (1908) was about a *caipira*, or yokel, visiting Rio for the first time. A few years later in Argentina, another rural film, *Nobleza gaucha* (1916), by Martínez y Gunche Cía, achieved that country's greatest film success of the era. In Chile Latin America's first woman film-maker, Gabriela Bussenius, produced *La agonía de Arauco* (1917), about the exploitation of the Indians by ruthless capitalists. In 1908, the same year as *Nhô Anastácio*, *Os estranguladores* appeared in Brazil, the first of many Latin American films of the era to portray 'sensational' crimes on the North American model. The leading exponents in Brazil were the Botelho brothers. In Chile in 1916, the Argentinian Salvador Giambastiani produced his controversial picture, *La baraja de la muerte*, about a local society murder case, whilst in Mexico in 1919, the great pioneer Enrique Rosas and the Alva brothers produced *La banda del automóvil gris*, a gangster film generally recognized as the outstanding Mexican production of the silent era.

The Brazilian case was perhaps the most interesting at this time, since it is there that the most vigorous autochthonous cinema developed. In Brazil also one can see most clearly the cinema's tendency to reproduce, in an extraordinarily condensed and foreshortened time-scale, the historical development of the novel in the national period. Many of the early Brazilian films, indeed, were actually based on novels, especially such popular romantic works as Taunay's *Inocência* (1914) and Alencar's *A viuvinha* (1914), *Iracema* (1917), *Ubirajara* (1919), all transferred to the screen by Luís de Barros. Alencar's best-known work, *O guarani* was filmed by Antônio Botelho in 1920. Shortly after, films based on naturalist works like Azevedo's *O mulato* appeared, followed by similar social dramas such as *Exemplo regenerador* (1919), *Perversidade* (1921), *A culpa dos outros* (1922), and the masterpiece *Fragmentos de vida* (1929), all by the Italian immigrant Gilberto Rossi and his collaborator José Medina. The greatest Brazilian film-maker of the era, however, Humberto Mauro, from Minas Gerais, was, like Portinari, Lins do Rêgo or Villa-Lobos (with whom he worked on *O descobrimento do Brasil*), one of the great Brazilian artistic masters of the era and the principal forerunner of critical realism in the Brazilian cinema. He directed a number of films, from *Valadião, o cratera* (1925), on banditry in Minas, through *Tesouro perdido* (1927) and *Sangue mineiro* (1933), to his masterpiece, the silent classic *Ganga bruta* (1933), a stunning synthesis of expressionist, lyrical romantic and documentary realist techniques not dissimilar to Graciliano Ramos's later novel *Angústia* (1936). In 1934 Mauro produced the rather more sentimental *Favela dos meus amores*, thereafter to become enveloped, like other Brazilian and Mexican artists of the era, in bureaucratic diversions. Other notable Brazilian films of the period included *São Paulo: sinfonia de uma metrópole* (1929), by Adalberto Kemeny and Rodolfo Lustig, and Mário Peixoto's now legendary avant-garde *Limite* (1930), Brazil's equivalent to *Un Chien andalou*, on the conditionings which limit human freedom.

It was in the 1920s that the manufacture and exhibition of moving pictures became the United States' largest industry. The United Artists Corporation, founded in 1919, undertook an aggressive marketing penetration in Latin America.[39] Wherever the film went, trade followed; and much else besides. Film magazines proliferated and Sunday supplements were full of news and pictures of Hollywood stars. Hispanic cultural forms like the *zarzuela* or the bullfight appeared suddenly old-fashioned and fell into decline, as the North Americanization of Latin American culture and misrepresentation of Latin American realities went on apace. The demonstration effect began to stir even the smallest towns and villages, beginning – it was said – with the imitation of crimes and sexual mores seen in movies from the United States.

Nowhere was this impact more dramatic, nor more resented, than in Mexico. There, the pre-1910 tradition of historical film dramas was continued during the Revolution. In 1914 an important documentary about the *zapatistas*, *Sangre hermana*, was widely exhibited, and in 1916 a Yucatecan company produced *1810 o los libertadores de México*, the country's first full-length film. As in Brazil, many popular nineteenth-century novels were filmed: in 1918 alone, for example, the romantic classics *María* and *Tabaré*, and the naturalistic *Santa*, were all filmed, and by the late 1930s many of Mexico's best-known novels had been turned into film scripts. But in the early 1920s, while Mexico was producing perhaps ten movies a year, Hollywood's annual output of five hundred features was saturating the international market and, quite incidentally but all the more insultingly, routinely purveying an image of the Mexican either as 'greaser' or as a dangerously uncontrollable and wild-eyed

---

[39] See G. S. de Usabel, *The high noon of American films in Latin America* (Ann Arbor, 1982) for a comprehensive analysis.

revolutionary. (When talking pictures arrived, further insult was added to injury when Mexican characters were heard speaking in accents from Madrid or Buenos Aires.) It was at this point that a Mexican self-image, equally caricaturesque, began to be built in opposition to such external characterizations. The Mexican revolutionary governments of the 1920s, although frequently responding to insults with censorship and expropriation, shared little of the awareness of Lenin and Lunacharsky of the cinema's political potential. The key film-maker of the era was, in fact, the rather stolid Miguel Contreras Torres, an ex-soldier who did perceive the importance of building a new historical tradition based on revolutionary myths, with films such as *El sueño del caporal* (1922), *De raza azteca* (1922), *Fulguración de la raza* (1922), *Almas tropicales* (1923), or *Atavismo* (1923). All of them were suffused by a rather double-edged patriotic fervour, with a unifying impulse which anticipated the great nationalist cinema of the 1930s in Mexico. Other leading film-makers were Jorge and Carlos Stahl, who began a series of works with *La linterna de Diógenes* in 1925. Gamboa's *Santa*, already filmed in 1918, became the first talkie in 1931, starring Lupita Tovar as the country girl who becomes a city prostitute, and a Mexican myth. Meanwhile Mexican actors like Antonio Moreno, Ramón Novarro and, above all, Dolores del Río, were beginning to star in Hollywood movies in heart-throb roles in the era of Valentino and *El Zorro*. In contrast, Eisenstein arrived in 1930 to begin *¡Que viva México!*. His obsessively hieratic and meticulous 'expressive realist' style had a lasting impact on Mexican cinema, and was appropriated by populist film-makers such as Emilio 'El Indio' Fernández and his collaborator, the great cameraman Gabriel Figueroa, to communicate a dramatic 'national essence' in a succession of monumental movies.[40]

As in Brazil, it was in 1933 that Mexican cinema began to find its defining national style. Arcady Boytler's *La mujer del puerto*, based on a Maupassant story and similar in many regards to Maura's *Ganga bruta*, was the first truly outstanding Mexican cinematographic production. Even more important historically, however, was Fernando de Fuentes's *El compadre Mendoza*, released in the same year, a subtle satire on the way in which the landowning class had managed to survive the Revolution and build new alliances, a perspective not altogether dissimilar to that of the novelist Martín Luis Guzmán and implicitly critical of the post-revolutionary order. With already characteristic subtlety, the govern-

[40] See J. Ayala Blanco, *La aventura del cine mexicano* (3rd edn, Mexico, 1985), 34–42.

ment was moved to begin to subsidise this new style of cinema. In 1934 Zinnemann's *Redes* and Navarro's *Janitzio*, two scripted fictionalized documentaries, were financed by the Ministry of Education, with music by Chávez and Revueltas, the film technique itself a mixture of Eisenstein, Murnau and Flaherty, and with Emilio Fernández in the cast. In 1935 the Cárdenas government subsidized Fernando de Fuentes himself, and he produced the serious, disillusioned and again implicitly condemnatory *¡Vámonos con Pancho Villa!*. Incongruously yet appropriately enough, this was followed in 1936 by his celebrated *Allá en el Rancho Grande*, starring North America's favourite Mexican Tito Guízar, a film that was picturesque, melodramatic and self-indulgent, but the solution to many nationalist contradictions and the prototype of many essentially conservative *comedias rancheras* to come: the consecration of the Mexican as *mariachi* for the tourist trade, both to attract foreign visitors and to export a new brand of Latin movies to the rest of the continent.

CONCLUSION

In retrospect, it is easy to see that the 1920s and early 1930s, the age of the avant-garde and of modern art, were less a beginning than an end, and not only in Latin America. Although the artistic expression of the period shocked both the complacent bourgeoisie and the man in the street – himself a 'modern' phenomenon – and appeared to confront them with something either entirely new or threateningly alien, it was in reality the climactic moment of Western development since the Renaissance. Modernity was not, despite appearances, a new phase – one which might, implicitly, last for ever ('this is it', 'we've arrived') – but the end of the previous one, not a departure but a climax, a finale. Since that moment we have not known exactly where we are going, or what to say about it, which is why terms like post-modern have been coined, to indicate perhaps the current sense of a vision lost, or rather of an illusion recognized.

In the 1930s, following the slump, when fascism in Europe rose to challenge communism and culminated in the Second World War, the avant-garde itself rapidly lost momentum and gave way to movements dominated by the socialist realist doctrine: objectivist, documentary and sociological. In Spanish America, as a result, and by way of illustration, the only universally acknowledged historic narrative of the 1930s was Icaza's *Huasipungo*. This was an age of politics, not of poetry.

It was during the inter-war period, though most acutely up to 1930, that Latin American culture became at once more complicated and more coherent than ever before. Leading artists and major cities at last caught up with European trends, modes and models at precisely the moment when the United States, their continental neighbour, rose to economic, cultural and eventually political supremacy. Latin America became 'American' as it became modern, but its new American identity was a continental one which at once unified the Latin American nations themselves as never before, yet also incorporated concepts which aligned the new national cultures with United States patterns. In that sense, paradoxically, Latin America became truly modern earlier than the great European nations, whilst, of course, also remaining overwhelmingly underdeveloped. The dramatic tension and contrast determined by such historical contradictions began to give Latin American artists, who before the First World War had found it so difficult to *see* even their own national realities, a vision at once cosmopolitan, continental and national which has characterized Latin American art since that time. Painters like Rivera, Torres García or Portinari, musicians like Chávez and Villa-Lobos, architects like Costa, Niemeyer and Villanueva, novelists and poets like Vallejo, Huidobro, Mário de Andrade, Borges, Carpentier, Asturias and Neruda, were able, in the age of mass culture, to use the dynamic relationship between modern city and 'traditional' – slower moving – countryside, between their own American reality and European models, to develop distinctive forms of art which rank with the most important of the century.

12

THE CATHOLIC CHURCH IN LATIN AMERICA, 1830–1930

INTRODUCTION: THE POST-COLONIAL CHURCH

The Church in Latin America after independence bore the marks of its Iberian and colonial past. From Spain Catholics inherited a tradition of strong faith, a basic doctrinal knowledge and an enduring piety. Observance itself was a medium of knowledge, for in the Mass, the Litanies and the Rosary the people learnt the doctrines, the scriptures, and the mysteries of the Catholic faith. Portugal too transmitted an orthodox Catholicism, but with less doctrinal knowledge and a lower degree of observance. Everywhere, religion in Latin America was a religion of the people, and the Church continued to receive the adherence and the respect of the Indians, *mestizos* and other popular sectors. Ruling groups were less committed, and the great fear of the Church in the nineteenth century was the apostasy of the elites, not the desertion of the masses. The Iberian tradition in religion favoured a privileged and a state-controlled Church. After independence, however, the wealth, influence and privileges of the Church were viewed by the new states as a rival focus of allegiance, an alternative power and a source of revenue. The threat of state control appeared in a new form. The Church had to look to its own resources – and these in the early nineteenth century were diminishing.

Independence administered a great shock to the Church. To many it was the end of an epoch, the collapse of an entire world, the triumph of reason over faith. If Iberian power was broken, could the Catholic Church survive? Independence exposed the colonial roots of the Church and revealed its foreign origins. Independence also divided the Church. While some of the clergy were royalists, many were republicans, a few were insurgents, and most were influential in encouraging mass support for the new order once the last battle had been won. The hierarchy was less divided by independence, but its unity was hardly a source of strength. A few bishops accepted the revolution. The majority rejected it and remained loyal to the crown. They might justify themselves in religious terms but they could not disguise the fact that they were Spaniards, identified themselves with Spain, and had, in effect, abandoned the American Church. From Rome they received little guidance. The papacy, pressed by Spain and the Holy Alliance, refused to recognize Latin American independence. This was a political error, fruit of human judgement and not of church doctrine. But it was a costly error, and when the irrevocability of independence and the need to fill vacant sees forced the papacy, from 1835, to recognize the new governments, great damage had been done.[1]

The Church moved from Spain and Portugal to Rome in the nineteenth century, from Iberian religion to universal religion. While this avoided the emergence of national churches, it did not remove the threat of state control of the Church. The *patronato* (*padroado* in Brazil), the royal right of presentation to ecclesiastical benefices, was now claimed by the national governments and placed in the hands of liberal and agnostic politicians. The issue was fought over for many years. In Mexico, after prolonged and unyielding debate, the question subsided after 1835, though the government continued to insist on its claim. In Argentina in the 1820s Bernardino Rivadavia established almost complete state control over the personnel and property of the Church, a tradition which Juan Manuel de Rosas continued and bequeathed to succeeding governments. It was only gradually that the secular states came to see the *patronato* as an anachronism and closed the issue by separating church and state.

In the years after 1820 it became clear that independence had weakened some of the basic structures of the Church. Many bishops had deserted their dioceses and returned to Spain. Others had been expelled. Others died and were not replaced. The responsibility for empty dioceses was shared between Rome, which dragged its feet over recognition, and liberal governments, which would accept their own nominees or none. In Mexico after the death of the bishop of Puebla in April 1829 not a single resident bishop remained. The archdiocese of Mexico was vacant

---

[1] For a brief discussion of the Catholic Church and the independence of Latin America, see Bethell, *CHLA* III, Note to Part One. On the Church in Spanish America in the period after independence, see Safford, *CHLA* III, chap. 9, *passim*.

between 1822 and 1840. Honduras was without a resident bishop for 43 years, Cuenca in Ecuador for 41 years. Bolivia at independence did not have a single bishop and had to rely on distant Peru, where there were only two bishops, in Cuzco and Arequipa. With the hierarchy gone, no one was left to speak for the Church. The absence of a bishop meant the loss of teaching authority in a diocese, lack of government and decline of ordinations and confirmations. Shortage of bishops was inevitably accompanied by shortage of priests and religious. By 1830 the total number of priests in Mexico had been reduced by one-third, through execution of insurgents, expulsion of Spanish priests and the gradual decrease of local clergy. Many parishes were left unattended, Mass and the sacraments no longer available, sermons and instruction discontinued. In Bolivia eighty parishes were vacant at independence. In Venezuela in 1837 there were two hundred priests less than in 1810.

The economic assets of the Church were also shrinking. Tithes were reduced during the wars of independence and discontinued afterwards, in Argentina in 1821, in Peru in 1856. In 1833–4 a liberal government in Mexico ended government sanction for the collection of tithes and sought to limit the fiscal independence of ecclesiastical corporations. The new rulers, conservatives and liberals alike, coveted church property and income, not necessarily to reinvest them in welfare or development but as a rightful revenue of the state. And they wanted not only diocesan property but also that of the religious orders, which now came under attack in Argentina (1824), Bolivia (1826) and Nicaragua (1830). These measures inaugurated the gradual erosion of church property in the nineteenth century and the cancellation of loans and annuities owed to the Church. Bishops, priests and religious organizations came to rely for their income not on independent church revenues but on the contributions of the faithful or a subsidy from the state.

Yet the Church survived, its mission defended if inert, its assets real if diminished, its offices intact if often unfilled. This was not a Church in decline, and, if it was temporarily weak, the state was weaker. Here was a paradox and a problem. In the aftermath of independence the Church was more stable, more popular and apparently more wealthy than the state. The state reacted by seeking to control and to tax the Church and to restore the balance in its own favour. After a period of relatively conservative government in Spanish America, from 1830 to 1850, the advent of the liberal state heralded a more basic rupture with the past and with the Church. The principle behind liberal policy was individualism, a

belief that the new states of Latin America could only make progress if
the individual were freed from the prejudice of the past, from corporate
constraints and privilege, privilege which in the case of the Church was
accompanied by wealth in real estate and income from annuities. These
gave the Church political power, retarded the economy, and stood in the
way of social change. The Church was thus seen as a rival to the state, a
focus of sovereignty which should belong to the nation alone. These
assertions were not necessarily true, but they were the liberal perceptions
of the time. And liberalism represented interests as well as principles. In
Mexico, for example, where typical mid-century liberals were young
upwardly mobile professionals, these considered the Church as a major
obstacle not only to nation-building but also to their own economic and
social ambitions.

The post-colonial Church, therefore, encountered from specific social
groups a hostility which it had never experienced before. For the first
time in its history, in the period 1850–80, the Latin American Church
acquired enemies who hated it with an intensity born of frustrated
conviction. It is true that not all liberals shared these convictions.
Some were simply seeking to reform the state, to constitute the rule of
law for all and to modernize the economy. None of these objects were
necessarily a threat to religion. But more radical liberals went beyond an
attempt to establish the appropriate autonomy of the state: they favoured
an all-out attack on the Church's wealth, privileges and institutions, for
they believed that without the destruction of ecclesiastical power and the
death of its accompanying dogma no real change could be made. So
secularization in the nineteenth century took various forms and drew
various responses, some of them violent. The battle was fought over the
right to appoint bishops, over ownership of property, over the legal and
political sanctions of religion and over education. And secularism had a
social base, among the elite or those aspiring to the elite. The masses, it
seemed, preferred their ancient beliefs.

In reaction the Church sought allies where it could. Throughout Latin
America Catholic political thought became more conservative in the
mid-nineteenth century. Churchmen aligned themselves with civilian
conservatives in the belief that religion needed a political defence. In turn
the dominant ideology of conservatism was Catholicism, and a belief that
the alleged irrationality of man created a need for strong government
supported by the Church and the sanctions of religion. The conservative
political philosophy was not essentially religious but an interest and an

ideology. Conservatives believed that without the restraint of religion people would be turbulent and anarchic, a defence of religion on the grounds not of its truth but of its social utility. The alliance was harmful to the Church, for it placed it among a complex of interests identified as obstacles to change by liberals and progressives, and it shared in the reverses of its associates.

Gradually, in the last quarter of the nineteenth century, the Church emerged from the age of privilege and persecution, adjusted itself to the secular state and began a process of independent development. This took the form of modernizing its institutions and resources, increasing the number and improving the training of its priests and demanding a greater commitment from the laity. The movement of internal reform can be dated from approximately 1870 and lasted to 1930 and beyond. Religious renewal was followed by greater social awareness, as immigration and economic growth posed new problems for the Church and forced it to come out of the sacristy. Social Catholicism did not synchronize exactly with the movement of church reform, and there was a time-lag during which traditional attitudes endured and the religious mission of the Church was closely identified with conservatism. But from about 1890 Catholic social action can be observed in a number of countries, and by 1930 the Church had begun to speak out more clearly on the duties of capital, the rights of labour and the role of the state.

PRIESTS, PRELATES AND PEOPLE

The structure of the Church mirrored in part that of secular society. Bishops and higher clergy were of the elites, alongside landowners, office-holders and merchants. Many of the lower clergy belonged to the poor rather than the rich, but they accepted church and society as they found them, seeking to improve rather than transform. There was no class struggle in the Church; it was a social as well as a mystical body, one which contained various opinions and interests but remained ultimately united around its leaders. The clergy traditionally derived their income from *capellanías* (endowed benefices), fees from masses, baptisms, marriages and funerals, and tithes and first fruits. The decline and abolition of tithes reduced the Church's revenue and the clergy became more dependent on fees from masses and other services and perhaps more engrossed in the economic aspects of their work. But there were great inequalities of income between upper and lower clergy, between wealthy city benefices and poor parishes in the country. In rural societies priests were often younger sons whose land inheritance prospects were poor and who found an alternative career in the Church. This created a reserve of recruits for the clergy and was an asset to the Church, though it did not in itself produce good vocations or ensure that priests kept their vows.

Peru began its independence with about 3,000 priests for a population of some 2 million, a very favourable ratio which steadily declined. Most of the Peruvian clergy were of middle class origin, coming usually from professional families and educated along with other elite groups in college or university. For theology some priests went to a seminary, Santo Toribio in Lima, San Jerónimo in Arequipa, or the seminary in Trujillo, while others went to the College of San Carlos in Lima, and many others received no seminary education. The system produced a relaxed and somewhat secular-minded clergy, whose character was further affected by the clerical conventions of the time. Many priests did not reside in their parishes but appointed a vicar who was paid a portion of the parish income but whose qualifications were usually untried. Celibacy, moreover, was frequently ignored. Many priests in Lima, and probably more in the sierra, lived with women, a practice accepted by society though not by the ecclesiastical authorities. Yet the Peruvian Church was not unique in its condition and was probably typical of the unreformed Church of the first half of the nineteenth century. This was why the Latin American bishops at the First Vatican Council (1869–70) were so concerned to raise clerical standards. The Peruvian bishop, Manuel Teodoro del Valle, referred to those clerics who cast aside their cassock 'in order to enter the world of business or to attend more easily public spectacles and houses of prostitution'.[2] Clerical reform was overdue but it had to await the efforts of a later generation. Meanwhile vocations to the religious orders in Peru had greatly declined, and by the middle of the nineteenth century new entrants were extremely rare. The reason for decline was not economic, for the orders were well endowed. It was rather the lack of a distinct identity and mission, at a time when the dioceses had sufficient secular clergy and the orders no longer had Indian parishes or frontier missions.

In Mexico statistics tell a story of more vigorous survival and growth. After the losses at independence, the number of clergy remained fairly

---

[2] Quoted in C. J. Beirne, 'Latin American bishops of the First Vatican Council, 1869–1870', *The Americas*, 25 1 (1968), 273.

constant throughout the nineteenth century. There were 3,463 in 1826, 3,232 in 1851, 3,576 in 1895, 4,015 in 1900, and 4,533 in 1910. Assuming that the number of nominal Catholics was almost co-terminous with the population, this meant that in 1895 (total population 12.6 million) there were less than 3 priests for every 10,000 inhabitants, and in 1910 (total population 15.1 million) just over 3. The number of churches grew from 9,580 in 1895, to 12,225 in 1900, to 12,413 in 1910. The training available for priests was also expanded during this period. Diocesan seminaries increased in number from 9 in 1826 to 10 in 1851, 29 in 1910. The Conciliar Seminary of Mexico City was raised to the Pontifical University in 1896, with authority to grant degrees in theology, canon law and philosophy. In 1907 the old Palafox Seminary became the Catholic University with faculties of theology, philosophy, canon law and civil law, medicine and engineering. These changes were characteristic of the period 1880–1910, years of growth and renewal for the Church in Mexico after a time of conflict and contraction.

Beyond the statistics, the qualitative life of the Church and the standards of the clergy were also changing. During the first decades of independence many Mexican priests, like their Peruvian counterparts, were a source of scandal rather than sanctity, and in the 1850s Pope Pius IX commissioned the bishop of Michoacán to reform the clergy, especially the regulars. A process of reform and renewed evangelization is observable in the fifty-year period from 1860 to 1910. The revival was at its strongest in rural Mexico, in Michoacán, Guanajuato and Jalisco, and it was here that the new priests found the greatest response. A typical Mexican priest was a country priest, though, since the failure of the College of Tlatelolco in the sixteenth century, not normally recruited from the Indian communities. Most priests came from the middle class, and many vocations were found among the families of prosperous ranchers and store-keepers. They were products of the local diocesan seminary, where they learnt Latin, scholastic philosophy and theology, and were instilled with strict moral values and a deep hostility to liberalism. They embarked on pastoral work with their new seminary ideals, exhorting their parishioners to regular attendance at Mass and the sacraments, organising catechism classes, encouraging observance of Lent, and inculcating in their people 'a deep awareness of sin, a heightened sense of shame, and avoidance of sex outside marriage'.[3] On

[3] Luis González, *Pueblo en vilo. Microhistoria de San José de Gracia* (Mexico, 1968), 164.

an already firm religious base the new priests built a more fervent Catholicism and became the leaders of a spiritual and moral renewal in the Mexican countryside. The priest lived among the peasants and the rural poor. In many places he was the centre of their life, the provider of Mass and the sacraments, a source of information and a medium of rural culture.

The religious orders in Mexico experienced the vicissitudes of the rest of the Church – post-independence recession, mid-century anti-clerical-ism and eventual renewal. In 1851 there were only 8 religious orders in Mexico. By 1910 the number had grown to 18. Of the older religious orders the Jesuits were the most dynamic and recovered most rapidly from persecution. In 1910 they had 338 members, thirteen churches, fourteen colleges for middle class entrants and thirty schools for poor children; in addition they worked in a number of mission fields. Women's orders also grew, from 9 in 1851 to 23 in 1910. The increase was mainly due to the advent of the new nineteenth-century urban and teaching orders, without whom the Church in Mexico could not have maintained its position in the field of education. The Jesuits, for example, had thirty primary schools in 1900, the Marist Brothers thirty-five; while the development of vocational schools for working-class boys was due almost entirely to the teaching orders.

In Mexico and Peru the post-colonial Church inherited a distinct infrastructure on which it could later build. In Argentina, on the other hand, the Church was less developed and the crisis of the clergy correspondingly greater. Standards began to decline at independence, when diocesan sees were left vacant, in Buenos Aires from 1812 to 1834, in Córdoba from 1810 to 1831, in Salta from 1812 to 1860. Following the exodus of Spanish priests, the Church had to rely on local recruits of inferior quality at a time when seminary training was virtually extinct. This weakened Church was a willing victim of the *rosista* state and it was quickly reduced to a group of functionaries and propagandists. Decline outlasted Rosas. In 1864 in the vast diocese of Buenos Aires there were only 35 secular priests, whose theological training, spiritual formation, not to mention general education, were not equal to the demands of the time. Between 1868 and 1874, as a result of the republican revolution in Spain, some two hundred Spanish priests migrated to Argentina, but it was a native clergy whom Argentina most needed. At the time of national organization Argentina did not have a 'national' clergy, and the Church was lagging behind the state in structure, morale and growth. In many areas of national life it did not even have a presence. The provision of basic things such as the Mass, sermons, and sacraments was notoriously deficient in many urban centres and virtually non-existent in rural areas. The religiosity of the common people somehow survived this prolonged neglect, especially outside Buenos Aires. But there were unmistakable signs of crisis, as ignorance and indifference concerning religion spread rapidly through society, but especially among the educated elite groups; and this was the greatest challenge to religion during the following hundred years.

In due course the Church began to modernize itself, following the example of the nation. From about 1860 new seminaries were created, with some state support. The seminary in Buenos Aires had only 42 students in 1868, 45 in 1872, not all of whom were native Argentines; 6 were ordained in 1873, an exceptionally high number at the time. For the twelve parishes in the city of Buenos Aires and for the fifty-four in the rest of the diocese (which then included the whole of the littoral and Patagonia) there were only 84 priests in 1880. The diocese of Salta, serving the whole of the north-west, had even more ground to make up. But slowly results began to show. Thanks in part to the Conciliar Seminary, which the Jesuits took over in 1874, the number of priests increased in the years 1880–1914, as the population itself did. Even more notable was the growth of religious orders, many entering the country from Europe and the United States for the first time towards the end of the nineteenth century, the Passionists (1883), Redemptorists (1883), Fathers of the Divine Word (1894), Capuchins (1897), the Christian Brothers (1889) and the Marists (1903). Among the various women's orders were the Sacred Heart Sisters (1880), Sainte Union (1883), the Sisters of the Good Shepherd (1885), Marie Auxiliatrice (1883) and the Daughters of the Child Jesus (1893). Many of these orders were dedicated not only to the contemplative life but also to welfare and education, and they helped to fill a gap in the social provisions of the conservative republic.

Between 1880 and 1914, in an age of massive immigration and economic growth, Catholicism underwent great expansion in Argentina. In Buenos Aires there were nineteen parishes in 1900 compared to seven in 1857. But the countryside too was Christianised. José Gabriel Brochero, a worthy rural priest in the tradition of the *cura criollo*, built churches, chapels and schools in the hills near Córdoba and spread the practice of the Spiritual Exercises throughout the province. Attendance at Mass was reported to be increasing, even among men, and in 1901 5,000 men participated in the annual pilgrimage to Luján.

Brazil too shared in the church growth characteristic of the rest of Latin America. Here as elsewhere, the clergy of the old regime failed to meet the needs of society. The ecclesiastical power of the state inherited from the colonial regime and closely guarded by the Brazilian monarchy from 1822 to 1889 produced a breed of 'political priests' who owed their preferment to politicians and became in effect government servants and social parasites. Priests of this kind tended to be hostile to Rome, advocates of a fashionable liberalism and Jansenism, servants of the elite and not always even faithful to their vows. During the empire there were only about 700 secular priests, almost all of whom had been educated in state-controlled seminaries, to minister to 14 million people. As for the religious orders they were virtually suppressed by a government hostile to the idea of contemplative life; in 1855 a circular from the Minister of Justice, José Tomás Nabuco de Araújo, specifically prohibiting the entry of novices into the orders threatened them with eventual extinction. The decline and fall of the monarchy gave the Church the opportunity to free itself from direct political influence and to look to its own renewal. Dioceses were established, seminaries founded, and a new and more dedicated clergy emerged, zealous for Catholicism, loyal to the bishops and to Rome, and orthodox in their faith and morals.

While the faithful relied on priests for Mass and sacraments, priests depended upon bishops for selection and ordination, and the Church depended on them as teachers and administrators. According to canon law and Catholic tradition a bishop has virtually absolute power in his diocese, subject only to the pope. How he used that power, of course, varied from bishop to bishop. The Latin American episcopacy was not entirely homogeneous, either in ideas or in social status. The majority of the bishops came from the same middle ranks of society which supplied the priests, from traditional Catholic families in Mexico and Peru, from immigrant families in modern Argentina. They made their way in the Church through their superior qualifications, moral character and powers of Christian leadership rather than through social or political interests. Where the state retained an element of patronage, as in Argentina, episcopal appointments tended to be the results of compromise between the government and Rome and to produce a conventional episcopacy unlikely to disturb church or state. The Latin American episcopacy underwent significant change in the course of the nineteenth century. The regalism and complacency inherited from the colonial and early national regimes gave way to a more insistent orthodoxy, reformist and Rome-orientated. This is often characterized as 'ultramontanist'. In some contexts this refers to no more than an intellectual background, as when it is said that all five of Brazil's bishops in the mid-nineteenth century were ultramontanist, mainly because they had been educated in Europe or had travelled there. But the word has acquired a pejorative and polemical sense, to denote a contrast to liberal or national positions in religion, and as such it is of limited value to the historian. It is true that the Latin American episcopate now looked to Rome for leadership and direction, but in most cases this signified reform and independence for the Church and became the Catholic norm rather than the extreme.

In general the bishops took a cautious and middle way, more prone to defence than to initiative, to compromise than to conflict. But during times of crisis they varied between intransigents and those seeking a consensus with society and the state. In Mexico there were, on the one hand, men like Eulogio Gillow, archbishop of Oaxaca (1887–1922) and Ignacio Montes de Oca, bishop of San Luis Potosí (1884–1921), both from wealthy families, both educated abroad, Gillow in England, Montes de Oca in Rome and both true princes of the Church, though not less pastoral because of that. On the other hand, there was Eduardo Sánchez Camacho, bishop of Tamaulipas, who aroused much indignation among Mexican Catholics for his attempt to reconcile the laws of the Church and those of the liberal Reform, and for his opposition to the cult of Our Lady of Guadalupe. He was dismissed by Rome from his see and died without the sacraments. Pelagio Antonio de Labastida y Dávalos, archbishop of Mexico, one of the principal supporters of the French intervention in 1861 and of accommodation with the Porfiriato, was succeeded in 1892 by Próspero María Alarcón, rumoured, though incorrectly, to be a liberal.

The political thinking of the Colombian bishops was almost entirely conservative. In their response to liberal policy the prelates recognized their obligation to submit to secular authority, but there was a qualifying condition. In a pastoral letter of August 1852 issued on the eve of his departure for exile following opposition to liberal laws, Manuel José Mosquera, archbishop of Bogotá, told the faithful that religion commanded them to obey the civil laws and respect and love the magistrates, as the pope said in his encyclical of 9 November 1846, 'those who resist authority resist the Divine Plan and will be condemned, and therefore the principle of obeying authority cannot be violated without sinning unless something contrary to the laws of God and the Church is required'.[4] So there was a right of resistance to liberal measures when they attacked the inherent God-given rights of the Church. The Colombian bishops, like many of their Mexican colleagues, argued that disamortization was contrary to the inalienable rights of the Church and its legal power to own property and income.

The dramatic conflicts with the liberal state in which many Latin American bishops were involved tend to obscure the spiritual and pastoral functions of their office, though these were essential ingredients of church reform. Every diocesan bishop was obliged to make pastoral visits to the parishes within his jurisdiction, so that the whole of the diocese was visited at least every five years. The object was to sustain faith and morals, promote religious life, encourage the parish clergy and inspect the organization, buildings and accounts of the local church. The *visita pastoral* was the point of encounter between ecclesiastical authority, pastoral care and the life of the people, and it was the high water mark of the local religious calendar. It was then that the priest reported on the spiritual life of his parish. Some drew attention to levels of observance, fidelity to prayers, Lenten devotions and visitation of the sick. Others emphasised the *vicios principales* of the parish, usually alcohol and sex. In general, and especially in the period of renewal from the 1870s onwards, bishops complied scrupulously with the obligation of pastoral visitation, in spite of distance, poor communications and adverse weather. It was through these visits that bishops gained direct knowledge of religious conditions in all parts of the diocese. And the *libros de visitas pastorales*, when they are available, are a prime source for the religious history of Latin America.

Lay membership of the Church in the nineteenth century covered a multitude of saints and sinners, and ranged over a wide spectrum of religious belief and practice, from those who went to Mass every Sunday and received the sacraments regularly, to those whose only contact with religion was at birth, first communion, marriage and death, and those whose Catholicism was primarily social and political. There was, however, an ingrained Catholicism in the mass of the people which was not easily measured by external practice, but was part of national and popular culture.

[4] Quoted in Robert J. Knowlton, 'Expropriation of church property in nineteenth-century Mexico and Colombia: a comparison', *The Americas*, 25 1 (1968), 395.

The laity knew the Church as a parish, and their most immediate contact with organized religion was through their parish priest. The Church had a strong pastoral presence in the older cities and provincial towns of Latin America, where numerous churches, schools and other institutions served the various religious needs of the urban populations. In the countryside the framework of religion was spread more widely and often more thinly, and the services provided by the Church depended very much upon individual priests. Yet the firmness of peasant commitment to the Church was never in doubt. The Mexican Indians, though in the past neglected and to some extent exploited by the Church, were more inclined to accept the legitimacy of the clergy's authority than that of civil officials and politicians. Almost all peasants regarded themselves as Catholics, but few seem to have felt any sense of identity with the new republic and even fewer had any awareness of national identity. The peasants of central Mexico, like the Church, were victims of liberal policy and they resented attacks on communal landholding and other threats of modernization. They were the natural allies of the Church, though it cannot be said that the Church went out of its way to cultivate their support or to provide the priests and resources for distant communities. Some of the Indian communities of central Mexico fought for religion against its liberal enemies, or provided indirect support throughout the years of persecution. They did not voluntarily support all conservative causes, but they would be moved to action in defence of traditional practices such as pilgrimages and processions, or by the appeal of a particular priest or caudillo.

The Peruvian Indians traditionally suffered from many exploiters, including clerics, whose extortionate behaviour frequently went far beyond the just collection of fees for church services, and who had often behaved more like predators than pastors. Yet, in Indian rebellions of the later nineteenth century in the central and southern Andes, church leaders in the diocese of Puno and elsewhere defended the interests of the Indians or at least acted as mediators between the rebels and the government. The Indians responded to these initiatives and reaffirmed their attachment to religion and respect for its ministers. In pacifying the Indians, of course, priests sometimes served government interests rather than those of the rebels, and it is difficult to assess the balance of church action in the sierra. The majority of priests in the Indian areas were white or *mestizo*, though many spoke Quechua or Aymara. The Church did not seriously seek vocations to the priesthood among the Indians themselves. But the allegiance of the Indians to traditional Catholicism endured even during times of revolution, and there is no evidence that religion was used as a palliative or became an inhibiting factor in the Indians' long struggle against abuses.

The laity, then, were part of the ecclesiastical structure, grouped in parishes and dioceses, but they also had organizations of their own. The most significant of these were traditionally, in Spanish America, the *cofradías*. These confraternities, or lay brotherhoods, were inherited from Spain and were established in churches and parishes by different social groups, to organize communal religious activities, such as honouring particular saints, conducting festivals, or maintaining a church in good repair. Confraternities were not only for the elite. Urban, Indian and *mestizo* sectors also had their confraternities. Some comprised different social classes, uniting them in corporate activity and emphasising the vertical bonds within society; others reinforced stratification and social hierarchy. In Brazil the *irmandades* of blacks and mulattos served as a shelter in a white-dominated society, a source of religious service and instruction, a welfare system and a focus of corporate identity. In Spanish America, too, the confraternities had an economic role; they were often mutual aid societies, owners of capital and property, and a source of employment and income for parish priests.

The life of the parish was acted in great measure around this socio-economic system. The *mayordomo* of a confraternity was a man of minor substance and probity within a community. It was his duty to organize the fiestas and the cult of Our Lady or the saint under his care, to guard the cult's material assets such as clothes, jewels, flowers and money, to supervise processions and to allocate the funds needed for these and the accompanying food and drink. The confraternity offices were often closely linked to municipal offices. A single hierarchy operated in communities at a political and religious level. It was also a family network. *Mayordomos* were assisted by their wives and children, and the whole kinship lived in reflected glory, especially at times of fiesta and processions.

The confraternities were essentially lay organizations, administered by the laity for the laity. They were autonomous in their structure and finance, and they did not allow bishop or priest to interfere in their affairs; when they needed the services of a priest, say for a Mass, they requested them and paid for them. This independence caused tension with ecclesiastical authorities, who considered that they had ultimate jurisdiction; and the reformed Church of the later nineteenth century sought to control the confraternities on grounds of religious discipline. Criticism focused on maladministration of property, neglect of religion and preference for entertainment. Many of the religious fiestas of the confraternities were becoming profane celebrations; processions and vigils, according to some parish priests, were idolatrous in their excesses, and often the occasion for all-night drinking and dancing. So the church authorities sought to scrutinize the accounts, nominate the officers and supervise the activities of the confraternities, though not with complete success. In any case events were moving against the confraternities and reducing their significance in the life of the Church. The economic and social changes of the late nineteenth century transformed the world in which the Church had to live and made the traditional confraternities, if not an anachronism, less relevant to the social requirements of the time; the Church now needed more outward-looking organizations to confront an increasingly secular world.

ROME, REFORM AND RENEWAL

The doctrinal heritage of Latin American Catholicism was not different from that of the rest of the Church. Bishops and priests received and transmitted traditional Catholic theology and scholastic philosophy. Whatever its past service to religion in reconciling faith and reason, scholasticism had become inert and repetitive. It failed to respond to the ideas of the Enlightenment, and in the nineteenth century Latin American Catholicism did not have the intellectual tools to confront the utilitarians, liberals and positivists, with the result that the Christian argument went by default. The Bolivian priest, Martín Castro, complained of the education given in the seminaries and of the dominance of scholasticism 'which is rightly banned by modern civilisation'.[5] The Church relied not on new philosophical expression of religious dogma but on dogmatic restatement of ancient beliefs.

The doctrinal inspiration of the Latin American Church in the nineteenth century came from Rome and standards were set by Pope Pius IX (1846–78), who, in December 1864, published the Encyclical *Quanta Cura*, with its annex, the *Syllabus of Errors*. The Syllabus condemned liberalism, secularism, freedom of thought and toleration. It specifically

5 Josep M. Barnadas, 'Martín Castro. Un clérigo boliviano combatiente combatido', *Estudios Bolivianos en homenaje a Gunnar Mendoza L.* (La Paz, 1978), 189.

condemned lay education and the idea that state schools should be freed
from ecclesiastical authority. It condemned the proposition that 'in our
age it is no longer expedient that the Catholic religion should be regarded
as the sole religion of the State to the exclusion of all others', and it
condemned, too, the proposition that 'the Roman Pontiff can and should
reconcile and harmonize himself with progress, liberalism and recent
civilisation'. The attitude of the papacy, of course, had a philosophical
and historical context. The liberalism of the time was seen as an assertion
of man's emancipation in relation to God and a deliberate rejection of the
primacy of the supernatural. As Rome was bound to deny a rationalist
and purely humanist conception of man, so it opposed the political
conclusions which liberals drew from this. The papacy, moreover, was
itself beleaguered by the Piedmontese government which, as it annexed
the papal states, systematically applied a secular regime and imprisoned
priests and bishops who opposed it. The Syllabus was a defence reflex.
Even so, it was a crude and uncompromising compendium.

The Syllabus was a weight round religion's neck, a burden which
damaged its prospects of peaceful growth in Latin America. Catholic
moderates seeking a middle way were embarrassed by its intransigence.
Conservative Catholics could appeal to it against moderates. And liberals
could cite it as proof of the danger from the Catholic Church. As applied
to Latin America the policy of Pius IX can be seen in his reaction to the
Peruvian liberal priest, González Vigil, who attacked papal power and
advocated a new national and liberal organization for the Church. Pius
IX banned his book and excommunicated the author for denying that the
Roman Catholic faith was the only true belief, for proclaiming religious
toleration and for preferring clerical marriage to celibacy. Some of these
views would have been regarded as heterodox in any age of the Church
and were probably unrepresentative of Catholic opinion. The policy of
Pius IX, therefore, did not introduce a new or 'romanized' faith and
morals to Latin America but, after a period of regalism and laxity,
defined more clearly doctrines and discipline as they were and asserted
the primacy of Rome. It was papal definitions which were new, not papal
authority.

What were the instruments of papal influence in Latin America?
Ultimately it depended upon the respect of Catholics for the successor of
St Peter. But it also had a number of more worldly agents. First, Rome
sought to retain the nomination or confirmation of bishops, and only
those who looked to Rome for authority were considered. In this context

it has been remarked that Rome did not always get the bishop it preferred, but it never permitted a bishop it disapproved.[6] A second means of influence was the Catholic media in Latin America; the papal position was propagated in the Catholic press and by individual writers and clerics. A third power base were the seminaries, bastions of orthodoxy, where the faith and morals of future leaders of the Church were formed. In 1858 Pius IX established the Latin American College in Rome, and future graduates of the Gregorian University would return to Latin America as an ecclesiastical elite. Fourthly, the new religious orders, many emanating from Europe, were key agents of Rome and took modern Catholicism to the length and breadth of the subcontinent. Finally, the Holy See had its own representatives in Latin America, though its diplomatic presence was not consistently strong. In Mexico, for example, there were no representatives of the Holy See from 1865 to 1896, in spite of requests to Rome from the Mexican church, because the government would not establish diplomatic relations. In 1896 Pope Leo XIII sent an Apostolic Visitor to Mexico and, after two such appointments, began to send Apostolic Delegates.

Meanwhile the Latin American bishops came into direct contact with the new Catholicism at the First Vatican Council in 1869–70. They comprised 48 of the 700 prelates who participated in that gathering, which was called to discuss clerical discipline, plan a universal elementary catechism, clarify relations between faith and reason and define papal infallibility. The Latin American bishops adopted fairly conservative positions on matters of faith and morals. And almost without exception they supported the definition of papal infallibility. Although they urged local autonomy on some issues, they championed the authority of the Holy See, partly out of principle, partly as a lever against national governments.

Thirty years later the Latin American episcopate had a further opportunity of affirming their allegiance to the Holy See when Pope Leo XIII convoked the first Latin American Plenary Council. This was held in Rome in 1899, and out of a total episcopate of 104, 13 archbishops and 41 bishops attended, though regional theologians were not called upon to play a part. The council deliberated on problems of paganism, superstition, ignorance of religion, socialism, masonry, the press and other perceived dangers to religion in the modern world. There were 998

---

[6] Frederick B. Pike, 'Heresy, real and alleged, in Peru: an aspect of the conservative-liberal struggle, 1830–1875', *Hispanic American Historical Review* (*HAHR*), 47 1 (1967), 50–74.

articles for the reorganization of the Church in Latin America, most of them inspired by Roman theology and canon law rather than Latin American traditions, and more designed to conserve and defend than to increase and initiate. But one aspect of this meeting has been underlined as 'the rebirth of a collegial consciousness among the Latin American episcopate, which would yield fruit in the future'.[7] This took the form of a specific instruction urging conferences of bishops to be held every three years in the ecclesiastical provinces of Latin America.

Within Latin America itself planning for reform was undertaken by regional councils and synods. Provincial councils directed and promoted the work of the Church in each country, and it was from these that the local churches received information and instructions on faith, morals and Catholic practice. The synods legislated on the particular needs of clergy and people at a diocesan level. With the encouragement of Rome the Mexican Church held five provincial councils between 1892 and 1897, which also served as a preparation for the Latin American Plenary Council in Rome. Seven synods were held in Mexico between 1882 and 1910.

The organization of religion was thus improved and expanded in the period 1870–1910. The Latin American Churches were now integrated more closely into the universal Church, from which they received direction and many of their personnel. The papacy, it should be said, did not so much take over the Latin American Church as move into a vacuum of ecclesiastical power which neither the national governments nor Churches were capable of filling. In the process the Latin American hierarchy and clergy began to discard the regalism and laxity of the past, and to conform more closely to the Roman ideal of religious vocation. Orthodoxy and reform tended to go hand in hand. Diocesan seminaries began to chose candidates more carefully and to train them in moral virtue as well as orthodox doctrine; some were sent to Rome and Paris for further study, and these were often the bishops of the future. The new priests were soon to be agents of reform throughout the Latin American Church.

The process can be observed in Brazil. In spite of the regalism of Pedro II, his opposition to Rome and his indifference towards Catholicism, he had to acknowledge that the reformed and orthodox clergy were the most worthy candidates for preferment. The new bishops then had to

[7] Enrique D. Dussel, *Historia de la iglesia en América Latina. Coloniaje y liberación (1492–1973)* (3rd edn, Barcelona, 1974), 175–6.

face the hostility first of liberal politicians and, after 1870, of republicans who were suspicious of Rome and wanted to strip the Church of state support. The separation of church and state in 1890–91 (see below) was a blessing in disguise, for the Church now had to generate its own resources. Attention was first focused on reorganizing the structure of the Church through the creation of new dioceses. In 1891 the Brazilian Church consisted of only 12 dioceses. By 1900 there were 17, in 1910 30, in 1928 58. The bishops chosen to occupy the new sees were selected by Rome, and they first concentrated on two tasks, the restoration of the material fabric of the Church, such as churches, chapels and other shrines of religion, and the renewal of the religious mission of the Church through the establishment of seminaries for training good priests and, in an increasingly secular world, the founding and reopening of monasteries and convents. Because of the reluctance of middle class families to enter their sons to the priesthood and the consequent shortage of religious vocations in Brazil, the Holy See encouraged European orders to dispatch priests, nuns and brothers to replenish the religious houses or undertake parish work. This accounts for the large number of foreign priests in Brazil from then onwards.

The growth of the so-called bureaucratic or organizational Church in the period 1870–1930 has been characterized as the introduction of a European model largely irrelevant to Brazilian life. According to this interpretation, the establishment of Catholic schools for the middle classes, of various pious groups and associations, of a standard liturgy and other elements of reform were more appropriate to an urban, bourgeois society than to the needs of Brazil, which remained predominantly rural and underdeveloped.[8] In the process the Brazilian Church became middle class and European, alien to the mass of the people, whose 'popular Catholicism' deriving from the colonial period was now marginalized by the 'orthodox' Catholicism of the reformed Church. The analysis is largely invalid. In the first place, the reform movement did not direct itself exclusively to the middle classes but also sought out the popular sectors. The new priests from Europe did not all remain in the towns; some went into the country and helped to organize rural parishes to minister to peasants and labourers. A frontier-type network took shape: two or more priests were often grouped in a parish house from

8 Thomas C. Bruneau, *The Church in Brazil. The politics of religion* (Austin, 1982), 18, 31; see also Roger Bastide, *The African religions of Brazil: toward a sociology of the interpenetration of civilizations* (Baltimore, 1978).

which they periodically visited a number of chapels situated throughout the rural area of a *município*. The system functioned more effectively when it was in the hands of the religious orders, whose members were accustomed to working from a community base, but secular clergy, too, had a presence in the rural sector. Primary education, often provided by nuns, also reached a wider social group than the local middle classes. These developments are not surprising, for in Europe itself – in Italy, France, Spain and Portugal – the Church had experience of rural societies, and if it did export a 'model' to Brazil it was not exclusively an urban or developed one. In any case, Brazil, like other parts of Latin America, was undergoing immigration and urbanization and the Church had to respond to a new environment, not necessarily an elitist one.

In Argentina a Catholic revival could be observed from about 1880. Under the leadership of some effective bishops the Church began to emerge from its state of depression and to employ modern methods of organization, evangelization and propaganda. First, religious teaching was improved and extended. Monsignor León Federico Aneiros, auxiliary bishop of Buenos Aires from 1870, worked for improved preaching and instruction, and to the pulpit he added the press, with the foundation of Catholic newspapers and periodicals, *La Religión, El Orden, El Católico Argentino, La Unión* and *La Voz de la Iglesia*. Reform could also be seen in the improvement and extension of seminaries, especially from 1858 when it was accepted that there should be one for each diocese, and the government undertook to finance the support of poor seminarists. In 1860 President Derqui requested Pius IX and the General of the Society of Jesus to send Jesuits to Argentina. They returned to Santa Fe in 1862 and in 1868 they opened in Buenos Aires the Colegio del Salvador, an object of some controversy in its early years culminating in 1875 when it was attacked and burnt by an anti-Jesuit mob. Meanwhile, at the request of Bishop Aneiros, St John Bosco, founder of the Salesian Fathers, sent ten of his order to Argentina in 1875; they opened their first college in San Nicolás, and in 1877 founded the first School of Technical Studies, later the Pius IX College.

Education was a source of fierce controversy between church and state in Latin America, and Catholic expansionism clashed with the determination of liberals and positivists to free education of all religious content and bring it under the control of the secular state. In the second half of the nineteenth century secularization won the day in almost the whole of Latin America, though the rate and degree of change varied from country to country. In Argentina the law of secular education of 1884 seemed to settle the matter and remove Catholic religion from the schools, but this was not the end of the subject. The religious issue in education reappeared periodically, in Argentina and elsewhere, and in some countries there was a return to religious teaching in state schools, though as an optional subject. In most cases, however, the Church lost the battle for influence in public education and had to fall back on providing an alternative school system of its own, often though not invariably for those who could afford to pay. The Church also attempted to compete with the state at a university level, and Catholic universities were created parallel to the state system. Such creations were more characteristic of the period after 1930, but in Argentina the idea of a Catholic university was already frequently mooted by the episcopacy and in Catholic congresses. At last the time seemed right, and in 1910 the Catholic University of Buenos Aires was founded; its rector was Monsignor Luis Duprat, and it offered courses in the faculty of law and social sciences. It began to seek official recognition for its courses and degrees; but the proposal was strongly opposed by the University of Buenos Aires and this was fatal, for without real degrees to offer it could not attract students and it ceased to function in 1920. As an alternative the so-called Courses of Catholic Culture were established in 1922, designed to provide formal instruction in Catholic doctrine to university students, graduates and other people, an indication of Catholic concern over the loss of the elite rather than a great experiment in higher education.

A living Church seeks to grow, and a measure of growth is its success in taking the Gospel beyond the converted into new mission fields. After the closure of the colonial missions and the post-independence vacuum, it took some time to regain momentum. From the second half of the nineteenth century, however, the Latin American Church began to expand its frontiers once more, and the first stage was the gradual return of the friars. Andrés Herrero, Franciscan commissioner general of the missions in Spanish America, formed a group of twelve Franciscans in 1834 to undertake evangelical work among the Indians of Bolivia. Soon they were joined by another 83 friars, and colleges in Peru, Chile and Bolivia were opened. In 1843 the Dominicans returned to Peru.

Pius IX, who had visited Latin America as a young canon, took a particular interest in expanding the Latin American missions and it was he who negotiated the political framework which made this possible, signing a series of concordats, with Bolivia in 1851, Guatemala and Costa

Rica in 1852, Honduras in 1861, and Nicaragua, Venezuela and Ecuador in 1862. The Church managed to obtain material help from some governments to carry out the missionary work of Propaganda Fide. In 1848 12 Capuchins were assigned to evangelize the Araucanians of Chile. In 1855 24 Franciscans and in 1856 14 more went to Argentina to establish similar missions. Bishop Aneiros predictably played a leading role in the evangelization of the Indians of the south, a purely ecclesiastical enterprise which owed nothing to the government. He formed a commission of clergy and laity to provide backing and requested the Lazarist Fathers to undertake the task. These established mission stations in Azul, Patagones, Bragado and elsewhere, concentrating scattered groups into communities for easier access. Between 1878 and 1884 Monsignor Mariano Antonio Espinosa, later archbishop of Buenos Aires, travelled over the great part of the south in the company of the first Salesian missionaries. It was these who, from 1879, were responsible for evangelizing the whole of Patagonia, the Araucanians and the Indians of Tierra del Fuego, as well as in the south of Chile. Other Churches were not so dynamic. In Rome's eyes Peru lagged behind, and Pope Leo XIII called upon the Peruvian bishops in 1895 to make a greater effort among the Indians, who comprised 57 per cent of the population. The first group of Augustinian missionaries arrived there in 1900. In Mexico missionary expansion took place in the early twentieth century and owed much to Jesuit efforts. Fr Magallanes of Totatiche renewed contact, broken since the eighteenth century, with the Huicholes, placing a mission post at Azqueltán under Fr Lorenzo Placencia and taking the Gospel into the sierra itself.

In Colombia serious missionary effort was delayed until the last decade of the nineteenth century. The Augustinians arrived in 1890, the Monfortians in 1903, the Lazarists in 1905, the Claretians in 1908, the Carmelites and Jesuits in 1918. But it was the Capuchin missions in southern Colombia which made the most dramatic advances, working mainly among the Inga and Sibundoy Indians. National legislation of the 1890s, particularly the renewal of the 'Convention of the Missions' in 1902, conceded absolute authority to missionary orders, including the Capuchins, to govern, police, educate, and generally control the Indians of the interior; about 75 per cent of the national territory was thus placed under missionary rule. Between 1906 and 1930 a group of Catalan Capuchins under the direction of Fray Fidel de Montclar established themselves as the dominant political and economic power in the

Sibundoy region and worked to win converts and influence among the Indian population. Soon the territory of the Capuchin missions underwent further expansion, backed by a programme of economic development and one of civilizing the Indians. The missions became owners of extensive landholdings and built an infrastructure of roads and services for trade and access, as well as towns where the Indians were obliged to settle. And in the process the Capuchins became a combination of priests, magistrates and entrepreneurs.

The Capuchin missions in Colombia have been criticized as a state within a state, a theocratic dictatorship which usurped the land and freedom of the Indians in exchange for a spurious civilization. These are value judgements reminiscent of the charges levelled against the Jesuits in Paraguay in the eighteenth century, and like them they fail to do justice to the religious motivation of the missionaries and their need for a protective framework. They also fail to establish whether alternative and probably inevitable forms of contact – with merchants, landowners, officials, anthropologists – would have been superior to that of the missionaries or provided better material prospects for the Indians. Throughout Latin America the methods and the results of evangelization were probably mixed; it is clear that mistakes were made and the failure rate was high. Doubts are expressed as to the true Christianity of Indian converts and there is a tendency to see only syncretism and 'idols behind the altars' in convert communities. But these are superficial judgements. Many Indians were real Catholics. Others were not. But it was a juxtaposition of different religious systems rather than a debased syncretism.

THE RELIGION OF THE PEOPLE

How Catholic were the people of Latin America? Faith in a personal God is a matter of individual conscience and this is not easily judged or quantified. The religion of a people, however, can be tested by outward observance, by attendance at Sunday Mass, reception of the sacraments and fulfilment of Easter duties, and these can be measured, as sociologists have done for parts of Europe, though less so for Latin America. According to modern surveys of attendance at Mass in Brazil, the Church can claim no more than a minority of the people, perhaps 10–15 per cent, at the most 20 per cent. These are orthodox Catholics. The majority of Brazilians are informal Catholics who may pray to the saints but do not go to Mass. The historical stages of this decline in religious observance, however, are not known, nor is the original base. For other parts of Latin America statistics are available for the 1960s. In Mexico 95 per cent of the population were baptized, and the average attendance at Easter Communion was 50 per cent. In Venezuela the average attendance at Sunday Mass was 13 per cent, in Colombia 15 per cent, in Peru 12 per cent. But these contemporary figures are not a sure guide to the past, or to the rate, the geography and the sociology of decline in religious practice. At what point, for example, did Peruvian Catholicism begin to recede from the high attendance figures at the time of independence to the low levels of the 1960s?

A religious sociology of Latin America would indicate a number of significant variations. Among the Indian populations attendance at Mass on Sundays and reception of the sacraments were important but irregular, yet they had great respect for the clergy, for saints and for religious ceremonies and pilgrimages. Blacks were not notably Catholic, though they were religious after their own fashion, while the extensive mulatto populations of Brazil, Venezuela and the Caribbean were largely indifferent to organized religion. The *mestizo* population was the real base of orthodox Catholicism and it was in zones of *mestizo* settlement that the full life of the Church was best observed. The elites, on the other hand, produced the lapsed Catholics of the nineteenth century, who moved into freethinking, masonry and positivism, though it would be common in many of these families to have a pious wife of an agnostic husband. The professional and academic classes of contemporary Latin America are the recognizable heirs of these sectors. Among economic groups, small proprietors and tenant farmers would be more likely to be religious than ranchers and cattlemen. There also appear to have been regional differences in the map of religion, places where regular churchgoers predominated, others where seasonal Catholics were the norm. Thus, Mendoza was more religious than Buenos Aires, Lima than Trujillo, Popayán than Cartagena, Mérida than the *llanos*, Michoacán and Jalisco than the Mexican north. But outward conformity does not tell the whole story or penetrate to the degree of commitment either among fervent Catholics or among apparently nominal ones, nor does it indicate the influence of political and social pressures on belief. Moreover, there is a chronology of growth and renewal among Catholics in the nineteenth century as they responded to the Church's progress from inertia to reform. And in some places this was a movement from informal to formal religiosity.

In the plateau of Michoacán in the 1860s and 1870s lack of instruction and even of public worship did not prevent the people from remaining obedient to ecclesiastical government and faithful to the practice of religion. 'Most people could recite from beginning to end the Our Father, the Creed, the Hail Mary, the Ten Commandments, the Magnificat, the Litanies, and many other prayers. No one doubted a single article of faith. For these country people, heaven, hell and purgatory were as real as day and night'.[9] The informed minority of Catholics knew the catechism by heart, accepted it and lived by it. They believed in the mystery of the Trinity and had an eschatalogical view of life and destiny. The great majority, no less Catholic, possessed a more simple and very personal faith, spoke directly to Christ and the saints, frequently broke the commandments, especially the sixth and ninth, and, although the remnants of primitive religions had long been Christianized, retained still a few superstitions from the past.

Catholic priests in Mexico and Central America had no misgivings about the faith of their parishioners, only about their morals. As reported by parish priests in El Salvador, the greatest moral problems were alcoholism and concubinage. In some parishes, two-thirds of sexual unions were informal, blessed by neither church nor state. They blamed this on growing religious indifference, especially among men, who failed to attend Mass or fulfil their Easter duties. 'Yet in spite of this, the faith is preserved intact and there is much religious enthusiasm'.[10] And on special occasions such as fiestas, or during pastoral visitations, or at times of personal crises, the Church would be full of people, the confessionals packed with penitents. So the priests made a distinction between morality and piety: their people were pious but immoral, relying in the end upon Confession and looking to the Church as a refuge of sinners. This gap between faith and morals was a source of great scandal to non-Catholic opinion and to those for whom religion was little more than a code of ethics at the service of society, but in the final analysis it simply represented the perennial tension between the city of God and the earthly city. It was expressed in a perverse way by Manuel, in *The Children of Sánchez* (1961), who was tempted towards North American Protestantism with its strict moral values and orderly behaviour, but confessed 'I remained a Catholic, because I didn't feel strong enough to obey the Commandments, and to carry out the strict rules of the Evangelists.

---

9 González, *Pueblo en vilo*, 110.
10 Quoted in Rodolfo Cardenal, S.J., *El poder eclesiástico en El Salvador* (San Salvador, 1980), 163.

I would no longer be able to enjoy smoking, or gambling, or fornicating . . .'[11]

The reformed Church turned its gaze more intently towards the faithful after about 1870. There was a growth in the number of clergy, and a change in character as they became more ardent, more evangelist, more hungry for souls, as it was said. The parish priests no longer passively accepted religious inertia but actively worked to spread belief and piety. The change in ecclesiastical style was typified by the ministry of a parish priest in El Salvador. He arrived in Arentas in 1855, when there was 'no sign of a parish', only an old church with no ornaments or missals and one chalice. After twenty-three years' work, he had built five new churches for the region, could claim some success in raising faith and morals, and confessed 'while there are sins and excesses still, these must be considered an inevitable consequence of the world around us'.[12]

Reform bred a certain rigidity and produced a kind of model parish, where closer definition and greater discipline were imposed than hitherto. The parish priest said Mass, on Sundays and holy days to a mixed congregation, on weekdays to a small group of women. He preached sermons, recited the decades of the Rosary, held a catechism class for the young, heard the confessions of women and children, and administered the Last Sacraments to those who required them. This was the Latin American parish around 1900. But the majority of men escaped the Church's net and people often referred to those who went to church as '*beatas*'. By defining religion more closely, reform narrowed the door to the Church and many did not enter. It is true that there were signs of a fresh spurt of renewal in the early twentieth century, with devotions to the Blessed Sacrament and the Sacred Heart, but still within the model. Eucharistic devotions, originally designed to make reparations for insults to Jesus Christ from liberals, freemasons and others, led to more frequent Communions and an effort to convert the state itself. Individuals, families, parishes, entire countries were consecrated to the Sacred Heart, in recognition of the sovereignty of Jesus over society, and June was the special month of devotion to the Sacred Heart. There was also a renewal of the cult of Our Lady, and special months, May and October, were devoted to Mary. With March and April came Lent and Holy Week, and so the whole liturgical year unfolded, newer devotions being added to ancient practices.

[11] Oscar Lewis, *The Children of Sánchez* (New York, 1961), 332–3.
[12] Cardenal, *El poder eclesiástico en El Salvador*, 167.

The new religiosity directed from the dioceses and preached from the pulpits was an attempt to bring the people back to Christ and the Church, and there was a response from the mass of Catholics. The people, the parish priests still said, were faithful to religion but prone to evil. This was the limit of reform. The Church could not conquer sin or convert the people to good ways. The secularization of society completed what nature began, and the consequences of original sin were plain to see. From the pulpit the priests attacked the modern world and its snares and urged more frequent recourse to the sacraments. Yet they had to be satisfied with formal observance, private piety and individual morality. This was the object of the Redemptorist missions, which became popular throughout Latin America from the early years of the century; it was also of course part of the Church's mission, to bring people to personal holiness. Yet there was a sense in which the Church turned in upon itself and away from the modern world. There was little sign yet, from priest or people, of a public conscience or social awareness. This had to await a later generation.

Religion did not necessarily bring people together across social barriers. As the parish priest of San Miguel in El Salvador reported in 1878, 'there exists a deep division between the top families and the common people, a division which produces hatred and resentment'.[13] Yet there was a social unity in the Church as well as a unity of belief. The Catholic religion was implanted not only on the coasts but in the highlands, not only in the towns but in the country, among peasants, miners and artisans. It has been said of Peru: 'From Spanish cities to the most primitive Indian communities in the bleak *altiplano* the same signs and symbols of the Christian faith were recognized and revered, pointing to a unity of religious belief that cut across steep economic, social and linguistic barriers'.[14]

The historian can reconstruct the sacred as well as the economic landscape of Latin America, and bring into view the local world of images and relics, patron saints, vows, shrines and miracles, and all the other spiritual aids which these urban and rural communities invoked against the scourges of plague, earthquake, drought and famine. The religion of the people was expressed in various ways, vows to Our Lady and the saints, relics and indulgences, and, above all, the shrines and sacred sites of local religious life. These were the scenes of cures, miracles

---

13 *Ibid.*, 163.
14 Jeffrey L. Klaiber, S.J., *Religion and revolution in Peru, 1824–1976* (Notre Dame, 1977), 2.

and visions, the holy places where prayers were said and heard, the objects of processions and pilgrimages, part of the landscape of the people. Everyday life was pervaded by religion, which appeared to the people in metaphysical truths and physical forms; it answered their questions and satisfied needs which nature itself could not. The great religious processions, Christ of the Miracles in Lima, Our Lady of Chapi in Arequipa, the Lord of Solitude in Huaraz, Our Lady of Copacabana in Bolivia, Our Lady of Luján in Argentina, Our Lady of Guadalupe in Mexico, these testify to the popular base of the Church and the strength of popular religiosity.

How far is it justifiable to speak of a 'popular' religion as distinct from another kind of religion, of a popular Church as distinct from an official Church? Was there a religious sub-culture independent of the institutional Church, the expression of marginal sectors of society, and existing alongside and perhaps in opposition to the orthodox religion of the priests and bishops? The concept of popular religion has been favoured by modern theologians and historians anxious to see signs of liberation in the more distant past. But its validity is open to question. In the first place, popular Catholicism did not invent a new religion. Its characteristic practices expressed the Church's teaching on saints, indulgences, the holy souls, prayers for the dead, the veneration of relics and wearing of medals; all these were orthodox practices and not 'autonomous' in any discernible way. Moreover, the new 'official' religiosity of the late nineteenth century, especially the Marian devotions and the Rosary, fused easily with previous popular practices, which already contained a traditional cult of the Virgin Mary. This is an example of the unity of the universal Church, for such devotions were basically the same everywhere and attested to the Catholicity of Latin American religion. The Rosary, for example, which encouraged meditation on the great mysteries of religion, was a means of instruction in the universal faith. The Rosary led the mind to Christ and the Virgin, but the Virgin to which Latin America prayed was the universal Mary, and the cult of Our Lady of Guadalupe was doctrinally the same as that of Our Lady of Walsingham or Our Lady of Częstochowa.

Popular religiosity and lay organizations were not inherently anticlerical. They had developed to some degree in response to the absence of priests, not in opposition to them. It is true that the reformed Church looked askance at the traditional confraternities and sought either to control them or to set up alternatives such as pious, charitable or

fund-raising organizations under ecclesiastical tutelage. The confraternities had outlived their usefulness and tended to withdraw from the centre
of parish life. They had never been exclusive to the popular sectors. Nor
was popular religion confined to any one social class. It was urban as well
as rural, artisan as well as peasant, clerical as well as lay. The Church
obviously existed within the prevailing social structure, where the poor
were more prone to disease and starvation and more likely to invoke
their special saints than were the rich. But the Latin American Church
was far from homogeneous and appeared to comprehend a variety of
people and movements. It was not so much two levels of religion,
popular and official, local and universal, practised and prescribed, as
many expressions. And in the ultimate analysis the beliefs and practices
of popular Catholicism represented no more than the people's attempts
to make the abstract more concrete, to redefine the supernatural in terms
of the natural environment in which they lived.

The variety of religious experience could be seen in Brazil, where the
Church was a combination of pure Catholicism, partial Catholicism and
marginal deviants. Pure Catholicism was expressed in dogma, the Mass,
the sacraments, and the orthodox cults of the Virgin Mary. Partial
Catholicism tended to comprise prayers to the saints, processions,
images and prayers for the dead, practices which supplied many religious
needs in the absence of priests and parishes. This religious sub-culture
was long tolerated by the Church because it could keep religion alive
without a numerous clergy and elaborate institutions, and was really a
reflection of weak infrastructure rather than defective belief. The
influence of Spiritism, on the other hand, was less orthodox, and in its
more extreme form basically irreconcilable with Catholicism. African
religions in Brazil were not preserved in their original form but
underwent a process of development and adaptation. *Candomblé*, for
example, was a popular form of Spiritism which used prayers and rituals
borrowed from Catholicism but developed into a system of beliefs over
which the Church had no control. Anthropologists describe the process
in terms of syncretism, or even the Africanization of Brazilian religion,
though what the Church was witnessing was the development of a
different religious system outside Catholicism among a people who had
been only superficially converted to Christianity in the first place.

Messianism was yet another strand of Brazilian religious experience,
and in this period found expression in two religious movements in the
Brazilian north-east – Canudos and Joaseiro – each of which formed

around a messianic leader and looked for deliverance from catastrophe into a heavenly city. These are now seen not as isolated phenomena of the backlands but as part of a wider national and ecclesiastical problem, in which the people of the north-east are at once actors and victims. The area was one of comprehensive church reform from the 1860s, a typical product of which was the founding of numerous Houses of Charity, part orphanages, part schools, staffed by lay brothers (*beatos*) and sisters (*beatas*). Economically the north-east was a declining area, losing its labour to coffee and rubber booms in other regions and faced with a declining agriculture. The ability of the new messiahs to attract pilgrims to the north-east where they remained as workers gave them some political leverage, and it also meant that they were able to deliver votes. Thus, they came to be cultivated by local political elites.

The movement known as Canudos was led by the mystic, Antônio Conselheiro. His 'holy city' of about 8,000 *sertanejos* flourished in the Bahian town of Canudos from 1893 until its destruction by Brazilian federal troops four years later. Conselheiro was a layman but a *beato*, a 'wandering servant of the Church', who helped local priests and organized the rebuilding of churches.[15] But he also preached from church pulpits, and this brought him into conflict with the archbishop of Bahia, whose programme of clerical reform had no place for amateur preachers. His defenders claimed that he was an orthodox Catholic, and did not question the doctrines of the Church or pretend to be a priest. Indeed his criticisms of the Republic were made from the standpoint of traditional Catholicism and were directed against a secular state which had just disestablished the Church, introduced religious toleration and removed ecclesiastical jurisdiction over marriage and burial. The Republic, however, was supported by the bishops; under political pressure themselves, they urged the priests of the north-east to abandon Conselheiro, and so he lost his religious base. But he also had some local political support because of his influence over labour. In 1893 he campaigned against the tax policies of the Republic and after a skirmish with the police he and his followers retreated to the hills of Canudos. Messianism of this kind lent itself to political manipulation by local interests and could suffer either from their support or their hostility. In the event federal troops were dispatched to destroy Canudos in 1897.

Messianism travelled further from its origins in the movement of

---

[15] Ralph della Cava, 'Brazilian messianism and national institutions: a reappraisal of Canudos and Joaseiro', *HAHR*, 48 3 (1968), 407.

Joaseiro. Cícero Romão Batista was a priest, one of the first products of the seminary at Fortaleza and, when appointed to Joaseiro in Ceará, was a prototype of the new priests in the backlands, orthodox, zealous, promoter of the St Vincent de Paul Society and a friend of the community of *beatos* and *beatas*. In March 1889 the Communion host which he gave to a *beata* of Joaseiro was transformed into blood, thought to be the blood of Christ. A miracle was proclaimed by priests and people, soon pilgrims were making their way to Joaseiro, and a popular cult came into being comprising the priests of the backlands, landowners and middle sectors, and the Catholic masses. The bishops, on the other hand, denied the miracle and suspended Padre Cícero; his supporters appealed to Rome and the miracle was condemned there too in 1894. Padre Cícero then sought a political bargain with local *coronéis*, requesting support in return for his neutrality. But although he wanted to keep Joaseiro a city of God, the miracle engendered wealth and growth, as miracles often do, and so he was drawn inexorably into public life. Soon he acquired a political adviser, Dr Floro Bartholomeu, a physician from Bahia, campaigning for Joaseiro's autonomy and elevation to *município* status in 1914. And the next step for Padre Cícero was support for armed action to defend his holy city, and then entry into national politics. There was a tendency in messianism to abandon the sacred for the profane.

PROTESTANTISM, POSITIVISM AND CATHOLIC RESPONSES

Popular religiosity, fringe Catholicism, messianism, these and other manifestations of religious enthusiasm took place more or less within the boundaries of the Catholic faith. The nineteenth century, however, saw the growth of another religion in Latin America, one which did not accept the jurisdiction of the Catholic Church or the primacy of the pope. The first Protestants in Latin America were foreign diplomats, merchants and residents who, from the early years of independence, settled in the capitals and ports of the subcontinent, protected directly or indirectly by the British trade treaties with the new nations. Congregations and churches of Anglicans, Presbyterians and Methodists appeared in this form. These were tolerated enclaves and did not represent missionary expansion. The next phase was the arrival of representatives of Bible Societies, who sought to reach beyond the foreigners to the Catholic population. The Catholics of Latin America were not ignorant of the sacred scriptures, for they had long encountered them in the Epistles and

Gospels of the Mass. But the Bible Societies met the needs of some and led to a further phase, that of evangelization among Catholics and unconverted Indians by missionaries, especially from the United States and including now Episcopalians and Baptists. The numbers of clergy and followers increased, especially in countries like Argentina and Brazil which received large immigrant populations in the late nineteenth century and where the Catholic Church did not immediately respond to their existence. To survive the new churches and sects had to rely on liberal policies of religious toleration and separation of church and state. This affinity between liberalism and Protestantism further alerted the Catholic Church and caused it to rely even more on protection and privilege, determined to keep control of registration of births, marriages and deaths. In Catholic eyes Protestantism became equated with secularization and illustrated the danger of religious toleration; it also strengthened the Church's alliance with conservatives and reliance upon Concordats between the Holy See and the national governments, in which control of church patronage was often traded for a special position for the Church in the state. Meanwhile, continuing mass immigration led to further expansion of the immigrant churches. From the early twentieth century, and especially from 1914, United States' trade and investment in Latin America made great advances, accompanied by increased political and sometimes military presence. The opportunities for American Protestantism also expanded: new groups appeared, the Quakers, Salvation Army, Seventh Day Adventists, and new missionary movements, such as the Free Church Missions and the Evangelical Union of South America, added to the Protestant presence and to Catholic indignation. Yet, even after a century of growth Protestantism was a rare and exotic phenomenon in Latin America. In the struggle for minds the Catholic Church had a more potent rival.

The main intellectual challenge to the Catholic Church came not from Protestantism but from positivism, which, following earlier waves of utilitarianism and liberalism, succeeded in dominating the thinking of the Latin American elite in the last decades of the nineteenth century.[16] The philosophy of Auguste Comte was based on 'positive' knowledge, that is knowledge which could be scientifically demonstrated. In place of revealed religion he established rational and empirical principles. These would yield a theory of social structure and change from which a system

[16] See also, Hale, *CHLA* iv, chap. 10.

of social planning could be developed. The political framework for this was a dictator based on popular consent, ruling for life with the aid of a technocratic elite, and promoting economic progress in an ordered society. Positivism arrived relatively late in Latin America, at a time when it was already out of favour in Europe, but it took root from the 1870s and came to exert a dominant influence in a number of countries for the rest of the century and beyond. It struck an instant response in those who were seeking to explain the political and economic backwardness of Latin America and who welcomed its promise of renewal and modernization and its challenge to the influence of the Catholic Church over the minds of the masses. To government elites and technocrats it offered legitimacy for the prevailing economic model and its authoritarian framework. To the middle sectors it was a reassuring mixture of reformism and conservatism, promising material progress without threatening the social structure. Academics, schoolteachers, the military and other groups interested in modernization, development and the improvement of society, all absorbed in some degree positivist philosophy and pointed an accusing finger at religion and the Church.

Positivism was presented as an alternative to religion, and its scientific methods were greeted with enthusiasm in countries such as Brazil, Chile and Mexico and regarded as a key to unlock the door of progress. In Brazil it made its presence felt in the central government and also among state governors. In Mexico Gabino Barreda, minister of education after the restoration of the Republic in 1867, sought to reorganize higher education and give it a uniform curriculum based on Comte's hierarchy of the sciences. In Chile, too, positivists believed that education should be restructured and the power of Catholicism destroyed. Everywhere positivism appeared to speak clearly and look confidently towards the future. As the Brazilian Catholic publicist, Jackson de Figueiredo said, 'Positivism knows how to say what it wants for the general good in the midst of this enormous confusion of ideas'.[17]

Intellectual conflict was even more bitter in Peru. There the attack on religion and the Church was spearheaded by the atheist Manuel González Prada (1848–1918), who in the decades after the War of the Pacific (1879–83) waged a relentless war of words on Catholicism and everything it stood for. He condemned Catholicism as one of the worst obstacles to progress in Peru; he wanted to eliminate the Church from all public life

---

[17] Quoted in Robert G. Nachman, 'Positivism, modernization, and the middle class in Brazil', *HAHR*, 57 1 (1977), 22.

and substitute science, 'the only God of the future'.[18] González Prada went beyond positivism. He sought revolutionary change in Peru through an alliance of intellectuals and workers who would overthrow the Catholic Church, the Hispanic tradition, and Peruvian conservatism. His espousal of anarchism gave him further intellectual ammunition, which he aimed at the state as well as the Church: 'In Peru there are two great lies: the Republic and Christianity'.[19] According to González Prada there was a triple alliance of priest, official and landlord to oppress the Indian and keep him in ignorance and poverty, offering him religious processions instead of material progress. He did not want the integration of the Indians into Peruvian society but the restoration of their separate identity, aloof from Hispanic and Catholic culture. The crude anti-clericalism of González Prada was not shared by José Carlos Mariátegui (1894–1930), who travelled a more spiritual path in his journey from the traditional Catholicism of his youth to become the founder of Marxism in Peru. Mariátegui was still a believer in 1917 when, at the age of twenty-three, he wrote 'I believe in God, above all things and I do all things devoutly and zealously in his holy name', and he respected the popular manifestations of Peruvian Catholicism. But he returned from Europe a convert to Marxism, convinced that the end of organized religion was near.

How did the Catholic Church respond to positivism? From pulpit and press the Church rejected the new philosophy, denied that religion was a thing of the past and demanded a place for Catholicism in public education. In Mexico the educational and political content of positivism was attacked as contrary to freedom of conscience and alien to the country's religious tradition. In Chile Catholic writers rushed to the defence of the faith, inspired by Pius IX's denouncement of liberalism, rationalism, science and progress. In Brazil Jackson de Figueiredo (1891–1928), who had abandoned the Church of his youth in favour of agnosticism and then undergone a new conversion, went over to the offensive, appalled by positivism's conquest of the educated classes and their total indifference to religion. In the pages of his review *A Ordem* he presented a Catholic position on the leading issues of the day and sought to stir the Church out of its intellectual lethargy to lead a great crusade against materialism. Catholics also fought positivism politically, in alliance with conservative groups, in order to procure governments

---

[18] Klaiber, *Religion and revolution in Peru*, 34.
[19] *Ibid.*, 40.

open to their influence, to thwart legislation hostile to religion and, in general, to preserve the public position of the Church. In Chile, for example, they worked through their political club, *Los Amigos del País*, lobbying for Catholic causes, and in particular for Catholic education, usually one of the first targets of reformers, and they succeeded in forcing the resignation of positivist, Diego Barros Arana, from the headship of the Instituto Nacional. In short, the Church fought positivism as a political battle over relative influence in public life. Its methods were a mixture of polemical journalism and pressure group tactics, and the results were mixed: in Colombia, after setbacks, complete success; in Chile a losing battle; in Mexico almost total failure. Everywhere, the reliance on public privilege and state sanctions to secure the survival of the Church against positivist attack was probably pernicious in the long run.

Intellectually, the Church did not respond to positivism and the debate was never joined, at least at the level of Comte's philosophy. There was eventually an intellectual reaction against positivism in Latin America, but this was not specifically Catholic in its inspiration. It is true that a number of Catholic writers proved themselves to be effective apologists for religion and brought religious discussion out of the Church and into the media. In Brazil Jackson de Figueiredo and Alceu Amoroso Lima widened the terms and improved the quality of politico-religious debate, but their writings impress for their polemical rather than their philosophical content. Moreover, Figueiredo and especially Amoroso Lima took Brazilian Catholic thought along the wrong road. Their search for 'order' in politics, society and thought was a throwback to positivism itself, adding to it a new base of Catholic morality. Other ideas they derived from reactionary Catholic thinkers such as Joseph de Maistre, Charles Maurras and Donoso Cortes, clothed them in Brazilian nationalism, and produced a political thought which was critical not only of materialism and capitalism but also of democracy. Yet, if the Church lost the elites and some of the arguments, it would not be correct to conclude that it lost the conflict with positivism. The philosophy of Comte was received in Latin America as an action system rather than a sociological theory. The political and economic model which it helped to legitimize was in due course overtaken by criticism, change and collapse, while positivism itself became discredited. The social consequences of positivist models remained to be resolved, and at this point social Catholicism emerged to take the argument a stage further and give religion a new dimension. The intellectual struggle had been one for the minds of the elites not those of the masses. The Church had never lost its base among the popular sectors and it outlived positivism to speak more directly to them in the course of the twentieth century, as will be seen. Before that happened, however, the Church had to redefine its relation to the state.

CHURCH AND STATE IN A SECULAR AGE

The Catholic Church was traditionally opposed to the separation of church and state and demanded for itself the position of officially established religion; in the nineteenth century this was regarded as the only defence against liberalism, positivism and other secular enemies. To preserve its privilege the Church cultivated governments and associated with conservative elites, who in turn exploited the Church for political or financial advantage. This made its opponents the more determined to curb its powers or even to restrict its religious freedom. The system had its critics even within the Church. In France around 1830 the Abbé Lamennais struggled to secure the independence of the Church from the state in opposition to the Gallican tradition, and to persuade the Church freely to renounce the compromising protection which it received from the state. Pope Gregory XVI reacted (*Mirari vos*, 1832) by denouncing liberalism, liberty of the press, separation of church and state, and, in particular, the notion that liberty of conscience ought to be guaranteed. These views were confirmed and enlarged by Pope Pius IX and were transmitted to the Latin American Church if not as articles of faith then as the authoritative teaching of the Church. This led the Church into absolutist positions and delayed its integration into the modern world. Liberalism too became intolerant, and even conservatives took material advantage of the Church's difficulties; thus relations between the two powers deteriorated amidst bitter recriminations.

Attacked by its enemies and ill-served by its friends, the Church in Latin America had to accept the loss of temporal power and privilege and the triumph of the secular state in the second half of the nineteenth century. The pace of change, and the degree, differed from country to country, however. In some cases anticlericalism was so strong that not only was the Church disestablished but limitations were even imposed on its religious functions. In other countries a compromise was reached, and the Church continued to be subsidized by the state and also dependent upon it. In yet other countries the Church remained more or less established but had to accept state control over the appointment of bishops. How can we explain the wide variations of church–state relations in the different countries of Latin America? One factor was the different national histories and traditions, and the contrasting experiences of state-building in the nineteenth century. Another was the character of particular governments or caudillos, and the nature of their beliefs. But perhaps the most important factor was the relative power and wealth of the Church. Where the Church was large, in clergy and resources, it was more likely to provoke anticlericalism and envy, both political and personal; it was also in a stronger position to defend itself. The ensuing conflict would probably be bitter and violent, and the settlement more decisive, one way or the other. Where the Church was poor and weak it did not provoke overt hostility; but nor could it defend itself, and gradually, without dramatic conflict, it would find its privileges eroded. And in some cases there was a balance of power.

The experience of the Church in Brazil was perhaps the most traumatic of all, for in the space of a few years it passed simultaneously from monarchy to republic, from a Catholic state to a secular state, from an established Church to a disestablished one. The political independence of Brazil brought no independence to the Church. The almost absolute power of the Portuguese crown over the colonial Church was inherited intact by the empire. Pedro II, who had a purely political attitude to religion, retained full powers of patronage and rights of intervention between Rome and the Brazilian Church. He nominated bishops, collected tithes, paid the clergy. But the problem went deeper than the personal policy of the emperor. The advent to power of a conservative ministry in 1868 signalled a growth in the power of the state and in its expenditure. Church lands and properties were now viewed by politicians with keener interest, and the Church was subject to yet greater pressure. The progress of religion thus came to depend upon the favour or fear of the monarchy rather than the inner resources of the Church. When, in the course of reform, the Church began to behave more truly as a Church and less as a department of state then it brought swift retribution upon itself.

The so-called Religious Question began in March 1872, when a priest in Rio was suspended for refusing to abjure freemasonry. The penetration of religious institutions by freemasonry undoubtedly compromised the Church and was a matter of legitimate concern to its leaders. In December 1872 Dom Frei Vital M. Gonçalves de Oliveira, bishop of Olinda (later joined by Dom Antonio de Macedo Costa, bishop of Pará) ordered all Catholics who were masons to be expelled from the confraternities. These, dominated as they were by masons, refused to comply, and when placed under an interdict they appealed to the emperor, demanding that the bishop be restrained by the imperial power of patronage. The papal encyclicals invoked by the bishops had never been approved by the government and were therefore not legally valid in Brazil. So this was a conflict not only between Church and monarchy, but between the monarchy and Rome. Pope Pius IX retreated from his earlier position of support for the bishops after the Brazilian government intervened. But the government was not so willing to hold back and it brought the two bishops to trial in 1874, when they were found guilty of impeding the will of the executive power and sentenced to four years' imprisonment, though they were subsequently amnestied. These spectacular events have tended to overshadow the more prosaic but not less persistent pressure on the Church by the successive administrations of the time. When the liberals came to power in 1878 they began a sustained attack on church institutions, while the radicals in their midst were convinced that the Church, along with slavery, was a major obstacle to modernization in Brazil. Clauses in a number of budgets restricted the Church's right to hold rural and urban property; they sought also to establish a civil registry and to limit the Church's opportunity to 'promote ignorance' in education.

The Church learnt little from this experience. In spite of the Religious Question and the subsequent liberal legislation, Catholics continued to support the monarchy against republicanism, trusting in the alliance of the altar and the throne against the enemies of God and the emperor. But the monarchy fell and the republicans came to power. This was a bewildering experience for the Church, helpless without its familiar supports. It had no influence with the new political leaders, who for their part were not anxious to see a repeat of the Religious Question of 1874. They took prompt and decisive action. In 1890 the Church was separated from the state and disestablished; and the process was completed and ratified by the constitution of 1891. Freedom of worship, civil marriage, secular education, all were now instituted; there was a ban on government subsidy of religious education, and after a year government financial support for the clergy was withdrawn. There was an inevitability about secularization which the Church had to accept, though it suspected the motives of the republicans, and not without reason, for the latter were gratuitously illiberal towards religion when they decreed that members of religious orders who were bound by a vow of obedience were to be disenfranchised.

Yet 1891 was a vital date in the history of the Brazilian Church, the date of its independence. This was not exactly how the hierarchy saw it, for they did not appreciate the long-term advantages of disestablishment; convinced that liberalism and positivism had taken over Brazil, they hankered after state support and still pursued public influence through political power. But these were now denied the Church, and it had to look to Rome for leadership and to its own resources for survival. In the event the period 1889–1930 was one of institutional growth for the Church, as it slowly recovered from the shock of separation and adjusted itself to the world of the First Republic. New dioceses were founded, more clergy recruited, religious orders encouraged and, by 1930, reinforced by foreign priests and new funds, the Church had become an independent and well-organized institution, yet even now still ready to claim a legal as well as a moral pre-eminence in the nation.

The Brazilian Church in these years was personified by Sebastião Leme da Silveira Cintra (1882–1942), priest, archbishop of Olinda, archbishop of Rio de Janeiro, cardinal and statesman of the Church. Dom Leme was inspired by two goals: to improve the religious life of priests and people, and to gain for the Church a greater place in the affairs of the nation. He could not accept that in an 'essentially Catholic country' like Brazil the Church should have so little influence, and in a resounding pastoral letter in 1916 he lamented: 'we are a majority who count for nothing'.[20] Dom Leme fought on various fronts, against spiritism, secularism and positivism. He sought to make the faith of Brazilians more orthodox and better informed by introducing European priests and pastoral methods, and by great public manifestations of religion. This was a time of jubilees, religious feasts, Eucharistic Congresses and, in 1931, the elevation of Christ the Redeemer above Rio de Janeiro. Meanwhile Dom Leme was applying political pressure to obtain the return of religious education in state schools, to block any move to legalize divorce and to secure the election of politicians sympathetic to the Church. Finally, he sought to rechristianise the Brazilian elite, especially the intellectuals, and then to make them the activists of the lay

[20] Irmã Maria Regina do Santo Rosário, *O Cardeal Leme (1882–1942)* (Rio de Janeiro, 1962), 66, 68.

apostolate. There had already been distinguished precursors, Julio Cesar de Morais Carneiro, who became a Redemptorist priest and ended all his sermons with the cry 'We must make Brazil Catholic', and Joaquim Nabuco, who was influenced by John Henry Newman and English Catholicism. Now, in 1917, the young writer Jackson de Figueiredo made his peace with the Church and began to do battle with its rivals and detractors. How, he asked, could the Catholic majority allow the minority to impose its opinions on the nation? Materialism and secularism drew strength from religious ignorance, for which Catholics themselves were responsible; so he started a periodical *A Ordem*, and set up the Dom Vital Centre to study Catholic doctrine and mobilize Catholic intellectuals. Dom Leme regarded his new recruit as the model of a lay apostle and supported him in all his work until his untimely death in 1928. Meanwhile he himself, in 1922, founded the Catholic Confederation, the prototype of the later Brazilian Catholic Action, to form militant laymen in the service of the Church. To a later generation of Brazilian Catholics no doubt Dom Leme has become an exemplar of the triumphalist tradition in the Church, and it is true that rather than re-think the Church's position in the world he preferred to seek temporal power to safeguard religion. Yet he brought the Brazilian Church out of the crisis of disestablishment, strengthened its structures and imposed it upon the attention of the nation.

The Argentine Church had a long tradition of regalism though its experience of this differed from that of Brazil. The Constitution of 1853 obliged the state to 'support' the Catholic religion without 'professing' it. The support was real enough but it could also be seen as intervention, even though in practice each side respected the other. The crucial issue was the power given to the government to control important ecclesiastical appointments. The president was given 'the rights of the national patronage in the appointment of bishops for the Cathedral Churches, selected from three names proposed by the Senate'. The papacy did not recognize these rights, but in practice resigned itself to the process and appointed the person presented by the president. So the Argentine state began and continued its history with a firm control of patronage and a bias towards a national Church, though formally recognizing Rome. There was another way of resolving church–state relations, to free the Church through separation, as the Brazilian Church was freed, but in Argentina this was very much a minority view. In any case the Church enjoyed advantages under the system, even if they were short-term.

Argentina had a tradition of religious toleration, and the 1853 Constitution embodied freedom of conscience and freedom of worship. This toleration, however, was an expedient rather than a principle and it did not mean that the Catholic Church had been converted to true toleration. Though the assurance of toleration was given to all faiths, they were obviously not all equal. Catholicism was seen as the traditional religion of the nation, and its majority position was reinforced in these years by mass immigration from Catholic Europe. Moreover, while Catholics subscribed to the basic freedoms of thought, speech and religion, they were favoured by the bias in the Constitution and were reluctant to share their rights with non-Catholics. Yet the constitutional position was not altogether clear. Did support for the Catholic religion oblige the state to provide religious instructions in schools or to sanction Catholic marriage laws?

These questions came to a head in 1884 when the secular trends of the Roca government, already under attack from the Catholic hierarchy, culminated in a new education law; following pressure from professional teachers, the government removed religious instruction from the regular curriculum in state schools. A great national debate followed. The government criticised Catholics for wanting to impose their own beliefs on everyone; it also took the view that bishops were officers of state and could not attack government policy. Certain bishops were threatened with legal action for opposition to the government; the Apostolic Delegate was expelled; and steps were taken to remove a bishop from his see. The lay spokesman for the Catholic position was the scholar and publicist José Manuel Estrada, who at the Catholic Congress convoked in August 1884 to mobilise opinion asked: 'To what extent did the policy of the government interpret the general will, Catholic for the most part?'.[21] Now he argued that religious instruction was a traditional part of education for the overwhelmingly Catholic population of Argentina. Such instruction need not be imposed, but it should be available to those who wanted it. The government was not impressed and Estrada was dismissed from all his academic posts for speaking against his employer's policy.

Another clash of opinion occurred over marriage law. The Civil Marriage Law of 1888 did not prohibit a religious ceremony for marriage, but required that it be preceded by a civil ceremony and this

21 Quoted in Guillermo Furlong, S.J., 'El catolicismo argentino entre 1860 y 1930', Academia Nacional de la Historia, *Historia Argentina Contemporánea 1862–1930*, II, Primera Sección (Buenos Aires, 1964), 273.

was obligatory for all marriages. The new legislation, like that on religious education, was part of a policy of secularization applied by the Roca and Juárez Celmán administrations (1880–90) in the interests of individual freedom, a policy which had much support in Argentina, but which Catholics regarded as a comprehensive attack on religion and its place in society. These administrations were succeeded by those of Pellegrini, Sáenz Peña and Uriburu, which could afford to be more tolerant towards Catholics because the basic positions had now been won. By the end of the nineteenth century laicization was largely complete and Argentina was a secular state. This result had been achieved without violence or civil unrest and was accepted by Catholics who were now concerned to show that there was no incompatibility between Catholicism and a secular state, though, as in Brazil, there was a conservative wing which still fought for old causes. But the basic reason for accommodation between church and state was that the Argentine Church was neither wealthy nor powerful, and in a position neither to provoke nor to defend.

The Church in Uruguay had even less power than that in Argentina and the Uruguayan hierarchy even less influence in national affairs. In 1984 only 3.8 per cent of the country's 3 million inhabitants were practising Catholics, and there was only one priest for every 4,300 persons. At what point in the modern period this de-Christianization took place it is difficult to say, but it evidently had its origins in the past. In the course of the nineteenth and twentieth centuries Uruguay abandoned religion and converted to secularism.

Conflict between church and state began in 1838 when Fructuoso Rivera suppressed Franciscan convents and confiscated their properties. In subsequent years the Jesuits were expelled, readmitted and expelled again, allegedly for meddling in state affairs but really for being independent of the state, at a time when the latter was seeking to build its power and authority against all rival institutions. When Bernardo Berro came to power in 1860 the government became even more hostile and took a number of laicizing measures. Berro, who was a freemason, expressed the opinion that Christianity was a means of domination and oppression, and he used his power to weaken the Church and reduce its place in civil life. There was a reaction under his successor Venancio Flores who, among other things, re-admitted the Jesuits to Uruguay. In the following decades, however, the Church came under increasing pressure, especially on education and marriage, the two issues which arose throughout Latin America at this time. In 1885 a new law made civil marriage compulsory and the only legally binding form of marriage. And state subsidies to the Church were gradually eroded. From 1904 José Batlle y Ordóñez dealt the final blow to official church–state relations. He was actively anticlerical, a mason, and did not hide his contempt for religion. He removed all signs of religion from public life and buildings. He established the country's first divorce laws and was hostile to any form of religious education; in 1909 the teaching of religion in state schools was prohibited. The government even replaced religious feasts by secular holidays, the Epiphany by Children's Day, Holy Week by Tourist Week, the Immaculate Conception by Beach Day, Christmas by Family Day, no doubt an extreme example of a certain liberal mentality but one which helps to explain the Catholic reaction to liberalism in Latin America. By now there was so little opposition from Uruguayan Catholics – and so few real Catholics – that the state had little difficulty in completing the work of secularization in the new Constitution of 1 March 1919, when the Church was disestablished and the separation of church and state became formal. This freed the Church and left it to survive by its own resources in a largely indifferent society. Its resources were not impressive; in the 1920s there were only eighty-five churches and 200 clergy. Weak as it was, however, the Church in Uruguay was stronger than that in neighbouring Paraguay, where the Church emerged from the horrors of war in 1870 hardly less diminished and demoralized than the rest of the population. For the next decades the Paraguayan Church lay prostrate and usually silent, neglected by conservatives, occasionally attacked by liberals and largely ignored by history.

The Church in Chile, unlike those in the rest of the southern cone, had a significant voice in public affairs, yet it did not become a cause of great division in the nation. In the nineteenth century there was a steady erosion of the Church's privileges rather than a total confrontation. Freedom of religion existed in fact, if not in the constitution; given Chile's commercial interests and the influx of foreigners it could hardly have been otherwise. In 1865 all denominations were granted legal permission to worship and establish schools. Later, when Liberal and Radical parties dominated the government, the Church lost a number of other positions. Clerical immunity was abolished in 1874; cemeteries were secularized in 1883, civil marriage was made compulsory and all civil records were placed in the hands of the state in 1884. Although the

Church conducted a rearguard action against all these measures, there was no stopping the advance of the secular state; for the next forty years the two powers co-existed and the state continued to subsidise the Church.

The Church in Chile was not wealthy either in land or property, and could not be identified by liberals as an obstacle to economic progress. During the late nineteenth century, however, it acquired some controversial political friends and became closely identified with the Conservative party, its protector, exploiter, and divider. For Conservative support the Church had to pay at elections, in funds, words and votes, and the alliance brought divisions into the Church, between bishops and priests, priests and laity, and among the laity themselves. And it was very shortsighted. During the years 1891 and 1920 Chile was ruled by a strong parliamentary government based on an alliance of Conservatives and traditional Liberals. The regime was impervious to the growth of new middle sectors in commerce and industry and of an industrial working class in the mining areas of the north, and it ignored demands for a change. While the Church did not clearly read the signs of the times, it The lesson for the Church should have been clear: the social base of Conservatism was shrinking and the political structure was ready for change. While the church did not clearly read the signs of the times, it could not fail to see the flaws in the Conservative alliance.

The circumstances were thus right for a final understanding with the state. Arturo Alessandri, a Radical and reforming president, who first came to power in 1920, wanted separation of church and state: the policy was traditional to his party and it might also yield the political bonus of detaching the Church from the Conservatives and strengthening the middle ground. Archbishop Crescente Errázuriz also wanted a church independent of the state and free from exploitation by the Conservative party. While not all bishops agreed, many people in the Church followed the archbishop and believed that disestablishment would give the Church freedom of action and make for an impartial clergy. Rome appeared to share these views. Alessandri consulted Pope Pius XI and his secretary of state, Cardinal Gasparri and gained acceptance of his proposals subject to certain conditions. Rome had experience of church–state conflict and had learnt that it was a losing battle which could only damage the Church, as it did in Mexico. A separation peacefully negotiated, on the other hand, which would give freedom to the Chilean Church and control of patronage to Rome, would be better by far than one accepted under duress. So the Vatican instructed the Chilean hierarchy to accept.

The Constitution of 1925 disestablished the Church. It provided for the free exercise of all religions, but it recognized the legal personality of the Roman Catholic Church and guaranteed it rights to own property exempt from taxation, as it did for all religions. The government's rights of ecclesiastical appointments and of veto over papal communications were abolished. The Church was allowed to establish dioceses, seminaries and religious communities without congressional approval, and to maintain its own education system. State payment of salaries to clerics and other subsidies for the Church were ended, though the government eased the transition by paying the Church an annual sum of 2.5 million pesos for five years. The balance of clerical and lay opinion in the Church was in favour of disestablishment. No doubt there were still right-wing Catholics who supported the Conservative alliance or went even further along the road of reaction. But the days of a privileged Church were over.

Peru took a different path to that of the southern cone, preferring a close union of church and state, the one legally privileged, the other officially Catholic. In Peru liberal anticlericalism was relatively mild and was never a popular issue: the endurance of Spanish culture and tradition among the elite and of religious enthusiasm among the masses prevented this. In terms of clerical wealth and presence Peru occupied a middle position in the league of Churches, enough to arouse interest but not to provoke conflict. In the first decades after independence liberals managed to close many convents and reduce the number of priests and nuns; and in the liberal constitution of 1856 the ecclesiastical *fueros* and tithes were abolished. This seemed to satisfy the majority of Peruvians. In 1860 President Ramón Castilla introduced a new constitution designed as a compromise between conservatism and liberalism. It declared that the state protected the Roman Catholic religion and did not permit the public exercise of any other; it safeguarded the Church's wealth and property; and it assured the Church autonomy and freedom from political control. But the constitution suppressed the ecclesiastical (and military) *fueros* and ended state collection of tithes, replacing them by an annual government subsidy. It also provided for a system of public education which would end the monopoly of the Church. So this constitution gave something to the Church and to the liberals, and it lasted, with the exception of a brief 'pure' liberal interlude in 1867, until

1920. The Church accepted it as a good arrangement, as indeed it was, giving it security, authority and wealth. From this base it improved its structures, orientated itself towards Rome and became a strong force in the life of the nation.

But it was not a permanent victory. From the 1870s the Church lost influence among intellectuals and statesmen, as secular values began to prevail and positivism and more radical influences began to replace traditional liberalism in the minds of the elites. What the Church lost among the privileged it tried to recoup among the poor. Its influence among the Indians and *cholos* of the sierra continued uninterrupted, but now it sought a new constituency among urban workers. Incipient industrialization and the emergence of an industrial working class introduced the issue of workers' rights into political debate and generated the first attempts at labour organization. Here too the Church sought a role. In Arequipa, for example, it played a part in early forms of trade unionism, and the most influential of the local mutual aid societies was the *Círculo de Obreros Católicos* formed in 1896. But the Church was not the only voice speaking for the Indians, peasants and workers of Peru, and here too it found it was challenged. The reformist movement APRA began life in the 1920s as an enemy of the church and religion, and only later invoked the social message of the Gospels and the role of Christ as a reformer in order to pre-empt official religion and divert the religiosity of the lower classes towards its own party. APRA was also hostile to the political associates of the Church. The model of development favoured by President Augusto B. Leguía (1919–30) – unrestricted foreign investment and a primary export economy – was criticised by APRA but not by the Church, which had close and compromising relations with the regime. In a pastoral letter of 25 April 1923 Archbishop Emilio Lisson declared that he was going to consecrate Peru to the Sacred Heart of Jesus in a ceremony in the Plaza de Armas in Lima. He also invited Leguía to preside over the ceremony as 'patron of the Church'. The proposal was a pious and polemical idea, embarrassing to many Catholics, outrageous to secularists, and a bonus to the dictatorship; it was denounced as an abuse of the union of Church and state and an affront to freedom of conscience; and the voices in its favour were not very convincing. A protest movement led by future APRA leaders gained momentum, and in the face of violence on the streets the archbishop suspended the ceremony, which he claimed had been turned into a campaign 'against the legitimately established government and social institutions'.[22] Among the various models of church–state relations the episode was an example and a commentary.

The historical relation of church to state in Bolivia is not easy to categorize. In the nineteenth century there was a prolonged dispute between the Vatican and the Bolivian government over the control of ecclesiastical patronage, and attempts to resolve this by concordats failed in 1851 and 1884. The national government continued to nominate bishops and the Vatican, reluctantly, to confirm them. The Church in Bolivia drew strength less from government policies and current resources than from its centuries-old presence in the country and from the continuing, if irregular, demand for its sacramental services from those Indians who had been Christianised. In the course of the nineteenth century the Church received contradictory signals from the state. If the liberals were normally hostile, conservatives were unpredictable and not automatically allies of the Church. In 1880 the Church lost tithes and first fruits and was assigned instead a state subsidy; this was accompanied by tax exemption for church property. After two decades of conservative rule the Liberal party returned to power in 1898, and in 1906 it decreed liberty of worship, to the alarm of Catholics but without greatly increasing the number of Protestants. The Church also lost its control over cemeteries, which were secularized in 1908. And in 1911 a new marriage law was enacted which recognized only civil marriage as binding, though this could be followed by the religious ceremony. With the fall of the Liberals the Church recovered some of the positions which it had lost. In 1920, by common demand of clergy and Indians, the religious marriage of Indians was allowed to fulfil civil requirements. Throughout the 1920s the Church underwent institutional growth, and in 1928 it regained a place for religious instruction in state schools.

It has been suggested that the imperatives of state-building, political convictions and church power can combine to produce tension and conflict in church–state relations and a change in the balance of power. In Colombia, where conflict developed amidst great bitterness and occasional violence, it was the Church rather than the state which eventually emerged triumphant. The initiative was taken by the Liberals. While some simply wanted to secure religious toleration, others were deter-

[22] Quoted in Klaiber, *Religion and revolution in Peru*, 133.

mined to establish state control over the Church to prevent it fighting back. Among these was Tomás Cipriano de Mosquera (1845–9, 1866–8), who was responsible for perhaps the fiercest anti-Church policy of the nineteenth century and an assertion of the state's right of 'tuition' over the Church. Mosquera's Liberal party enacted the Constitution of Rionegro (1863), which may be regarded as the high water mark of liberal policy towards the Church. It declared freedom of religion, barred the clergy from federal offices and prohibited the Church from interfering in political matters, reasonable statements in themselves but open to anticlerical application. Moreover, in the wake of similar legislation in Mexico (see below), it prohibited ecclesiastical corporations from acquiring and possessing real estate. In addition the decree of 9 September 1861 disamortized corporate property and enforced its sale in public auction. The government hoped to bring property into the market and make it more accessible to individuals. In the event these measures simply concentrated property still more, and tended to replace the Church as a landowner and creditor by more acquisitive individuals. The Church itself did not co-operate. It defended its right to own property, condemned those who denied it and punished clergy who compromised it. The faithful were warned against liberalism and forbidden to take the oath to the Constitution of 1863, except in a form excluding the anticlerical parts. And Rome supported the Colombian Church. In an encyclical addressed to the Colombian bishops in 1863 Pius IX condemned the 'sacrileges' committed by the Liberal government in opposing the doctrines and rights of the Catholic Church.

From 1870 relations between church and state entered another period of crisis when the government undertook a long overdue reform of education. In the Decree of Primary Education (1 November 1870) provision was made for free and obligatory primary education throughout Colombia; the state would not provide religious instruction but this could be given by priests within schools. Some of the hierarchy, notably the moderate archbishop of Bogotá, Vicente Arbeláez, were willing to accept the secular schools and indeed to work for general reconciliation with the state. But conservative Catholics rejected compromise. In Cauca, whose 'neo-Catholic fanaticism' was denounced by liberals, clerical opposition was intransigent. In Pasto Catholics rallied to the defence of religion against atheism and liberalism. Monsignor Carlos Bermúdez, bishop of Popayán, citing the Syllabus of Errors and insisting on Catholic control of schools, forbade parents to send their children to state elementary schools under pain of excommunication. On the other side liberal fanatics also drew up their battle lines and contributed their share to the political hysteria. Caught between conservatives and liberals, moderate churchmen were unable to establish a middle ground as reason gave way to reaction. Thus, opposition to educational reform contributed to a conservative-Catholic revolution in 1876 and the civil war of 1876–77.

The revolution began in Cauca, and here it took on the appearance of a religious crusade as well as a political struggle. Conservatives exploited religion for political ends, and this was well known. A captured conservative colonel was reported as saying 'If we had not taken the pretext of religion, we would not have had even half of the people in arms'.[23] Such attitudes were doubly provocative to opponents of the Church, and after the war the Liberal Congress decided to end clerical interference in politics once and for all by legislating to complete the secularization of Colombia and to prevent clerical opposition to federal and state laws; and four prelates were exiled for ten years for allegedly fomenting revolution.

A further cycle of conflict led to the conservative revolution of 1885, and in 1886 a centralist and authoritarian constitution was promulgated which, together with a new Concordat with the Vatican, established the Catholic Church in a position of primacy and privilege. While guaranteeing the Church 'its own independence', the new order authorized a number of specific measures which favoured the Church for many years to come, in particular the control and enforcement of religious education in universities, colleges and schools, the recognition of the Catholic marriage ceremony as valid in law for Catholics, and a statement recognizing the Holy See's right of nominating to vacant sees but granting precedence to the wishes of the Colombian president. And President Rafael Núñez, formerly a leading proponent of disamortization and now a pro-clerical conservative, restored to the Church all property not actually alienated and agreed to pay the Church an annual subsidy to the value of the property sold. Conservative Catholics – and these were the majority of Colombian Catholics – were satisfied that political intervention and military action had been justified by their success. As Monsignor Ezequiel Moreno, bishop of Pasto, said in a pastoral letter in 1900, 'priests can and should intervene in politics and

23 Jane Meyer Loy, 'Primary education during the Colombian Federation: the school reform of 1870', *HAHR*, 51 2 (1971), 275–94.

support an essentially Catholic political party against a liberal one'. And in spite of a papal prohibition of clerical participation in civil wars (12 July 1900), Bishop Moreno insisted that the clergy could exhort Catholics 'to take up arms in a just war, such as that now being waged against liberal and masonic revolutionaries'.[24] The same bishop left instructions in his will that during his funeral there should be displayed a large placard bearing the words 'Liberalism is a sin'.

From 1886 to 1930 the Catholic Church in Colombia consolidated its position in the state and presented an object lesson in the preservation and exercise of power. In the first place, it gave support and political legitimacy to the government and in return earned important privileges. Second, the superior education and administrative expertise of clerics made them indispensable to the functioning of local government in areas where the state's presence was weak. Third, the Church controlled education and therefore the career prospects of many Colombians. Finally, the power of the Church to open – and close – newspapers gave it the means of influencing the media and silencing its enemies, and allowed it a peculiar advantage in the battle for public opinion. The Church in Colombia had achieved this success partly through its own inherent strength, partly through the weakness of the state. A similar formula could be applied to Ecuador, though in this case the Church overstepped the bounds of what was politically possible.

The high point of church influence in Ecuador was reached in the years 1860–75, when Gabriel García Moreno, already an ardent Roman Catholic, enemy and victim of liberalism, defender of the Jesuits and admirer of Pius IX, made himself dictator of Ecuador and placed his government under the tutelage of the Church. García Moreno believed in the truth of religion, but he also valued it for its perceived political and social utility, as a force for stability in government and order in society. He calculated that the only way to govern Ecuador was through the Church, acting as the senior partner of the state, and employing a reformed clergy to preach obedience to the government as well as to God. In the light of political alternatives in Ecuador and the experience of state-builders elsewhere in Latin America he could claim some legitimacy for his experiment. The first step was a concordat with the papacy (1863), which gave the Holy See the exercise of ecclesiastical patronage, placed education, from university to primary school, under

---

[24] Fernán E. González G., *Partidos políticos y poder eclesiástico* (Bogotá, 1977), 161–2.

the complete control of the Church, confirmed the Church's right to tithes, guaranteed the Church's right to own and acquire property, and obliged the government of Ecuador to propagate the faith and aid the missions within its territory. The concordat was followed, in 1869, by a constitution modelled on the Syllabus of Errors, in which the power of the president was only exceeded by that of the Church. The Roman Catholic religion was declared to be the religion of the state, and Catholicism was made a requisite for citizenship. García Moreno's ideal of the Church, it has to be said, was that of a reformed church, and under his regime there was specific improvement in ecclesiastical organization, seminary training and clerical discipline. Moreover, there was some validity in his belief that 'Religion is the sole bond which is left to us in this country, divided as it is by the interests of parties, races, and beliefs'.[25] Yet, in the ultimate analysis, this small clerical state was no more than a temporal paradise. The Church was deluged with rights, privileges, powers, but all this depended upon its benefactor and did not lead to autonomous development. The dictatorship was personalist and finite. García Moreno was assassinated in a Quito square on 6 August 1875.

The Church did not immediately suffer from the loss of its patron, and for the next twenty years the conservative structure remained more or less intact. When a liberal revolution in 1895–6 threatened to oust the clerical alliance and to put the *cholo* Eloy Alfaro into power, the Church raised a call to arms. Bishop Schumacher led a small army against Alfaro with the battle-cry 'God or Satan'. The archbishop of Quito denounced liberalism as 'the great whore of Babylon' and urged Catholics to fight for religion. Not all the clergy subscribed to these views and not all liberals were fanatics. The new Constitution of 1897 confirmed the Roman Catholic religion as that of the state to the exclusion of all others. But mutual antagonism raised the temper of debate and the Church paid for its intransigence in a new wave of anticlericalism. A new patronage law in 1899 gave the state right of presentation of archbishops and bishops, whereupon the Vatican broke off diplomatic relations. In 1902 civil marriage and divorce were introduced. In 1904 religious toleration was guaranteed, the tithe was discontinued, the establishment of new religious orders was prohibited and the Church's use of its own income was restricted. In 1906, in yet another constitution, church and state were

---

[25] Quoted in J. Lloyd Mecham, *Church and state in Latin America* (rev. edn, Chapel Hill, 1966), 151.

separated, and religion was removed from state schools, though the Church was not prevented from developing an education system of its own. As for the property of the Church, in 1908 its land was disamortized and nationalized. Thus the liberals propelled Ecuador into the twentieth century, secularized the state and deprived the Church of temporal power. Such was the norm in the modern world and there was no looking back. But this was elite politics and the mass of the people, who were undoubtedly Catholics, were not consulted.

Venezuela, too, was governed by caudillos representing an elite of landowners, merchants and office-holders, and it was only after 1935 that the process of nation-building was gradually extended to the popular sectors. The ecclesiastical policies of successive governments, therefore, were not the result of national debate and consultation but of the decisions of individual dictators backed by the particular coalitions which they put together. Yet it would be a mistake to attribute the decline of the Venezuelan Church to the anticlerical policies of caudillos such as Antonio Guzmán Blanco. The logic of events appears to have been different. The Church in Venezuela *began* from a low base in the years after 1830, and it was the inherent weakness of the Church, in structure, personnel and resources, which enabled the state to treat it as it willed. Venezuela had been on the margin of the Spanish empire and Church and much of it was hardly Christianised. Now the missions were destroyed, the *llanos* empty of priests. Even the centre-north lacked episcopal direction, parish priests and new vocations, while shortage of funds were a basic constraint on the Church's mission. Yet while the Church had no power, it still had a voice, and clerics expressed their political preferences for one side or another, not always the same side, and rarely from a position of independence. For the clergy were drawn into caudillo politics and the patron-client relationships which were characteristic of nineteenth-century Venezuela. For partisanship of this kind they would be severely punished.

The Church emerged from the first decades of the republic relatively intact. Religious freedom had been declared in 1834, the tithes suppressed and ecclesiastical patronage placed firmly in the hands of the government, but the Church received an annual budget from the state, and President José Antonio Páez had even accepted a pro-clerical concordat from Rome shortly before his fall in 1863. Now all this was changed with the advent of Antonio Guzmán Blanco (1870–88), Liberal-Federal leader, dictator in the 'order and progress' mould, mason and anticlerical. He made it clear from the beginning that he would not tolerate clergy who supported conservatives in press or pulpit. Archbishop Silvestre Guevara of Caracas took up the challenge, refused Guzmán Blanco a *Te Deum* and resisted attempts to appoint clergy according to party political opinion. He was immediately exiled to Trinidad and there he remained until, at the suggestion of Pius IX, he resigned and ended the impasse. Behind this apparently trivial clash of wills lay the determination of Guzmán Blanco, a personalist caudillo, to allow no alternative focus of allegiance, no rival leader. He followed this with a torrent of anticlerical legislation. In 1873 the Church was deprived of clerical immunity, of registration of births, marriages and deaths, of jurisdiction over cemeteries; and civil marriage was made the only legal form and given precedence over the religious ceremony. In 1874 the dictator abolished all monasteries, convents, colleges and other religious institutions, suppressed seminaries, confiscated church property, suspended the Church's subsidy, and issued a law of lay education. The mentality of Guzmán Blanco could be seen not only in what he did but in what he wanted to do and failed. He sought to legalize the marriage of the clergy and even to establish a national church free from Rome. But he allowed no one to prevent his building a Masonic Temple in Caracas. By the end of the regime the Church had been almost legislated out of existence. In 1881 in the whole of Venezuela there were only 241 priests for 639 parishes with a total of over 2 million parishioners.

The Church recovered some lost ground under subsequent caudillos. Cipriano Castro (1899–1908) yielded to no one in his absolutism, but he was more benevolent towards the Church and did not enforce all the anticlerical legislation. A number of religious orders began to return and seminaries to reopen. In the constitution of 1904 the Roman Catholic religion was declared to be the national religion and the state contributed to its support. Juan Vicente Gómez (1908–35) was mildly tolerant to the ecclesiastical establishment but any churchman who dared to criticize soon felt the dictator's displeasure. Thus, by the end of this period, at the pleasure of the caudillos, the Venezuelan Church had undergone some renewal at least in public, though how deeply its message penetrated into society was open to question. Among the elite many were seduced by positivism and a sociology of dictatorship. Among the lower sectors the survival of cults to María Lionza, to the Negro Primero, to the Negress Matea and to the twentieth-century folk-doctor José Gregorio Hernández was evidence of a religious void in the lives of the people which the Church had not yet begun to fill.

In Central America the Church had varied experience in adjusting to the liberal state of the nineteenth century. In Guatemala the attack on the temporal power of the Church was begun in the first flush of liberal enthusiasm in 1825–38, when intemperate anticlerical measures antagonized the Catholic masses and were then followed by conservative reaction from 1839 to 1865 under Rafael Carrera. Far from being a mere tool of the priests, Carrera was a populist caudillo who led a popular and successful Indian rebellion against the European-style government of the liberals. Carrera was a *mestizo*, though more Indian than white. He understood the Indian communities, recognized the *ejidos*, protected their lands and reduced their taxes. It was within this context that he restored the traditional influence and privilege of the Church and maintained good relations with Rome; there is no evidence that the mass of the people wanted otherwise. But clerical association with conservative attempts to regain power after 1871 brought more radical elements into prominence within the liberals, and in 1873 these insisted on a complete anticlerical programme. Justo Rufino Barrios became president in 1873: he suppressed religious orders and stripped the Church of its economic and political influence. Civil marriage was declared legal, and education was secularized. The constitution of 1879 confirmed these measures and completed the formation of a secular state with the disestablishment of the Church. While the Church thus lost its temporal power, the expulsion of many priests reduced its actual presence in Guatemala and its activities were rarely free of interference from the government.

Guatemala was typical of the Church's experience in Central America, where there was a standard pattern of treatment, fanatical liberalism of the post-independence period, followed by a conservative reaction to about 1870, which was succeeded by liberal regimes imposing classical secularism. In Honduras the liberals were in power from 1880. In the same year church and state were separated, church property was taxed and reduced to actual churches and houses of the clergy. In Nicaragua the conservative regime of 1857–93 allowed the Church to survive with its privileges intact, and it was not until 1893–1904, under José Santos Zelaya, that church and state were separated, religious orders suppressed, bishops and priests exiled. In El Salvador the liberal party, which was dominant from 1871 to 1945, produced a constitution which separated church and state, provided for civil marriage and also for divorce and lay education; and here too religious orders were proscribed. In Costa Rica freedom of worship existed from 1864, and in 1884 a liberal government ordered the expulsion of the Jesuits and of the bishop of San José; lay education and other stock features of liberalism were introduced, without, however, seriously damaging the Church or its relations with the state.

In Mexico, where the Church was stronger than the state and priests were more privileged than politicians, relations between the two powers were resolved by war, and one war did not suffice. Classical liberal policy culminated in the Laws of Reform of 1856–7. The Juárez Law of 23 November 1855 abolished clerical immunity. The Lerdo Law, or Law of Disamortization of 25 January 1856, ordered church corporations to dispose of their real estate, to be sold to tenants or at public auction. On 5 February 1857 a new constitution was issued by a Constituent Congress dominated by professional liberals and unrepresentative of Catholic opinion. This established freedom of press and speech; the clergy were barred from election to Congress; government intervention in worship was allowed; and the Juárez and Lerdo Laws were confirmed. The Lerdo Law did not rob the Church; it simply diverted its land and wealth into capital and mortgages. To reject this was probably an error of judgement, one which the papacy also shared. The result was to plunge the country into civil war between 'Religión y Fueros' and 'Constitución y Reforma', which lasted from 1858 to 1860 and which involved the Church as one of the belligerents.

The Church lost even more by war, as each side plundered its wealth for the war effort. In 1859 the liberal government nationalized church property, separated church and state, and suppressed all male religious orders. This was followed by a civil marriage law and civil registry law; and in 1860 religious liberty was established. With victory in 1861 the liberals applied the Reform Laws and secularized schools, hospitals and charitable institutions of the Church. The most dramatic victory was over church property. The wealth of the Church available for appropriation amounted to something between $100 million and $150 million, much less than the sums existing in the imaginations of politicians and public.[26] Perhaps the greatest damage to Mexico was the loss of income by schools, hospitals and charities, which left a gap in the social services for many years to come. Yet adversity was not complete. The Church reacted to the liberal victory by promoting the intervention of France, hoping to regain from a Catholic prince what it had lost to Mexican

---

[26] See Robert J. Knowlton, *Church property and the Mexican Reform, 1856–1910* (DeKalb, 1976), 121.

liberals. But it was soon disillusioned. Napoleon III and the Archduke Maximilian had no intention of cancelling the Reform Laws or restoring church property; and when France withdrew in 1867 the Church was more vulnerable than ever before.

The Restored Republic was not a happy time for Catholics. After the tolerant government of Juárez (1867–72), the government of Sebastián Lerdo de Tejada (1872–6) was oppressively anticlerical. Catholics had often predicted that the liberals would not be content to disestablish the Church but would then proceed to attack its religious functions. Lerdo now proved them correct. The campaign against religious orders was intensified in 1873, as many of their members were forced out of their houses and others were imprisoned; 10 Jesuits, 6 Passionists, 2 secular priests and a Pauline father, all foreigners, were expelled from Mexico; and priests were prosecuted for administering the sacraments without prior civil registration. These incidents were just the beginning of an anticlerical drive which included an oath of allegiance to the constitution for officials, the expulsion of the Sisters of Charity, the incorporation of all the Reform Laws into the constitution (25 September 1873), and, finally, the Organic Law of Reform (14 December 1874) reaffirming the anticlerical laws on property, education, clerical dress and the holding of religious activities outside churches.

How did Catholics react to these relentless measures? The bishops protested strongly and censured those who complied with the anticlerical laws, but otherwise recommended that Catholics adopt an attitude of resignation to the law, at most 'passive resistance', and exhorted them to piety and prayers, and to work for the Society of St Vincent de Paul and other charities. But conservative Catholics, stung by the intolerant policy of Lerdo's government, looked around for political alternatives, either by alliances with dissident factions of the liberal party or, in the course of 1874–5, by staging minor armed rebellions, the so-called *Religioneros*, in which a few local clergy and Catholic peasants took part. When all else failed, there was only one lifeline, the Porfiriato. And for his part Porfirio Díaz believed that to govern in peace he needed the support of Catholics.

Porfirio Díaz regarded himself as a Catholic 'in private and as head of family', but 'as Head of State' he professed no religion, because the law prohibited it. His regime was based on conciliation and from the beginning he made it clear that while he adhered to the constitution he offered also a policy of toleration: 'the individual conscience ought to be respected even when it errs'.[27] This also made political sense, for he was aware that a hostile Church could destabilize the regime. So he cultivated good personal relations with the bishops and turned a blind eye when Catholics began to venture out from underground. This is not to say that anticlericalism was dead during the Porfiriato. It was active in the press, in Congress and among some officials, and it seemed that only Díaz stood between Catholics and their enemies.

The nationalization of church property continued to its completion; politically and practically it was not possible to reverse this or to undo the transfer of property already made. On the other hand, Díaz allowed the Church to acquire wealth once more in forms not strictly prohibited by law, such as holdings in railroads, mining, telegraph systems and manufacturing, and, it was said, even in pre-Reform types of mortgages and real estate. This was often done through the agency of trustworthy laymen and lawyers or by other means. Many of these charges were exercises in propaganda and the truth may never be known. But the Church took advantage of the Díaz years in other ways than wealth. Processions were held outside churches, clerical dress was worn in public, Catholic marriages were celebrated. And this was a time of reconstruction. Religious orders unobtrusively re-established themselves, and a number of new Mexican orders were founded, often specializing in charitable work. The Jesuits returned, with Spanish and other foreign priests, and grew in numbers and prestige as they attracted Mexicans to their ranks. The Church opened schools of its own and provided various social services. New dioceses were created, and the number of Catholic churches increased from 4,893 in 1878 to 9,580 in 1895. The new position of the Church in the Porfiriato was epitomized in 1895 with the Coronation of the Virgin of Guadalupe when a great gathering of bishops, priests and laity was organized to symbolize the unity of Mexico around the idea of the moral grandeur of its Christian people.

Yet while the Church made progress, it could not recover anything like the power and influence of the years before 1856. In 1895 there were less than three priests for every 10,000 inhabitants, and in 1886 140,000 children attended Catholic schools compared to 477,000 in secular schools. The Fifth Mexican Provincial Council in 1896 ordered priests to remain aloof from politics in all matters where the Church allowed

---

[27] Quoted in Jorge Adame Goddard, *El pensamiento político y social de los católicos mexicanos, 1867–1914* (Mexico, 1981), 101.

freedom of opinion. As for Catholic conservatives, after a useless effort to participate in the elections of 1877, they withdrew from political activity. And the policy of conciliation, while it did not satisfy the absolute claims of the Church, left the revolutionaries after 1910 with a pretext for attacking the Church, to confiscate its property again and to restore the work of the Reform.

In the period 1870–1930 the Church in most of Latin America lost the support of the state and ceased to rely on legal and political sanctions for the promotion and protection of religion. Catholics did not at first welcome their new status or respond positively to conditions of religious toleration, social pluralism and political independence, but continued to look backwards to a Christian state and collaborating Church as the ideals against which to judge the secular trends of the age. But gradually adjustment was made and the Church exchanged external support for inner renewal. The state's appropriation of the civil registry left the Church with pure sacraments – baptism and marriage – for which Catholics now had to opt. The secularization of state education forced Catholics to improve their own schools or devise other ways of Christian instruction. This sharpened the distinction between believers and unbelievers and made religion more of a choice and less of a habit. The result was a drop in the real numbers of Catholics but an increase in the spiritual life of the Church. Moreover, withdrawal from the state was a precondition of independent social action, a new role demanded of the Church by the force of events.

RELIGION, REFORM AND REVOLUTION

The independence and reform of the Church took place at the same time, 1870–1930, as society itself was undergoing profound change under the impact of mass immigration, foreign investment and international trade. There was a time-lag, however, between the onset of church reform around 1870 and the emergence of Catholic social awareness in the 1890s. It required the dramatic impact of social conditions and urgent prompting from Rome to alert the Church to the need for change. Immigration seriously tested church institutions in a number of countries. At the same time incipient industrialization created an urban working class largely unknown to the Church. The effect of economic change and population growth on organized religion was most obvious in large cities. The populations of Buenos Aires, Rio de Janeiro, Lima and Mexico City grew rapidly in the period 1870–1930. The influx of new immigrants and the migration of people from the countryside into expanding capitals presented the Church with unfamiliar pastoral problems at a time when it could no longer count on the economic resources of the past. How could the Church establish contact with the isolated and impoverished masses who filled the working class suburbs and shanty towns? While city centres had well-endowed older parishes and the services of religious orders, the marginal areas might not have a church within miles. Gradually the great cities of Latin America were transformed and often de-Christianised.

This was the society into which the new working class was born, semi-industrial and semi-pagan. The Church was not alone in failing to 'win' the working class. Socialism too had a limited impact and failed to become a mass movement. Anarcho-syndicalism had some influence among manual and skilled labour, but it was a foreign movement, persecuted by the state and handicapped by its failure to revolutionize the workers. The Church had as much chance as any movement, if it seized the opportunity. But this required a visible presence in the new society in competition with its rivals. In the early twentieth century there was a reaction in Latin America against nineteenth-century thought and in particular against positivism.[28] Not all the reaction was Christian in inspiration, but it was more favourable to a religious view of life and it meant that Catholic thought was no longer struggling against a single orthodoxy, as the influence of Bergson, Unamuno, and through him Kierkegaard, and Husserl joined that of neo-Thomism to replace positivism in the universities.

The restoration of Thomist philosophy in Catholic seminaries and colleges was urged in the early encyclicals of Pope Leo XIII. The teachings of St Thomas Aquinas on the nature of liberty, the origins of authority, laws, obedience and charity were recalled to Catholics in opposition to modern philosophy and revolutionary solutions. Scholasticism had a new lease of life in Latin America in the early twentieth century and provided a link between traditional and social Catholicism. Not all Catholic thought was progressive. Some of it, perhaps the papal encyclicals themselves, still owed much to Spain, to Jaime Balmes and Donoso Cortes, partial to corporatist structures and vertical social organization, and was more anxious to avoid revolution than promote

---

[28] See Hale, *CHLA* IV, chap. 10.

reform. But there was a further influence from Europe. The industrial revolution had stimulated the emergence of Catholic social movements in France and Germany, where Bishop William Ketteler had pioneered a new approach. There was in Catholic tradition a bias towards guild organization or corporatism in industry. The Germans, however, provided a new ingredient for Catholic thought, a clear commitment to state intervention to mitigate the consequences of capitalism, and an argument for effective trade unionism.

These influences converged in the encyclical *Rerum Novarum* issued by Pope Leo XIII in 1891. Here was a new statement of Catholic social thought, in a modern context and confronting actual problems. It was a reaction rather than an initiative, and fear of the competing claims of socialism for the support of the masses obviously underlay many of the papal preoccupations of the time. But it was new for a pope to proclaim the rights of workers and the injustices of the liberal system. *Rerum Novarum* recognized the existence of conflict between employers and workers, deriving from the growth of industry, the concentration of wealth and the impoverishment of the masses. As against socialism, it defended the right of private property and urged the concept of a just wage from which workers too could profit and save, and the gap between rich and poor would close through peace and justice. But the encyclical also advocated a degree of state intervention in favour of the workers to guarantee adequate conditions of life and labour. Leo XIII issued a call to action. He urged Catholics to take up the struggle for social justice, and in particular to organize congresses, establish newspapers and create worker associations.

In Latin America *Rerum Novarum* received a varied response, in some countries prompt and serious, in others slow and timid, among the lower clergy with some enthusiasm, among the hierarchies less so. In Mexico there was a positive reaction. In El Salvador it was thirty years before the encyclical was studied and applied. Yet the primitive capitalism which the encyclical described, if it no longer prevailed in Europe, was precisely that which existed in Latin America. Many Catholics recognized this. The Jesuits in most countries responded actively to papal initiatives and regarded Catholic social action as an indispensable strategy to preempt working class organization and establish a Catholic presence in factories and unions.

The objects and limits of Catholic social action could be seen in Argentina. In the years around 1900 the political preoccupations of

Catholic pressure groups were joined by a new type of activity more concerned with social work than with public policy, and pragmatic rather than ideological in its approach. In 1892 a German Redemptorist Friedrich Grote, founded the *Círculo de Obreros* in Buenos Aires, drawing on his experience of working men's clubs in his own country. Between 1892 and 1912 77 groups were founded, with 22,930 members and 21 buildings of their own, and capital of one million pesos. In 1898 the Círculos organized the first Catholic Worker Congress, and began to send to the National Congress proposals for labour legislation of a reformist kind which coincided with a number of socialist proposals and were in fact carried into law. Fr Grote was also instrumental in founding a Catholic daily newspaper, *El Pueblo* (1900), and in 1902 a weekly *Democracia Cristiana*. It would be misleading to cite this action as typical of the Catholic Church in Argentina at the time. Although the initiatives of Fr Grote corresponded precisely to the social teaching of *Rerum Novarum*, many Catholics including the hierarchy impeded his work and condemned it as subversive. But what he had begun others continued. Dr Emilio Lamarca projected the foundation of a *Liga Social Argentina*, based on the German model which he had studied at first hand, and this was sanctioned by the Congress of Argentine Catholics in 1907. By 1914 the League had 5,743 members, 184 centres, and was publishing *Semana Social* and numerous pamphlets, and making a significant contribution to Catholic workers' education and organization. The Catholic Congresses themselves were a new development which gave a further impetus to Catholic social action, and generated yet further organizations such as Catholic Youth Congresses and Catholic Students Centres.

The proliferation of Catholic groups caused the bishops to take more positive action and also to exercise some control. At the end of the First World War they sponsored the formation of the *Unión Popular Católica Argentina*, which later, in 1928, gave way to *Acción Católica*. The UPC was a lay organization which sought to form a Catholic social conscience by appealing to employers and other ruling groups to improve conditions of the working classes; to this extent it had a distinctly paternalist message, though it also sought to encourage labour organization and to provide a house-building programme for workers. Its leading spokesman was Bishop Miguel de Andrea who, in the years following the *Semana Trágica* of 1919 played a national and in many ways progressive role in the working class movement, including the organization of women workers and the provision of low-cost housing. Against these positive achievements, however, must be set another feature of Catholic social thinking in Argentina. In a search for a way between capitalism and socialism many Catholics such as Bishop Andrea opted for corporatism, which in the political context of the 1930s would lend itself to exploitation by those who advocated fascist solutions.

In Mexico the Catholic social movement began in the 1890s. *Rerum Novarum* was published there in May 1891. At first it attracted little comment, and it was not until March 1895, when the journalist Trinidad Sánchez Santos publicized the document, that Catholic leaders began to respond and to demand action to improve labour conditions, raise wages and create Catholic trade unions. Of the bishops most committed to social Catholicism, José Mora y del Río, Ramón Ibarra González, José Othón Núñez, Francisco Orozco Jiménez, all had studied at the Colegio Pio Latinoamericano in Rome and were graduates of the Gregorian University. Of the priests three were Jesuits, Bernardo Bergöend, Alfredo Méndez Medina and Carlos María Heredia, and one, José Castillo y Piña, studied at the Gregorian University. Méndez Medina had the most systematic training in religious sociology, having studied in Burgos, Louvain and Paris, as well as visiting England, Holland and Germany. But on the whole Mexican Catholics produced activists rather than theoreticians. *La cuestión social en México* (1913) by Fr Méndez was virtually the only serious and scholarly work on the Catholic side comparable to the writings of the secularists. Catholic journalism, however, was effective and realistic. It took a critical view of the prosperity and progress claimed by the Porfiriato, especially from 1906; it drew attention to the poverty and hunger of the popular sectors, to the lag of wages behind prices, to the lack of opportunities for the middle classes, with 'railways, industries and trade in foreign hands'.[29]

In 1903 the first Mexican Catholic Congress met in Puebla. The delegates recommended the creation of worker organizations with religious and technical training programmes. A young Jalisco lawyer, Miguel Palomar y Vizcarra, who had re-converted to Catholicism after a liberal interlude, proposed the establishment of credit co-operatives and subsequently experimented with these on a regional basis. The assembly resolved that landowners should provide schools, medical and other social services for rural labourers. At a second Catholic Congress, in

---

[29] *La Voz de México*, 10 Nov. 1906, in Adame Goddard, *Pensamiento político y social*, 205.

Morelia in 1904, demands were made for primary education for the working class, for technical schools, worker, employer and craft guild associations, and an end to oppressive labour contracts. A third Congress at Guadalajara in 1908 reaffirmed previous proposals and in addition demanded schools for workers' children and just wages for labourers, to be paid in cash not company tokens. These congresses were not revolutionary gatherings; they were essentially religious but with a new social awareness. Like *Rerum Novarum*, Mexican Catholic thought rejected the class struggle and deplored revolutionary change, but it did advocate state intervention to protect the most vulnerable in society. The reforms proposed for the industrial sector were fairly comprehensive. But did the Church have a policy on the all-important agrarian problem?

Three Agricultural Congresses were held, though they concentrated on practical matters, not structure, and they were attended by *hacendados* as well as rural workers. Their object was to find specific ways of improving the moral and material conditions of rural labourers. The discussion included wages but not as yet land redistribution. Even Fr Méndez Medina, who sought to establish Catholic trade unions 'to defend salaries and working conditions, procure jobs, and speak for the working class', was paternalist on agrarian problems, advocating only that 'the industrious and worthy peasant be assured as far as possible the possession or most secure use of sufficient land to maintain his family decently'.[30] And the *Liga Social Agraria* formed in 1913 with the blessing of Archbishop Mora y del Río was designed not as an instrument of agrarian reform but for the improvement and growth of agriculture, and it was dominated by landowners, large and small. Nevertheless, this pointed the way to a church version of agrarian reform, based on reducing haciendas in favour of smaller properties.

By 1910 therefore the Catholic social movement had begun to produce specific results, the most significant perhaps being the formation of the Catholic Workers Circles. By 1911, with more than 43 branches and a total membership of 12,332, the movement was strengthened by the formation of the Confederation of Catholic Workers. The Confederation's second national convention in January 1913 was attended by delegates from 50 branches representing 15,000 members. It was decided to organize an independent Catholic labour movement. The first Mexican trade union was founded in the same year by Fr Méndez Medina

[30] *Ibid.*, 244.

in Mexico City. The Church was now ready to challenge its rivals for influence among workers and by the early 1920s the National Catholic Labour Confederation competed with the CROM, the Mexican Workers Confederation, especially among rural workers.

The onset of the Mexican Revolution changed the situation for the Church. Catholics were hopeful but wary of Madero; some suspected that his credentials were too liberal, others that he was not a social reformer. In the circumstances it seemed logical to form a Catholic political party. With the blessing of the archbishop and on the model of the German Centre Party, the National Catholic Party was formed in May 1911, not to participate in the old regime nor to give unconditional support to Madero, but to be in a position to support the Church in the new democratic conditions, and in particular to promote Catholic social reform in the interests of the rural and industrial poor. In 1911–13 the party gave a good account of itself, winning the election of 29 federal deputies, 4 senators and governors of four states. In Jalisco it was responsible for significant social and labour legislation.

The final years of the Porfiriato and the brief regime of Madero, therefore, were a time of renaissance for Mexican Catholicism, when it regained its strength, confidence and purpose. Then, suddenly, disaster came and from 1913 the Church endured a great persecution far beyond anything it had experienced under liberalism and totally unpredictable in its process and results. How can we explain this strange reversal? In the first place the very success of the Church was its undoing. It had not only begun to reform itself but it had actually recovered some political space and seemed poised to make even further gains. Meanwhile the state too had been growing more powerful; in the years after 1910 the revolutionaries inherited the authoritarian and secular state of the Porfiriato and began to eliminate all rivals. The revolutionary state came into collision not with an abject Church but with a reformed and militant Church, which had its own policy for labour organization and agrarian reform, and offered in effect an alternative to the Mexican Revolution, one which might appeal to many Mexicans and which an all-absorbing state could not tolerate. Moreover the revolutionaries were not the same as the liberals. They were intolerant, absolutist and sought the destruction of the Church and the obliteration of religion. They saw their chance and seized it. The fall of Madero brought a struggle for power between two extremes, Huerta leading the old military and Carranza the revolutionaries. The Church was caught in a trap. Its traditional reputation and new popular appeal made it an object of attack by Carranza and the Constitutionalists. Their onslaught on Catholic priests and property drove Catholics closer to Huerta. The Church was then accused of supporting the counter-revolution. As the revolution spread in the course of 1913–14, bishops, priests and nuns were jailed or exiled, church property was seized and Catholics were attacked by local caudillos as enemies of the revolution.

The Church was therefore the victim of its own success, of revolutionary ideology and of the conjuncture of 1913–14. From then on it was the enemy of the Revolution, and the Revolution was its tormentor. In the course of prolonged religious conflict there were a number of peaks, and the first was the Constitution of 1917. This repeated earlier Reform laws such as the prohibition of religious vows and of church ownership of real estate. But it went further. The Church was deprived of any legal status. Public worship outside church buildings was banned, and the state would decide how many churches and how many priests there would be. The clergy were denied the right to vote and the religious press was forbidden to comment on public affairs. All primary education had to be secular. The Mexican bishops protested. The government was adamant. It was a state of war.

The response of the Church was far from united. The most advanced position was taken by young activists, often inspired by Jesuits and grouped in the Catholic Association of Mexican Youth (ACJM), who concentrated first on spiritual formation, then on Catholicizing society and in the final stage on political or even armed action. This tendency was anti-revolutionary and to some extent anti-democratic. The middle ground was occupied by the Mexican bishops, united in opposition to the Revolution but divided into intransigents and moderates, the latter looking for an accommodation with the Revolution and hoping for peace from Carranza and later from Obregón. The response of Rome itself was perhaps least 'Catholic' of all. The Vatican sought to reduce tension and reach an understanding with Obregón, to appoint non-political bishops, to encourage an exclusively spiritual mission, and thereby perhaps abandon Mexican social and political Catholicism. But the Revolution did not respond, and in turn the ACJM and other militant organizations intensified their opposition and denounced the Mexican government as the enemy of the Church. They seemed to have proved their point when, on 1 December 1924, Plutarco Elías Calles succeeded to the presidency.

Calles was the proponent of a new nationalism, a monolithic state and a perpetual Revolution in which there would be no alternative allegiances, least of all the Church; in fact he was determined to 'defanaticize the masses', and to exterminate religion in the interests of state power and national progress. His government inaugurated a new purge of religion and even an abortive attempt to contrive a schism and a national church. These initiatives alerted Catholic activists such as Palomar y Vizcarra and brought them together from various groups to form the National League for the Defence of Religious Liberty in March 1925, to win religious freedom by means which would be 'constitutional' and also 'those required by the common good'. This soon became a political movement and then an underground organization. For in the course of 1925–6 the regime deliberately escalated the conflict. In October the state of Tabasco ended Catholic worship; Chiapas, Hidalgo, Jalisco and Colima increased anti-religious measures. In February the government started to close churches in the capital to the accompaniment of street protests. Events culminated in the 'Calles Law' of July 1826 specifying strict application on a national scale of the laws on religion with severe penalties for infringements. For Catholic militants this was the breaking point. The bishops too saw it as a crisis, for the decree requiring compulsory registration of the clergy would take appointments out of the hands of bishops and give to the government the right to appoint and dismiss priests. So, with the approval of the Vatican, the Mexican bishops stopped all public worship and withdrew the clergy from the churches. On Sunday 1 August 1926 no priest celebrated Mass in the parishes churches of Mexico. Calles was unimpressed: calling it 'the struggle of darkness against light', he determined to fight on.

There was still another option open to the League militants, insurrection. After 1 August calls for action became insistent, and in some states local Catholics, suffering perhaps from a specific application of the Calles Law and shocked by the suspension of services, went beyond prayers and penance into armed action. Late in September the League decided to lead the incipient rebellion, and in November in response to the argument that tyranny justified rebellion the bishops gave their informal approval. The rebellion, which came to be called that of the 'Cristeros', was activated on 1 January 1927 with risings in various parts of the country. It managed to take root in Jalisco, Guanajuato, Michoacán, Querétaro and Colima, and in the course of the year it became an effective resistance movement.

The rebellion was a severe test for Catholic principles. League support and initial episcopal acquiescence were said to be based on traditional doctrine and neo-Thomist ideas: there exists a right to resist tyranny, if all other ways have failed and there is a chance of success. These are not necessarily valid inferences from scholastic philosophy and most of the bishops had misgivings and remained aloof from the movement. Some denied that the Cristeros had a right to rebel, while the few who supported them were reprimanded by Rome. Many Catholics defended the action of José de León Toral in killing ex-president Obregón after his re-election in July 1928 because they believed that it was legitimate to kill a tyrant. Their views were strengthened by the subsequent execution, without trial, of the Jesuit underground priest Fr Miguel Pro. Some of the Cristero groups were led by priests who acted as fighters as well as chaplains and had no doubt that armed resistance was justified. As for the Cristeros themselves, they believed that the cause of Christ the King and the Virgin of Guadalupe was inherently just, legitimized by its nature and its aims. Rome did not share these views, convinced as it was that armed force would not succeed and would compromise the Church in future. So it ordered the Mexican bishops to distance themselves from the rebellion and work for a negotiated settlement. Through the mediation of the United States the bishops reached a compromise with the Revolution in January 1929 and formally withdrew the Church from the conflict. Their action has been described as cynical and opportunist, but they were faced with a real dilemma: they had a wider Church to govern, a future to think of and no bishop in the twentieth century would willingly lead a war of religion. But the settlement was worthless to the Church. As the rebels demobilized so the government pressed harder. Catholics gained freedom to practise their religion but no other rights. The government presented this as the surrender of the Church, and so it was. The Revolution had finally crushed Catholicism and driven it back inside the churches, and there it stayed, still persecuted, throughout the 1930s and beyond.

The Cristeros were dismayed, but they laid down their arms and accepted the amnesty for what it was worth. 'It was a tragic thing', recalled Palomar y Vizcarra, 'completely bewildering to us, the greatest proof Mexican Catholics have given to the Holy See of their firm adhesion to the Vicar of Christ, in spite of this terrible blow to their hopes'.[31] This was the voice of the middle-class political leadership. In the countryside, where the Cristeros were a peasant movement as well as

---

[31] Miguel Palomar y Vizcarra, in James W. Wilkie and Edna Monzón de Wilkie, *México visto en el siglo veinte: entrevistas de historia oral* (Mexico, 1969), 447.

a Catholic resistance, the defenceless rebels were massacred at the end of the war, a war in which 90,000 combatants had died. The Cristeros were never condemned by the Church and in time they came to occupy an honourable place in Catholic history. But if these events had any message it was to draw for Catholics a distinction between reformism and revolution, and to demonstrate that the Church could not sanction violent ways to power.

THE CHURCH IN 1930: BETWEEN TRADITION AND MODERNITY

The years 1870–1930 were decisive for the Church in Latin America, the time when it gained its independence, established real as distinct from nominal union with Rome, and undertook its own modernization, the time indeed when it became the 'institutionalized' and 'triumphalist' Church rejected by many contemporaries and scorned by later Catholics. It would be inappropriate to compare the progress of the Church in 1870–1930 too closely with that of secular institutions of the time and unhistorical to apply to it the religious and social criteria of more recent decades. The Church, like other institutions, has to be judged in the context of the age and according to its own nature and purpose. Definitions of these may vary. Bishop Bossuet defined the Church as Christ extended in time and space. In the Catechism of Christian Doctrine Latin Americans learnt that the Church was the union of all the faithful under one head. To agnostics the Church appeared a collection of myths, privileges, buildings and money, which once it had been purged of power might still serve an ethical function in society. But how can the historian establish external norms to judge the progress of the Church, assess its mission, appraise its influence in society? Church attendance can be measured, and changes in organization and social action described, but such indicators provide only an approximation.

Judged by these standards the Church suffered some decline in the years around 1900. It lost a large number of adherents, first among the elite then among the urban working class, as they drifted into secularism or indifference. Rural Catholicism was more tenacious, though perhaps less assiduously served by the Church, which was thin on the ground outside the towns. And many Latin Americans were not only indifferent to religion but positively hated it and would try to destroy it, an unnerving experience for the Church. Traditional Catholics blamed these adversities on the withdrawal of state support and resources, and they did not always take advantage of the opportunities which this presented for religious innovation, unsure whether they were victors or victims of the secular state. The Church had not yet generated the inner resources to compete with other philosophies in a pluralist society, to appeal to conscience not to power. Catholics may have accepted religious toleration as a lesser evil or an opportunist adaptation to the modern world, but not as a doctrine or a principle.

Yet the Church in Latin America had adjusted to change. At the beginning of the nineteenth century it was a colonial Church, dependent on a metropolis, Spain or Portugal. A century later it was truly independent, compatible with the nation state yet part of the universal Church. It still fulfilled a basic responsibility of a Church, to bring people to God, and it preserved intact Christian doctrine and religious observance for transmission to future generations. To any one who asked: God, where are you? Cardinal Leme had a confident answer. Moreover, the compromising alliance of the altar and the throne, of the church and the state, was gone for ever, thanks less to Catholics than to liberals, but in any case leaving the Church free for the future, as it learnt that it had less to fear from Nero than from Constantine. This new independence had a number of implications. It enabled the Church to speak more clearly to the poor and oppressed. It sharpened the division between religionists and secularists, as Catholics had to choose to be Catholics and the Church to compete with other beliefs. At the same time the Church expanded materially, increasing its own revenue and strengthening its own institutions. These institutions, or 'structures' as they came to be called, became a cause of scandal to later theologians, who condemned them as impediments to true religion, but who forgot too readily, perhaps, that the Church was human as well as divine and needed institutions as society itself did. By 1930 the institutions were in place, the bishops were in their dioceses, the priests at the altars, the faithful at prayer. But there were many outside who would never enter and many who would only return to die. The question was still relevant, and the answer is still uncertain. How Catholic was Latin America?

BIBLIOGRAPHICAL ESSAYS

LIST OF ABBREVIATIONS

The following abbreviations have been used for works which occur repeatedly in the bibliographical essays:

CHLA	*Cambridge History of Latin America*
HAHR	*Hispanic American Historical Review*
HM	*Historia Mexicana*
JIAS	*Journal of Inter-American Studies and World Affairs*
JLAS	*Journal of Latin American Studies*
LARR	*Latin American Research Review*
L-BR	*Luso-Brazilian Review*
TA	*The Americas*

I. LATIN AMERICA AND THE INTERNATIONAL ECONOMY, 1870–1914

Scholars working on the economic history of Latin America in the period 1870–1914 are singularly fortunate in that much, indeed most, of what they need to locate is identified in Roberto Cortés Conde and Stanley J. Stein (eds.), *Latin America: a guide to economic history 1830–1930* (Berkeley, 1977). The editors, in their introduction, provide a helpful overview of problems and issues, while each country section of the masterfully annotated bibliographies on Argentina, Brazil, Chile, Colombia, Mexico and Peru is also prefaced by an interpretive and evaluative essay from a noted scholar. With such an exceptionally valuable resource listing over 4,500 items already available, this essay will concentrate on studies from the more recent years which deal with the international matrix of Latin American regional development, with

597

occasional mention of works written earlier but not included in the aforementioned comprehensive bibliography. Particular emphasis is given to doctoral dissertations. There are a number of other bibliographies which deal with individual countries: for example, Enrique Florescano *et al. (*eds.*), Bibliografía general del desarrollo económico de México, 1500–1976* (Mexico, 1980), an excellent work.

A very good place to begin understanding the period is with more general works on the engagement of Latin America in the international economy. Pascal Arnaud, *Estado y capitalismo en América Latina: casos de México y Argentina* (Mexico, 1981) represents one type of approach; based on the experience of two large countries in the 1820–1910 era, the author attempts to develop a general, perhaps too sweeping, picture of the transition to capitalism in Latin America. More satisfying, for being closer to the evidence, are the eleven studies contained in D. C. M. Platt (ed.), *Business imperialism, 1840–1930: an inquiry based on British experience in Latin America* (New York, 1977). See also Irving Stone, 'The composition and distribution of British investment in Latin America, 1865 to 1913' (unpublished Ph.D. thesis, Columbia University, 1962).

Other works that explicitly focus on foreign penetration, usually with a country focus, are Joseph B. Romney, 'American interests in Mexico: development and impact during the rule of Porfirio Díaz, 1876–1911' (Ph.D. thesis, Utah, 1969); B. W. Aston, 'The public career of José Yves Limantour' (Ph.D. thesis, Texas Tech, 1972); Kennett S. Cott, 'Porfirian investment policies, 1876–1910' (Ph.D. thesis, New Mexico, 1979); Robert J. Deger, Jr, 'Porfirian foreign policy and Mexican nationalism: a study of cooperation and conflict in Mexican-American relations, 1884–1904' (Ph.D. thesis, Indiana, 1979); Robert H. Lavenda, 'The first modernizing attempt: modernization and change in Caracas, 1870–1908' (Ph.D. thesis, Indiana, 1977); Charles E. Carreras, 'United States economic penetration of Venezuela and its effects on diplomacy' (Ph.D. thesis, North Carolina, 1971); Benjamin A. Frankel, 'Venezuela and the United States, 1810–1888' (Ph.D. thesis, Berkeley, 1964). George E. Carl, *First among equals. Britain and Venezuela 1810–1910* (Ann Arbor, 1980) shows how foreign interest centred, before the rise of a major export enclave, on the local market for imports and on transport, banking and public utilities. Vera B. Reber, *British mercantile houses in Buenos Aires, 1810–1880* (Cambridge, Mass., 1979), just reaches into the decades under review, but provides a particularly clarifying view of the preparatory period for the *fin-de-siècle* expansion. See also, Heraclio

Bonilla, *Gran Bretaña y el Perú: los mecanismos de un control ecónomico*, V (Lima, 1977); Dale W. Peterson, 'The diplomatic and commercial relations between the United States and Peru from 1883 to 1918' (Ph.D. thesis, Minnesota, 1969); Charles G. Pregger-Roman, 'Dependent development in nineteenth century Chile' (Ph.D. thesis, Rutgers, 1975); James Ferrer, Jr, 'United States–Argentine economic relations, 1900–1930' (Ph.D. thesis, Berkeley, 1964); Daniel W. Zimmerman, 'British influence in the modernization of Chile, 1860–1914' (Ph.D. thesis, New Mexico, 1977). Steven Topik, 'State intervention in a liberal regime: Brazil, 1889–1930', *HAHR*, 60/4 (1980), 593–616, an authoritative revisionist article, points out how much the government manipulated economic conditions in what is commonly supposed to be a liberal epoch. Useful statistics and interpretation relevant to the international economy and Mexico, Argentina, Brazil and Peru appear in the four volumes of Laura Randall, *A comparative economic history of Latin America* (Ann Arbor, 1977). These are complemented, for Colombia, by Miguel Urrutia and Mario Arrubla (eds.), *Compendio de estadísticas históricas de Colombia* (Bogotá, 1970); José Antonio Ocampo, 'Desarrollo exportador y desarrollo capitalista colombiano en el siglo XIX', in *Desarrollo y sociedad* (1979), 139–44, and 'Las exportaciones colombianas en el siglo XIX', *Desarrollo y sociedad* (1980), 165–226; Frank Safford, *Aspectos del siglo XIX en Colombia* (Medellín, 1977), and *The ideal of the practical* (Austin, 1976), both of which stress the Colombian response to external stimuli. On Argentina, see in particular Roberto Cortés Conde, *El progreso Argentino, 1880–1914* (Buenos Aires, 1978), and on Peru, Rosemary Thorp and Geoffrey Bertram, *Peru 1890–1977: growth and policy in an open economy* (London, 1978).

Although major countries have understandably tended to receive the bulk of scholarly attention, the experience of some of the smaller countries has also been examined. For example, on the Central American Republics, Thomas L. Karnes, *Tropical enterprise: the Standard Fruit and Steamship Company in Latin America* (Baton Rouge, 1978), which deals mainly with Honduras in years after 1923; Benjamin Teplitz, 'The political and economic foundations of modernization in Nicaragua; the administration of José Santos Zelaya, 1893–1909' (Ph.D. thesis, Howard, 1973); Kenneth V. Finney, 'Rosario and the election of 1887; the political economy of mining in Honduras', *HAHR*, 59/1 (1979), 81–107; Thomas R. Herrick, 'Economic and political development in Guatemala during the Barrios Period, 1871–1885' (Ph.D. thesis,

Chicago, 1968); David J. McCreery, 'Economic development and national policy, the Ministerio de Fomento of Guatemala, 1871–1885' (Ph.D. thesis, Tulane, 1972); Charles A. Brand, 'The background to capitalistic underdevelopment: Honduras to 1913' (Ph.D. thesis, Pittsburgh, 1972); Edward D. Hernández, 'Modernization and dependency in Costa Rica during the decade of the 1880s' (Ph.D. thesis, UCLA, 1975); and Mitchell A. Seligson, *Peasants of Costa Rica and the development of agrarian capitalism* (Madison, 1980).

The transport sector, and especially railways, which attracted so much foreign capital and entrepreneurship, has not surprisingly been the focus of much research. See, for instance, Thomas K. O'Horo, 'American foreign investments and foreign policy: the railroad experience, 1865–1898' (Ph.D. thesis, Rutgers, 1976); James H. Neal, 'The Pacific age comes to Colombia: the construction of the Cali-Buenaventura route, 1854–1882' (Ph.D. thesis, Vanderbilt, 1971); Delmer G. Ross, 'The Construction of the railroads in Central America' (Ph.D. thesis, California at Santa Barbara, 1970); Hugo DeClerco, 'The development of the communications and transportation infrastructure of Argentina's more advanced economy, 1850–1914' (Ph.D. thesis, Florida, 1973); William J. Flemming, Jr, 'Regional development and transportation in Argentina: Mendoza and the Gran Oeste Argentino Railroad, 1885–1914' (Ph.D. thesis, Indiana, 1976); Paul B. Goodwin, 'The Central Argentine Railway and the economic development of Argentina, 1854–1881', *HAHR*, 57/4 (1977), 613–32; Colin Lewis, *British Railways in Argentina, 1857–1914* (London, 1983); Robert B. Oppenheimer, 'Chilean transportation development: the railroad and socio-economic change in the Central Valley, 1840–1885' (Ph.D. thesis, UCLA, 1976); Dawn A. Wiles, 'Land transportation within Ecuador, 1822–1954' (Ph.D. thesis, Louisiana State, 1971); Robert H. Mattoon, Jr, 'Railroads, coffee, and the growth of big business in São Paulo, Brazil', *HAHR*, 57/2 (1977), 273–95; John G. Chapman, 'Steam, enterprise, and politics; the building of the Veracruz-Mexico City Railway, 1837–1880' (Ph.D. thesis, Texas, 1971); Arthur P. Schmidt, 'The social and economic effect of the railroad in Puebla and Veracruz, Mexico, 1867–1911' (Ph.D. thesis, Indiana, 1974); and, most notably, John H. Coatsworth, *Growth against development: the economic impact of railroads in Porfirian Mexico* (De Kalb, 1981).

Other sectors, especially export industries, have also attracted the attention of scholars: see, for example, Walter Gómez-D'Angelo, 'Mining in the economic development of Bolivia, 1900–1970' (Ph.D.

thesis, Vanderbilt, 1977), and David A. Denslow, Jr, 'Sugar production in Northeastern Brazil and Cuba, 1858–1908' (Ph.D. thesis, Yale, 1974). Other studies of the minerals sector include Kenneth V. Finney, 'Precious metal mining and the modernization of Honduras: in quest of El Dorado (1880–1900)' (Ph.D. thesis, Tulane, 1973); Joanne F. Przeworski, 'The decline of the copper industry in Chile and the entrance of North American capital, 1870–1916' (Ph.D. thesis, Washington University, 1978); John P. Olinger, 'Dreyfus Frères, guano and Peruvian government finance: 1869–1880, a chapter in economic imperialism' (Ph.D. thesis, SUNY-Binghamton, 1973), which deals with the vexed question of how effectively Peru used this export boom; Charles H. McArver, 'Mining and diplomacy: the United States interests at Cerro de Pasco, Peru, 1876–1930' (Ph.D. thesis, North Carolina, 1977). The Chilean nitrate experience has been a particularly favoured field of study. See, for example, an early study, Joseph R. Brown, 'The Chilean nitrate industry in the nineteenth century' (Ph.D. thesis, Louisiana State, 1954); Markos J. Mamalakis, 'The role of government in the resource transfer and resource allocation process; the Chilean nitrate sector, 1880–1930', in Gustav Ranis (ed.), *Government and economic development* (New Haven, 1971); Thomas F. O'Brien, Jr, *The nitrate industry and Chile's critical transition, 1870–1891* (New York, 1982), 'The Antofagasta Company: a case study of peripheral imperialism', *HAHR*, 60/1 (1980), 1–31, and 'Chilean elites and foreign investors: Chilean nitrate policy 1880–2', *JLAS*, 11/1 (1979), 101–21; Michael Monteón, *Chile in the nitrate era. The evolution of economic dependence 1880–1930* (Madison, 1982); Michael A. Meeropol, 'On the origins of the Chilean nitrate enclave' (Ph.D. thesis, Wisconsin, 1973); and Harold Blakemore, *British nitrates and Chilean politics 1886–1896* (London, 1974). Pierre Vayssiere, *Un siècle de capitalisme minier au Chile, 1830–1930* (Paris, 1980) is broader in scope but deals with some of the same themes.

On export agriculture, Charles W. Berquist, *Coffee and conflict in Colombia, 1886–1910* (Durham, 1978) examines the stresses generated when the export sector is domestically owned. Marco Palacios, *Coffee in Colombia 1850–1970: an economic, social, and political history* (Cambridge, 1980) shows the constant need for disaggregation in analysis by portraying the different impacts on land tenure the coffee boom had in different regions of the same countries. Other inquiries into Latin American agriculture include Jeffrey A. Lamia, 'Money, sheep, and economic crisis in Argentina, 1852–1900' (Ph.D. thesis, New York

602 Bibliographical essays

Univ., 1979); Rolf Sternberg, 'Farms and farmers in an estanciero world, 1856–1914: origin and spread of commercial grain farming on the humid pampa' (Ph.D. thesis, Syracuse, 1971); Noemí M. Girbal de Blacha, *Los centros agícolas en la provincia de Buenos Aires* (Buenos Aires, 1980); William A. Svec, 'A study of the socio-economic development of the modern Argentine estancia, 1852–1914' (Ph.D. thesis, Texas, 1966); Richard D. Weigle, 'The sugar interests and American diplomacy in Hawaii and Cuba, 1893–1903' (Ph.D. thesis, Yale, 1939); Mauricio Domínguez, 'The development of the technological and scientific coffee industry in Guatemala, 1830–1930' (Ph.D. thesis, Tulane, 1970); David J. McCreery, 'Coffee and class: the structure of development in liberal Guatemala', *HAHR*, 56/3 (1976), 438–60; Thomas H. Holloway, *The Brazilian coffee valorization of 1906: regional politics and economic dependence* (Madison, 1975). Like Holloway, Eugene W. Ridings also tries to tie economic phenomena to the social context in 'Class sector unity in an export economy: the case of nineteenth-century Brazil', *HAHR*, 58/3 (1978), 432–50. Also useful is Ivar Erneholm, *Cacao production of South America: historical development and present geographical distribution* (Gothenburg, 1948).

At times almost the same as a sectoral study but often more complex in scope of coverage are a number of regional histories that illuminate the empirical aspects of export expansion theories – and caution against premature or unqualified generalizations. Three such studies which were planned as deliberate parallels have to do with Brazil: Robert M. Levine, *Pernambuco in the Brazilian Federation, 1889–1937* (Stanford, 1978); Joseph L. Love, *São Paulo in the Brazilian Federation, 1889–1937* (Stanford, 1980); and John D. Wirth, *Minas Gerais in the Brazilian Federation, 1889–1937* (Stanford, 1977). No such comparative analyses like these have yet been made at the regional level elsewhere in Latin America, but local and regional histories rich in insight have been done for other parts of the continent: Mark Wasserman, *Capitalists, caciques and revolution: elite and foreign enterprise in Chihuahua, 1854–1911* (Chapel Hill, 1984); Alexander M. Saragoza, 'The formation of a Mexican elite: the industrialization of Monterrey, Nuevo León, 1880–1920' (Ph.D. thesis, Calif. at San Diego, 1978); Allen Wells, 'Family elites in a boom-and-bust economy: the Molinas and Peóns of Porfirian Mexico', *HAHR*, 62/2 (1982), 224–53; Harry E. Cross, 'The mining economy of Zacatecas, Mexico, in the nineteenth century' (Ph.D. thesis, Berkeley, 1976); Kenneth A. Hardy, 'Access and differentiation: the case of Buenos Aires province, Argentina, 1880–1914' (Ph.D. thesis, North Carolina, 1978); Donna J. Guy, 'Politics and the sugar industry in Tucumán, Argentina, 1870–1900' (Ph.D. thesis, Indiana, 1978); Arthur F. Liebscher, 'Commercial expansion and political change: Santa Fe province, 1897–1916' (Ph.D. thesis, Indiana, 1975); David C. Johnson, 'Social and economic change in nineteenth-century Santander, Colombia' (Ph.D. thesis, Berkeley, 1975); and Richard P. Hyland, 'A fragile prosperity: credit and agrarian structure in the Cauca Valley, Colombia, 1851–87, *HAHR*, 62/3 (1982), 369–406.

Still another group of works deal with the widespread changes in labour and working conditions, partly from the effects of immigration and partly attributable to the nature of the new patterns of economic activity. Friedrich Katz, *Servidumbres agrárias en México del porfiriato* (Mexico, 1977) and 'Labor conditions on haciendas in Porfirian Mexico', *HAHR*, 54/1 (1974), 1–47. For a more detailed discussion of the bibliography on rural labour in Spain America in this period, see *CHLA* IV, bibliographical essay 5. On Brazil, see in particular Michael M. Hall, 'The origins of mass immigration in Brazil, 1871–1914' (Ph.D. thesis, Columbia, 1969) and Thomas H. Holloway, *Immigrants on the land. Coffee and society in São Paulo, 1886–1934* (Chapel Hill, 1980). There are important contributions in Kenneth Duncan and Ian Rutledge (eds.), *Land and labor in Latin America: essays on the development of agrarian capitalism in the nineteenth and twentieth centuries* (Cambridge, 1977). For a discussion of the bibliography on urban labour in this period, see *CHLA* IV, bibliographical essay 9.

2. LATIN AMERICA AND THE INTERNATIONAL ECONOMY FROM THE FIRST WORLD WAR TO THE WORLD DEPRESSION

This essay concentrates on material concerning Latin America as a whole, and on certain works of particular use from a comparative point of view. For individual countries in this period, see bibliographical essays, *CHLA* V. The period is one of increasing integration with the world economy, particularly in the 1920s. It is therefore no surprise to find that most of the richest contemporary material is foreign in origin, and produced in English. It is also, typically, only the foreigner who perceived 'Latin America' as a whole. Both factors are reflected in this review of the secondary literature; the material of foreign origin is exceptionally valuable as long as its context is borne in mind.

The outstanding book on U.S. expansion in this period, both for data and qualitative information, is C. Lewis, *America's stake in international investments* (Washington, 1938); also important are M. Winkler, *Investments of U.S. capital in Latin America* (Boston, 1929), J. F. Normano, *The struggle for South America* (Boston, 1931), H. Feis, *The diplomacy of the dollar* (Baltimore, 1950) and M. Wilkins, *The maturing of multinational enterprise: American business abroad from 1914 to 1970* (Cambridge, Mass., 1974). An excellent comparative study is U.N., ECLA *Foreign capital in Latin America* (New York, 1955). On the expansion of banking, C. W. Phelps, *The foreign expansion of American banks* (New York, 1927) and David Joslin, *A century of banking in Latin America* (London, 1963) are the key secondary sources. Excellent sources on Kemmerer's role in several Latin American countries are R. N. Seidel, 'American reformers abroad: the Kemmerer missions in South America 1923–1931', *Journal of Economic History* 32/2 (1972) and P. Drake's forthcoming work of which one chapter has been published: 'The origins of United States economic supremacy in South America: Colombia's dance of the millions 1923–33', Wilson Center Working Paper, no. 40 (1979). M. Marsh, *The bankers in Bolivia* (New York, 1928) is worth mentioning for the exceptional interest of the work, though it covers only one country.

Underpinning foreign interest was a great expansion in the flow of information from the U.S. Department of Commerce. There are countless handbooks and special studies for this period which are invaluable and, since the same author often studied several different countries, of great comparative use. Especial mention should be made of the 'Commercial and Industrial Handbooks' in the 1920s, the various country studies by C. A. McQueen published in the Trade Promotion Series, e.g., *Peruvian Public finance* (Washington, 1926), which were followed by various 'Tariff Handbooks'. *Commerce Reports* are less ample in the 1920s than the 1930s but worth using. On the British side, the Department of Overseas Trade Reports ('Economic Conditions in . . . .') are one of the best sources of information on economic conditions in individual countries, with a fair amount of statistical information. In many countries the local English-speaking community had a flourishing business periodical at this period, which is worth seeking out (e.g., *Review of the River Plate*, *West Coast Leader*). The *South American Journal* published in London is an invaluable source of financial and commercial data.

There are two pathbreaking general economic histories of Latin

America as a whole which include some discussion of this period: W. P. Glade, *The Latin American economies* (New York, 1969) and Celso Furtado, *The economic development of Latin America* (Cambridge, 1970). An exceptional book for its combination of conceptual framework, interdisciplinary character and empirical content remains F. H. Cardoso and E. Faletto, *Dependencia y desarrollo en América Latina* (Mexico, 1971); Eng. trans., *Dependency and development in Latin America* (Berkeley, 1979). A series useful for comparative work because of the similar methodology is UN, *Análisis y proyecciones*; the different country studies were published in the late 1950s and early 1960s and contain excellent statistical appendixes. The ECLA *Economic survey of Latin America 1949* is a particularly useful volume because of its long historical series. J. W. Wilkie, *Statistics and national policy*, supplement 3, UCLA *Statistical abstract of Latin America* (1974), also provides a good and uniform data source. Books specifically on industrialization include UN *Process of industrialisation in Latin America* (1966), G. Wythe, *Industry in Latin America* (2nd edn, New York, 1949), D. M. Phelps, *Migration of industry to South America* (New York, 1936) and F. S. Weaver, *Class, state, and industrial structure: the historical process of South American industrial growth* (Westport, 1980). R. Thorp (ed.), *Latin America in the 1930's: the role of the periphery in world crisis* (London, 1984) is a recent study of the effect of the 1929 depression, which contains much material on the two preceding decades and attempts to combine comparative analysis with detailed country studies by Enrique Cárdenas and E. V. K. Fitzgerald on Mexico, Victor Bulmer-Thomas on Central America, Flavio Versiani and Marcelo de Paiva Abreu on Brazil, Arturo O'Connell on Argentina, José Antonio Ocampo, Rosemary Thorp and Carlos Londoño on Colombia and Peru and Gabriel Palma on Chile.

A number of macro-economic country studies look at the relationship to the international economy and give enough attention to this period to be particularly useful for a comparative perspective.

On Brazil, see W. Dean, *The industrialisation of São Paulo 1880–1945* (Austin, 1969); Celso Furtado, *Formação econômica do Brasil* (Rio de Janeiro, 1959); Eng. trans., *The economic growth of Brazil* (Berkeley, 1963). Stanley J. Stein, *Brazilian cotton manufacturing* (Cambridge, Mass., 1957); A. V. Villela and W. Suzigan, *Política do governo e crescimento da economía brasileira, 1889–1945* (Rio de Janeiro, 1973); Eng. trans. 'Government policy and the economic growth of Brazil 1889–1945', *Brazilian Economic Studies* No. 3, I.P.E.A. (Rio de Janeiro, 1975); C. M. Palaez, 'An economic analysis of the Brazilian coffee support program 1906–1945: theory, policy and measurement', in C. M. Palaez (ed.), *Coffee and economic development* (São Paulo, 1973); N. Villela Luz, *A luta pela industrialização no Brasil* (São Paulo, 1961); F. R. Versiani and M. T. R. O. Versiani, 'A industrialização brasileira antes de 1930: uma contribuição', *Estudos Económicos*, 5/1 (1975); F. R. Versiani, 'Industrial investment in an "export" economy: the Brazilian experience before 1914', *Journal of Development Studies* 7/3 (1980); A. Fishlow, 'Origins and consequences of import substitution in Brazil', in L. Di Marco (ed.), *International economics and development: essays in honor of Raul Prebisch* (New York, 1974); Wilson Cano, *Raízes da concentração industrial em São Paulo* (São Paulo, 1977).

On Argentina, see C. Díaz-Alejandro, *Essays on the economic history of the Argentine Republic* (New Haven, 1970); G. Di Tella and M. Zymelman, *Las etapas del desarrollo económico argentino* (Buenos Aires, 1967); J. Fodor and A. O'Connell, 'La Argentina y la economía atlántica en la primera mitad del siglo XX, *Desarrollo Económico* 13 (1973), 13–65; E. Gallo, 'Agrarian expansion and industrial development in Argentina 1880–1930'; Raymond Carr (ed.), *Latin American Affairs, St. Antony's Papers, No. 22* (Oxford, 1970).

On Mexico, J. Womack 'The Mexican economy during the Revolution, 1910–1920: historiography and analysis', *Marxist Perspectives*, 1/4 (Winter 1978), is a superb guide and survey article of an extensive literature; C. W. Reynolds, *The Mexican economy: twentieth century structure and growth* (New Haven, 1970) and L. Solís, *La realidad mexicana* (Mexico, 1970) are particularly solid economic histories of the period. See also Lorenzo Meyer, *Mexico y los Estados Unidos en el conflicto petrolero, 1917–1942* (Mexico, 1972); Eng. trans., *Mexico and the United States in the oil controversy, 1917–1942*, (Austin, 1977).

On Chile, see O. Muñoz, *Crecimiento industrial de Chile 1914–1965* (Santiago, 1968); J. G. Palma, 'Growth and structure of Chilean manufacturing industry from 1830 to 1935' (unpublished D.Phil. thesis, Oxford, 1979); H. W. Kirsch, *Industrial development in a traditional society: the conflict between entrepreneurship and modernisation in Chile* (Gainesville, 1977).

On Colombia, see L. Ospina Vásquez, *Industria y protección en Colombia 1810–1930* (Medellín, 1955); M. Palacios, *El Café en Colombia 1850–1970: una historia económica, social y política* (Bogotá, 1979); Eng. trans., *Coffee in Colombia 1850–1970: an economic social and political history* (Cambridge, 1980); J. A. Ocampo and S. Montenegro, 'La crisis mundial de los años treinta en Colombia', *Desarrollo y sociedad* 8 (1982); S. Montenegro, 'Historia de la indústria textil en Colombia 1900–1945' (unpublished M.A. thesis, Universidad de Los Andes, Bogotá, 1982); J. A. Bejarano, 'El fin de la economia exportadora y los orígenes del problema agrario', *Cuadernos Colombianos* 6, 7, 8 (Medellín, 1975); W. McGreevey, *An economic history of Colombia, 1845–1930* (Cambridge, 1971).

On Venezuela, see B. S. McBeth, *Juan Vicente Gómez and the oil companies in Venezuela, 1908–1935* (Cambridge, 1983).

On Peru, see R. Thorp and G. Bertram, *Peru 1890–1977: growth and policy in an export economy*, (London, 1978); P. Klarén, *Modernisation, dislocation and Aprismo: origins of the Peruvian Aprista Party* (Austin, 1973); C. Boloña, 'Protectionism and liberalism in Peru 1880–1980', (unpublished D.Phil. thesis Oxford, 1981); and R. Miller, 'British business in Peru 1883–1930' (unpublished Ph.D. thesis, Cambridge, 1979).

On Cuba, see H. C. Wallich, *Monetary problems of an export economy. The Cuban experience, 1914–1947* (Cambridge, Mass., 1950).

On Bolivia, see L. Whitehead, 'El impacto de la Gran Depresión en Bolivia', *Desarrollo Económico* (1972).

On Uruguay, see M. H. J. Finch, *A political economy of Uruguay since 1870* (London, 1981). And on Central America, see Ciro F. S. Cardoso and H. Pérez Brignoli, *Centroamérica y la economía occidental (1520–1930)* (San José, 1977).

A relatively unexplored area is the role of the state. But, on Brazil, see, for example, Steven Topik, 'The evolution of the economic role of the Brazilian state, 1889–1930', *JLAS* 11/2 (1979) and 'State intervention in a liberal regime: Brazil 1889–1930', *HAHR* 60/4 (1980), and S. Schwartzman, 'Empresarios y política en el proceso de industrialización. Argentina, Brasil, Australia', *Desarrollo Económico* (1973). A similar neglect is typical of all issues concerning the internal economy: there is virtually no material of a comparative or continental basis – partly because the secondary material on individual countries is not yet very strong for this period. The number of solid individual case studies is growing fast, however, as the bibliographical essays for individual countries in *CHLA* v make clear.

Finally, on the international economy itself there is a rich secondary literature. On this period, see, for example, G. Hardach, *The First World War 1914–1918* (London, 1977); D. H. Aldcroft, *From Versailles to Wall Street 1919–1929* (London, 1977); and C. P. Kindleberger, *The world in depression 1929–1939* (London, 1973). The bibliographical references in each are an excellent source for earlier works. Standard books which have made major contributions are M. T. Copeland, *A raw commodity revolution* (Harvard Business Research Studies no. 19, Cambridge, Mass., 1938); H. B. Lary, *The United States in the world economy* (U.S. Dept. of Commerce, Washington, 1943); J. F. Rowe, *Primary commodities in international trade* (Cambridge, 1965); and P. L. Yates, *Forty years of foreign trade: a statistical handbook with special reference to primary products and underdeveloped countries* (London, 1959). An older study of especial value for the 1920s is W. A. Lewis, *Economic survey 1919–39* (London, 1949).

3. LATIN AMERICA, THE UNITED STATES AND THE EUROPEAN POWERS, 1830–1930

An invaluable guide with over eleven thousand listings is David F. Trask, Michael C. Meyer and Roger R. Trask (eds.), *A bibliography of United States–Latin American relations since 1810* (Lincoln, Nebraska, 1968). See also Michael C. Meyer (ed.), *Supplement to a bibliography of United States–Latin American relations since 1810* (Lincoln, Nebraska, 1979). Several countries have guides to the secondary literature for their diplomatic history. One of the best is Daniel Cosío Villegas, *Questiones internacionales de México* (Mexico, 1966). A good overall introduction to the history of international relations of Latin America is Harold Eugene Davis, John J. Finan and F. Taylor Peck, *Latin American diplomatic history: an introduction* (Baton Rouge, 1977). A more theoretical analysis of the international dilemma of Latin America is Leopoldo Zea, *Latin America and the world*, translated by Frances Hendricks and Beatrice Berler (Norman, Oklahoma, 1969). This should be read in conjunction with another classic interpretation, Arthur P. Whitaker, *The western hemisphere idea: its rise and decline* (Ithaca, N.Y., 1954). For questions of international organization and law one should consult John C. Dreir *et al.*, *International organization in the western hemisphere* (Syracuse, N.Y., 1968), and C. Neale Ronning, *Law and politics in inter-American diplomacy* (New York, 1963).

For a more detailed presentation of United States relations with Latin America, see Graham Stuart and James Tigner, *Latin America and the United States* (6th edn, Englewood Cliffs, N.J., 1975). See also Gordon Connell-Smith, *The United States and Latin America: an historical analysis of inter-American relations* (London, 1974) and, a more general treatment from a different perspective, Lloyd C. Gardner, Walter LaFeber and T. McCormick, *The creation of the modern American Empire. U.S. diplomatic history* (London, 1973), as well as the various works of William Appleman Williams. Wilfrid Hardy Callcott, *The western hemisphere: its influence on United States policies to the end of World War II*, (Austin, 1968), is a well balanced account of hemispheric relations and the international context. The basic study of the Monroe Doctrine remains Dexter Perkins, *A history of the Monroe Doctrine* (Boston, 1955). For specific studies of Latin American relations with the United States, see, for example, Frederick Pike, *Chile and the United States, 1880–1962* (Notre Dame, Ind., 1963) and *The United States and the Andean Republics: Peru, Bolivia, and Ecuador* (Cambridge, Mass., 1977); Karl Schmitt, *Mexico and the United States, 1821–1973: conflict and co-existence* (New York, 1974); and Sheldon Liss, *Diplomacy and dependency: Venezuela, the United States, and the Americas* (Salisbury, N.D., 1978). Joseph S. Tulchin, *The aftermath of war: World War I and U.S. policy toward Latin America* (New York, 1971), provides a good analysis of American policy in the wake of changing power relationships. An excellent analysis of power rivalries in Mexico during the revolution is presented in Friedrich Katz, *The secret war in Mexico: Europe, the United States and the Mexican Revolution* (Chicago, 1981).

For power rivalries in the Caribbean the most extensive study is Lester Langley, *Struggle for the American Mediterranean: United States–European Rivalry in the Gulf-Caribbean, 1776–1904* (Athens, Ga., 1976) and *The United States and the Caribbean in the twentieth century* (Athens, Ga., 1982). The British position for the nineteenth century is given excellent coverage in several essays in R. A. Humphreys, *Tradition and revolt in Latin America, and other essays* (London, 1969). These are complemented by Joseph Smith, *Illusions of conflict: Anglo-American diplomacy toward Latin America, 1865–1896* (Pittsburgh, 1979); and Warren Kneer, *Great Britain and the Caribbean, 1901–1913* (East Lansing, Mich., 1975). A short survey of European possessions in the twentieth century is presented in Sir Harold Mitchell, *Europe in the Caribbean: the policies of Great Britain, France, and the Netherlands towards their West Indian territories in the twentieth century* (Stanford, 1963). Detailed studies emphasizing the strategic interpretation of U.S. policy in the Caribbean are Dana Munro, *Intervention and dollar diplomacy in the Caribbean, 1900–1921* (Princeton, 1964), and *The U.S. and the Caribbean Republics, 1921–1933* (Princeton, 1974). Hans Schmidt, *The United States occupation of Haiti, 1915–1934* (New

Brunswick, N.J., 1971), stresses racist and cultural factors, and is most critical of the United States. For a well-balanced presentation, see also David Healy, *Gunboat diplomacy in the Wilson era: the United States in Haiti, 1915–1916* (Madison, Wis., 1976). The economic aspects of U.S. policy towards Cuba during the 1920s can be found in Robert Freeman Smith, *The United States and Cuba: business and diplomacy, 1917–1960* (New York, 1960). A study utilizing the dependency theory is Jules Benjamin, *The United States and Cuba: hegemony and dependent development, 1880–1934* (Pittsburgh, 1974). Lester Langley utilizes the 'colonial wars' theme in *The banana wars: an inner history of American empire, 1900–1934* (Lexington, KY, 1983). On Panama and the United States, see W. LaFeber, *The Panama Canal* (New York, 1978).

The economic involvement of Great Britain is covered in two excellent studies by D. C. M. Platt, *Latin America and British trade, 1860–1914* (London, 1972), and *Business imperialism 1840–1930: an inquiry based on British experience in Latin America* (New York, 1977). The classic study of American investments for the period is Cleona Lewis, *America's stake in international investments* (New York, 1938). Important recent studies include Mira Wilkins, *The emergence of multinational enterprise: American business abroad from the colonial era to 1914* (Cambridge, Mass., 1974) and *The maturing of multinational enterprise: American business abroad from 1914 to 1970* (Cambridge, Mass., 1974). The influence of the idea of the Open World and the diplomatic concept of reciprocity as factors in U.S. Latin American policy are analysed in Robert Freeman Smith, 'Reciprocity', in Alexander DeConde (ed.), *Encyclopedia of American foreign policy: studies of the principal movements and ideas*, III (New York, 1978). Various case studies with differing approaches are presented in Marvin Bernstein (ed.), *Foreign investment in Latin America: cases and attitudes* (New York, 1966). Robert Freeman Smith, *The United States and Revolutionary Nationalism in Mexico, 1916–1932* (Chicago, 1972), covers the American reaction to the economic nationalism of this revolution. See also Lorenzo Meyer, *Mexico and the United States in the oil controversy 1917–42* (Austin, 1977). A good discussion of economic relations with Colombia after 1920 can be found in Stephen J. Randall, *The diplomacy of modernization: Colombian–American relations, 1920–1940* (Toronto, 1977). For U.S.–European rivalry over aviation see Wesley Phillips Newton, *The perilous sky: U.S. aviation diplomacy and Latin America, 1919–1931* (Miami, Florida, 1978).

Rollie E. Poppino, *International communism in Latin America: a history of the movement, 1917–1963* (Glencoe, Illinois, 1964) is a good survey. This can be reinforced by the fine collection of documents edited by Stephen Clissold, *Soviet relations with Latin America, 1918–1968: a documentary survey* (London, 1970).

4. THE POPULATION OF LATIN AMERICA, 1850–1930

In the absence of a general analysis, except for the relevant chapters of Nicolás Sánchez-Albornoz, *The population of Latin America: a history*, (Berkeley, 1974), 2nd Spanish edn, *La población de América latina: desde los tiempos precolombinos al año 2000* (Madrid, 1977) which have been updated here, the reader should follow the development of the population of Latin America in the period from 1870 to 1930 in books and articles on the individual countries. For Argentina, CELADE (Centro Latinoamericano de Demografía), *Temas de población de la Argentina: aspectos demográficos* (Santiago de Chile, 1973) and Zulma Recchini de Lattes and Alfredo E. Lattes (eds.), *La población de Argentina* (Instituto Nacional de Estadística y Censos, Buenos Aires, 1975) have compiled parallel studies which provide an overall view of the principal demographic variables from 1889 onwards. *La población de Cuba*, (Centro de Estudios Demográficos, Havana, 1976) was conceived in the same way, but is not backed up by such detailed previous research. For Brazil from 1800, T. W. Merrick and D. H. Graham, *Population and economic development in Brazil: 1800 to the present* (Baltimore, 1979) attempts to achieve a balance between chronological presentation and a diachronic discussion of themes. The Centro de Estudios de Población y Desarrollo in Lima has, for its part, made a notable attempt at historical reconstruction in its *Informe demográfico del Perú: 1970* (Lima, 1972). However, there was not one single census report in Peru between 1876 and 1940, which means that the study can only be of limited use. On Mexico the two volumes by Moisés González Navarro, *Población y sociedad en México (1900–1970)* (Mexico, 1974), although amply documented, lack the analytical technique used by demographers in the other books already mentioned.

Compilations of statistics on demographic history may be found for Chile in M. Mamalakis, *Historical statistics of Chile*, vol. II (Westport, Conn., 1980), and for Uruguay in J. Rial, *Estadísticas históricas de Uruguay, 1850–1930* (Centro de Informaciones y Estudios del Uruguay, Cuaderno no. 4, Montevideo, 1980), which should be supplemented with J. J.

Pereira and R. Trajtenberg, *Evolución de la población total y activa en el Uruguay, 1908–1957* (Instituto de Economía, Publicación no. 26, Montevideo, 1966). J. Rial and J. Klaczko, *Uruguay: el país urbano* (Montevideo, 1981), although it focuses on the process of urbanization, at present constitutes the best alternative to the population history of Uruguay which we still lack. The first population history of a Latin American country, El Salvador, was written as early as 1942: R. Barón Castro, *La población de El Salvador: estudio acerca de su desenvolvimiento desde la época prehispanica hasta nuestros días* (Madrid, 1942; repr. Universidad Centroamericana Simeón Cañas, 1978). Although the work is dated, it has not yet been replaced. Panama has a recent general study by O. Jaén Suárez, *La población del istmo de Panamá del siglo XVI al XX: estudio sobre la población y los modos de organización de las economías, las sociedades y los espacios geográficos* (Panama, 1978). For the other Central American countries, see Ciro F. S. Cardoso and H. Pérez Brignoli, *Centroamérica y la economía occidental (1520–1930)* (San José, 1977). For Venezuela, J. Paéz Celis, *Ensayo sobre la demografía económica de Venezuela* (Dirección General de Estadística y Censos Nacionales, Caracas, 1974), though dealing specifically with more recent years, contains some retrospective references. F. Moya Pons, 'Nuevas consideraciones sobre la historia de la población dominicana: curvas, tasas y problemas', in *Seminario sobre problemas de población en la República dominicana* (Santo Domingo, 1975), 37–63, deals briefly with the population growth of Santo Domingo, while A. Averanga Mollinedo, *Aspectos generales de la población boliviana* (La Paz, 1974) does the same for Bolivia. D. M. Rivarola, *et al.*, *La población del Paraguay* (Centro Paraguayo de Estudios Sociológicos, (Asunción, 1974) provides, somewhat unsystematically, precise data on Paraguay.

The following studies have rectified various previous estimates of the population of Latin America for 1850, 1900 and 1930: R. Barón Castro, 'El desarrollo de la población hispanoamericana (1492–1950)', *Journal of World History*, 5 (1959), 325–43; C. A. Miró, *La población de América latina en el siglo XX* (CELADE, Santiago de Chile, 1965); CELADE, 'América latina: población total por paises. Año 1970', *Boletín demográfico*, 6 (1970); see also *Boletín demográfico*, 32 (1983).

Among the components of demographic change, the factor of international migration has attracted most research. Much of this literature is of a commemorative type and is mostly of marginal interest. With regard to the size of the flow, W. F. Willcox, *International migrations*

(National Bureau of Economic Research, New York 1929), though dated, is still useful, but should be complemented by more recent research, such as Z. L. Recchini de Lattes and A. E. Lattes, *La población de Argentina*, for Argentina, and M. S. Ferreira Levi 'O papel da migração internacional na evolução de população brasileira (1872–1972)', *Revista de saúde pública*, 8 (suppl.) (1974), 49–90, for Brazil. Giorgio Mortara, 'Pesquisas sôbre populaçoẽs americanas', *Estudos brasileiros de demografia* 1 (1947), 1–227, and Gino Germani, 'Mass immigration and modernization in Argentina', in I. L. Horowitz (ed.), *Masses in Latin America* (New York, 1970), 289–330, among others, have discussed numerically various aspects of the effect which immigration had on the demography of Latin America. Chiara Vangelista, 'Immigrazione, struttura produttiva e mercato del lavoro in Argentina a in Brasile (1876–1914)', *Annali della Fondazione Luigi Einaudi*, 10 (1975), 197–216 and *Le braccia per la fazenda. Immigrati e 'caipiras' nella formazione del mercato del lavoro paulista (1850–1930)* (Milan, 1982), and R. Cortés Conde, *El progreso argentino, 1880–1914* (Buenos Aires, 1979) also explore the socioeconomic conditions which prompted European emigration. Although both authors rely on information from one country, namely Italy, their approach is a general one. Thomas H. Holloway, *Immigrants on the land. Coffee and society in São Paulo, 1886–1934* (Chapel Hill, N.C., 1980), for its part, examines immigration in the specific context of São Paulo.

Migration studies referring to ethnic groups are plentiful, although in an inverse proportion to their importance as a group. There are no thorough histories of Italian, Spanish, or Portuguese migration, but on the migration of Germans to Chile, see G. F. W. Young, *The Germans in Chile: immigration and colonization* (Center for Migration Studies, New York, 1974), and to Rio Grande do Sul, see J. Roche, *A colonização alemã no Rio Grande do Sul* (2 vols., Porto Alegre, 1969); on the Welsh to Patagonia, see G. Williams, 'The Structure and process of Welsh emigration to Patagonia', *Welsh History Review*, 8 (1976), 42–74; on the Irish to the province of Buenos Aires, see J. C. Korol and H. Sábato, '*The Camps': inmigrantes irlandeses en la provincia de Buenos Aires, 1870–1890* (Buenos Aires, 1979); and on the French to Uruguay, see M. Marenales Rossi and G. Bourdé, 'L'immigration française et le peuplement de l'Uruguay (1830–1860)', *Cahiers des Amériques latines*, 16 (1977), 7–32.

Among the migration of non-Europeans, a considerable amount of research has been devoted to the Japanese, above all in Brazil: Hiroshi Saito, *O japonês no Brasil: estudo de mobilidade e fixação* (São Paulo, 1961),

Teiiti Suzuki, *The Japanese immigrant in Brazil* (2 vols., Tokyo, 1969), J. T. Cintra, *La migración japonesa en Brasil (1908–1958)* (Mexico, 1971), and A. Rocha Nogueira, *A immigração japonesa para a lavoura cafeira paulista (1908–1922)* (Rio de Janeiro, 1973). Chinese settlement in Latin America has also been the subject of several articles: for example, E. Chang-Rodríguez, 'Chinese labor migration into Latin America in the nineteenth century', *Revista de Historia de América*, 45–6 (1958), 375–97, and J. Pérez de la Riva, 'Demografía de los culíes chinos en Cuba (1853–1874)', *Revista de la Biblioteca Nacional José Martí*, 57 (1966), 3–32. Although the focus of his work is centred on Santo Domingo, José del Castillo, *La inmigración de braceros azucareros en la República dominicana, 1900–1930* (Santo Domingo, 1978), offers a general panorama of migration in the Antilles at the beginning of the present century. For Cuba, this should be complemented with H. Pérez de la Riva, 'La inmigración antillana en Cuba durante el primer tercio del siglo XX'. *Revista de la Biblioteca Nacional José Martí*, 66 (1975), 75–88.

With regard to African immigration during the last century, apart from the estimates in Philip D. Curtin, *The African slave trade. A census* (Madison, 1969), see Franklin W. Knight, *Slave society in Cuba during the nineteenth century* (Madison, 1970), for Cuba; Robert Conrad, *The destruction of Brazilian slavery, 1850–1888* (Berkeley, 1972) for Brazil; and J. V. Lombardi, *The decline and abolition of negro slavery in Venezuela 1820–1854* (Westport, Conn., 1971), for Venezuela. In addition, R. W. Slenes, 'The demography and economics of Brazilian slavery: 1850–1888' (unpublished Ph.D. thesis, Stanford University, 1976) has studied internal migration and the demographic characteristics of black slaves in Brazil.

Among the various works on Mexican emigration to the United States, the most detailed study on the period prior to 1930 is Lawrence A. Cardoso, *Mexican emigration to the United States, 1897–1931: socio-economic patterns* (Tucson, 1980).

In the absence of figures for internal migration, as precise as those which exist for international flows, scholars need to reconstruct this internal flux. Either one begins by examining the discrepancy between place of birth and residence, as recorded in census forms, or one starts with the tables of survival, or finally, one compares growth rates between two censuses. All these methods require the existence of census reports, which were not always carried out. So far these methods have been applied to only two countries, Argentina and Brazil; see Z. L.

Recchini de Lattes and A. E. Lattes, *Migraciones en la Argentina. Estudio de las migraciones internas e internacionales, basado en datos censales, 1869–1960* (Instituto Torcuato di Tella, Buenos Aires, 1969) and D. H. Graham and S. Buarque de Hollanda Filho, *Migration, regional and urban growth and development in Brazil. A selective analysis of the historical record, 1872–1970* (Instituto de Pesquisas Econômicas, São Paulo, 1971). Jorge Balán deals instead with internal migration from a comparative point of view in 'Migrações internas no desenvolvimento capitalista no Brasil: ensai histórico-comparativo', in J. Balán (ed.) *Centro e periferia no desenvolvimento brasileiro* (São Paulo, 1974), 109–84, or considers one region in 'Migraciones, mano de obra y formación de un proletariado rural en Tucumán, Argentina, 1870–1914', *Demografía y economía*, 10/2 (1976), 201–34. On Chile, see Ann Hagerman Johnson, 'Internal Migration in Chile to 1920: its relationship to the labor market, agricultural growth, and urbanisation' (unpublished Ph.D. thesis, University of California, Davis, 1978). M. E. Castellanos de Sjostrand, 'La población de Venezuela. Migraciones internas y distribución espacial, 1908–1935', *Semestre histórico*, 1 (1975), 5–62, examines the issue in relation to Venezuela.

With respect to the determinants of natural growth, the evolution of life expectancy has permitted Eduardo A. Arriaga, at first with the collaboration of Kingsley Davis, and later alone, to follow the course of mortality in Latin America: see E. A. Arriaga and K. Davis 'The pattern of mortality change in Latin America', *Demography*, 6 (1969), 223–42, and E. A. Arriaga, *Mortality decline and its effects in Latin America* (Institute of International Studies, University of California, Berkeley, 1970). Using the same method, Jorge L. Somoza has focused on Argentina in *La mortalidad en la Argentina entre 1869 y 1960* (Instituto Torcuato di Tella, Buenos Aires, 1971). For the great epidemics of cholera and yellow fever, see J. S. Ward, *Yellow fever in Latin America: a geographical study* (Centre for Latin American Studies, University of Liverpool, Monograph Series no. 3, 1972), and D. B. Cooper, 'Brazil's long fight against epidemic disease, 1849–1917, with special emphasis on yellow fever', *Bulletin of the New York Academy of Medicine*, 51 (1975), 672–96. There is a lack of detailed research on crop variability and nutrition, as well as on the incidence of the most common diseases and the progress in medicine and sanitation. On fertility, O. Andrew Collver, *Birth rates in Latin America: new estimates of historical trends and fluctuations* (Institute of International Studies, Berkeley, 1965), elaborates a general scheme for the twentieth century, but there is nothing on the nineteenth century. On a national level, it is worth noting Maria S. Müller's work on Argentina, *La mortalidad en Buenos Aires entre 1855 y 1960* (Buenos Aires, 1974).

The interaction of several demographic variables in a specific area has not been studied to any great extent. But see, for example, J. Casey Gaspar, *Limón: 1880–1940. Un estudio de la industria bananera en Costa Rica* (San José, 1979), on the area of Limón in Costa Rica, and Z. L. Recchini de Lattes, *La población de Buenos Aires. Componentes demográficos del crecimiento entre 1855 y 1960* (Instituto Torcuato di Tella, Buenos Aires, 1971), on the city of Buenos Aires.

5. RURAL SPANISH AMERICA, 1870–1930

The study of Spanish American rural history, virtually ignored after a short burst of work in the 1930s, has impressively expanded in the past two decades. This has been due, in the first instance, to an enthusiasm for the process of modernization and more recently to laying bare the roots and mechanism of dependency. The colonial epoch, from the sixteenth to the eighteenth centuries, has attracted most attention and, traditionally, the best scholars, while the post-Second World War period became the scene of intense work by anthropologists, economists and sociologists as well as historians. In between, the understanding of nineteenth- and early twentieth-century rural history improves but remains relatively under-developed; it is, however, now on a sufficiently firm footing to permit discussion.

Three international congresses have yielded collections of papers. *Les problèmes agraires des Amériques Latines* (Paris, 1967); Enrique Florescano (ed.), *Haciendas, latifundios y plantaciones en América Latina* (Mexico, 1975); and Kenneth Duncan and Ian Rutledge (eds.), *Land and labour in Latin America* (Cambridge, 1977). Apart from a handful of essays in these volumes that attempt to embrace the area as a whole, very few scholars, undoubtedly humbled by the formidable variety and discontinuity of Latin America, have attempted broad, comparative analyses. C. Kay, 'Comparative development of the European manorial system and the Latin American hacienda system' (unpublished Ph.D. thesis, University of Sussex, 1971), Shane Hunt, 'The economics of haciendas and plantations in Latin America,' unpublished MS (1972), and the well-known Eric Wolf and Sidney Mintz, 'Haciendas and plantations in Middle America and the Antilles', *Social and Economic Studies*, 6/1 (1957),

380–412, are some who have endeavoured to rise to a level of abstraction above the monograph. Magnus Mörner has always been concerned with the broad view and his 'The Spanish American hacienda: a survey of recent research and debate', *HAHR*, 53/2 (1973), 183–216, and 'A comparative study of tenant labor in parts of Europe, Africa and Latin America 1700–1900', *LARR*, 5/2 (1970), 3–15, are excellent points of departure. A. J. Bauer, 'Rural workers in Spanish America: problems of peonage and oppression', *HAHR*, 59/1 (1979), 34–63, and the discussion which follows in the Forum section of the same journal, *HAHR*, 59/3 (1979), 478–89, reviews some of the issues and recent work. Alain de Janvry, *The agrarian question and reformism in Latin America* (Baltimore, 1981), treats the broader issues for the recent years and his work has theoretical implications for the period 1870–1930.

In Mexico, the best current work on rural history turns around the scholarly centre of the Dirección de Estudios Históricos (INAH) in Mexico City. The 'Informes Generales' of that Institute are good guides to publications. Volume 91 of the *Revista mexicana de ciencias políticas y sociales* (Jan.–March 1978) is devoted to the Mexican hacienda in the nineteenth and twentieth centuries; the *Historia Mexicana* contains a great many articles on this subject. Among other work, the most recent proceedings of the periodic Reunion of Mexican and North American Historians. *El trabajo y los trabajadores en la historia de México* (Mexico and Tucson, 1979), and especially within that volume the essays by John Womack, Jr, and Enrique Florescano are valuable. D. A. Brading (ed.), *Caudillo and peasant in the Mexican Revolution* (Cambridge, 1980) is an important contribution, and the following monographs, selected from a large recent literature, are excellent: Arturo Warman, *Y venimos a contradecir: los campesinos de Morelos y el estado nacional* (Mexico, 1976); Jan Bazant, *Cinco haciendas mexicanas* (Mexico, 1975); John Womack, Jr, *Zapata and the Mexican Revolution* (New York, 1969); Jean Meyer, *La Cristiada*, 3 vols. (Mexico, 1974); Luis González, *Pueblo en vilo* (Mexico, 1968); Paul Friedrich, *Agrarian revolt in a Mexican village* (Englewood Cliffs, 1970); Frans J. Schryer, *The rancheros of the Pisaflores* (Toronto, 1980); and Moisés González Navarro, 'La vida social', in Daniel Cosío Villegas, *Historia Moderna de México; el Porfiriato* (Mexico, 1957). Friedrich Katz, 'Labour conditions on haciendas in Porfirian Mexico: some trends and tendencies', *HAHR*, 54/1 (1974), 1–47, is indispensable.

Scholarly work on Guatemala and Central America is often not possible and understandably not abundant. Severo Martínez Peláez, *La patria del criollo* (Guatemala, 1971) has some material on the nineteenth century. Also useful are David Browning, *El Salvador, landscape and society* (Oxford, 1971); Ciro F. S. Cardoso, 'La formacíon de la hacienda cafetalera costarricense en el siglo XIX' in Enrique Florescano (ed.), *Haciendas, latifundios, y plantaciones*; and David J. McCreery, 'Coffee and class: the structure and development in liberal Guatemala', *HAHR*, 56/3 (1976). The research of Julio Castellanos Cambranes is beginning to appear in print.

Work on Peru has benefited from the recently created *Archivo del Fuero Agrario* (*AFA*) in Lima, a repository of hacienda and plantation records confiscated during the 1969 agrarian reform, and the scholarly leadership of Pablo Macera at the University of San Marcos and José Matos Mar of the Institute of Peruvian Studies. Because the best records in the *AFA* were kept by the north coast sugar plantations, work has tended to concentrate on that zone; but students from France, Britain and the U.S.A. as well as the new generation of Peruvians are creating a rural history where none existed. Among the most useful are: Henri Favre, Colin Delavaud, José Matos Mar, *La hacienda en el Perú* (Lima, 1967); Juan Martínez-Alier, *Haciendas, plantations and collective farms* (London, 1977); Benjamin Orlove and G. Custred (eds.), *Land and power in Latin America: agrarian economies and social processes in the Andes* (New York, 1980); Jean Piel, 'A propos d'un soulèvement rural peruvien au début de vingtiéme siècle: Tocroyoc (1921)', *Revue d'Histoire Moderne et Contemporaine*, 14 (1967); Wilfredo Kapsoli, *Los movimientos campesinos en Cerro de Pasco 1880–1963* (Lima, 1972). For the north coast plantation, see: Pablo Macera, *Cayaltií 1875–1920: organización del trabajo en una plantación azucarera del Perú* (Lima, 1975); Bill Albert, *The Peruvian sugar industry 1880–1920* (Norwich, 1976); Peter Klarén, 'The social and economic consequences of modernization in the Peruvian sugar industry, 1870–1930', in Duncan and Rutledge (eds.), *Land and labour*; Peter Blanchard, 'The recruitment of workers in the Peruvian sierra at the turn of the century: the enganche system,' *Inter-American Economic Affairs*, 33/3 (1980); Michael J. Gonzalez, *Plantation agriculture and social control in northern Peru, 1875–1933* (Austin, 1984). Also see, Florencia C. Mallon, *The defence of community in Peru's Central Highlands. Peasant struggle and capitalist transition, 1860–1940* (Princeton, 1983). Work parallel to this in the sugar zone of Tucumán, Argentina, is Donna Guy, 'The rural working class in nineteenth century Argentina: forced plantation labor in Tucumán',

LARR, 13/1 (1978) and Jorge Balán, 'Migraciones, mano de obra y formación de un proletariado rural en Tucumán, Argentina, 1870–1914', *Demografía y Economía*, 10/2 (1976).

On Ecuador and Colombia, see Rafael Baraona, 'Una tipología de haciendas en la sierra ecuatoriana', in Oscar Delgado (ed.), *Las reformas agrarias en la América Latina* (Mexico, 1965); Michael Taussig, 'The evolution of rural wage labour in the Cauca Valley of Colombia, 1700–1970', in Duncan and Rutledge (eds.), *Land and labour*; Malcolm Deas, 'A Colombian coffee estate: Santa Bárbara, Cundinamarca, 1870–1912', in *ibid.*,; David C. Johnson, 'Economic and social change in nineteenth century Colombia: Santander, 1850–1885' (unpublished Ph.D. thesis, Berkeley, 1977); Pierre Gilhodes, 'Agrarian struggles in Colombia', in R. Stavenhagen (ed.), *Agrarian problems and peasant movements in Latin America* (Garden City, N.Y., 1970); Marco Palacios, *Coffee in Colombia, 1850–1970* (Cambridge, 1980); William P. McGreevey, *An economic history of Colombia* (Cambridge, 1971); Charles Bergquist, *Coffee and conflict in Colombia, 1886–1910* (Durham, N.C., 1978); Catherine Legrand, 'From public lands into private properties: landholding and rural conflict in Colombia, 1870–1936' (unpublished Ph.D. thesis, Stanford University, 1980).

New work on Bolivia includes Ramiro Condarco Morales, *Zarate 'El Temible' Wilke: historia de la rebelión indígena de 1899* (La Paz, 1965); Erwin P. Greishaber, 'Survival of Indian communities in nineteenth-century Bolivia: a regional comparison', *JLAS*, 12/2 (1980); Silvia Rivera Cisicanqui, 'La expansión del latifundio en el altiplano boliviano: elementos para la caracterización de una oligarquía regional', *Avances* (La Paz), 2 (1978); Andrew Pearse, 'Peasants and revolution: the case of Bolivia', *Economy and Society*, 1/3 (1972). For Chile, see C. Kay already cited; Brian Loveman, *Struggle in the countryside: politics and rural labor in Chile, 1919–1973* (Bloomington, 1976); A. J. Bauer, *Chilean rural society from the Spanish Conquest to 1930* (Cambridge, 1975); and Maurice Zeitlin, *The Civil Wars in Chile: the bourgeois revolutions that never were* (Princeton, 1984).

6. PLANTATION ECONOMIES AND SOCIETIES IN THE SPANISH CARIBBEAN, 1860–1930

For a discussion of the bibliography on the history of sugar in Cuba, Puerto Rico and the Dominican Republic in the period *c.* 1860–1930, see *CHLA* v, bibliographical essays 5, 6 and 7.

7. THE GROWTH OF LATIN AMERICAN CITIES, 1870–1930

By way of introduction, several important studies on Latin American cities, which range beyond the period 1870–1930, are particularly useful: Jorge Enrique Hardoy (ed.), *Urbanization in Latin America: approaches and issues* (New York, 1975), especially the articles by Hardoy and by Richard M. Morse; Richard M. Morse (ed.), *Las ciudades latinoamericanas* (2 vols.; Mexico, 1973), I, *Antecedentes*. II, *Desarrollo histórico*; and José Luis Romero, *Latinoamérica: las ciudades y las ideas* (Mexico, 1976). In addition, useful items appear in the following collections: Institut des Hautes Études de l'Amérique Latine, *Villes et régions en Amérique Latine* (Paris, 1970; Spanish transl., Mexico, 1973), with studies on Cuzco, Medellín, Guadalajara and the Brazilian cities of Minas Gerais; and Richard P. Schaedel, Jorge E. Hardoy and Nora Scott Kinzer (eds.), *Urbanization in the Americas from its beginnings to the present* (The Hague, 1978), especially the articles by Alejandro Rofman, Richard M. Morse, James R. Scobie, Roberto Cortés Conde and Nancy López de Nisnovich, Spencer L. Leitman and Jorge Balán.

For general background on the problems and issues of urbanization in this period, readers will find insights from disciplines outside history to be extremely helpful. The sociologists have been the most productive, starting with early influential studies such as Andrew H. Whiteford, *Two cities of Latin America: a comparative description of social classes* (Beloit, Wisconsin, 1960), a stimulating comparison of Popayán, Colombia, and Querétaro, Mexico, which has since been refocused on Popayán alone in *An Andean city at mid-century: a traditional urban society* (East Lansing, Michigan, 1977); Phillip M. Hauser and Leo F. Schnore (eds.), *The study of urbanization* (New York, 1965), especially the chapters by Gideon Sjoberg and by Schnore; and Gerald Breese (ed.), *Urbanization in newly developing countries* (Englewood Cliffs, N.J., 1969). Other significant work by sociologists includes John Walton, *Elites and economic development: comparative studies on the political economy of Latin American cities* (Austin, 1977), and Bryan Roberts, *Cities of peasants. The political economy of urbanization in the Third World* (London, 1978), as well as the more specialized studies of José Luis de Imaz, *Estructura social de una ciudad pampeana* (2 vols., Buenos Aires, 1965) and Mary C. Megee, *Monterrey, Mexico: internal patterns and external relations* (Chicago, 1958). Useful case studies by economists that measure contemporary developments against an historical background include Arthur S. Morris, 'Urban growth patterns in Latin America with illustrations from Caracas', *Urban Studies*, 15/3 (1978), 299–312; Pedro Pinchas Geiger, *Evolução da rede urbana brasileira* (Rio de Janeiro, 1963), and Martin T. Katzman's chapter in John D. Wirth and Robert L. Jones (ed.), *Manchester and São Paulo: problems of rapid urban growth* (Stanford, 1977). Anthropological insights are effectively summarized in Richard P. Schaedel, 'The anthropological study of Latin American cities in intra- and interdisciplinary perspective', *Urban Anthropology*, 3/2 (1974), 139–70. In an important early work, *Town and country in Brazil* (New York, 1956), Marvin Harris made interesting use of anthropological field work to produce an historical analysis of society in a small Brazilian town. Similar studies include Ruben Reina's analysis of a provincial capital in *Paraná: social boundaries in an Argentine city* (Austin, 1973) and Eugene A. Hammel, *Power in Ica: the structural history of a Peruvian community* (Boston, 1969). Another model case study has been provided by a geographer, Charles S. Sargent, *The spatial evolution of Greater Buenos Aires, 1870–1930* (Tempe, Arizona, 1974). Studies by architects and city planners naturally contribute valuable information on urban developments. Representative studies include Peter W. Amato, *An analysis of the patterns of elite residential areas in Bogotá, Colombia* (Ithaca, 1968); Carlos Altezar and Hugo Barachini, *Historia urbanística y edilicia de la ciudad de Montevideo desde su fundación colonial hasta nuestros días* (Montevideo, 1971); José Xavier Martini and José María Peña, *La ornamentación en la arquitectura de Buenos Aires* (2 vols., Buenos Aires, 1966–67), I, *1800–1900*, II, *1900–1940*; and Carlos Martínez, *Bogotá: sinopsis sobre su evolución urbana, 1536–1900*. I (Bogotá, 1976).

Extremely useful for orientation, both for bibliography and for thematic and methodological suggestions, are the series of articles by Richard M. Morse in the *LARR*: 1/1 (1965), 35–74; 6/1 (1971), 3–52; and 6/2 (1971), 19–75. Several other helpful articles by Morse include 'The development of urban systems in the Americas in the nineteenth century', *JIAS*, 17/1 (1975), 4–26; 'Latin American cities; aspects of function and structure', *Comparative Studies in Society and History*, 4 (1961–2), 473–93, and 'Trends and patterns of Latin American urbanization, 1750–1920' in that same journal, 16/4 (1974), 416–47; 'Primacia, regionalización, dependencia: enfoques sobre las ciudades latino-americanas en el desarrollo nacional', *Desarrollo Económico*, 11/41, (1971), 55–85; and 'A prolegomenon to Latin American urban history', *HAHR*, 52/3 (1972), 359–94. Eugene F. Sofer and Mark D. Szuchman have added another provocative piece with 'City and society: their connection in Latin American historical research', *LARR*, 14/2 (1979), 113–29. An important departure point for general bibliographical information is provided by Martin H. Sable, *Latin American urbanization* (Metuchen, N.J., 1971). The investigator needs also to refer to ongoing publications, including *Latin American urban research* (6 vols., Beverly Hills, 1971–78); *Urban history yearbook* (Leicester, 1974–); *Urbanism past and present* (Milwaukee, 1976–); and the *Journal of Urban History* (Beverly Hills, 1974–).

The numbers and definitions for urban populations, as has been suggested (see *CHLA* iv, chap. 7, note 2), prove exasperatingly elusive. The investigator will first want to consult the following valuable efforts to piece together sources and evaluate materials: the previously mentioned Vol. ii of *Las ciudades latinoamericanas*, edited by Morse, which provides information on the major cities of Argentina, Brazil, Chile, Colombia, Cuba, Mexico, Peru and Venezuela between 1750 and 1920; Richard E. Boyer and Keith A. Davies, *Urbanization in nineteenth-century Latin America: statistics and sources* (Los Angeles, 1973), with data on major cities in Argentina, Brazil, Mexico, and Peru; and Jorge Enrique Hardoy and María Elena Langdon, 'Análisis estadístico preliminar de la urbanización de América Latina entre 1850 y 1930', *Revista Paraguaya de Sociología*, 42–43 (1978), 115–73, which provides discussion and tables of average national growth rates, growth of major cities and indexes of primacy involving the four largest cities. Nicolás Sánchez-Albornoz, *The population of Latin America. A history* (Berkeley, 1974) is a thorough analysis by an outstanding historian and demographer of general population trends. Other useful guides to more specialized problems include Alejandro Moreno Toscano, 'Cambios en los patrones de organización en México, 1810–1910', *HM*, 22/2 (1972), 160–87; Richard E. Boyer, 'Las ciudades mexicanas: perspectivas de estudios en el siglo XIX', appearing in the same issue of *HM*, 22/2 142–59; Richard W. Wilkie, 'Urban growth and the transformation of the settlement landscape of Mexico, 1910–1970', in James Wilkie and Michael Meyers (eds.), *Contemporary Mexico* (Berkeley, 1976), 99–134; Keith A. Davies, 'Tendencias demográficas urbanas durante el siglo XIX en México', *HM*, 21/3 (1972), 481–524; and Zulma L. Recchini de Lattes, *Aspectos demográficos de la urbanización en la Argentina, 1869–1960* (Buenos Aires, 1973).

General works on individual Latin American countries often contain considerable information on urbanization patterns. Among works that should be consulted in this regard are William P. McGreevey, *An economic history of Colombia, 1845–1930* (Cambridge, 1971); Rory Miller, Clifford T. Smith and John Fisher (eds.), *Social and economic change in modern Peru* (Liverpool, 1976), especially the articles by Rosemary Thorp and Geoffrey Bertram, and by Bryan B. Roberts; Carlos F. Díaz Alejandro, *Essays on the economic history of the Argentine Republic* (New Haven, 1970); Ricardo M. Ortiz, *Historia económica de la Argentina, 1850– 1930* (2 vols., Buenos Aires, 1955); James R. Scobie, *Argentina: a city and a nation* (2nd edn, New York, 1971); Manuel Diégues Júnior, *Imigração, urbanisação e industrialização* (São Paulo, 1964); Richard Graham, *Britain and the onset of modernization in Brazil, 1850–1914* (Cambridge, 1968); Tulio Halperín Donghi, *Historia contemporánea de América Latina* (Madrid, 1969); and T. Lynn Smith, *Brazil, people and institutions* (4th edn, Baton Rouge, 1972).

A number of urban histories of Latin American cities cover a more extended period than that treated in this chapter. Among those that have chapters or sections dealing with the years 1870 to 1930 are Richard M. Morse, *From community to metropolis: a biography of São Paulo* (Gainesville, 1958; reprint, New York, 1971; Portuguese transl., São Paulo, 1970); Guy Bourdé, *Urbanisation et immigration en Amérique Latine: Buenos Aires* (Paris, 1974); the works by José Luis de Imaz and Ruben Reina, already cited, dealing with the Argentine cities of Río Cuarto and Paraná; Claude Bataillon, *Ville et campagnes dans la région de México* (Paris, 1971; Spanish transl., México, 1973); Claude Bataillon and Hélène Rivière d'Arc, *Les grandes villes du monde: México* (Paris, 1973; Spanish transl., México, 1973); Hélène Rivière d'Arc, *Guadalajara et sa région* (Paris, 1971; Spanish transl., Mexico, 1973); Theodore E. Nichols, *Tres puertos de Colombia: estudio sobre el desarrollo de Cartagena, Santa Marta, y Barranquilla* (Bogotá, 1973); and Yves Leloup, *Les villes du Minas Gerais* (Paris, 1970).

Books which deal largely with the years 1870 to 1930 include Warren Dean, *The industrialization of São Paulo, 1880–1945* (Austin, 1969); Mark D. Szuchman, *Mobility and integration in urban Argentina: Córdoba in the liberal era* (Austin, 1980); Richard M. Morse (ed.), *Lima en 1900: estudio crítico y antología* (Lima, 1973), which focuses on excerpts from Joaquin Capelo's major study, *Sociología de Lima* (4 vols., Lima, 1895–1902); James R. Scobie, *Buenos Aires, plaza to suburb, 1870–1910* (New York, 1974; Spanish transl., Buenos Aires, 1977); and Eugene F. Sofer, *From Pale to Pampa: The Jewish immigrant experience in Buenos Aires* (New York, 1980). See also the following articles: Bainbridge Cowell, Jr, 'Cityward migration in the

nineteenth century: the case of Recife, Brazil', *JIAS*, 17/1 (1975), 43–63;
E. Jeffrey Stann, 'Transportation and urbanization in Caracas, 1891–
1936', in the same issue of *JIAS*, 82–100; Gerald M. Greenfield,
'Dependency and the urban experience: São Paulo's public service
sector, 1885–1913', *JLAS*, 10/1 (1978), 37–59; and Emília Viotti da
Costa, 'Urbanización en el Brasil del siglo XIX', in Francisco de Solano
(ed.), *Estudios sobre la ciudad iberoamericana* (Madrid, 1975), 399–432.

8. INDUSTRY IN LATIN AMERICA BEFORE 1930

A notable impulse to the study of the early history of industry in Latin
America was given by the official reports and policy documents
published by the United Nations Economic Commission for Latin
America (*Comisión Económica Para América Latina*) during the 1950s,
1960s and after. Another was given by the dependency debate launched
during the 1960s, partly in response to ECLA (*CEPAL*) structuralist
approaches to the subject. Although much has been written in recent
decades, Celso Furtado, *Economic development of Latin America: historical
background and contemporary problems* (2nd edn, Cambridge, 1977) remains
the most succinct statement of *cepalista* hypotheses. Establishing the
primacy of the 1930s as a departure point in Latin America's process of
industrialization, Furtado absorbs elements of the revisionist challenge
to this chronology and demonstrates the achievements of manufacturing
in the larger economies by 1929. Comprehensive national studies of the
same school are: Aldo Ferrer, *The Argentine economy* (Berkeley, 1967);
Celso Furtado, *Economic growth of Brazil* (Berkeley, 1965); Aníbal Pinto,
Chile: un caso de desarrollo frustrado (Santiago, 1962). An early strident
presentation of the dependency perspective is set out in André Gunder
Frank, *Capitalism and underdevelopment in Latin America: historical studies of
Chile and Brazil* (New York, 1969) which argues that the world
depression of 1929 shattered Latin America's foreign trade sector and
triggered the drive to industrialize. For similar, but distinct, emphases
see the excellent continental survey by Ciro F. S. Cardoso and H. Pérez
Brignoli, *Historia económica de América Latina*, II (Barcelona, 1979) and
the now classic text J. V. Levin, *The export economies: their pattern of
development in historical perspective* (Cambridge, Mass., 1960). Located
within a dependency framework, F. H. Cardoso and E. Faletto,
Dependency and development in Latin America (Berkeley, 1979) stresses

formative developments in manufacturing during the phase of export-led growth.

Much of this scholarship addresses themes far beyond industry and industrialization. However, structuralist and dependency writing provoked a response from all sides. Rooted in classical economics and copiously endowed with statistical material is the *ad hoc* series published at New Haven by the Yale University Press under the auspices of the Economic Growth Center: W. Baer, *Industrialization and economic development in Brazil* (1965); T. B. Birnberg and S. A. Resnick, *Colonial development: an econometric study* (1975); C. F. Díaz Alejandro, *Essays on the economic history of the Argentine Republic* (1970); M. J. Mamalakis, *The growth and structure of the Chilean economy: from independence to Allende* (1976); C. W. Reynolds, *The Mexican economy: twentieth-century structure and growth* (1970). But the new revisionism in the debate about industry and industrialism in Latin America can be more precisely dated with the appearance of the seminal study by Warren Dean, *The industrialization of São Paulo, 1880–1945* (Austin, 1969). Dean argued plausibly that the pace of pre-Second World War industrialization proceeded most rapidly during periods of export-led growth and sparked a controversy which has yielded a large corpus of literature concerned either to vindicate earlier views or to sustain revisionist hypotheses. Notable contributions are A. Fishlow, 'Origins and consequences of import substitution in Brazil', in E. Di Marco (ed.), *International economics and development: essays in honour of Raul Prebisch* (New York, 1972); W. Cano, *Raízes da concentração industrial em São Paulo* (São Paulo, 1977); J. M. Cardoso de Mello, *O capitalismo tardio: contribução à revisão crítica da formação e desenvolvimento da economía brasileira* (São Paulo, 1982); and F. R. Versiani, 'Before the depression: Brazilian industry in the 1920s', in R. Thorp (ed.), *Latin America in the 1930s: the role of the periphery in world crisis* (London, 1984). Also linking the emergence of a manufacturing base to the dynamic coffee sector are descriptive studies like A. C. Castro, *As empresas estrangeiras no Brasil, 1860–1913* (São Paulo, 1979) and S. Silva, *Expansão cafeeira e orígens da indústria no Brasil* (São Paulo, 1976). These works represent an advance upon dated but valued examples of an earlier historiographical tradition such as N. Vilela Luz, *A luta pela industrialização do Brasil, 1808 à 1930* (São Paulo, 1961). Noteworthy industrial case-studies written from a revisionist perspective have also appeared, for example F. R. Versiani, *Industrial investment in an 'export' economy: the Brazilian experience before 1914* (London, 1979), which adds a quantitative dimension to pioneering work by S. J. Stein, *The Brazilian cotton manufacture: textile enterprise in an underdeveloped area, 1850–1950* (Cambridge, Mass., 1957) and A. P. Canabrava, *O desenvolvimento do algodão na província de São Paulo, 1861–1875* (São Paulo, 1951).

The quality of the discourse, and indeed the length of the bibliography, relating to the early industrial expansion of Brazil is matched only by that of the writing on Chile. Since the 1960s several texts have been published which directly address the question of manufacturing and industrial expansion before 1930. Most, though not all, argue that the First World War was an important watershed for Chile. See M. Carmagnani, *Sviluppo industriale e sottosviluppo economico il caso chileno, 1860–1930* (Turin, 1971); C. Hurtado, *Concentración de la población y desarrollo económico: el caso chileño* (Santiago, 1966); H. W. Kirsch, *Industrial development in a traditional society: the conflict of entrepreneurship and modernization in Chile* (Gainesville, 1977); R. Lagos, *La industria en Chile: antecedentes estructurales* (Santiago, 1966); O. Muñoz, *Crecimiento industrial de Chile, 1914–1965* (Santiago, 1968) and *Proceso de la industrialización chilena* (Santiago, 1972). Several of these studies may be described as either neo-structuralist or 'late' dependency.

For other countries the literature is less direct, more diffuse. In addition to the material cited above, general information on Mexican industry during the period before 1930 may be gleaned from W. P. Glade and C. W. Anderson, *The political economy of Mexico* (Madison, 1963) and L. Solís, *La realidad económica mexicana: retrovisión y perspectivas* (Mexico, 1970). In addition two excellent collections of essays, written from different perspectives, contain valuable statistical material: C. Cardoso (ed.), *México en el siglo XIX (1821–1910)* (Mexico, 1980) and E. Pérez López (ed.), *Mexico's recent economic growth: the Mexican view* (Austin, 1967). For an earlier period the exemplary study by R. A. Potash, *El Banco de Avío de México: el fomento de la industria, 1821–46* (Mexico, 1959) indicates what may be accomplished. As in Brazil, the textile industry has absorbed scholarly interest: see, for example, D. Keremitis, *La industria textil en el siglo XIX* (Mexico, 1973).

Diffusionist precepts permeate much of the recent general work on Argentina: see Díaz Alejandro, *Essays*, cited above; R. Cortés Conde, *El progreso argentino, 1880–1914* (Buenos Aires, 1979); R. Cortés Conde and E. Gallo, *La formación de la Argentina moderna* (Buenos Aires, 1967); E. Gallo, 'Agrarian expansion and industrial development in Argentina

1880–1930', in Raymond Carr (ed.), *Latin American Affairs. St Antony's Papers, No. 22* (Oxford, 1970); V. Vázquez-Presedo, *El caso argentino: migración de factores, comercio exterior y desarrollo, 1875–1914* (Buenos Aires, 1971) and *Crisis y retraso* (Buenos Aires, 1978); and G. Di Tella and M. Zymelman, *Las etapas del dessarrollo económico argentino* (Buenos Aires, 1967). These works locate the modern origins of Argentine industry firmly in the phase of export expansion. Di Tella and Zymelman, drawing upon modernization theories prevalent during the 1950s and early 1960s, attempt to create a revised Rostovian stage theory for Argentina, arguing that the pre-conditions for industrialization already existed by 1914, but that self-sustained development did not take place until after 1930. Other authors take a less negative view of the 1920s.

Elsewhere the literature is even more fragmented and the subject of industry has been addressed only obliquely. Reflecting the small size of the manufacturing sector, little specific material is contained in an otherwise excellent collection of monographs on Colombia: R. Brew, *El desarrollo económico de Antioquia desde la independencia hasta 1920* (Bogotá, 1977); D. Chu, *The Great Depression and industrialization in Colombia* (Santa Monica, 1977); W. P. McGreevey, *An economic history of Colombia, 1845–1930* (Cambridge, 1971); M. Palacios, *Coffee in Colombia, 1870–1970: an economic, social and political history* (Cambridge, 1980); Frank Safford, *The ideal of the practical: Colombia's struggle to form a technical elite* (Austin, 1976). Disputing the hypothesis of Levin in *The export economies*, cited above, S. J. Hunt, *Growth and guano in nineteenth-century Peru* (Princeton, 1972) presents a more positive analysis of the environment within which manufacturing may have emerged in Peru by the turn of the century. Differing assessments of Peru's industrial potential are available in H. Bonilla, *Guano y burguesía* (Lima, 1973) and E. Yepes del Castillo, *Perú 1820–1920: un siglo de desarrollo capitalista* (Lima, 1972). See also Thorp and Bertram, *Peru 1890–1977*, cited below.

Several authors have sought to integrate structuralist and dependency maxims with post-Dean revisionism (and even earlier descriptive accounts of manufacturing and industrialization). The most successful is F. S. Weaver, *Class, state and industrial structure: the historical process of South American industrial growth* (Westport, 1980). Equally impressive national surveys elaborated from diverse methodological and ideological frameworks are R. Thorp and G. Bertram, *Peru 1890–1977: growth and policy in an open economy* (London, 1978) which presents much valuable data on the condition of manufacturing, and J. G. Palma, 'External disequilibrium and internal industrialization: Chile, 1914–1935', in C. Abel and C. M. Lewis (eds.), *Latin America, economic imperialism and the state: the political economy of the external connection from independence to the present* (London, 1985). Less concerned to integrate, and more inclined to refute, earlier perceptions is N. H. Leff, *Underdevelopment and development in Brazil* (2 vols., London, 1982) who juxtaposes a number of interpretations of Brazilian history.

These recent works have revived interest in the neglected writings of Latin American scholars who either detailed manufacturing developments or advanced programmes to promote industrialization during the period before 1930. Notable examples of such scholarship include A. E. Bunge, *La economía argentina* (4 vols., Buenos Aires, 1928–30) and *Los problemas económicos del presente* (Buenos Aires, 1920); F. A. Encina, *Nuestra inferioridad económica* (Santiago, 1912); and A. Molina Enríquez, *Los grandes problemas nacionales* (Mexico, 1909) which commanded continent-wide attention. Of national significance were works such as F. Alayza Paz Soldan, *La industria: estudio económico, técnico y social* (Lima, 1933); P. L. Gonzalez, *Chile industrial* (Santiago, 1916); A. Garland, *Reseña industrial del Perú* (Lima, 1902); J. Martínez Lamas, *Riqueza y pobreza del Uruguay* (Montevideo, 1930); O. Morató, *La industria manufacturera en el Uruguay* (Montevideo, 1927). See also A. Dorfman, *Evolución de la economía industrial argentina* (Buenos Aires, 1938) and R. C. Simonsen, *A indústria em face da economía nacional* (São Paulo, 1937).

Contemporary studies often drew upon an expanding body of statistical data compiled by various government agencies. Although most Latin American states did not begin to accumulate macroeconomic data on a regular basis until the 1930s, earlier national censuses such as those taken in Argentina in 1895 and 1914, or in Brazil in 1890 and 1920 contained valuable – if not always reliable – information. Equally, partial industrial surveys were conducted during the early decades of the twentieth century, such as that taken in Medellín, Colombia, in 1922. Similar material is available in official surveys and reports of the period produced by the British Board of Trade and the U.S. Department of Commerce. These data were occasionally incorporated into texts such as F. L. Bell, *Colombia: a commercial and industrial handbook* (Washington, D.C., 1923); W. H. Koebel, *South America: an industrial and commercial field* (London, 1919); D. M. Phelps, *Migration of industry to South America* (New York, 1936); G. Wythe, *Industry in Latin America* (New York, 1945); and L. J. Hughlett (ed.), *Industrialization of Latin America* (New York, 1946).

A number of specific themes have tended to dominate revisionist approaches to the subject. Much has been written, for example, about the consequences of the First World War. In addition to the studies on Brazil and Chile listed above, see R. Miller, 'Latin American manufacturing and the First World War: an exploratory essay', *World Development*, 9/8 (1981) for a cautious appraisal. Discussions of even earlier exogenous shocks feature in, for example, J. C. Chiaramonte, *Nacionalismo y liberalismo económicos en Argentina, 1860–1880* (Buenos Aires, 1971). The effect of the Baring Crisis is addressed in the writing of Cortés Conde, Gallo and others cited above. There is some discussion of government policy and the growth of manufacturing in G. Ranis (ed.), *Government and economic development* (New Haven, 1971) and in various other works, not least Weaver, *Class, state and industrial structure*. However, the most outstanding investigation of policy is A. V. Villela and W. Suzigan, *Política do governo e crescimento da economía brasileira, 1889–1945* (Rio de Janeiro, 1973) which offers a model analysis and establishes a framework that has a general significance for countries other than Brazil. Potash, *El Banco de Avío de México* is equally valuable for the early nineteenth century. On Argentina, see also D. J. Guy, 'Carlos Pellegrini and the politics of early industrialization, 1873–1906', *JLAS*, 11/1 (1979). Many policy issues are addressed in several excellent essays in Thorp (ed.), *Latin America in the 1930s*. Tariffs, money supply and exchange rates are areas of policy formation that have received specific attention. Dated, but nevertheless outstanding in the field, is L. Ospina Vásquez, *Industria y protección en Colombia* (Medellín, 1955). J. C. Nicolau, *Industria argentina y aduana, 1835–54* (Buenos Aires, 1975) is an important study as is Chiaramonte, *Nacionalismo y liberalismo*. On Brazil, besides the work of F. R. Versiani, see also M. T. R. O. Versiani, *Proteção tarifária e o crecimento industrial brasileiro dos anos 1906–1912* (Brasília, 1981). The influence of money supply and currency policy upon the general level of economic activity is addressed by C. M. Peláez and W. Suzigan, *História monetária do Brasil: análise da política, comportamento e instituições monetárias* (Rio de Janeiro, 1976). Also useful are J. Pandía Calógeras, *A política monetária do Brasil* (São Paulo, 1960); C. M. Peláez, *The economic consequences of monetary, fiscal and exchange orthodoxy in Brazil, 1889–1945* (Rio de Janeiro, 1971) and E. A. Cardoso, 'Exchange rates in nineteenth-century Brazil: an econometric model', *Journal of Development Studies*, 19/2 (1983). See also essays in E. Fernández-Hurtado (ed.), *Cincuenta años del banco central* (Mexico, 1976) for some discussion of monetary policy and manufacturing in Mexico during the 1920s. Conventional currency and banking histories exist for most Latin American republics but are less direct. Brazil is exceptional in the quality of the material relating to money supply, the exchange and industry.

Complementing the institutional focus of policy-orientated studies is O. Ianni, *Industrialização e desenvolvimento social no Brasil* (Rio de Janeiro, 1963) which, although largely outside the period, offers some insights into societal aspects of industrialization. Also useful in this respect are Weaver, Kirsch and Bonilla, cited above. Orthodox accounts that stress the role of immigrant entrepreneurs and external influences in early manufacturing are provided by Díaz Alejandro, *Essays*; R. Graham, *Britain and the onset of modernization in Brazil, 1850–1914* (Cambridge, 1968); and V. B. Reber, *British mercantile houses in Buenos Aires, 1810–1880* (Cambridge, Mass., 1979). And see Dean, *Industrialisation of São Paulo*. National contributions to early industrial growth are emphasized by L. Ortega, 'Nitrates, Chilean entrepreneurs and the origins of the War of the Pacific', *JLAS*, 16/2 (1984), as well as by Cano and Cardoso de Mello, cited above. Yet much remains to be done on the social origins and membership of industrial organizations like the Club (later Unión) Industrial Argentina, founded in Argentina in 1875, and Chile's Sociedad de Fomento Fabril, organized in 1883, which were established in most Latin American countries by the turn of the century. More has been achieved in terms of labour, despite the post-1930 focus of most writing, the non-industrial emphases of several works and the novelty of the subject, all of which preclude generalization. And the debate about labour and industrial growth has expanded to include direct discussion of wage rates and salaries, factors that influenced the elasticity of demand for manufactures. For the bibliography on the urban working class and the early labour movements in Latin America, see *CHLA* IV, bibliographical essay 9.

9. THE URBAN WORKING CLASS AND EARLY LATIN AMERICAN LABOUR MOVEMENTS, 1880–1930

There are several general histories of the Latin American labour movements that cover the pre-1930 period. Among the more recent are Hobart A. Spalding, Jr, *Organized labor in Latin America* (New York, 1977), and Julio Godio, *Historia del movimiento obrero latinoamericano* (2 vols., Mexico City, 1980–3). The first volume of the work by Godio deals with the movements in Argentina, Mexico and Chile up to 1918, while the second treats communism and nationalism for the region as a whole between 1918 and 1930. Robert Paris and Madeleine Rebérioux provide an informative shorter survey, 'Socialisme et communisme en Amérique latine', in *Histoire générale du socialisme*, Jacques Droz (ed.) (Paris, 1978), IV, 165–255.

The most comprehensive bibliography remains Carlos Rama, *L'Amérique latine: 1492–1936* (Mouvements ouvriers et socialistes, V, Paris, 1959). There is a later German edition: *Die Arbeiterbewegung in Lateinamerika. Chronologie und Bibliographie, 1492–1966* (Bad Homburg, 1967). Additional material can be found in Kenneth Paul Erickson, Patrick V. Peppe and Hobart A. Spalding, Jr, 'Research on the urban working class and organized labor in Argentina, Brazil, and Chile: what is left to be done?', *LARR*, 9/2 (1974), 115–42.

The largest collection of the early Latin American labour press is to be found at the International Institute of Social History in Amsterdam. The holdings for the larger countries are described in Eric Gordon, Michael Hall and Hobart A. Spalding, Jr, 'A survey of Brazilian and Argentine materials at the International Instituut voor Sociale Geschiedenis in Amsterdam', *LARR*, 8/3 (1973), 27–77, and in Raymond Buve and Cunera Holthuis, 'A survey of Mexican materials at the International Instituut voor Sociale Geschiedenis in Amsterdam', *LARR*, 10/1 (1975), 155–68.

Works on specific topics which deal with Latin America as a whole include Carlos M. Rama (ed.), *Utopismo socialista, 1830–1893* (Caracas, 1977), which reprints several important documents of the early period. Alfredo Gómez attempts a continent-wide survey of anarchism and anarcho-syndicalism in his *Anarquismo y anarcosindicalismo en América Latina* (Paris, 1980). There are two general treatments of the Communist movement, both of which include considerable information on the pre-1930 period: Robert J. Alexander, *Communism in Latin America* (New Brunswick, 1957), and Boris Goldenberg, *Kommunismus in Lateinamerika* (Stuttgart, 1971).

The main currents of the Argentine labour movement are represented in several informative, though sometimes highly partisan works. Diego Abad de Santillán describes the anarchist movement in *La F.O.R.A., ideología y trayectoria del movimiento obrero revolucionario en la Argentina* (Buenos Aires, 1933; 2nd edn, 1971). Sebastián Marotta presents a syndicalist view in *El movimiento sindical argentino, su génesis y desarrollo* (2 vols., Buenos Aires, 1960–61). The most influential socialist history is Jacinto Oddone, *El gremialismo proletario argentino* (Buenos Aires, 1949). On the socialists, see also Dardo Cúneo, *Juan B. Justo y las luchas sociales en la Argentina* (Buenos Aires, 1956) and Richard Walter, *The Socialist Party of Argentina, 1890–1930* (Austin, 1977).

The most helpful bibliography is Leandro Gutiérrez, *Recopilación bibliográfica y de fuentes para el estudio de la historia y situación actual de la clase obrera argentina* (Instituto Torcuato di Tella, Buenos Aires, 1969). Documents dealing with various aspects of the labour movement are reprinted in Hobart A. Spalding, Jr (ed.), *La clase trabajadora argentina. Documentos para su historia, 1890–1912* (Buenos Aires, 1970). Guy Bourdé, *Urbanisation et immigration en Amérique Latine: Buenos Aires (XIXe et XXe siècles)* (Paris, 1974), James R. Scobie, *Buenos Aires: plaza to suburb, 1870–1910* (New York, 1974), and José Panettieri, *Los trabajadores en tiempo de la inmigración masiva en Argentina 1870–1910* (Buenos Aires, 1967) include considerable information on living and working conditions. Donna J. Guy analyses the role of women in 'Women, peonage, and industrialization: Argentina, 1810–1914', *LARR*, 16/3 (1981), 65–89.

On the early period of the labour movement, see José Ratzer, *Los marxistas argentinos del 90* (Córdoba, 1969), and Gonzalo Zaragoza Ruvira, 'Anarchisme et mouvement ouvrier en Argentine à la fin du XIXe siècle', *Le mouvement social*, 103 (1978), 7–28. An important local study is Hilda Iparraguirre and Ofelia Pianetto, *La organización de la clase obrera en Córdoba, 1870–1895* (Córdoba, 1968).

Iaacov Oved provides a very well-documented account of the anarchist movement at the beginning of the twentieth century in *El anarquismo y el movimiento obrero en Argentina* (Mexico City, 1978). Among the several works of Osvaldo Bayer on aspects of anarchism in Argentina, see especially *Severino di Giovanni, el idealista de la violencia* (Buenos Aires, 1970), and *Los vengadores de la Patagonia trágica* (2 vols., Buenos Aires, 1972).

For the period after 1917, see Julio Godio, *La semana trágica de 1919* (Buenos Aires, 1971), Emilio J. Corbière, 'La fundación del P.C., 1917–1920', *Todo es historia*, 106 (1976), 7–31, and David Rock, *Politics in Argentina, 1890–1930* (Cambridge, 1975).

There are several general accounts of the early Brazilian labour movement: Boris Fausto, *Trabalho urbano e conflito social (1890–1920)* (São Paulo, 1976), Francisco Foot Hardman and Victor Leonardi, *História da indústria e do trabalho no Brasil: das orígens aos anos vinte* (São Paulo, 1982), and Sheldon Maram, *Anarquistas, imigrantes e o movimento operário brasileiro, 1890–1920* (Rio de Janeiro, 1979). Maram's work is also available in English in his articles: 'Anarchosyndicalism in Brazil', *Proceedings of the Pacific Coast Council on Latin American Studies*, 4 (1975), 101–16; 'Labor and the Left in Brazil, 1890–1921: a movement aborted', *HAHR*, 57/2 (1977), 254–72; 'The immigrant and the Brazilian labor movement, 1890–1920', in Dauril Alden and Warren Dean (eds.), *Essays concerning the socioeconomic history of Brazil and Portuguese India* (Gainesville, 1977); and 'Urban labor and social change in the 1920s', *L-BR*, 16/2 (1979), 215–23.

Several earlier works retain their importance. Everardo Dias, *História das lutas sociais no Brasil* (São Paulo, 1962; 2nd edn, 1977) is a combination of memoir and narrative history by a participant in many of the struggles of the pre-1930 period. Considerable information is also to be found in the various books by Edgar Rodrigues, particularly *Socialismo e sindicalismo no Brasil* (Rio de Janeiro, 1969), and *Nacionalismo e cultura social* (Rio de Janeiro, 1972). Azis Simão, *Sindicato e estado: suas relações na formação do proletariado de São Paulo* (São Paulo, 1966) remains an influential sociological interpretation of the São Paulo labour movement.

The most extensive bibliography is Ronald Chilcote, *Brazil and its radical Left: an annotated bibliography of the Communist movement and the rise of Marxism, 1922–1972* (Millwood, N.Y., 1980). There are two collections of documents: Paulo Sérgio Pinheiro and Michael M. Hall (eds.), *A classe opéraria no Brasil, 1889–1930* (2 vols., São Paulo, 1979–81), and Edgard Carone (ed.), *O movimento operário no Brasil, 1877–1944* (São Paulo, 1979). Yara Aun Khoury, *As greves de 1917 em São Paulo e o processo de organização proletária* (São Paulo, 1981) contains an important selection of documents from the 1917 São Paulo general strike.

Sílvia Magnani, *O movimento anarquista em São Paulo (1906–1917)* (São Paulo, 1982), provides a well-documented, though highly critical, study of early anarchist and anarco-syndicalist currents in São Paulo. Francisco Foot Hardman, *Nem pátria nem patrão: vida operária e cultura anarquista no Brasil* (São Paulo, 1983) concentrates on working-class culture. Maria Valéria Junho Pena, *Mulheres e trabalhadoras: presença feminina na constituição do sistema fabril* (Rio de Janeiro, 1981) furnishes information on women workers in the early phases of industrialization. See also Maria Valéria Junho Pena and Elça Mendonça Lima, 'Lutas ilusórias: a mulher na política operária da Primeira República', in Carmen Barroso (ed.),

Mulher, mulheres (São Paulo, 1983), 17–33. Ethnic divisions among workers are analysed in Michael M. Hall, 'Immigration and the early São Paulo working class', *Jahrbuch für Geschichte von Staat, Wirtschaft und Gesellschaft Lateinamerikas*, 12 (1975), 393–407.

The history of the Brazilian Communist Party has received considerable attention. John W. F. Dulles, *Anarchists and Communists in Brazil, 1900–1935* (Austin, 1973) is a lengthy narrative history, with emphasis on the leaders of the party in the 1920s. Many of the early writings of Astrogildo Pereira have been republished in Michel Zaidan (ed.), *Construindo o PCB (1922–24)* (São Paulo, 1980). Edgard Carone (ed.), *O P.C.B. (1922–1943)* (São Paulo, 1982), includes a number of documents from the first years of the party. Memoirs by several important figures in the Communist movement have also appeared: Octávio Brandão, *Combates e batalhas* (São Paulo, 1978), Heitor Ferreira Lima, *Caminhos percorridos: memórias de militância* (São Paulo, 1982), and Leôncio Basbaum, *Una vida em seis tempos (memórias)* (São Paulo, 1976), among others. The review *Memória e História* devoted numbers 1 and 2 (1981 and 1982) to the early history of the PCB, including previously unpublished material from the Astrogildo Pereira archives. Edgar de Decca, *1930: o silêncio dos vencidos* (São Paulo, 1981), provides an important interpretation of the BOC.

The series under the general editorship of Pablo González Casanova, *La clase obrera en la historia de México* (Mexico, 1979–), to be completed in 17 volumes, provides a comprehensive survey of the history of the Mexican working class and labour movement. Several of the individual volumes are noted below. Other valuable surveys include Jorge Basurto, *El proletariado industrial en México (1850–1930)* (Mexico, 1975), and Luis Araiza, *Historia del movimiento obrero mexicano* (4 vols., Mexico, 1964–5).

The Centro de Estudios Históricos del Movimiento Obrero Mexicano (CEHSMO) publishes a journal, *Historia Obrera* (1974–), a monograph series, and a collection of reprints and documents under the general title 'Cuadernos Obreros'. The CEHSMO has also produced a bibliography, *El movimiento obrero mexicano: bibliografía* (Mexico, 1978). For additional references, see José Woldenberg, 'Características de los estudios sobre la clase y el movimiento obrero en México: 1970–1978', *Memorias del encuentro sobre historia del movimiento obrero* (Puebla, 1980), I, 13–47.

The anarchist movement is treated in John M. Hart, *Anarchism and the Mexican working class, 1860–1931* (Austin, 1978). There is an excellent account of the labour movement during the 1860s and 1870s in Juan

Felipe Leal and José Woldenberg, *Del estado liberal a los inicios de la dictadura porfirista* (*La clase obrera en la historia de México*, vol. II, Mexico, 1980). For the following period, Ciro Cardoso, Francisco González Hermosillo and Salvador Hernández, *De la dictadura porfirista a los tiempos libertarios* (*La clase obrera en la historia de México*, vol. III, Mexico, 1980) provides elements for an understanding of the Porfiriato and includes a valuable study of the PLM. David Walker, 'Porfirian labor politics: working class organizations in Mexico City and Porfirio Díaz, 1876–1902', *TA*, 37/3 (1981), 257–89, emphasizes the co-optive rather than the coercive aspects of the Díaz regime.

The outstanding study of the working class and labour movement at the end of the Díaz period is Rodney D. Anderson, *Outcasts in their own land: Mexican industrial workers, 1906–1911* (DeKalb, 1976). Anderson is rather sceptical about the influence of the PLM among Mexican workers. For another view, see James D. Cockcroft, *Intellectual precursors of the Mexican Revolution, 1900–1913* (Austin, 1968). Armando Bartra has republished a selection of writings from the PLM's newspaper in *Regeneración, 1900–1918: la corriente más radical de la revolución mexicana de 1910 a través de su periódico de combate* (Mexico, 1977). Some of Ricardo Flores Magón's writings are available in English in David Poole (ed.), *Land and liberty: anarchist influences in the Mexican Revolution, Ricardo Flores Magón* (Sanday, Orkney, 1977).

A particularly valuable survey of labour covering the revolutionary period and the 1920s is Barry Carr, *El movimiento obrero y la política en México, 1910–1929* (2 vols., Mexico, 1976, 2nd edn in 1 vol., 1981). See also Ramón E. Ruiz, *Labor and the ambivalent revolutionaries: Mexico, 1911–1923* (Baltimore, 1976), and Pablo González Casanova, *En el primer gobierno constitucional (1917–1920)* (*La clase obrera en la historia de México*, vol. VI, Mexico, 1980) and A. Knight, 'The working class and the Mexican Revolution, 1900–20', *JLAS* 16/1 (1984), 51–72.

Marjorie Ruth Clark, *Organized labor in Mexico* (Chapel Hill, 1934), remains an influential study on the 1920s. For anarcho-syndicalism in the period, see Guillermina Baena Paz, 'La Confederación General de Trabajadores', *Revista Mexicana de Ciencias Políticas y Sociales*, 83 (1976), and José Rivera Castro, 'Le syndicalisme officiel et le syndicalisme révolutionnaire au Mexique dans les années 1920', *Le Mouvement social*, 103 (1978), 31–52. Useful on the Communist Party are Manuel Márquez Fuentes and Octavio Rodríguez Araujo, *El Partido Comunista Mexicano (en el período de la Internacional Comunista: 1919–1943)* (Mexico, 1973), and

Barry Carr, 'Marxism and anarchism in the formation of the Mexican Communist Party, 1910–19', *HAHR*, 63/2 (1983), 277–305.

The CROM has received critical attention in Favio Barbosa Cano, *La CROM: de Luis N. Morones a Antonio J. Hernández* (Puebla, 1980), and Rocío Guadarrama, *Los sindicatos y la política en México: la CROM, 1918–1929* (Mexico, 1981). See also Arnaldo Córdoba, *En una época de crisis (1928–34)* (*La clase obrera en la historia de México*, vol. ix, Mexico, 1980) for an account of the decline of the CROM and the subsequent struggle to co-opt and control labour.

Works dealing with broad periods in the history of the Chilean labour movement include Hernán Ramírez Necochea, *Historia del movimiento obrero en Chile, siglo XIX* (Santiago, 1956), Jorge I. Barría Serón, *Los movimientos sociales de Chile desde 1910 hasta 1926* (Santiago, 1960), the same author's *Breve historia del sindicalismo chileno* (Santiago, 1967), and Luis Vitale, *Génesis y evolución del movimiento obrero chileno hasta el Frente Popular* (Caracas, 1979).

Peter De Shazo, *Urban workers and labor unions in Chile, 1902–1927* (Madison, 1983), is an important study which provides considerable information on anarcho-syndicalism. See also his article, 'The Valparaíso maritime strike of 1903 and the development of a revolutionary labor movement in Chile', *JLAS* 11/1 (1979), 145–68. For the background of labour struggles in the north, see Michael Monteón, *Chile in the nitrate era: the evolution of economic dependence, 1880–1930* (Madison, 1982).

The complex figure of Recabarren is treated in Julio César Jobet, *Recabarren: los orígenes del movimiento obrero y del socialismo chileno* (Santiago, 1965). See also Julio César Jobet, Jorge I. Barría Serón, and Luis Vitale (eds.), *Luis Emilio Recabarren: obras escogidas* (Santiago, 1965). On the Communist Party, there is Hernán Ramírez Necochea, *Orígen y formación del Partido Comunista de Chile* (Santiago, 1965), and the memoirs of its leader, Elias Lafertte, *Vida de un comunista* (Santiago, 1956). James O. Morris, *Elites, intellectuals and consensus: a study of the social question and industrial relations system in Chile* (Ithaca, 1966), treats the origins of the labour legislation of the 1920s.

Valuable works dealing with the Peruvian labour movement include Denis Sulmont, *El movimiento obrero en el Perú, 1900–1956* (Lima, 1975), Peter Blanchard, *The origins of the Peruvian labor movement, 1883–1919* (Pittsburgh, 1982), Piedad Pareja Pflucker, *Anarquismo y sindicalismo en el Perú (1904–1929)* (Lima, 1978), and Wilfredo Kapsoli, *Las luchas obreras en el Perú, 1900–1919* (Lima, 1976).

For Uruguay, see Franciso R. Pintos, *Historia del movimiento obrero del Uruguay* (Montevideo, 1960), and Héctor Rodríguez, *Nuestros sindicatos (1865–1965)* (Montevideo, 1965). On Paraguay, there is Francisco Gaona, *Introducción a la historia gremial y social del Paraguay* (Asunción and Buenos Aires, 1967). The most helpful work on Bolivia is Guillermo Lora, *A history of the Bolivian labour movement, 1848–1971*, trans. Christine Whitehead (Cambridge, 1977). Colombian developments are treated in Miguel Urrutia, *The development of the Colombian labor movement* (New Haven, 1969). For Venezuela, there is Julio Godio, *El movimiento obrero venezolano, 1850–1944* (Caracas, 1980).

Among works dealing with the Caribbean region, see especially Evelio Tellería Toca, *Los congresos obreros en Cuba* (Havana, 1973), and the work prepared by the Instituto de Historia del Movimiento Comunista y la Revolución Socialista de Cuba, *El movimiento obrero cubano: documentos y artículos*, vol. I (1865–1925), vol. II (1925–35) (Havana, 1975). On Puerto Rico, there is Angel Quintero Rivera, *Workers' struggle in Puerto Rico: a documentary history* (New York, 1976), and Yamila Azize, *Luchas de la mujer en Puerto Rico, 1898–1919* (San Juan, 1979). For Guyana, see Walter Rodney, *A history of the Guyanese working people, 1881–1905* (Baltimore, 1981), and Ashton Chase, *A history of trade unionism in Guyana, 1900–1961* (Georgetown, 1964).

There is information on pre-1930 developments in Central America in the following works: Luis Navas, *El movimiento obrero en Panamá (1880–1914)* (San José, 1979), Mario Posas, *Luchas del movimiento obrero en Honduras* (San José, 1981), Rafael Menjívar, *Formación y lucha del proletariado industrial salvadoreño* (San Salvador, 1979), and Arístides Augusto Larín 'Historia del movimiento sindical de El Salvador', *La Universidad*, 4 (1971), 136–179.

10. POLITICAL AND SOCIAL IDEAS IN LATIN AMERICA, 1870–1930

The principal sources for this chapter are the writings of the *pensadores*, those Latin American intellectual leaders who were in part men of letters, in part journalists, in part social or political theorists, and most often also politicians or bureaucrats. They were rarely professional academic scholars, in the present-day sense, and they lacked the leisure, the library resources and the training to engage in extensive empirical research. Thus, the *pensadores* were not isolated thinkers; they were usually respected and influential public figures. The close tie between the intellectual and governmental elite of the era makes the study of ideas an important approach to political history, particularly to the assumptions that underlay policy. Though spokesmen for the establishment receive most attention, dissenters, both inside and outside the governing group, have also been treated. The choice of individuals and works to be included for discussion has been governed in part by the chapter's organization, which is thematic and not biographical. Latin American thought cannot be considered in isolation from Europe; frequent reference has been made to European intellectual and political currents. However, limitations of space dictate that only the secondary literature on Latin America is discussed here.

Three principal bibliographical problems were encountered in preparing this chapter. The first is the paucity of general, and particularly comparative, studies which go beyond national boundaries and/or which treat the years 1870 to 1930 as a whole. Especially scarce are studies that compare ideas in Spanish America and Brazil. The second problem is the lack of bio-bibliographical studies, even on major figures. To analyse ideas in context, it is essential to establish the genesis and publication history of specific texts, which can be complex. Books usually appeared first as articles or speeches and often reappeared several times in slightly revised form. One welcomes such painstaking works as José Ignacio Mantecón Navasal, *et al.*, *Bibliografía general de don Justo Sierra* (Mexico, 1969), Peter J. Sehlinger, 'El desarrollo intelectual y la influencia de Valentín Letelier: un estudio bibliográfico', *Revista chilena de historia y geografía*, 136 (1968), 250–84, and Guillermo Rouillon, *Bio-bibliografía de José Carlos Mariátegui* (Lima, 1963); just as one laments the lack of similar works for other figures, such as Ingenieros, Molina Enríquez, or Oliveira Vianna.

The third bibliographical problem is that the analysis of political and social ideas does not fall into an established category of scholarship. It must draw on both the study of the literary and philosophic essay by humanists, and of political elites, social movements and ideologies by social science-oriented historians. Not only do the two groups often emphasize different intellectuals, but the former tend to be less concerned with political and social context and the latter less concerned with the analysis of ideas themselves. Moreover, their respective inquiries are often guided by distinct questions and methodological assumptions.

Probably the two best general studies of ideas, both by humanists who *do* have a sense of historical context, are Alberto Zum Felde, *Índice crítico de la literatura hispanoamericana: los ensayistas* (Mexico, 1954), and Martin S. Stabb, *In quest of identity: patterns in the Spanish American essay of ideas, 1890–1960* (Chapel Hill, 1967). It is lamentable that neither work has been reprinted. For the nineteenth century, Leopoldo Zea, *Dos etapas del pensamiento en hispanoamérica* (Mexico, 1949, Eng. trans., *The Latin American mind*, Norman, Okla., 1963), is valuable, despite the author's philosophical opposition to historical detachment. The only general synthesis that treats Brazil and Spanish America is Jean Franco, *The modern culture of Latin America: society and the artist* (2nd edn, London, 1970). François Bourricaud, 'The adventures of Ariel', *Daedalus*, 101 (1972), 109–36 offers numerous insights. The standard manual of *pensadores* is William R. Crawford, *A century of Latin American thought* (2nd edn, Cambridge, Mass., 1961); also useful is Harold E. Davis, *Latin American thought: a historical introduction* (Baton Rouge, 1972). A superb, comprehensive essay treating educational ideas from the sixteenth to the twentieth century is Mario Góngora, 'Origin and philosophy of the Spanish American university', in Joseph Maier and Richard W. Weatherhead (eds.), *The Latin American university* (Albuquerque, 1979), 17–64.

Other comparative studies that touch tangentially on ideas include Carl Solberg, *Immigration and nationalism in Argentina and Chile, 1890–1914* (Austin, 1970), Hobart A. Spalding, Jr., *Organized labor in Latin America* (New York, 1977), and Thomas E. Skidmore, 'Workers and soldiers: urban labor movements and elite responses in twentieth-century Latin America', in Virginia Bernhard (ed.), *Elites, masses, and modernization in Latin America, 1850–1930* (Austin, 1979). Though not explicitly comparative, J. Lloyd Mecham, *Church and state in Latin America* (Chapel Hill, 1934), remains a standard guide. The work of Claudio Véliz, most recently his *The centralist tradition of Latin America* (Princeton, 1980), has proved valuable on the central theme of this chapter, despite his one-dimensional view of liberalism. On corporatism, see the essays by Philippe C. Schmitter and Ronald C. Newton in Frederick B. Pike and Thomas Stritch (eds.), *The new corporatism* (Notre Dame, 1974), and James M. Malloy, introd. to *Authoritarianism and corporatism in Latin America* (Pittsburgh, 1977).

Substantive national coverage in this chapter is limited to Argentina, Brazil, Chile, Mexico and Peru. Among the few national studies that are general in scope, see, for Argentina, José Luis Romero, *Las ideas políticas en Argentina* (3rd edn, Buenos Aires, 1959), Eng. trans. *Argentine political thought* (Stanford, 1963), and particularly *El desarrollo de las ideas en la sociedad argentina del siglo xx* (Mexico, 1965). Alejandro Korn, *Influencias filosóficas en la evolución nacional* (Buenos Aires, 1936) is a primary source that can also be used as an authority. *Historia argentina contemporánea, 1862–1930* (2 vols., Buenos Aires, 1963) is a valuable reference work for the non-specialist. David Rock, *Politics in Argentina, 1890–1930: the rise and fall of radicalism* (Cambridge, 1975) is fundamental. Since most Argentine intellectual expression took place in the capital, James R. Scobie, *Buenos Aires: from plaza to suburb, 1870–1910* (New York, 1974) is invaluable. On Brazil, see T. E. Skidmore's *Black into white: race and nationality in Brazilian thought* (New York, 1974) and João Cruz Costa, *A history of ideas in Brazil* (Berkeley, 1964). For Chile, Frederick B. Pike, *Chile and the United States* (Notre Dame, 1963) treats ideas and politics comprehensively and includes prolific notes for further study. On Peru, *La literatura política de González Prada, Mariátegui y Haya de la Torre* (Mexico, 1957) by Eugenio Chang-Rodríguez is a thorough study of ideas. F. B. Pike, *The modern history of Peru* (New York, 1967) is a good reference, as is Jorge Basadre's monumental *Historia de la república del Perú* (5th edn, 6 vols., Lima, 1961–2).

More specific works that are useful include, for Argentina, the studies of university reform by Richard C. Walter, *Student politics in Argentina* (New York, 1968) and 'The intellectual background of the 1918 university reform in Argentina', *HAHR*, 49/2 (1969), 233–53. H. Spalding's brief 'Sociology in Argentina', in Ralph L. Woodward (ed.), *Positivism in Latin America, 1850–1900* (Boston, 1971), makes some interesting points. Sandra F. McGee, 'The social origins of counterrevolution in Argentina, 1900–1932' (unpublished Ph.D. thesis, University of Florida, Gainesville, 1979) breaks new ground in treating the political Right of the 1920s. For the Uruguayan, José E. Rodó, Gordon Brotherston's introduction to his edition of *Ariel* (Cambridge, 1967) is excellent.

On Brazil Fernando Azevedo, *Brazilian culture* (New York, 1950) is valuable for positivist educational thought. See also Robert G. Nachman, 'Positivism, modernization, and the middle class in Brazil', *HAHR*, 57/1 (1977), 1–23. Robert Conrad's English edition of, and commentary on, Joaquim Nabuco, *Abolitionism* (Urbana, 1977), is a boon to the non-expert. Richard Graham, 'Landowners and the overthrow of the empire', *L-BR*, 1 (1970), 44–56 places abolitionist ideas in social and political context, and his 'Joaquim Nabuco, conservative historian', *L-BR*, 17 (1980), 1–16 is valuable, despite some doubts about the use of the label 'conservative'. W. Douglas McLain, Jr, 'Alberto Torres, ad hoc nationalist', *L-BR*, 4 (1967), 17–34, is a useful précis of ideas, though the best study is now Adalberto Marson, *A ideologia nacionalista em Alberto Torres* (São Paulo, 1979). Joseph L. Love illuminates the political system of the Old Republic in *Rio Grande do Sul and Brazilian regionalism, 1882–1930* (Stanford, 1971).

Chilean sources are varied. Alejandro Fuenzalida Grandón, *Lastarria i su tiempo* (Santiago, 1893) and Luis Galdames, *Valentín Letelier y su obra* (Santiago, 1937) are intellectual biographies by disciples. Ricardo Donoso, *Las ideas políticas en Chile* (Mexico, 1946) covers the pre-1891 period. Simon Collier, 'The historiography of the "Portalian" period (1830–1891) in Chile', *HAHR*, 57/4 (1977), 660–90, is an excellent guide. Allen Woll treats several facets of the change in ideas in *A functional past: the uses of history in nineteenth-century Chile* (Baton Rouge, 1982). A good reference for political events of the pre-1891 era is Francisco A. Encina, *Historia de Chile* (20 vols., Santiago, 1941–52). Harold Blakemore, *British nitrates and Chilean politics, 1886–1896: Balmaceda and North* (London, 1974) is indispensable for its period, as is Julio Heise González, *Historia de Chile. El período parlamentario, 1861–1925*, 1 (Santiago, 1974), for the twentieth century. Jean-Pierre Blancpain, *Les Allemands au Chili, 1816–1945* (Cologne, 1974) is an exhaustive treatment. Arnold Bauer provides a valuable characterization of the Chilean elite about 1910 in *Chilean rural society* (Cambridge, 1975). Brian Loveman's *Chile: the legacy of Hispanic capitalism* (New York, 1979), gives the non-specialist a good sense of the social bases of politics in the twentieth century. Frederick M. Nunn properly stresses the role of the military in *Chilean politics, 1920–1931: the honorable mission of the armed forces* (Albuquerque, 1970). Julio César Jobet, *Luis Emilio Recabarren* (Santiago, 1955) is a sympathetic treatment. James O. Morris, *Elites, intellectuals, and consensus. A study of the social question and the industrial relations system in Chile* (Ithaca, 1966), is an authoritative study of the Labour Code of 1924.

For late nineteenth-century ideas in Mexico, see Charles A. Hale, '"Scientific politics" and the continuity of liberalism in Mexico, 1867–1910', in *Dos Revoluciones. Mexico y los Estados Unidos* (Mexico, 1976), 139–52. L. Zea, *El positivismo en México* (3rd edn, Mexico, 1968) is a standard work, but should be complemented by W. Dirk Raat, *El positivismo durante el Porfiriato* (Mexico, 1975). Moisés González Navarro, *Sociología e historia en México* (Mexico, 1970) is a ready summary of the ideas of several figures treated in the chapter. M. S. Stabb, 'Indigenism and racism in Mexican thought: 1857–1911', *JIAS*, 1 (1959), 405–23 elucidates the subject. Daniel Cosío Villegas, *et al.*, *Historia moderna de México* (9 vols. in 10; Mexico, 1955–72) is an indispensable reference. On the Ateneo group, Juan Hernández Luna's introduction to *Conferencias del Ateneo de la Juventud* (Mexico, 1962) and Patrick Romanell's philosophical, *The making of the Mexican mind* (2nd edn, Notre Dame, 1967) are useful. Enrique Krauze, *Caudillos culturales en la revolución mexicana* (Mexico, 1976) illuminates the intellectual generation of 1915 and Henry C. Schmitt, *The roots of lo Mexicano: self and society in Mexican thought, 1900–1934* (College Station, Texas, 1978) highlights the ambiguous relation between social reform and humanism. John Womack's *Zapata and the Mexican Revolution* (New York, 1969) is unsurpassed. James D. Cockroft, *Intellectual precursors of the Mexican Revolution, 1900–1913* (Austin, 1968) and John M. Hart, *Anarchism and the Mexican working class, 1860–1931* (Austin, 1978), are complementary works on anarchism and the P.L.M. Ramón E. Ruíz, *Labor and the ambivalent revolutionaries: Mexico, 1911–1923* (Baltimore, 1976) elucidates government policy, as does Barry Carr, 'The Casa del Obrero Mundial, Constitucionalismo and the Pact of February 1915', *El trabajo y los trabajadores en la historia de México* (Mexico and Tucson, 1979), 603–32. Jean Meyer revises much of the history of the 1910–30 era in *La révolution mexicaine* (Paris, 1973), emphasizing the growth of the revolutionary state. Arnaldo Córdova, *La ideología de la revolución mexicana* (Mexico, 1973) is a stimulating interpretation from the Left. Another approach to the authoritarian state is Peter H. Smith, *Labyrinths of power: political recruitment in twentieth-century Mexico* (Princeton, 1979).

Besides the general works on Peru, J. Basadre's essay on Francisco García Calderón in the anthology *En torno al Perú y América* (Lima, 1954) is superb. Jesús Chavarría, *José Carlos Mariátegui and the rise of modern Peru, 1890–1930* (Albuquerque, 1979), illuminates the national context for Mariátegui's thought, John M. Baines, *Revolution in Peru: Mariátegui and the myth* (Alabama, 1972) the European sources. Peter F. Klarén, *Modernization, dislocation, and Aprismo: origins of the Peruvian Aprista Party, 1870–1932* (Austin, 1973) is a model study, emphasizing Aprismo's tie with the Trujillo region. Thomas M. Davies, Jr, 'The Indigenismo of the Peruvian Aprista Party: a reinterpretation', *HAHR*, 51/4 (1971), 626–

45, is a critical analysis, as is François Chevalier, 'Official *Indigenismo* in Peru in 1920', in Magnus Mörner (ed.), *Race and class in Latin America* (New York, 1970), 184–96. Steve Stein, *Populism in Peru. The emergence of the masses and the politics of social control* (Madison, 1980) provides excellent context for understanding Haya de la Torre. Robert J. Alexander (ed.), *Aprismo. The ideas and doctrines of Victor Raul Haya de la Torre* (Kent, 1973) is a useful English version of the key texts, together with an uncritical study of Haya. See also Jeffrey L. Klaiber, S.J., 'The popular universities and the origins of Aprismo, 1921–1924', *HAHR*, 55/4 (1975), 693–716.

11. THE LITERATURE, MUSIC AND ART OF LATIN AMERICA 1870–1930

The problems of preparing a bibliographical review of Latin American culture flow directly from the problems of the existing bibliographical materials themselves: fragmentary in nature, with few standard works, and many of those inaccessible. Even in literature, by far the most researched of the arts in Latin America, there are few classic histories either of the continent's literary production as a whole or of that of individual republics. On music, painting, architecture and film, the existing material for most periods is very sparse indeed. In addition, most works about 'Latin American' culture exclude Brazil. Although this review of the period 1870–1930 is intended to stand alone, the reader will also find it useful to consult bibliographical essay 18 on the period 1810–70, in *CHLA* III.

General works on cultural history

Pedro Henríquez Ureña, *Historia de la cultura en la América hispánica* (Mexico, 1947; trans., with a suppl. chapter, by G. Chase: *A concise history of Spanish American culture*, New York 1947), although barely more than an annotated check-list, remains the most useful of the general surveys. Also invaluable, if less objective, is G. Arciniegas, *El continente de siete colores* (Buenos Aires, 1965; Eng. trans. *Latin America: a cultural history*, New York, 1966). S. Clissold, *Latin America: a cultural outline* (London, 1965), has appeal for the non-specialist beginner, whilst J. Franco's title, *Society and the artist: the modern culture of Latin America* (London, 1967), has flattered a generation of readers only to deceive them, but remains a stimulating literary introduction. Specifically on Brazil, F. de Azevedo,

A cultura brasileira (Rio de Janeiro, 1943; Eng. trans. *Brazilian culture*, New York, 1950), remains an essential introduction. See also N. Werneck Sodré, *Síntese da cultura brasileira* (Rio de Janeiro, 1970), and W. Martins' monumental *História da inteligência brasileira* (São Paulo, 1981).

On Latin American thought and its influence on culture, see M. S. Stabb, *In quest of identity* (Chapel Hill, 1967), esp. useful on the 1890–1930 period; L. Zea, *El pensamiento latinoamericano* (2 vols., Mexico, 1965), and *The Latin American mind* (Norman, Okla., 1963), indispensable for an understanding of nineteenth and twentieth-century cultural trends, as are two other works by self-styled *pensadores: Radiografía de la pampa* (Buenos Aires, 1933) by Ezequiel Martínez Estrada, and *El laberinto de la soledad* (Mexico, 1950) by Octavio Paz. On Brazil, see J. Cruz Costa, *Contribuição à história das idéias no Brasil* (Rio de Janeiro, 1956; Eng. trans. *A history of ideas in Brazil*, Berkeley, 1964), and I. Lins, *História do positivismo no Brasil* (São Paulo, 1964).

The Ayacucho collection of Latin American classic texts published from Caracas includes *Pensamiento conservador, 1815–1898*, ed. by J. C. and L. A. Romero, 1978; *Utopismo socialista, 1830–1893*, ed. by C. M. Rama, 1977, and *Pensamiento positivista latinoamericano*, ed. by L. Zea, 2 vols., 1980. These volumes have excellent chronological appendixes (an innovation propagated in Latin America by the Cuban publishing house, Casa de las Américas), which provide very helpful background for students of culture.

Architecture

The most useful outline work is L. Castedo, *A history of Latin American art and architecture from Precolumbian times to the present* (New York, 1969), though sketchy and in no sense a handbook. Similar works are F. Bullrich, *New directions in Latin American architecture* (New York, 1969), for the later part of our period, J. E. Hardoy, *Las ciudades en América Latina* (Buenos Aires, 1972), and R. Segre (ed.), *América Latina en su arquitectura* (Mexico and Paris, 1975). The integrationist approach is taken by D. F. Damaz, *Art in Latin American architecture* (New York, 1963), and P. M. Bardi, *História da arte brasileira: pintura, escultura, arquitetura, outras artes* (São Paulo, 1975).

Valuable national surveys are I. E. Myers, *Mexico's modern architecture* (New York, 1952), S. Moholy-Nagy, *Carlos Raúl Villanueva and the architecture of Venezuela* (New York, 1964), and J. Arango and C.

Martínez, *Arquitectura en Colombia* (Bogotá, 1951), for Spanish America; and for Brazil, H. E. Mindlin, *Modern architecture in Brazil* (New York, 1956), E. Corona, *Dicionário da arquitetura brasileira* (São Paulo, 1972), with unique coverage in both breadth and depth, and A. de Souza, *Arquitetura no Brasil: depoimentos* (São Paulo, 1978), brief, but with well-focused insights into Warchavchik, Costa, Niemeyer, etc.

Painting and sculpture

Curiously – no doubt there is an economic explanation – more general works on Latin American art exist in English than in Spanish or Portuguese. For panoramic syntheses, see Castedo, *History of Latin American art and architecture* and S. L. Catlin and T. Grieder, *Art of Latin America since independence* (New Haven, 1966). Specifically on the contemporary period, see G. Chase, *Contemporary art in Latin America* (New York, 1970), both knowledgeable and readable, and works by the two most prominent Latin American critics of recent times, M. Traba, *La pintura nueva en Latinoamérica* (Bogotá, 1961), and D. Bayón, *Aventura plástica de Hispanoamérica* (Mexico, 1973). See also, D. Bayón (ed.), *América Latina en sus artes* (Mexico-Paris, 1974), another structured overview produced under the aegis of Unesco.

On Mexico, see B. Smith, *Mexico: a history in art* (London, 1979), and the sumptuous *Cuarenta siglos de plástica mexicana*. Vol. III: *Arte moderno y contemporáneo* (Mexico, 1971), lavishly illustrated and edited by E. O'Gorman *et al.*, with chapters by J. Fernández on the nineteenth century and L. Cardoza y Aragón on the art of the Revolution. See also Fernández's *Arte moderno y contemporáneo de México* (Mexico, 1952) and Cardoza y Aragón's *Pintura mexicana contemporánea* (Mexico, 1953), both essential reading on the topic. Other useful works are B. S. Myers, *Mexican painting in our time* (New York, 1956), J. A. Manrique, 'El proceso de las artes, 1910–1970', in *Historia general de México*, IV (El Colegio de México, 1976), 285–301, E. Báez Macías, *Fundación e historia de la Academia de San Carlos* (Mexico, 1974), O. Paz, *La pintura mural de la Revolución Mexicana* (Mexico, 1960), Jean Charlot, *The Mexican mural renaissance, 1920–1925* (New Haven, 1966), an authoritative view from one who was there, A. Reed, *The Mexican muralists* (New York, 1966), O. S. Suárez, *Inventario del muralismo mexicano* (Mexico, 1972), a brilliantly multifaceted study by a Cuban practitioner of the art, and R. Tibol, *Documentación sobre el arte mexicano* (Mexico, 1974), invaluable source of background materials. E. W. Weismann's *Mexico in sculpture* (Cambridge, Mass., 1950) gives insight into the art for our period.

On Cuba, see J. Gómez Sicre, *Pintura cubana de hoy* (Havana, 1944), by a former member of the Parisian avant-garde, and L. de la Torriente, *Estudio de las artes plásticas en Cuba* (Havana, 1954). On Venezuela the leading authority is A. Boulton: see his *Historia de la pintura en Venezuela* (3 vols, Caracas, 1972); also J. Calzadilla and P. Briceño, *Escultura, escultores: un libro sobre la escultura en Venezuela* (Caracas, 1977), indispensable in its field. On the Andean countries, see G. Giraldo Jaramillo, *La pintura en Colombia* (Mexico, 1948), T. Núñez Ureta (ed.), *Pintura contemporánea* (2 vols, Lima, 1975), which divides Peruvian artistic history into the periods 1820–1920 and 1920–1968, providing illustrations unavailable elsewhere, M. Lauer, *Introducción a la pintura peruana del siglo XX* (Lima, 1976), particularly helpful on indigenism, and J. Sabogal, *Del arte en el Perú y otros ensayos* (Lima, 1975), by the standard-bearer of artistic nationalism himself. M. Ivelic and G. Galaz, *La pintura en Chile desde la colonia hasta 1981* (Valparaíso, 1981), beautifully illustrated, is the best guide to Chilean art of all periods.

On Argentina, see esp. R. Brughetti, *Historia del arte en la Argentina* (Mexico, 1965), A. Pellegrini, *Panorama de la pintura argentina contemporánea* (Buenos Aires, 1967), polemical and individualist but essential reading, and C. Córdova Iturburu, *Ochenta años de pintura argentina* (Buenos Aires, 1978). The most useful work on Uruguayan art is J. P. Argul, *Proceso de las artes plásticas del Uruguay desde la época indígena al momento contemporáneo* (Montevideo, 1958).

Brazil is particularly well provided with dictionaries and handbooks on modern and contemporary art, with the 1920s – as in Mexico – and particularly the São Paulo Modern Art Week of 1922, providing the focal point of departure. See R. Pontual, *Dicionário das artes plásticas no Brasil* (Rio de Janeiro, 1969), C. Cavalcanti, *Dicionário brasileiro de artistas plásticos* (5 vols, Brasília, 1973), P. M. Bardi, *O modernismo no Brasil* (São Paulo, 1978), very good on both the 1920s and 1930s, with invaluable insights into the contribution of architects to the new wave, and A. Amaral, *Arte y arquitectura del modernismo brasileiro, 1917–1931* (Caracas, 1978), as good an anthology of critical articles and original documents as can be found in any Brazilian publication. Finally, A. Amaral, *Tarsila, sua obra e seu tempo* (3 vols, São Paulo, 1975), makes the whole period come alive.

Music

The three best known works in English are N. Slonimsky, *Music of Latin America* (New York, 1945), eccentric but still enjoyable reading, G. Chase (again), *A guide to Latin American music* (New York, 1955), and G. Béhague's much more detailed and scholarly *Music in Latin America: an introduction* (New Jersey, 1979). Indispensable, for Latin America as elsewhere, is the admirable *New Grove dictionary of music and musicians* (20 vols, New York and London, 1980), to which Chase and his student Béhague have again both contributed extensively. O. Mayer-Serra, *Música y músicos de Latinoamérica* (2 vols, Mexico, 1947), still retains much of its usefulness for this period. See also I. Aretz (ed.), *América Latina en su música* (Mexico-Paris, 1977), and M. Moreno Fraginals (ed.), *Africa en América Latina* (Mexico-Paris, 1977), both useful Unesco publications.

On individual republics, starting with Mexico, see O. Mayer-Serra, *Panorama de la música mexicana* (Mexico, 1941), and R. M. Stevenson, *Music in Mexico* (New York, 1952), by one of the greatest authorities on music in the Americas. For Cuba, A. Carpentier's *La música en Cuba* (Mexico, 1946) remains the classic statement. Also helpful are J. Ardevol, *Introducción a Cuba. La música* (Havana, 1969), by a well-known practitioner, and E. Martín, *Panorama histórico de la música en Cuba* (Havana, 1972), a very general survey.

For Colombia, see J. I. Perdomo Escóbar, *Historia de la música en Colombia* (Bogotá, 1938), and A. Pardo Tovar, *La cultura musical en Colombia* (Bogotá, 1966), whilst S. Claro Valdés and J. Urrutia Blondel, *Historia de la música en Chile* (Santiago, 1973), achieve a persuasive synthesis of the Chilean experience. V. Gesualdo's *Historia de la música en la Argentina* (Buenos Aires, 1961), and R. Arizaga's *Enciclopedia de la música argentina* (Buenos Aires, 1971), are both indispensable. Uruguay's most important work is S. Salgado, *Breve historia de la música culta en el Uruguay* (Montevideo, 1971), particularly helpful on the period covered here.

On Brazil, Mário de Andrade's *Ensaio sôbre a música brasileira* (1928) retains all its historical importance, whilst R. Almeida's *História da música brasileira* (1942) is also revealing as a document of its times. More contemporary perspectives are offered by L. H. Correia de Azevedo, *150 anos de música no Brasil, 1800–1950* (Rio de Janeiro, 1956), and M. A. Marcondes (ed.), *Enciclopedia da música brasileira: erudita, folclórica e popular* (2 vols, São Paulo, 1977), a vast and invaluable resource albeit weak on bibliographical support.

Cinema

The most comprehensive general work is C. Hennebelle and A. Gumucio-Dragón (eds.), *Les cinémas de l'Amérique Latine* (Paris, 1981), whilst E. B. Burns, *Latin American cinema: film and history* (Los Angeles, 1975), was a pioneering work. G. S. de Usabel, *The high noon of American films in Latin America* (Ann Arbor, 1982), charts the penetration of Latin American markets and cultures by Hollywood in the early decades of the movies.

Mexican cinema is particularly well covered, above all by E. García Riera's monumental *Historia documental del cine mexicano* (10 vols., Mexico, 1968–), both exhaustive and scrupulous. Also useful was his earlier *El cine mexicano* (Mexico, 1963), and a similar work by J. Ayala Blanco, *La aventura del cine mexicano* (Mexico, 1968). More specifically historical in orientation are A. de los Reyes, *Los orígenes del cine mexicano, 1896–1900* (Mexico, 1983), and *Cine y sociedad en México, 1896–1930* (2 vols, 2nd edn, Mexico, 1983), invaluable background to our period, and the standard work in English, C. J. Mora, *Mexican cinema: reflections of a society, 1896–1980* (Berkeley-Los Angeles, 1982).

A. Gumucio-Dragón has recently provided an informative *Historia del cine boliviano* (Mexico, 1983), whilst Chile is well served by M. Godoy Quesada, *Historia del cine chileno* (Santiago, 1966), thorough and detailed, and the excellent C. Ossa Coo, *Historia del cine chileno* (Santiago, 1971). On Argentina, see D. di Nubile, *Historia del cine argentino* (Buenos Aires, 1959), E. Dos Santos, *El cine nacional* (Buenos Aires, 1971), somewhat populist in approach, M. Bottone, *La literatura argentina y el cine* (Buenos Aires, 1964), very useful for our purposes, and J. M. Couselo, *El Negro Ferreyra: un cine por instinto* (Buenos Aires, 1969), on the increasingly recognized precursor film-maker of the early period.

On Brazil, see A. Gonzaga and P. E. Salles Gomes, *Setenta anos de cinema brasileiro* (São Paulo, 1966), G. Santos Pereira, *Plano geral do cinema brasileiro* (Rio de Janeiro, 1973), rambling but indispensable, R. Johnson and R. Stam (eds.), *Brazilian cinema* (E. Brunswick, 1982), a vital resource for all students of Latin American cinema, and P. E. Salles Gomes, *Humberto Mauro, Cataguases, 'Cinearte'* (São Paulo, 1974), an appraisal of the greatest director of the early period, relating him illuminatingly to 1920s *modernismo*.

Literature

This bibliography is devoted almost exclusively to secondary sources of continental or national scope, rather than to individual authors, however distinguished. No attempt has been made here to offer a guide to critical editions of major texts, nor to record even the most important translations. The reader is referred to B. A. Shaw, *Latin American literature in English translation: an annotated bibliography* (New York, 1976).

Among the most useful bibliographical works are: S. M. Bryant, *A selective bibliography of bibliographies of Latin American literature* (Texas, 1976), with 662 entries covering the entire range of scholarly endeavour; P. Ward (ed.), *The Oxford companion to Spanish literature* (Oxford, 1978), with good coverage of Spanish America; W. Rela, *Guía bibliográfica de la literatura hispanoamericana, desde el siglo XIX hasta 1970* (Buenos Aires, 1971); A. Flores, *Bibliografía de escritores hispanoamericanos. A bibliography of Spanish American writers, 1609–1974* (New York, 1975), a most useful select practical guide; J. Becco, *Fuentes para el estudio de la literatura hispanoamericana* (Buenos Aires, 1968), a superb concise list in 64 pages; Unesco, *Bibliografía general de la literatura latinoamericana* (Paris, 1972); and Pan American Union, *Diccionario de la literatura latinoamericana* (Washington, 1958–), of which, regrettably, only the volumes on Bolivia, Central America, Chile, Colombia and Ecuador appeared.

National bibliographies: D. W. Foster, *Mexican literature. A bibliography of secondary sources* (Metuchen, NJ, 1983), is essential, as also A. M. Ocampo and E. Prado Velázquez (eds.), *Diccionario de escritores mexicanos* (Mexico, 1967), using a careful bio-bibliographical approach. Since 1979 the leading publishing house, Fondo de Cultura Económica, has been publishing facsimile editions of major *Revistas literarias mexicanas modernas*, providing a priceless bibliographical resource for scholars.

For the Caribbean area, see D. W. Foster, *Puerto Rican literature. A bibliography of secondary sources* (Westport, Conn., 1982), Biblioteca Nacional José Martí, *Bibliografía de la poesía cubana en el siglo XIX* (1965), and L. Cardoso and J. Pinto, *Diccionario general de la literatura venezolana* (Mérida, Venez., 1974).

On the Andean region, see J. E. Englekirk and G. E. Wade, *Bibliografía de la novela colombiana* (Mexico, 1950); J. M. Barnadas and J. J. Coy, *Realidad histórica y expresión literaria en Bolivia* (Cochabamba, 1977); F. and L. Barriga, *Diccionario de la literatura ecuatoriana* (Quito, 1973); D. W. Foster, *Peruvian literature. A bibliography of secondary sources* (Metuchen,

NJ, 1983), another indispensable contribution; *idem, Chilean literature. A working bibliography* (Boston, 1978); and E. Szmulewicz, *Diccionario de la literatura chilena* (Santiago, 1977).

As usual, the River Plate region is well served: J. H. Becco, *Contribución a la bibliografía de la literatura argentina: bibliografía, antología, historia y crítica general* (Buenos Aires, 1959), is vast in scope, while D. W. Foster, *Argentine literature. A research guide* (New York, 1983), is yet another outstanding contribution from the indefatigable bibliographer, whilst P. Orgambide and R. Yahni provide a very businesslike *Enciclopedia de la literatura argentina* (Buenos Aires, 1970). On Uruguay, see W. Rela, *Contribución a la bibliografía de la literatura uruguaya* (Montevideo, 1963); and on Paraguay, neglected as ever, see R. Maxwell and J. D. Ford, *A tentative bibliography of Paraguayan letters* (Cambridge, Mass., 1934).

Finally, on Brazil, the *Introdução ao estudo da literatura brasileira* (Instituto Nacional do Livro, Rio de Janeiro, 1963), a critical synthesis and bibliography, and the *Dicionário literário brasileiro* (5 vols, São Paulo, 1969) by R. de Menezes, with references to 4,000 writers, deserve mention.

Anthologies in Spanish and English include A. Flores, *Historia y antología del cuento y la novela en Hispanoamérica* (New York, 1967), a point of reference for all later anthologists; A. Flores and H. M. Anderson (eds.), *Masterpieces of Spanish American literature* (2 vols, New York, 1974), perhaps the most attractively produced of all the anthologies; M. Benedetti and A. Benítez Rojo (eds.), *Un siglo del relato latinoamericano* (Havana, 1976); S. Menton (ed.), *El cuento hispanoamericano: antología crítico-histórica* (2 vols, Mexico, 1964); C. Ripoll and A. Valdespino (eds.), *Teatro hispanoamericano: antología crítica* (New York, 1972); J. Lafforgue (ed.), *Teatro rioplatense, 1886–1930* (Caracas, 1977); C. Ripoll, *Conciencia intelectual de América: antología del ensayo hispanoamericano, 1836–1959* (New York, 1961); Gordon Brotherston (ed.), *Spanish American modernista poets* (Oxford, 1968), J. E. Pacheco (ed.), *Antología del modernismo, 1884–1921* (2 vols, Mexico, 1970), different in scope but both excellent; G. Zaid (ed.), *Omnibus de poesía mexicana* (Mexico, 1971); A. de María y Campos, *La Revolución Mexicana a través de los corridos populares* (2 vols, Mexico, 1962), A. Castro Leal (ed.), *La novela de la Revolución Mexicana* (2 vols, Mexico, 1960), the classic collection; D. Agustín del Saz (ed.), *Antología general de la poesía argentina* (Barcelona, 1969); G. Ara (ed.), *Suma de poesía argentina, 1538–1968: crítica y antología* (2 vols, Buenos Aires, 1970). The most valuable anthology of Brazilian literature for non-Brazilians is undoubtedly C. Hulet (ed.), *Brazilian literature* (3 vols, Washington, 1974), with texts in Portuguese, commentaries in English, and excellent bibliographical listings.

History and criticism

The outstanding synthesis of Latin American literary history remains Pedro Henríquez Ureña, *Las corrientes literarias en la América hispánica* (Mexico, 1949), which included Brazil and appeared first in English as *Literary currents in Hispanic America* (Cambridge, Mass., 1945). Henríquez Ureña's judgements have acquired permanent authority. Also invaluable is Luis Alberto Sánchez, *Historia comparada de las literaturas americanas* (4 vols, Buenos Aires, 1976), which includes Brazil, Haiti and the United States. Other well-known general histories in English include J. Franco, *An introduction to Spanish American literature* (Cambridge, 1969), and her *Spanish American literature since independence* (London, 1973), both useful outlines, and the somewhat peremptory 'Spanish American literature' by D. P. Gallagher, in P. E. Russell (ed.), *Spain: a companion to Spanish studies* (London, 1976), 429–71. The best of the general works in Spanish, in addition to those mentioned, are E. Anderson Imbert, *Historia de la literatura hispanoamericana* (2 vols, Mexico, 1954), an outstanding synthesis and critical guide, also available in English, and A. Zum Felde, *Índice crítico de la literatura hispanoamericana* (2 vols, Mexico, 1959), universally admired. Also worthy of note, finally, are B. G. Carter, *Historia de la literatura hispanoamericana a través de sus revistas* (Mexico, 1970), and the imaginative collective critical history commissioned by Unesco and edited by C. Fernández Moreno, *América Latina en su literatura* (Mexico-Paris, 1972).

Specifically on fiction, the best-known works are L. A. Sánchez, *Proceso y contenido de la novela hispanoamericana* (Madrid, 1953), F. Alegría, *Historia de la novela hispanoamericana* (Mexico, 1959), J. Loveluck (ed.), *La novela hispanoamericana* (Santiago, 1969), an outstanding critical anthology whose influence is still felt, and K. Schwartz, *A new history of Spanish American fiction* (2 vols, Miami, 1972). A. S. Visca, *Aspectos de la narrativa criollista* (Montevideo, 1972), gives the best insight into this continent-wide regionalist movement, whilst T. Pérez (ed.), *Tres novelas ejemplares* (Havana, 1971), provides a selection of seminal critical texts and bibliographical guides to *La vorágine, Don Segundo Sombra* and *Doña*

Bárbara. L. Leal, *Historia del cuento hispanoamericano* (Mexico, 1966), is still the best work on this topic.

On Spanish American poetry there are surprisingly few general works. Among the best are S. Yurkievich, *Fundadores de la nueva poesía latinoamericana* (2nd edn, Barcelona, 1984), on the later part of our period, and G. Brotherston, *Latin American poetry* (London, 1975), which begins with *modernismo*. See also M. H. Forster, *Historia de la poesía hispanoamericana* (Clear Creek, Ind., 1981). There is a large bibliography on *modernismo*, of which the standard works are M. Henríquez Ureña, *Breve historia del modernismo* (Mexico, 1954), a classic, and I. A. Schulman, *Génesis del modernismo* (Mexico, 1966). J. Giordano, *La edad del ensueño* (Santiago, 1970), and A. Rama, *Rubén Darío y el modernismo* (Caracas, 1970), both place Darío's work in its cultural context and are essential reading for all critics, as are F. Pérus, *Literatura y sociedad en América Latina: el modernismo* (Mexico, 1976), and N. Jitrik, *Las contradicciones del modernismo* (Mexico, 1978), a fashionable symptomatic reading. Perhaps the best known study of an individual modernist poet is I. A. Schulman's *Símbolo y color en la obra de José Martí* (Madrid, 1960). There are fewer general works on Spanish American avant-garde poetry (unlike the case of Brazil). The most valuable is probably O. Collazos (ed.), *Los vanguardismos en la América Latina* (Havana, 1970), whilst G. de Torre, *Historia de las literaturas de vanguardia* (Madrid, 1965), remains essential general reading. On individuals, see A. de Undurraga's excellent introduction to his anthology, *Vicente Huidobro, poesía y prosa* (Madrid, 1967), and T. Running, *Borges' Ultraist movement and its poets* (Lathrop, Michigan, 1981).

On theatre, see J. J. Arrom, *Historia del teatro hispanoamericano* (2nd edn, revd., Mexico, 1967), and F. Dauster, *Historia del teatro hispanoamericano, siglos XIX y XX* (Mexico, 1966). Finally, as useful general background to all the foregoing, see R. G. Mead and P. G. Earle, *Breve historia del ensayo latinoamericano* (Mexico, 1962), A. Sacoto, *El indio en el ensayo de la América española* (New York, 1971), R. L. Jackson, *The black image in Latin American literature* (Albuquerque, 1976), and A. Pescatello (ed.), *Female and male in Latin America* (Pittsburgh, 1973), which contains sections on both Spanish American and Brazilian fiction.

National literatures

On Mexico, the authoritative work on the nineteenth-century novel is J. L. Martínez, *La expresión nacional. Letras mexicanas del siglo XIX* (Mexico,

1955). *Idem*, 'México en busca de su expresión', in *Historia general de México*, III (El Colegio de México, 1976), 283–337, is invaluable, as is its sequel in *ibid.*, IV, by C. Monsiváis, 'Notas sobre la cultura mexicana en el siglo XX', 303–476, a brilliant synthesis. See also J. Brushwood, *Mexico in its novel* (Austin, 1966), and A. M. Ocampo (ed.), *La crítica de la novela mexicana contemporánea* (Mexico, 1981), a judicious anthology of critical studies of twentieth-century output. The best works on the novel of the Mexican Revolution are A. Dessau, *La novela de la Revolución Mexicana* (Mexico, 1972), Marxist in orientation but the unrivalled classic; J. Rutherford, *Mexican society during the Revolution. A literary approach* (London, 1971); and R. Rodríguez Coronel (ed.), *Recopilación de textos sobre la novela de la Revolución Mexicana* (Havana, 1975), an outstanding collection of key critical texts on this important literary phenomenon.

For the Caribbean region, see M. Henríquez Ureña, *Panorama histórico de la literatura dominicana* (Santo Domingo, 1966), D. Sommer, *One master for another: populism as patriarchal rhetoric in Dominican novels* (Santo Domingo, 1983), an astringent feminist view which could be more widely applied to Latin American fiction as a whole; and on Puerto Rico, J. L. González, *Literatura y sociedad en Puerto Rico* (Mexico, 1976). For Cuba, see J. A. Portuondo, *Bosquejo histórico de las letras cubanas* (Havana, 1960), by the critic who has most influenced Cuban literary culture since 1959, and R. Lazo, *Historia de la literatura cubana* (Mexico, 1974). Curiously, the revolutionary rewriting of Cuban literary history remains to be undertaken, and no definitive new version has yet appeared. The single most important work on Central America is R. L. Acevedo, *La novela centroamericana* (Río Piedras, P.R., 1982), sober and comprehensive.

On Venezuela, see M. Picón Salas, *Formación y proceso de la literatura venezolana* (Caracas, 1940), and J. Liscano, *Panorama de la literatura venezolana actual* (Caracas, 1972); and on Colombia, A. Gómez Restrepo, *Historia de la literatura colombiana* (Bogotá, 1956), and D. McGrady, *La novela histórica en Colombia*, 1844–1959 (Bogotá, 1962).

On Ecuador, see I. J. Barrera, *Historia de la literatura ecuatoriana* (Quito, 1960), R. Descalzi, *Historia crítica del teatro ecuatoriano* (Quito, 1968), and A. Rojas, *La novela ecuatoriana* (Mexico, 1948). On Bolivia, see F. Díez de Medina, *Historia de la literatura boliviana* (Madrid, 1959), and E. Finot, *Historia de la literatura boliviana* (La Paz, 1964).

Bolivia has gradually inched its way, thanks above all to the 1952 Revolution, to the prospect of an agreed national culture; whilst in Peru, perhaps the most violent and bitter cultural battlefield in the whole of Latin America, the struggle goes on, particularly through the continuing debate on indigenism. Best general works are by L. A. Sánchez, *Introducción a la literatura peruana* (Lima, 1972), and *La literatura peruana: derrotero para una historia cultural del Perú* (5 vols, Lima, 1966). The indigenist debate is unavoidable, however, going back to Mariátegui, Valcárcel, etc. in the 1920s and returning with a vengeance in the 1970s and 1980s. See X. Abril *et al.*, *Mariátegui y la literatura* (Lima, 1980), L. E. Tord, *El indio en los ensayistas peruanos, 1848–1948* (Lima, 1978), and two outstanding works of recent years, A. Cornejo Polar, *Literatura y sociedad en el Perú: la novela indigenista* (Lima, 1980), and *Hermenéutica y praxis del indigenismo: la novela indigenista de Clorinda Matto a José María Arguedas* (Mexico, 1980), by Julio Rodríguez-Luis.

Chile, the home of some of Latin America's greatest poets, has also produced many of her most outstanding literary critics and historians, most of whom have given their attention not only to Chile but to the continent as a whole; see R. Silva Castro, *Panorama literario de Chile* (Santiago, 1961), A. Torres Rioseco, *Breve historia de la literatura chilena* (Mexico, 1956), F. Alegría, *La literatura chilena del siglo XX* (Santiago, 2nd edn, 1967), and J. Promis, *Testimonios y documentos de la literatura chilena, 1842–1975* (Santiago, 1977).

There is a profuse coverage of Argentine literature for all periods, though the nineteenth century is better served in terms of synthesis than the twentieth, which is wracked by dissension and personalism, the result being a stream of political and sociological readings of narrative, poetry and theatre which, on the whole, promise more than they can deliver. The outstanding history of our period is R. Rojas, *Historia de la literatura argentina: ensayo filosófico sobre la evolución de la cultura en el Plata* (9 vols, Buenos Aires, 1957), a continental classic. Other important general works are A. Yunque's pathbreaking *La literatura social en la Argentina: historia de los movimientos literarios desde la emancipación nacional hasta nuestros días* (Buenos Aires, 1941), J. C. Ghiano, *Constantes de la literatura argentina* (Buenos Aires, 1953), E. Carilla, *Literatura argentina, 1800–1950: esquema general* (Tucumán, 1954), G. Ara, *Los argentinos y la literatura nacional* (Buenos Aires, 1966), A. Prieto, *La literatura autobiográfica argentina* (Buenos Aires, 1966), and N. Jitrik, *El fuego de la especie* (Buenos Aires, 1971). The period of consolidation in the last decades of the nineteenth century, and in particular the 1880 Generation, have received renewed attention since the late 1960s. See A. Rama, *Los gauchipolíticos rioplatenses* (Buenos Aires, 1976), which treats the relation between gauchesque poetry and politics throughout the nineteenth century, E. Fishburn, *The portrayal of immigration in nineteenth-century Argentine fiction, 1845–1892* (Berlin, 1981), an illuminating survey of authorial ideology, L. Rusich, *El inmigrante italiano en la novela argentina del 80* (Madrid, 1974), and a series of somewhat unstructured but indispensable populist-Marxist works by D. Viñas: *Literatura argentina y realidad política: de Sarmiento a Cortázar* (Buenos Aires, 1971), *Apogeo de la oligarquía* (Buenos Aires, 1975), *Indios, ejército y frontera* (Mexico, 1982), and *Grotesco, inmigración y fracaso* (Buenos Aires, 1973), which takes the work of the immigrant writer A. Discépolo as its point of departure. Similar contributions are A. R. Cortázar (ed.), *Indios y gauchos en la literatura argentina* (Buenos Aires, 1956), A. Prieto, *Literatura y subdesarrollo* (Buenos Aires, 1968), and J. Hernández Arregui, *Imperialismo y cultura* (Buenos Aires, 1973). On the later period, see M. Scrimaglio, *Literatura argentina de vanguardia, 1920–1930* (Rosario, 1974).

On Uruguay, rich beyond its size and population in literary creation, see A. Zum Felde, *Proceso intelectual del Uruguay* (3 vols, 1941; 3rd edn revd., Montevideo, 1967), S. Bollo, *Literatura uruguaya, 1807–1965* (2 vols, Montevideo, 1965), J. E. Englekirk and M. E. Ramos, *La narrativa uruguaya: estudio crítico bibliográfico* (Berkeley, 1967), and W. Rela, *Historia del teatro uruguayo, 1808–1968* (Montevideo, 1969); and on Paraguay, for which the reverse is true, see H. Rodríguez-Alcalá, *La literatura paraguaya* (Buenos Aires, 1969), J. Plá, *Apuntes para una historia de la cultura paraguaya* (Asunción, 1967), and *idem, El teatro en el Paraguay* (Asunción, 1967).

On Brazil, A. Coutinho, *Introdução à literatura no Brasil* (Rio de Janeiro, 1955; Eng. trans. *An introduction to literature in Brazil*, New York, 1969), is the outstanding general introduction, setting Brazil's literary production in the international cultural context with consummate power of synthesis, and ending with *modernismo* in the 1920s. The most readable works in English remain E. Veríssimo's idiosyncratic *Brazilian literature: an outline* (New York, 1945), which plays to the English-speaking gallery, and S. Putnam's enthusiastic and enduringly civilized *Marvelous Journey: a survey of four centuries of Brazilian writing* (New York, 1948), which effectively returns the compliment. Other essential general works are A. Cândido, *Brigada ligeira* (São Paulo, 1945), *Formação da literatura brasileira, 1750–1880* (2 vols, São Paulo, 1959), and *Presença da literatura brasileira* (São Paulo, 1964), N. Werneck Sodré, *História da literatura brasileira: seus fundamentos econômicos* (Rio de Janeiro, 1940; revd edn São Paulo, 1982), and A. Bosi, *História concisa da literatura brasileira* (São Paulo, 1972). On the early part of our period, see J. C. de Andrade-Muricy, *Panorama do movimento simbolista brasileiro* (2 vols, Brasília, 1973); for the period as a whole A. L. Machado Neto, *Estrutura social da República de Letras* (São Paulo, 1973), invaluable background for our purposes; and for the period preceding *modernismo*, see A. Bosi, *O pré-modernismo* (3rd edn, Rio de Janeiro, 1969).

Brazilian *modernismo* is attracting ever-increasing critical attention, on a scale far beyond that accorded to its Spanish American equivalents. See W. Martins, *O modernismo* (3rd edn, Rio de Janeiro, 1969); R. Bopp, *Movimentos modernistas no Brasil, 1922–1928* (Rio de Janeiro, 1966), by one of the participants; G. Mendonça Telles, *Vanguarda européia e modernismo brasileiro* (Petrópolis, 1972); L. Ivo, *Modernismo e modernidade* (Rio de Janeiro, 1972); F. Teixeira de Salles, *Das razões do modernismo* (Rio de Janeiro, 1974); and S. Castro, *Teoria e política do modernismo brasileiro* (Petrópolis, 1979). M. R. Batista, T. P. A. Lopez and Y. S. de Lima, *Brasil: primeiro tempo modernista, 1917–1929. Documentação* (São Paulo, 1972), is invaluable as a source book. Important reviews like the *Revista de Antropofagia* (São Paulo 1976, reprint) and *Klaxon* (São Paulo, 1974, reprint) have been republished, serving Brazilian criticism in the way that reprints of *Amauta* and *Contemporáneos* have served Spanish American criticism in recent years.

Finally, for the very end of our period, see A. Filho, *O romance brasileiro de 30* (Rio de Janeiro, 1969).

12. THE CATHOLIC CHURCH IN LATIN AMERICA, 1830–1930

The historiography of the Church in Latin America in the period 1830–1930 is variable in coverage and quality and does not compare with the standard of historical writing in other aspects of Latin American history. One of the objects of the Comisión de Historia de la Iglesia en América Latina (CEHILA) is to remedy this situation and the results of its work will be seen in the multi-volumed *Historia general de la Iglesia en América Latina* (*HGIAL*) under the general editorship of E. D. Dussel, individual volumes of which have already begun to appear. CEHILA has published a useful compendium on the sources and methods of church history, *Para una historia de la Iglesia en América Latina. I Encuentro Latinoamericano de CEHILA en Quito (1973)* (Barcelona, 1975), which compensates to some extent for the lack of basic bibliographies.

General histories of the Church in Latin America are few in number. Enrique D. Dussel, *Historia de la iglesia en América Latina. Coloniaje y liberación (1492–1973)* (3rd edn, Barcelona, 1974) provides a framework of the subject, and Hans-Jürgen Prien, *Die Geschichte des Christentums in Lateinamerika* (Göttingen, 1978) is a substantial history. For a synthesis of the modern period see François Chevalier, *L'Amérique Latine de l'Indépendance á nos jours* (Paris, 1977), 415–53.

Individual countries have their church histories, often traditional in character but indispensable as sources of information. The following are a selection. Cayetano Bruno, *Historia de la Iglesia en la Argentina* (Buenos Aires, 1966–71), vol. VII onwards for post-1800; Juan Carlos Zuretti, *Historia eclesiástica argentina* (Buenos Aires, 1945); Guillermo Furlong, S.J., 'El catolicismo argentino entre 1860 y 1930', Academia Nacional de la Historia, *Historia Argentina Contemporánea 1862–1930*, II, *Primera Sección* (Buenos Aires, 1964), 251–92. João Faguades Hauck and others, *História da Igreja no Brasil (HGIAL*, II-2, Petrópolis, 1980); Thales de Azevedo, *O catolicismo no Brasil* (Rio de Janeiro, 1955); João Alfredo de Sousa Montenegro, *Evolução do Catolicismo no Brasil* (Petrópolis, 1972). Felipe López Menéndez, *Compendio de historia eclesiástica de Bolivia* (La Paz, 1965). Rubén Vargas Ugarte, *Historia de la Iglesia en el Perú* (5 vols., Burgos, 1962) ends in 1900. Rodolfo Ramón de Roux, *Colombia y Venezuela (HGIAL*, VII, Salamanca, 1981); Mary Watters, *A history of the Church in Venezuela, 1810–1930* (Chapel Hill, 1933). Ricardo Blanco Segura, *Historia eclesiástica de Costa Rica* (San José, 1967), José Gutiérrez Casillas, S.J., *Historia de la Iglesia en México* (Mexico, 1974). There are a large number of social science studies of the modern Church, only a few of which have a historical dimension. See, for example, Henry A. Landsberger (ed.), *The Church and social change in Latin America* (Notre Dame, 1970), and Thomas C. Bruneau, *The Church in Brazil. The politics of Religion* (Austin, 1982).

The post-colonial Church can be reconstructed from various studies of particular themes. On economic aspects of the Church, see A. Bauer, 'The Church in the Economy of Spanish America: *Censos* and *Depósitos* in the Eighteenth and Nineteenth centuries', *HAHR* 63/4 (1983), 707–33. R. F. Schwaller, 'The episcopal succession in Spanish America 1800–1850', *TA*, 24/3 (1968), 207–71, provides data on the bishops, and Antonine Tibesar, 'The Peruvian Church at the time of Independence in the light of Vatican II', *TA*, 26/2 (1970), 349–75, on the Peruvian clergy. On the Mexican episcopacy see Fernando Pérez Mener, *El episcopado y la Independencia de México (1810–1836)* (Mexico, 1977). Michael P. Costeloe deals with two different sources of conflict in Mexico, *Church wealth in*

Mexico. A study of the 'Juzgado de Capellanías' in the Archbishopric of Mexico, 1800–1856 (Cambridge, 1967), and *Church and State in independent Mexico: a study of the patronage debate, 1821–1857* (London, 1978).

There are hardly any monographs on the clergy and laity and their organizations. Various aspects of clerical thinking and activities can be studied in the following: C. J. Beirne, 'Latin American bishops of the First Vatican Council, 1869–1870', *TA*, 25/1 (1968), 265–80; Josep M. Barnadas, 'Martín Castro. Un clérigo boliviano combatiente combatido', *Estudios Bolivianos en homenaje a Gunnar Mendoza L.* (La Paz, 1978), 169–220; José Gutiérrez Casillas, S. J., *Jesuítas en México durante el siglo XIX* (Mexico, 1972); Frederick B. Pike, 'Heresy, real and alleged in Peru: an aspect of the conservative-liberal struggle, 1830–1875', *HAHR*, 47/1 (1967), 50–74; and the same author's 'Spanish origins of the social-political ideology of the Catholic Church in nineteenth-century Spanish America', *TA*, 29 (1972), 1–16. See also T. G. Powell, 'Priests and peasants in Central Mexico: social conflict during "La Reforma"', *HAHR*, 57/2 (1977), 296–313.

On religious thought and practice the bibliography is sparse, but what exists is good. Jeffrey L. Klaiber, S. J., *Religion and revolution in Peru, 1824–1976* (Notre Dame, 1977), questions the old stereotype of a conservative Church and brings out the role of popular religious beliefs. Rodolfo Cardenal, S. J., *El poder eclesiástico en El Salvador* (San Salvador, 1980), covers among other things parish life, confraternities, pastoral visitations and church reform in the nineteenth and early twentieth centuries. Luis González, *Pueblo en vilo. Microhistoria de San José de Gracia* (Mexico, 1968), a classic of community history, with insight into the Catholic revival of the late nineteenth century in Mexico and into the Cristero rebellion. Two related studies of messianic movements throw light on the Brazilian Church in general: Ralph Della Cava, 'Brazilian messianism and national institutions: a reappraisal of Canudos and Joaseiro', *HAHR*, 48/3 (1968), 402–20; and the same author's *Miracle at Joaseiro* (New York, 1970). On other aspects of the religion of the people in Brazil see Eduardo Hoornaert, *Verdadeira e falsa religião no Nordeste* (Salvador, 1973), and Roger Bastide, *The African religions of Brazil: toward a sociology of the interpenetration of civilizations* (Baltimore, 1978).

Modern missionary work is less well known than that of the colonial period; Victor Daniel Bonilla, *Servants of God or masters of men? The story of a Capuchin mission in Amazonia* (London, 1972), is essentially polemical. For examples of the available bibliography on Protestantism, see Robert

Leonard McIntire, *Portrait of half a century: fifty years of Presbyterianism in Brazil (1859–1910)* (Cuernavaca, 1969); Emilio Willems, *Followers of the new faith. Culture change and the rise of Protestantism in Brazil and Chile* (Nashville, 1967); and Arnoldo Canclini, *Jorge A. Humble. Médico y misionero patagónico* (Buenos Aires, 1980). On Positivism, see *CHLA* IV, bibliographical essay 10. Sister M. Ancilla O'Neill, *Tristão de Athayde and the Catholic social movement in Brazil* (Washington, 1939) is an example of Catholic reaction against positivism.

Church and state have been comprehensively studied, perhaps because relations between the two powers are of interest to historians working outside the purely ecclesiastical field. The standard general work is that by J. Lloyd Mecham, *Church and state in Latin America. A history of politico-ecclesiastical relations* (Chapel Hill, 1934, rev. edn. 1966); on regional aspects see Frederick B. Pike, 'Church and state in Peru and Chile since 1840: a study in contrasts', *AHR*, 73/1 (1967), 30–50; and Robert J. Knowlton, 'Expropriation of church property in nineteenth-century Mexico and Colombia: a comparison', *TA*, 25, 1 (1968), 387–401. Argentina can be studied for the period 1870–1930 in John J. Kennedy, *Catholicism, nationalism, and democracy in Argentina* (Notre Dame, 1958), and the Catholic rearguard action in the 1880s in Néstor Tomás Auza, *Católicos y liberales en la generación del ochenta* (Buenos Aires, 1975). Studies of church-state relations in Brazil have concentrated on the last decades of the empire, though the following are of more general interest: Milo Pereira, *Conflitos entre a igreja e o estado no Brasil* (Recife, 1970); Brasil Gérson, *O regalismo brasileiro* (Brasília, 1978); and Thales de Azevedo, *Igreja e estado em tensão e crise: a conquista espiritual e o padroado na Bahia* (São Paulo, 1978). On the 'religious question' of 1872–5 and its aftermath in Brazil, see Sister Mary Crescentia Thornton, *The Church and Freemasonry in Brazil, 1872–1875, a study in regalism* (Washington, 1948); Roque Spencer M. de Barros, 'A questão religiosa', *História Geral da Civilização Brasileira*, VI (São Paulo, 1971), 317–65; David Gueiros Vieira, *O Protestantismo, a Maçonaria e a questão religiosa no Brasil* (Brasília, 1980); George C. A. Boehrer, 'The Church and the overthrow of the Brazilian monarchy', *HAHR*, 48/3 (1968), 380–401. For a more general account of the Church in Brazil during the empire, see George C. A. Boehrer, 'The Church in the second reign 1840–1889' in Henry H. Keith and S. F. Edwards (eds.), *Conflict and Continuity in Brazilian Society* (Columbia, S.C., 1969), 113–40. See Oscar Figueiredo Lustosa, *Reformistas na igreja do Brasil-Império* (São Paulo, 1977), for church reform, and Irmã Maria

Regina do Santo Rosário, *O Cardeal Leme (1882–1942)* (Rio de Janeiro, 1962) for a documented study of the great post-disestablishment churchman. For Chile, Brian H. Smith, *The Church and politics in Chile: challenges to modern Catholicism* (Princeton, 1982), is a political science study but it gives a good account of church-state relations in the constitution of 1925. Ecuador can be studied in Richard Pattee, *Gabriel García Moreno y el Ecuador de su tiempo* (Quito, 1941), and J. I. Larrea, *La iglesia y el estado en Ecuador* (Seville, 1954). Church and state is a major theme of Colombian history: see, for example, Fernán E. González G., *Partidos políticos y poder eclesiástico* (Bogotá, 1977); Helen Delpar, *Red against Blue: the Liberal Party in Colombian politics, 1863–1899* (Alabama, 1981); Jane Meyer Loy, 'Primary education during the Colombian Federation: the school reform of 1870', *HAHR*, 51/2 (1971), 275–94. On the anti-clerical liberal caudillo in Guatemala, see Hubert J. Miller, *La iglesia y el estado en tiempo de Justo Rufino Barrios* (Guatemala, 1976). The conflict of church and state in nineteenth-century Mexico has been exhaustively studied: Jan Bazant, *Alienation of church wealth in Mexico: social and economic aspects of the Liberal Revolution, 1856–1875* (Cambridge, 1971); Robert J. Knowlton, *Church property and the Mexican Reform, 1856–1910* (DeKalb, Illinois, 1976); Karl M. Schmitt, 'The Diaz conciliation policy on state and local levels, 1876–1911', *HAHR*, 40/4 (1960), 513–32; after Díaz the problem becomes that between the church and the Mexican Revolution.

Catholic social reformism was best exemplified in Mexico; at any rate this is the most fully documented case. Catholic thought is described and interpreted by Jorge Adame Goddard, *El pensamiento político y social de los católicos mexicanos, 1867–1914* (Mexico, 1981). Robert E. Quirk, *The Mexican Revolution and the Catholic Church 1910–1929* (Bloomington, 1973) and David C. Bailey, *¡Viva Cristo Rey! The Cristero Rebellion and the church-state conflict in Mexico* (Austin, 1974), in addition to dealing with their main themes also take account of the Catholic social movement. So, too, does Jean A. Meyer, *La Cristiada* (3 vols., Mexico, 1973–4), a richly detailed study of which there is a shorter English version, *The Cristero Rebellion: the Mexican people between church and state* (Cambridge, 1976). J. Tuck, *The Holy War in Los Altos: a regional analysis of Mexico's Cristero Rebellion* (Tucson, 1982) is a more local study. James W. Wilkie and Edna Monzón de Wilkie, *México visto en el siglo veinte: entrevistas de historia oral* (Mexico, 1969) contains (pp. 411–90) an interview with the veteran Catholic reformist Miguel Palomar y Vizcarra.

INDEX

Labour Nationalization Decree (1933), Cuba, 221

Lam, Wilfredo (b. 1902), Cuban painter, 483

Lamarca, Emilio, Argentine Catholic leader, 587

land:
clerical debt, 178; cultivation, 26–7, 32, 56; ownership, 27–33, 167–70, 185, 214–15, 262–4; role of the state, 175–8; supply, 25–6, 169–70; *see also* agriculture; haciendas

Lang, Francisco Curt (b. 1903), musicologist, 493

Lansing, Robert, American secretary of state, 107, 110, 111

Lastarria, José Victorino (1817–88), Chilean statesman and writer, 369–70, 374, 385, 389–90

Lavín, Carlos (1883–1962), Chilean composer, 492

Le Bon, Gustave, racial theorist, 398–400

League of Nations, 118

leather, 272

Leguía, Augusto, Peruvian president (1919–30), 65, 264, 432, 572

Leguizamón, Martiniano (1858–1935), Argentine dramatist, 455

Leme da Silveira Cintra, Sebastião (1882–1942), Brazilian cardinal, 565, 595

León, Tomás (1826–93), Mexican composer, 471

Lerdo de Tejada, Sebastián, Mexican president (1872–6), 371–2, 377, 582

Letelier, Valentín (1852–1919), Chilean educationalist, 385, 386, 390–1, 392, 426, 438

Levy, Alexandre (1864–92), Brazilian composer, 471

liberalism:
decline of, 373–82; heritage of, 367–9; revolt against, 369–72

Licht, F. O., sugar brokers, 197

Liga Patriótica Argentina, 439–40

Lillo, Baldomero (1867–1923), Chilean writer, 496

Lima:
housing and health, 257, 335; industry, 329; population of, 244, 245, 249–50; strikes (1919), 359; yellow fever in, 141

Lima Barreto, Afonso de (1881–1922), Brazilian writer, 504

Limantour, José Yves, Mexican finance minister, 395

Lins do Rêgo, José (1901–57), Brazilian writer, 506

Lisson, Emilio, Peruvian archbishop, 572

List Arzubide, Germán (b. 1898), Mexican writer, 511

literature:
avant-garde (20th c.), 509–20; *modernismo*, 445, 455, 456–65, 477, 495, 507, 510; newspapers and periodicals, 465, 486, 511, 513, 516, 546, 587; novels (19th c.), 446–53; novels (20th c.), 494–506; Parnassianism, 449, 460, 467; poetry (19th c.), 456–69; poetry (20th c.), 506–9

Llorens Torres, Luis (1878–1944), Puerto Rican poet, 464

Lobato, José Bento Monteiro (1880–1948), Brazilian writer, 504–5

Lodge, Henry Cabot, American senator, 93, 99

Lopes Neto, João Simões (1865–1916), Brazilian writer, 504

López, Luis Carlos (1883–1950), Colombian poet, 508

López, Luis V. (1848–94), Argentine writer, 451

López Buchardo, Carlos (1881–1948), Argentine composer, 493

López y Fuentes, Gregorio (1897–1967), Mexican writer, 499

López Portillo, José (1850–1923), Mexican writer, 453

López Velarde, Ramón (1888–1921), Mexican poet, 507

Loveira, Carlos (1882–1928), Cuban writer, 512

Lugones, Leopoldo (1874–1939), Argentine poet, 440, 463, 497, 501, 516

Lynch, Benito (1885–1951), Argentine writer, 501

Macedo Costa, Antonio de, bishop of Pará 379, 564

Machado de Assis, Joaquim Maria (1839–1908), Brazilian writer, 449–50, 467

McKinley, William, American president, 95–6

Madeiros, José Maria de (1849–1926), Brazilian painter, 474

Madero, Francisco, Mexican president, 351, 421, 426, 590

Magallanes, Fr., Jesuit priest, 548

Malatesta, Errico, Italian anarchist, 345–6

Malfatti, Anita (1896–1964), Brazilian painter, 487

Malharro, Martín A. (1865–1911), Argentine painter, 475

Mansilla, Lucio (1831–1913), Argentine writer, 450

Manaus, 147, 254

mancomunales Chilean labour organizations, 348

Mora, José María Luis (1794–1850), Mexican writer, 378, 382
Mora y del Río, José, Mexican bishop, 588, 589
Morais e Barros, Prudente José de, Brazilian president (1894–8), 391
Morales, Melesio (1838–1908), Mexican composer, 469
Morelos, 153, 170, 174, 177, 430
Moreno, Ezequiel, bishop of Pasto, 575–6
Morones, Luis N., Mexican labour leader, 353, 354
Morrow, Dwight W., American ambassador to Mexico, 117
Mosquera, Manuel José, archbishop of Bogotá, 537
Mosquera, Tomás Cipriano de, Colombian Liberal leader, 574
Mosquito Indian coast, 87
mulattos, 402, 540, 550
municipal services, 21, 261
Murillo, Gerardo, *see* Atl, Dr
music:
  (19th c.), 469–73; (20th c.), 489–94
mutual aid societies, 337–9, 540, 572

Nabuco, Joaquim (1849–1910), Brazilian writer and statesman, 382, 391, 393, 421, 566
Nabuco de Araújo, José Tomás, Brazilian minister of justice, 536
Napoleon III, emperor of France, 84, 369, 582
National Industrial Recovery Act (1933), Puerto Rico, 226
Nepomuceno, Alberto (1864–1920), Brazilian composer, 471–2
Neruda, Pablo (1904–73), Chilean poet, 515
Nervo, Amado (1870–1919), Mexican poet, 465
newspapers, *see* literature
Nicaragua:
  population, 142; relations with USA, 88, 93, 108, 115–16; religious affairs, 580
nitrate industry:
  boom and decline, 254, 294, 337; exports, 13, 25, 67, 300; land ownership, 27–8; strike massacre (1925), 359; workers, 326, 337
Novo, Salvador (1904–74), Mexican writer, 511
Núñez, Rafael, Colombian president, 575

obrajes (workshops), 271
Obregón, Álvaro, Mexican president (1924–8), 351, 353, 354, 591, 593

O'Gorman, Juan (b. 1905), Mexican artist and architect, 478
oil, *see* petroleum
Oliveira, Alberto de (1859–1937), Brazilian writer, 467
Oliveira Lima, Manoel (1865–1928), Brazilian historian and diplomat, 422
Oliveira Vianna, Francisco (1885–1951), Brazilian jurist, 438
Olney, Richard, American secretary of state, 93, 94
Oquendo de Arnat, Carlos (1909–36), Peruvian writer, 514
Oriente province, Cuba, 149, 213–14, 220, 222
Orinoco river, 94
Orozco, José Clemente (1883–1949), Mexican painter, 482
Ortega, Aniceto (1823–75), Mexican musician, 469
Ortiz, Fernando (1881–1969), Cuban anthropologist, 491
Ortiz de Mantellano, Bernardo (1899–1949), Mexican writer, 511
Othón, Manuel José (1858–1906), Mexican poet, 464

Páez, José Antonio, Venezuelan president, 578
painting:
  (19th c.), 473–6; (20th c.), 480–8
Palacios, Alfredo L. (1880–1965), Argentine socialist, 429
Palacios, Nicolás (1854–1911), Chilean writer, 409, 439n
Palomar y Vizcarra, Miguel, Mexican lawyer, 588, 592, 593, 660
Pan American Union, 104
Panama Canal:
  agreements concerning, 87, 88, 100–1; compensation paid, 69; effect on area, 125; labour employed, 127, 138, 141; need for, 94–5; railway, 235
Paniagua, Cenobio (1822–82), Mexican composer, 469
Paraguay:
  agriculture, 27; the Church, 569; immigrants in, 127, 130; population, 124; War (1865–70), 372
Pareja Diezcanseco, Alfredo (b. 1908), Ecuadorian writer, 502
Parreiras, Antônio (1864–1937), Brazilian painter, 474
Partido Autonomista Nacional (PAN) (Argentina), 394, 395, 423
Partido Liberal Mexicano (PLM), 349, 350, 351, 429–30, 635

Index

673

Quesada, Ernesto (1858–1934), Argentine writer, 410, 411
Quiroga, Horacio (1878–1937), Uruguayan writer, 497
Quito, population of, 245, 248

Rabasa, Emilio (1856–1930), Mexican jurist and writer, 412, 413, 453
race-consciousness, 397–405
radio, 113
railways:
inter-city, 235; network development, 42–3, 53, 89, 285, 308; sugar transport, 201, 203; workers, 326, 346, 363; workshops, 279
Ramos, Samuel (1897–1959), Mexican writer, 512
Ramos Mejía, Francisco (1847–93), Argentine writer, 410, 411
Ramos Mejía, José María (1849–1914), Argentine positivist, 406, 408, 410
Rebolledo Hidalgo, Efrén (1877–1929), Mexican poet, 464
Rebouças, André, Brazilian abolitionist, 382
Recabarren, Luis E. (1876–1924), Chilean socialist, 343, 428
religion, see church
Rerum Novarum encyclical, 586–7, 588, 589
Reverón, Armando (1889–1954), Venezuelan painter, 483
Revueltas, Silvestre (1899–1949), Mexican composer, 490–1
Reyes, Alfonso (1889–1959), Mexican scholar, 420, 421, 512
Reyles, Carlos (1868–1938), Uruguayan writer, 450, 501
Ribeiro, Júlio César (1845–90), Brazilian writer, 448
Riccio, Gustavo (1900–27), Argentine poet, 508
Río Blanco textile workers' strike (1907), Mexico, 331, 336, 350
Rio Grande do Sul, Brazil, 303, 421
Rio de Janeiro:
coffee production, 252; housing, 257; immigrants in, 332–3; labour force, 326, 327, 348, 356; political parties, 364; population, 245, 248–50; yellow fever in, 141
Rionda, Manuel, Cuban sugar broker, 197
Riva-Agüero, José de la (1885–1944), Peruvian scholar, 417, 418
Rivadavia, Bernardino, 378, 528
Rivera, Diego (1886–1957), Mexican painter, 479, 481
Rivera, Fructuoso, Uruguayan president, 568

Rivera, José Eustasio (1888–1928), Colombian writer, 499–500
roads, 177
Roca, Julio A., Argentine president (1880–6, 1898–1904), 372, 394, 567
Rodó, José Enrique (1871–1917), Uruguayan litterateur, 118, 400n, 412n, 414–17, 476, 495
Rojas, Ricardo (1882–1957), Argentine writer, 408, 417
Roldán, Amadeo (1900–39), Cuban composer, 491
Roosevelt, Theodore, American president, 88, 97, 100, 101, 102
Root, Elihu, American secretary of state, 96, 97, 102, 104, 108
Rosario, 235, 245, 346, 488
Rosas, Juan Manuel de, Argentine dictator, 83, 371, 410, 411, 528
Rosas, Juventino (1868–94), Mexican composer, 471
Roy, M. N., Indian nationalist, 362
Ruatan island, 86, 87
rubber:
exports, 15, 18, 179; production, 147, 184–5, 254
Ruiz Espadero, Nicolás (1823–90), Cuban composer, 471
Russian Revolution, 355–6, 360

Sabogal, José (1888–1956), Peruvian painter, 484, 514
Sáenz Peña, Roque, Argentine president (1910–14), 395, 423
Saldias, Adolfo (1850–1914), Argentine writer, 410, 411
Salisbury, Lord, British foreign secretary, 93
Salta, 153, 182
San Diego, plan of, 108
San Gregorio massacre (1921), Chile, 358
San José (Costa Rica), 248
San José de Gracia (Mexico), 160, 163, 180
San Luis Potosí, 168, 169, 171
San Vicente sugar mill, Puerto Rico, 202
Sánchez, Florencio (1875–1910), Uruguayan dramatist, 455
Sánchez, Luis Alberto (b. 1900), Peruvian writer, 514
Sánchez Camacho, Eduardo, bishop of Tamaulipas, 537
Sánchez de Fuentes, Eduardo (1874–1944), Cuban composer, 489
Santa Cruz, Bolivia, 141
Santa Cruz, Domingo (b. 1899), Chilean composer, 492
Santander, Colombia, 171